FEDERAL TAXES ON GRATUITOUS TRANSFERS

ASPEN CASEBOOK SERIES

FEDERAL TAXES ON GRATUITOUS TRANSFERS

LAW AND PLANNING

JOSEPH M. DODGE

Stearns Weaver Miller Weissler Alhadeff & Sitterson Professor of Law
Florida State University College of Law

WENDY C. GERZOG

Professor
University of Baltimore School of Law

BRIDGET J. CRAWFORD

Professor
Pace Law School

Wolters Kluwer
Law & Business

Printed in the United States of America.

1 2 3 4 5 6 7 8 9 0

ISBN 978-1-4548-0240-2

Library of Congress Cataloging-in-Publication Data

Dodge, Joseph M., 1941-
     Federal taxes on gratuitous transfers : law and planning / Joseph M. Dodge, Wendy C. Gerzog, Bridget J. Crawford.
       p. cm.
     Includes index.
     ISBN 978-1-4548-0240-2
1.   Inheritance and transfer tax — Law and legislation — United States. 2.   Gifts — Taxation — Law and legislation — United States. 3.   Estate planning — United States.   I. Gerzog, Wendy C. II. Crawford, Bridget J. III. Title.

KF6572.D63 2011
343.7305′3 — dc22

2011006721

About Wolters Kluwer Law & Business

Wolters Kluwer Law & Business is a leading global provider of intelligent information and digital solutions for legal and business professionals in key specialty areas, and respected educational resources for professors and law students. Wolters Kluwer Law & Business connects legal and business professionals as well as those in the education market with timely, specialized authoritative content and information-enabled solutions to support success through productivity, accuracy and mobility.

Serving customers worldwide, Wolters Kluwer Law & Business products include those under the Aspen Publishers, CCH, Kluwer Law International, Loislaw, Best Case, ftwilliam.com and MediRegs family of products.

CCH products have been a trusted resource since 1913, and are highly regarded resources for legal, securities, antitrust and trade regulation, government contracting, banking, pension, payroll, employment and labor, and healthcare reimbursement and compliance professionals.

Aspen Publishers products provide essential information to attorneys, business professionals and law students. Written by preeminent authorities, the product line offers analytical and practical information in a range of specialty practice areas from securities law and intellectual property to mergers and acquisitions and pension/benefits. Aspen's trusted legal education resources provide professors and students with high-quality, up-to-date and effective resources for successful instruction and study in all areas of the law.

Kluwer Law International products provide the global business community with reliable international legal information in English. Legal practitioners, corporate counsel and business executives around the world rely on Kluwer Law journals, looseleafs, books, and electronic products for comprehensive information in many areas of international legal practice.

Loislaw is a comprehensive online legal research product providing legal content to law firm practitioners of various specializations. Loislaw provides attorneys with the ability to quickly and efficiently find the necessary legal information they need, when and where they need it, by facilitating access to primary law as well as state-specific law, records, forms and treatises.

Best Case Solutions is the leading bankruptcy software product to the bankruptcy industry. It provides software and workflow tools to flawlessly streamline petition preparation and the electronic filing process, while timely incorporating ever-changing court requirements.

ftwilliam.com offers employee benefits professionals the highest quality plan documents (retirement, welfare and non-qualified) and government forms (5500/PBGC, 1099 and IRS) software at highly competitive prices.

MediRegs products provide integrated health care compliance content and software solutions for professionals in healthcare, higher education and life sciences, including professionals in accounting, law and consulting.

Wolters Kluwer Law & Business, a division of Wolters Kluwer, is headquartered in New York. Wolters Kluwer is a market-leading global information services company focused on professionals.

To Molly

— JMD

To Harry and Alex, the two men in my life,
and to Amy, in sweet remembrance

— WCG

To Jonathan

— BJC

SUMMARY OF CONTENTS

CONTENTS

4 THE BASIC ESTATE   141

PREFACE

This book deals with the federal wealth transfer taxes and the federal income tax insofar as it bears on gratuitous transfers. The federal wealth transfer taxes as of 2011 consist of a unified estate and gift tax and a generation-skipping transfer tax. The federal transfer tax system is separate and apart from the federal income tax.

This coursebook differs (to a greater or lesser degree) from others in the same field in the following respects:

(1) pervasive use of problems as a pedagogical tool;
(2) emphasis on text, statutes, and regulations, rather than cases (especially cases that involve routine application of law to facts);
(3) integration of related income tax materials, including the income taxation of estates and trusts;
(4) relation of tax doctrine to tax planning strategies;
(5) focus on doctrine that influences the practice of estate and trust law, rather than doctrine for its own sake;
(6) integration, early on, of valuation issues into "taxability" material;
(7) reference to state law (including recent developments) as it bears on transfer tax issues, with full coverage of issues raised by community property systems; and
(8) "building block" organization, rather than segmented organization according to Code sections.

To elaborate on the last item, the first chapter operates as a transition from courses in Property, Individual Income Taxation, and Estates and Trusts. The second chapter provides an overview of the basic features of the federal transfer tax landscape. Thereafter, the book progresses from problems attendant upon routine or simple estates to those attendant upon wealthy estates with complex tax-oriented features. This organizational scheme renders it possible (if not optimally desirable) for the student to take this course concurrently with the basic courses in Income Tax and in Wills, Estates, and Trusts. The organizational format of this text entails the repetition of basic or important points and the relationship of the fine points to the basics. In general, the intent has been to create a fresh view of the subject as of the year 2011, as opposed to bringing a previous effort up to date.

The book incorporates both the "Tax Relief, Unemployment Insurance Reauthorization, and Job Creation Act of 2010" (2010 Tax Act), P. L. 111-312, signed into law Dec. 17, 2010, and the Joint Committee on Taxation's Technical Explanation of that legislation published for the U.S. Senate a week before the bill's passage. See JCX-55-10, pp. 39-53 (Dec. 10, 2010). Sections 301-304 of the

2010 Tax Act include the reinstatement of the estate tax, the repeal of carryover basis for assets in a decedent's estate, an election (with respect to decedents dying in 2010) to avoid estate taxes but to be subject to the carryover basis rules of §1022, new tax rates and exemptions, a new provision providing for portability of a deceased spouse's unused exclusion amount, and the extension of the EGTRRA Sunset until the end of the year 2012.

The emphasis on text, analysis, and problems also renders this text suitable for an LL.M. program in taxation. As the book progresses, it becomes more technical, with increased references to drafting issues and commentary on controversial legal issues.

The organization (simple to complex estates), the frequent references to state law and income tax provisions, the descriptions of transactions and their uses, and the elaborate discussion concerning the drafting and use of formula clauses in relation to the marital deduction combine to make this book suitable for a tax-oriented estate planning course.

A reason to study the federal transfer taxes is that many doctrines of state law come into play primarily in a tax context. A leading example is the law of disclaimers. In the absence of the federal transfer taxes, various kinds of trusts (and, within trusts, powers of appointment) would be used much less often. Indeed, much of the "law" concerning trusts and powers of appointment is to be found in cases involving the federal transfer taxes.

Study of the federal transfer taxes well serves the development of skills relating to statutory exegesis, transactional analysis, and planning. The very nature of the subject, the transfer of wealth to the natural objects of one's bounty and charity, is intrinsically forward-looking, as it is concerned with managing property around a future certain event — one's death (and thereafter).

A few editorial points. Cases and other sources are edited, often heavily, but in the interests of continuity omissions are not always indicated by periods or asterisks. Footnotes within cases and other excerpted materials are freely omitted; those retained have the same numbering as in the original. Any significant alterations of the original are set off in brackets. Brackets also are used to indicate editors' notes and explanations and, in cases, summaries of facts and arguments.

Citation form has been standardized. Citations given are not necessarily complete. Citations to parallel sources (such as L.Ed.) and to the prior history of a case are often omitted. Unless otherwise indicated, all section ("§") references are to the Internal Revenue Code of 1986 as amended or to Treasury regulations under said Code.

The abbreviations "H" and "W" are often used to refer to "husband" and "wife" respectively in examples and problems where spouses are involved in order to enhance reader comprehension. "A" and "B" would denote parties who are not married.

FEDERAL TAXES ON GRATUITOUS TRANSFERS

CHAPTER 1

SETTING THE STAGE: THE BASICS OF GRATUITOUS TRANSFERS

This chapter serves as a transition from prior or concurrent courses (Property, Estates and Trusts, Income Tax) to this course, which deals with the federal taxation of gratuitous transfers, with emphasis on the federal wealth transfer taxes. Accordingly, this chapter consists of a review of basic concepts (hopefully) covered in Property, Estates and Trusts, and of the federal income tax as it bears on gratuitous transfers, and concludes with some musings about the taxation of wealth and wealth transfers.

§1.1. Review of Property Concepts

This section will review basic property-law concepts as they bear on gratuitous transfers, first from a historical perspective and second by way of a glossary of basic terminology, which may come in handy as these terms are encountered in later material.

A. *History of Law of Gratuitous Transfers*

The history set forth below probably covers more ground than is necessary for a course in the current taxation of gratuitous transfers, but it is prudent not to omit important strands from the narrative.

Until the nineteenth century, most wealth was in land and its yield; accordingly, most of the relevant historical developments up to the nineteenth century pertain to land.

The American system of property law is derived from the English system, and the conventional date for beginning the tracing of English property law is that of the Norman Conquest, 1066, which saw the entrenchment of a national feudal system. Under the post-Conquest English feudal system, all title to land derived from the King. The King granted land to lords in exchange for pledges of service and loyalty, the breach of which could give rise to forfeiture. The lords in turn could grant land to knights or others on similar conditions, and so on down the line. The process whereby a person (grantor) granted land to a person below (grantee) in exchange for services, produce, or whatever, is called subinfeudation.

At first (and in theory), a grant of land was only for the grantee's lifetime, after which the land would revert to the grantor (or the grantor's successor). However, the grantor might consent to re-grant the land to the grantee's heir upon payment of a bargained-for fee, called a relief. The relief was the predecessor of estate taxation. A grantee could transfer his rights and obligations to another during his lifetime, but only with *his* grantor's consent and again with the payment of a fee (the predecessor of the gift tax), according to a process called substitution. Thus, in the post-Conquest period, there was no power either to make an *inter vivos* transfer of land by substitution or to pass property to one's heir or to anyone else at death, without the grantor's consent and payment of a fee (transfer tax). (Besides relief, there were other feudal incidents running to the grantor, viz., wardship and marriage.[1])

Later, under pressure from grantees who desired something less ephemeral than a tenancy for life, it became common to grant land to a grantee "and his heirs." An heir is the person prescribed by law to take land (and titles) upon the deceased's death. In feudal England, the heir, determined under the system of primogeniture, was the deceased's eldest son or, if he was dead, the eldest male (if any) produced by a complex system of tracing through descendants and ancestors. (Primogeniture was abolished in England only in 1925. In the U.S., primogeniture never took hold.) When a grant was made to "A and his heirs," the property passed upon A's death by "inheritance" to his heir, who assumed A's feudal obligations to A's grantor (and his heirs), and so on, for so long as there were heirs to take. The relief was still payable upon each event of succession, but it was a fixed fee set at the time of the original grant and not negotiated upon each succession. If an heir died without any heir, the property reverted (escheated) to the grantor (and his successors).

Subinfeudation was able to avoid the various feudal incidents, although it did not relieve a grantee of his obligations to his grantor. To preserve the value of the feudal incidents, the Statute *Quia Emptores*, enacted in 1290, forbade further subinfeudations. At the same time, the power of a grantor to deny consent to, and levy a fee upon, substitution was abolished. After *Quia Emptores*, land could be conveyed freely *inter vivos*. Land continued to pass at death to one's heir only by inheritance. Hence, a deceased had no power to make a disposition of land at death contrary to the law governing heirship. That is, the common law courts would not enforce an attempted devise of land by will. The situation was different for personal property: A person had freedom to dispose of personal property during

---

1. Wardship enabled the grantor and his successors to have possession of land, and to reap its profits without any duty to account, during the minority of the grantee's heir. Marriage gave a grantor the right to pick the marriage partner of an unmarried heir of the grantee. A prospective marriage partner of the heir would likely be willing to pay the grantor for being the chosen one.

life or after death. In fact, it was religious custom to do so at death through the medium of the last confession, and the ecclesiastical courts would enforce the terms of a "testament" of personal property.

To avoid the principle that a will devising land would not be recognized, landholders employed the device of the use: Land would be conveyed *inter vivos* by A to X and his heirs to the use of A, and after A's death to transfer the land to a person designated by A. The common law courts, of course, only acknowledged the passing of title to X and his heirs, and did not enforce the interest granted to (retained by) A and his successors. However, the Court of Chancery did enforce the use. The Chancery Court operated under the simple maxim that a person should act in accordance with moral command, rather than under legal rules as such, and the acceptance by X and his heirs of title with conditions attached was deemed to impose upon them the obligation to perform the stated conditions. Moreover, since the Chancellor was a high-ranking executive official in the King's "cabinet," the Court of Chancery could enforce its orders by imprisoning the disobeying party for contempt. Thus, in the conveyance described above A could instruct X and his heirs to convey the property to B at A's death free of the use and the claims of A's heir. The person to whom X (and his heirs) owed duties (A, and then B) was called the *"cestui que use."* The successive *cestuis* were "equitable" owners, just as the Chancery Court was a court of "equity."[2]

Inter vivos transfers might also be used as attempted will substitutes: The transferor could create various future interests which would operate to shift ownership from one person to another over time. Moreover, each shift would be free of the feudal incidents, especially relief, which only attached to transfers by inheritance. (The use of successive future incidents to avoid estate or inheritance tax was a problem for governments into the twentieth century, where it was finally dealt with in the U.S. by the generation-skipping transfer tax.) At old common law various doctrines existed to invalidate attempts to create certain kinds of future interests, such as the prohibition on springing and shifting interests, the doctrine of the destructability of contingent remainders, the Rule in Shelley's case, the Doctrine of Worthier Title, and the Rule Against Perpetuities. But these doctrines did not prohibit all future interests, and in some cases they could be finessed by the device of the use. A scenario that continues to raise issues under the current federal transfer taxes is that of an *inter vivos* transfer by A to A for life, remainder to B and his heirs, which is a clear attempt to dispose of property after one's death to a person other than one's heir while retaining possession or enjoyment during the rest of one's life. Under the old common law, such a

---

2. The Chancery Court also was involved in *inter vivos* transfers. Traditionally, a transfer of a freehold interest was accomplished by a ceremony called "livery of seisin." The "bargain and sale" was developed to avoid livery of seisin. Bargain and sale was simply a written agreement for the purchase of land, which recited that the purchaser had given consideration. The Court of Chancery treated the purchaser as the equitable owner — with the seller as legal owner — under a relationship essentially identical to that involving the use. (This relationship survives in modern property law, where a purchaser under a land contract has the right of specific performance.)

"testamentary" transfer was held to be ineffectual. A transfer by an owner of a present interest to himself was considered to be illogical, and a present transfer of a future interest to commence in the future (the "remainder" to B and his heirs), without any intervening interest in a person other than the grantor, was not recognized by the common law. Nevertheless, the use could be employed to achieve the desired result: A could transfer land to X and his heirs to the use of B and his heirs following the death of A. This device was called a "springing use," and was enforceable in Chancery.

The Statute of Uses, which became effective as of 1536, simply caused all equitable estates to be executed (converted into) legal estates. Thus, *cestuis* became legal owners or holders of legal future interests, and springing and shifting interests (called executory interests) were validated. Although an immediate consequence of the Statute of Uses was to curb the utility of the use as a device to effect a devise of land,[3] Parliament shortly (in 1540) dealt with that issue by enacting the Statute of Wills (1540), which permitted free devises of land if certain formalities of execution were satisfied.

The Statute of Uses applied by its terms to land only. Also, it was held not to apply to "active" uses — now called trusts — in which the legal owner — the "trustee" — is granted active duties, such as collecting and paying over rents to the *cestui* — now called the "beneficiary." The trustee's duties under arrangements not executed by the Statute of Uses continued to be enforced by the Chancery Court.

In modern times, distinctions between the law of real property and personal property have largely disintegrated to reflect the emergence of personal property (including interests in productive enterprise) as the principal form of wealth in modern industrial society. Legal and equitable jurisdiction has generally been merged, although in some cases special courts (probate, chancery, surrogate's) are given jurisdiction over matters pertaining to wills, trusts, inheritance, and guardianships. The entire system in the U.S. is now administered by courts rather than administrative officials or ecclesiastics.

At old common law, a woman could own land, but during marriage her husband had exclusive control over, and the right to the profits from, the land, including the power of sale and disposition. Upon his wife's death, if issue had been born to the marriage, the husband held an estate for life in all of the wife's lands, called an estate by curtesy. The wife had an estate for life in one-third of the husband's lands, called dower. Neither dower nor curtesy could be defeated by an *inter vivos* transfer unless the wife or husband joined in the deed, nor could it be defeated by will. At the same time, neither the husband nor the wife was the heir of the other. These rules have since been altered by statute: Women have use and control over their property; dower and curtesy have been abolished, modified, or replaced; and a surviving spouse is often an heir of the deceased spouse.

Because of the obsolescence of the feudal incidents, the law of transfer taxation has become separated from underlying property law. Most of the old common-law

---

3. The use was executed so as to give A a fee simple, putting A back to square one.

doctrines that were hostile to the creation of certain future interests have been repealed or loosened or can be avoided by the creation of trusts. Thus, the validity of future interests is rarely a problem. A transfer that is legally valid — such as A's creating an *inter vivos* trust, income to A for A's life, remainder in fee simple to B — can be (and is) reached by the current gift and estate taxes.

B. Glossary of Terms

At this point, it is desirable to set forth definitions of certain terms commonly used in the area of wills, trusts, and future interests; in some cases the legal significance of the term is indicated. Many of the terms should be familiar from Property, and the others are developed in the basic course on Wills, Estates, and Trusts. However, your Property course might not have covered future interests and the basics of trusts, and you might not have taken Wills, Estates, and Trusts. Accordingly, you can view the following as a kind of miniversion (or overview) of material that is ideally a prerequisite to this course but which you have not actually encountered.

This glossary is by no means exhaustive. Numerous additional terms will be dealt with in due course. Italicized words and phrases within definitions indicate that the word or phrase is defined elsewhere in this glossary. Terms like curtesy, dower, use, and *cestui*, which are described in §1.1.A, are not repeated here.

The glossary is presented alphabetically, rather than in the order you might encounter the terms in other courses, for ease of use as a reference tool. If you are a complete neophyte to the area of gratuitous transfers, you might consider starting with these terms in the following order: future interest, remainder, reversion, vested, inheritance, will, residue, probate, estate, trust, administration, beneficiary, fiduciary, corpus, income, and power of appointment.

Account. A written record of the financial transactions in an *administration*, such as receipts, disbursements, payments of claims and taxes, sales, investments, distributions, and so on. To "render an account" means to present the account to a court or to a *beneficiary*.

Administration. The management of an *estate, trust,* or *guardianship* by the *fiduciary*, called the *personal representative* or *executor* (in an estate), the *trustee* (in a trust), and the *guardian* (in a guardianship). Powers and duties include collecting and preserving assets, investing, collecting income, paying debts and expenses, effecting distributions to beneficiaries, and keeping an account of the foregoing. See *personal representative* and *executor*.

Administrator. The *personal representative* of an *estate* in the case where the decedent died *intestate* or failed to name an *executor*.

Annuity. A contractual right to have paid a fixed sum of money annually (or monthly) to a person for a fixed period or for the life of one or more persons. Social Security retirement benefits and, often, employee retirement plans pay benefits in the form of an annuity.

Beneficiary. Equitable owner of property in a *trust* or *estate*, to whom *distributions* of *income* or *corpus* are made from time to time during the *administration* of the trust or estate. In broad sense, the term also includes any person holding a *remainder* or *executory interest* in a trust. In the case of an estate, refers to any *legatee, devisee, heir*, and *next of kin*; that is, the ultimate distributees.

Bequest. Refers to the disposition of *personal property* at death pursuant to a will. See also *devise*. The person who receives a bequest is a *legatee*.

Community property. In jurisdictions having a community property system, property acquired during marriage (other than by gratuitous transfer) is held as community property, which is a kind of co-ownership by husband and wife. (The community-property idea supposedly originated in Germanic tribes, and was transmitted to the U.S. through Spain and France.) The states having community-property regimes are: Louisiana, Texas, New Mexico, Arizona, Nevada, California, Washington, Idaho, and Wisconsin. The law of the jurisdiction determines which spouse, or whether both spouses jointly, have the power to manage various items of community property. On the death of a spouse, that spouse can dispose of (by *will* or *intestacy*) only his or her half of the community property, because the surviving spouse already owns the other half. A few community-property states allowed the creation of "community property with right of survivorship" in specific property, with the result that the decedent spouse's share of the property item merges with that of the surviving spouse upon the decedent spouse's death. Property that is solely owned by one spouse is called "separate property." A state that does not have a community-property system is referred to as a "common-law property state."

Constructive trust. A form of equitable remedy to redress fraud and other wrongful or unjust accessions to property. When a court declares a constructive trust, the wrongdoer is required to convey the property to the aggrieved party. Not to be confused with a conventional (i.e., "express") *trust*.

Contingent (interest). See *remainder, vested*.

Corpus. The "principal" of an *estate, trust*, or *guardianship*, as distinguished from the *"income."* Transactions involving income or corpus that occur during the course of an *administration* are reflected in the *account*. The distinction between corpus and income is often important, because typically, under the terms of the trust or will or pursuant to state law, different *beneficiaries* are entitled to receive income and corpus and at different times. The leading example is a trust that requires "income" to be distributed to B for life, *remainder* to C. What is "income" for this purpose is determined by trust law (which usually defers to the settlor's intent if expressed in the trust instrument). The definitions of "income" under state or federal income taxes or under GAAP ("generally accepted accounting principles") for business accounting are not controlling.

Descent. Technical (archaic) reference is to the disposition of *real property* at death, usually to heirs in the case of intestacy. Basically the same as *inheritance*. See also *distribution*.

Devise. Refers to the disposition of real property at death pursuant to a will. See also *bequest*. The person who receives a devise is a "devisee."

Distribution. In technical (and archaic) sense, refers to the disposition of *personal property* at death, usually to *next of kin* upon *intestacy*. See also *descent*.

Now it simply denotes the payment of money and the transfer of property from an *estate* or *trust* to a *beneficiary*.

Equitable interest. An interest or right enforceable in a court of equitable jurisdiction with equitable remedies such as specific performance and injunction. *Beneficiaries* of *estates* and *trusts* possess equitable interests. See also *legal interest*.

Estate. The general meaning is "aggregation of property." There are several specific meanings, which are dependent on the context. (1) The aggregate wealth of a living person or a dead person without reference to any particular body of law. Thus, "estate planning" refers to planning with respect to any and all wealth owned by the decedent directly or indirectly and in whatever form. (2) The state of affairs following the death of a decedent where the property owned by the decedent at his death becomes subject to the control of the *personal representative* (who has authority to control and deal with the property, perhaps subject to court supervision) during the period of the estate's *administration*. In other words, the property of a decedent that is subject to administration by the decedent's personal representative. This is commonly referred to as the "probate estate." See also *probate*. (3) The property subject to a *fiduciary* relationship other than that described in (2), such as a "guardianship estate" or a "trust estate." (4) The aggregation of property subject to federal estate tax. (5) The separate taxable entity (distinct from the decedent, the personal representative's nonfiduciary existence, and the beneficiaries) for federal *income* tax purposes. The estate for federal income tax purposes commences with the death of the decedent and continues (typically) until the (probate) estate (see meaning (1), supra) is wound up. (6) Any of a number of interests in property, as in "life estate" and "estate in fee simple." This use of the term conveys little information. (7) A designation for the payment of a sum of money or a *distribution* of property to the *estate* of a deceased person. Thus, life insurance proceeds may be payable to "B's estate." Similarly, property might be transferred in *trust*, income to B for life, *remainder* to B's estate. In both cases, the money or property is paid, at the appropriate time, to B's estate as described in meaning (1) above. The effect of an "estate" designation is to treat the property somewhat as if it had been acquired by the decedent (B, in this case) just prior to his death. Thus, the property is subject to estate administration and passes to the beneficiaries of the estate according to the laws of *intestacy* or the decedent's *will*, as the case may be, just as if the decedent (B) had owned the property at the time of his death.

Executor. The *personal representative* of an *estate* named in a valid *will* and appointed by a court of *probate* jurisdiction.

Executory interest. A *future interest* in property that defeats or cuts short a *vested* interest (whether in the transferor or another). An example would be a transfer from A to B and his heirs, but if descendants of Elizabeth II cease to occupy the throne of England, then to C and her heirs. C has a "shifting" executory interest. If A transfers land to B for ten years, then to A, then to C upon reaching the age of 30, C has a "springing" executory interest. See also *remainder*. The distinction between executory interests and remainders has little significance at present.

Fiduciary. A person (including a legal person, i.e., a corporation, where authorized by state law) who owes duties (of loyalty, no self-dealing, etc., referred to as "fiduciary duties") to others. *Personal representatives* of *estates, trustees,* and *guardians* are fiduciaries, as are, for example, directors of corporations, agents, and receivers. The quality and extent of fiduciary duties depend upon the type of fiduciary relationship involved. In the case of *estates* and *trusts,* the fiduciary duties are owed to the *beneficiaries,* who can enforce such duties in a court of equitable jurisdiction.

Future interest. A present right, protected by law or equity, to future possession or enjoyment of property. Examples are *executory interests, remainders,* and *reversions.* A "present" interest is one currently in possession or enjoyment, as is typical with a *life estate.* See also *term for years.*

Gift. Inter vivos gratuitous transfer of money or property, usually effected by delivery combined with donative intent. For federal gift tax purposes, a gift is an *inter vivos* transfer for no (or insufficient) consideration in money or money's worth. A "gift *causa mortis*" is a gift of personal property made in expectation of imminent death, which is automatically revoked if the donor fails to die as anticipated, and is revocable by the donor prior to his death.

Governing instrument. Refers to the *will, trust* document, deed, contract, insurance policy, or other instrument that governs the situation at hand.

Guardianship. Arrangement involving a guardian. A "guardian of the person" is that person who has personal control of a minor or other person under legal disability. A "guardian of the property" is a person in charge of the *administration* of the property (the guardianship estate) of a minor or person under legal disability, who stands in a *fiduciary* relation to the minor or person under legal disability. A guardian of one under legal disability is sometimes referred to as a "committee," "conservator," or "curator." In theory, a guardian of the property must be appointed whenever a minor or person under legal disability has property other than consumables. A "guardian *ad litem*" is not a true guardian, but rather a person appointed by a court to represent minors, persons under legal disability, and persons unborn or unascertained in litigation that might affect their interests in money or property.

Heir. A person entitled to take real property under the law governing *inheritance* (i.e., where the decedent dies without an effective *will*). It is incorrect to refer to a person taking under a will as an "heir." See also *next of kin.*

Income. The income of an estate or *trust* consists of receipts, less expenses, etc., which are not treated as *corpus.* The rules, prescribed by state law or the *governing instrument,* for determining what is income for "trust (or estate) accounting purposes" (see *account,* supra) are very similar, but not identical, to those that define "taxable income" for federal income tax purposes. Thus, dividends and interest are typically income for both trust (or estate) accounting and federal income tax purposes, but capital gains (which are income for federal income tax purposes) are usually added to corpus for trust (or estate) accounting purposes. See also *corpus.*

Inheritance. Strictly speaking, refers to the disposition of property — usually *real property* — at death to *heirs* insofar as it is not controlled by a *will.*

Intestacy. Where a person dies without a valid will. Such person is said to die "intestate." Upon intestacy, property passes to the descendant's heirs and *next of kin* (except that which goes to creditors and is laid aside as dower or curtesy).

Issue. Refers to the descendants, as a group, of the person referred to. Modifying phrases such as "*per stirpes*" and "*per capita*" are aimed to identify certain persons within the group.

Joint ownership. Concurrent ownership of property by two or more persons, under which ownership passes automatically to the surviving "joint tenant(s)" upon the death of one by "right of survivorship." An interest in a joint tenancy, therefore, does not pass by *inheritance* or *will*. A "tenancy by the entireties" is a subcategory of joint tenancy that can only occur between husband and wife. A "tenancy in common" is a form of concurrent ownership without the right of survivorship; an interest in a tenancy in common passes by inheritance or will.

Legal interest. As contrasted to "equitable" interest, refers to present and future interests created by "outright" (not-in-trust) transfers, as where A deeds property to B for life, remainder to C and his heirs.

Legatee. The person receiving a *bequest*. The subject matter of the bequest (the property bequeathed) is often called a "legacy."

Life estate. An estate in *real property* or *personal property* that expires at a person's death (usually that of the owner of the estate). An "equitable" life estate is an income interest in a trust for a beneficiary's life, as opposed to a "legal" life estate in a non-trust conveyance. An estate to last during the life of another person ("to B for the life of A") is an "estate *per autre vie*."

Next of kin. Strictly speaking, refers to the person or persons who take *personal property* upon the death of the person without a *will*. See also *heir*.

Personal effects. This term, often used in *wills*, denotes "tangible *personal property*" for personal use, such as clothing and articles of personal adornment with a more-or-less "personal" connection; the term usually is not deemed to refer to articles of general utilitarian use, such as cars, consumer durables, and furniture.

Personal property. Refers to any property which is not *real property*. (Does not refer to property in personal use, such as a personal residence, car, or consumer durable.) "Intangible" personal property refers to stocks, bonds, debentures, notes, claims, partnership interests, options, patents, copyrights, beneficial interests in trusts and estates, choses in action, and other rights conferred by law or contract to receive or acquire money, property, or legal protection in carrying on an economically advantageous activity. Personal property is "tangible" when it consists of a physical object (other than an object that embodies intangible property, such as a stock certificate).

Personal representative. The person in charge of *administration* of an *estate*; she has a *fiduciary* relationship to the estate *beneficiaries*. See also *administrator* and *executor*.

Power of appointment. Although a precise definition of this term is elusive, in its current usage the term almost always refers to a discretionary distributive power pertaining to a trust held by a person who is not the settlor of the trust. A power of appointment is wholly discretionary, and is not subject to fiduciary constraints. A power of appointment may be held by a trustee, a beneficiary, or a person (other than the settlor) who is neither trustee nor beneficiary. A power of appointment is created by the trust instrument. A given trust may contain more than one power. The settlor of the trust is the "donor" of the power. The person who holds the power is the "donee" of the power. The persons to whom property can be appointed are the "objects" of the power, and the persons who receive the distributions pursuant to the exercise of the power are called the "appointees." The persons who take the property if the power is not exercised are the "takers in default." A power that can be exercised by the donee during the donee's lifetime is called an "*inter vivos* power" or a "power by deed." A power that can be exercised by donee only by the donee's *will* is called a "testamentary power." A power is a "general power" if it can be exercised in favor of the donee, the donee's estate, or the creditors of either. A power that is not a general power is called a "special power."

Present interest. See *future interest.*

Probate. (1) Specifically, the judicial procedure by which a decedent's *will* is given legal effect and validity as a result of proving that the requisite formalities were complied with. (The linguistic derivation of "probate," the Latin "*probare,*" means "to prove.") The process is called "admitting the will to probate." A will has no force and effect until it is probated. (2) In general, synonymous with *estate administration.* Thus, the phrase "avoiding probate" means avoiding the process of estate administration. (3) The term "probate *estate*" means the property of the decedent subject to estate administration, as contrasted with nonprobate dispositions — such as life insurance, *joint ownership*, employee death benefits, survivor annuities, and *trusts* — which are not subject to estate administration (and are sometimes called the nonprobate estate). Probate avoidance, then, involves use of these nonprobate methods of transferring wealth. (4) A probate court is a court dealing with the matters referred to above, plus testamentary trusts and (sometimes) *guardianships.* A court of probate jurisdiction is a court of general jurisdiction authorized to handle probate matters. See also *Uniform Probate Code.*

Real property. Land, buildings, fixtures, and interests therein. For some purposes and in some jurisdictions, leases, *terms for years*, and rights to extract or exploit minerals may be classified as realty.

Remainder. (1) A *future interest* in property that comes into possession or enjoyment upon the expiration of a prior interest, such as a *life estate.* See also *vested.* (2) In this book, in order to avoid "remainderman," the word "remainder" refers to a person owning a remainder interest.

Residue. In connection with a *will*, this term refers to the property in the probate *estate* that remains after *bequests* and *devises* of specific sums of money and specifically described property. It is sometimes called the "residuary estate." A "residuary bequest" is a provision in a will that disposes of the residue to one or more persons. A "residuary legatee" is a person designated to receive all or part of a residuary bequest. In most cases the residuary legatees are the primary *beneficiaries* of an estate.

Resulting trust. A "trust" imposed by law, requiring only the conveyance of property. A "purchase money" resulting trust arises by inference when a purchaser of real or personal property has title placed in the name of another party. Here the impression by a court of a resulting trust means that the other party must convey to the purchaser upon demand. The inference is negated if the grantee is a close relative of the purchaser or if there was evidence that a gift was intended. A resulting trust also arises if a conventional (express) *trust* fails, is declared void, or terminates, without direction on the part of the creator of the trust as to the disposition of the property: The trustee of the trust is said to "hold upon resulting trust" for the creator of the trust or his successors in interest — that is, he must convey the property to them and not keep the trust property himself. In operation, this type of resulting trust is the same as an implied *reversion*.

Reversion. That interest in property — usually in trust — which the transferor retains or has, in herself and her *successors in interest*, by virtue of transferring interests whose aggregate maximum duration is theoretically shorter than that of the interest that she had to begin with. An "express reversion" is one expressly retained, as where A transfers land to B for life, then to A and her heirs. An "implied reversion" exists where a transferor gives away less than she has. For example, if A transfers land to B for life, then to B's surviving children, A has an implied reversion because there may be no children of B surviving at B's death. See also *resulting trust*.

Rule Against Perpetuities. The rule of property law which, in its classic formulation, states that no *interest* in property is valid unless it must *vest*, if at all, within lives in being plus 21 years.

Successors in interest. The persons who own, or will own, property (or an *interest* therein) as the result of any combination of transfers by *gift, bequest, devise, inheritance*, or purchase — no matter how many such transfers are involved — starting with the original owner. Thus, the creator of a trust retaining a *reversion*, or a person holding a *remainder* or *executory interest*, can transfer the reversion, remainder, or executory interest by gift, sale, bequest, etc., and his transferee(s) can do the same, and so on, until the interest finally comes into possession, fails, or expires according to its terms. A sentence like "After the expiration of B's life estate the property will pass to C or his successor in interest" means that, when B dies, the property passes to C personally, if alive, or if C is dead or has otherwise disposed of the remainder, to those persons who then own it.

Tenancy (in common, by the entirety). See *joint ownership*.

Term for years. A present or future *interest* in which the duration of possession or enjoyment is described in terms of a fixed period of time. An example is a deed by A to B for five years, then to C and his heirs. A term for years in which the transferor has a *reversion* and the person in possession pays consideration for the right of possession is essentially a "lease." A leasehold is a non-freehold estate.

Testamentary. By way of a "testament," which is a synonym for *will* but implying that the property disposed of is *personal property*. A "testamentary disposition" is a transfer effectuated through a will, and a "testamentary *trust*" is a trust created by a will, as distinguished from an *inter vivos* trust.

Testate. Describes the situation where a decedent dies with a valid *will*; he is said to die "testate."

Testator. A person who dies *testate*.

Trust. Denotes a *fiduciary* relationship arising out of an expression of intent to create a trust. (The "intent" aspect distinguishes such "express" trusts from *constructive trusts* and *resulting trusts*, which are both essentially remedial devices imposed by courts.) An express trust can be created by will (a testamentary trust), *inter vivos* transfer to the trustee, or declaration of trust (declaring oneself as trustee). The fiduciary, called the "trustee," has legal title to the property in the trust (the trust *res* or, often, the "trust *estate*"), which he holds for the benefit of the *beneficiaries.* See also *administration.* The person creating the trust is often referred to as the "grantor" or "settlor," particularly in the case of *inter vivos* trusts. The grantor (settlor) is not precluded from being trustee himself. But to talk of a transfer in trust in such a case is rather awkward; instead, it is said that the grantor (settlor) has made a "declaration of trust." A grantor (settlor) can be a beneficiary of the trust, but the same person cannot create the trust, be sole beneficiary of the trust, *and* be sole trustee, all at the same time.

Uniform Probate Code. A model body of statutory provisions covering the law of *wills, inheritance,* and *estate administration.* First approved by the National Conference of Commissioners on Uniform State Laws (NCUSL), and by the American Bar Association, in 1969, and subsequently revived. Versions of the UPC have been adopted in whole or in part in several states (mostly in the Midwest and mountain West, plus Alaska and Hawaii), and has influenced law reform in some other states as well.

Uniform Trust Code. Another model code produced by NCUSL covering the law of express *trusts.*

Unitrust. A trust that pays a fixed percentage of the corpus, revalued annually, to the current beneficiary, who is said to have a "unitrust interest."

Vested. A vested *future interest* is one which will take effect in possession or enjoyment upon the expiration of prior interests and is subject to no contingency (as far as possession or enjoyment is concerned) other than the expiration of such prior interests. A future interest, the possession or enjoyment of which is contingent upon something other than (or in addition to) the expiration of a prior interest, is a *contingent interest. Executory interests* can never be vested in the technical sense; by definition they arise upon contingencies and cut off vested interests (that is, the prior interests do not expire). *Remainders* can be vested or contingent. *Reversions* are necessarily vested, since they take in possession, by definition, only upon the expiration of prior interests.

Ward. A person (usually a minor) subject to a *guardianship.*

Will. The expression of a decedent's intent as to the disposition of property by *bequest* and *devise,* the *administration* of her *estate,* the appointment of a *personal representative* to administer said estate, and the appointment of a *guardian* over her minor children, to take effect upon her death. A will has no operative effect prior to death — it is said to be "ambulatory" — and, indeed, it has no effect after death unless it is admitted to *probate.* The appointment of the personal representative and guardians is also subject to court approval independently of admitting the will to probate. See also *testamentary.*

Note the frequent parallelism in legal terminology: "devise and bequeath," "descent and distribution," "heirs and next of kin," "will and testament," and "executor and administrator." In modern dispositive-instrument (will, deed, and trust) drafting, such duplication is not necessary. It is sufficient in a will to say "I give my property to B," to refer to both bequests and devises as "bequests," and to make reference to "my personal representative." Accordingly, in this book profuse and duplicative terminology will be avoided. "Bequest" refers to both devises and bequests, "legatee" refers to recipients of devises and bequests, "heirs" denotes both heirs and next of kin, "personal representative" is used instead of "executor or administrator," and so on. Purely as a convention, the term "grantor" (rather than "settlor") is the term usually used to refer to the creator of an *inter vivos* trust.

Certain other terms that you might recall from property law, such as "fee tail," "fee simple determinable," and "possibility of reverter," do not appear in the glossary, partly because they do not play a significant role in modern estate planning, and partly because no particular purpose would be served by dealing with them at this time.

Some of the more relevant of the foregoing concepts to federal transfer taxation can be fleshed out. Suppose A deeds property to "B and his heirs," the phrase "and his heirs" merely defines the *quality* of B's estate: B has an estate in fee simple. B's heirs individually or collectively do not possess any "future interest" in the property. To be sure, an heir of B may in fact end up with the property by inheritance or otherwise, but he will take from B (or a successor in interest to B), not from A. Having an estate in fee simple, B can dispose of his interest in any way and to anybody that he desires by bequest, gift or sale, leaving his heirs empty-handed if he so decides. In other words, the phrase "B and his heirs" really means "B." (As a legal convention of fixed and long-standing meaning, the expression "and his heirs" is the one used in conveyancing.) By way of legal jargon, the words "and his heirs" are "words of limitation" — (again) describing the quality of B's estate — just as "for life" describes the quality of B's interest in "to B for life." Accordingly, for the sake of brevity, the phrase "and his heirs" will not be used to describe an estate in fee simple absolute. A bequest "to B" is sufficient to denote a fee simple interest in B.

The word "heirs" can also be used to describe the persons who own a future interest. Thus, if A conveys to "B for life, then to the heirs of C," C's heirs own a remainder interest, which is acquired from A immediately upon A's conveyance. Jargon again: "Heirs" are here used as "words of purchase"; that is, to denote the persons who have an interest. As is the case with all future interests, C's heirs acquire their remainder interest from A at the time of A's conveyance. By definition, a future interest is a *present right* to future possession or enjoyment. The heirs of C acquire nothing from C, who has no interest at all under this conveyance, and nothing from B, whose life interest (also acquired from A) expires at B's death.

To generalize, the holders of successive future interests do not acquire property from each other, but rather acquire "interests" from the original transferor. Interests for life or a term of years will expire. Remainder interests may be vested or contingent, and vested remainders may come into possession or not.

The foregoing has relevance to the federal transfer taxes. The estate tax applies to transfers by bequest or inheritance (as well as to certain *inter vivos* transfers that take effect at the transferor's death), but not to shifts in enjoyment that occur by reason of the succession of future interests. However, the latter may trigger the generation-skipping tax.

The distinction between contingent and vested remainder interests is also relevant to the transfer taxes. Vesting is not the same as "coming into possession." An interest is vested in a person if the person's *ownership* of the interest cannot be defeated by a condition precedent. Thus, a transfer to "B for life, remainder to C and her heirs" gives B a life estate and C a vested remainder. The *ownership* by C of this remainder interest is not conditioned on C outliving B (only C's *possession* is so contingent). C's vested remainder can be assigned and is descendible. Thus, if C predeceases B, C's remainder passes by bequest or inheritance, and is an asset that can be reached by the creditors of C's estate. By way of contrast, a transfer to "B for life, remainder to C if C survives B, but if C does not survive B then to D and her heirs," creates alternate contingent remainders in both C and D. The interest of C is conditioned on surviving B, and the interest of D is conditioned on C predeceasing B. If, after the initial transfer, C in fact predeceases B, C's interest expires, and D's interest vests. Alternatively, if (after the initial transfer) D predeceases both B and C, then D's contingent remainder descends to his legatees or heirs, because the event that would defeat it (C surviving B) has not yet occurred.

A current issue in the law of trusts and future interests is what language is required to create a vested remainder. At common law, there has been a constructional preference for vested interests. Thus, at common law, a transfer to "B for life, remainder to C" gives B a life estate and C a vested remainder. However, vested remainder interests are now somewhat disfavored in estate planning circles precisely because they (1) descend (perhaps inadvertently) to residual legatees and heirs, (2) are subject to the creditors of C's estate, and (3) are included in C's gross estate for estate tax purposes. The statutory law of certain states now treats a remainder "to C" as a remainder that is contingent on C surviving B, and, if C does not survive B then to the then living descendants of C as alternate contingent remainders (but, if there are no such living descendants, reversion to the settlor's successors in interest).[4] A remainder interest contingent on C's surviving B passes (if C predeceases B) to the alternate contingent remainders (or holders of the settlor's reversionary interest) from the settlor (not from C), and is neither subject to the creditors of C's estate nor is included in C's gross estate.

Nevertheless, the possible effect of state law on the characterization of remainder interests is beyond the scope of a book on wealth transfer taxation. Accordingly, examples and problems in this book should be construed to be "after" the application of applicable state law. Thus, an example or problem that refers to a remainder "to C" should be viewed as giving C a vested remainder in fee simple after the application of applicable state law.

Unless otherwise provided by law or the instrument of transfer (for example, under a "spendthrift" clause in a trust), present and future interests are freely

---

4. See §2-707 of the Uniform Probate Code (UPC).

alienable by gift, bequest, inheritance, pledge as collateral, and sale. The sole fact that an interest is "contingent" instead of "vested" is no curb on its alienability. (However, an interest that is contingent on one's own survival cannot be bequeathed or passed to one's heirs.) Of course, the contingencies may have a profound effect upon the *value* of an interest (what a potential buyer would be willing to pay for it). Even in the absence of contingencies, the market for future interests is very thin, and values are likely to be heavily discounted.

In modern estate planning, future interests are predominantly used in the context of trusts. "Legal" future interests (not in trust) posit conveyancing problems, because all holders of legal present and future interests must join in any transfer of the underlying property. In contrast, the trustee of a trust, conveniently, has the sole capacity to transfer title to the trust assets.

An instrument purporting to create a legal (i.e., non-trust) future interest may well raise problems having to do with the precise contours of the interest. For example, does the governing instrument give the life tenant the power to consume, give away, mortgage, or sell the property? A trust might also raise problems, such as what are the duties and powers of the trustee *vis-à-vis* the beneficiaries, but the powers of trustees (and beneficiaries) to sell and dispose of the property (and interests therein) are usually clearly set out under the terms of the trust and/or state law. Also, while both legal life tenants and trustees owe implied duties to remainders and beneficiaries respectively, those of the trustee are largely spelled out by the trust and if not, are supplied by state law, with which trustees are usually familiar. In contrast, holders of legal interests rarely are aware of their potential liabilities.

Therefore, following contemporary practice, most of the problems and examples in this book involving future interests explicitly refer, or should be deemed to refer, to trusts (rather than to legal future interests).

PROBLEMS

1. Describe the various interests involved in the following transfers, both in terms of jargon and in terms of when and who will derive what possession or enjoyment:
   a. A deeds Blackacre to B for life, then to C and his heirs. Can C make a gift or bequest of an interest in Blackacre? Can an heir of C make a gift or bequest of an interest in Blackacre?
   b. Same as item a except that the phrase "and his heirs" is omitted.
   c. A transfers cash and securities to the X Bank, as trustee, income to be paid to B for life, at which time the trust will terminate and the trust property be distributed, free of the trust, to C if living and if not to D if living.
2. a. Suppose that A by *inter vivos* instrument creates a trust, income to B for life, remainder to C. At the commencement of the trust, A transfers stocks and bonds to the trust. During B's lifetime, the trust receives dividends and interest; also, stocks and bonds are sold, resulting in capital gains and losses, and the proceeds are reinvested in other securities. Who, do you suppose,

gets what and when? (Precise answers are given by the state's version of the Uniform Principal and Income Act, but this does not have to be consulted to answer this problem.) What happens if the trustee fails to pay the income to B or fails to distribute the trust estate to the person(s) holding the remainder interest upon B's death? Are the results the same if A is trustee?

b. What if, instead, the trustee is given the discretion to pay income to B or accumulate income (and add it to corpus)? Who benefits (and loses) from an accumulation of income? A wholly discretionary power is subject to the fiduciary duty of good faith but not that of "impartiality" among beneficiaries. Thus, neither B nor C can enjoin the trustee's exercise of good faith discretion. Does the trustee in this case possess a "power of appointment?"

§1.2. Review of Basic Income Tax Concepts Relating to Gratuitous Transfers

Only those aspects of the federal income tax that bear on gratuitous transfers are discussed herein. The material below is intended primarily as a review of material that might have been covered in a basic income tax course. Additional income tax material will be presented from time to time hereafter.

A. Gratuitous Receipts

The following describes the basic income tax consequences of gratuitous transfers themselves.

1. Income Exclusions

The receipt of a gratuitous transfer is excludible from gross income under §102(a).

A parallel provision is §101(a), which excludes from gross income the proceeds of life insurance received by a beneficiary by reason of the insured's death. Life insurance proceeds are a "contractual" bequest effectuated through the medium of a third party (the insurance company).

The acquisition of a future interest or survivorship interest by gratuitous receipt is not only excludible, but it is also the case (as a broad generalization) that the subsequent vesting, coming into possession, expiration, or loss of such interest or right is not considered a realization event that can give rise to gain or loss to the holder of such interest or right.

2. Nondeductibility of Gifts

Gratuitous transfers by individuals are, in general, nondeductible personal and family expenses under §262. The notion that a decedent could obtain a deduction for a bequest is incoherent, since a taxpayer's income tax existence terminates at the moment of death.

Thus, as a general proposition, the "principal" of a gratuitous transfer is taxed only once under the federal income tax: to the transferor (by not being deductible), but not to the transferee.

3. *Basis of Transferee*

When property is transferred by gift or bequest, the gratuitous transferor (donor or decedent) generally does not realize gain or loss by reason of having disposed of the property. So, if gift or death is not a realization event, the issue then becomes that of whether such difference (the built-in gain or loss that had accrued to the transferor) disappears from the income tax system (by means of giving the transferee a fair-market-value-at-transfer basis), or whether it is passed along to the transferee (by carrying the transferor's basis over to the transferee). Under current law, the answer to this question is complicated indeed.

Since the beginning of the income tax, the rule, currently found in §1014, for property transferred at death is that such property obtains a basis equal to its fair market value on the "estate tax valuation date" which, in the vast majority of cases, is the date of the decedent's death. The §1014 basis rule applies not only to property included in the decedent's probate estate but also to almost all property transferred by the decedent during life which is included in the decedent's gross estate for estate tax purposes (e.g., property in a revocable trust created by the decedent). See §1014(b). Of course, §1014 attaches only at and after the decedent's death.

This §1014 basis rule, when combined with the principle that gains and losses are not reckoned until "realized," operates to permanently exclude from income tax unrealized gains accrued up to death and to cause unrealized losses to vanish from the income tax.

An extremely important rule for holders of community property (described in the glossary, supra) is §1014(b)(6), which applies the rule of §1014 not only to the decedent's property but also to the surviving spouse's share of the community property!

A potential tax-avoidance scheme would be to give appreciated property to a person just prior to the latter's death with the understanding that such person will bequeath the property back to the original owner. To prevent the original owner from obtaining a "laundered" stepped-up basis in this fashion, Congress enacted §1014(e). That section holds that, if a donor gives appreciated property to a decedent within one year of the latter's death and the donor (or the donor's spouse) receives the property back by bequest (etc.), the donor's basis shall be the same as the decedent's basis at the moment just prior to the decedent's death.

The §1015 basis rule for in-kind *inter vivos* gifts, in contrast to that of §1014, sets forth a general rule that the donee's basis shall be the same as the donor's basis. Section 1015 was enacted so that gains could not be "washed out" of the income tax system by means of gifts of appreciated property among family members. Thus, for appreciated property, the donor's basis (and hence the donor's built-in gain), is passed on to the donee.

However, this "carryover basis" rule for gifts is modified in the situation involving gifts of property with built-in losses; that is, where the value at the time of gift was lower than the donor's adjusted basis. The "except" clause of the first sentence of §1015(a) states that the donee's basis is the fair market value at the time of gift (rather than the donor's basis) "for the purpose of determining loss" (to the *donee*). Thus, if the donee after receiving the gift sells the asset for less than the fair market value at the time of gift, the donee will have a loss even if the donee's basis is the fair market value at the time of gift, and hence the donee's basis *is* such value. The purpose of this rule is to prevent the shifting of a loss to a high-bracket donee.

Section 1015(a) fails to explicitly provide for the situation where the amount realized by the donee (in a post-gift realization event) is higher than the fair market value at the time of gift but lower than the donor's adjusted basis. If the donee were given a "value" basis, then the donee would have a gain, but the "except" clause mandating a value basis applies only for determining loss. Yet, if the donee were to take the donor's basis, then the donee would indeed have a loss, which would throw the donee back into the value basis rule, but that would result in the donee having gain. Around and around we go. This conundrum is resolved by the example following Reg. §1.1015-1(a)(2): The donee's basis must equal the amount realized, so as to produce neither gain nor loss.

If (in the case of a gift with a built-in loss) the amount realized by the donee in a post-gift realization event is greater than the donor's basis, then the general carryover-basis rule applies, since the donee in that situation necessarily has a gain.

Under §1015(d)(6), the donee obtains an increase in basis equal to the gift tax, if any, which is allocable to any unrealized appreciation in the property (excess of value over donor's adjusted basis) at the time of gift. If the gift was made before 1977, the adjustment equals the entire gift tax on the property. In neither case, however, can the adjustment increase the basis to an amount greater than the value of the property at the time of gift. In other words, the adjustment is only available, if at all, for gifts of appreciated property.

Section 1015 does not apply to gifts between husband and wife. In that case, a straight carryover basis rule applies, with no adjustments. See §1041(b).

B. *Post-Transfer Income: Trusts and Beneficiaries*

Although gratuitous transfers received are excluded from the gross income of a recipient under §102(a), it is provided in §102(b) that income arising subsequent to the receipt of any excludible gratuitous transfer is not covered by the §102(a) exclusion. Thus, such income is includible by the party who owns the property (unless an exclusion other than §102 comes into play). Section 101 follows a similar scheme: Only the payable-on-death amount is excluded. Subsequent accretions are includible income.

The rule that post-transfer income is generally taxable poses the problem of how to tax trusts. Under §1(e), a trust is treated as a separate taxpaying entity, with its own rate schedule for trust taxable income. It is clear that, where a gift or bequest is made to a trust, the initial receipt is tax-free to the estate or trust. But a trust exists only to serve its beneficiaries, so the problem is then raised whether the post-transfer income of a trust should be taxed to the trust or to the beneficiaries. In the case of *inter vivos* trusts, the further issue arises of whether the post-transfer income might, at least in some cases, be attributed to the grantor (rather than to the trust or its beneficiaries). These issues are dealt with by the rules of Subchapter J of the Code (§§641-692).

To make a long story short, the grantor of an *inter vivos* trust is taxed on the trust income for so long as the trust is revocable by him, for so long as he possesses a reversionary interest worth more than 5 percent, for so long as the trust income or corpus can be distributed to him, or for so long as he retains certain powers over the administration or enjoyment of the trust. See §§671-677 (referred to as the "grantor trust rules").

If the grantor is not treated as the owner of the trust under the grantor trust rules, then the trust's taxable income is attributable to the trust or beneficiaries according to the following principles. First, if a beneficiary can obtain the trust corpus (or income) on demand, the trust income is attributable to such beneficiary. See §678. Such a trust is known as a "beneficiary-owned trust."

Second, if (as is usually the case) §678 does *not* apply, the trust taxable income is computed at the trust level in the same manner as for an individual, but the trust obtains a deduction equal to the amount of distributions made during the year to beneficiaries (but the deduction cannot decrease the trust's taxable income below zero). See §§642, 643, 651, and 661. The beneficiaries receiving distributions have gross income equal to the deductible distributions. See §§652 and 662. Thus, crudely speaking, trust taxable income (to the extent thereof) is allocated to beneficiaries receiving distributions, and undistributed current income ("accumulated income") is taxed to the trust under the §1(e) rate schedule. A trust taxed in this fashion on undistributed income is commonly referred to as a "Subchapter J trust." The §1(e) rate schedule is "highly compressed," meaning that taxable income attributed to the trust (or estate) rises very quickly to higher and higher marginal rate brackets. Thus, it is generally undesirable that significant amounts of income be attributed to a trust.

The foregoing is only a very rough outline of the income taxation of trusts. The general idea is that the trust is treated initially as an "accounting entity" that computes taxable income on an annual basis, and that this income is then apportioned on an annual basis among the grantor (if living), the trust as a taxable entity, and the individual beneficiaries according to various rules. The system is basically an income-allocation mechanism, and it follows that no "new" income comes into existence by reason of a trust, but neither does income disappear from the system by reason of using a trust (except for the modest "personal exemption" for trusts). In addition to deciding "which taxpayer(s)" are taxed on trust income, Subchapter J also controls as to *when* such income must be reported and what the "character" is of such income (as capital gains, ordinary income, tax-exempt income, foreign-source income, etc.). The details of the income taxation of trusts, grantors, and beneficiaries are described later in this book.

C. The Estate as an Income Tax Entity

An estate is an income tax "person" that is (generally) treated like a trust for income tax purposes. In general, the income tax estate commences on the death of the decedent and continues for the period of estate administration, and the property constituting the income tax estate is generally the property that is subject to estate administration (as opposed to nonprobate property). The property acquired by the estate from the decedent (the probate estate) is excluded from the estate's gross income under §102(a), but income arising after the decedent's death is taxable to one or more taxpayers according to the mandate of §102(b).

Since the "grantor" of the estate is, by definition, dead, the income tax estate cannot be subject to the grantor trust rules, nor can it be treated as a beneficiary-owned trust. In other words, the income tax estate is always treated as a "Subchapter J trust" with respect to income arising after death. Distributions from the estate in satisfaction of legacies would initially be treated as "distributions" for income tax purposes, which would be deductible by the estate (but not in excess of the taxable income therefrom) and (to the same extent as deductible by the estate) includible by the legatees. However, it is provided by §663(a)(1) that distributions in satisfaction of specific property bequests and of fixed dollar bequests (payable in no more than three installments) are not treated as "distributions" for estate income tax purposes. Thus, only distributions in satisfaction of residual bequests and of inheritances are treated as "distributions" for estate income tax purposes. As can be seen, the income tax treatment of an estate is affected by the drafting of the will, specifically, whether there are significant specific property bequests and fixed dollar bequests.

An estate, as an income tax entity, is subject to the highly compressed §1(e) rate schedule.

The income taxation of estates is discussed in greater detail in §4.3. In conclusion, it is crucial to realize that there is an "estate income tax" that is wholly separate from any estate tax (or other death or succession tax). Estate personal representatives have a duty not only to comply with any estate tax but also with any estate income tax.

PROBLEMS

1. Suppose D has securities that cost $40,000 and are now worth $100,000.
    a. Can D shift the built-in gain to a lower-bracket donee?
    b. Is it an even better plan to hold onto this property until D's death?
2. Suppose instead that D had paid $130,000 for the securities now worth $100,000.
    a. Can D shift the potential loss to a higher-bracket donee?
    b. Is holding onto the securities until death a good idea?
    c. What other possibility exists?
3. Suppose D creates an *inter vivos* trust in early 2009 with the securities (worth $100,000) referred to above. The trust names the X Bank as trustee and provides that income is to be paid to B or accumulated in the trustee's discretion, and upon B's death the trust is to terminate with the assets being distributed to C. In the remainder of 2009, the trust receives $7,000 of interest

and pays the trustee a commission of $1,000, and $2,000 is distributed to B. Who is taxed on how much if, in the alternative:

    a.   the trust is revocable by D (see §676);

    b.   the trust is irrevocable, and the trust provides that C can appoint the trust corpus to himself, free of any trust, by delivering a written request to the trustee (see §678); or

    c.   the trust is irrevocable, but C has no such power?

4. a.   Suppose T dies early in 2009, and his will leaves 100 shares of IBM stock to B, $10,000 to C, and the residue to R. During the rest of 2009, the estate has net income from interest and dividends of $40,000 and pays $8,000 of deductible expenses. Also in 2009, T's personal representative distributes the 100 IBM shares (worth $22,000) to B, the $10,000 to C, and $12,000 to R. What income tax results to the various parties?

    b.   Are the results in (a) optimal? What could T's personal representative have done to improve such results?

    c.   How might the income tax rules affect the drafting of wills? Consider especially the situation where the client desires to leave most or all of her property to one individual.

§1.3. Looking at the Big Picture

The federal transfer taxes are a component of the larger federal tax system. It is legitimate to ask if the existing form of wealth transfer taxes is a necessary or appropriate component of the system.

A. *Relation of the Transfer Taxes to the Income Tax*

The federal transfer taxes (gift, estate, and generation-skipping taxes) are taxes *on the value of property at the time of gratuitous transfer.* Thus, "basis" for income tax purposes is wholly irrelevant under the federal transfer taxes. In general, the federal transfer taxes (unlike the income tax) are imposed "on" the transferor, not the recipient, of gratuitous transfers.

Thus, the federal transfer taxes constitute a wholly separate tax system apart from the federal income tax. In general, the transfer tax system by definition is a tax on "capital" (previously taxed income). For example, wages, interest, dividends, rents, and royalties received before death are subject to income tax and, to the extent not consumed or wasted, subsequently to transfer tax. *It is, emphatically, not a legitimate argument to say that an item should be excluded from the federal transfer taxes just because the item was included in the income tax base.*

Thus, it initially appears that gratuitous transfers are taxed twice, once under the income tax and (at least) once under the transfer taxes. However, there are two main exceptions to the notion that gratuitous transfers are taxed twice. First, unrealized gains at death avoid the income tax thanks to §1014 (as does other excluded income). Second, the federal transfer taxes only reach a fraction of total gratuitously transferred wealth because of very generous exemptions, exclusions, and deductions from the tax base. These "gaps" do not coincide. Thus, much wealth avoids both taxes, and other wealth is indeed subject to both taxes.

B. *Typology of Wealth (Transfer) Taxes*

A wealth transfer tax may be viewed as a kind of proxy for taxing wealth itself. A pure wealth tax (as opposed to a wealth transfer tax) is a tax, levied periodically, on the value of property owned by the taxpayer. Most U.S. states impose taxes on wealth in the form of real property, and some impose taxes on various categories of tangible or intangible personal property. However, although wealth taxes have been used in the U.S. states as well as in other countries, a federal wealth tax in the U.S. is considered by most commentators to be a "direct tax" that would be unconstitutional *unless apportioned among the states in accordance with population*. Since apportionment of a wealth tax according to population is not feasible (unless the states were assessed directly by the federal government), a federal wealth tax has never gotten beyond the stage of abstract discussion (although apportioned federal real property taxes were essayed a few times in the early days of the Republic).

Wealth *transfer* taxes have passed constitutional muster as "indirect taxes" that are not subject to the apportionment requirement. In the abstract, a tax on transfers of wealth can take any of four forms:

(1) Integration with the income tax by including the receipt of gifts and bequests in the "income" of the recipient, contrary to present §102(a). Presumably, transfers made would continue to be nondeductible personal or family expenditures under §262. Otherwise, high-bracket transferors could shift "income" to low-bracket transferees.

(2) An *inheritance* tax, which applies a rate schedule to the aggregate bequests received by an individual from a *given* decedent. An inheritance tax is sort of like a separate income tax with a separate exemption and rate structure for a single type of income received in a single year, but it differs from an income tax in that the tax is payable by the estate. (Nevertheless, the tax "on" a bequest may well be taken out of the bequest, so that the burden of the tax may be born by the legatee.) An inheritance tax provides some tax incentive for the dispersion of wealth by the testator, since typically there are different rate schedules applicable to different categories of recipients, with the lowest rate schedule being applicable to bequests and inheritances received by "near" legatees such as spouses and children, a somewhat steeper rate schedule being applicable to those received by lineal descendents other than children, and the steepest rate schedule being reserved for those received by more remote relatives. The inheritance tax was the traditional form of state death taxation, and federal inheritance taxes were enacted occasionally in the nineteenth century to help finance various wars.

(3) An *accessions* tax (which is not in force in any state) would be a tax under a progressive rate schedule on the *cumulative* gratuitous transfers (*including gifts*) *received* over the recipient's lifetime from any and every donor and decedent.

(4) A tax, separate from other taxes, on the *transfer* (as opposed to the receipt) of wealth. The federal and state gift, estate, and generation-skipping taxes fall into this category. Under a typical estate tax, including the federal estate tax, the cumulative estate transfers of a decedent are subject to a progressive rate schedule. Thus, there is no dispersal-of-wealth incentive, except that bequests to spouses and charities can be favored by rendering such transfers deductible from the tax base. A gift tax is typically a tax on the cumulative lifetime gifts of a donor, with the tax being paid by the donor. The gift tax may be "integrated" with the estate tax, which is the case with the federal estate and gift taxes. Here, the tax base is the cumulative *inter vivos* and testamentary transfers of a donor-decedent.

The issue of tax base and rates must not be confused with the issue of who bears the economic burden of the tax. The donor usually pays the gift tax, and an estate or inheritance tax is usually paid out of the decedent's estate prior to distribution of bequests and inheritances. However, the decedent can usually allocate ("apportion") the tax among the various estate transfers in any way he or she desires, so long as such desire is set forth in his or her will. If such desire is not expressed in the will, or if there is no will, then state law (and to a minor degree federal law) will control the apportionment of taxes. It is only under an accessions tax or an inclusion-in-income system that the tax figured with respect to a gift or bequest will necessarily be borne in full by the recipient thereof.

C. Should the Federal Transfer Taxes Be Retained?

Although the federal transfer taxes have been around since 1916 (in the case of the estate tax), the possible repeal of them became a hot political issue during the presidency of George W. Bush (2001-2009). Wealth transfer taxation can be analyzed (a) on its own terms, (b) in relation to the larger scheme of federal taxation, and (c) in relation to the possible alternative modes of taxing wealth transfers discussed above. Taxes in general are commonly evaluated according to four "clusters" of norms, namely, (1) fairness norms, (2) norms relating to economic efficiency (meaning minimal distortion of decisions), (3) norms relating to social welfare (which includes the issue of distribution of wealth within society), and (4) "legal" norms, such as clean line-drawing, doctrinal coherence, and the like. Since taxes are a "given" in modern society, the issue is basically how well wealth transfer taxes compare to other kinds of taxes.

The issue of the optimal form of wealth transfer tax is discussed below.

Gerald Jantscher, Aims of Death Taxation

In *Death, Taxes and Family Property* (Edward Halbach, ed.) (1977)

Death Taxes as a Source of Revenue

It is unlikely that the sovereigns who imposed the earliest death taxes puzzled for long over the purpose of the tax. They required revenue and an inheritance tax was a convenient way of obtaining it. These authorities lacked the many alternative sources of revenue that are available to modern authorities. This justification for death taxation is clearly of no relevance today. The modern state has many alternatives to death and gift taxation. Indeed, in view of the small proportion of total receipts that these taxes contribute and the high cost of administering them, it is arguable that, if the taxes were only imposed to raise revenue, they ought to be abolished. In the U.S. the yield of the federal estate and gift taxes is not negligible [about $28 billion in fiscal year 2001, but only a little over 1.0 percent of total federal tax receipts]. The addition of just one percentage point to the full range of federal individual income tax rates would add an even larger sum to income tax receipts, at what presumably would be a minor addition to administrative and compliance costs.

A more sophisticated version of the revenue argument holds that even though these taxes may not be strictly necessary as revenue sources, they are a less costly way of raising [the given] revenue than the federal income tax if we define cost broadly enough to include not only administrative and compliance costs but also the effects of the tax on [economic] efficiency, investment, and so forth.

Consider first the effects of such a substitution on the many persons who save primarily for other reasons than to leave property to their survivors. They may save as a precaution against sudden illness or loss of work, or to provide income for their retirement years, or to enjoy nonpecuniary benefits such as pride, position, and respect. Or they may be habitual savers, as incapable of refraining from accumulation as some men are of restraining their ambition. Or they may have large incomes but modest tastes and be unable to consume all that they earn. In the case of all these persons a change in death tax rates is not apt to affect economic behavior.

If an equal-yield tax on income were substituted for a death tax the cost of saving would increase. The addition of a few percentage points to the income tax rates means that forgoing $1 of current consumption would net savers less than before, say $1.90 after ten years instead of $2. At least some persons would respond to this fall in the rate of return by reducing their saving and increasing their consumption, much as consumers respond to a selective increase in prices by curtailing their purchases of the more costly goods.

Now consider the response among persons who are strongly motivated to save for their survivors. An increase in income tax rates would have the same effects on their willingness to save as it would among the rest of the population. But the accompanying reduction in death tax rates would affect them differently. Bequests would become less costly, in the sense that $1 of saving would purchase a larger after-tax estate. Some savers would respond by curtailing their consumption in order to take advantage of the new, lower cost of making bequests. It is possible, however, that other persons would respond by curtailing their saving, on the ground that the reduction in death tax rates would make it possible to leave a bequest of a certain size from a smaller estate.

[In sum,] a reduction in death tax rates and increase in income tax rates that left total tax collections unchanged would be likely to have only slight effects on incentives to save and invest. Recall that the federal estate and gift taxes now contribute [about 1 percent] of annual federal revenues. Even if saving were depressed by a small fraction of this sum — the largest effect conceivable — it would be of little consequence. If authorities decide that saving is too low, other instruments are available for increasing it.

Taxing Capital Periodically

Death taxes are sometimes said to serve the purpose of imposing a periodic tax on capital — of imposing a once-a-generation tax on family wealth. According to this view, a death tax substitutes for a regular tax on the wealth of the living, a net wealth tax of the kind imposed annually in a number of foreign countries. This rationale for death taxation is regarded by some proponents as especially relevant in the U.S., where the prospect of ever imposing a federal net wealth tax is clouded by the constitutional prohibition on unapportioned direct federal taxes.

Apart from the constitutional question that the [net wealth] tax raises in this country, its attraction is considerably diminished by the formidable difficulty of administering it well. Death taxes are much easier to impose. They are an established part of the American tax structure and the problems they raise are familiar to tax administrators and taxpayers. Administrative costs are kept low both by the infrequency with which the taxes are imposed and by the fact that they are levied at a time when a person's property must be inventoried anyway.

The incidence of a death tax is apt to differ appreciably from that of a net wealth tax. The equity argument for net wealth taxation supposes that a wealth tax would be borne primarily by the owner of the property and would force him to curtail his consumption, his saving, or his leisure. Death taxes normally have either no effect or only a small effect on the owners of wealth and are borne instead by the heirs.

Furthermore, a tax on wealth that is imposed only once and is intended to substitute for an annual wealth tax should bear some relation to the average wealth of the person over his lifetime. A death tax does not — witness a person who accumulates much wealth during his life, dissaves in retirement, and dies owning nothing, or a person who dies suddenly in late middle age when his savings are greatest.

Perhaps a death tax would be a more attractive substitute for a periodic tax on net wealth if it were viewed as an impost on the wealth of heirs instead of an impost on the wealth of decedents. That is, rather than tax the inherited wealth of heirs annually at low rates, the government might tax it just once — at high rates when they receive it. There is then some justification for taxing transfers to remote descendants more heavily than transfers to near descendants, on the basis that the former are on average younger than the latter and that the stream of annual [wealth] taxes that the former avoid is greater in value and must be replaced by a larger death tax. This formulation invites the objection that it is hardly feasible to substitute a single tax for a stream of annual taxes without knowing how long an heir will retain his property.

If death taxes are intended to tax wealth once a generation, there is a clear case for exempting transfers between spouses. Transfers to one's parents should be tax-free, or even occasion a refund of tax but transfers to grandchildren should be charged at double the rate that applies to transfers to children.

In conclusion, the differences of result between a death tax and a periodic tax on net wealth are so substantial that I do not believe a death tax can be supported as a substitute for the other. If my view is correct, rate discrimination according to age or generational differences between the transferor and transferee is uncalled for. There may still be good reasons for exempting transfers between spouses from tax but not on the ground that death taxes should be imposed [only] once a generation.

Taxing Windfalls

One of the most common features of the inheritance tax is the graduation of rates according to the relationship between the decedent and the recipient. This feature is normally explained by reference to the "windfall aim of death taxation." Recipients of windfalls are perceived to have more ability to pay a tax than other persons who receive payments of a regular or recurring nature. [But] the justification for placing a heavy tax on windfalls is not convincing. Is it appropriate to take account of expectations, even indirectly, in determining a person's tax liability?

Taxing Concentrations of Wealth

In my opinion the one aim of a death tax that stands scrutiny is its anti-concentration aim. The federal income tax also erodes concentrations of wealth, and a net wealth tax would too. But death taxes have a role to play. If many of the country's largest fortunes are composed in the main of inherited wealth, a properly designed, well administered, progressive tax on inheritances ought to be an effective means of leveling wealth.

The word "leveling" should not be taken literally. The limitations upon the effectiveness of the tax must be acknowledged at once. Not all wealth is inherited wealth, and even if all inheritances were confiscated by the state the distribution of wealth in American society would still be unequal, though presumably less unequal than it is today. Furthermore, not all of one's inheritance — for many persons, not even the most important part of it — is received in the form of property rights. A study by John Brittain found among other things that gifts and bequests "explained" (in the statistical sense) very little of the economic status of sons. Another kind of "inheritance" explained much more: the inheritance of family background or socioeconomic status. The children of well-to-do families generally were themselves well-to-do even before their parents died and they received their patrimony. The number of years of schooling that the children had completed also explained more of their status than the material bequests they received.

Brittain's work confirms that other factors than inheritance help to explain why some persons are wealthy and others are not; but the plain evidence of our senses tells us that the persistence of many of the largest American fortunes over several generations is chiefly due to the institution of inheritance and not to the socioeconomic background of the owners.

I take it for granted here that a more equal distribution of wealth is desirable. Tastes differ, of course, and others may disagree. Nearly everyone would agree, however, that some limit ought to be placed on the amount of wealth that one man should control. Unreasonable inequality poses a particular danger to societies that prize a high degree of individual freedom and that lack many of the legal restraints to be found in more tightly controlled societies that limit the harm in equality may do. The alternative to greater equality may be more regulation.

Economists quite naturally have focused on the economic costs of promoting equality: the trade-off between equality and efficiency. Death taxes receive high marks for being less burdensome than alternative instruments of redistribution, principally the income tax and a hypothetical wealth tax. [Also,] death taxes have the merit of assailing concentrations of inherited wealth but not concentrations of "self-made" wealth, a discrimination that would be clumsy to incorporate into an income tax or net wealth tax. Is the influence of inherited wealth more pernicious than that of newly-created wealth, and would the substitution therefore be undesirable? The question is usually answered affirmatively; but I wonder whether a thoughtful reconsideration would leave us quite so sure that it ought to be.

If the anti-concentration aim of death taxation is paramount, the increase in the federal estate tax exemption [level] that Congress enacted in 1976 [and 1981] was not unwarranted. Concentrations of even a few hundred thousand dollars may be presumed to threaten no one, whereas concentrations of millions may not.

The anti-concentration aim calls for a death tax tailored to the circumstances of the recipient rather than to those of the decedent. Moreover, the tax should take account of the heir's separate wealth. Bequests received by wealthy persons should be taxed more heavily than bequests received by less wealthy ones. In practice, discrimination of this kind would be denounced as inequitable. One man's inheritance would be taxed differently depending on whether he received it early in life, when his savings were small, or later in life, when his savings were large. Probably the most highly developed form of inheritance tax that is a practical possibility is the "accessions tax." Each gift or bequest would be taxed at a rate that depended not only on its size but also on the size of all previous gifts and bequests that the person received. Unlike an estate tax an accessions tax would also encourage testators to distribute their property widely. Although proponents of the tax like to emphasize this feature, I am skeptical whether at current levels of taxation many persons would react to it. Many wealthy persons already distribute their property widely, and may not be able to distribute it more widely without passing it outside their families.

Notwithstanding the observations made above, the idea that the federal transfer tax is justified as a partial proxy for a wealth tax seems to be gaining some currency under the guise of the "one tax per generation" notion. Thus, since 1954, the estate of a decedent obtains a credit under §2013 against the estate tax based upon the estate tax imposed upon the person who transferred property or cash to the decedent by bequest, if the two deaths are less than ten years apart. The credit is equal to 100 percent of the prior estate tax on the same property if the two deaths occur within two years of each other, but the percentage declines, in 20 percent steps, to zero where the deaths are separated by more than ten years. Since 1948, there has been a *marital deduction* for qualified transfers between spouses. Since 1981, the marital deduction has been equal to 100 percent of the value of such transfers. Thus, transfers between spouses are generally exempt from transfer tax. The federal generation-skipping tax assures that transfer tax cannot be avoided by trusts that benefit successive generations of beneficiaries. Even outright transfers are subject to generation-skipping tax (in addition to the gift or estate tax) just because the transferee occupies a generation two or more generations below that of the transferor. These features (apart from §2013) are laid out in more detail in the next chapter.

Then again, these generational features are somewhat crude. There is no "negative tax" or exemption for transfers to ancestors or other higher-generation individuals, and the generation-skipping tax just referred to is the same whether the transferee is a grandchild or great-grandchild. The age or generational status of the spouses is not taken into account under the marital deduction or the generation-skipping tax. Finally, the estate tax credit only applies to property recently subject to *estate* tax, not gift or generation-skipping tax, and the ten-year phaseout period under §2013 is quite short.

Returning to the issue of the desirability of the federal transfer taxes relative to other federal taxes, a main line of criticism is that the taxes are complex and avoidable by the savvy, and that (therefore) they impose very high transaction costs relative to any social benefits (such as curbing excessive accumulations of wealth). Whether the federal transfer taxes are effective in curbing undue wealth accumulations is partly a normative question (i.e., is that a good thing?) and partly an empirical question which is difficult to answer, because it cannot be easily determined how wealth accumulations would have played out in the absence of the transfer taxes. Similarly, there is insufficient data to answer the charge relating to high transaction costs. Whether the taxes can be easily avoided by the sophisticated perhaps suggests that the taxes might be reformed to eliminate whatever loopholes exist, rather than jettisoning the taxes completely. But what are the problems and where are the loopholes, and can they (and will they) be fixed? These questions cannot be reasonably evaluated without a detailed knowledge of the operation and doctrine of the federal transfer taxes. That's what the rest of this book is for.

QUESTION AND NOTE

1. a. Estate taxes are ultimately borne by the donor/decedent's successors as a group. The donor/decedent has a good deal of leeway in apportioning the tax burden within this group, because of the decedent's power to allocate the tax burden and to adjust the relative sizes of estate transfers. Under an accessions tax or income-inclusion scheme, the tax (being imposed in the first instance on the recipient) would be borne by the recipient.

b. An annual wealth tax would "eat up" the property (and destroy the tax base) if the rate were higher than a conservative income yield. Most wealth and property taxes in the world have maximum rates that do not exceed (about) 1 percent of the value of the property. A high-rate wealth or property tax would invite avoiding ownership of taxable wealth.

2. **a.** Jantscher summarily dismisses the "windfall" idea by implying that expectations should play no role in taxation. Many would disagree. Expectations play a role in an individual's economic choices, and also in one's choice of lifestyle. A tax on wealth transfers would not affect the behavior of legatees, who aren't put to much of a choice, except perhaps to take it easy. As to transferors, the effect of the prospect of a future tax on behavior is hard to evaluate. The future tax base depends on investment outcomes, longevity, and lifestyle choices. Motives for accumulations of wealth vary, but surely a main one is to provide for retirement and old age, not for bequests.

   b. An accession tax (or an income-inclusion approach) creates an incentive for wealth dispersal (which is not the same as redistribution), whereas an estate tax provides practically no such incentive. However, dispersal among one's children is already the norm in the U.S.

3. The weight of academic opinion is against double taxation of wealth transfers under the income tax, but favors a wealth transfer tax in addition to an income tax. This body of opinion also tends to favor significant exemptions in the wealth transfer tax, say, in the range of $1M-$10M. Is there any objective basis or criterion for deciding an appropriate exemption level? Since the decedent is dead, should the exemption level be for transferees (as would occur under an accessions tax)?

4. If the transfer taxes were repealed, the retention of §1014 would be hard to defend politically. The repeal of the estate tax scheduled for 2010 was linked to a replacement of §1014 by a (complex) carryover basis regime. A carryover basis regime creates a disincentive to sell on the part of the transferee. An alternative approach (actually adopted by Canada and a few other countries) is to deem gratuitous transfers to be sales (for fair market value) at the time of transfer under the income tax. Transferees would then acquire a "legitimate" fair-market-value-at-transfer basis. Spousal transfers could be subject to a carryover basis.

CHAPTER 2

Overview of the Federal Transfer Taxes

This chapter presents the core features of the federal transfer taxes, accompanied by explanations of how these features evolved to their present state.

§2.1. Prelude

Unfortunately, federal transfer tax law and doctrine cannot be adequately understood without an awareness of its history, both in the big-picture sense and in the doctrinal sense. The material immediately below deals with the big-picture history insofar as it relates to the scope of the federal transfer taxes; that is, what gratuitous transfers are covered by it.

Taxes on the succession of property at death have antecedents in ancient Egypt and the Roman Empire, and the feudal "relief" (see §1.1) was a mainstay of Medieval and Renaissance England. Starting in the early nineteenth century, inheritance taxes were in place in the various U.S. states. Inheritance taxes were also used by the federal government from time to time to finance wars. The 1864 and 1898 inheritance taxes, enacted to help finance the Civil and Spanish-American Wars, respectively, were each held to be constitutional as an excise (or "indirect" tax), which is not subject to any requirement of apportionment among the states in proportion to population.[1] In contrast, the 1894 income tax was held to be unconstitutional as a nonapportioned "direct" tax in the notorious case of *Pollock v. Farmers' Loan & Trust Co.*, 157 U.S. 429, *on rehearing*, 158 U.S. 601 (1895).

By 1913, Populist Democrats and Progressive Republicans succeeded in passing and ratifying the 16th Amendment, which freed any federal income tax from the apportionment requirement. A progressive income tax was enacted by Congress the same year in conjunction with a reduction in tariffs. As mentioned

---

1. *Scholey v. Rew*, 90 U.S. (23 Wall.) 331 (1874); *Knowlton v. Moore*, 178 U.S. 41 (1900).

earlier, the income tax enacted in 1913 — unlike some of the earlier income taxes — provided that gifts and bequests received are excluded from gross income. The possibility of a federal inheritance tax was discussed in connection with the consideration of the 1913 income tax bill, but such a tax was not included in the final bill that became law. Nevertheless, in 1916, as pressures leading to the involvement of the U.S. in World War I mounted, a federal estate tax (but not a gift tax) was enacted. This tax (as subsequently amended) is the present-day estate tax.

§2.2. The Federal Estate Tax

The current estate tax is Chapter 11 of the Code, and consists of §§2001-2210. Under current law, the amount subject to tax is called the "taxable estate" (gross estate less deductions). See §2051. The federal estate tax applies to the taxable estate, wherever located, of U.S. citizens and residents. Nonresident aliens are subject to estate tax only on property situated in the U.S. pursuant to §§2101-2108 and 2208-2209. A former U.S. citizen or resident claiming nonresident alien status (an "expatriate") who is subject to §877 (by reason of sufficient income or wealth, during the ten-year period following expatriation) is subject to U.S. estate tax on worldwide net wealth if she is present in the U.S. for more than 30 days in the year of death. See §877(g). This book does not further delve into the estate tax treatment of nonresident aliens.

A. Net Estate Subject to Tax

The original 1916 version of the estate tax applied a modestly progressive rate structure ranging from 1 to 10 percent against the tax base, called the "net estate." The net estate was defined as the gross estate less a flat "exemption" of $50,000 and less deductions for the decedent's debts, mortgages, funeral expenses, estate administration expenses, and casualty losses occurring during estate administration. These deductions (representing amounts that never pass to legatees or heirs) have been carried forward to the present, and are found in §§2053 and 2054, discussed in §4.2, infra.

There has long been an unlimited deduction for certain gross-estate-included property that passes to charity. This deduction allows testators, in effect, to avoid estate tax by leaving their entire net estate to charity. This deduction is found in current §2055.

Early versions of the estate tax contained a modest per-estate fixed dollar exemption, so that "small estates" would be relieved of paying any estate tax (or filing an estate tax return). Nevertheless, since the exemption operated as a deduction, it benefited all estates.

B. Rates and Exemptions

The rate schedule for the estate tax, to be applied against the taxable estate, became more highly progressive in the 1930s and 1940s, and peaked during World War II and its aftermath. The maximum marginal rate for decedents dying in 2009 is 45 percent, and 35 percent for those dying in 2010-2012. There is an election for decedents dying in 2010 who can opt for a 0 percent rate combined with the §1022 carryover basis rules.

Since 1976, the exemption (deduction) was replaced by a "free" tax credit that operates to exempt small and moderate estates from tax. The credit (against the tax on the taxable estate figured under the §2001(c) rate schedule) is an amount equal to the tax (using the same §2001(c) rate schedule) on a taxable estate equal to the "exemption equivalent," which was $1M for estates of decedents dying in 2002 and 2003 but was subsequently ratcheted upward to $3.5M for estates of decedents dying in 2009 and to $5M for estates of decedents dying in 2010-2012. The $5M exemption will be indexed for inflation after 2011. See §2010(c).

The difference between an exemption (deduction) and an exemption-equivalent credit can be illustrated by assuming that testator T died in 2002 with a taxable estate (before any exemption) of $1,250,000. If the system operated on the basis of a straight exemption of $1M, the $1M would be subtracted (deducted) from the tax base, leaving a taxable estate of $250,000, which would produce a tax of $70,800 under the §2001(c) rate schedule. Under the actual 2002 law, which conferred a credit equal to an exemption equivalent of $1M, the taxable estate is $1,250,000 (unreduced by any exemption), which produces an initial ("tentative") tax of $448,300 under the §2001(c) rate schedule, which is then credited by $345,800 (the §2001(c) tax amount on the exemption equivalent of $1M), resulting in a net tax of $102,500 (which is 41 percent of $250,000).

To summarize, the exemption method taxes the $250,000 at the bottom rates (averaging to 28 percent), whereas the credit method taxes the same $250,000 at 41 percent, which is the marginal rate for a tax base over $1M but not over $1.25M. *Where the exemption equivalent for the credit is high enough, the estate tax is essentially a flat rate tax on the taxable estate in excess of the exemption equivalent amount.* The credit cannot reduce the net tax below zero (i.e., cannot entitle the estate to a tax refund).

Under an estate tax (as opposed to an inheritance tax or an "accessions tax"), the tax is payable by (and out of) the estate itself, not by the legatees and/or heirs. See §2002 (stating that the estate tax is payable by the "executor," which is defined in §2203). Since the estate tax is not deductible in arriving at the taxable estate, the estate tax base is said to be "tax inclusive."

C. Augmented Gross Estate

The provisions defining the gross estate in the 1916 Act, which were modeled on state inheritance taxes, included in the gross estate not only the value of property owned by the decedent at death (present §2033), but also the value of property transferred during life (a) "in contemplation of death," (b) as a joint tenancy with right of survivorship, or (c) in a way that had a testamentary effect. The 1918 Act added a provision that included the proceeds of life insurance on policies taken out by the decedent. These provisions have evolved to what is now §§2035-2040 and 2042.

The transfer-in-contemplation-of-death provision has been greatly watered down. What's left of it is located in §2035. The "testamentary effect" idea has undergone gradual evolution over the years, and has been dispersed over Code

§§2036-2039. Thus, the following nonprobate items attributable to *inter vivos* transfers are currently included in the gross estate:

(1) the proceeds of insurance on the decedent's life where the insured owned the policy and made a gift of it within three years of death (§2035(a));

(2) gift tax paid (or owed) on gifts made within three years of death (§2035(b));

(3) certain *inter vivos* transfers with *retained* interests for life (such as life estates, income interests, and reversions) (current §§2036(a)(1) and 2037);

(4) certain *inter vivos* transfers with retained powers (such as revocable trusts created by the decedent) (§§2036(a)(2) and 2038, and §2037 to a minor extent);

(5) survivorship benefits under annuities and employee retirement and deferred compensation plans (§2039); and,

(6) joint-tenancy property with right of survivorship, in the ratio that the consideration provided by the decedent bears to all consideration, with a special one-half inclusion rule for joint-tenancy property held by a married couple regardless of the decedent spouse's cost contribution (§2040).

Thus, the gross estate (since the beginning of the modern estate tax) has included the death-time value of property traceable to certain *inter vivos* transfers by the decedent. For example, an *inter vivos* transfer of the type that was mentioned in §1.1.A (A deeds Blackacre to A for life, remainder to B) is included in A's gross estate at A's death under current §2036(a)(1). The rationale of §2036(a)(1) is that this *inter vivos* gift by A to B, to take effect in B's possession at A's death, is testamentary in nature in effect. The *inter vivos* transfers that are included in the gross estate are included in an amount equal to their fair market value at the donor's death (not the value when the *inter vivos* transfer is made). These statutory provisions were initially thought to be necessary to prevent the avoidance of the estate tax in a context where there was no comprehensive gift tax. (The most obvious way to avoid a simple estate tax on the probate estate is, of course, to get rid of the property during life by way of gift.) Although a comprehensive gift tax was firmly in place by 1932, the provisions of the estate tax, described above, relating to inclusion of certain *inter vivos* transfers in the gross estate, were not repealed. Thus, *inter vivos* transfers may be "subject to" both the estate and the gift tax, and this phenomenon is what has "caused" much of the doctrinal complexity within the estate and gift taxes.

The gross estate also includes property transferred (in trust) *by another person* over which the decedent possessed (at death) a "*general* power of appointment," which is a power in the decedent to acquire (withdraw, draw down) the (trust) property. See §2041. (The term "power of appointment" is defined in the glossary, §1.1.B, supra.) Possession of a general power of appointment over the corpus or income of a trust created by another person is considered to be the equivalent of ownership of the corpus or income. (The income tax analogy is the doctrine of "constructive receipt.")

Current §2042, dealing with the inclusion of the proceeds of insurance on the decedent's life, is also based on a general-power-of-appointment principle (as opposed to a transfer-retention principle). Section 2042 includes the proceeds of life insurance in the *insured's* gross estate if (a) the proceeds are payable to the insured's "estate" or (2) where the insured possessed ownership rights ("incidents of ownership") over the policy at the moment just prior to death. Note that the identity of the payer of premiums is not relevant under §2042.

§2.3. The Federal Gift Tax

The gift tax, enacted in 1932 as a back up to the estate tax, is found in Chapter 12 of the Code, §§2501-2524. The gift tax applies to all gifts by U.S. citizens or residents regardless of where the property is located. Gifts by nonresident aliens are generally subject to gift tax only in the case of certain tangible property located in the U.S. However, in the case of a nonresident alien who is an expatriate subject to §877 (by reason of sufficient wealth or income, for the ten-year period following expatriation), the following gifts are subject to U.S. gift tax: (1) gifts of any property, wherever located, made in a year in which the expatriate was present in the U.S. for more than 30 days, (2) certain intangible property deemed by statute to be located in the U.S. (such as stock and debt issued by U.S. persons), and (3) stock of a controlled foreign corporation. See §§877(g), 2501(a)(3) & (5). The gift taxation of nonresident aliens is otherwise not covered in this book.

The gift tax is imposed on the cumulative lifetime taxable gifts of a donor, with the tax "on" the current year's taxable gifts being payable by April 15 of the following year. From 2002-2009, the first $1M of a donor's lifetime taxable gifts are effectively exempt from gift tax by reason of a free gift tax credit having an exemption equivalent of $1M. Note that the $1M-exemption-equivalent gift tax credit in 2009 was substantially lower than the $3.5M-exemption-equivalent estate tax credit. This disparity (which was phased-in commencing in 2004) is sometimes referred to as the "de-coupling" of the estate and gift taxes, which for a long time previously had a common (or "unified") exemption/credit amount (as well as a common rate schedule). This decoupling was a feature of the 2001 Act that provided for repeal of the estate tax for decedents dying in 2010. However, the gift tax was not scheduled to expire after 2009, because Congress thought that the gift tax could continue to play the meaningful role of backing up the income tax by imposing a toll charge on gifts of income-producing property that would shift income. In accordance with this rationale, the gift tax rate after 2009, assuming estate tax repeal, was scheduled to drop to an effective flat rate of 35 percent. The failure of the estate tax to disappear undermined the rationale for decoupling the gift and estate tax rates, and the gift and estate tax exemption amounts as well. Thus, the 2010 legislation reunified the gift and estate tax rate (35 percent) and the gift and estate tax exemption amounts ($5M) for 2011 and 2012, although the $1M gift tax exemption remains in effect for 2010.

A. What Is a "Gift" Under the Gift Tax?

The federal gift tax reaches all *inter vivos* transfers of any kind of property (or money) by gift, whether outright or in trust, and whether direct or indirect. §§2501(a)(1) and 2511(a). The gift tax does not reach economic waste, business and investment expenses and losses, taxes and fines, or the decreasing of one's wealth by personal consumption obtained in commercial transactions. See Reg. §25.2512-8. Along the same lines, the gift tax does not reach the provision of "support" under state law, the theory being that support is not "gratuitous" but sort of like the payment of a tax. Alternatively, support provided in kind can be viewed as a form of consumption by the provider, even though another party is the person who benefits from the support.

Nor does the gift tax reach situations where wealth is converted into another form. Thus, a transfer "for full and adequate consideration in money or money's worth" is beyond the reach of the gift tax, because there is no *net* depletion of the transferor's potential gross estate. See §2512(b). But a "purchase" for cash of love and affection would be a gift by the purchaser, since here the consideration, not being in money or money's worth, would not augment the purchaser's potential gross estate, nor would this transaction qualify for the "commercial transaction" exception to the concept of gift.

B. Incomplete Gifts

According to case law and Reg. §25.2511-2, an *inter vivos* gratuitous transfer may be *incomplete* because of the donor's retention of certain powers, such as a power to revoke the transfer. An "incomplete transfer" cannot be a gift — at least until the transfer becomes complete at a later time. However, if a gift becomes complete because of (or at) the donor's death — such as is the case with a revocable trust (because the donor's retained power to revoke expires at her death) — the transfer cannot be subject to *gift* tax, because the gift tax can only apply to a gift that becomes complete during the donor's lifetime. However, the transfer will be included in the gross estate for estate tax purpose under one or more of §§2036-2038. Thus, a retained-power transfer can only delay — but not avoid — federal transfer tax.

Under the 2001 Act, Congress provided that, if estate tax repeal takes effect, any transfer in trust will be treated as a completed gift unless the transfer is wholly incomplete for income tax purposes (under the grantor trust rules of §§671-677). See §2511(c). In other words, the gift tax would be triggered unless the trust transfer is *wholly* ineffective to shift income away from the grantor. The 2010 Act repealed §2511(c).

C. The Annual Exclusion

Section 2503 of the gift tax contains certain "exclusions," the most important being for (1) the direct payment of another person's tuition and medical bills and (2) gifts (except gifts of future interests) up to $13,000 per donee per year. This latter is known as the "annual exclusion." The per-donee per-year limit is to be adjusted upwards (in $1,000 increments) to reflect inflation.

D. Gift Tax Computation

Since the taxable estate is subject to progressive rates under §2001(c) of the estate tax, the gift tax, if it is to be an effective back-up to the estate tax, should also provide for progressive rates. But if the gift tax were computed on an annual basis (like the income tax), high marginal rates could be avoided by spreading gifts over numerous years. This problem of imposing progressive rates to gift-giving activity that occurs over several years could be solved by imposing the gift tax only at death on the donor's cumulative (aggregate) lifetime gifts. However, this method would entail long delays for the government in computing and collecting the tax and impose record-keeping burdens on taxpayers.

The solution to the problem of maintaining a progressive rate schedule for aggregate lifetime gifts, while at the same time imposing the gift tax on an annual basis, involves the following steps:

(1) computation of the tax, under the progressive rate schedule, on *cumulative* taxable gifts made through the *end* of the current year (i.e., current-year taxable gifts *plus* all taxable gifts for prior years); and

(2) Subtraction of the tax computed — by using the same rate schedule used in step (1) — on only the cumulative taxable gifts for years *prior* to the current year.

The result of the subtraction described above is the tax (before the credit) "on" the current-year taxable gifts figured at the appropriate marginal rates. This method is prescribed by §2502. The subtraction referred to in step (2) is not a true "tax credit," because it is not an amount of tax actually paid (which would have been "after" the gift tax credit). Rather, the amount subtracted is the *hypothetical* tax that would be due on an amount equal to the sum of all prior taxable gifts under an *assumption* of no available gift tax credit.

The gift tax credit is taken after the computation described above. Since the applicable credit amount is a "lifetime" (rather than an annual) credit, the credit that can actually be taken against the gift tax on the current year's taxable gifts is the donor's *remaining* credit, which is "the applicable credit amount" based on an exemption equivalent of $1M ($345,800 if the §2001 rate schedule is in effect)[2] reduced by the credits allowable against prior taxable gifts. (For post-2009 gifts, the credit deemed used up for prior gifts taxed at a rate greater than 35 percent is recalculated by using a maximum 35 percent marginal rate.) See §2505(a). Because the statute refers to credits previously "allowable" (rather than "allowed") a donor cannot hoard credit amounts for future use. Nevertheless, a donor making taxable gifts in excess of $1M before 2010 can use the full $4M of additional post-2009 exemption equivalent amount in calculating the gift tax for post-2009 gifts.

Example: Assume that the donor makes her first taxable gift in 2002 in an amount equal to $1M. Under the rate schedule found in §2001(c), the tax (before the gift tax credit) would be $345,800. The donor's applicable credit amount for 2002 was

---

2. The applicable credit amount is $330,800 in 2010, when the highest gift tax marginal rate is reduced to 35%. In 2011, when the exemption equivalent amount is $5M, the applicable credit amount is $1,730,800.

$345,800 (there having been no previously allowable credits). Hence, the donor's after-credit gift tax for 2002 is zero ($345,800 − $345,800). In 2007, the donor makes a second taxable gift of $250,000. The before-credit tax is figured as follows: (1) Start with the tax on the cumulative gifts through 2007 of $1,250,000, which is $448,300; (2) subtract the tax-rate-schedule tax on "prior taxable gifts" of $1M, which is $345,800. Thus, the before-credit tax "on" the $250,000 gift made in 2007 is $102,500 (i.e., at a marginal rate of 41 percent). The donor's remaining credit is zero ($345,800 lifetime applicable credit amount less $345,800 allowable credit against the 2002 taxable gift). Hence, the after-credit gift tax for 2007 is $102,500.

Before 1977, the system operated on the basis of a fixed dollar "lifetime exemption" that could (until exhausted) be subtracted as a deduction in arriving at taxable gifts. In other words, credits have been allowable only with respect to post-1976 taxable gifts. Section 2505(b) provides that the "applicable credit amount" is to be reduced by an amount equal to 20 percent of any exemption amount allowed with respect to gifts made after September 8, 1976 (and before 1977).

The gift tax base ("taxable gifts") is based on the amounts transferred to donees, and does not include the gift tax paid or owed. Thus, in contrast to the estate tax (where the estate tax does not reduce the taxable estate), the gift tax is said to be "tax exclusive."

The gift tax is to be paid by the donor (not the donees, although the donees have secondary liability for payment). See §2502(c).

PROBLEMS

1. a. Suppose Greta creates a revocable trust in 2001 with $1M, naming the X Bank as trustee. The trust provides that trust income and/or corpus is to be paid to Greta's child Bob or accumulated in the trustee's discretion; on the death of Bob (or the prior death of Greta) the trust is to terminate and the trust property is to be paid to Greta's grandchild Carrie. In 2006 the trust distributes $60,000 income and $40,000 corpus to Bob. In 2010, Greta dies, at which time the trust is worth $1.4M, and the $1.4M is paid over to Carrie. What are the transfer tax results of the foregoing to the various parties (including X Bank)? See Reg. §25.2511-1(g)(1) and §2511-2(c) & (f).
    b. What is the justification for the result in (a)? What undesirable result might occur if the creation of a revocable trust were subject to gift tax?
2. a. Sally (who is unmarried) sells Blackacre (which cost Sally $400,000), worth $1M, to her daughter, Bay, for $100,000 in 2011. What are the gift and income tax consequences of this transaction? What is Bay's basis in Blackacre? See Reg. §1.1015-4.
    b. Same facts as (a), and, in addition, Sally makes a gift of $200,000 to her son Dugald in 2012. What gift tax results to Sally?

§2.4. Husband and Wife: The Gift and Estate Tax Marital Deductions

Up to this point, the issue of husband and wife has been ignored. Are they "one" or are they "two?"

A. *Husband and Wife as Separate Taxpayers*

From the beginning of the estate and gift taxes, husband and wife have been considered separate taxpayers for estate and gift tax purposes. In determining which of husband and wife is the donor of a gift, or the person making an estate transfer by bequest or inheritance, the rules of property ownership (mostly state law) are followed. Thus, the gift or bequest is made by the spouse owning the property at the moment of gift or death. If the property is subject to co-ownership, the donor or decedent makes a gift or bequest of property to the extent of his or her ownership interest therein.

B. *Tax Advantages of Owning Community Property*

This ownership principle has favored couples owning community property over other couples, because community property wealth is owned 50-50 by husband and wife. (See the definition of "community property" in the glossary, §1.1.B, supra.) Thus, if the husband dies first, only one-half of the value of the community property is included in his gross estate (the other half already being owned by the surviving spouse). And any gift of community property (even if the gift is "made" by one spouse) is treated as a gift by *each* spouse of one-half of the value of the property. Furthermore, since husband and wife are separate taxpayers, each donor spouse can use any of his or her annual exclusion to reduce or wipe out the gift. Finally, each spouse can use his or her unused gift or estate tax credit (if any) to reduce or eliminate tax. The inherent advantage of community property can be illustrated by the following example.

Example: H and W together own $4M of community property. Assume no taxable gifts by either spouse. Suppose H dies in 2007, leaving everything (his half of the CP) to his children, and in 2008 W dies, leaving everything (her half of the CP) to her children. Assume no deductions. Under the §2001(c) rate schedule — and ignoring the exemption-equivalent credit — each of them has a taxable estate of $2M which produces a before-credit tax of $780,800 (or $1,561,600 combined). After the credit, each estate has a net tax of zero. (In 2007 and in 2008 the credit had an "exemption equivalent" of $2M.) If W owned the entire $4M (and H owned none of it), there would be no tax on H's death (and the credit available to H's estate would be worthless) but on W's death her estate would incur a net tax of $225,000 ($1,680,800 before-credit tax on $4M less credit of $1,455,800). Here the "second" $2M is subject to higher marginal rates than in the CP situation, and only one spouse's credit can be used.

It also needs to be mentioned that the creation of community property by the efforts of one party through (say) the earning of salary does not entail a gift for gift tax purposes of half of it to the other party, because community property law views the salary as being earned 50 percent by each spouse. Nor does a gift occur when separate property is changed to community property (or vice versa) by such events as marriage, divorce, or moving across state lines. These situations are not viewed as transfers by gift, but are transfers that occur by operation of law "incidentally" to a change of status that has ramifications beyond attempting to avoid estate or gift tax. In contrast, a gift results from the creation by one party of a joint tenancy (or tenancy in common) with another party.

C. The Gift-Splitting Election

To avoid the problems of geographical discrimination, Congress in 1948 decided to confer benefits on transactions not involving community property in an attempt to create parity between community property and common-law property. In §2513, Congress allows gifts by one spouse of non-CP property *to a third party* to be treated, pursuant to an election by both spouses on a gift tax return, as a gift of half of the property by each spouse. Section 2513 has survived to the present with virtually no changes.

Example: H, a resident of Florida (which is not a CP state) makes a gift of $26,000 to child C. H and W file a gift tax return on which the §2513 election is indicated. Accordingly, each of H and W is treated as having made a gift of $13,000, and (assuming no other gifts to C) each gift is fully excluded under each spouse's entitlement to the annual exclusion.

D. The Marital Deduction

Congress in 1948 also enacted the gift and estate tax marital deduction for qualifying gift and estate transfers from one spouse to another.

1. The Original Version

Under the 1948 gift tax marital deduction, only half of any gift (before any exclusion) to the other spouse was deductible. Thus, if W gave $30,000 cash to H, $15,000 was deductible under the marital deduction and $3,000 would have been excluded under the then annual exclusion, resulting in a taxable gift of $12,000. A gift of an interest in CP did not qualify for any marital deduction, on the theory that the donee spouse already owned half of the CP.

The 1948 marital deduction allowed an estate tax deduction for qualifying estate-included transfers to one's surviving spouse. The deduction could not exceed one-half of the decedent's "adjusted gross estate" (gross estate, not counting community property, less deductions for debts, etc.).

2. The Current Unlimited Marital Deduction

The 1948 system was criticized insofar as it created a tax disincentive to "leave everything to my surviving spouse." Thus, if H left all his net wealth to W, half would be deductible and half would be taxable, and all of it would be taxed again at the surviving spouse's death.[3] In order to allow the total avoidance of double taxation to husband and wife, the marital deduction was overhauled in 1981 by (1) removing all limitations on the maximum amount of the deduction and (2) removing any disability with respect to community property.

Thus, under current law, if H bequeaths all of his property to W, all of it is deductible, so that H's estate has a taxable estate of zero. All of the spousal wealth will be taxed on W's death (unless W consumes it). The overall effect of this scheme is (potentially) to defer tax on the wealth of the first spouse to die until (at the latest) the death of the second spouse. However, the scheme just described was undesirable in large estates through 2009, because H's exemption equivalent amount would have been wasted. Accordingly, the 2010 Act introduced "portability," whereby a deceased spouse dying in 2010 and thereafter can (in effect) transfer his or her unused exemption equivalent amount to his or her surviving spouse. The gift and estate tax marital deduction is available only for gift and estate transfers that "qualify" for the deduction under §§2056 and 2523. The qualification rules are too complex to be considered at this point, except to say that they are designed so that deductible property will appear in the transferee spouse's gift or estate tax base. Obviously, outright (non-trust) transfers of money and property to the other spouse qualify.

PROBLEMS

1. Under the "unlimited" marital deduction, why (before portability) was it not desirable to leave everything to one's surviving spouse? To help focus on this question, assume that H (who was likely to die first) had a net estate of $5M, that W has no wealth of her own, and that the exemption equivalent amount is $3.5M. Has portability solved this problem?
2. Under the same assumptions as in item 1, what move (prior to the enactment of portability) was considered optimal to deal with the possibility that W would die first?

§2.5. Relation of Estate and Gift Taxes

The 1932 gift tax was a separate tax from the estate tax. Each tax had its own exemptions and rate schedule. This system created a tax incentive to dispose half of one's wealth by gift and half by estate transfer, since both exemptions could be

---

3. If the deaths occurred close together, the §2013 credit would have been available to mitigate double taxation of the same property in the two estates. However, the §2013 credit phases out at the rate of 20% every two years following the death of the first spouse, and is completely lost after the tenth year.

used and taxable wealth could be shifted from high marginal estate tax rates to lower marginal gift tax rates. This incentive was aggravated by a gift tax rate schedule that was less steep than the estate tax rate schedule.

A. *Unification of Estate and Gift Taxes*

This problem was partially corrected in 1976, and again in 2010, by the "unification" ("integration") of the estate and gift taxes. Such unification was achieved by: (1) positing one rate schedule for both taxable gifts and taxable estate transfers; (2) having a single exemption (obtained through an exemption-equivalent credit, officially referred to as the "unified transfer tax credit"); and (3) under §2001(b)(1)(B), treating the taxable estate as if it were the "last taxable gift" of the decedent.

Example: Assume X has aggregate taxable wealth of $2M. Assume also that the unified transfer tax credit available to X (and X's estate) is $345,800, which equates to an exemption-equivalent of $1M. If X makes no gifts, X's taxable estate is $2M, and the net tax is $435,000 ($780,800 less $345,800 credit). Suppose instead X makes a taxable gift in 2002 of $1M. The net gift tax is zero ($345,800 less credit of $345,800). In 2003, X dies with a taxable estate of the remaining $1M. In the absence of unification, X's net estate tax would be zero, since the tax on $1M of $345,800 would be fully offset by a separate estate tax credit of $345,800. Under integration, however, the credit has been exhausted, and cumulative taxable gift and estate transfers are $2M. Thus, the net estate tax is $435,800. This is figured, *conceptually* (using the method prescribed by the gift tax), as follows: (1) Begin by ascertaining the tentative tax on a cumulative tax base consisting of the taxable estate *plus aggregate taxable gifts* (i.e., $2M), which is $780,800; (2) subtract the §2001(c) before-credit tax on aggregate taxable gifts of $1M, which is $345,800; and (3) subtract the remaining (i.e., unused) unified transfer tax credit, which is zero, because it was all used up against the gift tax.

Note that only post-1976 gifts are included in the cumulative tax base *for purposes of computing the estate tax*. In other words, estate and gift tax integration was prospective only. The *gift tax* cumulative tax base includes gifts made by the donor after June 6, 1932. See §2502(b).

The *statutory* method of computing the estate tax prescribed by §2001(b) deviates from the foregoing (the gift tax method), but it produces the same end result. A close reading of §2001(b) reveals that the estate tax is to be computed as follows (using the same numbers as in the example above): (1) Start with the before-credit tax on the cumulative tax base (= $780,800); (2) subtract the *after-credit* aggregate gift taxes on post-1976 gifts (= 0); and (3) subtract the *full* unified transfer tax credit amount (= $345,800). But the result (a net estate tax of $435,000) is necessarily the same as in the example set forth above, because the §2001(b) method and the gift tax method used in the example are algebraic equivalents: In the example, the previously used credit amount ($345,800) reduces the step three subtraction (the unused credit amount), whereas under the §2001(b) method the same previously used credit amount reduces the step-two subtraction (after-credit taxes paid on post-1976 taxable gifts). The §2010(b) estate tax method can be described as a tax on the cumulative tax base (taxable estate plus post-1976 taxable gifts) reduced by two credits, the first being a credit for net gift taxes paid on post-1976 gifts, and the second being the full unified transfer tax credit amount.

Unification exists to the extent that (1) there is a single cumulative tax base that includes both lifetime taxable gifts and the taxable estate, (2) there is a single rate schedule, and (3) there is a single credit (that can be exhausted by making taxable gifts). As previously noted, this unification became somewhat uncoupled after 2003, because the exemption-equivalent amount for the gift tax credit was frozen at $1M, while that for the estate tax increased in steps to $3.5M (for decedents dying in 2009). Unification was restored by the 2010 Act beginning in 2011, when both the estate and gift tax have an exemption equivalent amount of $5M and a maximum marginal rate of 35 percent.

PROBLEM

Compute the federal estate tax for the estate of May, who died in 2008, where May's gross estate is $6M, and deductible estate debts, etc., are $250,000. May's will left $750,000 to the Z charity, $3M to her husband Sam, and the rest to her children. The adjusted taxable gifts of May, all made in 2004, were $1.5M.

B. Transfers Subject to Both Gift and Estate Tax

Unification only achieves *computational* integration of the gift and estate taxes. The *doctrine* relating to what is a "gift" and what *inter vivos* transfers are included in the gross estate was left untouched. Thus, an *inter vivos* transfer can be subject to both gift and estate tax. How this can occur will be revealed in subsequent discussions of doctrine (mainly in Chapter 8). (The possibility that an *inter vivos* transfer can avoid, in the doctrinal sense, both gift and estate taxes is very remote.)

Prior to unification in 1976, the problem of double estate and gift taxation of the same *inter vivos* transfer was accomplished by a complex credit against the estate tax for any gift tax on the "same" transfer. This provision, §2012, still exists, but it only applies with respect to pre-1977 gifts that are also included in the donor's gross estate.

For post-1976 gifts that are included in the donor's gross estate, the problem is dealt with by the rule that only "adjusted taxable gifts" (instead of "all" taxable gifts) are included in the cumulative tax base *for purposes of computing the estate tax*. See §2001(b)(1)(B). As already mentioned, "adjusted taxable gifts," as defined in the last sentence of §2001(b), excludes all pre-1977 taxable gifts, but it also excludes all post-1976 taxable gifts *that are included in the gross estate by reason of the form of transfer* (that is, by reason of the application of §§2035-2040). Thus, "testamentary" *inter vivos* transfers are ultimately included in the unified transfer tax base at their estate tax values. Their gift tax values are removed from the cumulative tax base.

If an after-credit post-1976 gift tax was paid on the twice-taxed transfer, this gift tax, being a prepayment towards the ultimate transfer tax liability, is creditable (along with other gift taxes paid) against the estate tax liability under §2001(b)(2), even though the gift (that triggered the gift tax) is not included in the "adjusted taxable gifts" total. The credit for post-1976 gift taxes cannot exceed the tax on the cumulative tax base.

Example: *To simplify this illustration, assume there is no unified transfer tax credit.* In 1977, Z creates an irrevocable *inter vivos* trust with $1M, reserving the right to income for herself for life, remainder on Z's death to R. A gift tax was paid on the net taxable gift of $300,000 in the amount of $120,000. In 2003, Z dies with a net probate estate of $1M, but Z's taxable estate is $2.7M, because the 1977 trust is included in Z's gross estate under §2036 at its 2003 value of $1.7M. The cumulative tax base is not $3M, but $2.7M (the taxable estate only), because the 1977 taxable gift amount of $300,000 is not an "adjusted taxable gift" (because the same property interest was ultimately included in the gross estate by reason of §2036). The §2001(c) tentative tax on $2.7M is $1,125,800, but the 1977 gift tax of $120,000 is credited against this figure, to arrive at $1,005,800. (Remember that the unified transfer credit is deemed not to exist in this illustration.)

The removal of twice-taxed post-1976 gifts from the "adjusted taxable gifts" total is hereinafter referred to as the "adjusted taxable gifts exclusion."

PROBLEMS AND NOTES

1. **a.** Suppose Jay (in 2001) purchases Blackacre (worth $1M), naming himself and daughter Kay joint tenants with right of survivorship, resulting in a taxable gift of $487K to Kay. Jay dies in 2005, having made no other taxable gifts, and the then value of Blackacre ($1.3M) is included in Jay's gross estate under §2040, along with $4M included in Jay's gross estate under other provisions. How does Blackacre figure into Jay's gift and estate tax bases and computations?

   b. Same basic facts as in (a), except that Jay makes an outright (fee simple) gift of Blackacre (worth $1M) to Kay in 2001. In 2005, Kay dies without a will, and Blackacre (now worth $1.3M) passes back to Jay by inheritance. In 2009, Jay dies holding Blackacre (now worth $2M) and $4M of other estate-included assets. What are the effects of these transfers on the transfer tax bases of the parties?

2. **a.** The "credit" for net taxes on post-1976 taxable gifts may exceed the net gift taxes actually paid, because §2001(b)(2) uses the word "payable" rather than "paid." Nevertheless, use of the word "payable" is justified. Unpaid gift taxes are either owed to the IRS or can't be collected due to the

running of the statute of limitations. If the term "paid" (instead of "payable") were used, §2001(b)(2) would improperly override the statute of limitations. To illustrate, assume a gift tax payable (but not paid, and barred by the statute of limitations) on a post-1976 gift of $1M and a taxable estate of $2M, and no gift or estate tax credit. If §2001(b)(2) had used "paid," the estate would pay tax on $3M, effectively overriding the statute of limitations barring collection of gift tax on the taxable gift of $1M. Because of the word "payable," the estate obtains, in effect, a credit against the estate tax for gift taxes that the IRS was once owed but is now barred from collecting. But note that the $1M taxable gift, the tax on which is barred, pushes the taxable estate into higher marginal rate brackets than if the gift were deemed not to have occurred at all. Cf. §2504(c).

b.   The §2001(b)(2) "credit" is for the gift tax that "would have been" payable if the estate tax rate schedule in effect at the decedent's death had been in effect at the date of gift. To illustrate the effect of the foregoing, assume a gift tax paid on a taxable gift of $1M in the amount of $300K (because of a flat 30 percent rate), a taxable estate of $2M, a rate of 40 percent on the cumulative tax base (raised from the former 30 percent) as of the donor's death, and no gift or estate tax credit. Without the cited language, the estate tax would be $900K ($1.2M − $300K), which results in an "incorrect" tax rate of 45 percent on the taxable estate. With the cited language, the estate tax is $800K ($1.2M − $400K), which correctly expresses the result of applying a 40 percent rate against a $2M taxable estate. The same rule also operates to prevent the taxpayer from obtaining the retroactive benefit of a rate reduction.

c.   The features of §2001(b)(2) described above are inherent in the gift tax computation, because §2502(a) computes the before-credit gift tax "on" the current year's taxable gifts by using the rate schedule found in §2001(c). The subtraction for the rate-schedule tax on prior taxable gifts is not conditioned on any actual payment of gift tax on prior taxable gifts.

C. Pros and Cons of Gifts

Despite unification, there are advantages and disadvantages of transferring property by gift rather than by a transfer included in the gross estate.

1. Gifts in Excess of the Reduced Gift Tax Exemption

Taxable gifts made after 2003 (but before 2010) that, when combined with prior taxable gifts, exceed the "decoupled" gift tax exclusion of $1M incurred unnecessary gift tax in cases where the same amounts, if included in the gross estate, would be sheltered by the larger estate tax exemption.

Example: D's prior taxable gifts are $1M. In 2004, D makes a taxable gift of $2M. Since the exemption amount was frozen at $1M, the gift produced a gift tax (at the 2004 maximum rate of 48 percent) of $915,000. On D's death in 2009, D has a taxable estate of $0.5M. The cumulative tax base at D's death is $3.5M, which equals the 2009 exemption amount of $3.5M. There is no estate tax. *The gift tax for 2004 was wholly unnecessary*, since, if the 2004 gift had not been made (and would have been included in D's gross estate at a value of $2M), there would have been no gift tax and no estate tax (on the same cumulative tax base of $3.5M). D's estate does not obtain a refund of the unnecessary gift tax.

The gift tax paid on a post-1976 taxable gift is not always lost in this fashion. If the cumulative tax base exceeds the exemption equivalent amount, the gift tax on post-1976 taxable gifts will be credited against the tax on the cumulative tax base, but it cannot produce a tax refund. Thus, if (in the example above) D had a taxable estate of $1.5M (instead of $0.5M), the cumulative tax base on D's death in 2009 would have been $4.5M (instead of $3.5M), and the resulting tentative tax of $1,905,800 would be reduced not only by the unified transfer tax credit amount of $1,455,800 under §2010 but also by so much of the $915K gift tax as would reduce the net estate tax to zero.

2. The Taxability of the Gift Tax Paid

A way in which the 1976 unification was incomplete has to do with the fact that the gift tax is generally "tax exclusive" (meaning that the gift tax paid or owed is not included in the tax base) whereas the estate tax is "tax inclusive" (meaning that the estate tax is not deducted from the estate tax base). The result is that the gift tax imposes less of a burden, net, on any given wealth transfer compared to the estate tax.

Any gift tax paid (or owed at death) not only is excluded from the gift tax base but economically reduces the donor's taxable estate. However, if the gift generating the gift tax paid (or owed) was made within three years of the decedent's death, *the gift tax amount* (not the value of the gift itself) is added back to the donor's gross estate under §2035(b). Thus, there is a tax advantage to gifts (not made within three years of death) that generate gift tax, compared to an equal amount included in the donor's gross estate.

Example: Assume that a 40 percent rate schedule applies for both gift tax and estate tax purposes, and that there are no gift or estate tax credits. X makes a taxable gift of $1M, which produces a tax of $400,000, payable by X (reducing X's future gross estate). If X were instead to die (after four years), a bequest of the same $1.4M would generate an estate tax of $560,000, leaving only $840,000 for the legatee (as opposed to $1M for the gift donee). If X makes the gift but dies within three years thereof, the $400,000 gift tax amount is added to the gross estate (without adding actual wealth to the gross estate), which generates an incremental estate tax liability of $160,000, reducing net gratuitous receipts to $840,000, the same net result as occurs with an estate-included transfer of $1.4M.

Section 2035(b) is something of a compromise. Some commentators have totally disapproved of the favoritism towards gifts resulting from not including the gift tax in the gift tax base. But, in order to equalize gifts and bequests (that is, in order to make the gift tax "tax inclusive," like the estate tax), any taxable gift amount would have to be "grossed up" by the gift tax thereon. But this is difficult, because the grossed-up tax base includes the tax, but one cannot figure the tax without knowing the tax base. This "circularity" problem can be resolved by a formula. But, rather than subject gift-giving taxpayers to the formula, and perhaps to leave some transfer tax inducement for the making of gifts, Congress has declined to systematically adopt a rule that would require the grossing up of gifts. Instead, Congress adopted a rule that causes only gifts made within three years of death to be tax inclusive. Since the time of death cannot be predicted in advance, this system can only be applied once the date of the donor's death is ascertained. Rather than retroactively applying the gross-up formula to prior gifts and requiring the filing of amended gift tax returns, Congress adopted the far more simple approach of mandating the inclusion in the gross estate of the gift tax paid on gifts made within three years of death.

3. The Bracket Effect

In the case of property that is expected to produce future net economic yield (income and/or appreciation), there is a potential advantage of making gifts rather than holding onto the property until death. This advantage accrues where the expected economic yield will be subject to tax on account of the using up of the exemption equivalent of the estate tax credit. This advantage only holds if the exemption equivalent amount itself does not increase at the rate of appreciation and if the tax rates do not similarly decrease.

Example: Assume a permanent exemption equivalent of $4M for both gift and estate tax purposes and a permanent flat tax rate of 40 percent, and assume that X has already made taxable gifts of $3M. X can make a gift now of $1M that will avoid tax. If X were to hold onto the property now worth $1M until her death, at which time the property and its yield grow to a value of $3M, X will suffer an "avoidable tax" of $800,000 ($2M subject to tax x 40 percent).

This phenomenon is referred to as "the bracket effect" (or "bracket creep"), because the appreciation pushes taxable wealth into higher marginal rate brackets. In the example above, the movement is from an effective zero bracket (thanks to the available credit) to a 40 percent bracket.

Keep in mind that rates and exemptions are subject to politics, and therefore lack permanency (and future predictability). In fact, during the period from 2003 through 2012, the estate tax exemption increased at a much faster rate than any reasonable expectation of economic yield. That fact, combined with the freezing of the gift tax exemption at $1M during that period, created a strong inducement *not* to make gifts.

4. The Gift Tax Exclusions

Since there is no estate tax equivalent of the gift tax exclusions found in §2503, gifts that avoid tax by reason of these exclusions (and future yield thereon) are tax advantaged without regard to future changes in rate schedules and exemption levels.

5. Support Obligations

The satisfaction of support obligations also depletes the support-provider's estate during life without gift tax exposure. The support obligations of a person usually terminate at that person's death. Bequests (or other estate-included transfers) to persons to whom the decedent owed support obligations during life are taxable estate transfers (unless qualifying for the marital deduction). Thus, the lavish provision of support during life can avoid federal wealth transfer taxes.

Despite the fact that the support exclusion does not survive the decedent's death, certain required payments under divorce and separation orders and agreements can reduce the taxable estate. Specifically, payments from a decedent's estate to a person whom the decedent was obligated to support are deductible as estate debts under §2053 if (a) the payments are made pursuant to a divorce settlement that satisfies the requirements of §2516 of the gift tax (see §2043(b)(2)), (b) the payments are mandated by a court order, or (c) the obligation to make the payments was incurred for a full and adequate consideration in money or money's worth (see §2043(b)(1)).

QUICK QUESTION

Is the income tax a tax-inclusive tax like the estate tax or is it a tax-exclusive tax like the gift tax?

    A. The income tax is a tax-inclusive tax like the estate tax.
    B. The income tax is a tax-exclusive tax like the gift tax.
    C. Huh? I have no idea what those terms mean. Perhaps I should reread §2.5.C.2.

PROBLEMS

1. Gramps (unmarried) has three adult children and seven grandchildren. How can Gramps most readily deplete his estate (without committing economic waste)?
2. Uma is 50 years old, healthy, wealthy, and (hopefully) wise. State which of the following assets are the best candidates for the making of (nonexempt) gifts, considering only transfer tax savings:
    a. corporate bonds
    b. utility company stocks
    c. pharmaceutical stocks
    d. unimproved land
    e. an unproven copyright
    f. an interest in a family business
    g. an interest in a venture capital firm

§2.6. Overlapping Transfer Tax Jurisdictions

A given estate may be subject not only to federal transfer taxes but also state and/or foreign wealth transfer taxes.

A. State Death Taxes

A long-standing issue has been the manner in which the federal estate tax should accommodate state taxes imposed by reason of a person's death, which until fairly recent times have mostly been inheritance taxes.

1. The Credit for State Death Taxes

There was concern in the early days of the federal estate tax that, because the transmission of property at death was a matter "reserved" to the states, only the states could impose wealth transfer taxes. This argument was not accepted as a doctrine of constitutional law, but Congress was more sensitive to federalism concerns under the estate tax than under the income tax, which only allows a deduction for state taxes (and not all state taxes). Thus, the initial approach of Congress was to allow an estate to claim a credit under §2011 against any federal estate tax liability remaining after the §2010 unified transfer tax credit for the amount of state death taxes paid or payable.

However, the credit could not exceed the "limitation." The limitation prevented the states from appropriating the entire federal estate tax for their own treasuries. The first step in computing the limitation was to subtract $60,000 from the taxable estate, which produced the "adjusted taxable estate," against which the table found in §2011(b) was applied.

Although the inheritance tax was the historic norm for state death taxation, most states moved to what is known as the "pick-up estate tax," because such a tax played off the §2011 credit. The pick-up estate tax imposed by the state was the excess, if any, of (1) the maximum allowable §2011(b) credit for the particular estate over (2) other state death taxes (if any) on the estate. Thus, if the other state death taxes already exceed the maximum §2011 credit, there was no state pick-up estate tax. If there was no other state death tax, the state death tax would equal the maximum §2011(b) credit amount. A state pick-up estate tax costs the estate nothing; it merely shifts revenues from the federal treasury to the state treasury. This result derives from the fact that the federal credit is the lesser of the actual state death taxes (of all types) or the §2011(b) maximum credit for the particular estate.

Example: Assume that the maximum §2011 credit allowable to the estate of D is $30,000 and the federal estate tax after the §2010 credit but before any §2011 credit is $250,000. Assuming that the state imposes a pick-up estate tax, the amount of such tax will be $30,000 (the credit limitation amount under §2011(b)). The state now receives $30,000 which is credited against the federal estate tax, which is reduced to $220,000, but the total taxes paid are still $250,000.

The fact that the §2011 credit came "after" the §2010 credit, see §2011(f), meant that the large increases in the §2010 credit amounts after 1977 substantially reduced state pick-up estate tax revenues. For example, if the taxable estate of A (who died in 2002) is $1M, there is no state pick-up estate tax, since there is no net tax left to absorb any §2011 credit.

2. Transition to a Deduction System

The tax law that was enacted in 2001 phased out the §2011 credit for estates of decedents dying in 2002, 2003, and 2004. See §2011(b)(2). The credit expired for decedents dying after 2004. §2011(g). For decedents dying after 2004, the estate can claim a deduction (without limitation) for state death taxes. See §2058.

Since the 2001 Act itself is set to expire at the end of 2012, it is possible (as this book goes to press) that the credit system will revive.

The demise of the credit system (at least during the period 2005-2012) has the effect of suspending the operation of all state pick-up estate taxes. Some states enacted (or beefed-up) their stand-alone inheritance or estate taxes, and others abolished existing death taxes.

There is no deduction or credit against federal gift or estate tax for state gift taxes.

B. Credit for Foreign Death Taxes

As mentioned earlier, the federal estate tax applies to all property wherever situated of U.S. citizens or residents. The estate of a U.S. citizen or resident may be liable for foreign taxes imposed by reason of a person's death. To mitigate double death taxation, §2014 allows a credit against the U.S. estate tax in an amount equal to the foreign death taxes attributable to an estate-included (and nondeductible) item, provided that the property is situated in the foreign country. As with the other credits, the net U.S. estate tax liability cannot be reduced below zero. This credit is not available to the estates of nonresident alien decedents.

The U.S. has entered into death tax conventions with numerous countries. The main benefit provided by the treaties to the estate of a decedent who was a "resident" of the treaty country is to subject estate items to the death tax of only one of the contracting countries, thereby obviating the need for an estate tax credit in either country.

There is no credit for foreign gift taxes or foreign GST taxes.

§2.7. Credit for Prior Estate Transfers

This credit, provided by §2013, attempts to mitigate the tax burden resulting where property passes through the estates of two persons in close succession. Conceptually, the second estate obtains a nonrefundable credit equal to the earlier estate tax on the same property.

Perhaps the mechanics of this credit are excessively complex to be learned at this point in one's career, but for the sake of completeness the basic steps will now be sketched. First, the "tentative" credit is that portion of the estate tax of the prior decedent (the "transferor") attributable, on an "average rate" basis, to the transfer of wealth to the later decedent (the "decedent"). It is figured according to the following formula:

$$\frac{\text{tentative}}{\text{credit}} = \frac{\text{property transferred to decedent}}{\text{transferor's taxable estate}} \times \text{transferor's estate tax}$$

The term "property transferred to decedent" refers to the net *taxable* value of the property that passed to the decedent from the transferor; that is, the includible value reduced by any portion thereof that was deductible under §2056 (the marital deduction). It is worth noting that the "property transferred to decedent" need not be traceable to, or even included in, the decedent's gross estate. Thus, an income interest bequeathed to the decedent by the transferor qualifies for the §2013 credit if it can be valued pursuant to actuarial principles as of the transferor's death. By the same token, the credit can be lost for an interest that is subject to conditions or contingencies that preclude actuarial valuation.[4]

The tentative credit is "nonrefundable" by reason of the fact that it cannot exceed an amount equal to the decedent's estate tax attributable to the transferred property, figured (this time) on a "highest marginal rate" basis. Thus, the credit, at this point, is the lesser of the transferor's or the transferee's estate tax attributable to the transferred amount.

The nonrefundable credit amount is then reduced as the time between the two deaths increases by multiplying it by 80 percent if the deaths are three to four years apart, 60 percent if the deaths are five to six years apart, 40 percent if the deaths are seven to eight years apart, and 20 percent if the deaths are nine to ten years apart. If the transferor died more than ten years before the decedent, no §2013 credit is available to the decedent's estate.

PROBLEMS

1. Suppose the death tax statute of the state of Texas reads as follows: "There is hereby imposed on the estate of each decedent who dies domiciled in this state a tax equal to the maximum federal estate tax credit for state death taxes allowed for federal estate tax purposes on the estate of such decedent." How does this statute apply in 2011?

2. Suppose that Jay makes an outright (fee simple) gift of Blackacre (worth $2M) to Kay in 2001, resulting in net gift tax of $435K. In October, 2005, Kay dies without a will, and Blackacre (now worth $3M) passes back to Jay by inheritance. Kay's aggregate taxable estate was $6M, resulting in a net estate tax of

---

4. See *Holbrook v. U.S.*, 575 F.2d 1288 (9th Cir.1978).

$2.115M. In March, 2009, Jay dies holding Blackacre (now worth $4M) and $4M of other estate-included assets. What is the amount (if any) of the §2013 credit to Jay's estate?

§2.8. The Federal Generation-Skipping Transfer Tax

The estate tax can be avoided for future generations by the use of trusts with successive interests. Thus, if W creates a testamentary trust, income to child X for life, then to grandchild Y for life, remainder to great-grandchild Z, the trust is not included in the gross estates of X and Y at their deaths, since neither X nor Y transfer any interest owned by them at death. Rather, the interests of X, Y, and Z were all acquired from W at W's death, and the interests of X and Y simply expire at their deaths. (Recall the discussion of the operation of future interests in §1.1.B, supra.) Yes, the trust property was included in W's gross estate at W's death, because the trust was created by W (under her will) with property owned by W. But, if W had bequeathed the property to X outright (not in trust), and X had bequeathed it to Y outright, who in turn bequeathed it to Z outright, the property would also have been included in the gross estates of X and Y, because each of X and Y would have owned the property at their respective deaths. (The property augments Z's potential gross estate under either scenario, since Z acquires the property outright.) In this example, the generations of X and Y are said to be "skipped generations," since no estate tax is imposed between the first (W's) and the last (Z's) generations.

To plug this perceived gap in the estate and gift tax (which favored the very wealthy who are able to create long-term trusts), a federal generation-skipping transfer tax (GST tax) was enacted in 1976. Using the trust created by W described immediately above, the 1976 GST tax would have imposed a tax, at X and Y's highest marginal estate tax rates, on the value of the property in the trust as of X and Y's respective deaths. However, the 1976 GST tax was criticized as being too complex. So, in 1986 the 1976 GST tax was retroactively repealed and replaced by the current GST tax, which applies only to trusts (etc.) created after September 25, 1985. The current GST tax is found in Chapter 13 of the Code, consisting of §§2601-2664.

The current GST tax reaches three types of taxable events: (1) taxable terminations, (2) taxable distributions, and (3) direct-skip transfers. See §2611(a). In the trust described above, the deaths of X and Y would be "taxable terminations" under §2611(a), because in each case the interest *of a person (or persons) in the generation below that of the grantor* terminates, with the result that the next interest in possession is held by a still lower generation. In contrast, if it were the case that X, Y, and Z were all children of W, there would be no taxable terminations, because no generations would be skipped without incurring estate or gift tax. (The property would be subject to estate and gift tax to Z, but Z is in only the first generation below W.)

In a taxable termination, the entire property that encompasses the terminating interest (the corpus *and* undistributed income) constitutes the GST tax base. The GST tax with respect to a taxable termination is paid by the trustee out of the trust property.

The "taxable distribution" concept is really a variation on the taxable termination concept. Thus, in the trust described above, if the trustee properly makes a distribution to grandchild Y during child X's lifetime, *whether out of income or corpus*, the amount distributed is a taxable distribution, because the distributee occupies a generation below that of X, who is a current lower-generation beneficiary (relative to W). See §2612(b). A taxable distribution is a kind of "accelerated partial termination." Here only the distributed amount is subject to GST tax. The tax is paid by the distributee.

Unlike the repealed 1976 GST tax, the 1986 GST tax reaches "direct-skip" transfers, such as an outright gift or bequest to one's grandchild. See §2612(c). The idea is that such a transfer skips (avoids) estate or gift tax with respect to the intermediate generation (the child of the transferor who is the parent of the transferor's grandchild). Instead of imposing the tax on the transferee (the grandchild) or the intermediate generation (the child), the tax is here imposed on the transferor, *in addition to any gift or estate tax on the transfer*. This might appear to be unjustified double transfer taxation of the same transfer to the same transferor, but really the GST tax on any direct-skip transfer should be viewed as a "proxy" for a tax with respect to the skipped generation, which happens to be imposed on the transferor for the sake of convenience. Also, any gift or estate tax "on" a direct-skip transfer is excluded from the amount subject to GST tax. At the same time, any GST tax paid with respect to an *inter vivos* direct-skip *gift* is included (not removed) from the *gift tax* base, even though this amount was not received by the donee. §2515. This rule prevents *both* the gift tax *and* the GST tax on the direct-skip gift from being removed from the gift tax base.

The GST tax is imposed at a rate which is the rate obtained by multiplying the "applicable rate" times the "inclusion ratio." §2641(a). The "applicable rate" is that flat rate which is equal to the highest marginal estate tax rate (35 percent after 2010, but 0 percent in 2010) at the date of the generation-skipping transfer. §2641(b). The "inclusion ratio" is a decimal amount obtained by subtracting from the number "1.0" the "exclusion ratio," also expressed as a decimal (and not to exceed 1.0). The "exclusion ratio" is always constituted upon the initial transfer (creation of the trust or when the direct-skip transfer is made), and is obtained by dividing the "GST exemption" by the value of the transferred property (reduced by federal and state estate and death taxes and any amount that qualifies for the estate or gift tax charitable contribution deduction). See §2642(a). The "GST exemption" is an amount equal to the exemption-equivalent amount for the §2010 credit (i.e., rising to $5M in 2010). §2631(c).

Example: D makes an *inter vivos* gift of $2M to her grandchild in 2008. Assume that the GST exemption allocated to this gift is $2M. The *exclusion* ratio is the $2M GST exemption divided by the $2M gift, which comes out to 1.0. The *inclusion* ratio is 1.0 minus the exclusion ratio of 1.0, which equals zero. Zero times the 45 percent rate for 2008 produces a zero tax rate. Hence the GST tax is zero.

This system seems needlessly complicated, since the same result would be obtained by treating the exemption amount as a true exemption (deduction), producing a tax base of zero. The significance of the inclusion ratio idea becomes clear when it is applied in the context of taxable terminations (and taxable distributions), remembering that *the ratio is constituted as of the initial transfer* (not as of the later generation-skipping transfer). Thus, if the inclusion ratio is zero when the trust is created, it is always zero, so that future taxable distributions and terminations are exempt from tax, no matter their amount! This phenomenon is referred to as the "leveraging" of the GST tax exemption.

The exemption amount is a cumulative (lifetime and deathtime) exemption for each transferor. It is exhausted as it is used up. That is, it is not an annual or per-transfer exemption. There are rules and procedures by which a transferor (and the transferor's personal representative) allocate the transferor's available exemption among direct-skip transfers and transfers that may give rise to future taxable distributions and taxable terminations. See §§2631(a) & (b) and 2632.

Husband and wife are separate transferors, each with his or her full exemption amount.

Husbands and wives are *per se* deemed to occupy the same generation. It follows that marital gifts and bequests are not generation-skipping transfers.

A direct-skip gift transfer that is excluded under the annual gift tax exclusion (or the exclusion for direct payments of tuition and medical care) is excluded from the GST, and none of the GST tax exclusion has to be used up to the extent of such gift exclusion. See §2642(c).

The GST tax is discussed in greater detail in §7.4, infra, in the context of tax issues pertaining to long-term trusts.

QUICK QUESTION

Anita creates an irrevocable trust with income to her daughter, Brenda, for life, remainder to her granddaughter, Celine. Which one of the following statements is *FALSE*?

  A. Brenda is a non-skip person.
  B. Celine is a skip person.
  C. Celine holds a GST defined "interest" in the trust.
  D. When Brenda dies, there will be a taxable termination.

PROBLEMS, QUESTIONS, AND NOTES

  1. Suppose Peewee creates an irrevocable *inter vivos* trust (with $1M) in 2002, naming the X Bank as trustee, income to and among such of Pewee's issue as the trustee decides, but the trustee can decide to accumulate income, and upon the death of the last survivor of Pewee's children, the trust is to terminate

and the property distributed to such of Pewee's issue as are then surviving, per stirpes. The trustee distributes $100,000 to Pewee's oldest son Dennis in 2002. In 2005, the trustee distributes $40,000 to Pewee's granddaughter Elvira. Pewee dies in 2006, at which time the trust is worth $1.4M. The trust terminates in 2009, it being then worth $5M, which is distributed among various grandchildren of Pewee. What are the gift, estate, and generation-skipping tax results of the foregoing to the various parties? See Reg. §25.2511-2(a).

2. The GST tax is not wholly uncontroversial. Consider the following arguments:
   a. "The GST tax (in the case of taxable terminations and taxable distributions) is not legitimate because it imposes *additional* transfer taxes on interests in property that were already subject to gift or estate transfer tax with respect to the original donor or decedent."
   b. "The GST tax (on taxable terminations and taxable distributions) is not required in the name of 'equity,' because a trust beneficiary (such as the holder of an income interest) is not the equivalent of a fee simple owner of property, and any distributions to a trust beneficiary augment the beneficiary's potential gross estate."
   c. "The GST should not encompass direct-skip transfers, because nobody occupying the generation between the transferor and the transferee has been in possession or enjoyment of the property so as to justify a double transfer tax in this type of case."

3. It is debatable whether the federal transfer taxes should be designed so as to reach all gratuitous transfers of wealth regardless of the generation-assignments of transferors and transferees, or whether they should be designed so as to approximate a once-per-generation wealth tax. What features of the existing system (noted so far) are modeled on the latter approach?

4. What caused the marital deduction to be enacted in 1948 was to allow spouses in common law states to achieve a measure of parity with their community property counterparts. Since 1981, the marital deduction has been expanded beyond that original rationale, but with no stated rationale other than that people supposedly want to leave everything to their spouse. However, that sentiment is not common among the very wealthy, who are now the only ones subject to the federal transfer taxes!

§2.9. The 2001 and the 2010 Acts

The Economic Growth and Tax Relief Reconciliation Act of 2001 (the "2001 Act," sometimes referred to as "EGTRA") contained major provisions affecting not only the transfer taxes but also the income tax as well. These provisions were to take effect for transfers made in 2010. However, to comply with 2001 budgetary rules, the entire 2001 Act was to self-destruct at the end of 2010 (under a "sunset" provision in the Act), and in 2011 the entire system as it existed in 2001 would be revived. On December 17, 2010, the Tax Relief, Unemployment Insurance Authorization and Job Creation Act of 2010 (the "2010 Act") was passed delaying the 2001 Act sunset until the end of 2012. The 2010 Act continues (1) the system existing in 2009 in most respects through 2012 and (2) the uncertainly as to the law that will ultimately apply after 2012.

The 2010 Act reinstated the estate tax for 2010-2012, with an election out for decedents dying in 2010 combined with a so-called carryover basis system as provided under §1022 (described in C. below). The Act also reunified and reduced estate and gift tax rates, increased the exemption amount, repealed §2511(c), adopted a zero GST tax rate for 2010, and enacted a provision allowing for the portability of a deceased spouse's exemption to his surviving spouse.

A. Repeal of Estate and GST Taxes

The 2001 Act had provided that the estate tax would no longer exist for the estates of decedents dying after 2009, and that the GST tax would not apply to generation-skipping transfers (taxable terminations, taxable distributions, and direct-skip transfers) made or occurring after 2009. The federal gift tax was not repealed, on the theory that it was needed to inhibit *inter vivos* gifts that would shift income and gains from high-bracket taxpayers to low-bracket taxpayers, but the maximum gift tax rate was lowered to 35 percent, the same as the maximum income tax rate, and the exemption equivalent amount was to be $1M. Also, §2511(c) was added in the gift tax in order to conform the completed-gift rules of the gift tax to those of the income tax. Thus, any post-2009 *inter vivos* gift into a trust that shifts any income away from the grantor was to be a completed gift for gift tax purposes.

B. The 2002-2009 Transition Period

There are provisions of the 2001 Act that operated as a phase-out of the estate tax and the GST during the period 2002-2009 inclusive.

First, the maximum estate tax (and GST) rate was reduced to 50 percent in 2002 and was ratcheted down to 45 percent in 2007-2009.

Second, the unified transfer tax credit for *estate tax* purposes was keyed to an exemption equivalent of $1M for estates of decedents dying in 2002 and 2003, and was ratcheted upward to $3.5M for estates of decedents dying in 2009. The GST exemption also increased in lock-step with the estate tax exemption-equivalent from 2004 through 2009. However, the *gift tax* exemption equivalent remained at $1M during the entire transition period (as well as thereafter).

As previously stated, the credit for state death taxes was phased out and replaced by a deduction for state death taxes. Additionally, a deduction conferred by §2057 for certain interests in family-owned businesses was repealed.

C. Partial Repeal of Stepped-Up Basis

To the extent that the estate of a decedent dying in 2010 elects out of the 2011 estate tax regime and thus is not subject to estate tax, estate transferees are subject to increased income tax exposure. The increased income tax exposure would result from the repeal of §1014 and its replacement by §1022 in the case of property acquired from a decedent dying in 2010. For purposes of §1022, the term "property acquired from a decedent" includes (*inter alia*) property acquired by bequest or inheritance from the decedent and property in a trust created by the decedent which the decedent had the power to revoke, alter, or amend.

Section 1022(a) provides that the basis of property acquired from a decedent dying after 2009 is to be the lesser of the decedent's basis or the fair market value of such property at the time of death. Thus, appreciated property acquired from a decedent is to have a carryover basis, but depreciated-value property is to have a value-at-death basis.

Appreciated property acquired from a decedent will be eligible for three upwards basis adjustments:

(1) the amount of unused deductible losses, consisting of the sum of:
    (a) unused net operating loss (NOL) carryforwards,
    (b) unused capital loss carryforwards, and
    (c) with respect to each and every business and investment asset held at death, the excess (if any) of the decedent's basis at death over the value at death;
(2) an amount equal to $1.3M (per decedent); and
(3) an amount equal to $3M for qualifying transfers to the decedent's surviving spouse.

These adjustments can only be made to assets owned by the decedent at death, trusts both created by and revocable by the decedent, and the surviving spouse's share of community property. In the case of property in which the decedent held an interest as joint tenant with right of survivorship, the decedent is treated as owning half where the other joint tenant is the decedent's spouse; otherwise, the decedent is treated as the owner of the portion of the property that is attributable to the consideration supplied by the decedent.

The adjustments can only be made to appreciated property and can only bring the basis of any appreciated asset up to its value at the time of the decedent's death.

Subject to the above-mentioned constraints, the aggregate available basis adjustment can be allocated among appreciated assets in the discretion of the decedent's personal representative. Of course, the $3M basis adjustment relating to qualifying transfers to the decedent's surviving spouse can only be made to such transfers.

D. Deferred Sunset of the 2001 Act

As mentioned at the beginning of this section, the sunset provision of the 2001 Tax Act (not in the Code), providing that all of the provisions of the 2001 Act shall cease to apply after 2010, was (by the 2010 Act) deferred to the end of 2012. If sunset actually occurs at the end of 2012, the law will essentially revert to its 2001 form, meaning that the exemptions under the estate tax and the GST would shrink to $1M, the higher rates found in §2001(c) will revive, the credit for state death taxes will be restored (and the §2058 deduction for the same would disappear), and the §2057 deduction for qualified interests in family-owned businesses would have been restored.

In addition to postponing the sunset until the end of 2012, the 2010 Act basically continues the federal transfer taxes (and §1014) as they existed in 2009, with various modifications mentioned above, but summarized here.

1. For decedents dying in 2010, 2011, and 2012, the estate tax exemption equivalent amount is raised to $5M, and the maximum estate tax rate is reduced to 35 percent.

2. Decedents dying in 2010 can elect between the reduced estate tax or the carryover basis system of §1022.

3. The gift tax exemption amount stays at $1M for 2010 but is raised to $5M for 2011 and 2012, and the maximum rate stays at 35 percent. Thus, the estate and gift taxes are re-integrated in 2011 and 2012.

4. The GST exemption amount increases to $5M. The GST tax rate is zero for 2010, and 35 percent for 2011 and 2012.

5. Portability of a married person's unused exemption equivalent amount to his or her spouse is allowed for decedents dying after 2009.

6. Section 2511(c), which would have linked the gift tax completed-gift rules to the corresponding income tax rules, is repealed.

7. Technical changes are made to the gift tax computation rules to insure that a donor does not lose available exemption equivalent amounts due to the changes in the gift tax.

QUESTIONS AND NOTES

1. The basis adjustments provided in §1022 cannot be made to the following assets:
    a. Property acquired by the decedent by gift within three years of death. This rule does not apply in the case of gifts from the decedent's spouse, unless such spouse herself acquired the property by gift during the three-year period. See §1022(d)(1)(C).
    b. Stock in certain foreign corporations. See §1022(d)(1)(D).
    c. IRD rights. The term "IRD" refers to "income in respect of a decedent," which means income earned by the decedent prior to death but not actually received. See §691(a). The prototype IRD right is earned but unpaid salary, including any right to deferred compensation, whether funded or unfunded. Thus pension rights, including rights in "401(k) plans," are IRD rights, as are annuities and IRAs.
2. a. Section 1014 is based on the larger notion that a taxpayer's income tax attributes wholly disappear at death. Not only does unrealized appreciation and depreciation disappear at a decedent's death, but so also do loss carryovers of all types (which are really a form of unrealized depreciation).

Under a carryover basis system, a decedent's income tax attributes continue after death. That is the rationale for upward basis adjustments for certain unused loss carryovers of the decedent.

b. It is certainly questionable that features of the transfer tax (such as a large exemption) be carried over to the income tax, as occurs under §1022 by reason of the free basis adjustments of up to $4.3M per decedent. The $3M free upward basis adjustment for qualified spousal bequests amounts to a permanent income tax exemption, whereas the transfer tax marital deduction operates only as a tax deferral mechanism.

c. A carryover basis system poses procedural problems. One is that the IRS is unlikely to contest basis determinations by an executor at a time (the decedent's death) when no tax is at issue. (Basis affects income tax only if there is a disposition of the asset by the transferee, or depreciation is claimed.) Second, the IRS has no way of knowing when carryover-basis assets are being disposed of. Thus, the §1022 carryover-basis system appears to be essentially unenforceable.

d. Estate personal representatives and trustees are under a duty to act impartially, unless the governing instrument explicitly waives that duty, and even then any discretion conferred upon the fiduciary must be exercised in good faith. What fiduciary problem is raised by §1022?

CHAPTER 3

GIFT TAX BASICS

This chapter deals with the issues of "what is a gift" under the gift tax after exclusions, who is the donor of a gift, when a gift is deemed to occur, and the valuation of gifts. In other words, this chapter has to do with identifying a "gross gift," a term not found in the Code. Since the gift tax deductions (for marital and charitable transfers) are almost identical to their estate tax counterparts, they are dealt with in a later chapter.

A "gross gift," by definition, is net of "consideration offsets." The gross gift is then reduced (or eliminated) by applicable exclusions (such as the annual exclusion) and deductions (the charitable deduction and the marital deduction), to arrive at the "taxable gift," which is the amount subject to gift tax. As described in Chapter 2, a given donor's lifetime cumulative taxable gifts are subject to a progressive rate schedule, but the tax is due on a "pay as you give" annual basis.

§3.1. Transfers Subject to Gift Tax

According to §2501(a), the gift tax is imposed on any "transfer of property by gift." The term "property" includes cash and interests in property, but not the value of services.[1] Section 2511(a) states that the gift tax "shall apply whether the transfer is in trust or otherwise, whether the gift is direct or indirect, and whether the property is real or personal, tangible or intangible." An example of an "indirect" transfer is a transfer carried out through an intermediary.[2]

Beyond the foregoing, the statutory provisions of the gift tax (unlike the estate tax) are virtually silent on how the details of various transactions are to be treated.

---

1. See *Comm'r v. Hogle*, 165 F.2d 352 (10th Cir.1947); *Estate of Childers v. Comm'r*, 10 T.C. 566, 579-580 (1948). See also *Rev. Rul. 66-167*, 1966-1 C.B. 20 (advance waiver of executor's commissions that enhanced son's legacy held not to be a gift).
2. See Reg. §25.2511-1(h)(1)-(3).

Most of the doctrine pertaining to the existence and amount of gifts derives from court cases and Treasury regulations.

In trying to understand gift tax doctrine, keep in mind that the gift tax was conceived primarily as a back up to the estate tax (and secondarily as a back up to the income tax). An *inter vivos* transfer subject to the gift tax should be a transfer that reduces the donor's potential gross estate.

A. *Transfer of Wealth for Insufficient Consideration*

The initial starting point is that any transfer of money or property (or an interest in property), regardless of motive, constitutes a gift for gift tax purposes. See §2512(b), which states: "Where property is transferred for less than an adequate and full consideration in money or money's worth, then the amount by which the value of the property exceeded the value of the consideration shall be deemed a gift. . . ." Contrast this "objective" approach with the subjective approach under the §102(a) income tax exclusion, where the donor's motive is the determinative factor.[3] Under the gift tax the presence or absence of donative intent or a motive of "disinterested generosity" is not wholly dispositive as to the existence or nonexistence of a gift.[4] Thus, a transfer pursuant to a settlement of marital property rights can be a gift for gift tax purposes, despite the absence of donative intent.

The rule that there is no gift for gift tax purposes where a transfer is made for full and adequate consideration in money or money's worth follows from the estate-depletion principle. In such a case, there is no depletion of the potential estate, since the property or money transferred has been fully replaced by other property or money of equal value.

1. *Meaning of "Money's Worth"*

The consideration must be in money or "money's worth," since only money or money's worth adds to a donor's net estate. Thus, "consideration" for gift tax purposes is not to be confused with the term "consideration" in the law of contracts. For example, a transfer in consideration of love and affection is a gift because love and affection are not in money or money's worth. This was the holding of *Comm'r v. Wemyss*, 324 U.S. 303 (1945). Indeed, love and affection are the typical motives for effecting gratuitous transfers. Likewise, detriment to the donee does not constitute consideration for gift tax purposes because it does not replenish the donor's estate.

The surrender of a claim against the transferor qualifies as consideration "in money's worth," since the surrender augments the transferor's wealth by relieving him or her of a legal obligation to deplete it by making payments that would not themselves be subject to gift (or estate) tax. For example, if B owes L $10,000 as the result of having purchased services from L on credit, and B transfers property worth

---

3. See *Comm'r v. Duberstein*, 363 U.S. 278 (1960).
4. See Reg. §25.2511-1(g)(1).

$10,000 to L on condition that L surrender the claim against B, there is no net gift, because neither party has changed its wealth position.

But then, a surrender of a right or claim against the transferor fails to qualify as consideration in money or money's worth in cases where the satisfaction by the transferor of such surrendered right or claim would be subject to the estate or gift tax. Thus, if a person makes an *inter vivos* transfer in exchange for the surrender by the transferee of the latter's right to dower, curtesy, elective share, or other inheritance right, the surrender fails to qualify as consideration in money's worth, because any estate transfer in satisfaction of any of these rights would be subject to the estate tax. See §2034 (property is included in the decedent's gross estate even though the surviving spouse may have possessed the "pre-existing" right to take it under her dower rights). This rule that the surrender of inheritance (etc.) rights does not qualify as consideration in money's worth was initially codified in what is now §2043(b) of the estate tax, which was "carried over" to the gift tax by the decision in the case of *Merrill v. Fahs*, 324 U.S. 308 (1945), and is now found in §25.2512-8 of the gift tax regulations.

Merrill v. Fahs involved an ante-nuptial agreement. There the Supreme Court held that the estate and gift taxes should be construed *in para materia* with respect to "money's worth." Thus, a future estate-included transfer (e.g., the taking of dower at the transferor's death) is prevented from being "converted" into a tax-free "sale" in exchange for a surrender of the inheritance right.

Now suppose that H transfers property to W in exchange for W's surrender of her community property interest in specified property. In this case, the rights W surrenders would constitute valid consideration in money's worth, since W's community property interest is her own existing interest in property, as opposed to being a mere inheritance right to be satisfied in the future by property includible in H's gross estate.[5]

Similarly, if H makes a transfer to W in exchange for W's release of her right to be supported by H during her lifetime or to obtain H's property upon divorce, the surrender by W of her support or divorce rights qualifies as valid consideration in money or money's worth. This result flows from the fact that the payment by H of support, or the transfer by him of property upon divorce, would not be subject to gift tax (under doctrine to be discussed below).[6] In other words, the present transfer by H is excluded because it is essentially a substitute for what would eventually have been one or more tax-free transfers.

2. Transfers for Partial Consideration

Where there is consideration in money or money's worth, but such consideration is worth less than the value of what is transferred, the gift amount is the excess of the latter over the former. In other words, the partial consideration is an "offset" against the value of what is transferred, and only the "net" transfer constitutes a gift.

---

5. See, e.g., *Gregory v. Comm'r*, 39 T.C. 1012 (1963).
6. See, e.g., *Rev. Rul.* 78-379, 1978-2 C.B. 238.

A common example of a transfer for partial consideration is where a donor transfers property worth $100,000 to a donee and the donee assumes (or takes subject to) a mortgage on the property in the amount of $65,000. Here, there is a net gift of $35,000.[7]

Another example of a partial-consideration gift is the so-called "net gift" transaction, which refers to the situation where the donor's gift is made on condition that the donee pay any gift tax due. Since the donor of a gift is legally liable for the gift tax under §2502(c), and since the payment of the gift tax by the donor would not itself be a gift, the assumption by the donee of such liability is an economic benefit in money's worth to the donor.[8]

3. Below-Market Term Loans

A purported loan transaction with a relative can involve a partial-consideration gift. Suppose Alice makes an interest-free loan to her brother Bob in the amount of $100,000 repayable in full at the end of ten years. The transfer of $100,000 is a gift to the extent, if any, that the $100,000 exceeds the value of the consideration received, which is a claim to the $100,000 principal at the end of ten years. Although the total to be received by A will eventually total $100,000, the consideration must be valued at the time of the transfer of the $100,000. If the consideration is not valued at the time of transfer, it will be impossible to ascertain the amount of the net depletion (if any) of the donor's potential gross estate occasioned by the transfer.

At this point it is necessary to explain more precisely the valuation of the right to receive future amounts. A dollar in hand is worth more than a dollar in the future. A dollar in hand can be invested, in which case it will grow with the passage of time on account of earning interest, and the interest will compound. The calculation can be expressed algebraically as follows, where the future amount (A) is obtained by investing the principal amount (P) at a specified interest rate (r), expressed as a decimal, for the number of periods (n), such as years.[9] The compound interest formula is:

$$A = P(1 + r)^n.$$

The *present value* of a future amount is figured by simply working through the compound interest formula in reverse. The generic formula for deriving the present value (P_v) of a future amount (A) to be received at the end of n future periods (such as years), at periodical (such as annual) interest rate ("discount rate") r is:

$$P_v = \frac{A}{(1 + r)^n}.$$

---

7. See, e.g., *Estate of Levine v. Comm'r*, 634 F.2d 12 (2d Cir.1980).

8. See *Rev. Rul.* 75-72, 1975-1 C.B. 310.

9. If the interest is compounded on a more frequent basis than annually, the n and the r must be put on a par. Thus, if the interest on a 10-year investment is to be compounded quarterly, n is 40 (10 × 4), and r is 0.025 (0.1 annual rate divided by 4).

Thus, if one is to receive $100,000 at the end of three years, its present value (at an assumed discount rate of 4 percent compounded annually) would be calculated as follows:

$$P_v = \frac{\$100,000}{(1+0.04)^3}$$

$$P_v = \$88,899.64.$$

The technique of discounting to present value is objective, but it makes the simplifying assumption that the timely collection of future amounts is a sure thing. In reality, future payments are not certain of collection, and greater accuracy could be obtained by examining the facts of each case, which normally would result in further discounting to allow for risks of noncollection or delay. Nevertheless, in order to avoid the necessity for costly fact-finding in related-party loan transactions, the IRS has valued debt obligations by simply discounting them to present value. However, prior to 1984, the gift tax law provided no standard computational method for such discounting.[10] These computational issues were resolved when, in 1984, Congress added §7872 to the Code, and made it applicable (*inter alia*) to below-market gift loans made after June 6, 1984. A below-market gift loan for a period of time (a gift "term" loan) is one in which the amount loaned exceeds the present value of the repayment obligation using a discount rate which is the applicable federal rate (AFR) for the month in which the loan is made. See §7872(e). (Below-market "demand" loans are discussed shortly.) The AFR (which is derived from the prevailing interest rate on very secure federal obligations) varies from month to month, and is set forth in Revenue Procedures published by the IRS. The discounting is to occur on a semi-annual basis. See §7872(f)(1) and (2)(A). A below-market loan is *prima facie* a "gift" loan if made to a relative or close friend.

Section 7872 deals with the income, gift, and estate tax treatment of below-market gift loans. For gift tax purposes, the excess of the amount lent over the present value of the repayment obligation is treated as a gift in the year the loan is made. See §7872(b)(1) & (d)(2). There is an exception where the aggregate of the loans between the lender and the borrower does not exceed $10,000, but this exception does not apply if the "borrower" uses the below-interest loan to directly or indirectly purchase or carry income-producing assets.[11]

Applying §7872 to the example of the no-interest loan of $100,000 from Alice to Bob, and assuming an AFR of 4 percent per annum, the r in the present-value formula would be 0.04 divided by two (= 0.02), and the n would be "20" (there are 20 half-years). Thus, the value of the consideration supplied by B would be $67,297, resulting in a gift for gift tax purposes of $32,703 in the year the loan is made.

Section 7872 also applies for income tax purposes. A below-market gift loan can be used as an income-shifting device: The funds that the lender could have invested

---

10. See *Rev. Rul.* 73-61, 1973-1 C.B. 408, which basically ignored these fine-tuning issues.
11. See §7872(c)(2).

at a market rate of return are transferred to the borrower, who can invest the borrowed money at a market rate of return without having to pay market rate interest for borrowing the funds. To counteract the income-shifting potential of a below-market gift loan, §7872(a)(1) provides that there is a deemed interest payment running from the borrower to the lender equal to the "forgone interest" calculated by using the AFR on an annual basis. In the hypothetical involving the $100,000 interest-free loan from Alice to Bob, Bob would be deemed to pay interest to Alice at the AFR (4 percent per year, or $4,000). This deemed interest payment is includible in Alice's gross income. The deductibility to Bob under §163 depends on what Bob does with the borrowed funds. Thus, if Bob invests the $100,000 in a bank CD, the deemed interest payment by Bob would be characterized as deductible "investment interest" subject to the limitation provided by §163(d). If the loan does not exceed $100,000, the deemed interest payment from the borrower to the lender cannot exceed the borrower's net investment income for the year, unless one of the principal purposes of the arrangement is tax avoidance. See §7872(d)(1).

If the lender (Alice) in the transaction described above were to die before Bob repaid the loan, Alice's claim against Bob would be an asset of her gross estate. The general estate tax valuation rule is that of "fair market value at death," which (as applied to Bob's note) would result in a heavy discount from its face value. See Reg. §20.2031-4 (estate tax valuation of notes). However, under §7872(i)(2) the estate tax valuation of repayment obligations under gift term loans is to be carried out by using the valuation techniques provided by §7872. Since valuation under §7872 is carried out only by discounting to present value (and using a relatively low discount rate), the effect is to confer an unrealistically high value on Bob's note, but one that is consistent with the gift tax treatment.

4. Sham Loans

Notwithstanding §7872, the IRS can argue in any given case involving a loan to a relative or good friend that the repayment obligation of the borrower, although valid in form, lacks economic substance or is a sham.[12]

The Ruling set forth below involves an "installment" gift, where the object of the taxpayer is to make a gift of significant-value property not easily carved up into small bites in installments (over several years) in order to obtain maximum use of the gift tax annual exclusion under §2503(b). The exclusion is currently $13,000 (as indexed) per donee per year, but during the years covered by the Ruling it was $3,000 per donee per year. The facts in the Ruling indicated that the "buyer's" notes bore no interest. Under current law, this transaction could have been dealt with under §7872 so as to find a gift equal to a portion of the amount lent. However, the Ruling was issued before the enactment (and effective date) of §7872. In any event, the sham loan doctrine can be invoked in an effort to show that the repayment obligation is worth zero (or very little).

---

12. For income tax purposes, if a purported loan is really a gift, the loan is a nondeductible expense and not a capital expenditure of the lender, resulting in a zero income tax basis to the lender, which defeats any bad debt or other loss deduction of the lender.

Revenue Ruling 77-299

1977-2 Cum. Bull. 14

G had given A, G's grandchild, $3,000 per year at Christmas since A was 10 years old. When A was 21 years old and enrolled in graduate school, G proposed to give Blackacre, an unimproved tract of nonincome-producing real property with a fair market value of $27,000, to A. A had spent the money previously given him by G, did not have any other funds, and did not have an independent source of income. When informed of G's intent, G's attorney, in order to minimize G's Federal gift tax on the transfer, suggested a sale of the property to A in return for installment notes that would be payable in yearly amounts equal to the annual gift tax exclusion.

The plan was implemented in July 1972, at which time A received a package of instruments in the mail from G's attorney which contained a check from G for $50, a deed to Blackacre, a mortgage on the property, one note with a face amount of $2,950 and eight notes each in the amount of $3,000. A letter also accompanied the package explaining the transaction and indicating that G did not intend to collect on the notes, but intended to forgive each payment as it became due. A did not have prior knowledge of the transaction. There were no negotiations concerning the transaction, and G's attorney represented all of the parties to it. The notes were nonnegotiable. The notes provided that A owed $26,950 on Blackacre. The first note in the amount of $2,950 matured on January 1, 1973, and each additional note in the amount of $3,000 matured on January 1 of each succeeding year. The mortgages on the property were taken to secure the payment of the notes.

On December 25, 1972, G forgave the $2,950 due on January 1, 1973. On December 25 of 1973 and 1974, G forgave the $3,000 due on January 1 of the following years.

The question presented is whether the transfer of the property in return for the notes secured by a purchase money mortgage was a bona fide sale between the parties or whether the transaction was in substance a gift of the transferor's entire interest in the property structured to avoid the Federal gift tax.

In *Deal v. Comm'r*, 29 T.C. 730 (1958), the taxpayer transferred in trust a remainder interest in unimproved, nonincome-producing property to the taxpayer's children in return for unsecured demand notes. The taxpayer cancelled $3,000 of each child's indebtedness each year until the balance due was completely cancelled. The Tax Court held the notes executed by the children were not intended as consideration for the transfer and, rather than a bona fide sale, the taxpayer made a gift of the remainder interest to the children.

Thus, in the instant case, whether the transfer of property was a sale or a gift depends upon whether, as part of a prearranged plan, G intended to forgive the notes that were received when G transferred the property. It should be noted that the intent to forgive notes is to be distinguished from donative intent, which is not relevant. A finding of an intent to forgive the note relates to whether valuable consideration was received.

In the instant case, the facts clearly indicate that G, as part of a prearranged plan, intended to forgive the notes. Accordingly, for Federal gift tax purposes, G made a transfer by gift to A in 1972 in the amount of $27,000.

The Tax Court does not go along with the approach of *Rev. Rul. 77-299.* In *Haygood v. Comm'r*, 42 T.C. 936 (1964), the notes were for a fixed term and were secured by the transferred property.[13] The Tax Court cited *Wemyss v. Comm'r*, 324 U.S. 303 (1945), supra, for the proposition that the existence of consideration is to be determined by objective facts, and that donative intent is not controlling.

The Tax Court will insist, nevertheless, that the consideration must be bona fide in the objective sense for it to be allowed as an offset under the gift tax. In *Estate of Mitchell v. Comm'r*, T.C. Memo. 1982-185, the donor transferred property to a donee in return for the latter's unsecured promise to pay an annuity to the donor for the donor's life. The court ignored the purported "consideration," since the donee was unable and unwilling to pay the annuity, and the donor was terminally ill. The transaction was held to be simply a disguised gift.

The Service still adheres to its position as stated in *Rev. Rul. 77-299.* See *Rev. Rul. 83-180*, 1983-2 C.B. 169, which approved serial gifts to a donee of fractional interests (acres) in real property.

The installment gift technique will be aborted in mid-stream if the donor dies before all the payments have become due. One technique for carrying the gift through might be for the donor's will to contain a provision forgiving any balance due on the notes upon his death. However, the forgiveness will not avoid transfer tax. The notes are included in the donor's gross estate because they were owned by the decedent at death, and the forgiveness-by-will is simply an "indirect" bequest.

Another technique is to add a provision in the installment notes themselves that states that the obligations contained therein shall be void upon the seller's death prior to maturity. An obligation of this type is referred to as a self-canceling installment note (SCIN). The SCIN technique has the effect of avoiding inclusion of the installment notes in the gross estate of the seller/creditor, because the asset ceases to have any value at the seller's/creditor's death.[14] For gift tax purposes, a SCIN would (in principle) have to be discounted to reflect the self-cancellation feature, unless the periodic payments were adjusted upwards.[15]

5. Below-Market Demand Loans

One can avoid the "consideration" rule by structuring a below-market gift loan as a "demand" loan rather than a term loan. (In a gift term loan the consideration is

---

13. Accord, *Kelley v. Comm'r*, 63 T.C. 321 (1974) (*nonacq.*). Assets that expire or disappear at the owner's death have a value of zero for estate tax purposes.

14. See *Estate of Moss v. Comm'r*, 74 T.C. 1239 (1980) (*acq.*).

15. See *Estate of Costanza v. Comm'r*, T.C. Memo. 2001-128, where the Tax Court held that the exchange of two properties for a SCIN was not a bona fide sale for adequate and full consideration where only three untimely payments were made on the note, but rather a gift of the total value of those properties less the three payments made.

valued — and it will be less than the amount lent — because future amounts must be discounted to present value.) In a gift demand loan situation, the lender can demand the immediate repayment of the full principal. It follows that the repayment obligation is in the "present," and this avoids meaningful discounting. Thus, the consideration (the repayment obligation) approaches being "full and adequate"; that is, its value almost equals the amount lent.

The gift demand loan was first dealt with by the courts. In *Crown v. Comm'r*, 585 F.2d 234 (1978), the government argued that there were gifts *with the passage of time* equal to the interest forgone by the lender during each calendar year the loan was outstanding. The Seventh Circuit rejected this contention, stating:

> [T]o characterize the mere use of property as a transfer of a property right implies a broader concept of what constitutes a property right under the gift tax laws than has heretofore been recognized. The application of the Commissioners' theory to the case at bar is the equivalent to viewing the taxpayer as constructively receiving a hypothetical interest payment on the money loaned which he then constructively transfers to the borrower. This raises the problem of whether a tax is being imposed on what the lender could have done rather than what he did.

The Seventh Circuit decided that failing to earn income was not a depletion of the donor's potential estate and did not augment the donee's wealth.

The *Crown* case was subsequently overturned by the Supreme Court in *Dickman v. Comm'r*, 465 U.S. 330 (1984), which held that gifts occurred under a related-party no-interest demand loan with the passage of time in an amount equal to the forgone interest for the period (during any calendar year) in which the loan was outstanding. In *Dickman* the majority opinion stated:

> We have little difficulty accepting the theory that the use of valuable property — in this case money — is itself a legally protectable property interest. . . . The right to the use of $100,000 without charge is a valuable interest in the money lent, as much so as the rent-free use of property consisting of land and buildings. . . . The value of the use of money is found in what it can produce; the measure of that value is interest — "rent" for the use of the funds.

In opposition to the contention that the gift tax does not reach a voluntary decision to abstain from investing for gain, the majority opinion stated:

> It is certainly true that no law requires . . . that a transferor charge interest or rent for the use of money or other property. An individual may, without incurring the gift tax, squander money, conceal it under a mattress, or otherwise waste its use value by failing to invest it. Such acts of consumption have nothing to do with lending money at no interest. If the taxpayer chooses not to waste the use value of money, but instead transfers the use to someone else, a taxable event has occurred.

The *Dickman* case, decided in early 1984, was quickly superseded by §7872, supra, enacted later in the same year. As applied to gift demand loans, §7872 provides that the gifts for gift tax purposes occur with the passage of time in an amount equal to the forgone interest (which is figured by using the AFR). See §7872(a)(1)(A) and (e)(2). This result basically tracks *Dickman*. As mentioned earlier, there is also for income tax purposes a constructive interest payment from the lender to the borrower designed to curb the income shifting potential of such loans. See also the *de minimis* exception found in §7872(c)(2).

QUICK QUESTION

Although she normally rents her condo to vacationers, Grandma Gertie gave grandson Harry and his wife the use of her condo in Florida for two weeks. Which one of the following statements is *TRUE*?

    A. Gertie has made a taxable gift equal to the fair rental value of the condo for the two weeks.

    B. Because this is not a transfer of property, there is no taxable gift.

    C. Section 7872 does not reach that imputed gift and so there is no taxable gift.

    D. The annual exclusion probably covers it so it isn't an important issue.

NOTES AND PROBLEMS

1. a. *Rev. Rul. 77-299*, supra, may be on shaky ground in stating that the status of the consideration given by the transferee is ascertained by reference to the intent of the *donor* (and not the donee)? The Service's approach is not necessary to prevent transfer tax avoidance, because the uncollected notes will be included in the transferor's gross estate (and the personal representative of the estate will have a duty to enforce the notes). The transfer tax aim of the transferor is only to be able to use multiple annual exclusions.

    b. How would a SCIN be analyzed for gift tax purposes? Assume the same facts as in *Rev. Rul. 77-299*, supra, except that (1) the notes are self-canceling, (2) the seller (G) was 85 years old, and (3) the notes provide a market rate of interest?

2. a. The installment-gift technique does not produce very appealing results under the income tax. Normally, an installment sale of real property by an individual qualifies for the "installment method," which has the effect of deferring the reporting of the gain for income tax purposes. However, under §453B, virtually any disposition (including by way of a gift) of an installment obligation is deemed to be a realization event for income tax purposes, so that the potential income-tax gain inherent in the note is recognized to the transferor, whether or not the transferor received anything of value. The purpose of this rule is to assure that the purchaser's (donee's) "cost" basis in the property reflected the full recognition of gain to the seller (donor).

b. If an installment note is owned at death, the installment note is treated as an IRD right (right to "income in respect of a decedent"), meaning that the decedent's basis in the note carries over to the estate or legatee acquiring the note. In other words, the note does not obtain a stepped-up basis under §1014. See §§691(a)(4) and 1014(c).

c. A bequest (as opposed to a gift) of installment notes does not normally constitute a "disposition" immediately triggering installment-note gain under the income tax. See §453B(c). However, there is an exception for a cancellation of a note at death, whether it occurs under the decedent's will or by its own terms (as in the case of a SCIN). In case of a cancellation at death, the decedent's estate (or legatee) realizes gain in the same manner as would occur under a gift. See §691(a)(5). See *Rev. Rul.* 86-72, 1986-1 C.B. 253 (construing §691(a)(5)(C) to refer to a SCIN).

d. An installment "sale" to related parties raise income tax issues aside from §453B. First, if the property is sold to one's spouse, no gain or loss is recognized, and the transferee takes a carryover basis. §1041. Second, if the sale is at a loss to one's spouse, children, grandchildren, or parents, there is not only no installment reporting, but the loss is disallowed under §267(a)(1). Third, for any kind of property sold on the installment method to any of these relations, a sale or other disposition of the property by the purchaser within two years of the first sale will produce an acceleration of gain to the original seller. See §453(e) & (f).

e. Transactions of the type described above are basic exemplars of a form of estate planning device known as an "estate freeze." The idea of estate freeze transactions in general is to shift future appreciation to the younger generation while, in its place, retaining a fixed-income obligation that is not likely to change appreciably in value.

3. a. The majority opinion in *Dickman* held that the right to use money at the sufferance of the lender was a property interest, citing the tenancy at will as an analogous property interest. Is this not elevating terminology over substance? A tenant at will has no right to sell or sublease. Moreover, a tenancy at will is hard to distinguish from a revocable license to use property, which is not considered to be a property interest, but only an immunity from an action for trespass. A licensee has a revocable permission to use property, whereas a tenant at will has the revocable right to exclusive possession.

b. A borrower does not really acquire an "interest in" money, but rather the money itself. Therefore, the repayment obligation is consideration for the transfer that should be subtracted from the amount lent to arrive at the amount of the net gift. The value of the repayment obligation could be determined under the willing-buyer willing-seller test, in which case it would be worth somewhat less than its face amount on account of possible delays, legal defenses, and collection problems. But the government simply didn't want to suffer the inconvenience of this approach. Nevertheless, there is little or no estate tax avoidance in the demand loan scenario: The offset to the gift (the value of the repayment obligation) is precisely what would be included in the lender's gross estate if the lender died prior to repayment.

c. Section 7872 implicitly recognizes that there is no depletion of the lender's estate by treating an amount equal to the imputed gift (the foregone interest) as being repaid by the borrower to the lender as interest. Off-setting cash payments are transfers for full and adequate consideration for gift tax purposes. For income tax purposes the character of the cross-payments matters. (The gift/interest dyad shifts income back to the lender.) For gift tax purposes it does not.

d. A demand loan of money superficially resembles a revocable trust, where gifts occur when distributions are made from the trust to a beneficiary, free of the power to revoke. But neither *Dickman* nor the §7872 gift rule refer to distributed wealth, which in the demand loan scenario would be the yield from the investment, if any, of the borrowed money by the borrower. However, the revocable-trust analogy collapses, because the lender has no power to revoke (obtain) the investment property and its yield.

4. a. An interest-free *term* loan is an estate planning loser, because the value of the repayment obligation (which is an offset to the gift, but is included in the gross estate) increases with the passage of time.

b. A rent-free *term* "loan" of *property* is the equivalent of a gift of a term interest followed by a reversion in the donor. The value of the term interest is to be determined by using actuarial tables that are based on discounting future amounts to present value. Thus, a rent-free term loan to a relative would clearly entail a gift for gift tax purposes. It would be a bad estate planning move for the same reason as in (a).

c. Gifts of term interests in property to a qualifying charity are generally disqualified from the income tax, gift tax, and estate tax charitable deductions. See §§170(f)(3)(A), 2055(e)(2), and 2522(c)(2). However, §2503(g) comes to the rescue in the case of a rent-free term loan of *an art work to a museum* by treating the gift as a nullity for gift tax purposes, thereby achieving the same end result as a gift tax charitable deduction. At the same time, §2503(g) provides that any outstanding term interest of the museum in the art work cannot be subtracted from the lender's gross estate for estate tax purposes. (In the absence of §2503(g), the interest would be subtracted from the lender's gross estate, wholly apart from the charitable deduction issue, because it is an interest not owned by the decedent at death.)

5. Does *Dickman* mean that a rent-free *demand* loan of a vacation home or a yacht to a friend or relative results in a gift equal to the foregone rent? (The dissent in *Dickman* worried over this point, because the majority opinion strongly implied that a rent-free "demand" lease of commercial property to a natural object of one's bounty would be a gift.) Does the answer depend on whether the transaction is characterized as (a) a leasehold interest, (b) a tenancy at will, or (c) a license (or bailment), under state law? Whether the property produces income or is a personal-use asset? Cf. *Rev. Rul.* 70-477, 1970-2 C.B. 62 (positing distinction between lease and license for purposes of pre-1970 income tax charitable deduction). In fact, the IRS has not moved down this path.

6. a. Gifts of services are not gifts of wealth. But what if Kevin helps Georgia build a garage on Georgia's land?

    b. Does the gift (or estate) tax reach the following types of valuable transfers to relatives, friends, and neighbors: economically valuable genes (appearance, personality, intelligence); good upbringing and acculturation; influential family friends and business associates; stock market (or horse racing) tips; business and investment opportunities (as opposed to funds)?

7. a. A transfer for *partial* consideration can for income tax purposes be characterized as a part-gift part-sale. Nevertheless, according to Reg. §1.1001-1(e), the transferor recognizes gain in an amount equal to the excess (if any) of the amount realized over the *full* basis in the transferred property. However, no loss can be recognized. Otherwise, one could obtain an income tax deduction for a partial gift but not for a "whole" gift.

    b. A part-gift part-sale to charity involves a different rule under which the basis of the transferred property is allocated between the gift element and the sale element. See §1011(b). For example, if Agnes, holding property worth $100x with a basis of $40x, "sells" the property to the X Charity for $40x, 40 percent of the basis ($16x) is allocated to the sale portion — since the consideration equals 40 percent of the property's value — producing a gain of $24. In the noncharitable situation, supra, Agnes would have no gain. Which approach is preferable?

    c. As noted earlier in a part-gift part-sale (not to a charity), the transferee's basis is the greater of the consideration provided or the §1015 basis, not the sum of the two.

B. Non-Gift Wealth Transfers

Certain wealth transfers (not for full and adequate consideration) are beyond the reach of the gift tax.

1. Personal Consumption and Economic Waste

As the excerpt from the majority opinion in *Dickman* stated, it has always been understood that personal consumption and economic waste are not gifts for gift tax purposes. This rule is related to, but not the same as, the rule pertaining to "full and adequate consideration in money or money's worth."

In the case of economic waste (destroying or abandoning property), the rationale must be that there is no "transfer," which word denotes the enrichment of another party.

In the case of consumption that takes the form of a purchase of consumer goods, the rationale might be that the initial payment for goods is a "transfer" (to another party) but the transfer is for full and adequate consideration in money or money's worth (property), which is then "wasted" through consumption of the purchased property.

In the case of consumption that takes the form of a purchase of services, there is a transfer, but here there appears to be no consideration received "in money's worth" in the sense of money or property. On the one hand, it is true that the services literally possess "money's worth" in the sense that they were obtained in commerce at a market price. On the other hand, the value of services received does not augment the transferor's potential gross estate — just as the performance of services does not deplete the service-provider's gross estate.[16]

An alternative rationale for excluding the purchase of services as consumption is that there is a transfer but it is not "by gift," as required by §2501(a)(1). The phrase "by gift" is not elaborated upon in the regulations under §2501, but Reg. §25.2511-1(c)(1) suggests that a gift is a "gratuitous" *inter vivos* transfer. The idea of "gratuitousness" suggests a transfer in which the transferor does not receive a *quid pro quo* of an *economic* (as opposed to personal) nature. Reg. §25.2511-1(g)(1) muddies the waters by stating that "donative intent" is "not controlling," and that "[t]he application of the tax is based on the objective facts of the transfer and the circumstances under which it is made."

This equivocation is resolved under Reg. §25.2512-8, which (despite its redundancy with material presented earlier) is worth quoting in part:

> Transfers reached by the gift tax are not confined to those only which, being without valuable consideration, accord with the common law concept of gifts, but embrace as well sales, exchanges, and other dispositions of property for consideration to the extent that the value of the property transferred by the donor exceeds the value in money or money's worth of the consideration given therefor. However, a sale, exchange, or other transfer of property made in the ordinary course of business (a transaction which is bona fide, at arm's length, and free from any donative intent), will be considered as made for a full and adequate consideration in money or money's worth. A consideration not reducible to a value in money or money's worth, as love and affection, promise of marriage, is to be wholly disregarded. . . .

This "ordinary course of business exception" to the concept of gift does not necessarily refer to any business *of the taxpayer*, although arm's length transactions within the course of the taxpayer's business would certainly come within this exception. Rather, the "business" referred to is that of the payee or transferee, and may perhaps be better thought of as an exception for transactions in commerce, market transactions generally, and bargained-for exchanges of an economic (as opposed to "personal") nature. In any event, the exception includes the purchase of services in the market.

2. Political Contributions

The status of political contributions surfaced in the early 1970s as a result of *Stern v. U.S.*, 436 F.2d 1327 (5th Cir.1971), which held that a political contribution — presumptively a wealth-transfer gift for no consideration in

---

16. See *Comm'r v. Hogle*, 165 F.2d 352 (10th Cir.1947).

money's worth — could come within the "business transaction" exception if the proper circumstances were present. In *Stern*, the taxpayer established that the contributions were bona fide, at arm's length, without donative intent, and permeated with economic and business motives. However, the Service refused to follow *Stern*.

Subsequently, in *Carson v. Comm'r*, 71 T.C. 252 (1978) (*acq.*), *aff'd*, 641 F.2d 864 (10th Cir.1981), the Tax Court, in a reviewed decision, held that a political contribution by the taxpayer was not a "gift," without relying on the business-transaction exception:

> [The facts here] do not suggest a gift to the candidate, but the use of petitioner's resources to promote the social framework petitioner considered most auspicious to the attainment of his objectives in life. Petitioner focused on the social structure most conducive to his economic aspirations; others may focus on a social structure advancing their own notions of social justice, or conditions they deem essential for world peace or public order. In either case, the individual candidate may generally be viewed, for purposes of the gift tax, as the means to the ends of the contributor.

The Tax Court majority opinion also relied heavily on the notion that the gift tax was intended as a back-up to the estate tax, and that political contributions are rarely substitutes for bequests. Political contributions are not *objectively* "donative" (regardless of donative intent) insofar as they do not involve the transmission of wealth to the natural objects of the transferor's bounty.

Three judges involved in the Tax Court decision in *Carson* concurred on the theory that the political contributions were a form of personal consumption to promote the taxpayer's views.

Three other Tax Court judges agreed with the result on the ground that the gift tax should not be construed so as to interfere with the political process.

A dissenting opinion in the Tax Court argued that the language of the gift tax statute and regulations encompassed political contributions.

The Tenth Circuit basically followed the Tax Court majority opinion.

Section 2501(a)(4), added to the Code in 1974, exempts from gift tax contributions made by an individual after May 7, 1974, to a "political organization (within the meaning of §527(e)(1)) for the use of such organization." (The facts at issue in the *Stern* and *Carson* cases occurred prior to 1974.) The 1974 Senate Report stated: "The committee believes that it is inappropriate to apply the gift tax to political contributions because the tax system should not be used to reduce or restrict political contributions."

Section 84 of the Code, enacted at the same time as §2501(a)(4), provides that a political gift of appreciated property is a deemed realization event for income tax purposes, so that the transferor recognizes gain (and the organization acquires a cost basis). However, a donor cannot realize a loss on an in-kind political contribution.

3. *Transfers Mandated by Law*

Although no Code provision or Treasury regulation is directly in point, it has always been assumed that transfers compelled by law or arising from a legal obligation are not subject to gift tax. Common examples include the payments of taxes, fines, penalties, assessments, and legally mandated fees. Similarly treated are payments, purchases, and other transfers in satisfaction of support obligations, which are imposed by state law, usually for the benefit of spouses and minor children. The support concept under state law typically covers necessities such as food, clothing, housing, and basic medical care. State law may vary with respect to whether other items, particularly education, are included within the support concept.[17] The quantity of expenditures mandated by the duty of support may vary according to the provider's (or recipient's) resources and accustomed standard of living.

A somewhat tortured explanation of the gift tax exclusion for law-mandated transfers in general, and the support exclusion in particular, was provided by the case of *Harris v. Comm'r*, 340 U.S. 106 (1950). There the Supreme Court dealt with the gift tax implications of a property transfer from H to W pursuant to a separation agreement adopted by a divorce decree, where the rights surrendered by W (which were inheritance rights) did not qualify as consideration in money's worth under §2043(b)(1), which was imported into the gift tax as a result of *Merrill v. Fahs*, 324 U.S. 308 (1945), and is now incorporated by Reg. §25.2512-8. Therefore, another theory was needed in order to reach the conclusion that there was no gift.

The Court's analysis in *Harris* began with the proposition that the "consideration" notion comes into play under §2053(c)(1) of the estate tax, which allows a deduction against the gross estate for the estate's payment of debts and claims against the estate *that are founded upon a "promise or agreement"* only if the decedent received consideration in money or money's worth. The rationale of this rule is that the consideration received during life augmented the potential gross estate of the decedent, and the estate tax deduction merely offsets this inclusion. Viewed instrumentally, this rule prevents a decedent's will from clothing a bequest to a friend or relative as a deductible debt or claim.

The payment by the estate personal representative of a claim that did *not* arise out of a promise or agreement (such as an income or gift tax liability) is deductible by the estate under §2053(a)(3), even though the decedent received no consideration for having incurred the obligation. In other words, the payment of such a claim is not considered to be a gratuitous estate transfer.

Next, the Court in *Harris* observed (on the basis of prior decisions, including *Merrill v. Fahs*) that the gift and estate taxes are to be construed *in pari materia*. Thus, if the payment of a debt or claim not founded on a promise or agreement is not subject to estate tax, then it is not subject to gift tax either.

Finally, the Court then held that the transfer in question did not derive its efficacy from the agreement between H and W but rather from the divorce decree, because the court having jurisdiction over the divorce decree had the power to modify the agreement that had been reached by the parties. Therefore, the *inter*

---

17. See *Rev. Rul.* 54-343, 1954-2 C.B. 318.

vivos transfer, having been "founded upon" such a court decree, was exempt from gift tax, even though the transferor did not receive consideration in money's worth.

It might be said the *Harris* analysis is unduly formalistic in that ongoing support obligations to one's spouse (not mandated by a divorce decree), and perhaps to children of the marriage, really *are* founded upon a "promise or agreement," namely, the marriage contract, or possibly an ante-nuptial agreement. But the legalistic perspective is that the marriage contract only creates a "status," and the obligations (and rights) incident to this status are imposed by state law. (An ante-nuptial agreement would be unlikely to create new support obligations or add to existing ones.) Thus, payments and transfers that satisfy ongoing support obligations are not really contractual, and do not require consideration to avoid being gifts.[18]

The unlimited gift tax marital deduction, the §2503(e) exclusion for the direct payment of tuition and medical care bills incurred by any person, and the gift tax annual exclusion all render the distinction between "gift" and "support" of marginal consequence.

A situation analogous to a "mandated-by-law transfer" involves community property. The law assumes there is no gift where income earned (or property acquired) by one spouse becomes the community property of both spouses. In effect, the income or property is deemed to be owned *ab initio* one-half by each spouse.

4. Divorce-Related Transfers

Under the *Harris* case, supra, the "test" for whether a transfer is exempt from gift tax because founded on the divorce decree (rather than on any prior or contemporaneous agreement) is whether the divorce court retained the power to modify or alter the agreement. The mere fact that a divorce decree may "incorporate" an agreement between the parties is, therefore, not conclusive of whether the transfer is founded upon the decree. Thus, the *Harris* doctrine calls for an analysis of the applicable state law and the terms of the particular divorce in every case.

In order to achieve a uniform national rule, Congress enacted §2516, which holds that property transfers to a spouse or former spouse and transfers for the support of minor children, made pursuant to an agreement, are totally exempt from gift tax if a divorce occurs within three years after the date which is one year prior to entering into the agreement. The power of the divorce court under state law is not a relevant fact if the rather minimal conditions of §2516 are satisfied.

In approaching a gift tax issue involving a property transfer pursuant to a separation or divorce, one should look first to the *per se* exclusion provided by §2516. If §2516 encompasses the transfer, it is exempt, and no further analysis is necessary.

To the extent, if any, that §2516 does not exempt the transfer — for example, because the divorce decree was not timely obtained — the transferor should then look to the *Harris* doctrine. The latter does not apply, *inter alia*, where the divorce court retained no jurisdiction to modify the decree or if a divorce or separate maintenance decree never was obtained.

---

18. See *Converse v. Comm'r*, 5 T.C. 1014 (1945) (IRS concession), *aff'd*, 163 F.2d 131 (2d Cir.1947).

If neither §2516 nor *Harris* applies, the transferor can avoid gift characterization only to the extent that the transfer was made for consideration in money or money's worth. At this point, the critical distinction is between (a) the release of inheritance-type rights (which does not qualify as consideration in money's worth) and (b) the release of support-type rights (which qualifies as valid consideration). If the consideration qualifies, it then has to be valued and compared to the amount transferred.

Ongoing alimony and child-support payments in cash are exempt from gift tax under the "support" exclusion.

5. *Paying for Education and Medical Care*

Under §2503(e), added in 1981, the term "gift" excludes amounts paid "on behalf of an individual (A) as tuition to an educational organization described in §170(b)(1)(A)(ii) for the education or training of such individual, or (B) to any person who provides medical care (as defined in §213(e)) with respect to such individual as payment for such medical care."

Education and medical care are borderline gift/support items. The status of education as support varies widely among the states, and in many cases may not be clearly articulated. Section 2503(e) finesses this distinction by rendering all qualifying payments fully excludible. To come within §2503(e) the beneficiary of the payment need not be a legal dependent of the donor. Moreover, there is no dollar limit on this exclusion.

A related reason for the enactment of §2503(e) was the fact that many persons paying educational expenses for children or grandchildren (and medical expenses for parents or descendants) were probably unaware that the gift tax was involved. Enactment of §2503(e) rescued a large class from being tax evaders.

The exclusion for tuition is not restricted to degree candidates or by educational level, and it covers part-time study. The educational institution does not need to be tax exempt. It need only be one that "normally maintains a regular faculty and curriculum and normally has a regularly enrolled body of pupils or students in attendance at the place where its educational activities are regularly carried on."[19] The exclusion generally does not extend beyond tuition to the payment of fees and the purchase of books, supplies, room, board, and transportation. There is a possible exception for fees that are "required" of all students, payable to the school, and not related to living expenses.[20] Some education-related living expenses may come within the concept of "support," even where "education" is not considered to be support according to state law.

The following private letter ruling allows the tax-free removal of a large portion of assets from a dying taxpayer's estate by prepaying multiple years of private school tuition. There is a risk, of course, that the donor's issue may not actually enjoy the full benefit of the donor's largesse (they may drop out, move

---

19. §170(b)(1)(A)(ii).
20. See Reg. §25.2503-6(b)(2).

away, etc.) because the tuition payments cannot be refundable and are forfeited if the grandchildren do not attend that particular private school.

P.L.R. 200602002[21]

Donor has three children, Child 1, Child 2, and Child 3. Child 1 has two children, Grandchild 1 and Grandchild 2. Child 2 has 2 children, Grandchild 3 and Grandchild 4. Child 3 has two children, Grandchild 5 and Grandchild 6.

School is an educational organization described in §170(b)(1)(A)(ii) of the Internal Revenue Code.

Donor proposes to enter into a separate written agreement with School with respect to each of Grandchild 1–6. Under the terms of each agreement, Donor agrees to prepay the total annual tuition for the respective Grandchild for each grade level through graduation (grade 12.) The amount to be paid under each agreement is set forth on a schedule attached to the agreement and is determined based on the current tuition rates charged by School. Under the agreement, the Donor acknowledges that tuition may increase in subsequent years and the balance due after the application of the prepayment for that year will be paid by the Donor, or the parents of the respective grandchild (who will a sign a consent and joinder). The agreements provide that the tuition payments are non-refundable, and once paid become the sole property of School. Finally, the pre-payment does not afford the respective grandchild any additional rights or privileges over any other student, does not guarantee enrollment, and the School expressly reserves all rights under its standards policies and procedures.

Section 25.2503-6(c), Example 2, [of the Regulations] considers a situation where the Donor, A, transfers $100,000 to a trust the terms of which require the trustee to use the trust funds to pay tuition expenses for A's grandchildren. The example concludes that A's transfer to the trust is a completed gift for gift tax purposes and is not a direct transfer to an educational organization and does not qualify for the unlimited exclusion under section 2503(e).

Section 2611(b)(1) provides that the term "generation-skipping transfer" does not include any transfer which, if made *inter vivos* by an individual, would not be treated as a taxable gift by reason of §2503(e).

[W]e conclude:

1. The prepayments of tuition by Donor directly to School, as described above, constitute qualified transfers that are excluded from the gift tax under §2503(e);

2. Under §2611(b)(1), the prepayment of tuition by Donor directly to School, as described above, will not constitute generation-skipping transfers.

---

21. See *T.A.M. 199941013* (same).

QUICK QUESTIONS

1. Able wanted to marry Barbara and agreed to transfer $2M to her if she would marry him. Barbara was not really the marrying kind and would have had to give up her Miss North America crown and monetary goodies (worth $2M over her lifetime, since she had just signed an ad campaign contract that she'd lose if she lost her crown before her year's reign was up). Assume Barbara finally agrees to marry Able and Able transfers the $2M to her. Which one of the following statements is *TRUE*?

    A. Able has made a taxable gift to Barbara.
    B. Because Able has received adequate compensation from Barbara, Able has not made a taxable gift.
    C. Because there was an enforceable contract between them, there is no gift.
    D. Because a promise to marry constitutes consideration, there is no gift.

2. Mark and Winnie were divorced on June 30, 2010. The court awarded Winnie a $3M property settlement. Which one of the following statements is *TRUE*?

    A. Mark has made a taxable gift to Winnie.
    B. Because Winnie gave Mark the best years of her life (so far), there is consideration from Winnie.
    C. Transfers that occur pursuant to a divorce cannot be taxable gifts.
    D. Transfers ordered by a court that has the power to modify the terms of the property settlement are not taxable gifts.

PROBLEMS AND QUESTIONS

1. Which (if any) of the following are gifts by reason of *not* falling within the "ordinary course of business" exception:
    a. the payment of $1M to an art dealer for a "Van Gogh" that turns out to be a fake and worth only $2,000,[22]
    b. the payment of wages at the rate of $100/hour by a person owning a Burger King franchise to her daughter for serving as a short-order cook,
    c. the payment of wages to a "companion" for an elderly person (the companion is expected to be a kind of live-in friend, who also is required to help the elderly person function in society, such as by accompanying the elderly person to cultural events, parties, shopping ventures, and restaurants),

---

22. See *Estate of Anderson v. Comm'r*, 8 T.C. 706 (1947).

     d. the payment of a fee (at the going rate) to a psychic who also happens to be a close friend, and

     e. payments for the living expenses of a lover.

2. **a.** The dissent in *Carson* claimed that the decision therein rendered §2522 (the charitable deduction provision) superfluous. Do you agree?

     b. A campaign organization of the type referred to in §2501(a)(4) is not supposed to personally benefit the candidate, but only to promote their political career. Does §2501(a)(4) render *Carson* superfluous?

3. **a.** In the absence of a rule that excludes all support from gift tax, would the provision of support in kind (food, lodging in one's home, medical care, etc.) be a gift?

     b. *Should* "support" that takes the form of a wealth transfer (say, large cash payments) be excluded from gift tax?

     c. In *Harris*, why should the controlling fact be whether the divorce court has the power to modify the terms of the decree and settlement? (By the way, child support is always subject to modification by a court.)

     d. Does §2516 allow the avoidance of transfer tax by way of a "friendly divorce?" Alternatively, should the reach of §2516 be broadened?

     e. At least one kind of transfer mandated by law is a gift: The GST tax on an *inter vivos* direct-skip transfer is a gift for gift tax purposes under §2515.

4. **a.** Does the §2503(e) exclusion apply where the donor gives cash to the student or patient, either as reimbursement or with the understanding that the student or patient will turn around and pay the school or provider of medical care?

     b. Does §2503(e)(2)(B) cover the payment of medical insurance premiums? Of fees for psychiatric counseling? Birth control devices? Cosmetic surgery?

     c. Given the economic risks, as well as not obtaining any credit for prepaying future costs, what was the estate planning point of the transaction described in *P.L.R. 200602002*? Does the ruling reveal a loophole in §2503(e) that should be closed by Congress?

§3.2. Identifying the Donor

The gift tax is figured on the basis of aggregate taxable gifts made by a donor, and the donor is liable to pay the gift tax. Also, the annual exclusion is available on a per-donor basis. Finally, the marital deduction requires a transfer by one spouse to the other spouse. Thus, identification of the donor of a gift is critical, but in most cases it is obvious.

Certain issues pertaining to the "donor" issue have already been addressed in Chapter 2, namely, (1) husband and wife as separate taxpayers, (2) gifts of co-owned property (including community property), and (3) the gift-splitting election for husbands and wives under §2513. In this section are considered (1) gifts involving entities, (2) indirect gifts, and (3) constructive gifts.

A. Transfers by Entities and Fiduciaries

Only individuals are donors for gift tax purposes. Thus, an entity as such cannot be charged with gift tax.

However, a business entity can make a gift in the property law sense. For gift tax purposes, the gift is attributed to the shareholders, partners, or equityholders. See Reg. §25.2511-1(h)(1). A gift by shareholders, partners, or equityholders may occur, for example, where a death benefit is paid to an employee's spouse (or other relative) following the employee's death, where there was no contract between the employee and the employer and no pre-existing program or policy providing for such benefits.

A fiduciary of a trust or estate cannot be a donor for gift tax purposes solely by acting as fiduciary, for example, in making a trust distribution according to the terms of the trust. This is so because only a beneficial interest may be the subject of a gift, and the trustee *qua* trustee has no beneficial interest. See Reg. §25.2511-1(g)(1). Nevertheless, a trustee may happen to also have a beneficial interest in the trust. Therefore, if the trustee is an individual *who also possesses a beneficial interest in the trust*, a *discretionary* act by the trustee that has the effect of shifting or transferring the trustee's beneficial interest to another person entails a gift by the trustee, but only in her capacity as beneficiary and not in her capacity as trustee.

Example: Drucilla creates a trust, naming Elton as trustee, income to Elton for life, with the trustee having the power to pay corpus to Fiona in the trustee's discretion, remainder to Fiona. Here, any exercise by Elton of his power to invade corpus for Fiona's benefit will operate as a *pro tanto* reduction of Elton's own income interest and to that extent will be a gift of it.

However, there is no gift in this scenario if the trustee's power is limited by "a reasonably fixed or ascertainable standard which is set forth in the trust instrument," such as "education," "support," "maintenance," or "health." See Reg. §25.2511-1(g)(2). The theory here would be that the trustee-beneficiary in exercising the power is not acting "on her own" but pursuant to the direction of the grantor, enforceable by the corpus beneficiary.

B. Indirect Transfers

The notion of "transfer" reaches "indirect" transfers. The concept of "indirect" transfer is set forth in §25.2511-1(h)(2):

> The transfer of property [from A] to B if there is imposed upon B the obligation of paying a commensurate annuity to C is a gift to C.

This statement means that the creation of third-party-beneficiary contract rights involves a possible "transfer" to the third party (C) from the first party (A). The second party (B) is not the real transferor but simply a conduit or intermediary.

The indirect-transfer concept has been applied to employee benefits, as the following ruling indicates.

Revenue Ruling 76-490

1976-2 C.B. 300

Advice has been requested whether certain life insurance premiums paid by an employer with respect to a group term policy held by a trust created by an employee are subject to the gift tax as indirect transfers under section 2511 of the Code, under the circumstances described below.

In 1970, X Company entered into an agreement with an insurance company providing for a master group term insurance policy insuring the lives of its employees. By the terms of the insurance contract, premiums were to be paid monthly in advance, on the first day of each month, by X Company. On January 31, 1975, D, an employee of X Company, created an irrevocable trust and assigned thereto all right, title and interest in a group term life insurance policy on D's life issued pursuant to the master policy. Under the terms of the trust, the beneficiary or the beneficiary's estate was to receive the full proceeds of the policy immediately on D's death.

The policy assigned to the trust provided insurance coverage in an amount of 200x dollars until D reached age 65, or ceased employment with X Company, whichever occurred first. Neither D nor the trust had a contractual right to require X Company to maintain the group contract. The premiums paid by X Company with respect to D's group insurance coverage were not reported as gifts by D in 1975. D did not report such sums as gifts because of D's belief that, by reason of the assignment, X Company paid the premiums for the direct benefit of the trust beneficiary.

Section 25.2511-1(h)(8) of the regulations provides, in part, as follows:

> If the insured purchases a life insurance policy, or pays a premium on a previously issued policy, the proceeds of which are payable to a beneficiary or beneficiaries other than his estate, and with respect to which the insured retains no [incidents of ownership over the policy], the insured has made a gift of the value of the policy, or to the extent of the premium paid, even though the right of the assignee or beneficiary to receive the benefits is conditioned upon his surviving the insured. . . .

The interest in the group policy that the employee assigned to the irrevocable trust had no ascertainable value at the time it was transferred since the employer could have simply failed to make further premium payments. Therefore, no taxable gift occurred.

As to the payment of the premiums by the employer, it is well established for purposes of various estate tax provisions that, in an appropriate case, a transfer by an employee can take place where, in consideration of an employee's past and future services, the employer promises to pay a survivor's benefit. *Estate of Bogley v. U.S.*, 514 F.2d 1027 (Ct. Cl. 1975). Each time a premium was paid by X Company additional compensation was conferred on D. By irrevocably assigning the insurance policy to the trust and continuing participation in the group term life insurance contract, D caused the economic benefit of this additional compensation to inure to the assignee as each payment was made.

Accordingly, in the instant case, each premium payment made by the employer for group term life insurance on the life of D, where D irrevocably assigned the policy to the trust, is deemed an indirect transfer by D to the assignee of the policy for purposes of section 2511 of the Code, and subject to the gift tax imposed by section 2501.

———————————

The Ruling above also held, without explanation (but correctly), that the gift qualified for the annual exclusion.

Most transfers involving employee benefits are not subject to gift tax, because, where (as is usually the case) the employee has the power to change the beneficiary, the gift is incomplete for gift tax purposes, as will be explained in §3.3.A, infra. Nevertheless, the "transferor" issue arises under estate tax §§2036-2038, and, in addition to *Estate of Bogley*, cited in *Rev. Rul. 76-490*, there are numerous authorities holding that employee benefits involve indirect transfers by employees under these sections.[23]

A gift to an existing entity is an indirect gift to its equityholders. See *Shepherd v. Comm'r*, 115 T.C. 376, 388 (2000), *aff'd*, 283 F.3d 1258, 1261 (11th Cir.2002). In contrast, a transfer of property to an entity in exchange for an equity interest that represents the transferor's proportionate contribution to the entity, followed by a gift of the equity interest, is a gift of the interest (not of the underlying property), and the gift of the interest may be subject to lack-of-marketability and minority-interest valuation discounts that would not be available to the gifts of the underlying property. In the family limited partnership (FLP) area, several cases have considered the factual issue of which occurred first, the gift of the FLP interest or the transfer of property to the partnership. For example, in *Senda v. Comm'r*, 433 F.3d 1044 (8th Cir.2006), the court applied the step-transaction doctrine to find that a gift of FLP interests was really a gift of the underlying property, so that entity-interest discounts were denied. Accord, *Linton v. U.S.*, 638 F. Supp. 2d 1277 (W.D. Wash. 2009). But then, in *Holman v. Comm'r*, 130 T.C. 170 (2008), the Tax Court found that the FLP was formed and funded with property prior to the gifts of the FLP interests. The Tax Court held that the six days that separated the two events was meaningful, because the donor bore the risk of valuation changes during that period. Accord, *Gross v. Comm'r*, T.C. Memo. 2008-221. This issue is revisited in Chapter 9.

PROBLEMS, QUESTIONS, AND NOTES

1. **a.** Fatma creates a revocable trust, income to Gisella for life, remainder to Heinrich upon the death of Gisella. The original transfer into trust is not a completed gift, due to Fatma's power of revocation. What gift tax results

———————————

23. *Estate of Fried v. U.S.*, 445 F.2d 979 (2d Cir.1971), *cert. denied*, 404 U.S. 1016 (1972); *Kramer v. U.S.*, 406 F.2d 1363 (Ct. Cl. 1969); *Nevin v. Comm'r*, 11 T.C. 59 (1948) (*acq.*); *Rev. Rul. 78-15*, 1978-1 C.B. 289; *Rev. Rul. 76-304*, 1976-2 C.B. 269.

(if any) when income is distributed to Gisella? Upon Gisella's death (prior to that of Fatma)? Does it matter whether the trustee is Fatma or the X Bank?

   b. Ingrid creates an irrevocable trust, income to Jared for life, with the trustee in its discretion having the power to pay corpus to Jared, remainder to Katia upon Jared's death. What gift tax results? Does it matter if the trustee is Ingrid, Jared, Katia, or the X Bank?

2. a. *Rev. Rul. 76-490* involved "term" insurance. Pure term insurance has no "savings element," that is, there is no cash surrender value. Rather, each year's premium supports that year's right to proceeds in case of death. However, a group term policy typically provides a right to renew coverage annually.

   b. *Rev. Rul. 76-490* states that the term insurance policy assigned to the irrevocable trust had no value (due to the possibility that the employer might discontinue the insurance), and "Therefore, no taxable gift occurred." But if the trust or its beneficiaries received nothing on account of the transfer of the employee's rights in the policy, how could they have received anything on account of the premium payments? Or did the gifts of premiums possess an ascertainable value to the trust and beneficiaries? (Could the employer cancel the policy after the premium was paid for that policy year?)

C. Constructive Transfers

A constructive transfer can occur for estate and gift tax purposes where (1) the first party allows a second party to dispose of the first party's property or (2) the second party refuses to accept a gratuitous transfer where such refusal results in the property passing to a third party. In both situations, a person is really giving up ownership by passive means.

A constructive-transfer scenario involves giving up actual ownership or a right to ownership, and is thereby distinguishable from a scenario where a person gives up an active power to obtain property owned by another, which is called a "general power of appointment." General powers of appointment, usually embedded in trusts, are discussed in later chapters, particularly Chapter 8. Since the constructive transfers discussed below do not involve general powers of appointment, they do not implicate §2041 of the estate tax and §2514 of the gift tax, which expressly deal with general powers of appointment.

1. Allowing Another to Dispose of One's Property

If one passively sits by and allows another to dispose of one's property to a third party or a trust, one may be said to have made a constructive transfer for gift and estate tax purposes. Of course, such a situation may amount to theft, and losing property by theft would not be a gratuitous transfer for estate and gift tax purposes. However, if the third party is a natural object of one's bounty, and the possibility of theft is negated (e.g., by consent or knowing acquiescence), then there is a gift, and the donor is the person whose property is being transferred, not the person who actively causes the latter's property to move to a third party.

A simple example of a constructive transfer is where H, having (it is assumed) sole management power over certain community property, makes a gift transfer of both H and W's interests in such community property to an adult child of theirs. In effect, W is a constructive transferor of her half interest in the community property.

Another situation involving a constructive transfer of this type is referred to as the *spousal election will*. Here the will of the first spouse to die (usually the husband) purports to dispose not only of his property but also the property of the surviving spouse. Spousal election wills are not uncommon where community property is involved. Under the state law doctrine of "election," the survivor (the wife) can elect to assert her ownership rights over her own property, but in doing so must forfeit any benefits proffered to her under the decedent's will. The other option is to acquiesce in the decedent's will, resulting in the constructive transfer of her own property. The survivor is not likely to acquiesce in the decedent's will unless the will provides substantial benefits to the survivor and to the natural objects of the survivor's bounty. For this reason the decedent is not likely to "order up" a will of this type without prior consultation with the survivor and an understanding that the survivor will acquiesce in the will. At this point the whole transaction begins to assume aspects of an "exchange" rather than "gratuitous transfer."

In any event, it is well settled that the acquiescence by the survivor in a will of this type constitutes a constructive transfer by the survivor of the survivor's own property for gift and estate tax purposes. See, e.g., *Estate of Vardell v. Comm'r*, 307 F.2d 688 (5th Cir.1962). At that point, further tax issues arise that are too complex to pursue here.

A situation akin to that of the spousal election will can be presented by *contractual wills*. Contractual wills are an arrangement, usually involving a married couple, whereby each spouse's will bequeaths his or her estate to (or for the benefit of) the other, but if the other does not survive, then to their common descendants, and the two wills (which are called "joint wills," if memorialized in a single instrument, or, if not, "reciprocal wills") are accompanied by a contract providing that, on the death of one, the survivor's will becomes irrevocable. In *Pyle v. U.S.*, 766 F.2d 1141 (7th Cir.1985), *cert. denied*, 475 U.S. 1015, the husband died first, and the surviving wife took his net estate under an obligation to bequeath the combined estates to their children. The Seventh Circuit held that the surviving wife made a gift, at the time of the husband's death, of the entire marital property, reserving a life estate therein, with remainder to their descendants. Not only was there a gift of a remainder interest, but the transfer with a reserved life estate would cause the property to be included in the surviving wife's gross estate under §2036(a)(1).[24]

In a case based on very similar facts, *Estate of Lidbury v. Comm'r*, 800 F.2d 649 (7th Cir.1986), the Seventh Circuit held that, although the contract existed, there was no gift, because the surviving spouse did not give up the right to consume or dispose of the property. It is not entirely clear if the holding here is one of "no

---

24. See *Estate of Grimes v. Comm'r*, 851 F.2d 1051 (7th Cir.1988) (also following *Pyle* on the gift issue).

transfer" or instead one of "incomplete transfer" (due to a power to revoke). In a Tax Court case based on similar facts, *Hambleton v. Comm'r*, 60 T.C. 558 (1973), the holding appears to be that there was no transfer, because a will, even if irrevocable, speaks only at death. It might also be said that, since a will only governs whatever property is owned at death, a contract not to revoke a will is not a restriction on (and cannot be a transfer of) property currently owned, unless (as in *Pyle*) part of the agreement is that the survivor cannot dispose of currently owned property.

It appears that the *Pyle* problem arises only in Illinois, because in other states a contractual will does not restrict the survivor from spending or disposing of her property. Additionally, the law of most states contains a presumption against finding that joint or reciprocal wills create a contract not to revoke. In the rare case where a transfer for gift and estate tax purposes results from a contractual-will situation, there might be additional tax issues, but they are not well developed in the tax literature.

2. Refusing to Accept a Gratuitous Transfer

An heir, legatee, donee, or beneficiary may refuse to accept a gratuitous transfer, with the result that the property will pass to another. Such a scenario involves a classic constructive transfer for transfer tax purposes, but such a transfer will be "exempted" if it constitutes a "qualified disclaimer" under §2518 or occurs as a result of a bona fide settlement of a contest to the validity or construction of a dispositive instrument (usually a will).

(a) Disclaimers

Suppose Lily dies, leaving a bequest of $40,000 to Meg and the residue of her estate to Nesta. Under state law, Meg and Nesta can disclaim their legacies. Essentially, a disclaimer is a refusal to accept a gratuitous transfer. Most of the states have enacted disclaimer statutes, which lay out the procedures for effectuating disclaimers. A disclaimer is accomplished, typically, by delivering a written notice of disclaimer to the personal representative, trustee, donor, or other agent of the transferor, and filing a copy of the same in court within a prescribed period of time of the transfer. (If no time is prescribed by statute, it is usually a "reasonable" period of time.)

The usual effect of a disclaimer under state law is to treat the disclaimant as having predeceased the decedent (in the case of a bequest or other death-time transfer) or as having died prior to the time the transfer took place (in the case of a nontestamentary transfer). Thus, in the example above, if Meg disclaimed her general legacy, the $40,000 would pass to any substitute takers under any applicable anti-lapse statute (usually, the descendants of Meg), but if there is no anti-lapse statute or takers under it, or if all such takers in turn disclaim the legacy, the gift would fail and (in this example) fall into the residue, thereby augmenting the bequest to Nesta. The same sort of analysis would apply if Nesta disclaimed her residuary legacy: Here the disclaimed legacy would pass to Lily's heirs if no anti-lapse statute applied.

State law would also be consulted to determine whether, and to what extent, a "partial" disclaimer is allowed. Examples of partial disclaimers are: (1) a disclaimer of 60 percent of an income interest for life; (2) a disclaimer, from an outright transfer in fee, of the remainder in such property following the disclaimant's life, leaving a life estate in the disclaimant; and (3) a disclaimer, with respect to a general power of appointment, of the power to appoint to oneself, one's estate, or the creditors of either, leaving a special power of appointment.

Turning to the federal gift (and estate) tax consequences of a disclaimer, it is clear that, in principle, a disclaimer results in a constructive transfer by the disclaimant. However, it was settled early on that it was an exempt transfer, the theory being that the ultimate taker received the property from the initial transferor rather than from the disclaimant. The leading case on this point was *Brown v. Routzahn*, 63 F.2d 914 (6th Cir.1933), *cert. denied*, 290 U.S. 641. The question then became what disclaimers "qualified" for the exemption, and the answer was determined primarily on the basis of whether the disclaimer was valid under state law. These requirements created uncertainty and geographical variation, and (to some extent) these issues were addressed by Treasury regulations. In *Jewett v. Comm'r*, 455 U.S. 305 (1982), the Supreme Court held that, to be valid, a disclaimer must not only be valid under state law but must also, in accordance with the then Treasury regulations, be effected within a reasonable time after the *creation* (rather than the "vesting" or coming into possession) of the future interest being disclaimed. Accordingly, an attempted disclaimer of a contingent remainder upon the expiration of an income interest that had run for 33 years was invalid and hence resulted in a gift for federal gift tax purposes.

Effective January 1, 1977, Congress superseded prior doctrine (including *Jewett*), which now applies only to disclaimers with respect to pre-1977 transfers, by providing that a disclaimer cannot be valid for federal gift tax purposes unless it conforms to §2518 of the Code. (In the estate tax, §2046 simply states that the rules of §2518 shall apply for estate tax purposes, and, in the GST tax, §2652(a) defines a "transferor" as one who was subject to gift or estate tax on the initial transfer.) *If a disclaimer is invalid under §2518, the disclaimant is deemed to be the (constructive) transferor of the disclaimed property for federal transfer tax purposes.*

The 1977 version of §2518 provided that, for a disclaimer to be effective for a post-1976 transfer:

(1) the disclaimant must make an unqualified and unequivocal refusal to accept an interest in the property;

(2) such refusal must be in writing;

(3) the written instrument of disclaimer must be received by the transferor or his representative no later than nine months after the day "the transfer creating the interest in such person is made" (or, if later, the date the disclaimant reaches 21); and,

(4) as a result of the disclaimer the interest does not come back, in whole or in part, to the disclaimant (unless the disclaimant is the transferor's spouse).

In addition, a *partial* disclaimer is valid only if it is of an "undivided" portion of an interest or power. This rule invalidates "carved-out-interest" disclaimers out of bequests received in fee simple absolute and attempts to "reduce" a general power of appointment to a special power of appointment. See Reg. §25.2518-3.

In *Walshire v. U.S.*, 288 F.3d 342 (8th Cir.2002), the court upheld the validity of Reg. §25.2518-3(b) insofar as it invalidated an attempt to disclaim a remainder interest in property while retaining a life interest in that property. According to *Walshire*:

> [A]n undivided portion of an interest is a portion that does not separate out the bundle of rights associated with the interest being apportioned. Thus, if a disclaimant is bequeathed a fee interest, as was Walshire, an undivided portion of that interest would have to include all of the rights associated with the fee. The purpose of [§2518] is to avoid a second transfer tax where the intended recipient steps back and allows the property to bypass him. By retaining the income from his share of his brother's estate, Walshire did not step back, but benefitted from the property during his lifetime.

The court held that the regulation was a reasonable interpretation of the statute since, by enjoying the income interest, the disclaimant received some of the benefits of the property in violation of the statutory language of §2518.

Notwithstanding a desire to "federalize" the disclaimer issue, the 1977 version of §2518 continued to depend somewhat on state law, especially under the requirement that, as a result of the disclaimer, the interest must pass to a person without any direction on the part of the disclaimant. Property will likely so pass only if there is a valid disclaimer under state law. In 1981, Congress responded by providing for a "transfer" form of disclaimer. Under §2518(c)(3), a transfer (not purporting to be a state law "disclaimer") will have the tax effect of a qualified disclaimer if: (i) the transfer satisfies the requirements of §2518(b)(1), (2), and (3) as to writing, timing, and nonacceptance of benefits, and (ii) the property goes to the person or persons who would have received the property under a valid state law disclaimer. This alternative "federal" disclaimer "must be of all of the transferor's interest in the property." Thus, partial disclaimers cannot be effected under this provision.

In sum, there are three sets of rules, depending on whether the interest being disclaimed was created: (a) before 1977 (see the discussion of *Jewett*, supra), (b) after 1976 but before 1982 (the original version of §2518), and (c) after 1981 (adding the "transfer" form of disclaimer).

The disclaimer is an important tool of post-mortem estate planning, especially insofar as it can be employed to decrease or increase the size of the marital or charitable deduction in the estate of the decedent without tax cost to the person effecting the disclaimer. Such tax-oriented disclaimers can be "fine tuned" where state law and §2518 permit partial disclaimers with respect to bequests of property.

A qualified disclaimer may alter the "facts" of a gratuitous transfer in a way that affects the application of the GST tax. A relevant rule in this context is that, to be a "transferor" under the GST tax, the person must be subject to gift or estate tax with respect to the property. §2652(a). Consider the following illustration.

Example: Suppose that Herwig makes a bequest to his son Igor, and Igor makes a qualified disclaimer so that the property passes to Igor's granddaughter Janelle.

Igor has not made a gift, nor has he effected a direct-skip transfer for GST tax purposes (even though Janelle is two generations below Igor), since Igor has not been deemed to have made a transfer subject to gift tax. At the same time, however, the disclaimer by Igor means that the bequest from Herwig to Igor — clearly not a generation-skipping transfer as such — is transformed into a direct-skip generation-skipping transfer by Herwig to his great-granddaughter Janelle.

Thus, a disclaimer that is qualified for estate and gift tax purposes can create a generation-skipping transfer where none existed previously. In a likely scenario, where one makes a gift or estate transfer to one's child, a valid disclaimer by the child produces a direct-skip transfer to the extent the property passes to the child's children (or descendants).

(b) Settlement of a Dispute over Succession

The heirs or legatees of the decedent may enter into an agreement that effectively "rearranges" the decedent's dispositive plan and/or supersedes the intestacy statute. Any such agreement must be acceded to by all interested parties. If any of them are minors, they will have to be represented by a guardian *ad litem*, and the agreement must be approved by a court. Whether or not minors are involved, it is advisable to obtain court approval for any settlement agreement.

The settlement in most cases is motivated by a desire to resolve a contest over the validity of a will or trust, an action to construe a will or trust, or a dispute over heirship. Nevertheless, it may be motivated by other concerns, as is illustrated by the case set forth below, involving the heirs of the Hiram Walker whisky fortune. This case also shows that a settlement might, depending on the circumstances, raise numerous tax problems.

Commissioner v. Estate of Vease

314 F.2d 79 (9th Cir.1963)

Before HAMLEY and DUNIWAY, Circuit Judges, and CROCKER, District Judge.
HAMLEY, Circuit Judge.

The Commissioner asserted an estate tax deficiency against the estate of Elizabeth Walker Vease. Elizabeth died testate in 1952 at the age of 49.

[The testator's father, J. Harrington Walker,] died testate on December 16, 1919, a resident of Detroit, Michigan. His survivors were his wife, Margaret T. Walker, who was then 57 years old, and five children, as follows: Elizabeth, 16; Mary, 25; Harrington, 35; Hiram, 33; and F. Caldwell, 29. Walker executed his will on June 24, 1918. It was prepared by his attorney, Z.A. Lash. Walker died suddenly in New York City. His estate, located in the U.S. and Canada, had a net value before taxes of slightly in excess of $4M. A few days before his death, Walker had worked out with Lash some modifications which he wished to make in his will. Lash prepared a new will incorporating these modifications but Walker died before it could be executed.

On December 28, 1919, twelve days after Walker's death, Lash went to Detroit to meet with Walker's widow and five children. Neither the executed will nor the unexecuted will was presented to the family at this meeting. Lash told them that there was both an executed will and a later unexecuted will and, without disclosing the contents of either document, asked them what they wanted to do under the circumstances. Their unanimous decision was that they wanted to do everything possible to carry out and comply with Walker's last wishes as evidenced by the unexecuted will. Lash immediately wrote an agreement [to that effect], which the members of the family then signed. [Eventually the executed will was admitted to probate and the agreement was formally signed by the parties, a guardian having been appointed to represent Elizabeth.]

The executed will directed [that various benefits be provided to the widow, and various other bequests,] including bequests of bonds of the par value of $150,000 to the two daughters. The residue of the estate was left in trust to be divided into five equal parts, one part for the benefit of each of Walker's five children, who were to receive the income. The principal of their respective shares was payable to them on attaining 30 [or upon prior death according to a special power of appointment or, if no appointment, to takers in default].

Under the terms of the unexecuted will, [a different package of benefits was to be provided for the widow, and other bequests were made,] but no specific bequests were made to Walker's daughters. The residue of the estate [passed so that 25 percent] was to be held [in trust, with Elizabeth receiving the income for life plus being given a special power to appoint the remainder among her children, but if no appointment was made by Elizabeth the trust would pass free of the trust to takers in default].

[In due course, parallel Canadian and American trusts were set up in accordance with Walker's unexecuted will.]

The Commissioner determined that the trusts [of which Elizabeth was beneficiary] had resulted from a transfer of property made by Elizabeth during her lifetime. He further determined that since Elizabeth had retained a life interest in the property, its value is includible in her gross estate [under the 1939 Code predecessor of §2036(a)(1)].

The Tax Court concluded that the trusts are a result of transfers made from the estate of Elizabeth's father, Walker, by reason of Elizabeth's status as Walker's heir. The Tax Court relied primarily upon the principle announced in *Lyeth v. Hoey*, 305 U.S. 188 (1938), that a receipt of property assumes the nature of the underlying claim upon which it is based. Property received by a disinherited heir in settlement of a will contest is property received by inheritance [for purposes of §102 of the income tax]. And so, it is not taxable to the recipient as income. The principle has been expanded into the fields of federal estate and gift taxation. For estate tax purposes the property received in settlement of a will contest is received from the decedent's estate; it is not transferred by the other parties to the settlement. *Estate of Reed v. Comm'r*, 171 F.2d 685 (8th Cir.1948).

In our view the Tax Court erred. One who has standing as an heir by intestacy, or as a beneficiary under a previous will, may make such standing the basis for a challenge of the will. Property received from the estate in settlement of a bona fide challenge of this kind, in whatever amount and however conditioned, may properly be said to be received by reason of such standing. But Elizabeth, her sister, brothers and mother were all named in the executed will, which was the only will ever executed by Walker, and none of them challenged that will or any provision thereof. The basis of the family agreement was therefore not the standing of heirs to contest the will. Rather, it was the standing of each, as a beneficiary under the executed will, to agree upon a disposition of the property bequeathed and devised to all of them thereunder in a manner different from that provided in the will. The resulting agreement was nothing more than a voluntary rearrangement of property interests acquired under an admittedly valid will, concluded without duress of unsatisfied claims.

Respondent [next] urges that Elizabeth did not accept, and so could not have transferred, her share under Walker's will because the family entered into its agreement before the will was admitted to probate. [However,] Elizabeth did not purport to renounce [i.e., disclaim] her share in favor of the other will beneficiaries. She bartered with them. It is one thing to say that a testamentary beneficiary may reject a part of his gift, without making a transfer to the residuary beneficiary. Leaving a larger estate to be shared by others need not constitute a transfer in any sense of the word. But it is another thing to say that a will beneficiary may exchange his fee interest in a fifth of the estate for a life interest in a quarter, and at the same time create remainder interests in persons who would not otherwise have shared, without having accepted or transferred anything. We hold that during her lifetime the decedent, Elizabeth Vease, made transfers of the property which constitutes the *corpora* of the trusts under consideration.

The case must be remanded for a determination of the extent to which the trusts are a result of transfer made by Elizabeth and the extent to which they are a result of transfers made by other parties to the agreement.

CROCKER, District Judge (dissenting).
I would affirm the Tax Court for the reasons set forth in its opinion.

QUICK QUESTION

Debby creates a revocable trust in 1995, income to Babs for life, remainder to Ronald if living, but if Ronald is not then living, to Sally. Debby dies in 2000 and Babs dies in 2001. When must Sally disclaim (within nine months of which one of the following significant dates)?

A. When the trust was created in 1995.
B. When Debby died in 2000.
C. When Babs died in 2001.
D. When Ronald dies.

PROBLEMS, QUESTIONS, AND NOTES

1. **a.** Both spousal election wills and contractual wills are devices to unify the estate plans of married couples. They also are a way of imposing dead hand control by the first spouse to die (usually the husband) over the surviving spouse's own property, which is likely to be substantial in a community property state. Which of these techniques is more effective to accomplish these nontax purposes? Don't they raise issues for attorneys on account of the potential conflict of interest in representing both spouses?

    b. The spousal election will is fraught with tax issues beyond that of constructive transfer. One issue is loss (in whole or in part) of the estate tax marital deduction on the death of the first spouse by reason of §2056(b)(4)(B) and Reg. §20.2056(b)-4(b), Ex. (3). Loss of the marital deduction, however, is typically unimportant in a community property scenario, where the aggregate marital (community) estate is already split 50-50. Income tax issues also exist.

    c. Spousal election wills have been used by wealthier couples as devices to avoid transfer taxes: The idea is that, although the half of the community estate of the first spouse to die is fully taxed, the half of the surviving spouse (placed in trust but included in her gross estate under §2036(a)(1) or §2038) will be reduced (or eliminated) by a consideration offset (namely, the interest received from the estate of the first spouse).

    d. Contractual wills have not been "sold" as a *tax*-planning device, but more as a device to restrict the surviving spouse's (widow's) control over the marital property. In a *Lidbury*-type scenario, the surviving spouse makes no completed transfer that can attract a consideration offset. A scenario that plays out like *Pyle* involves a constructive transfer by the survivor of the entire marital estate, but *Pyle* and cases following it do not mention consideration offsets. An alternative to a contractual will (as far as dead-hand control is concerned) is a trust.

2. **a.** Despite attempts by Congress to enact, in §2518, uniform federal disclaimer rules for gift and estate tax purposes, state law is still occasionally relevant. For example, there may be no disclaimer statute, and an heir of an intestate decedent might be barred (under common law) from disclaiming. Another example would be where state law provides that a disclaimer of a future interest must be filed within a certain period after the interest becomes indefeasibly vested, a time that could be too late for qualification under §2518 (which requires that the disclaimer be made within nine months of the "transfer"). Here recourse must be had to the "transfer" disclaimer provided by §2518(c)(3).

    b. Yet another scenario where state law is relevant would be where (as is usually the case) state law provides that a disclaimer can be made by a guardian, etc., of a minor or incompetent. If state law also provides a fixed time period for making a disclaimer, then the waiting-until-21 exception to the nine-month rule cannot be used (i.e., the delayed disclaimer would not be effective under state law). The choice here is to have a guardian make the disclaimer under the nine-month rule or to have the minor legatee make a "transfer" disclaimer under the waiting-until-21 exception.

3. a. Suppose Yoko inherits Blackacre in fee simple. Under state law, she disclaims a remainder interest in Blackacre, keeping a life estate. Is this a qualified disclaimer? See Reg. §25.2518-3(b) & (d) (Ex. 2). (If not, the gift and estate consequences to Yoko and her estate would be disastrous.)

    b. One of the requirements for qualification under §2518 is that the disclaimant must not accept any benefits under the transfer. An exception to this rule is provided by §2518(b)(4)(A), which allows a surviving spouse to disclaim in such a manner that some or all of the disclaimed property comes back to the disclaimant. For example, if H leaves $1M to W outright and the residue to a trust, income to W for life, remainder to C, W can disclaim part of the pecuniary bequest and have the disclaimed amount fall into the residue from which W benefits. The purpose of this particular disclaimer would probably be to cut down on an excessive marital deduction for H's estate.

    c. Suppose H's will leaves $2M to C, and the residue in a trust that is designed to qualify for the marital deduction. C is a child of H, having two children, and a disclaimer is contemplated to increase the marital deduction. What is the practical problem here?

    d. In the disclaimer area, attention must not only be paid to the state law of disclaimers but also to the drafting the dispositive instrument which might be effectively altered (in effect) by disclaimers. Sophisticated dispositive instruments often contain clauses (called "disclaimer clauses") that provide for alternate dispositions if a disclaimer is made by a legatee. How might the problem described in (c) be avoided by the drafting of H's will?

4. Section 2503(f) holds that a waiver of future survivor benefits by the beneficiary thereof is not to be treated as a gift for gift tax purposes. This rule applies only to vested survivor benefits held by an employee's spouse of the type mandated by ERISA for certain tax-qualified retirement plans. Technically, this scenario does not fall under §2518, because (a) the waiver is a creature of federal law, (b) the waiver covers rights that will accrue in the future, and (c) the waiver is effected prior to the receipt of distributions. Where §2503(f) does not apply, a waiver of a right to a future amount is a gift if one or more another individuals (who are natural objects of the person's bounty) benefit by reason of such waiver. Of course, if the right itself is contingent (because, for example, it is not vested), the value of the gift may be very low or even zero. Waivers of survivor benefits apart from §2503(f) are uncommon.

5. a. In *Estate of Vease*, did Elizabeth "disclaim" her interest? Was there a bona fide settlement of a dispute concerning succession?

    b. By transferring the property into a trust (prepared for her father) that provided her with the income for life, and the power to alter the identity of the remainders, there was actually no completed gift by Elizabeth in 1920, the year of the settlement. However, transfers of this type are fully included in the transferor's gross estate not only under §2036(a)(1) but also §2038.

c. An issue not decided by the Ninth Circuit in *Vease* (and not evidenced by any report of a decision on remand) was the amount includible in Elizabeth's gross estate. The Ninth Circuit did not offer any suggestions as to how to figure this out, and the potential issues bearing on the amount includible would be numbingly complex (and certainly not worth pursuing in a chapter on the gift tax).

d. What is the moral of *Estate of Vease*?

§3.3. When Does a Gift Occur?

Not every donative transfer results in a gift at the time the transfer is made. The timing of the gift is delayed until the gift becomes "complete." Less commonly, a gift can be accelerated by entering into a binding agreement to make a future gift. A gift might be deferred under the "open gift doctrine" until it is capable of valuation. However, the legal status of the open gift doctrine is uncertain.

A. Completion of Gift

There is no gift unless the transfer by the donor is completed during the donor's lifetime. Incomplete transfers are those where the transferor has retained sufficient *powers* over the transferred property ownership to preclude the gift being considered final for gift tax purposes. The specifics of what retained powers cause a transfer to be considered to be incomplete for gift tax purposes have been worked out in the cases, the results of which are codified in Reg. §25.2511-2, *which is essential reading*. There are no Code provisions currently in effect that deal with the issue of what retained powers render a gift incomplete.

1. What Is an Incomplete Transfer?

Basically, a transfer is incomplete for gift tax purposes so long as the donor retains the power to revoke the transfer or to alter beneficial enjoyment of the transferred property. Incomplete transfers usually occur in the context of *inter vivos* trusts.

Suppose Abby creates a trust, income to Bruce for life, remainder to Clara, and Abby retains the power to revoke the trust. (The term "revoke" is limited to the situation where the *donor* can reclaim the property transferred.)[25] The creation of

---

25. If a person *other than the donor* can appropriate or withdraw the property, that power is called an "*inter vivos* general power of appointment" (and not a "power to revoke"). The tax consequences of the possession, exercise, and lapse of powers of appointment are discussed in Chapter 7 and elsewhere.

the trust is an incomplete transfer. Hence, it is not a gift at the time of the creation of the trust. This rule derives from *Burnet v. Guggenheim*, 288 U.S. 280 (1933), which held that a (completed) gift was made not when a revocable trust was created but when the grantor released (gave up) his power of revocation. These results have been "cemented" into Reg. §25.2511-2(b), (c), and (f).

The notion that a *revocable* transfer is not "complete" is obvious and straightforward, and is echoed by §676 of the income tax, which holds that the grantor of a revocable trust continues to be taxed on the income from the trust. The incomplete transfer rule also dovetails with §2038 of the estate tax, which holds that a transfer that was revocable by the grantor at the moment just prior to the grantor's death is includible in the gross estate of the grantor. In sum, *a revocable transfer is effectively ignored for income, gift, and estate tax purposes.* That is, the donor continues to be treated as the tax owner of the property.

Revocable transfers are extremely important in estate planning as will substitutes and to avoid estate administration, but not as tax avoidance devices. Irrevocable transfers that are completed gifts are usually thought of as devices that have the *potential* to avoid estate and income taxes. Thus, the literate estate planner needs to know what retained powers (apart from the power to revoke) are deemed to cause a transfer to be incomplete for gift tax (and also estate and income tax) purposes. Powers range along a continuum, and the problem facing the makers of tax law is where to draw the line between retained powers deemed sufficiently significant to cause a transfer to be incomplete, on the one hand, and retained powers too "minor" to negate the making of a gift, on the other. Since the gift tax statute is silent, the courts, the Treasury, and the IRS have undertaken the task of developing rules to determine when a transfer is incomplete. The formulation of such rules must take place under the constraint that any retained power that is significant enough to preclude the existence of a completed transfer had better be of the type that causes inclusion of the transfer in the transferor's gross estate. Otherwise, there would be transfers that would escape both gift and estate tax. On the other side, given the "adjusted taxable gift exclusion" for post-1976 estate-included gifts (and, for estate-included gifts made before 1977, the §2012 credit), there is no great harm is designing rules that occasionally result in transfers being subject to both gift and estate tax. (The income and estate tax rules bearing on incomplete transfers will be dealt with in due course; these rules, based on statute, are independent of the gift tax rules.)

The leading post-*Guggenheim* gift tax case on the incompleteness issue, *Estate of Sanford v. Comm'r*, 308 U.S. 39 (1939), arose for a taxable year in which §2038 of the estate tax required inclusion in the gross estate of any transfer over which the transferor, at the moment just prior to death, held the power to "revoke, alter, or amend" the transfer. See §2038(a)(2). In *Sanford*, the Supreme Court held that a trust subject to a retained power to alter or amend was incomplete for gift tax purposes mainly on the basis of the fact that the property would be includible in the gross estate.

In the case of a transfer in trust, the notion of a power to revoke, alter, or amend refers to the trust estate; that is, the property that is held by the trust from time to time, rather than (narrowly) to the specific property transferred to the trust by the donor, which may be sold by the trustee (with the proceeds of sale being reinvested). Thus, the crucial inquiry is whether the donor has the power to revoke, alter, or amend *the trust* (as opposed to the specific assets originally transferred to the trust).

A retained power to "amend" a trust is a power in the donor (contained in the trust instrument) to change the dispositive provisions of the trust. A retained power to "alter" refers *to a power in the donor to alter (change) the beneficial enjoyment of the trust* apart from being able to amend the provisions of the trust. A power to alter beneficial enjoyment typically occurs *where the donor is the trustee, and the trustee (under the terms of the trust) has one or more discretionary powers that can alter the beneficial enjoyment of the trust income or corpus.*

Example: Jamie creates an irrevocable trust with $1M, naming herself as sole trustee. The trust instrument provides that income and/or corpus is payable to or among Jamie's issue as the trustee determines in its sole discretion. Upon the death of the last to survive of Jamie's children living at the time of the trust's creation, the trust is to terminate and its assets are to be distributed to Jamie's then living issue. Here the donor, Jamie, as trustee, has the discretionary power to alter the beneficial enjoyment of both income and corpus. Thus, the entire gift into trust is incomplete because of Jamie's power to alter the beneficial enjoyment of both income and corpus. (At Jamie's death, if that occurs before the termination of the trust, the trust will be included in Jamie's gross estate under §§2036(a)(2) and 2038.)

A power to alter may pertain only to the income interest or only to the corpus (remainder) interest. In that case, the gift in trust may be complete as to one or more trust interests and incomplete as to the others. Such a transfer is treated as a "retained interest" transfer, which is dealt with in Chapter 8.

Not every power that affects beneficial enjoyment is considered to be a power to "alter." Under Reg. §25.2511-2(d), an *inter vivos* transfer subject to a retained power to merely "change the time or manner of enjoyment" is treated as a completed gift.

Example: Paula creates a trust with $400,000, naming herself as trustee. The trust instrument provides that the income of the trust is to be distributed to Quincy or accumulated in the trustee's discretion. When Quincy reaches the age of 35 (or dies prior to reaching such age), the trust is to terminate, and the trust assets are to be distributed to Quincy if then living, or, if not, to Quincy's estate. Here Quincy is the sole beneficiary. (Quincy's "estate" is an extension of Quincy.) Hence, Paula's retained power over income is a power that only affects the time or manner of the enjoyment of the income, and Paula has made a gift of the full $40,000. See Reg. §25.2511-2(d).

Similarly, a grantor's power, as trustee, to affect beneficial enjoyment is not a power to "alter" (does not cause the transfer to be incomplete) if the power "is a fiduciary power limited by a fixed or ascertainable standard." Reg. §25.2511-2(c)(2).

Section 25.2511-1(g)(2) of the regulations discusses the issue of what standards are fixed or ascertainable. Thus, "education," "support," "maintenance," "comfort," and "accustomed standard of living" are fixed or ascertainable, whereas "pleasure," "desire," or "happiness" are not viewed as ascertainable standards in this context. (Transfers of this type are generally not included in the transferor's gross estate.)

Does the ability of a person to rescind a *voidable* gratuitous transfer constitute a power to revoke the transfer? The answer would generally be "no," because rescinding a voidable transfer would usually entail the uncertainty of a court action, in which case there would be no revocability "on demand" as a matter of unequivocal right. That is, the power would be viewed as a "contingent" power, and a transfer subject to a contingent power would be deemed to have passed beyond the donor's control.

In *Smith v. Shaughnessy*, 318 U.S. 176 (1943), the donor created an irrevocable trust that was destined for inclusion in the grantor's gross estate under the predecessor of §2037 due to the fact that the grantor retained a contingent reversion. The Supreme Court flatly rejected the taxpayer's argument that there could be no gift for gift tax purposes solely on account of the fact that the trust would be includible in the grantor's gross estate, noting that the grantor did not retain any *power* to alter beneficial enjoyment. In other words, the Court held that there was no *per se rule* to the effect that future inclusion in the gross estate rendered the transfer an incomplete gift.

2. *Completion of Incomplete Transfers*

A transfer that is initially incomplete can later become complete (in whole or in part) when the property ceases, during the transferor's lifetime, to be subject to the retained power. See Reg. §25.2511-2(f). Thus, if Angela creates a revocable trust in 2000 but releases the power to revoke in 2003, the gift becomes complete in 2003, and the amount of the gift is the value of the trust property at the moment the power is released.

Alternatively, if Angela continues to hold the power to revoke, and the trustee during Angela's life distributes income or corpus to any person other than Angela, such distribution constitutes a completion of the earlier incomplete transfer in an amount equal to the amounts distributed.

If Angela dies holding the power to revoke, her power is extinguished, but the gift tax cannot apply, because the gift becomes complete only at Angela's death. (The gift tax only reaches transfers completed prior to the donor's death.) However, the then value of the trust is includible in Angela's gross estate under §2038.

It should be mentioned that existing powers cannot be the subject of gifts, nor are powers descendible to heirs or legatees. In other words, any power held by an individual expires on that individual's death. Of course, a trusteeship power can extend beyond the death (or resignation) of an individual trustee, but such a power inheres in the office and passes to the successor under the terms of the trust or by court order, not by reason of a gratuitous transfer by the deceased or resigning holder of the power.

3. Jointly-Held Powers

The issue posed here is whether a power (under the instrument of transfer) in the grantor to revoke, alter, or amend the trust renders the transfer incomplete if the power is held jointly with another person. The traditional rule under the law of trusts is that, unless the trust instrument provides to the contrary, a joint trustee power can be exercised only with the unanimous consent of all persons who jointly hold it, but in some states the power can be exercised by majority vote. If there are two co-trustees, unanimity is the universal rule, unless the trust instrument assigns the particular decision to one trustee. It is probably the case that the two-trustee scenario is a lot more common than the scenario of three or more trustees.

The leading case on joint powers is *Camp v. Comm'r*, 195 F.2d 999 (1st Cir. 1952). In that case, the taxpayer created a trust on February 1, 1932, prior to the enactment of the gift tax later in that year. To simplify the facts somewhat, the trust income was payable to the taxpayer's wife Alida for her life, remainder to the taxpayer's surviving issue, but if no issue survived to X. Taxpayer retained the right to revoke (in whole or in part) or amend the trust jointly with X. In 1937, the taxpayer together with X amended the trust so as to substitute Alida in place of X as co-holder of the grantor's power to revoke or amend. The taxpayer argued that the transfer was a completed gift in full on February 1, 1932, and therefore was beyond the reach of the gift tax. The Tax Court had held instead that it was a completed gift in full in 1937, and thus subject to gift tax. The First Circuit panel took a middle course. After discussing the *Guggenheim* and *Estate of Sanford* cases, the court noted that a transfer may be complete as to some interests but not others, and continued by quoting extensively from what is now Reg. §25.2511-2(e), which states:

> A donor shall be considered as himself having the power where it is exercisable by him in conjunction with any person not having a substantial adverse interest in the disposition of the transferred property or the income therefrom. A trustee, as such, is not a person having an adverse interest in the disposition of the trust property or its income.

The court then opined in *dictum* that if a power to revoke the entire trust (but not a part of the trust) is held jointly "with a designated beneficiary who is given a substantial adverse interest in the disposition of the trust property or the income therefrom," then the entire transfer in trust will be deemed to be a completed gift. However, this rule did not control the outcome in *Camp*, because there the power was one to revoke in whole or in part or amend. The court then opined that the gift of an *interest* (capable of monetary valuation) to such an adverse-party joint power holder would be complete, because a rationally self-interested (adverse) party would not agree to the defeat of his or her own interest. The First Circuit held that this "rule" applied even if the grantor (in the particular case) could reasonably expect the adverse party to acquiesce in the exercise of the power to defeat his or her own interest. As to the interests of the other beneficiaries, the gifts would be deemed to be incomplete, because the adverse party would have no direct economic stake in preserving those interests.

Presumably, then, the 1932 gift of the alternate contingent remainder interest to X was complete on February 1, 1932, because X had a direct economic interest adverse to defeating her own interests by the exercise of the power to partially revoke or amend the trust. But the transfers of the other interests were incomplete in 1932, because X had no direct economic stake in preserving such interests. However, the gift of the income interest to Alida did become complete in 1937, because Alida (who would be adverse to the defeat of her own interest) then became the joint power holder.

The concept of "adverse party" is based on the conclusive presumption that a person would not exercise a power, or would not acquiesce in the exercise of a joint power, in a way that would defeat the party's direct economic interest as beneficiary. The concept possesses significance not only under the gift tax but also under the income tax grantor trust rules. The existence of an adverse party as co-holder of a power that would otherwise cause the income to be taxed to the grantor under any of §§674-677 will instead cause the income instead to be taxed to the trust or beneficiaries.

But the concept of adverse party has no relevance under the estate tax (except for §2037, but that section is rarely a factor in retained-power cases). That is, a power held by a trust grantor even with an adverse party is treated under §§2036 and 2038 as if the power were held solely by the grantor.

QUICK QUESTION

Alfred transfers $100K in trust with income to Bonnie for life, and corpus to Christina. Alfred retains the power to withhold income temporarily from Bonnie, but all accumulated income will go to Bonnie at Alfred's death if not currently distributed. Which one of the following statements is *TRUE*?

    A. The gift is complete.
    B. The gift is incomplete.
    C. The gift of the corpus, but not of the income interest, is complete.

PROBLEMS, QUESTIONS, AND NOTES

1. a. Once the transfer of an interest is "complete" for gift tax purposes, any subsequent distribution of income or corpus pursuant to that interest is not a "gift." The gift-time value of the interest "includes" future income and appreciation. To tax the subsequent distributions (from a completed gift) under the gift tax would amount to double taxation under the same tax of money or property that was previously subject to tax. This is an all-or-nothing rule. There is (unlike the income tax) no "basis" mechanism in the gift tax to fix the precise amount of dollars that were previously taxed.

The gift tax is a one-time tax on the transfer of wealth, not a periodic tax on the acquisition of new wealth.

b. Assume a revocable trust which pays income to a beneficiary other than the grantor. Why is a distribution of "income," as well as of corpus, to a person other than the grantor a completed gift? Note that the aggregate amount of completed transfers subject to transfer tax will likely be greater in such a case than if the transfer into trust had been a completed gift.

c. Are distributions from a revocable trust to persons other than the grantor treated as present-interest gifts under the annual exclusion? Who is the donor? Does this suggest a possible tax advantage for incomplete trust transfers?

2. Ajax creates an irrevocable trust, naming the X Bank as trustee, income and/or corpus to be paid among Ajax's issue in the trustee's discretion, remainder after 20 years to the then living issue of Ajax, or if there are none to Britney. Is there a present gift, even though the interests of the various beneficiaries cannot be valued using actuarial tables? See Reg. §25.2511-2(a). Who (or what) is the donee or donees of the gift: (a) the trust, (b) the beneficiaries of the trust as a group, or (c) the beneficiaries individually? If the latter, what interests do the donees receive? To what extent is the identity of the donees relevant?

3. a. Miranda creates an irrevocable trust with $100,000, naming herself as trustee, income to Nathaniel for life, remainder to Rex, with the trustee having the power to invade corpus for the benefit of Nathaniel in the trustee's sole discretion. What gift tax results to Miranda? Consider Reg. §25.2511-2(d), which states that a power that only affects the time or manner of enjoyment of property (or an interest therein) does not render the gift incomplete. Does Miranda's retained power amount to a power to "alter" the enjoyment of both Nathaniel's income interest and Rex's remainder interest?

b. Same as (a), except that the trustee can invade corpus to "support Nathaniel in his accustomed standard of living."

4. a. Achille creates an irrevocable trust, income to Beatrice for life, remainder to Cassandra if living, but if not to David. Achille retains the power to change the remainder with Cassandra's consent. Is there a completed gift of anything?

b. Same as (a), except Achille can change the income beneficiary with Cassandra's consent.

c. In connection with the *Camp* case, the scenario (cited in *dictum*) in which the grantor (along with an adverse party) has *only* an all-or-nothing power over the whole trust is virtually unheard of, since a power to revoke implies a power to revoke or amend any portion or provision of the trust.

d. In *Camp*, did X make a gift in 1937 by releasing her power? X's power was not a power to revoke (only the grantor can have a power to revoke), but was a *special* power of appointment under §2514(c)(3)(A), and therefore the power and its release possessed no tax significance in itself to X. The question is whether the release of the power in X to protect X's alternative contingent remainder interest amounted to a gift by X on the theory that thereafter the grantor (together with Alida) could redirect X's interest elsewhere. In *Rev. Rul. 80-186*, 1980-2 C.B. 280, A gave B a two-year option to buy property from A at a price below fair market value. The ruling held that a gift occurred when the option was granted, not when it was exercised, provided that it then had an ascertainable value. What gift tax results, if any, if the option lapses without having been exercised? Does this ruling apply to the facts in *Camp*? Is the ruling correct? Or should the gift be deemed to occur only if and when the option is exercised?

5. In footnote 6 of the majority opinion in *Dickman* (the Supreme Court case involving an interest-free demand loan), there occurs the following passage (not mentioned earlier):

> In order to make a taxable gift, a transferor must relinquish dominion and control over the transferred property. . . . At the moment an interest-free demand loan is made, the transferor has not given up all dominion and control; he could terminate the transferee's use of the funds by calling the loan. As time passes without a demand for repayment, however, the transferor allows the use of the principal to pass to the transferee, and the gift becomes complete.

a.   Is a demand loan of cash really a revocable transfer, or is it an irrevocable transfer for consideration in money or money's worth (the repayment obligation)?

b.   If it is a revocable transfer of the lent cash, then any distribution therefrom to a person other than the donor would be a gift under Reg. §25.2512-2(f). Is there any such "distribution" here? The full version of the *Dickman* footnote does not cite this provision of the regulation.

c.   Does a gift demand loan entail a revocable transfer of something other than the lent cash? Is a gift demand loan similar to the following: A irrevocably in trust, income to B for life, reversion to A, but A retains the power to terminate B's interest at any time and accelerate the reversion? Here A has not made a gift of the reversion following B's expected death, and the gift of B's income interest is subject to a power to alter, and therefore is incomplete. Any income distributions to B (at A's sufferance) would be completed gifts from A to B. Is the "use value" of money equivalent to an income distribution?

B. Binding Agreement to Make Future Transfers

The timing-of-gift issue also arises where the donor manifests a present commitment to transfer money or property in the future (without retaining any interest or power). Here the general rule is that a transfer occurs for gift (and estate) tax purposes when a contract to make a future transfer becomes enforceable, not when the transfer subsequently takes place. This rule finds support from two (perhaps dubious) analogies. One is the idea that a right to future payments is itself "property" that can be transferred. The other is that one can make a gift of a future interest, such as a remainder interest, in property that one owns.

An example of the binding-contract rule is found in *Rev. Rul. 69-347*, 1969-1 C.B. 227. There, pursuant to an ante-nuptial agreement, the prospective husband made a binding promise to pay an annuity to his prospective wife (out of his own pocket) starting one year after the marriage. The Service held that the gift was made on the date of marriage, when the contract became binding, in an amount equal to the then present discounted value of the annuity. In this ruling, the Service referred to prior cases involving marital agreements[26] and concluded that the weight of authority favored the conclusion that the gift should be deemed to occur when the contract to make future transfers of specific sums of money becomes binding, at least if the present value of the obligation can be determined.

The Service, however, came to a different result in the companion ruling, *Rev. Rul. 69-346*, 1969-1 C.B. 227. There the wife agreed with her husband that, if he provided for her welfare in a testamentary trust of his share of the community property, she would transfer her half of the community property to the same trust. Under Washington law, the contract was binding when made even though the wife (obviously) could not make the transfer until the husband died and created the trust in question. The ruling held that there was no gift when the contract was entered into, because it could not then be determined what amount of the wife's community property interest would be the subject of the future transfer. Accordingly, the taxpayer was considered to have made a gift at the husband's death, when the amount to be transferred first became susceptible of valuation.

Somewhat supporting the result of *Rev. Rul. 69-346* is *Bressani v. Comm'r*, 45 T.C. 373 (1966), cited in the ruling, where a wife agreed with her husband, at the time the husband executed his will, that the wife's share of the community property would be disposed of in trust under the husband's will, and the Tax Court held that the gift by the wife to the trust beneficiaries occurred on the husband's death, not the earlier time when the agreement became binding. However, the Tax Court did not base its decision on the difficulty of valuation, but instead on the ground that the wife's transfer obligation was triggered by (conditioned on) the husband's death.

Rev. Rul. 77-359, 1977-2 C.B. 24, involved a present enforceable agreement that after-acquired "separate" property would automatically become "community" property as and when acquired. Without citing any of the authorities noted above, the ruling held that a series of gifts would occur as and when separate property is acquired (and instantly converted to community property).

These authorities have potential application in the situation where a survivor benefit is paid to a beneficiary under an employee retirement or benefit plan.

---

26. In support of the ruling are *Rosenthal v. Comm'r*, 205 F.2d 505 (2d Cir.1953) (gift under divorce settlement was present value of future cash payments); *Harris v. Comm'r*, 178 F.2d 861 (2d Cir.1949) (same), *rev'd on other grounds*, 340 U.S. 106 (1950) [discussed at p. 76], and *Estate of Copley v. Comm'r*, 15 T.C. 17 (1950), *aff'd* 194 F.2d 364 (1952) (ante-nuptial agreement requiring payment of sum of money after marriage).

(The term "survivor benefit" is a euphemism for "death benefit," a benefit payable by reason of death.) Employee plans are either funded or unfunded. A funded plan is one in which money (a fund) is set aside (usually by the employer) in a trust, or else a contract right (annuity or insurance policy) is purchased (by the employer) from a third party for the benefit of the employee's beneficiaries. An unfunded arrangement is basically a contract between the employer and employee providing for future benefits. In both scenarios, the Service takes the position, supported by *Rev. Rul. 76-490*, supra, and ample authority,[27] that the employee (not the employer) is the "transferor" of the survivor benefit to the third party. In most cases of this type, the transfer is incomplete for gift tax purposes, because the employee retains the power to change the beneficiary (which is a retained power to "alter"). In virtually all cases, the survivor benefit will be included in the employee's gross estate under §2039 (if the plan provided retirement benefits for the employee), §2038 (if the employee could have changed the beneficiary of the benefit), or §2037 (if the employee's estate was a contingent beneficiary of the benefit).

The gift tax issue had to be faced in *Rev. Rul. 81-31*, 1981-1 C.B. 475, because the facts were such that the survivorship benefit would not have been included in the employee's gross estate. There, the employee entered into a contract with an employer providing for a future irrevocable (but unfunded) survivor benefit payable to the employee's surviving spouse (with no alternate beneficiaries if there was no surviving spouse) that was contingent on the employee's continued employment and future salary level. The Service held that there was an indirect transfer by the employee during life to his wife, but that the value of it could not be determined until the employee's death (assuming the wife survived), and hence the gift became completed at such time.

The case below involved an unfunded survivorship benefit situation that was similar, but not identical, to the one dealt with by *Rev. Rul. 81-31*.

Estate of DiMarco v. Commissioner

87 T.C. 653 (1986)

Sterrett, Chief Judge: Anthony F. DiMarco (decedent) died on November 16, 1979, survived by his wife, Joan, and five children. He had been employed continuously by IBM as a full-time employee from 1950 until his death. At the time of his death, decedent was employed as an electrical engineer. He was not an officer and did not have a written employment contract. IBM maintained a noncontributory [and unfunded] Survivors Income Benefit Plan for the benefit of its regular employees. With the exception of fewer than 30 top executives, all

---

27. See *Estate of Bogley v. U.S.*, 514 F. 2d 1027 (Ct. Cl. 1975); *Estate of Tully v. U.S.*, 528 F. 2d 1401 (Ct. Cl. 1976); *Estate of Fried v. Comm'r*, 54 T.C. 805 (1970), *aff'd*, 445 F. 2d 979 (2d. Cir.1971), *cert. denied*, 404 U.S. 1016 (1972); *Estate of Nevin v. Comm'r*. 11 T.C. 59 (1948); *Rev. Rul. 76-304*, 1976-2 C.B. 269 (unfunded benefit).

regular IBM employees, including decedent, were covered automatically by the Plan. At the time of decedent's death, the amount of the benefit was equal to three times the employee's regular annual compensation. The benefit was payable only to an employee's surviving spouse, certain minor and dependent children, and dependent parents. Payments continued only so long as there remained at least one eligible survivor, and if the employee left no eligible survivor at death, no benefit was payable.

Decedent never had any power to alter, amend, revoke, or terminate the Plan in whole or in part. He had no power to select or change the beneficiaries; no power to change the amount, form, or timing of the payments; no power to substitute other benefits; and, other than by resigning his employment with IBM, no power to terminate his coverage under the Plan. However, IBM expressly reserved the right, in its discretion, to modify the Plan if it determined that it was advisable.

Decedent did not report the survivor income benefit as a gift on a gift tax return, and [his executor, the petitioner here] did not report it either as part of the gross estate or as an adjusted taxable gift on decedent's Federal estate tax return.

First, it appears that respondent [Commissioner] argues that decedent made a completed transfer of a property interest in the benefit for gift tax purposes on January 9, 1950, but that because the interest could not be valued at that time, it was necessary to treat the transfer as an open transaction and to value the transferred property and impose the gift tax on the date of decedent's death, when the property interest finally became subject to valuation. In the alternative, respondent appears to argue that decedent made an incomplete transfer of a property interest in the benefit on January 9, 1950, because the property interest could not be valued at the time, but that the transfer became complete on November 16, 1979, when decedent died, because the transfer could then for the first time be valued.

Respondent argues that decedent transferred a property interest in the survivor benefit for gift tax purposes on January 9, 1950. This transfer was either complete or incomplete. On the one hand, if the transfer was complete, we have little difficulty in disposing of this case because a completed transfer would have been a taxable gift that was made by decedent before 1977 [and, therefore, not an "adjusted taxable gift"]. On the other hand, if the transfer was incomplete for gift tax purposes, we do not believe that we can deem that it became complete at the time of decedent's death.

We recognize that respondent does not assert in this case that the alleged transfer on January 9, 1950, became complete because decedent's death terminated a power. In view of the fact that a transfer of property that becomes complete because the donor's death terminates a power is not subject to the gift tax, we decline to hold that a transfer of property that becomes complete because the donor's death makes it possible for the first time to value the transferred property is subject to the gift tax. We perceive nothing in the statute or the regulations that would justify such a result.

In addition, we believe that respondent has confused the issues of completion and valuation in this case. Respondent appears to argue that, because the value of the survivors income benefit could not be determined on January 9, 1950, when the alleged transfer occurred, the transfer should be treated as incomplete for gift tax purposes until the survivor benefit became susceptible of valuation. We question, however, whether the fact that the value of transferred property cannot be readily determined at the time of transfer is relevant in determining whether the transfer is complete for gift tax purposes. We have noted above that transfers of property are complete and subject to the gift tax at the time the donor relinquishes dominion and control over the transferred property. Nothing in the statute or the regulations suggests that, even if a donor relinquishes dominion and control over transferred property, the transfer is or can be considered to be incomplete for gift tax purposes if the value of the property is uncertain. The clear language of the statute and the regulations requires that transferred property be valued for gift tax purposes at the time the transfer becomes complete. Section 2512(a) provides that "the value thereof at the date of the gift shall be considered the amount of the gift." Property must be valued and the gift tax imposed at the time a completed transfer of the property occurs.

We also agree with petitioner that decedent never made a taxable gift because we find no act by decedent that qualifies as an act of "transfer" of an interest in property. Respondent argues, however, that decedent's simple act of going to work for IBM on January 9, 1950, constituted an act of transfer. None of the cases cited by respondent hold that, without more, the simple act of going to work for an employer that has an automatic, nonelective, companywide benefit plan constitutes the "transfer" of an interest for either estate or gift tax purposes. We doubt that it can be maintained seriously that decedent began his employment with IBM (when he was 24, unmarried, and without dependents) for the purpose of transferring property rights in the survivors income benefit. While we agree with respondent that a taxable event may occur without a volitional act by the donor, as in a case where an incomplete transfer of property becomes complete because of the occurrence of an event outside the donor's control, we do not believe that there can be an act of transfer unless the act is voluntary and the transferor has some awareness that he is in fact making a transfer of property. See *Harris v. Comm'r*, 340 U.S. 106 (1950) [supra, p. 76].

Moreover, we question whether decedent ever owned a property interest in the benefit that he was capable of transferring during his lifetime. The categories of beneficiaries, the determination whether a claimant is an eligible beneficiary, and the amounts payable to the beneficiaries all were controlled directly by the provisions of the Plan and indirectly by IBM, and payments were made directly to the beneficiaries by IBM. Furthermore, the benefits were payable out of the general assets of IBM, not out of any fund in which decedent had a vested interest, and the benefits did not accrue until decedent's death. Most importantly, IBM had the power and the right to modify the Plan and the survivor benefit at any time and in its sole discretion. Under these circumstances, we have little difficulty in concluding that decedent never acquired enforceable property rights in the benefit that he was capable of transferring during his lifetime.

The IRS did not appeal *DiMarco*, and has acquiesced in the result, 1990-2 C.B. 1, but only insofar as *DiMarco* held that a gift for gift tax purposes cannot be deemed to occur at or after the transferor's death.

QUESTIONS AND NOTES

1. The notion that a gift "occurs" upon the entering into of a binding contract but becomes "complete" only at such later time as it can be valued is often called the open-gift doctrine. The larger issue is whether such a doctrine survives *DiMarco*, and, if so, what are the proper contours of such a doctrine.

    a. In the context of a trust (or non-trust property) transfer, the inability to value one or more interests on account of contingencies does not preclude the existence of a gift of the underlying property. The *DiMarco* case is unusual in that there was no transfer of a fund, and no alternate takers. The only transfer was to Mrs. DiMarco, and that was subject to contingencies. If Mrs. DiMarco received anything during her husband's life, was it a "conditional gift" or a "defeasible interest?"[28] Does this distinction matter under the gift tax? Can the transaction be called a gift of a defeasible interest only if it is funded (which was not the case in *DiMarco*)?

    b. Was the death benefit a "gratuity" on the part of IBM? As an aside, it may be worth noting that at one time the prevailing theory under employment law and contract law — now discredited — was that employee benefits were indeed employer gratuities. Realistically, the death benefit was part of the deceased's compensation package, so that it can be posited that the deceased suffered a reduced salary. But the reduced salary only produced the death benefit if certain contingencies were satisfied.

    c. So, when did the transfer occur? The government argued that it was when the employment contract was entered into, citing rulings and cases involving a binding promise to make future transfers *of money*. Is this approach sound? Does the giving of one's own IOU entail a present transfer of wealth? Are analogies to gifts of notes and of future interests in property one owns persuasive? Under the income tax, a cash method taxpayer cannot deduct an IOU, even if it is payable on demand. See *Don E. Williams Co. v. Comm'r*, 429 U.S. 569 (1977). More to the point, does the giving of a gratuitous IOU deplete the giver's gross estate? Is the amount owed under the IOU (if enforceable) excluded from the gross estate? Deductible as a claim? See §2053(c)(1).

    d. The scenario of a present agreement to make future transfers of not-yet-identified *property* would appear to raise similar issues as an agreement to make future transfers of cash, but here such authorities as *Bressani* and *Rev. Rul. 77-359* have held that the gift occurred only when the event conditioning the transfer occurred. This approach appears to be distinct

---

28. See, e.g., *Farkas v. Williams*, 125 N.E.2d 600 (Ill. 1955) (holding that a remainder beneficiary of a revocable trust has a defeasible "interest," rather than a mere expectancy).

from the difficulty-of-valuation rationale that underlies the open-gift doctrine as advanced in *Rev. Rul. 69-346, Rev. Rul. 81-31*, and *DiMarco*.

e. The Service appears to be moving towards the conditional-transfer approach, but without explicitly abandoning the open-gift approach. See *Rev. Rul. 77-359*, supra. In *Rev. Rul. 79-384*, 1979-2 C.B. 344, a promise to make a cash gift conditioned on the donee finishing college was held to occur on the date the donee graduated, the Service stating: "[W]here one promises to transfer property in the future, the gift tax consequences of the promise are judged as of the first date on which it is possible to determine that the transfer must be made and that the transfer will be of a determinable amount." In *Rev. Rul. 98-21*, 1998-1 C.B. 975, the Service ruled that a gift of a non-vested stock option occurred when the option vested (the earliest time it could be exercised, not the earlier date when the option became binding.) Does the situation in *DiMarco* somewhat resembles that described in *Rev. Rul. 98-21*? If so, when would the transfer take place? Does this help the IRS?

2. The following items bear collaterally on the doctrinal viability of the open-gift doctrine.

a. The open gift doctrine has ample parallel under the income tax as an application of the "realization" principle. See *Comm'r v. LoBue*, 351 U.S. 243 (1956) (valuation problems cause deferral of income realization); *M. E. Blatt Co. v. U.S.*, 305 U.S. 267 (1938) (same); *Burnet v. Logan*, 283 U.S. 404 (1931) (deferred realization of gain where consideration received on sale was contingent). Is the income tax doctrine persuasive in the gift tax context? Can the income tax handle deferral better than the gift tax? Consider the outright gift of an unproven royalty right, the economic life of which can continue after the death of the donor. Such a right was involved in *Burnet v. Logan*, and the Supreme Court noted that said right had to be valued for estate tax purposes on the owner's death, notwithstanding its contingent nature. Is the same true of gifts? How would the open-gift doctrine play out in this type of case?

b. In *Carpenter v. U.S.*, 7 Cl. Ct. 732 (1985), the donor argued that a contingent *retained* interest should be held "open" until its value was ascertained, and then that amount should be discounted back to the date of gift and subtracted from the amount then transferred, but the court held that the inability to value the retained interest at the time of the gift meant that it could not be subtracted at all.

c. Was the IRS doomed in *DiMarco* by Reg. §25.2511-2(b), which states: "As to any property . . . of which the donor has so parted with dominion and control as to leave to him no power to change its disposition, . . . the gift is complete." Does this sentence mean that a retained power is the *only* fact that might cause a gift to be incomplete? If so, can the government place the open-gift concept on sound footing by amending the regulations? Or is legislation required?

d. Does *Dickman*, supra, p. 69, implicitly adopt the open-gift theory? The majority opinion in *Dickman* cited *Rev. Rul. 69-346*, supra, with approval, and the holding of *Dickman* is that a gift demand loan produces gifts that occur with the passage of time equal to the use value of money. Curiously, the *DiMarco* case, decided after *Dickman*, did not cite the latter, perhaps because there is language in *Dickman* suggesting (erroneously) that a demand loan involves a revocable (incomplete) transfer, whereas the death benefit in *DiMarco* was not revocable in the gift tax sense.

3. a. Is the binding (or enforceable) agreement doctrine itself misconceived, even as modified to require the fulfillment of conditions? Shouldn't the gift be treated as occurring at the time of actual payment or transfer? Generally speaking, money or property is not excluded from the obligor's gross estate on account of an unexecuted obligation to make a gift of it. The obligation, if any, of the estate to execute the promised transfer would raise the issue of whether the claim against the estate is deductible under §2053. However, an obligation is not deductible for estate tax purposes as a claim against the estate unless it was contracted bona fide and for a full and adequate consideration in money or money's worth. See §2053(c)(1)(A). There is rarely adequate consideration in these cases. (Consideration in money or money's worth that would support the deduction would also have served to exclude any gift.) The whole point of §2053(c)(1)(A) is to prevent the conversion of unexecuted gifts into estate tax deductions. The *Harris* decision by the Supreme Court (discussed at p. 76) relies on just this kind of analysis.

b. Under the facts in *DiMarco*, the death benefit escaped inclusion in the employee's gross estate. Sections 2036-2039 did not apply, because the decedent did not (according to the judge's opinion in *DiMarco*) make a transfer of property or, if he had, did not retain any interest or power. (The power of the employee to cause the benefit to be forfeited by quitting his job is not considered to be a power to revoke for estate or gift tax purposes.) The employee himself had no "interest" in the survivor benefit that would require inclusion under §2033. Finally, a survivor benefit is not "life insurance" under §2042. Thus, *DiMarco* is a rare example of a transfer that avoided both gift and estate tax.

c. Under an accessions tax, the only relevant fact is what the donee receives as the result of a gratuitous transfer by the donor.

§3.4. Valuation of Gifts

The general standard of valuation is the "fair market value" of the property at the time of the gift. §2512(a). Income tax basis or cost is irrelevant, and appraisals for state property tax purposes are given little weight.

A. *The Willing-Buyer Willing-Seller Test*

The general rule for valuation under the federal gift tax (as well as under the estate tax and the GST tax) is stated in Reg. §25.2512-1:

> The value is the price at which the property would change hands between a willing buyer and a willing seller, neither being under any compulsion to buy or sell and both having knowledge of relevant facts.

The regulation goes on to say that the price is that in the market where the public usually obtains the item, which in most cases would be the retail market. Of course, the retail market is itself heterogeneous, and includes such low-price sectors as "wholesale outlets" and Internet vendors. In any event, the value is not one based on a "forced sale" price.

The willing-buyer willing-seller test is objective and hypothetical. It does not, in principle, depend on any of: (1) the existence of an actual willing buyer (or willing seller), (2) the actual knowledge (or lack thereof) of the parties, (3) the existence of a market, (4) the likelihood of sale by the donee, or (5) the personal situations of either the donor or the donee.

Valuation is an issue of fact. Where the retail price is not readily ascertainable, numerous factors can be considered, as appropriate, such as: (1) sales of similar property (or the property itself), (2) bids and offers for the particular property, (3) present valuation of estimated future net yield, (4) appraisals by experts, and (5) replacement cost (reduced by actual depreciation).

The fact that valuation is a question of fact has the consequence that most valuation disputes are settled between the donor and the Internal Revenue Service, and the few cases that go to court are seldom appealed, because the likelihood of reversal on appeal is small. Valuation disputes involving legal issues, as well as techniques for depressing the value of assets, mostly cluster around the estate tax. Accordingly, certain valuation issues are dealt with in later chapters.

The regulations under §2512 discuss such particular valuation scenarios as stocks and bonds, business interests, and notes, which would be tedious to quote here, because they basically state what facts are relevant. The estate tax has a similar set of valuation regulations under §2031, and these regulations sometimes delve into more detail than the corresponding gift tax regulations.

There are a few legal rules in this area worth noting. Reg. §25.2512-6(a) provides special rules for the valuation of gifts of unmatured life insurance and annuity contracts issued in commerce. The general rule is one of "replacement cost." However, the replacement-cost rule is hardly ever applied to life insurance policies, because insurance products change frequently. The backup rule here is one of interpolated terminal reserve plus the portion of the donor's premium payment for the current policy year that has not yet expired. "Interpolated terminal reserve" is a figure that is related, but not identical, to cash surrender value, and must be obtained from the insurer. In the case of pure term insurance, the gift is simply in the amount of the unexpired premium already paid by the donor.

Another special rule applies to shares in mutual funds: The value is the redemption price rather than the higher (if there is a "load") asking price.[29] This rule reflects a taxpayer victory on this issue in *U.S. v. Cartwright*, 411 U.S. 546 (1973).

Closely-held business interests can claim a *lack-of-marketability discount* where the value of the enterprise is initially valued by way of comparisons with publicly traded enterprises, because interests in publicly traded enterprises benefit from a liquidity premium, which is reflected in (higher) stock-market prices.[30] The lack-of-marketability discount (which is really a lack-of-liquidity-premium rule) can also be taken if the value of the enterprise is initially computed by adding up the value of the constituent assets of the entity.[31]

The *blockage discount rule* should be mentioned here, although its application is far more common in the estate tax. That rule, as codified in Reg. §25.2512-2(e), dealing with the valuation of stock, states:

> If the donor can show that the block of stock to be valued, with reference to each separate gift, is so large in relation to the actual sales on the existing market that it could not be liquidated within a reasonable time without depressing the market, the price at which the block could be sold as such outside the usual market, as through an underwriter, may be a more accurate indication of value than market quotations.

The blockage rule has also been applied in cases involving estates of prominent artists[32] or even the estate of a major art collector.[33] In the gift tax, the blockage rule is applied to each separate gift.[34]

The value of a gift is reduced by any mortgage, lien, or charge that is taken over by the donee.

There is a conflict in the circuits about whether post-gift facts may be used to determine gift tax value. The Federal Circuit and the Sixth and Eighth Circuits allow relevant probative post-valuation-date data, such as sales shortly after the transfer date. See *Polack v. Comm'r*, 366 F.3d 608 (8th Cir.2004); *Gross v. Comm'r*, 272 F.3d 333 (6th Cir.2001); *Krapf v. U.S.*, 977 F.2d 1454 (Fed. Cir.1992). In *Okerlund v. U.S.*, 365 F.3d 1044 (Fed. Cir.2004), the court observed:

> Valuation must always be made on the donative date relying primarily on *ex ante* information; *ex post* data should be used sparingly. As with all evidentiary submissions, however, the critical question is relevance. The closer the profile of the later-date company to that of the valuation-date company, the more likely *ex post* data are to be relevant (though even in some cases, they may not be).

---

29. Reg. §25.2512-6(b).

30. E.g., *Estate of Jung v. Comm'r*, 101 T.C. 412 (1993).

31. In *Knight v. Comm'r*, 115 T.C. 506 (2000), the court, although skeptical of much of the taxpayer's proof on the point, allowed some lack-of-marketability discount for interests in a family limited partnership that held real estate and securities.

32. See *Estate of [David] Smith v. Comm'r*, 57 T.C. 650 (1972), *aff'd on this issue*, 510 F.2d 479 (2d Cir.1975); *Estate of [Georgia] O'Keefe v. Comm'r*, T.C. Memo. 1992-210.

33. See *Janis v. Comm'r*, 461 F.3d 1080 (9th Cir.2006).

34. *Rushton v. Comm'r*, 498 F.2d 88 (5th Cir.1974) (blocks of stock); *Calder v. Comm'r*, 85 T.C. 713 (1985) (gifts of numerous works of Alexander Calder by his widow).

The greater the significance of exogenous or unforeseen events occurring between the valuation date and the date of the proffered evidence, the less likely *ex post* evidence is to be relevant — even as a sanity check on the assumptions underlying a valuation model.

The most vocal opponent for considering *any* post-gift events is the Fifth Circuit, as seen, for example, in *McCord v. Comm'r*, 461 F.3d 614 (5th Cir.2006), discussed in §3.4.D, infra.

This controversy also manifests itself in the estate tax area not only in connection with the valuation of assets but also with respect to the deduction for claims against an estate under §2053. See Chapter 4, section 4.2.

B. Can the Gift Itself Affect Its Value?

As a general matter, the value of property or a fund does not change by reason of the making of an *inter vivos* gift. Nevertheless, this issue occasionally arises, as the ruling set forth below demonstrates. The principal question in the ruling is whether the creation of minority interests (out of a controlling interest) by reason of the gift itself requires the imposition of *minority interest discounts* in valuing the gifts. The concept of *minority interest discount* is based on the notion that a minority interest in a closely-held business entails downside risks that would cause a willing buyer to bid less for this interest than an amount based on the *pro rata* share of the enterprise represented by the interest.[35] The minority interest discount has long been recognized, and it has even been applied to fractional interests in real estate.[36] At issue in the ruling is whether minority discounts can be "created" by the act of gift itself. Another issue dealt with by the ruling is whether any such discount should apply where the donees of minority interests are all members of the same family.

Revenue Ruling 93-12

1993-1 C.B. 202

Facts

P owned all of the single outstanding class of stock of X corporation. *P* transferred all of *P*'s shares by making simultaneous gifts of 20 percent of the shares to each of *P*'s five children, A, B, C, D, and E.

Issue

If a donor transfers shares in a corporation to each of the donor's children, is the factor of corporate control in the family to be considered in valuing each transferred interest?

---

35. See *Ward v. Comm'r*, 87 T.C. 78, 106 (1986).
36. E.g., *Propstra v. U.S.*, 680 F.2d 1248 (9th Cir.1982).

Law and Analysis

Section 25.2512-1 of the Gift Tax Regulations provides that, if a gift is made in property, its value at the date of the gift shall be considered the amount of the gift. The value of the property is the price at which the property would change hands between a willing buyer and a willing seller, neither being under any compulsion to buy or to sell, and both having reasonable knowledge of relevant facts.

Section 25.2512-2 (a) of the regulations provides that the value of stocks and bonds is the fair market value per share or bond on the date of the gift. Section 25.2512-2 (f) provides that the degree of control of the business represented by the block of stock to be valued is among the factors to be considered in valuing stock where there are no sales prices or bona fide bid or asked prices.

Rev. Rul. 81-253, 1981-1 C.B. 187, holds that, ordinarily, no minority shareholder discount is allowed with respect to transfers of shares of stock between family members if, based upon a composite of the family members' interests at the time of the transfer, control (either majority voting control or *de facto* control through family relationships) of the corporation exists in the family unit.

[The ruling then cites several estate cases that disregarded family relationships in awarding minority discounts.] In *Estate of Bright v. U.S.*, 658 F.2d 999 (5th Cir.1981) (*en banc*), the decedent's undivided community property interest in shares of stock, together with the corresponding undivided community property interest of the decedent's surviving spouse, constituted a control block of 55 percent of the shares of a corporation. The court held that, because the community-held shares were subject to a right of partition, the decedent's own interest was equivalent to 27.5 percent of the outstanding shares and, therefore, should be valued as a minority interest, even though the shares were to be held by the decedent's surviving spouse as trustee of a testamentary trust. *Estate of Andrews v. Comm'r*, 79 T.C. 938 (1982), and *Estate of Lee v. Comm'r*, 69 T.C. 860 (1978), held that the corporation shares owned by other family members cannot be attributed to an individual family member for determining whether the individual family member's shares should be valued as the controlling interest of the corporation.

After further consideration of the position taken in *Rev. Rul. 81-253*, and in light of the cases noted above, the Service has concluded that, in the case of a corporation with a single class of stock, notwithstanding the family relationship of the donor, the donee, and other shareholders, the shares of other family members will not be aggregated with the transferred shares to determine whether the transferred shares should be valued as part of a controlling interest.

In the present case, the minority interests transferred to A, B, C, D, and E should be valued for gift tax purposes without regard to the family relationship of the parties.

Holding

If a donor transfers shares in a corporation to each of the donor's children, the factor of corporate control in the family is not considered in valuing each transferred interest for purposes of section 2512 of the Code. Consequently, a minority discount will not be disallowed solely because a transferred interest, when aggregated with interests held by family members, would be a part of a controlling interest. This would be the case whether the donor held 100 percent or some lesser percentage of the stock immediately before the gift.

Effect on Other Documents

Rev. Rul. 81-253 is revoked.

———————————

Oddly, the ruling does not discuss the basis for treating the transfer for valuation purposes as five separate gifts of minority interests, as opposed to being a gift of a controlling interest, which would have obtained a valuation premium.[37] The sentence from Reg. §25.2512-2(e), quoted above, dealing with the blockage rule, only states that the *blockage rule* in the gift tax context is to be applied to each separate gift, a rule that is disadvantageous to the taxpayer. There is no similar statement in the regulations that gifts are generally to be valued separately. Nevertheless, there was some direct (if old) authority for the ruling's conclusion on this point.[38]

C. Actuarial Tables

The regulations have long provided that income, annuity, unitrust, and remainder (or reversionary) interests in trusts (or property), as well as annuity promises of individuals, are to be valued using actuarial tables. See Reg. §25.2512-5. Actuarial tables should be understood as an exception, grounded on considerations of administrative convenience, to the willing-buyer willing-seller test. Actuarial tables, based on mortality statistics and present-value calculations, avoid the necessity of having to determine the fair market value of these rights and interests on a case-by-case basis. Because the market for trust interests is very thin (or, in the case of spendthrift interests, nonexistent), and because potential buyers would be at an information disadvantage relative to sellers, the market value of a trust interest (or an unsecured promise to pay an annuity) would normally be heavily discounted relative to present values. The use of actuarial tables (which are figured solely by reducing future amounts to present value) results, therefore, in the systematic overvaluation of trust interests.

1. Construction and Use of the Tables

Section 7520 of the Code now *requires* the use of actuarial tables in the aforementioned situations, and goes on to prescribe a discount rate (rounded to the nearest 0.2 percent) equal to 120 percent of the federal mid-term rate for the month in which the transfer is made.

———————————

37. See, e.g., *Estate of Jung v. Comm'r*, 101 T.C. 412 (1993).
38. See *Whittemore v. Fitzpatrick*, 127 F. Supp. 710 (D. Conn.); *Heppenstall v. Comm'r*, T.C. Memo. 1949-34.

Reg. §20.7520-3(b) sets forth certain situations where the tables will not apply, such as (1) an income interest where the principal is committed to nonproductive investments, (2) an interest that can or will be cut down pursuant to the exercise of a power held by another, and (3) an interest dependent on the life expectancy of a person suffering from an incurable illness that is at least 50 percent likely to cause death within 12 months. In other cases where actuarial valuation is possible but the published tables are inadequate (say, because a reversion is contingent on the chances that one person shall survive another), the taxpayer can request the assistance of the Service.

In situations where the actuarial tables are to be used (and can be used), the tables supply "factors," expressed as decimal numbers, for income interests and annuity interests (expressed as a fixed dollar amount per period) lasting for a term of years or for the life of a person of a certain age, and for remainder (including reversionary) interests following an income or annuity interest. A legal life estate is treated as an income interest for life. The actuarial factor applicable to a particular interest is multiplied against the total amount of the gift creating that interest. The tables are comprehensively found in IRS Publication 1457, portions of which may often be found in an appendix to editions of the Code and regulations intended for law student use. See Reg. §§25.2512-5T (gifts on or after May 1, 2009), -5A (gifts before May 1, 2009).

The first step is to select the table "for" the appropriate "§7520 interest rate." Thus, one begins with the mid-term federal rate for the month (published in a Revenue Procedure), and then one multiplies that rate by 1.2. Thus, if the applicable mid-term rate for the month the gift is made is 6 percent, then 120 percent thereof is 7.2 percent, and one would refer to the table that is based on that rate.

It is worth understanding how the tables for the various possible §7520 interest rates are constructed. Basically, if an income interest is involved, the table is constructed by first figuring out the present discounted value of a remainder interest in $1 after a term of years (Table B) or a person's life expectancy (Table S), using the §7520 interest rate, compounded annually, as the discount rate. The factor for the income interest is the number "one" minus the actuarial factor of the remainder interest. The relevant factor is then multiplied by the value of the fund or corpus at the date of gift.

Example: Andy creates a trust with $80,000, income to Bob for 15 years, remainder to Carrie. After exactly five years, Bob makes a gift of his now ten-year income interest to Donna. If the applicable mid-term rate for the month in which the gift is made is 5 percent, then the §7520 interest rate is 6 percent. Using the 6 percent column under Table B (because the income interest is for a fixed term of years), the applicable actuarial factor for a ten-year term interest is 0.441605. Note also that the factor for the remainder interest after the remaining ten-year term interest is 0.558395. Note finally that the two factors together add up to 1.0 (100 percent). The income interest factor is multiplied by $100,000, the value of the trust at the date of gift. Therefore, the amount of the gift from Bob to Donna is valued at $44,160.50.

Where an annuity is involved, one selects the annuity factor from Table B or Table S and multiplies that factor by the annual payment. (If the payments are made more frequently than annually, the factor has to be adjusted.) The remainder following an annuity interest in trust is worth the current value of the fund or property reduced by the value of the annuity. Further complications arise if the annuity payout rate is high enough to produce a likely exhaustion of the corpus.

The valuation of unitrust interests (a right to a fixed percentage of corpus, valued annually) is governed by Reg. §1.664-4T(e)(7).

Some observations are worth making. First, the sum of the factors for all interests created by a gift is 1.0 (100 percent). Moreover, the 1.0 equates to 100 percent of the *existing* fund. Thus, the income interest is worth the current value of the fund minus the present discounted value of the remainder interest, and vice versa. This approach is often referred to as the "subtraction method." The subtraction method overlooks the possibility that fractionalization of interests might increase or decrease the aggregate value of the interests in a given trust. (Cf. *Rev. Rul. 93-12*, supra, where "spatial" fractionalization in the case of multiple gifts of pieces of the pie to different donees was held to reduce the aggregate value of the property.) Additionally, a more sophisticated method of valuation than that found in the tables would be based not on the current value of the fund, but rather on its expected future value at the relevant future date. If the fund is expected to grow (or shrink), the actuarial tables would undervalue (or overvalue) both the income and remainder interests on account of the constant-value-of-the-principal assumption.[39] In short, the actuarial tables opt for simplification over accuracy, a fact that is the basis for certain tax savings devices to be discussed in Chapters 8 and 9.

The higher the discount rate, the lower the value of remainder (and reversionary) interests and the higher the value of income, unitrust, and annuity interests. Although the discount rate used in the tables is 120 percent of the applicable federal mid-term rate, the latter rate is for a very safe investment, and 120 percent thereof is probably still too low a discount rate to apply to trust interests generally (relative to market discounts).

2. Retained-Interest Gifts

In the example set forth above, Bob gave away all he had (an income interest for ten years). But the same valuation principles have long applied in cases where a donor, owning property (or a fund), makes a gift (usually in trust) of one or more interests therein, while retaining one or more other interests. (A retained power to revoke, amend, or alter a particular transferred interest results in that interest being treated as a retained interest by reason of its incompleteness.) It is a commonplace observation that one cannot (conceptually speaking) make a gift to oneself. Thus, the actuarial value of the retained interest is not included in the gift. The conventional way of stating this rule is that the amount of the gift is the value of the amount transferred (usually in trust), less the value of the retained interest.[40]

---

39. Thus, if the present amount grows into a larger amount at the same (compound) rate as is used for discounting, the present value of the (increased) future amount is the same as its current value.

40. See Reg. §25.2511-1(h)(7).

Example: Elena (at age 60) creates a trust, in 2010, with $1M, income to herself for life, remainder to Geraldo. If the applicable mid-term rate for the month in which the gift is made is 5 percent, then the §7520 interest rate is 6 percent. Using the 6 percent column under the post-2009 version of Table S (because the income interest is for a person's life), one notes that the remainder factor for a person aged 60 is 0.35033, so that the factor for the retained income interest must be 0.64967, and the value such interest must be $649,670, and the value of the gift of the remainder must be $350,330. In this case, it is easier to simply figure out the gift of the remainder interest directly, rather than figuring out the value of the retained income interest and subtracting that from the amount transferred.

The tables are only used in this context where the retained interest can be valued by actuarial methods. In *Robinette v. Helvering*, 318 U.S. 184 (1943), the Supreme Court held that only the value of a retained interest that is capable of valuation under generally accepted valuation principles can be subtracted from the amount of the gift. In *Robinette*, the retained interest was a reversion contingent on a person's unmarried daughter dying without any issue attaining the age of 21. This rule is codified in Reg. §25.2511-1(e).

The subtraction-method approach to retained-interest gifts was radically altered by the enactment of §2702, generally effective since 1992. That section *disallows any subtraction for retained interests*, with certain exceptions too complex to delve into here. Section 2702, in other words, imposes a gift tax on what is not really a gift. Additionally, transfers with retained interests are likely (if not certain) to be included in the gross estate under one or more of §§2036-2038, as more fully analyzed in Chapter 8. Therefore, *a retained-interest transfer is now considered "poison," to be avoided at all costs, unless it can be made to fit into one of the §2702 exceptions and also to avoid estate tax*. Because of the complexity of (a) §2702 and its exceptions, (b) the retained-interest aspects of §§2036-2038 of the estate tax, and (c) the consideration-offset rules under both the gift and estate tax, the topic of retained-interest transfers is deferred to Chapter 8.

D. Defined-Value Clauses

A defined-value clause is a clause contained in an instrument of transfer that is designed to fix the amount of a gift or bequest at a fixed-dollar amount or pursuant to a formula. Formulas are routinely employed to fix the amount of the marital-deduction transfers for estate tax purposes, as is explained in §6.3.A, infra. The use of defined-value clauses in connection with gifts has sometimes provoked controversy.

In *Comm'r v. Procter*, 142 F.2d 824 (4th Cir.1944), *cert. denied*, 323 U.S. 756, a clause in the instrument of gift transfer (an *inter vivos* trust) provided that, in the event a court determined the transfer constituted a taxable gift, the amount of such gift would revert to the donor. The court in *Procter* held that this type of defined-value clause was a condition subsequent, and void as against public policy, because the clause (if given effect) would discourage the collection of tax, require a court to determine a moot issue, and effectively negate the court's decision.

In *McCord v. Comm'r*, 461 F.3d 614 (5th Cir.2006), *rev'g*, 120 T.C. 358 (2003) (reviewed), in January 1996 the donors executed an instrument of gifts of their interests in a family limited partnership (FLP) as follows (to somewhat simplify the facts): (1) to four GST trusts for their sons in an amount equal to the donor's unused GST tax exemptions; (2) directly to the sons in the amount of the excess (if any) of $6.9M over the gifts to the GST trusts; and (3) to charities. Anything passing to charity was deductible under §2522. The FLP in question (as is the case with most FLPs) was a holding company that contained assorted investments. In general, FLPs pose difficult valuation issues, which are discussed in Chapter 9. In *McCord*, about a month after the gift instrument was executed, an appraisal was made to determine the gift-date value of the FLP interests. When the formula contained in the instrument of gift was applied to this amount, the date-of-gift values that the various donees were entitled to became fixed. About a month after the appraisal, the donees entered into an agreement in which such dollar values were converted into percentage interests in the FLP. The charities in fact received interests worth about $460K, but, pursuant to a call right in the FLP, these interests were repurchased (redeemed by the FLP) for about $480K a few months later.

The effect of the arrangement was to create a disincentive for the IRS to contest the value of the gifted FLP interests, because any gift amount in excess of $6.9M would go to charity and avoid gift tax. In the trial before Tax Court Judge Foley, the Commissioner invoked *Procter*, supra. However, Judge Foley, in holding for the taxpayer, distinguished *Procter* on the ground that the gifts were final as of January 1996, and nothing hinged on a subsequent court determination. Judge Foley's opinion was withdrawn on account of the Tax Court review, which resulted (without relying on *Procter*) in an increase in the value of the gift, but without allocating all of the increase to the charitable gift.

The Fifth Circuit, in turn, reversed the Tax Court (in a rather sharp opinion), holding in effect that the Tax Court decision was improperly based on post-gift events, namely, what the charitable donees ended up with. The Fifth Circuit chastised the Tax Court majority for exhibiting "a palpable hostility to the dollar formula of the defined value clause in that donation agreement." The circuit court adopted the taxpayer's valuation, and approved the defined-value clause.

In *Estate of Christiansen v. Comm'r*, 586 F.3d 1061 (8th Cir.2009), *aff'g* 130 T.C. 1 (2008), the principal legatee disclaimed such amount of her bequest as "is finally determined for federal estate tax purposes" in excess of a fixed-dollar amount. Pursuant to a disclaimer clause, 25 percent of the disclaimed amounts went to charity. A disclaimer of a fixed-dollar amount out of a non-fixed-dollar bequest is not *per se* disqualified. See Reg. §25.2518-3(c). The Tax Court's holding that this clause was not void as against public policy was affirmed. The Tax Court had distinguished *Procter*, because in *Christiansen*, the formula clause would not negate the transfer, but would only reallocate the value of the property transferred among the legatee and other donees. The clause would not, as in *Procter*, make the court decide a moot issue nor destroy the finality of the court's decision. However, the Eighth Circuit "agree[d] with the Commissioner that the Tax Court's ruling in this case may marginally detract from the incentive to audit estate returns," while noting that this possibility did not apply to the actual facts in *Christiansen*.

PROBLEMS, QUESTIONS, AND NOTES

1. **a.** Apart from the exceptions alluded to above, the actuarial tables might be unavailing because the contingencies are too numerous to sort out, or the contingencies might not be capable of actuarial estimate. As mentioned above, in a hard case, the taxpayer can request actuarial-valuation assistance from the Service. If all else fails, presumably the party interested in valuation could try to prove a value under the willing-buyer willing-seller test. See Reg. §25.7520-3(b)(1)(iii).

    b. Try using the tables yourself. Take the scenario where A (age 55) creates an irrevocable *inter vivos* trust with $1M, income to B (age 32) for life, remainder to C (age 8). Twenty years later, C makes a gift of her remainder interest to D, in a month when the federal mid-term rate is 4 percent.

    c. A reversionary interest arises as a matter of law if the transferor fails to dispose of all of her interests in the property. An example lies where A creates an irrevocable *inter vivos* trust, income to B for life, remainder to the living issue of B, because, if B dies without issue, then the trust property would revert to A (or A's successors) on B's death. Even if this reversion could be calculated under actuarial methods, it could not be subtracted from the amount of the gift by reason of §2702. Additionally, the value (if any) of the reversion at the grantor's death would be includible in her gross estate. The retention of a reversion (express or implied) might cause all or a portion of the trust (other than the reversionary interest itself) to be included in the gross estate under §2037, *even if the reversion does not come into possession or even if the reversion (immediately before the grantor's death) is worth only slightly more than 5 percent of the corpus.* Finally, retention of a reversion worth more than 5 percent at the creation of the trust causes the trust income to be taxed to the grantor under §673. To complicate matters, the statutory law of some states might operate to convert a vested remainder into a contingent remainder, thereby resulting in the unintended creation of an implied reversion! In short, the estate planner contemplating the creation of an irrevocable *inter vivos* trust should *avoid the creation of reversions* unless they are well-versed in §§673, 2037, and 2702. What simple drafting technique can be used to avoid the inadvertent creation of a reversion?

    d. An issue in *McCord* (discussed in §3.4.D) was whether the donors' gifts had to be discounted to reflect the donees' agreement to pay any additional tax under §2035(b) should the donors die within three years of their gifts. The agreement can be viewed as giving the donor a contingent retained interest, or, alternatively, as constituting contingent consideration for the transfer. The issue was whether this agreement gave the donor a right that was capable of valuation under accepted valuation principles, under the *Robinette* doctrine. The Tax Court denied the adjustment on the ground that its value was speculative, explaining that "the dollar amount of a potential liability to pay the 2035 tax is by no means fixed; rather, such amount depends on factors that are subject to change, including estate tax rates and exemption amounts (not to mention the continued existence of the estate tax itself)." The Fifth Circuit reversed on this issue, holding "we are convinced as a matter of law that a willing buyer would insist on the willing seller's recognition that — like the possibility that the applicable tax law, tax rates, interest rates, and actuarially determined life expectancies of the Taxpayer could change or be eliminated in the ensuing three years — the effect of the three-year exposure to §2035 estate taxes was sufficiently determinable as of the date of the gifts to be taken into account."

2. a. The rules for mutual funds and blockage discounts are arguably inconsistent with the willing-buyer, willing-seller test. Also, they assume post-transfer events that may never occur. Nevertheless, these rules are firmly embedded in current law.

    b. Suppose your client owns garden-variety publicly traded investments. What move can be taken to obtain a potential lack-of-marketability discount in this situation? Should the move be respected? See *Strangi v. Comm'r*, 115 T.C. 478, *aff'd on this issue*, 293 F.3d 279 (5th Cir.2002).

3. a. *Estate of Bright v. U.S.*, an *en banc* decision of the Fifth Circuit cited in *Rev. Rul. 92-13*, essentially put an end to attempts by the Service to disallow minority interest discounts by taking family relationships into account. What (if any) is the legal basis for disregarding such relationships? Family minority discounts have been attacked by commentators, and one curative legislative proposal has been to introduce family attribution rules. Can the Treasury change this landscape by amending the regulations?

    b. Is the fractionalization holding of *Rev. Rul. 93-12* justified? The estate tax result is different: A decedent cannot obtain minority discounts for estate tax purposes by breaking up a controlling interest by bequest. This result allegedly follows from statements in early Supreme Court decisions (dealing with other issues) that the estate tax is on what the decedent had, not what the various legatees individually receive.[41] Shouldn't the gift tax be construed in relation to the estate tax?

    c. In *Driver v. U.S.*, 76-2 (CCH) USTC ¶ 13,155 (W.D. Wis. 1976), the court combined two gifts of minority interests, made to the same donee three days apart (but in two calendar years), into a single majority interest gift. Basically, this is an application of the step-transaction doctrine familiar from the income tax. Should the result be the same even if the two gifts to the same donee are not closely proximate or not pursuant to a prearranged plan? More generally, the question is whether a minority discount should be allowed where the gift of a minority interest results in the donee having a majority interest immediately following the transfer.

---

41. *Edwards v. Slocum*, 264 U.S. 61, 62 (1924); *Ithaca Trust Co. v. U.S.*, 279 U.S. 151, 155 (1929). The most cited case for this proposition is *U.S. v. Land*, 303 F.2d 170 (5th Cir.1962).

    d. Suppose X owns 70 percent of the stock of a closely-held business entity, and makes a gift of 21 percent of the entity's stock to Y, and then dies bequeathing her remaining 49 percent interest to Z. What gift and estate tax results? What if the bequest is also to Y? What if the gift is made shortly before death by a terminally ill person? See *Estate of Murphy v. Comm'r*, T.C. Memo. 1990-472.

4. a. In rejecting evidence of any post-death events (such as sales shortly after the transfer date) as affecting valuation, the Fifth Circuit has relied on *Ithaca Trust Co. v. U.S.*, 279 U.S. 151 (1929), which rejected reference to a person's actual (short) life span in lieu of the actuarial table's reference to actuarial estimates of life spans. *Ithaca Trust deals with the priority between statistical valuation and the willing-buyer, willing-seller test, an issue now resolved by §7520 and the regulations thereunder.*

    b. In *McCord*, when was the date of "transfer?" Was it the date the gift instrument was executed, or when the donees "took" their percentage interests in the FLP about two months later? (Is this a question of fact or law?) What of the fact that gifts of equity interests in an entity can *only* take the form of percentage interests (as opposed, in the case of debt instruments, fixed dollar amounts). Was *McCord* really an open-gift case? (This point does not appear to have been raised.)

    c. Formula clauses, such as that in *McCord*, are supposed to operate as of the date of transfer. (In *McCord*, the clause was supposed to operate as of the date of the gift instrument.). It appears that the percentage interests actually received by the transferees were "incorrect" with reference to the formula as applied to the date-of-transfer values. That is, the charities got too little and the noncharitable donees too much, leading to the charge that charitable deductions were obtained for "phantom" gifts to charity. (The charitable donees, who would have benefited by a higher appraisal than the one obtained by the estate, did not hire their own valuation expert.) The Tax Court trial judge found no evidence of collusion by the donees. (Can collusion be implied from the result? Should the Fifth Circuit have remanded on this issue?) What theory can the government pursue if the error was an honest mistake? Did the charity's failure to take its proper share amount to a disclaimer on its part, resulting in an additional gift from the donor to the noncharitable donees? (Again, this theory does not appear to have been raised.)

    d. Defined-value clauses in the context of *estate* transfers typically relate to values as finally determined for federal estate tax purposes. In such a case, distributions in satisfaction of the affected transfers would be postponed if there is a valuation dispute, because executors and trustees are under a fiduciary duty to distribute the correct amounts. In the case of an *inter vivos* gift, there is no such "natural" wait-and-see mechanism, and no neutral third-party monitors. The donees would have to fight it out if the gift amounts were later determined to be incorrect. Charitable donees, which are happy to receive anything, are unlikely to pursue their interests aggressively (as happened in *McCord*.)

e. In *McCord and Christiansen*, the government's concern was that the defined-value clauses (with excess amounts passing to charity) amounted to a "poison pill" created to discourage audit of the gifts. In these two cases, the courts appear to be limiting the public-policy doctrine of *Procter* to situations that nullify court decisions. Is a clause that nullifies agency action and enforcement any less of a violation of public policy?

§3.5. The Annual Exclusion

Unlike sales or payroll taxes, the gift tax cannot be designed to be comprehensively enforced by third parties, and most gifts (unlike deaths and probate) are not a matter of public record. Cooperation of donors (or donees) is necessary. Unfortunately for the government, many people are not even aware that gifts are subject to tax. Payments for the support of spouses and minor children are exempt from gift tax, but the differences among legal support, support in the moral sense but not the legal sense, routine gifts occasioned by custom (holidays, birthdays, weddings), and true wealth-transfer gifts may not be clear to a donor.

A. *General Outline of the Annual Exclusion*

Because of problems of the type just described, Congress has long provided the annual exclusion, which is located in §2503(b) and (c). The annual exclusion provides an exemption for a given donor, on a per-donee, per-year basis. Since 2002, the exclusion has been indexed for inflation. The exclusion amount for various years is indicated below:

Years	Exclusion Amount
1932-38	$ 5,000
1939-42	$ 4,000
1943-81	$ 3,000
1981-2001	$10,000
2002-05	$11,000
2006-08	$12,000
2009-	$13,000

For simplicity of presentation in examples and problems, the exclusion amount will be assumed to be $13,000 for any year in question after 2008.

The exclusion is not on a per-gift basis; it is on a per-year basis. Thus, if Adam makes two $8,000 outright gifts to Bea in 2009, $13,000 of the $16,000 total is excluded. But if the two gifts are split between 2009 and 2010, and if Adam makes no other gifts to Bea in those years, the entire $16,000 is excluded. This per-year aspect of the exclusion is the driving force behind an "installment gift" transaction of the type presented earlier.

The exclusion is also "per donee." Thus, the results described above can be replicated for as many donees as Adam makes gifts to in a given year. For example, if Adam makes ten $13,000 gifts to ten different donees, the entire $130,000 total is excluded. (Husband and wife are separate donees for this purpose.)

Finally, the exclusion is also "per donor." Thus, if the donor is married, it can be doubled for transfers to anyone other than the donor's spouse by means of §2513 gift splitting. Gifts of community property automatically entail a doubled exclusion, because each spouse is the donor of one-half of the gift.

The annual exclusion comes after the other §2503 exclusions, because the other exclusions are basically exemptions from the definition of "gift," whereas the annual exclusion is an exclusion of *amounts* that are conceded to be gifts. Any allowable marital and charitable deductions are taken "after" the annual exclusion, because the annual exclusion amounts reduce the amounts of (gross) gifts. See §2524.

Gift tax returns do not have to be filed for gifts that are wholly excluded by one or more of (1) the exclusion of payments for medical care and tuition under §2503(e), (2) the annual exclusion, and (3) the marital deduction. See §6019. However, a gift tax return has to be filed for gift splitting under §2513, because gift splitting requires the consent of both spouses. See Reg. §25.2513-2.

Qualification for the exclusion can be obtained *either* through §2503(b), applicable to present-interest gifts, *or* under §2503(c), applicable to certain gifts to minors.

B. Exclusion for Present-Interest Gifts Under §2503(b)

The exclusion under §2503(b) is only available to the extent of the value of a "present interest" transferred to an identifiable donee. Accordingly, a gift of cash or a gift of property in fee simple qualifies in full as a present-interest gift.

No exclusion is available for gifts of future interests, such as remainder interests and executory interests. This rule typically comes into play with respect to gifts in trusts, because trusts provide for future (as well as present) interests, and the "donees" for purposes of §2503(b) are the trust beneficiaries rather than the trustees or the trust itself.[42] Thus, if Xavier creates an *inter vivos* trust, income to Yvonne for life, remainder to Zach, Xavier has made a gift of an income interest to Yvonne and a gift of a remainder interest to Zach, and the latter clearly does not qualify as a present interest.

For purposes of constituting a "present" interest under §2503(b), *all* of the following must be satisfied with respect to the particular interest in question:

(1) possession or enjoyment (as well as legal or equitable title) must be obtained by the donee immediately upon the making of a gift,

---

42. See *Helvering v. Hutchings*, 312 U.S. 393 (1941).

(2) each present interest must attach to a single identifiable donee, and

(3) each such interest must be capable of valuation.

Requirements (2) and (3) logically derive from the fact that the exclusion is limited to present interests on a per-donee basis. That is, the exclusion cannot be greater than the value of the present interest of a given donee. For example, if Abel (who is not married) during the year transfers $20,000 into a trust, income to Ben for life, remainder to Cain, and the value of Ben's income interest is $8,000, the $8,000 is fully absorbed by the exclusion, but the unused $2,000 does not carry over to the remainder interest worth $12,000 (which is fully taxed). In the alternative, if Ben's income interest is worth $14,000 and the remainder is worth $6,000, the amount of Abel's gift is $7,000 [($14,000 − $13,000 for the present interest) + $6,000 for the future interest].

In practice, valuation of interests is not necessary where the value of a present interest clearly exceeds $13,000. In that case the entire gift is simply reduced by $13,000.

Valuation of present and future interests (in trust or otherwise) is, as has previously been explained, to be carried out with the use of actuarial tables supplied by the Treasury. See §7520. Actuarial factors only work for interests that depend on terms of years, life expectancies, the chances that one person will outlive one or more other persons, and, in the case of current interests, those that entail regular payouts expressed in terms of income, a fixed dollar amount, or a fixed percentage of corpus. The tables are relevant under §2503(b), as the following example illustrates.

Example: Andy creates a trust with $10,000, income to Bob for ten years, remainder to Carrie. Assume the §7520 discount rate is 6 percent. The applicable actuarial factor for a ten-year term interest under Table B is 0.441605 and the factor for a remainder interest after a ten-year term interest is 0.558395. Note that the two factors together add up to 1.0 (100 percent). These factors are multiplied by $10,000, the amount of the gift into trust. Bob's income interest is worth $4,416.05, and Carrie's remainder interest is worth $5,583.95. The gift to Bob is of a present interest, and all of it is excludible (assuming no other present-interest gifts to Bob from Andy during the year). The gift to Carrie is not excluded, because it is a gift of a future interest.

Interests that are dependent upon the exercise of discretion (by a person not holding the interest) are not susceptible to actuarial valuation.

Example: Same as the previous example, except that the trustee has the discretion to pay income to Bob or to accumulate the income and add it to corpus during the ten-year trust term. Neither interest is capable of valuation, because the trustee's discretion can be exercised so as to prevent Bob from receiving any income, and Carrie's interest will be increased by any accumulated income (Carrie, as holder of the remainder interest, receives the corpus at the end of the ten-year trust term). Bob's interest is not a present interest, because (1) he is not assured of immediate enjoyment, and (2) his interest cannot be valued using actuarial tables. Therefore, the entire gift is taxable. See Reg. §25.2503-3(c), Ex. (1).

Since there is no present-interest exclusion in the estate tax, the exclusion is extremely important in pre-mortem estate planning. Use of it over time allows for the making of substantial tax-free wealth transfers, especially if there is a plentiful supply of donees.

Of course, temptation creates situations where families have tried to multiply their exclusion limits beyond the amounts allowed under the statute. In *Sather v. Comm'r*, 251 F.3d 1168 (8th Cir.2001), siblings transferred stock in their family candy distribution business to each others' children as well as to their own children. The Eighth Circuit affirmed that part of the Tax Court's decision, T.C. Memo. 1999-309, that applied the reciprocal trust doctrine, discussed in Chapter 8, which resulted in re-allocating all of each parent's gifts to their own children (and not to the nephews and nieces). Accord, *Estate of Schuler v. Comm'r*, 282 F.3d 575 (8th Cir.2002).

The case below dealt with disqualification under §2503(b).

Maryland Nat'l Bank v. United States

609 F.2d 1078 (4th Cir.1979)

Before BUTZNER and HALL, Circuit Judges, and JOSEPH H. YOUNG, District Judge, sitting by designation.

BUTZNER, Circuit Judge:

Maryland National Bank, executor of the estate of Katherine L. N. Willis, deceased, appeals the District Court's denial of claims for refund of gift taxes based on the disallowance of seventeen $3,000 exclusions. We affirm.

By assignments in 1971 and 1972, Mrs. Willis transferred her one-half interest in a partnership owning real estate into an *inter vivos* trust for the benefit of seventeen members of her family. One tract was a farm; the other was waterfront property which contained recreational facilities. Both contained rental housing. Mrs. Willis had rented one of the houses on the waterfront property for a number of years before and after placing her interest in trust. Despite gross receipts from rents and farming, between 1968 and 1976 the partnership produced a net income of only $774.91 in 1971. That income was not distributed to the partners. All other years showed net losses.

The Willis trust directed the trustees to disburse "the entire net income of the trust" at least annually among the beneficiaries in set proportions. The trustees were given broad powers to invest in or retain nonproductive assets. They were required to disburse within three years rather than reinvest the net proceeds received from any sale of the partnership's land unless the proceeds were "used to purchase an additional or increased interest in [the original holdings]." Thus, the trustees could not convert the unproductive real estate into other holdings. The trustees had no duty to make the property generate income.

Only gifts of "present interest" are eligible for exclusion under §2503(b). The unqualified right to receive profits from the operation of the partnership's business presents the only arguable circumstance for holding that the beneficiaries received a present income interest.

The executor insists that Mrs. Willis was entitled to the exclusions because the trustees absolutely must disburse annually to the beneficiaries all the income from the partnership interest. In response, the government says one must probe deeper: that before the executor can rely on the disbursal clause of the trust, the executor must prove that income will be available for distribution. Lacking such proof, the government continues, the beneficiaries have only a future interest.

The Code does not define either future or present interest. The Service, however, has stated that "future interest" is a legal term, and includes "reversions, remainders, and other interests or estates, whether vested or contingent, and whether or not supported by a particular interest or estate, which are limited to commence in use, possession, or enjoyment at some future date or time." In contrast, a present interest is "an unrestricted right to the immediate use, possession, or enjoyment of property or the income from property." Reg. §25.2503-3. The Supreme Court in *Fondren v. Comm'r*, 324 U.S. 18 (1945), held that the distinction turns on whether the donor conferred a real and immediate benefit upon the donee:

> It is not enough to bring the exclusion into force that the donee has vested rights. In addition he must have the right presently to use, possess or enjoy the property. These terms are not words of art, like "fee" in the law of seisin, but connote the right to substantial present economic benefit. The question is of time, not when title vests, but when enjoyment begins.

The Code's "present interest" differs from the technical concept of a present estate for life or a term of years, because even a vested interest may be considered a "future interest" for gift tax purposes if the donee gets no immediate use, possession, or enjoyment of the property.

These principles are exemplified by *Comm'r v. Disston*, 325 U.S. 442 (1945). There the trust had income, but it placed such limitations on disbursement that the Court concluded that only a future interest was created. The absence of a steady flow of ascertainable income to the beneficiary can result just as surely from a lack of any prospect of income as it can from restrictions on the trustees' power to disburse income. *Disston* places a dual burden on the taxpayer. The taxpayer must show that the trust will receive income, and, second, that some ascertainable portion of the income will flow steadily to the beneficiary.

Application of these principles to the facts of this case presents little difficulty. The executor has failed to prove that the partnership has produced any income for distribution to the beneficiaries, that steps have been taken to eliminate the losses it has sustained annually, or that there will be any income in the foreseeable future. Moreover, the trust authorizes the trustees to hold this unproductive property, and it bars them from reinvesting the proceeds from the sale of partnership real estate, which is the trust's only significant asset, into stocks, bonds, or other real estate to generate income.

The executor, however, urges that this hiatus in the proof can be filled by use of the actuarial tables. [But] the tables are appropriate only when there is proof that some income will be received by the trust beneficiaries. The tables are designed to calculate the value of a present interest, not create it.

Rosen v. Comm'r, 397 F.2d 245 (4th Cir.1968), is readily distinguishable. In that case, the evidence disclosed, and the government acknowledged, that a gift in trust of publicly-traded corporate stock conferred a present interest, even though the stock had never paid dividends. The corporation was a profitable enterprise, and it had retained its earnings for growth. The trustees intended to hold the stock, although they had authority to sell, because they anticipated that dividends would be paid in the future and the stock would enhance in value. The income component of the gift was currently reflected by the stock's growth. Pointing out that the present income interest had value, we concluded that use of the tables would not "result in an unrealistic and unreasonable valuation."

Unlike the corporation in *Rosen*, the Willis partnership was not a profitable enterprise. It consistently operated at a loss. The executor's use of the tables, if allowed, would create an income value from assets that have never shown any capacity to produce income for the trust. This legerdemain would surely transgress the statutory ban on the exclusion of future interests.

HALL, Circuit Judge, dissenting:

The majority's holding is contrary to the rule of *Rosen*, where we held that a bona fide right of income from valuable property qualifies for the exclusion regardless of its past earnings. Here, the right is given, the underlying asset is very valuable and we should apply the actuarial value set forth in the Commissioner's tables.

In this case the trust asset is valuable real property which steadily appreciates in value each year it is held without sale. It is valuable for multiple dwelling residential development; however, at the time of the gift, it was used as a family rental estate and farming operation which together did not produce enough income to meet expenses. If the business use of the property by the trustees were to change, its profit potential would change.

Rosen teaches that we should not second-guess how trustees will elect to manage valuable trust assets, nor should we attempt to predict the future income of those assets on a case-by-case basis. Instead, we should turn to the actuarial tables promulgated. The tables index these present rights to the fair market value of the assets rather than to their profit histories. Implicit in such an approach is that the present value of all gifts of income should be set by the use and value of the asset to any willing purchaser. Such a theoretical user would put it to its most valuable potential use in the marketplace.

Contrary to *Rosen* (the earlier Fourth Circuit decision discussed in *Maryland Nat'l Bank*) is *Berzon v. Comm'r*, 534 F.2d 528 (2d Cir.1976), involving non-dividend-paying stock that the trustee was prohibited from selling, where the exclusion was denied. In *Berzon*, the corporation was inherently profitable, but dividends were not paid because of a management decision to undertake a program of expansion. Thus, the Second Circuit did not buy into the position that the exclusion is saved if the non-income-producing property is "potentially" capable of generating income.

The exclusion can be denied even for outright gifts of non-income-producing property that the donee is prohibited from assigning. See *Hackl v. Comm'r*, 119 T.C. 279 (2002), *aff'd*, 335 F.3d 664 (7th Cir.2003); *Rev. Rul. 76-360*, 1976-2 C.B. 298. However, in *Ltr. Ruling 8121003* (Jan. 26, 1981), the Service held that an outright gift of unproductive stock subject only to a right of first refusal, requiring the donee to offer the stock to certain parties before selling it to a proposed buyer, qualified for the exclusion.

Returning to the trust scenario, the terms of the trusts in *Maryland Nat'l Bank* and *Berzon* were somewhat unusual for locking in unproductive assets. An issue is whether a trustee's ability to get out from under such a restriction, or a beneficiary's ability to force a trustee to do so, would remove the gift tax disqualification. A trustee or beneficiary might obtain a court order to modify the trust on account of unforeseen circumstances or to compel diversification of investments, or a trustee might have the power to allocate principal to income (under a statutory power of equitable adjustment) or the statutory power to convert an "income" trust to a "unitrust" (a trust that is to pay out a fixed percentage of corpus valued annually). However, these possibilities are likely to be unavailing under §2503(b), because they are dependent on the outcome of litigation or on the trustee's discretion.[43] Thus, although the Treasury in 2001 issued regulations under various income, estate, and gift tax, and GST tax provisions to the effect that the word "income" in these provisions, when referring to trust accounting income, includes any 3-5 percent unitrust interest or corpus that is allocated to income under the law of any state that allows such an adjustment, no amendments were made to the §2503(b) regulations. A regulation issued in 1999, Reg. §20.7520-3(b)(2)(v), Ex. 1 & 2, seems to confirm the conclusions reached above.

---

43. Thus, in *Calder v. Comm'r*, 85 T.C. 713 (1985), the widow of the artist Alexander Calder made gifts of Calder art works to a trust, and the trustee had the power, and perhaps the duty, to (eventually) convert the art into income-producing assets. The Tax Court denied the exclusion, distinguished *Rosen* on the ground that there the Commissioner had conceded the existence of an income interest, so that the tables were invoked only on the valuation issue. The Tax Court noted that, even if the trustee had a duty to sell the art and to reinvest the proceeds, it was in no hurry to do so, and therefore the income beneficiaries lacked an immediate income flow. See also *McManus v. Comm'r*, T.C. Memo. 1980-296, *aff'd without opinion* (6th Cir.1982), where the Tax Court denied the exclusion where the trust was funded with unimproved land, even though the trustee possessed the power of sale. In *Rev. Rul. 69-344*, 1969-1 C.B. 225, cash and other property was transferred to a trust, with the terms of the trust authorizing investment in productive or nonproductive assets. The trustee actually invested the funds in life insurance policies, a type of investment that does not generate a current income yield. The exclusion was denied on the theory that the transaction as a whole indicated an intent not to transfer a present interest to the donee.

C. Gifts to Minors

Most gifts in a sustained gift-giving program attempting to take maximum advantage of the annual exclusion would be made to the donor's children or grandchildren. However, outright gifts to minors and young adults may not be desired. The donor may fear dissipation or mismanagement of the gift property. Also, a donee who is a minor will lack the capacity to sell or otherwise deal with the property.[44] A guardian of the property would have to be appointed, but guardianships involve expenses, obtaining court permission to deal with assets, and court accountings.

The donor can avoid these problems by the use of a custodial gift. A custodianship arrangement involves an outright transfer of cash, securities, life insurance policies, or other eligible property to a minor, but the property is under the control of the "custodian" (who may be the donor or other party with legal capacity). The terms of the custodianship are fixed by the version of the Uniform Gifts to Minors Act or Uniform Transfers to Minors Act in effect in the state where the donor resides, under which the custodian manages the property and can accumulate the income or pay to (or apply for the benefit of) the minor income and/or principal for the minor's "support, maintenance, education, and benefit." Although the custodian performs trustee-like functions, the custodian is not a trustee, does not have any kind of ownership interest, and is free of court supervision and oversight. The minor is the fee simple owner of the property. When the minor reaches the applicable age of majority, the property will be delivered to him, or if he dies before attaining the age of majority the property will pass to his estate.

A custodianship arrangement is more convenient than a court-supervised guardianship, but the minor must obtain the property outright at an early age. Also, if the minor dies prior to reaching majority, the property will become part of her probate estate, and under the applicable intestacy statute such property may well revert to the donee's parents.

A transfer to a custodial account will qualify for the present-interest exclusion under §2503(c).[45] Indeed, §2503(c) was added to the Code in 1954 to cover just this type of transfer, as well as an outright transfer to a minor to be administered by a guardian. Section 2503(c) was thought necessary because §2503(b) would bar the exclusion on account of the custodian's power to withhold (accumulate) income.

The beauty of §2503(c) is that *the entire qualifying gift is deemed to be of a present-interest*, as in the case of an outright gift. That is because the minor is the fee owner of the property under both guardianship and custodial arrangements. It is not necessary to carve up the transfer into present and future interests, as would be the case under §2503(b).

If the donor makes a custodial gift to a person two or more generations below him (e.g., grandchild, grandniece), a direct-skip type of generation-skipping transfer occurs.

---

44. In *Rev. Rul. 54-400*, 1954-2 C.B. 319, the Service held that an outright gift to a minor qualified for the §2503(b) exclusion notwithstanding the minor's disabilities and regardless of whether a guardian had been appointed.

45. *Rev. Rul. 59-357*, 1959-2 C.B. 212.

A trust arrangement may be preferred to a custodial gift. A trust might delay distribution to the child until a later age than the age of majority. Also, unlike a custodial gift, the dispositive and investment terms of a trust are not rigidly prescribed by statute. If the minor dies, the property can pass to a person other than the grantor or the child's estate.

The grantor of a minor's trust may attempt to qualify under §2503(c). If qualification is to be obtained under §2503(c), the first task is to conform the dispositive provisions of the trust to the terms of that provision. Reg. §25.2503-4(b)(1) states that the exclusion is lost if the trustee's discretion to expend for the "benefit" of the minor is subject to "substantial restriction." Thus, a transfer did not qualify where the trustee was required to consider the minor's situation and resources before applying funds for his benefit.[46] But a trust for the minor's "support, care, education, comfort, and welfare" passed muster, because standards like "welfare," "happiness," and "convenience" impose no objective limitations on the trustee's discretion.[47] In general, it seems that a trust will not be disqualified where the trustee's discretion as to the application of income and principal is at least as broad as that of a guardian under applicable state law.[48]

Qualification under §2503(c) will also requires that the gift be "vested" in the minor by provision for either the property's passing to her "estate" or according to the terms of a "general power of appointment," in case the minor dies prematurely. This requirement, however, presents only a slight problem. Inclusion of the property in the minor's estate for federal estate tax purposes will normally be without significance unless other substantial estate transfers are attributable to the minor. Probate of the property can be avoided — and control of devolution by the donor can be retained — by providing that the property is to pass pursuant to a general testamentary power of appointment and, in case of the nonexercise thereof, to takers in default. Such a power in most cases will never be exercised; in fact, the beneficiary will usually lack the legal capacity to exercise it, but this possibility will not disqualify the transfer from §2503(c). Thus, for all practical purposes, the property can be expected to pass to the takers in default.

A trust (but not a custodianship) can be set up to avoid termination when the donee reaches the age of majority and still qualify under §2503(c) by giving the donee the right to demand the trust property at age 21. The Service has acknowledged the effectiveness of this device, even where the beneficiary's right is exercisable only for a limited period of time and only by giving written notice to the trustee.[49]

---

46. See *Rev. Rul.* 69-345, 1969-1 C.B. 226.

47. See *Rev. Rul.* 67-270, 1967-2 C.B. 349.

48. See *Williams v. U.S.*, 378 F.2d 693 (Ct. Cl. 1967).

49. See *Rev. Rul.* 74-43, 1974-1 C.B. 285. In *Comm'r v. Herr*, 303 F.2d 780 (3d Cir.1962), the trust was to pay the income to the beneficiary for her maintenance or to accumulate the income, with any accumulated income being distributed to the beneficiary upon reaching 21, after which all the income was to be paid to the beneficiary; when the beneficiary reached 30, the trust was to terminate and was to be distributed to the beneficiary. In a dubious decision, it was held that the up-to-age-21 interest qualified under §2503(c), but the subsequent interests did not. Nevertheless, after further litigation on this issue, the Service acquiesced in *Herr.* See *Rev. Rul.* 68-670, 1968-2 C.B. 413. In estate planning, the *Herr*-type trust has been superseded by the Crummey trust, infra.

The beneficiary must be notified of his right to receive the property, and must be given a reasonable time to respond. Nevertheless, the donor may reasonably think that conferring a right on the beneficiary to demand corpus at an early age may cause the dispositive plan to be subject to an undue risk of disruption.

D. *Crummey Trusts*

It turns out that there is a way to qualify a transfer under §2503(b) in a way that produces a §2503(c) type result of qualifying the entire amount of the transfer for the exclusion. This goal is accomplished through a device commonly referred to as the "Crummey power" (or "Crummey trust"), named after the case of *Crummey v. Comm'r*, 397 F.2d 82 (9th Cir.1968). The Crummey power operates in the context of a trust for one or more beneficiaries who are (typically) considered too immature to be entrusted with fee ownership of property. Under the terms of the typical Crummey trust, the trustee is given the power to pay income to or among the beneficiaries or to accumulate the income, and the trust is to terminate when the beneficiaries have all reached a specified age. As described up to this point, the trust would not qualify under either of §2503(b) or §2503(c). Now we come to the Crummey power: Each beneficiary is given the power, exercisable annually, to withdraw from the trust an amount equal to the lesser of (a) the amount (if any) transferred to the trust by the grantor during that year or (b) an amount equal to the maximum annual exclusion. If the power is not exercised, the gift amounts become part of the trust corpus and cease to be subject to the demand power. In other words, the power of the beneficiary to withdraw corpus "lapses." The goal is for the amount transferred by the grantor into trust (up to $13,000 as indexed per beneficiary) to qualify in full for the §2503(b) exclusion on the ground that the beneficiary *had the right* to withdraw it during the same year. Of course, the beneficiary is discouraged from exercising the power, and in fact the power of withdrawal is practically never exercised.

In the *Crummey* case itself, the government's argument was basically that the minor beneficiary lacked the legal capacity or practical ability to exercise the withdrawal power conferred by the trust. Here is an excerpt from the Ninth Circuit opinion:

> A minor in California may own property. He may receive a gift. A minor of the age of 14 or over has the right to secure the appointment of a guardian and one will be appointed if the court finds it "necessary or convenient." A minor cannot sue in his own name and cannot appoint an agent. With certain exceptions a minor can disaffirm contracts made during minority.
>
> We do not feel that the appointment of an agent is a necessary prelude to the making of a demand upon the trustee. As we visualize the hypothetical situation, the child would inform the trustee that he demanded his share of the additions up to [the maximum amount]. The trustee would petition the court for the appointment of a guardian and then turn the funds over to the guardian. It would also seem possible for the parent to make the demand as natural guardian. This would involve the acquisition of property for the child rather than the management of the property. It would then be necessary for a legal guardian to be appointed to

take charge of the funds. The only time when the disability to sue would come into play would be if the trustee disregarded the demand and committed a breach of trust. That would not, however, vitiate the demand.

All this is admittedly speculative since it is highly unlikely that a demand will ever be made or that if one is made, it would be made in this fashion. However, as a technical matter, we think a minor could make the demand.

Under a test of examining everything and determining whether there is any likelihood of present enjoyment, the gifts would seem to be future interests. Although neither the trust nor the law forbid a demand by the minor, the practical difficulties of a child going through the procedures seem substantial. In addition, the surrounding facts indicate the children were well cared-for and the obvious intention of the trustors was to create a long-term trust. No guardian had been appointed. As a practical matter, it is likely that some, if not all, of the beneficiaries did not even know that they had any right to demand funds from the trust. Even had they known, the substantial contributions were made toward the end of the year so that the time to make a demand was severely limited. Nobody had made a demand under the provision, and no distributions had been made. We think it unlikely that any demand ever would have been made.

We decline to follow a strict [approach] in our situation because we feel that [it] is inconsistent and unfair. It becomes arbitrary for the I.R.S. to step in and decide who is likely to make an effective demand. Under the circumstances suggested in our case, it is doubtful that any demands will be made against the trust — yet the Commissioner allowed the exclusion as to the adult beneficiaries. There is nothing to indicate that it is any more likely that [the adult beneficiary] will demand funds than that any other beneficiary will do so. The only distinction is that it might be easier for him to make such a demand. Since we conclude that the demand can be made by the others, it follows that the exclusion should also apply to them. In another case we might follow the [strict] rule. We conclude that the result under the "right to enjoy" [test] is preferable in our case.

Despite the narrow "nondiscrimination" rationale in *Crummey*, the Service has acquiesced in the result, whether or not there are adult beneficiaries of the trust in addition to one or more minors.[50]

Nevertheless, the Service takes the position that the minor's right to demand must be meaningful. Thus, in *Rev. Rul. 81-7*, 1981-1 C.B. 474, a Crummey power was held not to qualify trust gifts for the exclusion, even though the beneficiary was not a minor, because the beneficiary received no notice of the additions to trust and had only three days to effect the withdrawal. The ruling stated that the donor's failure to inform the donee of the addition to the trust indicated an intent of the donor not to make a present-interest gift. In *Rev. Rul. 83-108*, 1983-2 C.B. 168, it was held that a 45-day period to exercise the right after receiving notice was reasonable time.

The Crummey power is a mainstay of estate planning, but it has been roundly criticized as being essentially illusory. Some proposals for eliminating the viability of the Crummey power have been introduced in Congress, but have not been enacted.

---

50. *Rev. Rul. 73-405*, 1973-2 C.B. 321.

QUICK QUESTION

Jennifer transfers $100k to a trust, with the bank as trustee. According to the terms of the trust, Cal is to receive all income annually and David is to receive the trust corpus at Cal's death. The trustee has the power to distribute principal to David at any time and in any amount. Does Jennifer's transfer qualify for the annual exclusion?

    A. Yes.
    B. Only the income interest qualifies.
    C. No, there is no present interest.
    D. No, the present interest is not ascertainable.

PROBLEMS, QUESTIONS, AND NOTES

1. A contribution to a qualified §529 state-sponsored college-savings plan in a given year can qualify for up to five exclusion amounts (in 2010, $65,000, or $130,000 if married). See §529(c)(2)(B). The contributions are completed gifts even if the donor is the plan owner or custodian who controls the funds and who can change the designated beneficiary (DB). See §529(c)(2)(A)(i). In addition, despite such retained control, a donor will generally not have any of the funds included in her gross estate. All states and the District of Columbia have such plans in the form of either or both of prepaid tuition plans and savings plans, called Qualified Tuition Programs (QTPs). Anyone (without income limitations) can contribute to the plans, but only in the form of cash. See §529(b)(2). Although there is no federal income tax deduction for a contribution, earnings that are used to pay eligible college expenses[51] are not subject to federal income tax. See §529(c)(3)(B). Some states provide state income tax deductions or credits for contributions. The plan DB can be anyone, even a nonrelative, and one can change the DB if the new beneficiary is in the DB's family, which is defined more broadly than most other Code sections and includes first cousins.[52]

---

51. Section 529(e)(3)(A) provides: "The term 'qualified higher education expenses' [QHEEs] means — (i) tuition, fees, books, supplies, and equipment required for the enrollment or attendance of a designated beneficiary at an eligible educational institution; and (ii) expenses for special needs services in the case of a special needs beneficiary which are incurred in connection with such enrollment or attendance." Also, reasonable room and board qualify as QHEEs for an eligible student as defined in §25A(b)(3), which requires that a student take at least half a course load at an eligible institution. See §529(e)(3)(B).

52. Section 529(e)(2) defines a family member of a *designated beneficiary* (DB) as including: "(A) the spouse of such beneficiary; (B) an individual who bears a relationship to such beneficiary which is described in subparagraphs (A) through (G) of §152(d)(2); (C) the spouse of any individual described in subparagraph (B) [of §529(d)(2)]; and (D) any first cousin of such beneficiary."

Congress has expanded §529 to include computer technology to the list of qualified higher education expenses, at least for 2009 and 2010. Recently, under the directive of §529(f), the IRS issued an advance notice of proposed rulemaking to prevent transfer tax abuses involving §529 plans.[53]

2. Is the §2503(b) exclusion available where:

   a. Sandra creates an irrevocable trust, income to Taz (a minor) for life or accumulated as the trustee decides, remainder to Ulrich? Can this trust be made to qualify under §2503(c)?

   b. Mel creates an irrevocable trust, all the income to Ned and/or Nedra in such proportions as the trustee decides for 20 years, remainder to Olive?

   c. Alan creates an irrevocable trust, income to Bill for life, corpus to Bill in the trustee's discretion, remainder to Chloe? The answer can be found in the second sentence of §2503(b)(1).

   d. Siegfried conveys a personal residence to Tristan, but Tristan agrees not to sell it for at least ten years?

   e. Gerhard owns a coupon bond, strips off the interest coupons (which he keeps), and gives the stripped bond (the right to the principal after ten years) to Peg? See Reg. §25.2503-3(a).

3. a. Assuming that income-producing property is transferred to a trust that provides for the payment of income to Otto, is the power in the trustee to invest in non-income-producing property (or to reduce income by exercising discretion over trust accounting decisions), even if *not* exercised, the equivalent to a power to accumulate? Does such a power result in disqualification under §2503(b)? Compare *Fischer v. Comm'r*, 288 F.2d 574 (3d Cir.1961) (broad array of such powers resulted in disqualification), with *Mercantile Safe Deposit & Trust Co. v. U.S.*, 311 F. Supp. 670 (D. Md. 1970) (routine boiler-plate discretion does not result in disqualification).

   b. Same as (a), except the trustee invests in high-tech stocks that produce a dividend yield of 1 percent of the value of corpus.

   c. What is the flaw in the dissenting opinion in *Maryland Nat'l Bank*?

4. a. Under the so-called "contract right" rule contained in Reg. §25.2503-3(a), an outright gift of a contract right that provides for future payments, such as a bond, note, annuity (to commence in the future), or life insurance policy, qualifies as a present-interest gift. Similarly, the payment of premiums on an annuity or life insurance policy is a present-interest gift to the owner thereof, if the owner is an individual. In both cases, qualification assumes that the individual donee or owner must possess the usual rights of an owner of such a contract right. See *Rev. Rul.* 55-408, 1955-1 C.B. 113.

   b. How can one explain the contract right rule? Consider the extreme case of a gift to an individual of a policy of term life insurance, which has no cash surrender value.

---

53. See *REG-127127-05* (advance notice), 73 Fed. Reg. 3441-3501 (Jan. 18, 2008).

    c. The contract right rule does not apply to gifts *in trust* of contract rights that provide only for future benefits. Similarly, it does not apply to the payment of premiums on life insurance policies held by trusts. Nevertheless, the annual exclusion might be obtainable on some other ground, such as the possession of a Crummey power by one or more persons (other than the grantor). Indeed, Crummey powers are a standard feature of irrevocable insurance trusts.

    d. In *Rev. Rul. 76-490*, set forth at p. 83, the Service held that the payment of premiums on term insurance held by an irrevocable trust for the benefit of a single named beneficiary was a gift that qualified for the annual exclusion. Is this ruling correct? Is it limited to term insurance?

5. a. Is the structure of §2503(b) flawed? Does the distinction between present and future interests make any sense relative to the purpose of the exclusion? (What purpose?) What about the fact that remainder interests can be sold for cash (unless the trust is a spendthrift trust)? Should the distinction be made between alienable and nonalienable interests? Cf. *Rev. Rul. 54-344*, 1954-2 C.B. 319 (spendthrift clause does not prevent qualification of income interest as a present interest).

    b. Various proposals have been made to reform the annual exclusion. One proposal would restrict it to outright gifts. A proposal made by the American Law Institute in 1969 would expand the exclusion to encompass gifts that involved immediate consumption by the donee. (Section 2503(e) was the eventual fruit of this proposal.)

6. a. Proposals have also been made to disarm the Crummey power by statute. Perhaps the easiest way would be to provide that a lapsing power of withdrawal is not deemed to be present enjoyment unless it is exercised within a short period of time after the gift.

    b. Is the *Crummey* case consistent with the line of cases (like *Maryland Nat'l Bank*) dealing with illusory present interests? These cases were based on objective facts, rather than findings as to intent or side-agreements. Is a Crummey power "objectively" inconsistent with a present interest? Can hindsight be used? (Virtually all Crummey powers lapse within a short period of time.)

    c. In *Estate of Cristofani v. Comm'r*, 97 T.C. 74 (1991), the Service unsuccessfully argued that Crummey powers given to persons who were not otherwise significant beneficiaries of the trust should not be recognized. (The donor's five grandchildren were contingent remainder beneficiaries.) In addition, the Crummey powers lapsed after a very short (15-day) period. Subsequently, the Service announced that it would disallow the exclusions in such cases on the basis of an understanding that the power not be exercised. However, in *Estate of Kohlsaat v. Comm'r*, T.C. Memo. 1997-212, the court declined to find an understanding simply by inference from the fact that the power was not exercised.

7. A Crummey power is a "general power of appointment" over the trust property subject to the power, because the power allows a person (who is not the grantor) to withdraw an amount from the trust. The possession of a general

power of appointment has numerous income, gift, and estate tax ramifications, which are discussed at §§7.1 and 7.2. The core idea is that such a power is the equivalent of ownership, by analogy to the "constructive" receipt doctrine under the income tax.

a. If the beneficiary holding the Crummey power dies while the power is exercisable, the amount then subject to demand is includible in the beneficiary's gross estate under §2041(a)(2). Since Crummey powers are generally noncumulative by reason of lapsing annually, the amount includible would normally be relatively insignificant.

b. Assuming that the beneficiary does not die, the annual lapse of the power results in the property "staying in the trust," which means that it is a "transfer" for gift (and estate) tax purposes by the beneficiary (back to the trust) *except to the extent of the greater of $5,000 or 5 percent of the property out of which the lapsed withdrawal power could have been satisfied.* See §2514(b) & (e). The portion of the lapsed amount in excess of the 5-or-5 amount may well constitute a taxable gift by the holder of the Crummey power. There would be no gift if: (a) the power is limited to the 5-or-5 amount; (b) the transfer is itself an "incomplete" transfer; (c) the holder of the Crummey power is the sole beneficiary of the trust; or, (d) the transfer (if complete) itself qualifies for the annual exclusion. Options (b) and (d) are improbable (why?), and option (c) is usually not desired. For all intents and purposes, the simplest and safest solution to this problem is to limit the withdrawal right to the lesser of (a) the annual exclusion amount or (b) the maximum 5-or-5 amount. A fancier approach is to limit the withdrawal power to the annual exclusion amount but to limit the lapse to the 5-or-5 amount. As a result, the power to withdraw the excess (if any) of the exclusion amount over the maximum 5-or-5 amount would "hang over" beyond the lapse. In estate planning jargon, this arrangement is referred to as a "hanging power."

c. A Crummey power results in treating the beneficiary as an owner of a portion of the trust for income tax purposes under §678, notwithstanding the lack of capacity or the nonappointment of a guardian. See *Rev. Rul. 81-6*, 1981-1 C.B. 385. Section 678 causes the owner of a portion of a trust to be taxed on the income therefrom. There is no 5-or-5 exception under §678. Having to pay incremental income tax by reason of *not* exercising a withdrawal power may well annoy an adult beneficiary. In the case of a minor beneficiary, the parent will probably pay the minor's incremental income tax, but this would count as an additional gift.

8. a. If a donor names himself custodian of a custodial gift for a minor and dies before the minor attains the age of majority, the property will be included in the donor's gross estate under §2038 because of the "retained" power in the grantor to "terminate" the custodianship by paying the property over to or for the benefit of the minor before the time the custodial account terminates. See *Rev. Rul. 57-366*, 1957-2 C.B. 618. For this reason, if the donor is a grandparent of the minor, the donor will typically name the minor's parent as custodian.

b. The minor, as owner of the custodial property, is taxed on the income therefrom. However, such income — along with other income taxed to the minor from (a) minor-owned investments, (b) under §678, or (c) as the result of trust distributions — is "unearned income," subject to the "kiddie tax." The term "kiddie tax" is the tax-jargon way of referring to §1(g) of the income tax Code, which has the effect of taxing a person under the age of 18 (or a student under age 24 whose earned income does not exceed half of the student's support) on unearned income at the highest marginal rates of that person's parents.

FURTHER NOTES ON GIFT TAX COMPUTATION AND PROCEDURE

1. Returns and payment:
    a. Under §6019, a gift tax return (Form 709) is due for each calendar year in which a donor makes a gift other than (a) a transfer which, before gift splitting, is wholly covered by the §2503 exclusions, or (b) a transfer deductible under §2523 (marital deduction), other than a transfer that qualifies under the so-called QTIP election. A gift tax return must be filed to elect (1) gift splitting under §2513 and (2) the marital deduction with respect to a QTIP transfer. See Reg. §25.6019-3 on whether a gift tax return needs to be filed for: (1) gifts deductible under §2522 (charitable deduction), (2) transfers exempt under §2516 (relating to divorce), and (3) transfers for full and adequate consideration in money or money's worth.
    b. The return is due by the April 15 of the year following the gift. An extension of time for filing an income tax return extends the time for filing the gift tax return. If gifts were made in the year of the donor's death, the gift tax return cannot be filed later than the time for filing the estate tax return (including extensions). See §6075(b).
    c. The gift tax must be paid by the due date of the return, without regard to extensions of time for filing the return. §6151(a). Nevertheless, an extension of time for payment of up to six months can be obtained under §6161(a)(1). Under §6161(b)(1), the time for payment of a gift tax deficiency can be extended for up to 30 months, but only if the donor would suffer "undue hardship" on account of being required to pay the deficiency when due.
    d. The gift tax is payable by the donor, of course. §2502(c). If the donor makes a gift on condition that the donee pay the tax, the amount of gift subject to tax is reduced accordingly, since the donee's payment of the net gift tax constitutes consideration in money's worth.
    e. Contrary to the usual ban on declaratory judgments in federal tax matters, the Tax Court can entertain a declaratory judgment action on a question of gift tax valuation, after administrative appeals are exhausted, even if a

gift tax is not due. See §7477. The amount of the gift (if made after 1976) would be an "adjusted taxable gift" that affects the computation of the estate tax.

2. The running of the statute of limitations bars the government from assessing a deficiency and bars the taxpayer from filing an amended return or claim for a refund.

   a. The statute of limitations for assessing a deficiency is three years starting from when the gift tax return was actually filed (or, if the return was filed early, from the due date of the return). See §6501(a) & (b)(2). The statute of limitations does not start to run if (a) no gift tax return is filed, (b) the return is fraudulent, or (c) the return fails to report or disclose a gift that is required to be reported. See §6501(c)(1), (3), and (9). The statute of limitations is suspended during the period from the mailing of a notice of deficiency to the date that is 60 days after the date any Tax Court decision becomes final.

   b. A taxpayer must file a claim for refund within three years of filing the return or, if later, two years from paying the tax. §6511(a). The timing of refund suits is dealt with in §6532.

3. The manner of computing the gift tax is discussed at pp. 36-38, supra.

   a. The general idea is that the gross tax on current-year taxable gifts (after taking the marital and charitable deductions) is the tax on the aggregate of current *and* prior taxable gifts reduced by the before-credit tax, using the same §2001(c) rate schedule, on prior taxable gifts. §2502(a). From the gross tax there is subtracted whatever of the exemption-equivalent credit as has not been used up in prior gift tax computations. §2505. There is no "option" to defer use of the credit. There are no credits against the gift tax other than the §2505 credit. The §2505 credit cannot exceed the §2502(a) tax; hence, the credit cannot produce a refund.

   b. The maximum credit amounts available after 1976, and their exemption equivalents, are found in the table below. After 1997, the credit amount is not stated in the statute except by reference to its exemption equivalent. No credit existed prior to 1977; instead there was a $30,000 lifetime "exemption."

Year	Credit Amount	Exemption Equivalent
1977	$ 30,000	$120,667
1978	34,000	134,000
1979	38,000	147,333
1980	43,500	161,563
1981	47,000	175,625
1982	62,800	225,000
1983	79,300	275,000
1984	96,300	325,000
1985	121,800	400,000
1986	155,800	500,000

Year	Credit Amount	Exemption Equivalent
1987-96	192,800	625,000
1997-98	—	625,000
1999	—	650,000
2000-01	—	675,000
2002-2010	—	1,000,000
2011	—	5,000,000
2012-	—	5,000,000 (indexed for inflation)

c. The maximum credit is reduced by an amount equal to 20 percent of the $30,000 exemption (if any) claimed on gifts made after September 8, 1976 and before January 1, 1977. This reduction constitutes a "penalty" for donors that rushed to use up their remaining exemption amount after it became known that it would expire and be replaced by a credit.

4. The computation of "prior taxable gifts" is somewhat dependent upon the law in effect when the gift was made. The rules are found in §2504 and the regulations. Keep in mind that these rules only affect the total of "prior taxable gifts" in computing the *current* gift tax liability. These rules do not affect the gift tax liability for any prior year on which the statute of limitations has run.

a. Transfers made prior to June 7, 1932, are totally excluded from the gift tax base, that being the date on which the modern gift tax became effective.

b. The annual exclusion is the same as the one in effect for the year of the gift. See §2504(b). See the table on p. 122 for the annual exclusion amounts for various years.

c. As already noted, prior to 1977 there was a cumulative per-donor lifetime exemption (deduction) of $30,000. This exemption was allowed by §2521, which was repealed as of January 1, 1977. Only $30,000 of gifts can be removed from the "prior taxable gifts" amount by reason of §2521, regardless of the amount exempt under prior law ($50,000 from 1932 through 1935 and $40,000 from 1936 through 1942). See §2504(a); Reg. §25.2504-1(b).

d. A gift incorrectly reported under the law then in effect should be removed from the prior taxable gifts total, even if the statute of limitations has run and even if the incorrectness resulted from a subsequent court decision or administrative rule. Similarly, a gift that was incorrectly excluded should be added to the prior taxable gifts total, even if the statute of limitations has expired on the gift tax liability itself. The same rule applies to deductions. Reg. §25.2504-1(d).

e. Prior to 1998, the *valuation* of prior taxable gifts was "fixed" only if the statute of limitations had run *and a gift tax was actually paid* with respect to the gift. Since the vast majority of taxable gifts avoid tax due to the unified transfer tax credit, this rule was viewed as creating too much uncertainty, and was changed by the 1997 tax act. Under current §2504(c), the value of prior taxable gifts is fixed if the statute of limitations for assessment has run, *the item was shown or disclosed on the return*, and the value was uncontested or the subject of a court judgment or settlement.

f.   The marital and charitable deduction rules are those in effect when the transfer was deemed complete. §2504(a)(4). The rules for split-interest charitable gifts were drastically revised for gifts after 1969. From 1948 through 1976, the marital deduction was an amount equal to 50 percent of the gift *before* the exclusion. From 1977 through 1981, the marital deduction computation became more complex: Roughly speaking, the first $100,000 of qualifying post-1976 gifts were fully deductible, the second $100,000 was not deductible at all, and amounts above a cumulative total of $200,000 generated a 50 percent deduction. During the 1948-1981 period, gifts of community property were not eligible for the marital deduction. The current unlimited marital deduction has applied to gifts made after 1981.

g.   Various provisions of the Code, including §2502(a), refer to "preceding taxable periods." This term is used because returns were filed on a calendar-quarter basis between 1976 and 1981 inclusive. See §2502(b).

CHAPTER 4

THE BASIC ESTATE

This chapter deals mainly with the question of what constitutes what might be called the federal estate tax "net estate," which is the property owned by the decedent at the death of the decedent (see §2033) reduced by the deductions for expenses and losses (see §§2053, 2054, and 2058). This material is followed by a section on the income taxation of estates. The chapter concludes with a discussion of estate tax valuation and procedural issues.

To set this chapter in a larger context, the gross estate consists not only of property owned by the decedent at death, but also:

(1) the amount of any gift tax paid or owed on gifts made within three years of death (§2035(b));

(2) the value of property "constructively" owned by the decedent at his death by reason of the possession (etc.) of a general power of appointment (§2041);

(3) the value of property transferred by the decedent during his lifetime with various retained interests and powers (§§2035-2040);

(4) the proceeds of life insurance policies under the decedent-insured's control at death (or within three years of death) or payable to the insured's estate (§§2035(a) & 2042); and,

(5) the value of property (not otherwise included) that had previously qualified for the gift or estate tax marital deduction by reason of a QTIP-election transfer made by the decedent's spouse (§2044).

These items (except the one for gift tax on gifts paid or owed within three years of death) are discussed in later chapters.

All gross estate items are valued, generally speaking, according to the same principles as are applied to gift tax valuation. The estate tax valuation date in the vast majority of cases is the date of the decedent's death, except where an election is made to use the "alternate valuation date" (shortly after the decedent's death).

§4.1. Property Passing by Will or Intestacy

The starting place for a discussion of the gross estate is, of course, that of property that the decedent owns at death *and* which passes to the decedent's legatees and heirs. The precise rule, found in §2033, is that the gross estate includes "the value of all property to the extent of the interest therein of the decedent at the time of his death." This provision can be viewed as a "continuation" of the previous chapter in that it deals with inclusion in the gross estate of property the decedent (1) did *not* make a transfer of prior to death, (2) did *not* expend on the purchase of annuities or life insurance, and (3) did *not* receive as employee compensation on account of being diverted to the provision of survivor benefits. In short, §2033 covers money and property still owned by the decedent at death. One of the messages to be delivered by this chapter is how inadequate §2033 has been as a lens for viewing the totality of testamentary transfers by a decedent.

The 1916 predecessor to §2033 referred to property of the decedent "which after his death is subject to the payment of the charges against his estate and the expenses of its administration and is subject to distribution as part of his estate," which is an elaborate way of saying "probate estate" (the estate subject to estate administration). This language was eliminated in 1926 in favor of the present language in order to cover property (commonly, real property), which, under applicable state law, passes directly to the legatee and is not subject to estate administration, or might possibly be subject to estate administration only if other assets are insufficient to pay claims.

"Nonprobate" testamentary-type transfers or (contractual) arrangements by a decedent, such as can be effected through *inter vivos* trusts (revocable or irrevocable), life insurance policies, annuity contracts, employee survivor benefits, and property (or an account) that passes to another person at the decedent's death by right of survivorship, are (generally) dealt with by Code provisions other than §2033. These provisions are covered in the next chapter.

A. What Is "Property" of the Decedent Under §2033?

The term "property" as used in §2033 is extremely broad and includes not only cash and conventional property but virtually anything of value that is entitled to legal protection and that can pass *from a decedent* by will, intestacy, or the operation of law. For example, in *Estate of Andrews v. U.S.*, 850 F. Supp. 1279 (E.D. Va. 1994), the gross estate was held to include the descendible right of publicity, protected by state law, that attached to a celebrity decedent's name. However, state law does not always create a descendible right of publicity.[1]

---

1. Additionally, the federal courts might misread state law on this and other issues. See *State ex rel. Elvis Presley v. Crowell*, 733 S.W.2d 89 (Tenn. App. 1987). See generally Mitchell Gans et al., *The Estate Tax Fundamentals of Celebrity and Control*, 118 Yale L.J. Pocket Part 203 (2008).

Government entitlements may come within §2033. Thus, it has been held that "rice acreage history" was property of the decedent under §2033, because it gave its owner a descendible claim to future rice production allotments under U.S. Department of Agriculture regulations.[2]

It is not necessary that the decedent have actually possessed the property or cash at death. It is enough that he owns it. A standard example is a vested remainder (or reversionary) interest that has not yet come into possession. Thus, if X creates an irrevocable trust, income to B for life, remainder to C, and C (the owner of a vested remainder) dies before B, the value of C's vested remainder interest is included in C's gross estate. Such value will be determined by actuarial tables (issued by the Treasury, as explained in Chapter 3) applied at the date of the decedent's death.

Another common example of a right that has not been reduced to possession or enjoyment is a right to salary, interest, dividends, etc., that was "earned" by a decedent before death but never received by him (but which is instead eventually received by the decedent's personal representative, a legatee, or a designated beneficiary).[3] In income tax jargon, such a right is known as an "IRD right" (a right to "income in respect of a decedent"). An IRD right is a §2033 asset for estate tax purposes, because the *right* to the income passes from the decedent to a legatee or heir. IRD rights pose a design problem under the *income tax* due to the twin fact that (1) individuals are mostly on the cash method of tax accounting and (2) the existence of an individual for income tax purposes terminates at death. Without a special income tax rule, the decedent would avoid income tax by reason of not having received the cash prior to death, and the successor would also avoid income tax by reason of §102(a) while at the same time obtaining a fair market value basis under §1014. One possible solution would be to put the decedent on the accrual method with respect to IRD rights, but Congress instead has opted to include the cash in the gross income of the person (legatee, heir, estate, beneficiary) who receives the cash following the decedent's death. This solution is accomplished by retaining the excludability of the right under §102(a) but at the same time placing such right outside of §1014, so that the decedent's basis (usually zero) carries over to the decedent's successor. See §1014(c). Then, the collection of the cash by the legatee (etc.) entails realized gross income (net of any carryover basis offset). See §691(a).

Example: Emil is an employee of Extron Corp, a recently formed high-tech firm. Emil has acquired accrued contractual deferred compensation rights worth $120,000, which has not yet been includible in Emil's gross income. Emil dies, and the deferred compensation right is part of Emil's residual estate, which is

---

2. *First Victoria Nat'l Bank v. U.S.*, 620 F.2d 1096 (5th Cir.1980). This property descended only to the devisees and heirs of the decedent who continued farming operations. The court treated the fact that the property was contingent on, *inter alia*, continuation of the government program as merely affecting the value, not the existence of a right.

3. The issue of when investment income has accrued is dealt with by Reg. §20.2032-1(d) & (e).

bequeathed to Fanny. This right is included in Emil's gross estate under §2033 at its value as of Emil's death, which is (say) $112,000. Several months later, the $120,000 is paid in cash by Extron to Emil's personal representative. Recall that the estate of Emil is an income tax entity. The estate acquired Emil's deferred compensation right under §102(a), but it is an IRD right that falls outside of §1014. Therefore, Emil's zero basis in the right carries over to his estate. The satisfaction of Emil's right for $120,000 cash produces $120,000 gross income to Emil's estate as an income tax entity.

IRD rights are rights to income that has been earned or accrued (but not received in cash or includible property). A right or claim, held by the decedent, to nonaccrued future payments (like a note) is garden-variety "property" within §2033, which does obtain a §1014 basis.

A right or claim is included even though future payment is subject to a condition precedent which might never occur. For example, the Tax Court has held that a contractual right to share in contingent legal fees in connection with pending litigation (not yet resolved) was includible under §2033.[4] Similarly, a decedent's outstanding claim for an income tax refund is property includible in her estate under §2033, even though the claim has not been resolved or settled.[5] However, it has been held that a potential claim to an insurance reimbursement was not includible where the right to the reimbursement depended on future discretionary acts of the decedent (which never occurred due to the decedent's death).[6]

In this type of contingent-right situation, the taxpayer will attempt to prove a greatly reduced *value* of the property on account of (1) the contingencies and (2) the futurity of payment, and in extreme cases a zero value may be established.

Contingent rights, which are "property," must be distinguished from "expectancies," which are not. Thus, if Jackson executes a valid will leaving Blackacre to Kendra, and Kendra dies before Jackson's death leaving "my interest in Blackacre" to LeeAnn, Kendra has no interest in Blackacre that can be included under §2033, because Jackson's will confers no rights on Kendra (or anyone else) until Jackson dies *and* Jackson's will is admitted to probate. Now suppose Jackson dies *after* the death of Kendra. Jackson has here made a bequest to Kendra that lapses (because Kendra was not alive at Jackson's death), but suppose that Blackacre passes to Kendra's sole surviving child, LeeAnn, under the applicable state anti-lapse

---

4. *Estate of Curry v. Comm'r*, 74 T.C. 540 (1980) (*acq.*). In valuing these claims, the court considered the extent to which the claims had been pursued, decedent's success in similar actions, and the probability of decedent's success in these claims as of the time of his death.

5. *U.S. v. Simmons*, 346 F.2d 213 (5th Cir.1965). In *Estate of Smith v. Comm'r*, 108 T.C. 412 (1997), *rev'd and remanded* (on the issue of valuation), 198 F.3d 515 (5th Cir.1999), both courts agreed that the decedent's right to §1341 claim of right relief was an asset of her estate includible under §2033.

6. See *Estate of Bull v. Comm'r*, T.C. Memo. 2001-92, wherein the insurer's obligation to reimburse decedent's residence-restoration costs after a fire was subject to the condition precedent of the completed reconstruction of her home. The court held that only the value of her 57%-completed residence was includible in her estate under §2033. The court also held that the estate could not deduct post-death costs of reconstructing the home.

statute. These facts do not alter the fact that Kendra had no interest in Blackacre at *her* death prior to that of Jackson. LeeAnn takes as a "substitute taker" (in lieu of Kendra) under Jackson's will as "amended" by the state anti-lapse statute. LeeAnn did not acquire any interest in Blackacre *from Kendra* by descent or otherwise.

An existing right capable of descent is considered property even though it is subject to a condition subsequent (other than the decedent's own death) or may be destroyed by the discretionary act of another. Thus, if Tracey creates a revocable *inter vivos* trust for 15 years, naming Ulmer as remainder, and Ulmer dies before Tracey, Ulmer owns an asset (a vested remainder interest subject to disfeasance) under §2033, even if Tracey subsequently revokes the trust, thereby causing Ulmer's remainder interest to be defeated. *Rev. Rul.* 67-370, 1967-2 C.B. 324.[7] Of course, the value of Ulmer's remainder would be quite low (or even zero) *because of* the possibility of disfeasance.

The distinction between an expectancy, on the one hand, and a defeasible interest or right, on the other, occasionally crops up in the context of employee survivor benefits. In general, the courts have held that discretionary benefits lie outside of §2033, even in cases where the employer made a practice of paying such benefits under predictable circumstances. Thus, in *Estate of Barr v. Comm'r*, 40 T.C. 227 (1963), the company, at its discretion annually declared a "wage dividend" (really, a bonus) to its employees and sometimes to survivors of deceased beneficiaries. The court held that the deceased employee had no right to the wage dividend (paid to a survivor).[8] On the other hand, if the death benefit is payable out of a fund that the employee could have withdrawn during life, then the death benefit is viewed as a §2033 asset.[9] Nevertheless, cases involving employer payments to survivors of an employee rarely fall within §2033, but inclusion in the deceased employee's gross estate may well occur under §2039 or, if §2039 is not applicable, under §2037 or §2038.

To come within §2033, the property must be owned beneficially. Ownership of property may be split between legal ownership and equitable ownership, as occurs in a trust. In such a case, a "legal" owner of property (the trustee) is not considered to be the owner for federal transfer tax purposes. The property is deemed owned by those having beneficial interests. Thus, assume that Allie creates a trust, naming her friend Thurgood as trustee, income to Brinley for life, remainder to Curt. If Thurgood dies before Brinley, the trust property is excluded from Thurgood's gross estate, because Thurgood lacks beneficial ownership. See Reg. §20.2033-1(a).

A discretionary power to control the beneficial enjoyment of property held (in trust or otherwise) by another is not an interest in property. Arguably, a power during life to obtain property held in a trust created by another might be

7. Accord, *Huggins v. U.S.*, 684 F.2d 417 (9th Cir.1982).

8. Accord, *Estate of Bogley v. U.S.*, 514 F.2d 1027 (Ct. Cl. 1975).

9. See, e.g., *Northern Trust Co. v. U.S.*, 389 F.2d 731 (7th Cir.1968); *Estate of Garber v. Comm'r*, 271 F.2d 97 (3d Cir.1959). As under the constructive receipt doctrine, §2033 will not apply where the right of withdrawal was subject to a significant penalty or restriction. *Estate of Brooks v. Comm'r*, 50 T.C. 585 (1968) (*acq.*), *Rev. Rul.* 80-158, 1980-1 C.B. 196.

considered a form of "constructive ownership" of the property. However, such a power (called an *"inter vivos* general power of appointment") has never been treated by state property law as the equivalent of fee ownership, even where creditors of the decedent or the decedent's estate could reach the property, and the Service has never successfully treated constructive ownership as actual ownership *under* §2033.[10] This scenario is now governed by a separate provision, §2041, that will be discussed in due course. The scenario where the decedent *retains* a power (including a power to revoke) over property transferred by the decedent herself *inter vivos* is likewise not controlled by §2033, but instead by §§2036, 2037, and 2038. A further obstacle to inclusion of property subject to a decedent's power under §2033 is the fact that the power expires at the decedent's death, because a power by its legal nature attaches to a person, and not to a thing.

B. Interests that Expire by Reason of the Decedent's Death

Section 2033 only applies to property that passes from a decedent to another party. This "passing" can only occur if (a) the same interest exists both before and after the decedent's death and (b) the survivor acquires the property *from the decedent* at the decedent's death (as opposed to by coming into possession of an interest acquired before the decedent's death). A right, interest, or power that expires with a decedent's death is not descendible, and avoids inclusion in the gross estate under §2033. The earlier discussion of publicity rights illustrates the rule that a right or interest of the decedent that expires at her death is not included in the gross estate under §2033. Or, perhaps such a right is included, but (if so) it would have a value of zero. Similarly, a power (by its legal nature) expires at a decedent's death.

Perhaps the leading example of an interest that expires at the death of a decedent is a life estate or its trust counterpart, namely, an income, annuity, or unitrust interest for the life of the decedent. Thus, if A creates an irrevocable trust, income to B for life, remainder to C, nothing passes or descends from B to C at B's death, and nothing is included in B's gross estate under §2033 (or any other provision). The remainder interest of C was acquired from A (not B) at the time A created the trust, and merely ripens (comes into possession) at B's death. (If A, B, and C occupy progressively younger generations, the death of B may well be subject to the GST tax.)

If A creates an irrevocable trust, income to *herself* for life, remainder to C, nothing is included in A's gross estate *under* §2033 by reason of A's death. Again, the remainder interest of C was acquired before A's death by *inter vivos* transfer from A. (Nevertheless, because A retained the income interest in herself for life, the trust will be includible in A's gross estate under §2036(a)(1).)

In a similar vein to the foregoing, if the decedent had purchased a single-life annuity providing for payments of $1,000 a month from the time of reaching age

---

10. See *Royce v. Comm'r,* 46 B.T.A. 1090 (1942).

65 until her death, at which time all payments cease, the annuity is not included under §2033 because it wholly expires at her death. Of course, any part of the *payments received* under the annuity that had not been consumed or given away would be part of the decedent's §2033 gross estate, but it would be incorrect to say that the annuity itself (as a property or contract right) is includible under §2033. In the case of an annuity contract purchased by Antoine that provides for payments to Antoine to life, then to Bertha for life, again nothing is included in Antoine's estate *under §2033*: Antoine's right expires at death, and Bertha's right was created by contract prior to Antoine's death. (However, the value of Bertha's annuity at Antoine's death will be included in Antoine's estate under §2039.)

Yet another example of an interest expiring at death is an interest contingent on the owner of the interest surviving the preceding estate. Thus, assume that A creates an irrevocable trust, income to B for life, remainder to C if C survives B, but if C does not survive B then to D, and assume further that C predeceases B. In this case, C's contingent remainder is not included in C's estate, because it expired by its terms on C's death prior to that of B.

As stated earlier, a power held by an individual necessarily expires (by reason of the legal nature of powers) at the holder's death, and therefore does not descend from the decedent to a person who succeeds to the power.[11] Thus, even if a power were treated as a property interest (which is not the case), it would avoid inclusion under §2033.[12]

C. Interests that Spring into Existence at the Decedent's Death

Just as interests that expire (etc.) at a decedent's death avoid §2033, so also do interests that spring up by reason of a decedent's death. Perhaps the cleanest illustration of this rule is with property that didn't even exist prior to a decedent's death, such as a right to a wrongful death recovery or *statutory* survivor benefit.[13] The rule holds true even if the decedent held an interest for life under the same arrangement, such as a retirement benefit or a right to withdraw the cash surrender value: The for-life interest avoids inclusion under §2033 because it terminates at the decedent's death, and the survivor benefit avoids inclusion under §2033 because it is a separate right in a different person that emerges at (or immediately after) the decedent's death.[14]

---

11. See, e.g., *Estate of Haggett v. Comm'r*, 14 T.C. 325 (1950).

12. See *Royce v. Comm'r*, 46 B.T.A. 1090 (1942) (pre-1942 power to withdraw corpus of a trust is not includible under §2033). Such a power is an *inter vivos* general power of appointment, which (if the power is created after 1942) causes inclusion in the gross estate under §2041(a)(2).

13. See, e.g., *Connecticut Bank & Trust Co. v. U.S.*, 465 F.2d 760 (2d Cir.1972) (wrongful death recovery); *Rev. Rul.* 82-5, 1982-1 C.B. 131 (survivor benefit payable under no-fault auto policy); *Rev. Rul.* 67-277, 1967-2 C.B. 322 (Social Security survivor benefit). Compare *Rev. Rul.* 83-44, 1983-1 C.B. 128 (holding that a decedent's right to medical-care benefits that survived the decedent is included in the decedent's gross estate under §2033).

14. See *Estate of Wadewitz v. Comm'r*, 39 T.C. 925 (1963), *aff'd on other grounds*, 339 F.2d 980 (7th Cir.1964).

Of course, "springing" benefits may be includible under some Code provision other than §2033. Thus, §2039 (as well as §§2037 and 2038) may apply to employee survivor benefits and survivor annuities, and §2042 may apply to life insurance proceeds.

D. Amounts Payable to the Decedent's Estate

In the abstract, if an already-existing fund or property is payable (under the terms of a contract or trust) to the decedent's estate upon the decedent's death, the property could be considered as having been owned by the decedent before death (as well as after death), because not only does the decedent exercise the right of testamentary disposition through her will (or the absence thereof), but in addition the decedent could have enjoyed the property during life by incurring debt that would be satisfied out of the money or property, which is available to the creditors of the decedent's estate.

It is not wholly clear, however, that §2033 applies in this scenario. Fortunately, the question is of virtually no consequence as a practical matter, because it is now dealt with by other Code provisions. However, the issue is worth discussing briefly, both for historical reasons and as an illustration of the highly technical flavor of estate tax doctrine.

A very closely analogous scenario for inclusion exists where a person has the power (under such person's will) to cause property (in a trust created by another) to be paid over to such person's own estate, and the person in fact exercises that power in favor of her estate. Such a power is referred to as a "testamentary general power of appointment." In the early case of *U.S. v. Field*, 255 U.S. 257 (1921), the decedent in 1917 exercised under her will such a power in favor of her descendants, rather than her estate. The Supreme Court, after noting that the assets appointed to the decedent's descendants were not owned by the decedent before death and were not merged with her probate estate assets after death, held that the predecessor of §2033 did not apply, despite the fact the decedent's creditors could have reached the appointed property if the probate estate had been insufficient. It is unclear from the opinion in *Field* if the result would have been different if the property had actually been appointed to the estate of the decedent.

The precise holding in *Field* was rendered obsolete by the enactment of §402(e) of the Revenue Act of 1919, effective only for powers created after enactment, which provided that any exercise of a testamentary general power of appointment (and certain exercises of *inter vivos* general powers of appointment) triggered inclusion of the appointed property in the estate of the person exercising the power, whether the appointment was to such person's estate or otherwise. (This provision is now §2041(a)(1) of the Code, which in turn is superseded by §2041(a)(2) for general powers of appointment created after 1942.) The decision in *Field* (dating from 1921) cited this 1918 enactment as evidence that the 1919 Congress must have been uncertain that the 1916 estate tax reached this scenario. That is, the Court felt that the 1919 Act did not merely codify or clarify prior law.

An additional lesson to be gleaned from this narrative is that Congress, when changing the law in this area, usually acts only prospectively (or with only modest retroactivity), out of concern that retroactive changes in the law affecting property raise the issue of a possible violation of the Due Process Clause of the Fifth Amendment.[15]

In *Helvering v. Safe Deposit & Trust Co.*, 316 U.S. 56 (1942), the Court characterized *Field* as holding that the exercise of a testamentary general power of appointment did not cause inclusion under §2033, regardless of the appointment, and that this result was implicitly confirmed by Congress in 1919 by enacting a separate provision to cover situations such as that presented in *Field*. The Court also held that the necessary implication of *Field* and subsequent legislative developments was that a *possessed* (but unexercised) testamentary general power of appointment would not cause inclusion, under §2033, of the property subject to the power. Finally, the Court held that the combination in the same person of an income interest for life with an unexercised testamentary general power of appointment did not "add up" to the fee ownership required by §2033, even though the combination encompassed most of the bundle of rights that a fee owner possesses.

Notwithstanding the foregoing, the government later took the position in litigation that a payment from a pre-existing fund (that paid income to the decedent for life) to the decedent's estate (pursuant to a beneficiary designation of a third party) was includible in the decedent's gross estate under §2033. However, this position was rejected in *Second Nat'l Bank of Danville v. Dallman*, 209 F.2d 321 (7th Cir.1954). There the father purchased insurance on his own life and designated a settlement option under which the daughter (the decedent) was to receive an annuity for life, and on her death the principal was to be paid to a beneficiary to be selected by the daughter, but, if the daughter failed to exercise this power, the principal was to be (and, in fact, was) paid to the daughter's estate. After holding that the daughter (1) did not have a testamentary general power of appointment and (2) did not exercise the power she had, as required under the 1919 Act provision previously alluded to, the court held that payment was not includible under §2033, because *she* did not own the fund prior to death. Although both the Fifth Circuit and the Service have disagreed with the power-of-appointment holding of this case,[16] the §2033 holding appears not to have been subsequently questioned.

The issue is of no practical importance any more, because since 1942 the *possession* at death of a general power of appointment (whether testamentary or *inter vivos*) causes the subject property to be included in the gross estate of the person possessing the power (if the power was created after 1942). A remainder to, or a payment by reason of a beneficiary designation to, a decedent's estate is the equivalent of giving the decedent a testamentary general power of appointment.

---

15. The most recent Supreme Court case dealing with the retroactivity of federal transfer tax legislation is *U.S. v. Carlton*, 512 U.S. 26 (1994), where the Court upheld 14-month retroactivity under what appears to be a test that balances the rationality of the legislation against the "harshness and oppressiveness" of the result.

16. See *Keeter v. U.S.*, 461 F.2d 714 (5th Cir.1972); *Rev. Rul. 55-277*, 1955-1 C.B. 456.

See Reg. §20.2041-1(b)(1). In short, if pre-existing property (or a fund) is paid to the estate of a decedent, the property (or fund) is included in the decedent's gross estate under §2041(a)(2), and the unresolved question of inclusion under §2033 is moot. (Powers of appointment are discussed in a Chapter 7.)

It has long been the rule, under what is now §2042(1), that the payment of life insurance proceeds to the insured's "executor" (i.e., the insured's estate) causes inclusion of the proceeds in the insured's gross estate.

An *inter vivos* transfer by a person that leaves or creates a reversion *in the donor or the donor's estate* can cause inclusion of the property (or interests therein) in the donor's gross estate under §2037 (discussed in Chapter 8), or, if the reversion is not contingent on the donor surviving a prior interest, the reversion (being the equivalent of a vested remainder) is included in the donor's gross estate under §2033 as an interest owned at death. An example of inclusion under §2033 would be where A creates a trust, income to B for 15 years, reversion to A, and A dies before the 15-year period expires.

E. *Property Owned by Another*

Property owned by another party is excluded from the decedent's §2033 gross estate. Thus, only one-half of community property is included in the gross estate of the first spouse to die under §2033, as the other half is already owned by the surviving spouse.

But then, rights of a surviving spouse to elect to take against the decedent's will out of the decedent's estate at the decedent's death, such as dower, curtesy, homestead, or elective share, are not deemed to be owned by the surviving spouse but instead by the decedent. §2034. "Interests" of this type might be said to be merely "forced heirship" rights that spring into existence at the decedent's death and merely affect who ends up with the decedent's property.

Joint tenancies with right of survivorship are not covered by §2033. All interests in joint tenancies are created by a prior transfer. The interests of the decedent joint tenant expire at death, and the survivor acquires possession pursuant to rights acquired under the terms of the instrument creating the joint tenancy. The survivor's interest is akin to a remainder (or reversionary) interest contingent on surviving the other joint tenant. All or part of the property may be included in the decedent's gross estate under §2040, however, which is covered in Chapter 5.

A personal representative might claim that an asset is not owned by a decedent at death either because it was not received before death or because it was given away or expended before death. On the receipt side, the general rule is that the crucial fact is the acquisition of the *right* to the cash or property, rather than the actual receipt of the cash or property. See Reg. §20.2033-1(d) (defining "included property"). If the right is to income, then it would probably be an IRD right, which was described earlier.

On the payment side, if an obligation is incurred prior to death to make a payment that will not (or does not) occur until after death, then the obligation is an item that may (or may not) be deductible under §2053, and it would be incorrect to both exclude the obligation and to deduct it. Therefore, the general rule here is that the obligation is excluded only if it was actually satisfied prior to death.

In the case of gifts by a decedent shortly before death, the issue is whether the gift has been actually completed before death. The general property-law rule for gifts of personal property is donative intent plus delivery. But an argument could be made that a gift of registered property is not effective until re-registration in the name of the donee. Nevertheless, for gift tax purposes a gift will be treated as effective upon delivery by the donor prior to re-registration, at least where re-registration is just a formality.[17]

A subcategory of the larger payment issue is that of checks written by the decedent but not cleared (not paid by the bank out of the decedent's account) before the decedent's death. Technically, prior to the clearing of the checks, the funds belong to the decedent, and the personal representative of the decedent's estate would have a duty to secure these funds by stopping all outstanding checks, after which the personal representative would seek to pay off valid claims. Of course, uncleared *gift* checks are not claims against the decedent's estate, and the personal representative should not allow these checks to clear. Reg. §20.2031-5 provides that checks outstanding at the decedent's death can be excluded from the gross estate where the checks relate to spending in commerce, presumably because exclusion in this case is a shortcut to an inclusion of the check amounts followed by a proper deduction for claims under §2053(c)(1). (Of course, if the check is excluded, the payment on the check cannot also be deducted.) A similar practice is followed for checks written to charities, because here inclusion of the checks would be offset by charitable deductions under §2055.[18] However, other outstanding checks (namely, those representing noncharitable gifts) are not excludible, because here there would be no offsetting deduction.[19]

Disclaimers can be used to avoid acquiring property by way of gratuitous transfer shortly before death. Suppose Obie's will leaves property to Petra, but Petra dies a few weeks after Obie's death. Here it is unlikely that the bequest was actually distributed to Petra while alive, and in that case it may be possible under state law for Petra's personal representative to effectively disclaim the bequest on behalf of Petra. If the disclaimer is valid under §2518 (discussed in Chapter 3), the disclaimer has the effect of preventing Petra's §2033 gross estate from being augmented by the bequest (or the right to the bequest) in a situation where Petra had no personal use for it (being dead).

---

17. See *Rev. Rul. 54-554*, 1954-2 C.B. 317 (delivery of shares of stock). The donee, having received the shares, has an equitable right to cause re-registration in her name. Compare *Rev. Rul. 54-135*, 1954-2 C.B. 205 (where the stock is held by a broker, and not capable of delivery, the date of gift is the date the stock is re-registered on the corporation's books).

18. *Estate of Belcher v. Comm'r*, 83 T.C. 227 (1984) (reviewed), *acq. in result*, A.O.D. 1989-014 (Nov. 13, 1989).

19. See, e.g., *Rosanna v. U.S.*, 245 F.3d 212 (2d Cir.2001); *McCarthy v. U.S.*, 806 F.2d 129 (7th Cir.1986). The relation-back doctrine, however, is applied where decedent was alive when the bank paid the check. See *Metzger v. Comm'r*, 38 F.3d 118 (4th Cir.1994); *Rev. Rul. 96-56*, 1996-2 C.B. 161.

F. The Role of State Law in Tax Disputes

Various matters dealt with so far pose the general problem of the relation between federal tax law and the substantive law of property, wills, trusts, contracts, torts, agency, and so on. For example, in *Safe Deposit & Trust Co.*, supra, the Supreme Court looked separately at each interest and power of the decedent, and held that none of them rose to the level of an interest that fell within §2033. The Court also refused to aggregate these state law property interests into a special category of "transfer tax substantial ownership." Nevertheless, it is possible that *state law itself* can combine interests. An example is where Rita deeds Blackacre to Simpson for life, giving Simpson the power to sell Blackacre and consume the proceeds. Unless it is clear that Rita's intent was truly to give Simpson only a life estate, the instrument might be construed under state law to create a fee simple, in which case the property is included in Simpson's gross estate under §2033.[20]

A body of tax law has developed on the interaction of state law (or nontax law generally) and federal tax law. The general and oft-cited rule is:

> State law creates legal interests or rights. The federal revenue acts designate what interests or rights, so created, shall be taxed. If it is found that an interest or right created by local law was the object intended to be taxed, the federal law must prevail no matter what name is given to the interest or rights by state law.

Morgan v. Comm'r, 309 U.S. 78, 80-91 (1940).

The application of nontax law to the facts of a given case may be unclear. In cases involving the law of gratuitous transfers, litigation may be instituted in state court to determine the respective interests and rights of various parties. Such a situation raises the problem of whether determinations by a lower-level state court pertaining to a particular taxpayer should be treated as being controlling for federal tax purposes, given that much estate and trust litigation is not truly adversarial. For example, a fiduciary might desire to have the administrative provisions of an instrument construed, and no beneficiary may have sufficient interest or awareness in the matter to take an opposing position. Or possibly the fiduciary has no particular interest in the outcome, but merely needs to have an issue resolved in order to avoid future disputes and potential liability. Or possibly the interests of all parties would be furthered by a certain outcome, namely, the avoidance of federal taxes.

The leading case in this area, *Comm'r v. Estate of Bosch*, 387 U.S. 456, 465 (1967), involved an issue under the federal estate tax. There the Supreme Court stated:

> When the application of a federal statute is involved, the decision of a state trial court as to an underlying issue of state law should *a fortiori* not be controlling. This is but an application of the rule of *Erie Rr. Co. v. Tompkins*, 304 U.S. 64 (1938), where state law as announced by the highest court of the state is to be followed. If there be no decision by that court then federal authority must apply

---

20. See Restatement Property 2d (Donative Transfers) §12.1 cmt. b.

what it finds to be the state law after giving "proper regard" to relevant rulings of other courts of the state. In this respect, it may be said to be, in effect, sitting as a state court.

In *Bosch*, the Court rejected a rule that would have given conclusive weight to even a state court determination in a genuinely adversary proceeding.

Contrast *Bosch* with *Rev. Rul.* 73-142, 1973-1 C.B. 405, where the Service gave effect to a state lower court decree that was inconsistent with the rule adopted by the state's highest court. The Service held that *Bosch* did not apply because: (1) the decree was final, the time for appeal having lapsed; (2) the decree bound the parties to the litigation; and (3) (and most importantly) the final determination of the property issue (whether the decedent held a certain power at death) occurred prior to the relevant taxing date (the decedent's death).

QUICK QUESTION

Cranky died in an auto accident caused by Danger. In a wrongful death action, Cranky's estate received $10M, of which $8M compensated his family for economic loss and $2M represented an amount for pain and suffering. Which one of the following statements is *TRUE*?

  A. $10M is included under §2033.
  B. Zero is included under §2033.
  C. $8M is included under §2033.
  D. $2M is included under §2033.

PROBLEMS AND NOTES

1. a. Would the following will clause have any estate tax effect: "I declare that all of my household furnishings have been and are the property of my beloved spouse?" See *T.D.* 2529 (1917) (household and personal effects presumed to be owned by spouse who dies first). What would be effective proof that the decedent did not own the furnishings?

    b. Community property is distinguishable from dower, curtesy, and a right to elect to take against the will, which confer no rights on the surviving spouse prior to the decedent spouse's death. These rights simply limit the decedent's freedom of testation. Any actual exercise by a surviving spouse of any such right would result in an estate transfer that could well qualify for the estate tax marital deduction.

    c. Is a gift *causa mortis* excluded from the donor's §2033 gross estate? See *Rev. Rul.* 74-365, 1974-2 C.B. 324.

    d. Ralph purchases property and places it in the name of Stephan, an unrelated party. Who owns the property for estate tax purposes? (What nontax legal issue is implicated by this transaction?) See *Rev. Rul. 78-214*, 1978-1 C.B. 285.

2. a. Dolly lends $3,000 to Esteban in 1999 for five years at 8 percent interest. In 2002 Dolly dies, at which time accrued but unpaid interest is $520. How much, if anything, is includible in Dolly's estate?

    b. Same as (a), except that Dolly's will expressly forgives and cancels Esteban's entire obligation? See *Rev. Rul. 81-286*, 1981-2 C.B. 177.

    c. Reg. §20.2033-1(b) states: "A cemetery lot owned by the decedent is part of his gross estate, but its value is limited to the salable value of that part of the lot which is not designed for the interment of the decedent and members of his family." What, if anything, might be the rationale for excluding the "family interment" portion of the lot?

    d. Is the value of jewelry and gold fillings interred with the decedent included under §2033?

    e. The will of Gustav, an artist, directed his executor to destroy certain works designated under her will. The executor carries out this provision. Are the art works included under §2033?

3. a. Suppose Abner creates a testamentary trust, income to Beulah for life, remainder to such of Beulah's children as are living at Beulah's death, share and share alike, but if Beulah is not survived by any of her children then to Dagmar. What result on Beulah's death? What result if Catherine, one of Beulah's children, predeceases Beulah? What result if Dagmar predeceases Beulah?

    b. If one creates an irrevocable *inter vivos* trust and fails to dispose of the entire estate, the grantor has a reversion, and reversions are descendible interests. An example would be an irrevocable *inter vivos* trust created by X, income to Y for life, remainder to Z if living at Y's death. If Z predeceases Y, the property passes to X (or X's successors) by way of reversion. The value of this reversion is includible in the gross estate of X (and any deceased successor of X) under §2033. Of course the reversion is extinguished if Y dies survived by Z.

    c. Suppose A creates an irrevocable *inter vivos* trust, in which the income is payable to B for life, and on B's death the trust is to terminate and all its assets distributed to A if living, but if not A's estate. Is anything included in A's gross estate under §2033, if A dies before B? In form, this appears to create the following: A in trust, income to B for life, then remainder to A if living, but if not to such persons as A appoints by her will, but if no such appointment then to A's heirs. In *Adriance v. Higgins*, 113 F.2d 1013 (2d Cir.1950), the court held that the effect of a very similar transfer was to give A a reversion includible in A's gross estate under §2033, rather than a remainder contingent on survival. The court made allusion to the Doctrine of Worthier Title (which converts a "remainder" in the grantor's heirs into a reversion). However, the Doctrine of Worthier Title has since been abolished in virtually all states, and it wouldn't seem to have applied, strictly speaking, in *Adriance*. Nevertheless, the holding here appears to be that that the various possibilities that could occur on B's death should be treated, in the aggregate, as a reversion, includible under §2033. (This trust, if at issue today, would *not* be included under §2041, because that section does not apply where a *grantor* holds a general power of appointment over a trust she created, but it would be included under §§2037 and 2038, dealing with *retained* powers over transferred property.)

    d.   Suppose Drago creates an irrevocable trust, income to Esmeralda for life, remainder to Esmeralda's estate. What result under §2033 on E's death? This transfer might conjure up memories of the Rule in Shelley's Case, which could (if applicable) operate to convert this into a fee simple interest in E, but the Rule has been abolished in all American jurisdictions. In any event, isn't this the same situation presented in *Second Nat'l Bank of Danville*? Here it cannot be claimed that Esmerelda has a "reversion." (Why not?) In any event, was *Second Nat'l Bank of Danville* wrongly decided on the §2033 issue? Does Esmeralda have the equivalent of a vested remainder? (Again this question is academic. Why?)

4. a.   Should a revocable trust created by the decedent be treated as a §2033 asset? In a throwaway line in *Burnet v. Guggenheim*, 288 U.S. 280 (1933), the important early case that held that a revocable transfer was an incomplete transfer, Justice Cardozo stated that a purported revocable outright gift of personal property would be void,[21] and therefore would not effect a transfer at all. In that case, the asset would be included in the purported donor's §2033 gross estate. A revocable transfer can be made in trust or under a contract right. Revocable transfers are incomplete gifts but are included in the donor's gross estate under §2038 so long as the donor held the power at (or within three years of) the donor's death.

    b.   Suppose Frida makes a gift to Ginny on the basis of a misrepresentation by Ginny that she is a fundraiser for a charity. The transfer is voidable by Frida. What result if Frida dies before asserting a claim against Ginny? If Ginny dies before being sued by Frida?

    c.   By definition, a power of appointment is a power created by a person (the grantor of the trust and "donor" of the power) *other than* the person holding the power (the "donee" of the power). A possible rationale for excluding an *inter vivos* general power of appointment from the reach of §2033 might be that the power, although representing constructive ownership during the donee's life, expires at the donee's death, and hence is equivalent to an interest for the donee's life. Is this rationale convincing? Is there any sense in which the property subject to the power passes from the decedent to other persons at the donee's death? Do these facts add up to "ownership?"

    d.   In *Second Nat'l Bank of Danville* the Seventh Circuit also held that the decedent did not possess (or exercise) a testamentary general power of

---

21. Justice Cardozo cited *Basket v. Hassell*, 107 U.S. 602 (1883), a nontax case.

appointment, which would have caused inclusion in the gross estate under §2041. The court analyzed the situation as one where the donee actually possessed only a nongeneral power, with the donee's estate being the "taker in default." This position was rejected in *Keeter v. U.S.*, 461 F.2d 714 (5th Cir.1972), involving facts similar to *Second Nat'l Bank of Danville*, where the court treated the combination of a nongeneral power and an "estate" taker in default as a testamentary *general* power under current §2041. Restatement of Property 2d (Donative Transfers), §13.1, cmt. c, now follows the *Keeter* approach.

e. In accord with *Keeter* is Reg. §20.2041-1(b)(1), which states that the term "power of appointment" is to be applied on the basis of substance and not form or nomenclature. Thus, a power held by the holder of a legal life estate in real property to sell the property and consume the proceeds is an *inter vivos* general power of appointment, as is an unfettered power of a person (other than the grantor) to consume the principal of a trust. And "a power of testamentary disposition over property in which [the donee] does not have an interest" is a testamentary power (which is "general" if the donee can appoint to her estate or its creditors).

5. a. Did the Court in *Safe Deposit & Trust Co.* get it right? That is, is the combination of "income to B for life, remainder to B's estate (or as B appoints by will)" the equivalent of fee ownership? What's missing?

b. *Safe Deposit & Trust Co.* is based on legislative history and congressional intent, rather than a blanket rejection of the substance-over-form doctrine. As stated in footnote 1 of the opinion:

> In declining to pass upon the [substantial ownership] issue, we do not reject the principle we have often recognized that the realities of the taxpayer's economic interest rather than the niceties of the conveyancer's art should determine the power to tax. Nor do we deny the relevance of this principle as a guide to statutory interpretation where, unlike here, the language of a statute and its statutory history do not afford more specific indications of legislative intent. *Helvering v. Clifford*, 309 U.S. 331 (1940).

The case of *Burnet v. Guggenheim*, 288 U.S. 280 (1933), holding that a revocable transfer is not a completed gift, embraced substance-over-form analysis, as did *Keeter* in item 2(c). Nevertheless, the doctrine is probably not as broadly applied in the estate and gift tax as it is in the income tax.

c. The cite (in the above quotation) to *Helvering v. Clifford* reminds us that the doctrine of "substantial ownership" exists for income-attribution purposes. In the income tax, the doctrine is used to choose which of two or more persons owns investment property, given that income from property is taxed to the owner. However, the income tax contains no *statutory* rules for determining ownership, other than the grantor trust rules (and the beneficiary-owned trust rules) of §§671-678, which were enacted subsequent to the *Clifford* decision.

6. In a split decision, relying in part on *Morgan*, cited in §4.1.F, above, which holds that state law defines property rights, the Tax Court in *Pierre v. Comm'r,*

133 T.C. 24 (2009) (reviewed), held that because, under New York law, on LLC formation and funding, the taxpayer no longer owned a property interest in the LLC's underlying assets, she made gifts of LLC interests despite the fact that she elected, under the "check-the-box" regulations, to have the LLC entity ignored "for federal tax purposes." The majority viewed the check-the-box rules narrowly, as a means of classifying the LLC for income tax purposes; the majority rejected the position that the regulations define the property interest the taxpayer transferred for gift tax purposes. Judge Halpern, in his dissent, interpreted *McNamee v. Dept. of the Treasury*, 488 F.3d 100 (2d Cir.2007), as holding that "federal law, in the form of the check-the-box regulations, does define the property rights and interests so transferred." In her dissent, Judge Kroupa took the different position that, despite state law classification of the entity, the regulations allow for a different federal tax treatment. "It therefore does not matter whether state law recognizes an LLC as a valid entity or provides that a member has no interest in any of the specific property of the LLC." Which interpretation is the correct one?

§4.2. Negative Assets: The Deductions Under §§2053, 2054, and 2058

The "taxable estate" is the gross estate, less deductions for debts, funeral expenses, administration expenses, casualty losses, and state death taxes, and for the net value of certain transfers to charities and to the decedent's surviving spouse. In this section are considered only the deductions with respect to the "negative assets" of the estate, namely, debts, funeral expenses, administration expenses, casualty losses, and state death taxes.

A. Overview

Section 2053 authorizes the deduction of (1) claims against the estate (debts and mortgages), (2) funeral expenses, and (3) estate administration expenses. Section 2054 authorizes a deduction for estate casualty losses. And, §2058 allows a deduction for state death taxes. *Estate administration expenses and casualty losses cannot be deducted for estate tax purposes if they are deducted for income tax purposes.* §642(g).

The treatment of the above can be approached by setting up an abstract model of how these items *should* be treated and comparing that model to the way in which such items are *actually* treated. The abstract model is based on five principles. First, an analytic distinction exists between "negative assets" of the decedent at death, on the one hand, and, on the other, claims and losses incurred by the estate attributable to post-death events, which can be viewed as costs of the decedent's successors in obtaining the decedent's property. Second, both categories are to be analyzed under both the income and estate taxes. Third, the analysis must take account of the general principle that the estate tax is a tax on "capital" (previously taxed income) or, to put it another way, that an item is not excluded from either the estate tax or the income tax just because the item was subject to the other of the two taxes. Fourth, a decedent's *income tax* existence terminates at death. Fifth, on the decedent's death, a completely new taxable entity for income tax purposes, the estate, comes into existence, and continues until estate administration is concluded.[22]

B. Claims Against the Decedent Arising Before Death

This section considers the negative assets of (claims against) the decedent acquired before death.

1. Estate Tax Treatment

If a decedent were to have paid all of the debts and claims against the decedent prior to death, the property in his §2033 gross estate would have been correspondingly reduced. Section 2053, which allows an estate tax deduction against the gross estate of the decedent on account of the decedent's debts, mortgages, and claims against the decedent which are properly allowable against the estate under state law (and eventually paid), can therefore be viewed as an appropriate modification of §2033 and necessary to arrive at a proper measure of a "net" estate of a decedent at death. Such debts are generally paid out of the probate estate by the decedent's personal representative, but, if the probate estate is insufficient, recourse might be had against revocable trusts created by the decedent and perhaps (although less likely) other nonprobate property passing from the decedent.

As noted earlier, those debts that are "founded on a promise or agreement" are not deductible except to the extent that the debt was contracted for on the basis of full and adequate consideration in money or money's worth. §2053(c)(1)(A). The purpose of this rule is to prevent a decedent from converting a taxable bequest into a deductible transfer by the expedient of agreeing with a contemplated legatee that the decedent "owes" the legatee money in a sum equal to the contemplated bequest. A "claim" of this type is nondeductible because the contemplated legatee failed to give the decedent consideration in money or money's worth. In contrast, a claim that is contracted for on the basis of consideration in money or money's worth ought to be deducted because the receipt by the decedent of the consideration in money or money's worth augmented the decedent's wealth (or allowed the decedent to avoid depleting it by way of gift). Thus, the deduction for the claim "offsets" the earlier augmentation of the §2033 gross estate, resulting in a "wash" to the taxable estate, rather than a net depletion of it. Alternatively, the claim is the residue of a transaction that occurred in the ordinary course of commerce, and would not have been a disguised gift.

Claims not founded on a promise or agreement, such as excise, gift, and income tax claims, tort claims, alimony and child support, fines, penalties, and

---

22. See §641(a) (estates and non-grantor trusts taxed under the same rules); Reg. §1.641(b)-3 (duration of estate as separate income tax entity).

the like, are not subject to the "consideration" rule. Such claims are typically incurred "involuntarily" and are not "bequest substitutes."

On the one hand, the debt or claim, to be deductible for estate tax purposes, must be a debt "of" the decedent (and not of another person). In *U.S. v. Stapf*, 375 U.S. 118 (1963), the Supreme Court held that only half of the "community" debts of a decedent subject to community property law was deductible by the estate of the decedent, even though the decedent's will directed the executor to pay the surviving spouse's share of the community debts. On the other hand, where the decedent was jointly and severally liable on a note, debt, or liability, the full amount can be deducted (if paid), but any right of contribution against solvent co-obligors would be included as a claim of the estate under §2033.[23] If the decedent's will waived any right of contribution against a co-obligor, such waiver would amount to a (nondeductible) bequest to the co-obligor. However, if the co-obligor is the decedent's spouse (or a charity), the bequest would be deductible under the marital (or charitable) deduction.

The treatment of mortgages on property owned by the decedent is bifurcated. If the decedent was personally liable on the mortgage, the proper procedure is to include the full value of the property and deduct the mortgage under §2053. Where the decedent was not personally liable on the mortgage, only the "equity" (the value reduced by the mortgage) is includible in the gross estate, and no separate deduction is allowed. The deduction or value reduction for mortgages must "track" with the amount includible. §2053(a)(4). Thus, if only half of the property is includible under §2033 (say, as a tenancy in common), only half of the mortgage can produce a deduction or value reduction.[24]

Any debt or claim must actually be paid to be deducted. Under the probate law of many states, claims against the estate must be presented within a specified short period after the appointment of the estate representative or they will be forever barred. Some states do not have such a special probate statute of limitations; however, it may be provided that, if a claim is presented to the estate representative and rejected, suit on it must be brought within a specified short period of time. In any event, if the statute of limitations runs on a claim against the estate, it cannot be deducted under §2053 even if the personal representative pays it in fact.

The due date for the estate tax return is nine months after the decedent's death, see §6075(a), at which time the payment of claims is unlikely to have been concluded. If a claim that will be paid is not due until some future date, the amount deductible is the date-of-death value of the claim, which typically entails discounting future sums back to the present. For existing claims that are uncertain in amount, an amount can be entered on the return if it can be estimated with reasonable accuracy.[25] Where a contingency goes to the *existence* of the claim (rather than to the amount), it cannot be deducted on the return unless and until the contingency is settled. The due date for filing the return can be extended by

---

23. *Parrott v. Comm'r*, 30 F.2d 792 (9th Cir.1929), *cert. denied*, 279 U.S. 870.
24. See *Estate of Fawcett v. Comm'r*, 64 T.C. 889 (1975).
25. See Reg. §20.2053-1(b)(3).

six months automatically or otherwise for good cause, but it appears that mere delay in paying or resolving claims is not good cause in itself.[26] A completed return is not absolutely final, as adjustments can be made on the basis of (a) further information communicated to the Service, (b) an audit of the estate's return, (c) the timely filing of a claim for refund, or (d) a timely petition to the Tax Court.

An issue is whether, in valuing a claim, post-death facts can be taken into account, in light of the Supreme Court's decision in *Ithaca Trust Co. v. U.S.,* 279 U.S. 151 (1929), which held that a bequest qualifying for the estate tax charitable deduction was to be valued at the time of death using actuarial tables, ignoring later events. Various positions have been advanced.[27] One (the current position of the Service) is that *Ithaca Trust* is limited to charitable deduction cases, and that consideration of post-death events is not *per se* improper.[28] Another is that *Ithaca Trust* is limited to cases involving actuarial tables.[29] A third approach is to follow *Ithaca Trust* and bar any consideration of post-death events.[30] A fourth approach would be adopt the same principle that applies (except in the Fifth Circuit) to valuing claims *of* the estate that are included under §2033, namely, to view the issue as an evidentiary question involving "relevance" from a date-of-death perspective.

To resolve the inconsistency among the circuits, which produced variant deductions dependent solely on the executor's residence, Treasury and the IRS in 2007 proposed regulations (and issued final regulations on October 20, 2009, see *T.D. 9468*) that state that valuation of a §2053 deduction must consider post-death events and that the §2053 deduction is limited to the amount the estate actually paid to satisfy the claim. The final regulations clarify that post-death events to be considered in determining a deductible claim and the extent of that deduction include those that occur up to the date for assessments under §6501 (including suspended periods); and that occur subsequently in connection with a refund claim for an estate tax overpayment under §6511(a). See §20.2053-1(d)(2). The regulations also provide rules for filing protective refund claims.

2. *Income Tax Treatment*

The basic income tax rule for the attribution of deductions among cash-method taxpayers is that a deduction can be taken only by the taxpayer who (1) is entitled to a deduction under the income tax law, (2) incurred (owes) the obligation, and (3) satisfies the obligation by payment.

---

26. See Reg. §20.6081-1.

27. See generally Wendy C. Gerzog, *Ithaca Trust and Section 2053: Smith, McMorris, and O'Neal,* 95 Tax Notes 570 (2002); *The Lottery Cases and Ithaca Trust,* 101 Tax Notes 289 (Oct. 10, 2003).

28. See A.O.D. 2000-04.

29. See *Estate of Van Horne v. Comm'r,* 720 F.2d 1114 (9th Cir.1983), *cert. denied,* 466 U.S. 980 (1984). In *Comm'r v. Estate of Shively,* 276 F.2d 372 (2d Cir.1960), it was held that the deduction for a contingent-amount claim could not exceed the amount actually paid, if the determination of the amount paid occurred before the return was filed.

30. The *Ithaca Trust* approach was followed in *Estate of McMorris v. Comm'r,* 243 F.3d 1254 (10th Cir.2001); *Estate of O'Neal v. U.S.,* 258 F.3d 1265 (11th Cir.2001); *Estate of Smith v. Comm'r,* 198 F.3d 515 (5th Cir.1999) (*nonacq.*).

As to the first requirement, the payment of any debt, claim, or mortgage by the decedent prior to his death would not have given rise to an income tax deduction if: (a) the payment was a repayment of loan principal or a refund of a nonincluded receipt, (b) the payment was a nondeductible capital expenditure, (c) the payment was a nondeductible expense (e.g., for personal consumption), or (d) a deduction for the payment was otherwise disallowed by the Code. An item that would not have been deductible by the decedent if paid by her does not become deductible for income tax purposes just because it is paid after death by another party. Indeed, in principle even an item that would have been deductible by the decedent if paid by her would cease to be deductible if paid by another party, including the estate (which is a separate taxpayer). Therefore, in the case even of debts or claims that were owed by the decedent and would have been deductible if paid before death, but are paid by the estate (or a successor of the decedent), it would appear that the item cannot be deducted either by the decedent (because not paid by her) or by the estate (or other party) who satisfies the debt or claim by payment (because not incurred by the payer).

At this point, two special "exceptions" come into play. First, medical expenses of the decedent's last illness, unpaid prior to death, *may* be claimed as an income tax deduction on the decedent's final return if paid by the *estate* within one year after death.[31] (Section 213 directly allows the decedent's spouse to claim the deduction for income tax purposes if the expenses are paid by such spouse.) However, if such a deduction is taken on the decedent's final return, a §2053 estate tax deduction for the same item cannot be claimed. §213(c).

Second, and of more pervasive significance, §691(b) allows the party actually paying the item to deduct the item if it falls within the category of deductions in respect of a decedent (DIRD). The concept of DIRD is the deduction counterpart to income in respect of a decedent (IRD). The DIRD category encompasses only items (other than medical expenses) that, if they had been paid by the decedent prior to death, would have been deductible, but §691(b) limits the DIRD category to items that would have been deductible by the decedent only under §§162, 163, 164, 212, and 611. This list excludes, for example, medical expenses (see above) and most other personal deduction items (except interest and taxes). Loss and depreciation deductions are removed from the possible reach of §691(b) by reason of the fact that the §1014(a) basis rule simply wipes out any losses accrued up to the estate tax valuation date.

In summary, a DIRD item is deductible both for estate tax purposes (if it meets the requirements of §2053) and on the income tax return of the actual payer, certain medical expenses are deductible either for estate tax purposes *or* on the decedent's final income tax return, and other debts and claims are deductible only for estate tax purposes.

---

31. Section 213 allows a payer to deduct medical expenses for himself, his spouse, and any dependents. Therefore medical expenses can be deducted under §213 if paid by the decedent's spouse.

3. The §691(c) Income Tax Deduction

Recall the concept of "IRD right," which is a right (included in the gross estate) to earned but unpaid pre-death income that passes from the decedent to a successor. If the IRD had (contrary to fact) been included in the gross income of the decedent prior to death, the estate tax base would have been reduced by the income tax paid (or due). Hence, in order to achieve parity with other property included in the decedent's gross estate, there should, it is thought, be a deduction for estate tax purposes under §2053 for the income tax actually paid with respect to such items, even though such income tax is not imposed upon the decedent himself because of the operation of §691(a). The problem is that such income tax cannot be known (or paid) until the IRD is received (by the estate, an heir or legatee, or by a beneficiary), which may not occur until several years after the decedent's death.

As a way out of this dilemma, the Code provides an *income* tax deduction for the IRD recipient under §691(c) (or under §691(d) where annuities are involved). The deduction is equal to the estate tax (if any) attributable to inclusion of the IRD right in the decedent's gross estate. This amount is figured by subtracting from the actual "net" federal estate tax (i.e., estate tax after credits) a "recomputed estate tax" calculated by excluding the value of net IRD (NIRD, which is IRD less DIRD) from the taxable estate.

Example: Assume that Forbes dies in 2009 with a taxable estate of $3.7M, including an IRD right valued at $200,000 for estate tax purposes which is received by Forbes' estate in the course of administration. The estate tax "on" the IRD right is $90,000, because all of the $200,000 falls within the highest marginal rate bracket applicable to Forbes' estate, which is 45 percent. The §691(c) income tax deduction to the estate, as an income tax taxable entity, is $90,000.

If there is more than one IRD recipient, the "total" §691(c) deduction, figured as outlined above, is then allocated among the various IRD recipients according to the ratio of the "gross" IRD amounts includible in their respective incomes to the total gross IRD amount. Where IRD is received by an estate or trust, in some cases all or a part of the §691(c) deduction is passed through to the beneficiaries.

Since the §691(c) deduction is not tied to any outlay or economic loss, it is easily overlooked by estates and beneficiaries.

C. Claims Against the Estate (Other than Death Taxes) Arising After Death

At the level of theory, if the estate tax is based on the idea of what the decedent had, then payments with respect to claims against the estate arising at or after death (funeral costs, estate administration costs, and taxes accruing by reason of, or after, death) would not be deductible for estate tax purposes. (Under an accessions tax, which is based on what the legatees or heirs receive from decedents and donors, payments on post-death claims against the estate would be deductible in principle.)

As far as the income tax is concerned, if the estate were not a separate entity for income tax purposes, funeral expenses would be nondeductible personal expenses of the decedent's family, and estate administration costs would be capital expenditures incurred to acquire gratuitous receipts. Since gratuitous receipts are excluded from income, the costs would neither be deductible as expenses[32] nor added to the free basis conferred by §1014.[33] However, since the decedent's estate *is* an income tax entity, administration expenses paid by the estate would (in theory) be partly capital expenditures for acquiring the decedent's property, partly expenses for obtaining estate income (deductible under §212(1)), partly expenses for managing income-producing property (deductible under §212(2)), and partly expenses for managing personal-use property (not deductible at all). Taxes would probably be deductible by analogy to §164, despite (in the case of death taxes) being inherently capital expenditures of obtaining the decedent's property. Funeral expenses, which benefit the family, would not be deductible in theory.

The actual picture bears little resemblance to the one just sketched. The basic rules are this: (1) Net funeral costs (that are a legal liability of the estate)[34] are deductible only for estate tax purposes (§2053(a)(1)), (2) estate administration expenses can be deducted either for estate tax purposes or for income tax purposes, but not both (see §§642(g) and 2053(a)(2)); and (3) state death taxes (but not the federal estate tax) can be deducted only for estate tax purposes (see §2058). Additionally, casualty and theft losses occurring during estate administration are also deductible for either estate tax purposes or income tax purposes but not both (see §§642(g) and 2054). By allowing all of these categories to be deducted for estate tax purposes, the estate tax concept is diluted, and the tax instead is on what the successors (collectively) receive, not what the donor had.

For income tax purposes, bona fide estate administration costs are viewed as being inherently deductible as "expenses" for the maintenance and conservation of income-producing property under §212(2),[35] if not deductible under a more specific provision. Administration expenses are not disallowed by reason of being a capital expenditure of obtaining estate property or of being an expense relating to non-income-producing property. Nevertheless, expenses allocable to tax-exempt income are disallowed under §265(a).

To be deductible for estate tax purpose as a bona fide administration expense, the item in question should be closely connected with the fact of death and the transmission of the property because of death, including the necessity of probating the decedent's estate. Otherwise, the category of items deductible would be too open-ended. Accordingly, the regulations take the position that administration expenses (especially those connected with selling assets) are allowable under §2053 only to the extent that the cost is justified to fulfill the functions of estate

---

32. See §245(a)(1) (disallowing expenses of obtaining exempt income).

33. See Reg. §1.1015-4 (basis of gift is greater of free carryover basis or cost of obtaining the gift, but not the sum of the two).

34. See, e.g., *Rev. Rul. 71-168*, 1971-1 C.B. 271 (California law).

35. See Reg. §1.212-1(i); *Trust of Bingham v. Comm'r*, 325 U.S. 365 (1945) (construing §212(2) to cover virtually all costs of the administration of a trust).

administration (paying claims and distributing legacies), but not insofar as such expenses are incurred for the convenience of legatees.[36] This distinction has generated much litigation of a fact-oriented nature.[37]

Income taxes on post-death income are not deductible for estate tax purposes;[38] state taxes on such income are deductible for income tax purposes under §164.

As far as estate administration expenses and casualty losses are concerned, §642(g) allows them to be deducted *either* for estate tax purposes *or* for income tax purposes but not both. The §642(g) election is made by the personal representative of the estate. It is not necessary that the estate representative take all such administration expenses in reduction of one or the other tax base. The personal representative can allocate the total (or even a particular item) between the two in any fashion.

D. Death Taxes

Death tax liabilities also reduce the amount received by legatees and heirs, and therefore pose the issue of deductibility for both estate and income taxes.

Federal estate tax liabilities are not deductible for income or estate tax purposes. See §§164(a)(1), 275(a)(3), and 2053(c)(1)(B). Although it would not be wholly illogical to deduct federal estate taxes for federal estate tax purposes, such a deduction would cause the computation of the tax to be circular. Deducting federal estate taxes for income tax purposes would make no sense, because the income tax "naturally" reduces the estate tax base.

A deduction for *state* death taxes is not allowed for income tax purposes. §§164(a)(1) and 275(a)(3), but deducting them for federal estate tax purposes would not pose a circularity problem, and indeed such a deduction is allowed under §2058. For decedents dying prior to 2005, there was a limited estate tax credit under §2011.

PROBLEMS, QUESTIONS, AND NOTES

1. a. Since items included in the gross estate are valued at the date of death (or alternate valuation date), with consideration of post-death facts being considered where they pass the evidentiary test of relevance (except in the Fifth Circuit), should the same approach be followed for the decedent's negative assets? Doesn't payment itself (a post-death event) *have* to

---

36. See Reg. §20.2053-3(d)(2); *Estate of Posen v. Comm'r*, 75 T.C. 355 (1980) (reviewed). This rule is not followed in the Seventh Circuit. *Estate of Jenner v. Comm'r*, 577 F.2d 100 (7th Cir.1978).

37. See, e.g., *Pitner v. U.S.*, 388 F.2d 651 (5th Cir.1967) (expenses of will contest); *Hibernia Bank v. U.S.*, 581 F.2d 741 (9th Cir.1978) (interest on loan to maintain home); *Estate of Wheless v. Comm'r*, 72 T.C. 470 (1979) (interest, accrued after death, on loan taken out by decedent).

38. See §2053(c)(1)(B).

be taken into account on the §2053 side? See §20.2053-1(b)(1) (2009). Could the government impose a discount on deductible amounts for which the delay in payment date (relative to the decedent's death) is known or can be estimated with reasonable accuracy?

   b. Unpaid income taxes of a decedent on pre-death income are deductible as claims against the estate, unless (as is the case with all claims) the statute of limitations has run against the government. The same is true of unpaid gift taxes of the decedent. Recall that gift taxes paid or owed on gifts made within three years of death are included in the gross estate under §2035(b).

   c. Although not founded on a promise or agreement, statutory allowances for the support of surviving spouses and minor children, including "widows' allowances" and "homestead" rights, are not deductible as estate debts, by analogy with §2043(b), holding that a release of inheritance rights is not valid consideration. Support and alimony claims by a former spouse or minor child that survive the decedent's death can be deducted for estate tax purposes if they (a) satisfy the requirements of §2516, (b) are founded on a court decree, or (c) are supported by valid consideration in money's worth. *Rev. Rul. 71-67*, 1971-1 C.B. 271.

   d. Since services performed for the decedent by another constitute consideration in money's worth sufficient to support a claim founded on a promise or agreement, it might be possible for intimate friends who are not (or cannot be) married to achieve an estate tax deduction somewhat similar to the marital deduction. Of course, in such a case the estate would have a heavy burden of showing the existence of a contract and the reasonable value of the services received by the decedent. See *Rev. Rul. 78-271*, 1978-2 C.B. 239. The other side of the coin is that the payment of any such "claim" by the estate would be characterized as compensation income to the recipient (as opposed to being a tax-free bequest under §102).

2. a. Why (do you suppose) are deductions for unpaid alimony and charitable pledges not included in the DIRD list? Are they deductible for estate tax purposes? Is the estate liable to pay them?

   b. Why (do you suppose) unpaid medical expenses are not deductible against both estate and income taxes in same fashion as DIRD items?

   c. The ability of the estate to take a deduction for unpaid medical expenses under §2053 assumes (as with any claim) that the estate succeeds to the decedent's liability to pay them. However, the expenses of a married woman's last illness may not be deductible by her estate under §2053 if state law imposes primary liability on the husband. Nevertheless, the deduction can still be obtained in that case if either (1) the wife's will directs her executor to pay such expenses (and the local court allows them out of the wife's estate) or (2) the husband is insolvent.[39]

3. a. In most estates, should the §642(g) deductions be taken for income or estate tax purposes?

---

39. See *Rev. Rul. 76-369*, 1976-2 C.B. 281.

b. A 1976 amendment to §642(g) holds that administration expenses that reduce gain (or increase loss) of the estate for income tax purposes (e.g., sales commissions) are to be treated the same as "deductions."

c. An estate elects to take an administration expense as an income tax deduction by filing a waiver of the right to claim an estate tax deduction. The waiver is filed with the income tax return or at any time prior to the expiration of the statute of limitations. Once filed, the waiver is irrevocable. Claiming the expense on the estate tax return does not preclude claiming it for income tax purposes, so long as the estate tax deduction is not ultimately allowed and the waiver is eventually filed. Reg. §1.642(g)(1). See also *Rev. Rul. 81-287*, 1981-2 C.B. 183.

4. a. Under §2053(c)(2), all §2053 debts and claims against the probate estate are deductible only up to the value of (a) the probate estate plus (b) amounts actually paid from nonprobate sources prior to the estate tax return date. This rule is an inducement to avoid the use of nonprobate funds to pay off probate claims, unless such is done prior to the estate tax return date.

b. Administration expenses need not be incurred by the personal representative to be deductible under §2053. They may be incurred by others — for example, by the trustee of a revocable trust established by the decedent. Expenses incurred in clearing title to joint property or expended by a beneficiary in obtaining life insurance proceeds also fall into this category (referred to as administration expenses of property "not subject to claims"). Under §2053(b), such expenses to be deductible must actually be paid before the statute of limitations expires. Administration expenses payable by the estate, in contrast, need not actually be paid within the limitations period, provided of course that they are eventually paid.

c. When a community property spouse dies, the entire community property estate is administered. As with other claims, only those amounts allocated to the decedent's estate, as determined under state law, are deductible under §2053. Expenses of determining the decedent's estate tax liability are allocated all to the decedent's share.

5. a. If the decedent were to have negative IRD (DIRD in excess of IRD), there should (in theory) be an increase in the estate tax base to reflect the fact that, if the deduction items had been taken by the decedent prior to death, the decedent's income tax would have been reduced, and the estate tax base increased *pro tanto*. However, the Code provides no such adjustment, probably because this scenario is uncommon.

b. For income tax purposes, net operating loss carryovers and capital loss carryovers expire at the decedent's death. This result is consistent in result with §1014, which erases accrued but unrealized losses and gains from the system.

c. Is the §691(c) deduction justified? It is based on a scenario (paying of the income tax by the decedent) that did not in fact occur. The income tax paid on IRD by the decedent's successors will reduce their gross estates.

§4.3. Income Taxation of Estates

As noted above, an individual taxpayer's income tax existence ends on the date of death. If the decedent is married, a joint income tax return can be filed for the short taxable year of the decedent and the full taxable year of the survivor. See §6013(a)(2) & (3). Additionally, the survivor can file under the §1(a) rate schedule for the two years following the year of her spouse's death if the requirements spelled out in §2(a) are satisfied.

Immediately following a decedent's death, a new taxable unit for income tax purposes, the decedent's "estate," springs into being and continues as a taxpayer for (roughly) as long as there is an estate administration with respect to the decedent under state law.[40] The representative of the estate is required to file the estate's income tax return (Form 1041). The estate is not a continuation of the decedent, and cannot file a joint return with the surviving spouse.

An election can be made under §645 to merge a revocable trust created by the decedent into the income tax estate, commencing on the decedent's death and lasting until the "applicable date" specified in §645(b)(2) (or the earlier date the estate is wound up). In the absence of this election, the revocable trust would, upon and after the death of the grantor have become a separate taxable entity.

A testamentary trust is also a separate taxable entity, distinct from the estate, but commencing when the trust is funded.

Under the income tax, there are four regimes governing estates, trusts, and their beneficiaries: (1) grantor trusts; (2) beneficiary-owned trusts; (3) "Subchapter J" trusts (sometimes referred to as "non-grantor" trusts); and (4) estates.

Grantor trusts (discussed at §8.4, infra) and beneficiary-owned trusts (discussed at §7.2, infra) are disregarded entities for income tax purposes, meaning that the income and deductions of such trusts are attributed directly to the "owner" (the trust grantor or beneficiary possessing an *inter vivos* general power of appointment, as the case may be) so long as such owner is alive. Since neither a grantor trust nor a beneficiary-owned trust is treated as a separate entity, the trust itself can owe no tax.

Estates and Subchapter J trusts are generally taxed alike, but there are a few significant differences, to be noted in due course. (Subchapter J trusts are discussed separately at §7.5, supra.) The income tax rules applicable to estates, Subchapter J trusts, and their beneficiaries are found Subparts A-D of Part I of Subchapter J of the Code (§§641 *et seq.*). The rate schedule applicable to the taxable income of estates (and Subchapter J trusts) is that found in §1(e), with the dollar figures defining the brackets being adjusted for inflation. This rate schedule is highly compressed: The lower marginal rate brackets are very narrow, and the highest marginal rate for ordinary income is reached very quickly. Therefore, it is undesirable that ordinary income be taxed to the estate (or Subchapter J

---

40. See Reg. §1.641(b)-3(a) for a discussion of the termination of an estate.

trust) if it is possible to divert the income to lower-bracket taxpayers. Since net capital gains are taxed pretty much at the same low rates wherever "located," diverting net capital gains to lower-bracket taxpayers is of secondary importance (or perhaps of no importance).

The estate (or Subchapter J trust) is a tax accounting entity, meaning that gross income, gains, deductions, losses, and so on, are initially "reckoned" (accounted for) at the level of the estate (or trust). As stated in §641(b): "The taxable income of an estate or trust shall be computed in the same manner as in the case of an individual, except as otherwise provided [herein]." The basic design issue under the income tax is whether (and to what extent) the resulting estate (or Subchapter J trust) net income is to end up being taxed to the estate (or trust) as a separate taxable entity or to one or more estate (or trust) beneficiaries. A person who can receive a distribution from an estate as a legatee, devisee, or heir is a "beneficiary" of the estate for income tax purposes. See §643(c).

The scheme of taxing estates and Subchapter J trusts (and their beneficiaries) also has to reckon with §102, which states that the receipt of gratuitous transfers is excluded from gross income, but that "income from" bequests, inheritances, and gifts is not excluded. Thus, the initial "funding" of the estate (or trust) with the decedent's property is not gross income to the estate by reason of §102(a). Additionally, §101(a) excludes from gross income the proceeds of life insurance payable by reason of death.

The gross income of an estate is typically composed of the income from investments, most commonly interest, dividends, and capital gains, and income from IRD rights. (Post-death income on specifically bequeathed property belongs to the legatee and not the estate.) Except in the case of IRD rights, the estate's income tax basis for all assets included in the gross estate is determined under §1014, which provides that the basis is equal to the fair market value on the estate tax valuation date. IRD rights carry over the decedent's basis, which is often zero. Assets *purchased* by the estate or trust take a §1012 cost basis, and property dispositions by the estate (whether of assets acquired by gratuitous transfer or by purchase) are dealt with at the estate or trust level according to the usual rules concerning sales, exchanges, basis, and so on.

The estate can deduct DIRD items it pays and (recalling §642(g)) those estate administration expenses (and casualty losses) as are not deducted for income tax purposes. Deductions not subject to the §642(g) election can be taken as a matter of course. Since an estate (or trust) has no "standard deduction," the distinction between "above the line" deductions and "itemized" deductions is unimportant except for the possibility that an itemized deduction can be a miscellaneous itemized deduction (MID) subject to the 2 percent-of-adjusted-gross-income floor. However, administration expenses unique to an estate (or trust) cannot be classified as MIDs. See §67(e). In *Knight v. Comm'r*, 552 U.S. 181 (2008), the Supreme Court held that a trust's investment advisory fees did not fall under this rule, because such fees are of the type that would be incurred if the property had not been held by a trust or estate.

In addition to the normal income tax deductions, an estate (or a Subchapter J trust) obtains a "distribution deduction," which is an amount equal to the *lesser* of (a) (actual) "distributions" to beneficiaries (regardless of source inside the estate or trust) *or* (b) the entity's distributable net income (DNI). See §661(a). Section 663(a)(1), however, provides that the term "distributions" (for purposes of computing the distribution deduction) *excludes* distributions in satisfaction of (a) specific property bequests and (b) "general" (i.e., pecuniary) bequests, if payable in not more than three installments. This rule mostly applies to estates, since specific property and pecuniary bequests are common features of wills, but it could apply to Subchapter J trust provisions mandating nonrecurring distributions of specific property or fixed dollar amounts. In any event, in the case of estates, *only distributions in satisfaction of residuary bequests and of inheritances are potentially deductible*.

Under §643(a), DNI is (leaving some complexities aside) equal to predistribution estate net income *less* net capital gains. However, the year in which the estate (or trust) terminates, net capital gains are included in DNI. A more exhaustive discussion of DNI is found at §7.5.C, infra.

An amount equal to the distribution deduction of the estate (or trust) is gross income to the distributees as a group. In an estate, this pool of gross income is allocated among the distributees in proportion to the "distributions" received by each during the taxable year of the estate or trust. See §662(a)(2). Recall that distributions in satisfaction of specific property bequests and pecuniary bequests do not count as "distributions," and therefore cannot carry estate income to distributees.

Since "distributions" and DNI can only be figured at the end of the taxable year, the requisite computations are performed at the end of the estate's taxable year. An estate (but not a trust) can report on a calendar-year or fiscal-year basis, as the personal representative decides. See §644. Income amounts allocated to beneficiaries are reportable by them in their taxable year in which the last day of the estate's taxable year falls. §662(c). For example, if an estate's taxable year ends on January 31, 2011, all of the estate income allocated to beneficiaries for the estate taxable year ending on that date is reportable by the (calendar-year) beneficiaries on their income tax returns for 2011, even though most of the income was earned by the estate in 2010. Notwithstanding the foregoing, under §663(b) the estate (or trust) can elect to treat distributions made during the first 65 days of the estate's (or trust's) taxable year as having been made in the prior taxable year of the estate (or trust).

This deduction/inclusion scheme has the effect of "shifting" current estate (or trust) income from the tax base (and marginal tax rate) of the estate (or trust) to the tax bases of one or more beneficiaries (and their marginal tax rates). This scheme neither adds income to the tax system nor removes income from the tax system, because the estate-level distribution deduction gives rise to a corresponding beneficiary-level gross income inclusion.

Current-year distributions in excess of the current-year DNI are not deducted by the trust, nor are they gross income to the beneficiaries. The noninclusion to the beneficiaries derives from the fact that any distribution in excess of DNI can only be "from" amounts taxed to the estate (or trust) in prior years and/or amounts received by the estate (or trust) tax free under §§101(a) and 102(a). An estate obtains a "personal exemption" deduction under §642(b) of $600.

Neither the distribution deduction nor the personal exemption can produce a net loss.

In-kind property distributions from estates (and Subchapter J trusts) raise issues concerning realization and basis. An in-kind estate distribution in satisfaction of a specific property bequest is not (under §663(a)(1)) a realization event or a "distribution" for income tax purposes, and the estate's basis carries over to the distributee. An estate distribution of in-kind property in satisfaction of a pecuniary bequest (payable in no more than three installments) is likewise not a "distribution" for income tax purposes, but here the estate realizes (and recognizes) gain or loss equal to the difference between the property's then FMV and its basis,[41] and the legatee (as a deemed "purchaser") takes a basis equal to the then FMV of the property. Finally an in-kind distribution on account of a residual legacy or inheritance (or its trust equivalent) is a "distribution" for income tax purposes subject to the following statutory default rules, to wit: (1) The "amount" of the "distribution" (for purposes of the distribution deduction and beneficiary inclusion) is the lesser of the property's basis or its FMV at the time of the distribution, (2) the estate does not recognize gain or loss on the distribution, and (3) the estate's basis in the property carries over to the distributee. However, the personal representative can elect to obtain the following set of results instead those provided by the default rules: (1) The distribution is deemed to be equal to the then FMV of the property, (2) the estate realizes gain or loss, and (3) the distributee takes the property with a FMV basis. See §643(e)(3).

Section 267(a)(1) disallows any loss on a "sale" between an estate and an estate beneficiary, but there is an exception for a loss arising from an in-kind distribution in satisfaction if a pecuniary legacy. See §267(b)(13). It appears that this loss-disallowance rule would apply to a loss arising from a §642(e) election, which is a "deemed" sale.

A testamentary trust is funded by a distribution from an estate. To the extent the distribution is in kind, the rules described in the preceding paragraph apply. Distributions from the estate to the trust (to the extent of estate DNI for the estate's taxable year) are gross income to the testamentary trust.

---

41. This is called the *Kenan* rule, after *Kenan v. Comm'r*, 114 F.2d 217 (2d Cir.1940). The theory is that the fixed-dollar legacy is a "debt" of the estate that is satisfied with the property distribution. In the case of certain farm real estate that is valued for estate tax purposes at a discount below FMV under §2032A, infra, the gain shall be computed as if the §1014 basis were the actual FMV at death. See §1040 (post-2010 version).

Look at §267 again. This is a loss disallowance section that disallows losses on sales between related parties as defined in §267(b). There is, however, a future benefit allowed by §267(d). Which one of the following statements is *TRUE*?

A. When a loss is disallowed to the transferor, the transferor can later get a tax benefit in §267(d).
B. The transferee can deduct the loss disallowed to the transferor when she later sells the property either at a loss or at a gain.
C. The transferee can reduce the amount of gain she receives on the sale of the property when she later sells the property at a gain.
D. The transferee can increase the amount of loss she receives on the sale of the property when she later sells the property at a loss.

1. Gordon dies in April of 2008. Gordon's will leaves his shares of General Electric stock to Hanna, the sum of $100,000 to Imelda, and the residue to Justin and Justine in equal shares. Gordon's executor selects a fiscal year for the estate that ends on March 31 of 2009 (and subsequent years). In July 2008, the executor distributes the GE stock, then worth $1M, having a §1014 basis of $980K, to Hanna. In January of 2009, the executor distributes (to Imelda) shares of Dell stock having a then value of $100K and a §1014 basis of $106K in full satisfaction of Imelda's legacy. In March, the executor distributes $60K to Justin. Apart from the foregoing, in the fiscal year ending on March 31, 2009, the estate has gross ordinary income of $100K and net capital gains of $20K, and pays deductible expenses of $12K.
    a. Based on the foregoing, what is the taxable income of the estate and the beneficiaries in the years in question? Also, what basis do the beneficiaries have in property received in kind?
    b. In April of 2009, Justine learns that Justin has received a distribution, and Justine asks the executor to distribute something to her too. The executor is thinking of distributing cash of $20K to Justine forthwith. Will this distribution, if it occurs, alter the results in item 1? Are any elections involved? If so, how should they be made?
2. Purely from a federal income tax angle, what are the *pros* and *cons* of the alternative will formats set out below? What additional facts would you like to know?
    a. "I bequeath my entire property and estate to my wife Gladys."

    b. "I leave my property and estate as follows:
        (1)   all my tangible personal property to my wife Gladys;
        (2)   my interest in any real property to my wife Gladys; and
        (3)   all the rest and residue of my estate to my wife Gladys."

3. **a.** Although loss carryovers of a decedent do not carry over to the estate (but instead expire at the decedent's death), loss carryovers of an estate (or Subchapter J trust) carry over to the termination distributees. See §642(h).

    b. Trust distributions of amounts expressed as an annuity (e.g., "$10K per year to P for life"), although expressed as a fixed dollar amount per year, are not treated as a "bequest of a specific sum of money" under §663(a)(1), because annuities are generally payable in more than three installments. Therefore, they are treated as "distributions."

    c. In computing the DNI of an estate (or trust), the default rule is that net capital gains (allocated to corpus for trust accounting purposes) are excluded from DNI, even though distributions during the year exceed estate (or trust) accounting income. There are some exceptions, one of which is that net capital gains are included in DNI in the year the estate (or trust) makes termination distributions. See §643(a)(3) and Reg. §1.643(a)-3. The effect of this rule is to tax net capital gains to the estate (or trust), except in the year of termination.

4. The income taxation of trusts and estates is a sufficiently broad and detailed topic that it typically constitutes a separate course in tax L.L.M. programs and even some J.D. programs, but the core concepts aren't particularly difficult, and every professional person dealing with tax, estate, and trust issues should be acquainted with these concepts. The description above leaves out many details, such as charitable distributions, refinements of the DNI concept, and the treatment of tax-exempt income. The income taxation of Subchapter J trusts involves further wrinkles, such as the distinction between simple and complex trusts and the distinction between first-tier and second-tier distributions. The taxation of grantor (and beneficiary-owned) trusts follows a different set of rules based on a pass-through approach. Further details of grantor, beneficiary-owned, and Subchapter J trusts are discussed in later chapters.

§4.4. Estate Tax Valuation

A substantial portion of estate practice is devoted to the problem of valuing property included in the gross estate. The basic valuation rules are found in the regulations under §2031. These rules apply to all property included in the gross estate, whether under §2033 or under other Code provisions. The same basic valuation principles that apply under the gift tax, discussed in Chapter 3 (such as the willing-buyer, willing-seller test and actuarial tables), also apply for the estate tax. Accordingly, the material below will consider only matter that is new or unique to the estate tax. Certain issues relating to valuation-reduction planning strategies (usually involving closely-held business interests) are reserved to Chapter 9.

A. *Estate Tax Valuation Date*

The first issue is the date of valuation. Pursuant to §§2031 and 2032, the estate tax valuation date is the date of the decedent's death. However, the estate representative can elect to value the entire corpus of gross estate assets on the alternate valuation date, if such election would result in both a lower gross estate total *and* a lower estate tax (after deductions and credits). (In other words, the alternate valuation date cannot be elected in order to obtain a higher income tax basis for gross estate assets under §1014.) The election to use the alternate valuation date applies to all assets in the estate; it cannot be elected on an asset-by-asset basis.

If the alternate valuation date is elected for the entire gross estate, the alternate valuation date for any particular asset is the earlier to occur of (1) the date the asset is sold, distributed, or otherwise disposed of, following the decedent's death, by the estate or legatee or (2) the date six months after the decedent's death. If an actuarial factor (or present-value calculation) is involved in the valuation, such factor is determined by reference to the date of the decedent's death and then applied against the value of the underlying property at the alternate valuation date.[42]

Under Prop. Reg. §20.2032-1(1)(f)(3), issued in 2008, only changes in market conditions are allowed to affect (depress) value on the alternate valuation date. Thus, if during the period between the decedent's death and the alternate valuation date (the interim period) shares of stock (owned by the decedent at death) lost value due to, for example, the imposition of restrictions on liquidity, those restrictions would be ignored.[43]

An election to use the alternate valuation date does not affect what items are includible in the gross estate. Thus, assuming the alternate valuation date is elected, dividends, interest, rents, royalties, and other items, earned or accrued during the interim period are excluded from the gross estate (and are referred to in the regulations as "excluded property").[44] Interest and rents accrued up to the date of the decedent's death are included. Dividends — even if "declared" prior to the decedent's death — are excluded if the "record date" falls after the decedent's death. Stock dividends, liquidation dividends, bond principal payments, and similar items representing a post-death severance of the before-date-of-death "principal" are categorized as "included" property — meaning both the original principal and the severed item are included if the alternate valuation date is

---

42. See Prop. Reg. §20.2032-1(f); Temp. Reg. §20.2032-1T(f)(1).

43. The proposed regulation follows the approach of *Flanders v. U.S.*, 347 F. Supp. 95 (N.D. Cal. 1972) (ignoring post-death restrictions of a conservation agreement) and specifically rejects the Tax Court's holding in *Kohler v. Comm'r*, T.C. Memo. 2006-152. See Prop. Reg. §20.2032-1(f)(3)(i), (ii), Ex. 1.

44. See Reg. §20.2032-1(d), (e). These regulations provide rules for when certain items are deemed to accrue or be earned, and is therefore relevant to what assets are included under §2033 (as well as other gross estate provisions).

elected. The same can be true of royalties relating to oil and gas in place at the date of the decedent's death but extracted before the estate tax valuation date.

B. Additional Valuation Rules

Most of the basic valuation rules were dealt with in the gift tax chapter. Here are some more.

Life insurance. If the proceeds of life insurance are included in the gross estate of the insured (under §2035(a)(2) or §2042), the amount includible is the proceeds, not the value of the policy just prior to death. If an unmatured policy is included in a person's gross estate (say, under §2033), the same valuation rule applies for the estate tax (Reg. §20.2031-8) as applies for the gift tax (Reg. §25.2512-6).

Ordinary household and personal effects. Reg. §20.2031-6(a) starts off by saying that values should be specified for every item. However, items in the same room can be grouped together if none of them has a value in excess of $100. In lieu of itemization, the executor can declare (under penalty of perjury) an aggregate value as appraised by a recognized appraiser or dealer.

Art works, antiques, and other valuable tangibles. Any items of artistic or intrinsic value, such as art works, jewelry, coins, antiques, silver, or the like, having a value (as an item or a collection) in excess of $3,000 must be appraised by a qualified reputable appraiser. See Reg. §20.2031-6(b). There is also an Art Advisory Panel of the Commissioner. Art valuation questions arising on audit *can* be referred to the Panel, and any item valued in excess of $20,000 *must* be referred to the Panel. The unsold work of a deceased artist (or even a large collection) might obtain a "blockage discount," as explained in Chapter 3.

Real estate. Real estate, being unique, requires appraisals, evidence of comparable sales, rentals, and so on.[45] Local real property tax appraisals are generally given little weight. For commercial real estate, capitalization of the future net income may be an important factor.[46] A fractional interest in real estate is likely to obtain a discount, in the neighborhood of 15 percent, from the percentage value of the entire property.[47]

Business interests listed on an exchange. The basic rules are set forth in Reg. §20.2031-2. For actively traded securities, the value (per share) is the mean between the highest and lowest selling prices on the estate tax valuation date. For less frequently traded securities, one computes a weighted average price based on the nearest sales before and after the estate tax valuation date. If actual sales can't be found but the securities are listed on some exchange, then the mean between bid and asked prices is used. At this point, the blockage rule (see Chapter 3) might come into play to depress the value. See Reg. §20.2031-2(e).

Nonlisted business interests. If the securities are unlisted, then one falls back on a facts-and-circumstances test as set forth in Reg. §20.2031-3 and *Rev. Rul. 59-60,*

---

45. See *Rev. Proc. 79-24,* 1979-1 C.B. 565.
46. See *Shepard v. Comm'r,* 283 F.3d 1258 (11th Cir.2002).
47. See, e.g., *Propstra v. U.S.,* 680 F.2d 1248 (9th Cir.1982).

1959-1 C.B. 237, as supplemented by later rulings.[48] Among the factors to be used are: future earning capacity, net worth, future dividend-paying capacity, the general economic outlook, the economic outlook in the industry, the corporation's position in the industry, and so on. If the entity is an investment holding company, primary weight is to be given to the market value of the constituent investments. In the case of ongoing businesses, §2031(b) of the Code specifically requires consideration of the value of listed securities in comparable companies. §2031(b).

If a major determinant of an enterprise's value is either publicly traded comparables or the aggregate value of its constituent assets, then a lack-of-marketability discount (discussed in Chapter 3) is available.

A minority-interest discount (also discussed in Chapter 3) might also depress the value. For purposes of ascertaining whether the decedent held a minority interest, interests of the decedent in the same entity are aggregated if they are included in the decedent's gross estate, even if different units are subject to different bequests or are included under different Code provisions.[49] However, aggregation does not encompass QTIP property included under §2044, because QTIP property was never really owned or transferred by the decedent.[50] There is no aggregation at the legatee level. Thus, if D, having a 40 percent interest in an entity, bequeaths that interest to E, who already has a 12 percent interest in the same entity, D's estate is not barred from obtaining a minority discount.[51]

The value of stock in a closely-held corporation may be discounted for potential income tax on the corporation's "inside gain" accrued to the date of transfer,[52] even if the corporation had no plan to liquidate or sell its assets.[53] However, the government has advised that discounting for the potential income tax liability does not apply to Series E U.S. Savings Bonds[54] (where there is only one buyer, the U.S. government) or to IRA proceeds.[55]

---

48. *Rev. Rul.* 65-193, 1965-2 C.B. 370; *Rev. Rul.* 77-287, 1977-2 C.B. 319; *Rev. Rul.* 80-213, 1980-2 C.B. 101; *Rev. Rul.* 83-120, 1983-2 C.B. 170.

49. See *F.S.A.* 200119013, citing *Ahmanson Foundation v. U.S.*, 674 F.3d 761 (9th Cir.1981), and *Estate of Curry v. U.S.*, 706 F.2d 1424 (7th Cir.1983).

50. See *Estate of Bonner v. U.S.*, 84 F.3d 196 (5th Cir.1996); *Estate of Mellinger v. Comm'r*, 112 T.C. 26 (1999), *acq.*, 1999-2 C.B. xvi; *Ann.* 99-116, 1999-2 C.B. 763. A QTIP trust is included in a transferee spouse's gross estate under §2044 solely because the transferor spouse (or his estate) obtained a marital deduction for the QTIP trust, in which the transferee spouse only has an income interest that expires at her death.

51. See *Estate of Bright v. U.S.*, 658 F.2d 999 (1981) (*en banc*).

52. For example, if a corporation owns one asset, unimproved land worth $10M, and the built-in gain on the land is $9M, the gain would produce a future corporate tax that would reduce the value of the corporation below its current value of $10M. Corporate income taxes on future corporate income cannot be taken into account because they depend on post-death events. In contrast, the amount of built-in corporate-level gain is a fact existing at the time of death.

53. *Eisenberg v. Comm'r*, 155 F.3d 50 (2d Cir.1998), *acq.* A.O.D. 1999-01 (holding that such a discount is not prohibited as a matter of law). The rule was otherwise until the Tax Reform Act of 1986 eliminated the possibility (the *General Utilities* doctrine) that a corporation could avoid built-in capital gain by liquidating. See *Estate of Jameson v. Comm'r*, T.C. Memo. 1999-43 (discounting estimated future taxes on accrued timber gains to present value).

54. *T.A.M.* 200303010.

55. *T.A.M.* 200247001.

C. Special Statutory Valuation Rules

There are special statute-imposed but elective estate tax valuation rules for real estate used in a farming (etc.) operation (or small business) and property subject to a qualified conservation easement.

1. Special Valuation Real Estate

The willing-buyer, willing-seller test as applied to real estate implies the "highest-and best-use" concept, which refers to the use that would generate the highest economic return regardless of how the land is presently used. Thus, low-return farm land would be valued by its potential income use for housing, commerce, or recreation — whichever would produce the highest value. Section 2032A, enacted in 1976, allows certain farm and small-business real property to be valued instead according to its less valuable current use. The term "farm" is defined broadly in §2032A(e)(4) to encompass virtually anything relating to the raising of plants, trees, and animals. Congress in enacting §2032A (by far the wordiest Code provision in the federal transfer taxes) wanted to encourage continued operation of farms and small businesses. It was asserted that a high valuation of such property might force the executor to sell the property just to pay the estate tax.

Strict requirements must be met before the favorable §2032A valuation rule can be used, but only a few will be mentioned here. One is that the "normal" fair market value of the aggregate farm or small business property (reduced by mortgages) must comprise 50 percent or more of the gross estate (reduced by mortgages). Also, at least 25 percent of the decedent's gross estate (reduced by mortgages) must be composed of the value of real property (reduced by mortgages) used in a family farm or business which passes from the decedent to a family member. Another is that the real property must have been owned by the decedent or a family member,[56] and one of them must have "materially participated" in the farm or business during at least five of the eight years immediately preceding the decedent's death, disability, or retirement. This provision is designed to ensure that only bona fide "family" operating farms and businesses receive favorable treatment.

Assuming the technical requirements are met, the estate's personal representative must elect §2032A within the time prescribed for filing the estate tax return. An agreement executed by all parties with an interest in the land must also be filed. This agreement amounts to a promise by the legatees to continue to operate a farm or other business on the property for ten years following the decedent's death, or, if they fail to do so, to bear personal liability for an additional estate tax to be imposed on the legatees keyed to the amount of taxes "lost" by the

---

56. Under §2032A(e)(2), a family member is one, who, in relation to the decedent, is an ancestor or spouse, or who is a lineal descendant (or spouse of such descendant) of the decedent, the decedent's spouse, or the decedent's parents.

Treasury due to the executor's use of the special valuation. This is often referred to as the "recapture tax." See §2032A(c).[57]

The aggregate gross estate reduction from the "normal" fair market value due to §2032A cannot exceed $750,000 adjusted for inflation after 1998.

2. Qualified Conservation Easements

The charitable deduction for income, gift, and estate tax purposes is generally not available for transfers of partial interests in property. §§170(f), 2055(e)(2), and 2522(e). However, there is an exception for qualified conservation easements as defined (elaborately) in §170(h). §§170(f)(3)(B)(iii), 2055(f), and 2522(d). Basically, a conservation easement is a transfer of development rights on property to a charity or government body for the purpose of perpetually preserving nature, wildlife,[58] open space, or historic real estate.[59] A conservation easement typically is only a surrender (virtual destruction) of development rights, and does not restrict the personal use of the property by the donor (and the donor's successors) for living, recreation, scenic enjoyment, and maintaining privacy and seclusion, nor does the property typically become available for public use.

Conservation-easement gifts are usually made *inter vivos* so as to obtain an income tax deduction, which is an amount equal to the loss in value of the land attributable to the granting of the easement. Objectively, the deduction amount can be quite large in relation to the value of the property, especially if the property is located near an urban area or other area that would be attractive for development. However, grants of easements can be made by testamentary instrument or even (under §2031(c)(9)) by a decedent's executor,[60] in which case they are deductible by the estate under §2055(f).

What is relevant for this chapter is the fact that §2031(c) gives an estate an elective valuation discount for the property subject to the qualified conservation easement. To state it as crudely as possible, the discount (called an "exclusion") is an amount equal to 40 percent (or a lesser percentage) of the value of the property net of the value of the easement (whether the easement was a creation of an *inter vivos* or testamentary transfer). However, the discount cannot exceed $500K. The discount (exclusion) is in addition to any estate tax charitable deduction for the grant of the easement. The operation of §2031(c) is illustrated by the following examples, which are shorn of such complicating factors as mortgages and retained development rights.

Example (easement granted before death): Suppose T owned a large-acreage estate, and made a qualified conservation easement. At T's death the property is

---

57. Where §2032A(c) triggers the recapture tax to increase both state and federal estate tax liabilities, the estate can increase its state death tax credit or deduction. *T.A.M. 199940005* (June 2, 1999).

58. See *Glass v. Comm'r*, 124 T.C. 258 (2005) (easement prohibited public from accessing significant habitat or ecosystem).

59. See *Turner v. Comm'r*, 126 T.C. 299 (2006) (disallowing qualification on this basis).

60. If the executor makes a timely easement donation that qualifies for the charitable deduction, the estate (as an income tax entity) must forego the income tax charitable deduction.

worth $1M (net of the easement) and the easement (owned by the Land Conservancy) is worth $1.4M. The valuation discount is the lesser of $400K (40 percent x $1M) or $500K. Hence, the amount includible is $600K. (Note: The 40 percent is reduced by a formula if the easement is worth less than 30 percent of the $2.4M, but that is not the case here.)

Example (easement granted at death): This time T dies with property worth $2.4M and grants (by will) a qualified conservation easement worth $1.4M. The initially included amount under §2033 is $2.4M, and the grant of the easement qualifies for an estate tax charitable deduction under §2055(f) of $1.4M. Under §2031(c), the estate gets an additional "exclusion" (valuation discount) of 40 percent (as before) of $1M (the value reduced by the charitable deduction), so again the amount remaining in the tax base is $600K.

Conservation easements are a classic "tax expenditure," and have been much used (or, in the opinions of some, abused). A specialized law practice has grown up around conservation easements.

QUICK QUESTION

Which one of the following statements is *FALSE*?

    A.   An estate may elect the alternate valuation date only when those alternate asset values in the aggregate reduce both the gross estate and the estate tax.

    B.   If property is sold during the six months after the decedent's death, the amount realized on the sale is the value to be used under the alternate valuation date statute.

    C.   A remainder interest owned by decedent is valued, for alternate valuation date purposes, at its value six months after decedent's death.

    D.   Decedent's stock is valued, for alternate valuation date purposes, at its value six months after decedent's death.

QUESTIONS AND NOTES

1. a. Section 6662(e) imposes a no-fault penalty for gift and estate tax purposes where any asset is valued at 65 percent or less of its value as ultimately determined. The penalty is 20 percent of the understatement of gift or estate tax attributable to the undervaluation. If an asset is valued at 40 percent or less of its value as ultimately determined, the penalty rate is 40 percent. This is a "no-fault" penalty, separate from negligence and civil fraud penalties.

b. Under §7517, a donor or the estate representative can demand a written statement explaining the Commissioner's method of valuation of any asset, including any appraisals, for gift and estate tax purposes. Such statement is not binding, however, on the Commissioner.

2. a. If the alternate valuation date is (properly) chosen, and an asset is sold, distributed, etc., prior to six months after the decedent's death, there will normally be no gain or loss to the estate for income tax purposes, because the amount realized will equal the §1014 basis, which is itself fixed under §1014 by the sale, etc. Nevertheless, the amount realized does not necessarily fix the fair market value; it is only good evidence thereof. See *Rev. Rul. 77-180*, 1977-1 C.B. 270.

b. For what constitutes a "distribution" for purposes of fixing the alternate valuation date of a particular asset, see Reg. §20.2032-1(c)(2). In *Rev. Rul. 78-378*, 1978-2 C.B. 229, the Service held that a devise of real estate that by-passed estate administration (but remained subject to claims against the estate) was not a distribution for this purpose. As mentioned earlier, a distribution from an estate to a testamentary trust carries estate income to the trust. In *Rev. Rul. 71-396*, 1971-2 C.B. 328, the Service, however, held that the creation of accounts by the executor in anticipation of testamentary trusts was not a distribution for this purpose. In contrast, the Service held, in *Rev. Rul. 73-97*, 1973-1 C.B. 404, that the division of an *inter vivos* trust (includible in the decedent's gross estate) into separate trusts following the decedent's death constituted a distribution from the single trust to the new trusts, but that a division of such a trust into "separate shares" was not a "distribution."

c. Although a corporate dividend is normally excluded from the gross estate if the "record date" falls after the date of death, the right to the dividend is to be taken into account if the stock was selling "ex-dividend" as of such date. Reg. §20.2031-2(i).

3. a. One can qualify for the special actual-use valuation rule of §2032A only if the farm (etc.) constitutes 50 percent or more of the decedent's gross estate (as reduced by mortgages). There is also a 25 percent-of-gross-estate rule for real property. A person owning a farm (etc.) might, therefore, contemplate making *inter vivos* gifts of nonqualified assets in order to facilitate qualification under §2032A. However, if the gifts occur within three years of death, they will be disregarded (i.e., pulled back into the gross estate) solely for purposes of the §2032A eligibility requirements. See §2035(c)(1)(B).

b. Under former §2057, in effect from 1997 through 2003, a deduction (not to exceed $675K) was granted for bequests of "qualified family-owned business interests." In this context, a deduction is the equivalent of an exclusion. The qualification rules under §2057 were closely modeled on those under §2032A.

c. Section 6166 (another long and complex provision) allows a five-year deferral, followed by ten years of installment payments, for the estate tax resulting from the inclusion in the decedent's gross estate of an "interest in a closely held business" as defined in §6166(a), which includes farms but excludes incorporated investment portfolios. Up to a certain limit, the interest rate on the deferred payments is only 2 percent. See §§6166(k)(4) & 6601(j). The benefits of §6166 are available where the business interest makes up more than 35 percent of the "adjusted gross estate" (gross estate less deductions under §§2053 and 2054). Gifts within three years of death of non-qualified property will be "brought back in" for testing purposes under §2035(c)(4). Deferral of tax can be obtained only for that portion of the estate tax that is attributable to the inclusion of the business interest in the gross estate. A declaratory judgment action can be brought to determine whether an estate is eligible for §6166 relief. See §7479.

d. Interest payable on deferred estate tax payments under §6166 is deductible for estate tax purposes under §2053 as an estate administration expense (if not deducted for income tax purposes). *Estate of Bahr v. Comm'r*, 68 T.C. 74 (1977) (*acq.*). However, the interest is deductible only as it accrues; no current deduction is allowed for future estimated interest payments, since their amount and timing are somewhat uncertain. *Rev. Rul. 80-250*, 1980-2 C.B. 276.

e. The reason for enacting §2031(c) was, according to S. Rep. 105-33 (1997), that:

> The Committee believes that a reduction in estate taxes for land subject to a qualified conservation easement will ease existing pressures to develop or sell off open spaces in order to raise funds to pay estate taxes, and will thereby help to preserve environmentally significant land.

Isn't the charitable deduction a sufficient tax benefit for conservation easements or, even better, an inducement for donating the entire property for use as (say) a public park? Additionally, property subject to a conservation easement could have been made eligible for §6166.

f. Another provision bearing on estate liquidity is §303, which gives the estate (succeeding to the decedent's shares of stock) full basis offset (and capital gains) on a redemption of the stock by the corporation. In the absence of this provision, the redemption proceeds might be treated as a dividend with no basis offset. Favorable treatment cannot exceed death tax liabilities plus §2053 expenses. To be eligible, the value of the decedent's stock included in the gross estate must exceed an amount equal to 35 percent of the decedent's gross estate net of deductions under §§2053 and 2054. For purposes of this eligibility formula, gifts of non-qualifying property made within three years of death are added back in. See §2035(c)(1)(A). If an estate is not eligible for §303 benefits, the same result might be obtained under §302.

g. In the case of partnership distributions to achieve liquidity for a partner's estate, several complex provisions, including §736, come into play.

4. a. Doesn't the blockage rule assume post-death events that might never occur (i.e., a liquidation sale by the buyer)? See *Estate of Prell v. Comm'r*, 48 T.C. 67 (1967) (blockage discount denied where there was

no evidence of an inactive market in the security, meaning that a skilled broker could have disposed of the stock at market prices over a reasonable period). Or does the "willing-buyer" concept imply consideration of future events that have a reasonable chance of occurring?

b. The valuation of an interest in a closely-held entity conventionally begins with the valuation of the entity itself, which value is then prorated among the various equity interests, with the third step being the imposition of discounts and premiums.

c. The opposite of a minority discount is a "control premium." Presumably, the notion that a valuation premium can attach to a majority interest would be based on the ability of an owner thereof to increase distributions to oneself, to pay oneself an inflated salary, to otherwise appropriate firm value from minority shareholders, and to engineer favorable mergers and buy-outs. However, the concepts of both minority discounts and control premiums raise the issue of "relative to what conception of the entity?" The standard could be any of: (a) entity owned by one person, (b) entity controlled by one person with family members as minority shares, (c) entity controlled by one person with arm's-length minority interests, (d) entity owned entirely by family with no single controlling interest, (e) entity with arm's-length minority shareholders but having a controlling coalition, or (f) entity with arm's-length minority shareholders with no stable coalition. The allowance of a discount or the imposition of a premium should be consistent with how the entity is valued in the first place. Cases imposing control premiums include *Succession of McCord v. Comm'r*, 461 F.3d 614 (5th Cir.2006); *Estate of Jung v. Comm'r*, 101 T.C. 412 (1993); *Estate of Newhouse v. Comm'r*, 94 T.C. 193 (1990).

5. a. The value of stock or a business interest can be discounted where the decedent was a "key man," on the theory that his absence depresses the value of the firm. See *Estate of Maddock v. Comm'r*, 16 T.C. 324 (1951); *Moskovitz v. U.S.*, 37 AFTR 2d 76-1519 (N.D.N.Y. 1975) (jury instruction allowing such a discount); *Brandt v. Comm'r*, T.C. Memo. 1949-89; *Rev. Rul. 59-60*, 1959-1 C.B. 237, §4.02(b).

b. Unlike the gift tax, minority interest discounts cannot, under the estate tax, be created by making fractionalized bequests of a controlling interest to various legatees. See *Ahmanson Foundation v. U.S.*, 674 F.2d 761 (9th Cir.1981) (no value reduction for carving up controlling interest into minority interests).

c. In *Ahmanson Foundation*, the Ninth Circuit stated in *dictum* that a valid direction in a decedent's will to destroy property would be effective to reduce or eliminate the value of the property from the gross estate. Is this position correct? At the moment of the decedent's death, it may not be clear if such a direction is valid, on account of the rule that a direction to destroy property would be invalid if, under the circumstances, the destruction of the property would be contrary to public policy. Is the property-destruction scenario different from a direction in the will to forgive a claim that the decedent had against a third party?

d.   Lack-of-marketability and minority-interest discounts, as well as other discounts, are staples of estate planning. Chapter 9, infra, is largely devoted to the practice of creating family holding companies (usually in the form of family limited partnerships (FLPs)) to hold securities and real estate so that the equity interests therein can obtain entity-related valuation discounts. The creation of family holding companies entails an apparent destruction of wealth in order to reduce transfer taxes. For outside reading, see Repetti, *Minority Discounts: The Alchemy in Estate and Gift Taxation*, 50 Tax L. Rev. 415 (1995); Fellows & Painter, *Valuing Close Corporations for Federal Wealth Taxes: A Statutory Solution to the Disappearing Wealth Syndrome*, 30 Stan. L. Rev. 895 (1978); Cooper, *A Voluntary Tax? New Perspectives on Sophisticated Estate Tax Avoidance*, 77 Colum. L. Rev. 161, 195-204 (1977). For a continuously updated treatise on all aspects of valuation, see J. Bogdanski, *Federal Tax Valuation*.

D. *The Effect of the Decedent's Death on Valuation*

An issue under the estate tax is whether death itself can affect value.

Estate of McClatchy v. Commissioner
147 F.3d 1089 (3d Cir.1998)

Before DOROTHY W. NELSON and A. WALLACE TASHIMA, Circuit Judges, and THOMAS S. ZILLY, District Judge.

TASHIMA, Circuit Judge:

Appellants (collectively, the "estate") contend that the Tax Court incorrectly held that stock owned by the decedent, Charles K. McClatchy ("McClatchy" or "decedent"), should be valued without regard to federal securities law restrictions on marketability that applied to McClatchy during his lifetime, but do not apply to the estate. We reverse.

The valuation of stock is generally a question of fact, reviewed for clear error. This case, however, was submitted on stipulated facts, raising only a question of law; therefore, we review *de novo*.

McClatchy was Chairman of the Board, Chief Executive Officer, and Editor of McClatchy Newspapers, Inc. (the "corporation") at the time of his death in 1989. The corporation had two classes of common stock: (1) Class A, which was publicly traded; and (2) Class B, which was not publicly traded, was convertible into Class A stock, and was subject to transfer restrictions set forth in a stockholders' agreement. McClatchy owned more than 2 million shares of Class B stock at the time of his death and had held them for more than three years. Because of his position with the corporation and his ownership interest, McClatchy was subject to federal securities law restrictions on the sale or distribution of his Class B shares as an affiliate of the corporation. These restrictions limited the marketability of McClatchy's shares, resulting in a value of $12.3375 per share before his death. Upon McClatchy's death, however, the shares passed to the estate, which was not an affiliate of the corporation. The estate therefore was not subject to the securities law restrictions applicable to decedent. The parties agree that, apart from the restrictions, the fair market value of the stock was $15.56 per share. The IRS [had] conceded that a "blockage discount" of 15 percent should be used in valuing the stock. The sole remaining disagreement was whether the stock should be valued subject to the federal securities law restrictions which had applied to decedent, but did not apply to the estate.

The Tax Court held that, because "the securities law restrictions evaporated at the moment of death, the shares must be valued free of the restriction, at $15.56 per share." 106 T.C. 206, 214 (1996).

The federal estate tax is a tax on "the transfer of the taxable estate of . . . decedent." §2001(a); see also *U.S. Trust Co. v. Helvering*, 307 U.S. 57, 60 (1939) ("An estate tax is not levied upon the property of which an estate is composed. It is an excise imposed upon the transfer of or shifting in relationships to property at death."); *Ithaca Trust Co. v. U.S.*, 279 U.S. 151, 155 (1929) ("The tax is on the act of the testator not on the receipt of property by the legatees."); *Young Men's Christian Ass'n v. Davis*, 264 U.S. 47, 50 (1924) ("YMCA") ("What this law taxes is not the interest to which the legatees and devisees succeeded on death, but the interest which ceased by reason of the death."). There is no question that the estate tax is on the transfer of property at death and that, therefore, the property to be valued is the interest transferred at death, "rather than the interest held by the decedent before death or that held by the legatee after death." *Propstra v. U.S.*, 680 F.2d 1248, 1250 (9th Cir.1982) (citing *Estate of Bright v. U.S.*, 658 F.2d 999, 1001 (5th Cir.1981) (*en banc*)). However, the Commissioner argues that, because the stock was transferred to a non-affiliate estate upon McClatchy's death, this is one of those rare cases in which death itself alters the value of the property. According to the Commissioner, then, the stock is to be valued at its higher value in the hands of the non-affiliate estate.

The Commissioner relies on *Ahmanson Foundation v. U.S.*, 674 F.2d 761 (9th Cir.1981), and similar cases where death itself alters the value of the decedent's property. In *Ahmanson*, the decedent held, through a revocable trust, a controlling interest (600 shares) in voting common stock of HFA, a holding company. Also in the trust were all 100 shares (99 nonvoting and one voting share) of Ahmanco, a corporate shell with no assets prior to the decedent's death. At the moment of death, Ahmanco became unconditionally entitled to the 600 shares of voting HFA common stock, Ahmanson Foundation became entitled to the 99 nonvoting shares of Ahmanco, [and] the voting share remained in the control of Ahmanson's family. The court stated that valuation must "take into account any transformations of the property that are logically prior to its distribution to the beneficiaries," and so the Ahmanco shares were to be valued based on the 600 shares of HFA that passed at death. The court noted that, although death itself does not usually alter the value of property owned by the decedent, in some instances, such as in the death of a key partner, death might change the value. Id. at 768 (citing *U.S. v. Land*, 303 F.2d 170, 172 (5th Cir.1962)). The Foundation argued that the

Ahmanco shares should be split into two blocks for valuation, with its 99 nonvoting Ahmanco shares valued separately from the voting share. The court declined to value the nonvoting shares separately from the voting share, [and] concluded that the 100 shares should be "viewed in the hands of the testator," not as two separate assets, because "nothing in the statutes or in the case law . . . suggests that valuation of the gross estate should take into account that the assets will come to rest in several hands rather than one." 674 F.2d at 768-769.

In *Land,* a partnership interest was restricted to two-thirds of its value during the partner's lifetime, but upon death, the surviving partners had to pay full value in order to purchase the interest. Because death "sealed the fact" that the interests would be purchased at full value, the court ruled that the full value controlled for estate tax purposes. In *Goodman v. Granger,* 243 F.2d 264 (3d Cir.1957), another case on which the Commissioner relies, an employment contract provided for the payment of benefits after the termination of employment, dependent upon contingencies which could cause forfeiture of the payments. Upon the employee's death, however, the possibility of any of the contingencies occurring was extinguished. The court reasoned that "death ripened the interest in the deferred payments into an absolute one"; consequently, the estate tax was measured by "the value of that absolute interest in property."

In these cases, death clearly is the precipitating event and is the only event required to fix the value of the property. Similarly, the death of a key partner can instantly decrease the value of a business. But in the instant case, death alone did not effect the transformation in the stock's value. The value of the stock was transformed only because the estate was a non-affiliate. Thus, contrary to the Commissioner's assertion, the property was not transformed prior to distribution to the estate. If the estate had been an affiliate, the securities law restrictions still would have applied. The affiliate or non-affiliate status of an estate depends on the status of the executor or other person who serves "in any similar capacity." The personal representatives for the estate were not issued letters testamentary until 25 days after McClatchy's death. The restrictions therefore did not evaporate at the moment of death.

Making the amount of estate tax dependent on the affiliate or non-affiliate status of the executor contradicts the principle that valuation should not depend on the status of the recipient. See *Estate of Bonner v. U.S.,* 84 F.3d 196 (5th Cir.1996) (the fact that decedent held a partial interest in property whose remaining interest was held in a trust that was included in decedent's estate did not allow the interests to be merged for 100 percent ownership of the assets by the estate); *Ahmanson,* 674 F.2d at 768 ("To take into account for valuation purposes the fact that the testator's unitary holding has become divided in the hands of two or more beneficiaries, would invite abuse."); *Bright,* 658 F.2d 999 at 1006 ("It would be strange indeed if the estate tax value of a block of stock would vary depending upon the legatee to whom it was devised."). The Commissioner's position would lead to the anomaly that, by using affiliate executors, a non-affiliate decedent [could reduce the estate tax valuation of stock by appointing an affiliate executor].

The Tax Court's holding contravenes the general principle that "the tax is measured by the value of assets transferred by reason of death, the critical value being that which is determined as of the time of death." *Goodman*, 243 F.2d at 269, quoted in *McClatchy*, 106 T.C. at 214. At the time of death, the stock belonged to McClatchy, an affiliate of the corporation, depressing their value to that reported by the estate. The Tax Code itself defines the value of the estate for estate tax purposes to include "the value of all property to the extent of the interest therein of the decedent at the time of his death." §2033.

Finally, the Commissioner's contention that the hypothetical "willing buyer willing seller" method of determining fair market value is determinative begs the question. The Commissioner argues that valuation depends on the hypothetical buyer purchasing the stock not from decedent but from the estate. However, the "willing buyer willing seller" method posits not only a hypothetical buyer, but also a hypothetical seller. In the instant case, the identity or status of that hypothetical seller is the very issue. We therefore agree with the estate that the "willing buyer willing seller" test "offers no guidance" in this case, especially since the parties agree on figures for fair market value, and the only question is which figure to accept.

The increase in the stock's value was occasioned, not by death, but by transfer to a non-affiliate estate; death alone did not alter the value. Therefore, the stock should be valued in the hands of the decedent. The decision of the Tax Court is REVERSED, with directions to enter a decision for the estate.

D.W. NELSON, Circuit Judge, Dissenting:

The federal estate tax is not assessed against the decedent, but against the decedent's estate. See §2001(a) ("A tax is hereby imposed on the transfer of the taxable estate of every decedent who is a citizen or resident of the United States."); *Estate of Curry v. U.S.*, 706 F.2d 1424, 1429 (7th Cir.1983) (holding that for estate tax purposes "property is to be valued as it exists in the hands of the estate"). In my view, it follows that McClatchy's stock was properly valued as it existed in the hands of his estate, rather than as it existed in his own hands. The Tax Court therefore did not err in deciding that the securities restrictions, which attached to the shares while in McClatchy's possession, vanished at the moment of death when the shares passed from McClatchy, an affiliate subject to the restrictions, to his non-affiliate estate.

Ahmanson Foundation v. U.S., 674 F.2d 761 (9th Cir.1981), is directly on point. In the words of the Ahmanson court: "The valuation should . . . take into account transformations brought about by those aspects of the estate plan which go into effect logically prior to the distribution of property in the gross estate to the beneficiaries." Applying the logic and language of *Ahmanson* to the instant case, McClatchy's death altered the value of his property by causing the shares to be passed to his non-affiliate estate, thereby voiding the restrictions that had previously attached on account of McClatchy's affiliate status. As in *Ahmanson*, the transformation at issue here — the lapse of the securities restrictions — went into effect prior to the distribution of McClatchy's property to his beneficiaries. Under *Ahmanson*, this pre-distribution transformation must be considered in determining McClatchy's estate tax liability.

The hypotheticals offered by the *Ahmanson* court to illustrate the difference between pre-distribution and post-distribution transformations in a decedent's property fully support the Tax Court's decision. For example, the *Ahmanson* court posed the following scenario: "If a public figure ordered his executor to shred and burn his papers, the value to be counted would be the value of the ashes, rather than the papers." Here, McClatchy's estate plan ordered that the stock be transferred to his executors prior to being distributed to his beneficiaries. Like the papers in the Ahmanson example, the stock should be valued in the aftermath of the pre-distribution transformation, free of the restrictions that attached while the stock was still in McClatchy's possession. The majority reasons that whereas the property transformation in the "ashes" example was occasioned by "death alone," the property transformation in the case at bar was occasioned by the non-affiliate status of decedent's estate. Given that the papers in the Ahmanson hypothetical were not burned and shred as a direct result of the decedent's death, but rather as the result of an order contained within the estate plan, I find the majority's distinction unconvincing.

Moreover, I believe that the Fifth Circuit's opinion in *U.S. v. Land*, 303 F.2d 170 (5th Cir.1962), only bolsters the Tax Court's reasoning. The *Land* court held that in determining the federal estate tax, restrictions applicable by virtue of the decedent's status in life must be disregarded:

> To find the fair market value of a property interest at the decedent's death we put ourselves in the position of a potential purchaser of the interest at that time. Such a person would not be influenced in his calculations by past risks that had failed to materialize or by restrictions that had ended. Death tolls the bell for risks, contingencies, or restrictions which exist only during the life of the decedent.

Id. at 173. Here, McClatchy's death "tolled the bell" for the securities law restrictions that existed only during his lifetime. In the words of the Tax Court, the restrictions "evaporated at the moment of death."

McClatchy maintains that "changes in the value of an asset which occur by reason of the identity and status of the recipient, not death, must be ignored for estate tax purposes." McClatchy's use of the generic term "recipient" blurs the line between the estate and the ultimate beneficiary of the decedent's property interest. Of course, it is well-established that changes in value resulting from distribution to beneficiaries or legatees are not accounted for in determining the federal estate tax. However, this court held in *Ahmanson* that there is a sharp distinction for estate tax purposes between pre- and post-distribution changes in the value of a decedent's property.

I believe that *Estate of Bright v. U.S.*, 658 F.2d 999 (5th Cir.1981), is inapposite. In that case, the Fifth Circuit held that property is to be valued for estate tax purposes in the hands of the estate, not in the hands of the legatee after distribution. The *Bright* court exclusively addressed the contrast between the pre-death moment and the post-distribution moment:

> The fact that Mr. and Mrs. Bright held their stock during her lifetime as a control block of 55% is an irrelevant fact. It is a fact which antedates her death, and no longer exists at the time of her death. Dictum in Land also suggests that the post-death fact — that the estate's 27.5% will pass to Mr. Bright as trustee of the testamentary trust — is also irrelevant.

Id. at 1002. Concerned only with the periods pre-death and post-distribution, Bright does not involve a pre-distribution value transformation like the one at issue in the present case.

The majority resolves this case by relying on the familiar distinction between the estate tax (a tax on the passing of property) and the inheritance tax (a tax on the receipt of property by the decedent's beneficiaries). This case, however, does not at all concern the moment of distribution or inheritance. Rather, it involves a pre-distribution value transformation resulting from the passing of shares to the decedent's estate, and should be considered in accordance with other cases of its kind.

E. Buy-Sell Agreements

In *Goodman v. Granger*, 243 F.2d 264 (3d Cir.1957), and *U.S. v. Land*, 303 F.2d 170 (5th Cir.1962), restrictions on property that lapsed at death were disregarded. Presumably the rule of these cases could be avoided by continuing the restrictions after death, and a way of doing this was through a buy-sell agreement. Typically, such an agreement prohibits the decedent from disposing of the closely-held business interest during life, and requires one or more persons (often family members) to purchase such interest after death at a below-fair-market-value fixed price or a price set by a formula (such as "book value"). Prior to the 1990 enactment of §2703, buy-sell agreements among family members were often (but not always) successful in fixing the value of the interest for estate tax purposes. The pre-1990 case law often validated these arrangements for estate tax valuation purposes solely on the basis of a finding of a business purpose to maintain family control. E.g., *Estate of Bischoff v. Comm'r*, 69 T.C. 32 (1977). However, the tide began to turn with *St. Louis County Bank v. U.S.*, 674 F.2d 1207 (8th Cir.1982), which held that such a business purpose would not preclude an inquiry into whether the agreement involved a "disguised bequest" element in an amount equal to the excess (if any) of the value of the interest (ignoring the agreement) over the price fixed by the agreement.

Section 2703 was enacted in 1990 to end abuses in this area.[61] Under the text of §2703, any right to acquire or use, or any restriction on the sale or use, of property,[62] contained in an agreement or entity structure,[63] that does not fall within the statutory exception of §2703(b) is disregarded for transfer tax valuation purposes.

---

61. Section 2703, enacted together with §§2701, 2702, and 2704 (which are separately discussed in Chapters 8 and 9), constitute Chapter 14 of the Code. Omnibus Budget Reconciliation Act of 1990, Pub. L. 101-508, Title XI, 11602(a), 104 Stat. 1388, 498. H.R. Conf. Rep. 101-964, 101st Cong., 2d Sess. 2838 (1990). See *Estate of True v. Comm'r*, T.C. Memo. 2001-167, *aff'd*, 390 F.3d 1210 (10th Cir.2004) ("These rules were enacted to . . . assure more accurate valuation of property subject to transfer taxes."); *Estate of Strangi v. Comm'r*, 115 T.C. 478, 487 (2000), *aff'd on this issue*, 293 F.3d 279 (5th Cir.2002).

62. See §2703(a); Reg. §25.2703-1(a)(2).

63. Reg. §25.2703-1(a)(3) provides: "A right or restriction may be contained in a partnership agreement, articles of incorporation, corporate bylaws, a shareholders' agreement, or any other agreement. A right or restriction may be implicit in the capital structure of an entity."

To fall within the exception of §2703(b), *all* three of the following conditions must be satisfied with respect to the right, restriction, option, or agreement:

(1) it must be a bona fide business arrangement;

(2) it must not be a device to transfer the property to members of the natural objects of the transferor's bounty for less than full consideration in money or money's worth; *and,*

(3) its terms must be comparable to similar arrangements entered into at arm's length and reaching a fair bargain.[64]

Thus, §2703 not only incorporates the rule of *St. Louis County Bank* but also added a third ("comparable terms") requirement.[65]

In the conference agreement, the conferees explained that the comparables requirement was not to be rigidly applied.[66] Taking this cue, Reg. §25.2703-1(b)(4)(ii) provides:

Evidence of general business practice is not met by showing isolated comparables. If more than one valuation method is commonly used in a business, a right or restriction does not fail to evidence general business practice merely because it uses only one of the recognized methods. It is not necessary that the terms of a right or restriction parallel the terms of any particular agreement. If comparables are difficult to find because the business is unique, comparables from similar businesses may be used.

The statute was intended not to replace prior case law,[67] but to codify and expand requirements in that area. Thus, the prior rules requiring that an agreement be binding during life and at death, and contain a fixed and determinable price, continue to apply.[68]

The regulations provide an exception for cases where more than 50 percent of the value of the property is owned (directly or indirectly through attribution rules) by individuals who are not natural objects of the transferor's bounty.[69]

---

64. §2703(b); Reg. §25.2703-1(b)(1) & (2).

65. The Senate Report states: ". . . the committee is aware of the potential of buy-sell agreements for distorting transfer tax value. Therefore, the committee establishes rules that attempt to distinguish between agreements designed to avoid estate taxes and those with legitimate business agreements. These rules generally disregard a buy-sell agreement that would not have been entered into by unrelated parties acting at arm's length." S. Rep. 3209, 101st Cong., 2d Sess. (1990), 136 Cong. Rec. §515, 629-04, at 15,681. See, e.g., *Estate of True v. Comm'r*, 390 F.3d 1210 (10th Cir.2004), *aff'g* T.C. Memo. 2001-167; *Estate of Blount v. Comm'r*, 428 F.3d 1338 (11th Cir.2005).

66. H.R. Conf. Rep. 101-964, 101st Cong., 2d Sess. 1137 (1990).

67. See *Estate of True v. Comm'r*, 390 F.3d 1210, 1218 (10th Cir.2004) (asserting that the arm's-length test was present, by negative implication, in the "testamentary substitute" concept).

68. See *Estate of Blount v. Comm'r*, 428 F.3d 1338, 1342 (11th Cir.2005), *aff'g on this issue*, T.C. Memo. 2004-116; *Estate of Amlie v. Comm'r*, T.C. Memo. 2006-76.

69. See Reg. §25.2703-1(b)(3). Although §2703(b)(2) refers to transfers to "members of the [sic] decedent's family," there is (unlike §§2701, 2702, and 2704) no statutory definition of this term in §2703. Thus, the regulations have replaced "decedent" by "transferor," and "member's of the . . . family" by "natural object of the transferor's bounty," while adding a safe-harbor exception.

In *Holman v. Comm'r*, 130 T.C. 170 (2008), the Tax Court applied §2703 to the restrictions on transferability the taxpayers placed in paragraph 9.3 of their family limited partnership (FLP) agreement. The court held that the agreement's restrictions did not assist a bona fide business arrangement of the taxpayers, and that the restrictions were a device to transfer property to their children for less than adequate consideration in money or money's worth. The Eighth Circuit affirmed the Tax Court's decision in *Holman* in an opinion that is excerpted below.

Holman v. Commissioner
601 F.3d 763 (8th Cir.2010)

Before MELLOY, BEAM, and GRUENDER, Circuit Judges.
MELLOY, Circuit Judge:
Restrictions on the sale or use of property generally tend to depress the value of the property. Oftentimes, such restrictions serve legitimate business purposes, impose actual and meaningful limitations on the use or transferability of property, and are accepted by parties dealing with one another in arm's-length transactions. When carefully crafted and applied in certain circumstances, however, such restrictions can minimize the tax consequences of gifts or transfers without imposing substantial additional limitations on the transferability or use of the property. This is particularly true in the context of family transfers where a donor may hold some degree of practical control over a recipient's actions, even in the absence of formal restrictions, and where transactions often do not occur at arm's length.

Because we conclude that the Tax Court correctly held the present restrictions are not "a bona fide business arrangement" in accordance with §2703(b)(1), we address only that [issue].

The Tax Court emphasized Mr. Holman's testimony in which he failed to identify any current or planned activity by the partnership other than holding passive investments without a clearly articulated investment strategy. In addition, he made clear that asset preservation meant preservation from dissipation by the children, not the pursuit of any particular investment strategy. Mrs. Holman emphasized the personal goals of educating the children as to financial responsibility.

In answering the question of whether a restriction constitutes a bona fide business arrangement, context matters. Here that context shows that the Tax Court correctly assessed the personal and testamentary nature of the transfer restrictions. Simply put, in the present case, there was and is no "business," active or otherwise. The donors have not presented any argument or asserted any facts to distinguish their situation from the use of a similar partnership structure to hold a passbook savings account, an interest-bearing checking account, government bonds, or cash. We and other courts have held that "maintenance of family ownership and control of [a] business" may be a bona fide business purpose. We have not so held, however, in the absence of a business.

In *Estate of Bischoff v. Comm'r*, 69 T.C. 32 (1977), the question was whether the price contained in a buy-sell agreement regarding limited-partnership shares was controlling for valuation purposes. In that case, the Tax Court stated, "the cases have held that the maintenance of family ownership and control constituted a legitimate business consideration." The underlying asset in *Bischoff* was "a pork processing business organized, controlled, and managed by three families" who sought "to assure their continuing ability to carry on their pork processing business without outside interference, including that of a dissident limited partner." In *Bischoff* then, there was a perceived risk of an outsider interfering with management.

There is no similarity between the facts of *Bischoff* and the present case, because the limited partners in the Holman partnership held little-to-no ability to interfere with asset management. Further, the donors have made no allegation that they, as the general partners, are skilled or savvy investment managers whose expertise is needed or whose investment philosophy needs to be conserved or protected from interference as might justify placement of stock assets into the partnership. Finally, the assets of the partnership, passively-held Dell Corporation stock, are not assets with which an outsider or dissident owner might interfere. In the quantities held by the partnership, the value of the underlying assets are largely unaffected by the individual actions of the general partners or other owners of relatively insignificant fractions of outstanding stock (unlike the actions of potentially dissenting co-owners of a pork-processing enterprise).

Arguably, the strongest cases for the donors are a line of cases involving investment entities with restrictions imposed to ensure perpetuation of an investment model or strategy. See *Estate of Black v. Comm'r*, 133 T.C. 15 (2009); *Estate of Schutt v. Comm'r*, T.C. Memo. 2005-126 (2005). These cases, however, are more nuanced than the donors assert, and each involves unique facts not present in our case. In *Schutt*, the Tax Court addressed a different code section, but one of the underlying questions at issue was similar: whether the transfer of publicly traded stock into a business trust was a bona fide sale for full and adequate consideration. Regarding the legitimate business purpose, the Tax Court ultimately concluded that the maintenance and perpetuation of a specific buy-and-hold investment strategy was, in that case, a legitimate business purpose. The court based its decision on an express factual finding that the transferor's primary objective was to preserve his very specific investment strategy. In so holding, however, the Tax Court appeared to recognize that it was approaching an outside limit as to the meaning of legitimate business purpose and noted the "unique circumstances of this case." In fact, the court noted the general position that "the mere holding of an untraded portfolio of marketable securities weighs negatively in the assessment of potential nontax benefits."

In *Estate of Erickson v. Comm'r*, T.C. Memo. 2007-107 (2007), however, the Tax Court distinguished *Schutt*, effectively illustrating an important difference between cases like *Schutt* and the present case:

> We have found a significant nontax purpose where the justification for the transaction was the decedent's personal views and concerns regarding the operation of an income-producing activity and not a business exigency. There is no significant nontax purpose, however, where a family limited partnership is just a vehicle for changing the form of the investment in the assets, a mere asset container.

Here, as in *Erickson*, the family partnership is "a mere asset container." The donors do not purport to hold any particular investment philosophy or possess any particular investing insight. The present partnership agreement does not require that the general partners retain the Dell stock held by the partnership and the donors apparently intend to diversify their investments, although they have articulated no time frame or strategy for doing so. The donors admit that holding Dell stock as the exclusive asset of the limited partnership is not part of an overall, long-term plan.

In the present case, looking at the entirety of the surrounding transactions — including the contemporaneous execution of wills, Mr. Holman's understanding of the potential tax benefits of his actions, Mrs. Holman's educational goals, and the absence of any business activity — we find ample support for the Tax Court's determination. When viewed in this context, there is little doubt that the restrictions included in the Holmans' limited partnership agreement were not a bona fide business arrangement, but rather, were predominately for purposes of estate planning, tax reduction, wealth transference, protection against dissipation by the children, and education for the children.

BEAM, Circuit Judge, *dissenting*.

The court majority halted its analysis after its discussion of §2703(b)(1), holding that the Holman partnership restrictions were not bona fide business arrangements. I, however, would hold that the restrictions safely satisfy §2703(b)(1)'s bona fide business arrangement test as well as the remaining tests in §2703(b)(2) and (3).

The court, like the Tax Court, essentially holds that "maintaining family control" is a legitimate business purpose for partnership restrictions only when the "control" being preserved is the right to manage an operating business or an actively-managed asset. While the court narrowly reads *Bischoff* to bolster its holding, congressional committees cited *Bischoff* to support much broader propositions. First, the Joint Committee on Taxation cited *Bischoff* for the proposition that maintaining family control is a legitimate business purpose for buy-sell agreements, "even when the 'control' being preserved is a right to receive income from investment assets." Furthermore, the parenthetical following the Committee's *Bischoff* citation explains that "maintenance of control is [a] business purpose even if the interest being sold is a limited partnership interest in a holding company." Finally, the Senate Finance Committee cited *Bischoff* for the proposition that "[c]ontinuation of family ownership" is a legitimate business purpose for buy-sell agreements "even when the 'control' being preserved is only the right to participate as a limited partner." Accordingly, I think the Holman partnership restrictions served the congressionally-recognized legitimate business purposes of maintaining family control over the right to participate as a limited partner and the right to receive income from the partnership's investment assets.

I now turn to §2703(b)(2)'s "device" test. Regulation §25.2703-1(b)(1)(ii) excises the phrase "members of the decedent's family" found in §2703(b)(2) and substitutes in its place the phrase "natural objects of the transferor's bounty," apparently because the Secretary of the Treasury interprets §2703(b)(2) to apply to both *inter vivos* transfers and transfers at death. Applying this regulation, the Tax Court held that the Holman partnership restrictions operate as a device to transfer property to the natural objects of the Holmans' bounty. The Holmans argue that Treasury Regulation §25.2703-1(b)(1)(ii) is invalid because it fails to give effect to §2703(b)(2)'s plain language. I agree.

The parties primarily dispute whether §2703(b)(2) is ambiguous. The Holmans assert that the term "decedent" unambiguously refers to a deceased person and, therefore, §2703(b)(2) asks only whether restrictions operate as a device to transfer property to family members at death. The Holmans point out that only the term "decedent," not the broader term "transferor," is used throughout §2703(b)(2)'s legislative history. Conversely, the Commissioner argues that the term "decedent" is ambiguous due to §2703's location in the Internal Revenue Code. Specifically, §2703 is located in Subtitle B of the Code, which includes three transfer taxes, the estate, gift and generation-skipping transfer taxes. More precisely, §2703 is located in Chapter 14, [where it] joins a set of special valuation rules targeting transfer tax avoidance schemes.

Therefore, Treasury Regulation §25.2703-1(b)(1)(ii) is invalid because it does not give effect to the plain language of §2703(b)(2). Since the Holmans are living persons, they are, by definition, not "decedents" and §2703(b)(2)'s device test is satisfied.

I now analyze the restrictions under §2703(b)(3)'s "comparable terms" test. While the Tax Court did not decide whether the restrictions satisfied the comparable terms test, it noted that both parties' experts "agree that transfer restrictions comparable to those found in [the Holman partnership agreement] are common in agreements entered into at arm's length." The Tax Court explained that this "would seem to be all that [the Holmans] need to show to satisfy section 2703(b)(3)." I agree, and I would hold that the Holman partnership restrictions satisfy §2703(b)(3)'s comparable terms test.

QUICK QUESTION

When Theodore died in 2002, he owned Blackacre. In the year before he died, Theodore leased Blackacre to his adult son. The terms of their lease were not comparable to similar leases in an arm's-length transaction. The lease is a restriction on the use of Blackacre. Which one of the following Code sections applies to determine the value of Blackacre for estate tax purposes?

    A. Section 2031(c)
    B. Section 2032
    C. Section 2032A
    D. Section 2703

QUESTIONS AND NOTES

1. **a.** The concept of the "moment of death" is illusive. Is the "valuation moment" the moment just prior to death? The moment just after death? The moment before distributions from the estate? Do statements about the nature of an estate tax resolve this issue? (Reg. §20.0-2(a) states that the federal estate tax "is a tax imposed upon the transfer of the entire taxable estate and not upon any particular legacy, devise, or distributive share.") Perhaps the most thorough discussion of this point is found in *U.S. v. Land*, 303 F.2d 170, 171-173 (5th Cir.1962), where it is stated that the value is determined at the date of death looking forward, and disregarding restrictions that lapse at the decedent's death. Facts and events that take effect immediately upon death are considered.

   b. Did the Ninth Circuit majority in *Estate of McClatchy* apply the correct principles incorrectly? If one disregards the effect of distributions and fractionalizing bequests, shouldn't one also disregard the identity of the executor? (Both the effectiveness of the will and the appointment of a personal representative are contingent on court action after the decedent's death.) Presumably there are willing buyers who would not be "affiliates." At the moment of death, is the hypothetical "willing seller" an affiliate? (What about the fact that, at such moment, there is no person with the authority to sell the stock?)

2. **a.** If estate tax valuation disregards restrictions that lapse at death, was the Service correct in insisting (in Reg. §20.2031-2(h)) that a prerequisite to the efficacy of a buy-sell agreement was that it be binding on the decedent prior to death? This point is also discussed in *Land*, 303 F.2d at 173, where it is stated that a restriction that is not binding on the decedent is the equivalent of a revocable (i.e., incomplete) transfer of a bargain-purchase right to a donee, and does not implicate valuation as such.

   b. If the restriction *is* binding on the decedent, is there not a completed gift of a bargain purchase right to a donee at the time the restriction was imposed? (How could the amount of the gift be determined?) If there was a completed gift, was *St. Louis Cty. Bank* wrongly decided? (If there was a completed gift, then an estate tax solution would have called for a statutory enactment, which occurred with §2703.)

   c. Doesn't the estate tax solution (of disregarding the restrictions) also imply a matching gift tax solution (which is to ignore the disguised gift)? Isn't that what §2703 provides? Section 2703(a), the operative provision, applies "for purposes of this subtitle," which is Subtitle B, dealing with all of the federal transfer taxes. The word "decedent" only applies for purposes of the §2703(b) exception. Therefore, in complete opposition to the dissenting opinion in *Holman*, it is the exception that cannot (literally) apply in a gift scenario. Nevertheless, the Treasury regulation allows the exception to be raised in the gift scenario. Treas. Reg. §20.2031-2(h), which long antedated the enactment of §2703, also referred to the "natural objects of his bounty." Finally, the term "members of his family" is not defined for purposes of §2703, as it is for §§2701, 2702, and 2704.

d. Does §2703 not go far enough? That is, if a buy-sell agreement involves family members, shouldn't the *only* inquiry be whether the price is less than the fair market value *at the date of death*? (Otherwise, doesn't the agreement have the objective effect of passing value to the natural objects of the decedent's bounty for less than a full and adequate consideration in money or money's worth?) The Tax Court, in cases arising before the effective date of §2703, allowed consideration of other factors existing at the time of the agreement, such as the fairness of the price at that time, the then health of the decedent, and the then state of family harmony. See, e.g., *Estate of Lauder v. Comm'r*, T.C. Memo. 1992-736. Isn't the whole point of these agreements (involving family members) the likelihood that the price under the agreement will be less than the value at death? See Reg. §20.2703-1(b)(4)(i).

3. a. How can a desire to keep a business within the family be a "business" purpose? Studies have shown that a substantial majority of family businesses do not long survive the death of the original entrepreneur, and either collapse or are sold off. Isn't the only rational business and family decision to allow the successors a choice in this matter?

b. The dissent in *Holman*, discussing the "a bona fide business arrangement," requirement, cites legislative history for its position. Can a congressional committee make an authoritative interpretation of case law? What about the actual holding of *Bischoff*, on which the committee reports purportedly rely? The distinction between "business" and "investment" is a fundamental structural feature of the income tax subtitle of the Internal Revenue Code.

4. a. In *Strangi v. Comm'r*, 115 T.C. 478 (2000) (reviewed), *aff'd on this issue*, 293 F.3d 279 (5th Cir.2002), the government argued that the limited partnership form itself constituted a restriction on the sale of the underlying assets in the partnership under §2703, with the result that the underlying assets should have been included in the gross estate (without entity-related valuation discounts). However, the Tax Court ruled that the "property" referred to in §2703(a) was the asset included in the gross estate (the interest in the limited partnership), not the assets that had previously been transferred into the limited partnership.

b. A buy-sell agreement needs to provide a means to value the business interest and a method to update that value. Despite the added cost, the parties may want to employ appraisers because of the greater probative weight attaching to third-party valuation. Different valuation methods are often used and they are sometimes averaged or weighted. Once computed, the valuation must be binding and enforceable both during life and at death. See, e.g., *Estate of Godley v. Comm'r*, T. C. Memo. 2000-242 ("We first note that the fixed price of the option, without any adjustment mechanism to reflect changing conditions, invites close scrutiny."); *Estate of Lauder v. Comm'r*, T.C. Memo. 1992-736 ("We are most concerned with the arbitrary manner in which Leonard, an experienced business-man, adopted the adjusted book value formula for determining the purchase price of the stock under the agreements. Leonard admitted that he arrived at the formula without a formal appraisal and without considering the specific trading prices of comparable companies. Nor does it appear that Leonard obtained any significant professional advice in selecting the formula price.").

5. a. In *Estate of Amlie v. Comm'r*, T.C. Memo. 2006-76, the decedent wanted her three children to share equally in her estate, and she therefore exe-cuted a will to that effect and appointed Rod, her son, executor. About ten years later, she had a conservator appointed to manage her finances. Her other children generally distrusted Rod. A large part of the decedent's assets consisted of minority interests in closely-held bank stock. An agree-ment executed in 1991 between the decedent (acting through her con-servator) and the controlling shareholder, Hill, and his holding company, Agri, was designed to restrict the marketability of decedent's shares and to allow Agri to purchase her shares. The conservator desired (1) to avoid a sale until decedent's death when the stock basis would be stepped up to its value at that time, (2) to fix the price of, and have a guaranteed buyer for, her minority interest in a closely-held company, and (3) to provide liquid-ity for her estate at her death. In 1994, Agri merged into FABG, which agreed to honor the 1991 agreement. The conservator then negotiated an agreement in 1994 to sell the decedent's stock after her death to FABG for $118. The conservator hired an expert to value the stock, and the latter found the $118 price to be fair, but when the conservator sought court approval, the court (after hearing disparate expert testimony) concluded that the $118 price was too low, and declined to approve the 1994 agree-ment. The conservator filed a motion for reconsideration and began to negotiate with the prospective heirs for an acceptable price for an agree-ment. In 1995, they executed a Family Settlement Agreement (FSA) guaranteeing decedent and the prospective heirs other than Rod a $118 price for the FABG stock, and preventing the decedent from transferring the stock without Rod's consent. The bequests to Rod would be satisfied in kind with FABG stock at the $118 value, but any remaining FABG stock in the decedent's estate would first be offered to Rod at that same price. The court approved the 1995 FSA. In 1997, Rod executed an agreement with FABG by which the latter agreed to pay $217.50 per share. In 1998, the decedent died at 96, and Rod's trust exercised its call option to purchase all of the remaining FABG in her estate, in excess of the stock bequeathed to him. Rod then sold the stock to FABG for about $1.5M per the 1997 agreement. Of the $1.5M, the estate ended up with about $1M and Rod the other $0.5M.

    b. The Tax Court in *Amlie* held that the 1995 FSA satisfied both the pre-1990 case-law requirements as well as the additional requirements of §2703, noting that the agreement set a floor as well as a ceiling in price that was effective during the decedent's life and after her death and that the arrangement was approved by the local court. The Tax Court held that the agreement served valid business reasons including risk reduction and providing liquidity for her estate. It was not a testamentary device in that, at the time the FSA was executed, the decedent received fair consideration for her shares of FABG stock. Finally, its terms were comparable to similar agreements concluded in arm's-length transactions, since the terms were the same as those in the 1994 agreement negotiated between the conservator and FABG, the interests of the prospective heirs other than Rod conflicted with his interests, and the 1994 price was "based on a survey of comparables."

c. The net effect of the arrangement was (1) to obtain estate liquidity for illiquid minority interests at the cost of entering into a bad bargain with the controlling interests, and (2) allowing Rod to profit at the expense of the other legatees. Arguably, these results flowed from three arm's-length bargains: (1) between the decedent and the controlling shareholder, (2) among Rod and his siblings, and (3) Rod and FABG. Should there be evidence that the family members *acted* like unrelated parties, such as hiring individual attorneys to represent their separate interests, or employing their own experts to value the stock? Did the local court act improperly in approving the 1995 FSA? Did this arrangement amount to a disguised bequest to Rod — or was Rod's profit the result of his own acuity?

§4.5. Estate Tax Procedure

The coverage in this chapter of property owned at death and aspects of estate administration relating to deductions (debts, claims, funeral and administration expenses, and death taxes) prompts a brief description of the basics of estate tax procedure.

A. *Returns*

Pursuant to §6018(a)(1) & (4), an estate tax return (Form 706) must be filed where the date of death value of the gross estate exceeds the applicable exclusion amount for the year of death reduced by the sum of "adjusted taxable gifts."

The return must contain a detailed list of the property in the gross estate as well as the claims against it. *It also must indicate all transfers of $1,000 or more within three years of the decedent's* death and all *inter vivos* gifts, whenever made, of a value of $5,000 or more. If any of such transfers were in trust, a copy of the trust instrument must be submitted. See generally Reg. §20.6018-3 and -4.

Under §7602, the Service can compel examination of books, records, documents, etc., and compel testimony.

The Form 706 is to be filed within nine months after the decedent's death. §6075(a). This period can be extended for up to six months pursuant to §6081(a).

The return, once filed, may be amended so long as the statute of limitations for refund claims has not expired.

B. Payment

Payment of the tax must be in cash, and is to be made within nine months of the decedent's death. Although the §6081(a) six-month extension does not apply to the payment requirement, see §6151(a), there are exceptions. Under §6161(a)(1), the Service can extend the time for payment for a period of up to 12 months. In addition, the Service, pursuant to §6161(a)(2), upon a showing by the estate of reasonable cause, may postpone all or part of the payment for up to ten years after the original due date. "Reasonable cause" is described in Reg. §20.6161-1(a)(1) in terms of nonliquidity, such as an inability to borrow cash at a reasonable interest rate, the existence of uncollected liquid assets, difficulties in selling nonliquid assets, and so on. Deferral (as a matter of right) of the tax "on" closely-held business interests has already been mentioned.

The tax is to be paid by the "executor," §2002, which term is broadly defined in §2203 to mean the personal representative of the estate. The executor is personally liable to pay the estate tax. In practice, this rule creates a strong inducement for the executor not to distribute the estate property until the estate tax has been paid. The executor can obtain a discharge from personal liability under the procedures prescribed in §2204. If the executor cannot (or does not) pay all or a portion of the estate tax, the decedent's transferees can be personally liable for the tax. Also, a lien attaches to the estate assets for a ten-year period. See §§6324 & 6901.

C. Burden of the Estate Tax

The federal rules designed to assure collection of the tax, supra, should not be confused with the rules as to who is ultimately to bear the burden of the tax. The burden issue is principally a matter of state rather than federal law. Basically, the burden of the estate tax (and state death taxes) is determined by reference to the decedent's intent as expressed in his will. If no tax apportionment provision is made in the decedent's will, the state law of apportionment controls. Under the Uniform Death Tax Apportionment Act, which has been adopted (more or less) in many of the states, death taxes are apportioned among all estate-included assets (including nonprobate assets, but not including assets that are deducted under the marital and charitable deductions) according to their gross estate values. In some states, the statutory default rule is that death taxes are charged against the residue of the estate.

Federal tax apportionment law preempts state law (but only in the absence of a direction in the decedent's will) in four situations: (1) life insurance proceeds (§2206), (2) power-of-appointment property (§2207), (3) property includible under §2044, relating to the marital deduction QTIP election (§2207A), and (4) property included in the gross under §2036 (§2207B). The allocation under §§2206, 2207, and 2207B is not made to amounts deductible under §2056 (the marital deduction).

The burden-of-tax rules guide the personal representative as far as what legacies, nonprobate transfers, etc., are to "ante up" prior to distributing the estate. However, if the tax is not paid "out of" the proper sources in advance of distribution, the federal government can extract payment from the personal representative "personally" or the transferees of the estate. The state and federal burden-of-tax rules give the estate (and its transferees) the right of contribution or reimbursement against the persons and property charged with bearing the burden of the tax. Code §2205 assures that the burden-allocation rules of state law (and the governing instruments) will be respected except to the extent that §§2206, 2207, 2207A, and 2207B override them. Thus, if the decedent's will provides that death taxes shall be paid from the residue, but the taxes are in fact collected by the IRS from a specific-property legatee, the latter can proceed for reimbursement against the estate, or if that has been distributed, against the residual legatees.

NOTES

1. The Service will not issue rulings "on matters relating to the application of the estate tax to property or the estate of a living person." Estate tax rulings can be obtained only with respect to estates of decedents after the date of death and before the estate tax return is filed. In contrast, rulings will be issued on proposed gift transactions.

2. Suppose the estate tax return involves an issue that has been generating controversy. For example, the issue may have been decided in favor of the government by a lower court and is currently on appeal. Or perhaps there is disagreement among the Circuits. Or, the issue may be one in which the Service's publicized position is known — through word of mouth — to be under attack by another taxpayer. If the estate does not wish itself to litigate the matter to the bitter end, it may obtain a "free ride" by the expedient of paying the tax with respect to the disputed item, filing a "protective" *claim* for refund at the last minute, see §6511(a), and hoping that the legal issue will be resolved in the estate's favor due to the efforts of another litigant before the statute of limitations on filing a refund *suit* has expired, see §6532(a).

CHAPTER 5

NONPROBATE TRANSFERS

This chapter covers the gift, estate, and income tax treatment of the standard nonprobate devices, namely, revocable trusts, jointly-held property with right of survivorship, annuities, employee survivor benefits, and life insurance.

§5.1. Revocable Trusts

Funded revocable trusts are the classic will substitute that avoids estate administration. However, unlike some of the other nonprobate devices, revocable trusts cannot be used by the grantor to avoid her creditors.

A trust is "revocable" for tax purposes if the grantor of the trust can, by her own efforts, re-obtain the trust property free of the trust.

A description of the tax treatment of revocable trusts is as simple as simple can be:

(1) the creation and funding of a revocable trust is an incomplete transfer, but distributions, during the grantor's lifetime, to persons (other than the grantor) are completed (present-interest) gifts;

(2) the value of the trust at the decedent's death is included in the decedent's gross estate at the decedent's death under §2038; and,

(3) the grantor is treated as the owner of the trust property for income tax purposes under §676, resulting in the attribution of the trust income and deductions to the grantor.

In short, funded revocable trusts offer no tax advantage relative to direct ownership of property.

In order for §2038 to apply, the power to revoke must be held by the grantor at the moment just prior to death.[1] In order to prevent avoidance of §2038 by obvious strategies to take advantage of this rule, Congress has provided two "constructive possession at death" rules. First, if a power to revoke was relinquished by the grantor within three years of the grantor's death, the relinquishment will effectively be disregarded. See §2038(a). Second, under §2038(b), the power is deemed to exist at death even though it could not have been exercised without prior notice or if the revocation (etc.) would be delayed after the exercise of the power.

Is there any *tax* advantage to an arrangement whereby the power to revoke is held by the grantor jointly with a person having an economic interest adverse to the exercise of the power to revoke (an "adverse party")?[2] The gift tax aspect of this issue was dealt with in Chapter 3, where it was revealed that an adverse party could cause all or a portion of the transfer to be a completed gift. However, there is no doctrinal consistency with the estate tax on this point, because §2038 expressly states (in the phrase "by the decedent alone or in conjunction with any person") that the existence of co-holders of the power is to be disregarded. Stated simply, a co-holder (adverse or non-adverse) of the power to revoke does not negate the application of §2038.

A power to revoke does not disappear because the holder of the power is adjudged to be incompetent prior to her death. An agent of the incompetent (under a durable power of attorney or person appointed by a court) can exercise the power on the incompetent's behalf.

Under §672(e) of the income tax, a power held by the grantor's spouse to revoke the trust will be attributed to the grantor. Furthermore, the grantor is treated as the owner of the trust under §676 if a non-adverse party (acting alone) has the power to re-vest the trust property in the grantor. However, a power to re-vest held only by an adverse party, or a power to revoke held by the grantor (or grantor's spouse) jointly with an adverse party, will negate attribution of the trust income to the grantor under §676. (In that case, assuming that the trust income is not attributed to the grantor under another provision, such as §677(a), the income tax treatment of the trust and beneficiaries will be governed by rules similar to those applicable to the income taxation of estates discussed in Chapter 4.)

Non-revocable transfers with retained powers are discussed in Chapter 8.

---

1. Where a decedent's power is, at his death, subject to a contingency beyond his control, §2038 does not apply, because the decedent did not actually possess the power at death. Reg. §20.2038-1(b). See, e.g., *Estate of Yawkey v. Comm'r*, 12 T.C. 1164 (1949), *acq.* 1949-2 C.B. 3 (where at decedent's death none of the beneficiaries was 30 years old, the precondition to his having the power to transfer principal to them had not occurred; therefore, §2038 was inapplicable).

2. The income tax definition of adverse party is found in §672(a). There is no *statutory* definition of adverse party for purposes of the gift, estate, or GST taxes.

1. a. In *Helvering v. Helmholz*, 296 U.S. 93 (1935), the Supreme Court held that a trust is not to be considered "revocable" solely because of the rule of trust law that allows a grantor, together with all of the beneficiaries, to terminate a trust and agree on the disposition of the trust property. The Court made a distinction between a reserved power and "a condition which the law imposes." However, the Court did not explain why this distinction should make a difference, especially since §2038 (then and now) did not require that the grantor have "reserved" or "retained" the power. Both §§2036 and 2037 expressly require that the decedent have "retained" the requisite interest or power in conjunction with the transfer.

    b. In the companion case to *Helmholz* of *White v. Poor*, 296 U.S. 98 (1935), the trustees (which initially did not include the grantor) had the power to cause all or a portion of the corpus to be paid to the grantor. One year later, the grantor was appointed by the other trustees to fill a vacancy in the trusteeship. Not surprisingly, the Supreme Court held that §2038(a)(2) did not apply because the grantor did not reserve the power in herself.

    c. In 1936, Congress added §2038(a)(1), effective for transfers after June 22, 1936. The 1936 change added three phrases: (1) "(in whatever capacity exercisable)," (2) "(without regard to when or from what source the decedent acquired such power)," and (3) "terminate." The clear intent of the first two insertions was to overturn the result of *White v. Poor*. Does the first parenthetical phrase also overturn the result of *Helmholz*? It is assumed in the estate planning community that *Helmholz* is still good law, and the result of *Helmholz* is, in fact, codified in Reg. §20.2038-1(a)(2). Does this violate the clear language of the statute? Is there a better rationale for *Helmholz* than what was offered by the Court in 1935?

2. What are the income, gift, and estate tax consequences of the following?

    a. Deirdre creates a trust, retaining the power to revoke until she reaches the age of 70, after which the trust is non-revocable and is to continue until and after Deirdre's death; assume that Deirdre dies at the age of 72.

    b. X declares an irrevocable trust over securities. (In a declaration of trust, the grantor is the sole trustee.) The trust provides that the income is payable to Y for life, remainder to Z, but that the trustee can distribute corpus to X in the trustee's discretion.

    c. H creates an irrevocable trust, naming the X Bank as trustee. The trust is to accumulate income until H's death, after which the trust is to continue for the benefit of those of H's issue who are living from time to time. W (H's wife) is, under the terms of the trust, given the power (so long as she is married to H) to re-vest all or a portion of the trust property in H. If W dies or ceases to be married to H, this power devolves on H's oldest child C. In fact, H and W divorce, and C (then having the power) outlives H.

    d. Agnes executes a durable power of attorney giving Boris legal authority "to manage and dispose of my property." Three months before Agnes' death,

Boris writes, signs, and delivers checks from Agnes' account in the amount of $13,000 to each of 30 of Agnes' family members. Under state law, a durable power of attorney is not interpreted to include the power to make gifts unless the document expressly provides that power in writing.

§5.2. Jointly-Held Property

Property and money in an account that passes by right of survivorship avoids estate administration. Real estate held in joint tenancy with right of survivorship avoids the creditors of the estate of a joint tenant, but the situation may be otherwise with respect to a decedent's share of a joint bank or brokerage account. Unless the context indicates otherwise, all of these arrangements described above will be referred to simply as "joint tenancies," and the persons with interests therein will be referred to as "joint tenants." Community property and tenancies in common lie outside of the realm of joint tenancies.

The creation and termination of jointly-held property is governed by general gift tax principles. Section 2040 is the estate tax provision dealing with all forms of concurrent undivided ownership of specific property with rights of survivorship.

A. Effect of State Law

Joint tenancies are typically created unilaterally by one person (the donor) purchasing property and putting it in the name of two or more joint tenants, one of which is typically the donor. The joint tenants other than the donor are referred to as the "donee" joint tenants. Alternatively, a joint tenancy can be created with pro rata contributions by all of the persons designated as joint tenants.

The survivorship right of a joint tenant in specific property is akin to a contingent reversion or contingent remainder following the expiring interests of the decedent joint tenant. Other features of joint tenancies depend upon the peculiarities of controlling law. The prevailing rule is that each tenant has an equal right to the possession or the income from the property during life. Except in the case of a "tenancy by the entireties" between husband and wife, each co-tenant possesses the right of "severance"; that is, to set off his or her aliquot fractional "share" of the property.

Joint bank (and brokerage) accounts come in various forms, but to be treated as jointly-held property for tax purposes each joint tenant must have the power (against the bank or broker) to withdraw the funds or property, and, on the death of one joint tenant the fund or property must be payable to the surviving joint tenant(s). The fact that a joint tenant who withdraws more than what she contributed (plus interest attributable thereto) may be liable over to the other co-depositor does not disqualify the arrangement from being a "joint tenancy" for tax purposes.

Whether a joint tenancy has been effectively created in the first instance is normally a question of property law. The description of title in the deed or other instrument is not necessarily conclusive. The intent of the creator(s) of the tenancy, perhaps ascertained by subsequent conduct, may ultimately be controlling. Nevertheless, state law provides various presumptions to fill evidentiary gaps concerning intent. Thus, if husband and wife create a joint tenancy in realty, the law might well presume a tenancy by the entireties. The litigated tax cases involve recitals in a deed or contract that the property is a joint tenancy, with the taxpayer arguing that the property is not really jointly-held property despite a state law presumption in favor of the efficacy of the recital. Most of the cases have held that the state law presumption favoring the joint tenancy was not overcome by evidence to the contrary.[3] In *Estate of Young v. Comm'r*, 110 T.C. 297 (1998), the issue was whether property designated as a joint tenancy under the deed was really community property. A state lower court decision held that it was community property, but the Tax Court held that the decision was erroneous under California statutory law, which required changes in the status of property made after 1984 to be in writing. In the case of U.S. Savings Bonds, registration as joint tenants is conclusive.[4]

An apparently unresolved issue is whether community property with right of survivorship (CPwRS) between husband and wife is jointly-held property or community property for tax purposes. The distinction is probably of little consequence for estate tax purposes, because half of the property would be included in the decedent spouse's estate in either event, and that half will qualify for the estate tax marital deduction because it passes to the surviving spouse automatically. However, under the income tax the distinction is significant, because all of the community property obtains a stepped-up (or stepped-down) basis under §1014(b)(6), whereas in the case of jointly-held property only the portion (in this case, half) of the property that is included in the decedent's gross estate qualifies for a §1014 basis (with the remaining portion obtaining a carryover basis). Our view is that CPwRS satisfies the requirements of §1014(b)(6), because (1) such property is community property up to the death of the first spouse to die (which essentially marks the termination of the community), and (2) half of the property will be included in the decedent spouse's gross estate.[5]

B. Gift Tax Treatment of the Creation and Termination of Joint Tenancies

Since any gift of an interest in a joint tenancy to one's spouse qualifies in full for the unlimited gift tax marital deduction under §2523, the gift tax treatment of the creation and termination of joint tenancies is significant only where a non-spousal joint tenancy is involved.

---

3. See *Lewis v. U.S.*, 485 F.2d 606 (Ct. Cl. 1973); *Wilson v. Comm'r*, 56 T.C. 579 (1971). But see *Estate of Chrysler v. Comm'r*, 361 F.2d 508 (2d Cir.1966).

4. *Chandler v. U.S.*, 410 U.S. 257 (1963) (*per curiam*).

5. In accord with this view is Jeremy Ware, *Section 1014(b)(6) and the Boundaries of Community Property*, 5 Nev. L.J. 704 (2005). But see Arthur Andrews, *Community Property with Right of Survivorship: Uneasy Lies the Head that Wears a Crown of Surviving Spouse for Federal Income Tax Basis Purposes*, 17 Va. Tax Rev. 577 (1998).

1. Creation of Joint-Ownership Property

There is no statutory provision prescribing how the creation of a joint tenancy in property is to be treated for gift tax purposes. (As used herein, the term "creation" also refers to improvements or additions, as well as to reductions of indebtedness.) Former Code §§2515 and 2515A dealt with specific situations involving joint tenancies, but these provisions were repealed in 1981 when the unlimited marital deduction was enacted. Thus, general gift tax principles currently control. Not surprisingly, the issue is approached by analyzing the various interests and powers that given away as opposed to those that are retained.

When a person purchases property in his and another's name as joint tenants in property, there is a "transfer" of the property subject to a "retention" (by virtue of the nature of a joint tenancy) in the donor of: (1) a retained right of survivorship (akin to a contingent reversion), (2) a retained right to current enjoyment as to one-half (or perhaps all or none) of the property, and (3) a retained power of severance (the setting aside of one-half in sole ownership). (The right of severance does not exist in a tenancy by the entireties between husband and wife, but tenancies by the entireties created by one spouse or both spouses do not raise gift tax issues because of the marital deduction.) In virtually all cases not involving spouses, the joint tenancy arrangement would entail rights of severance, and in that case the donor is deemed to make a gift of one-half of the property valued as of the time of gift. See Reg. §25.2511-1(h)(5) and -2(b)(1). The theory is that the donor has implicitly retained the right to "revoke" as to one-half, and, at the same time the donee has the power to obtain half of the property outright by exercising the right of severance.[6]

These rules are not affected by §2702 (dealing with retained-interest transfers), because that section only applies to "successive interest" transfers and not to "concurrent interest" transfers.[7]

Where two (or more) persons supply consideration for the purchase of property to be held by them as joint tenants, each person is effectively making gifts to the others to the extent their contributions exceed their pro-rata shares.

Example: A contributes $50K, B contributes $30K, and C contributes $10K for the purchase of Blackacre to be held by them as equal (one-third) joint tenants. Since the total purchase price is $90K, B paid exactly a third of the purchase price for a one-third interest, and is neither a donor nor a donee. A has made a gift of $20K to C.

Assuming (as is highly likely) that there is a right of severance, the gift qualifies for the present interest exclusion.[8]

---

6. See Reg. §25.2511-1(h)(5). In the rare case where rights of severance are absent, the value of the interest given away is computed by subtracting the actuarial value of retained interests. See Reg. §25.2512-2(b)(2).

7. See Reg. §25.2702-4(a).

8. If (as is highly unlikely) the right of severance does not exist, then the donee's current enjoyment interest must be valued for purposes of applying the exclusion. If the donee has no current enjoyment interest and possesses no right of severance, the exclusion is not available.

2. Creation of Joint Bank and Brokerage Accounts

Bank accounts with right of survivorship do not fit into the retained-interest-transfer mold of joint tenancies in property, because one or more persons have the power (against the bank or broker) to withdraw the entire fund during life. A brokerage account with right of survivorship registered in the name of a nominee of the brokerage firm is treated by the Service as being essentially the same (for tax purpose) as a bank account (and not as entailing interests in specific property).[9]

In some states it is possible to create a "self and survivor" bank account, in which only the depositor has a right of withdrawal during life. Here, there is no completed gift transfer, because the depositor can withdraw all of the funds and defeat the survivorship right, and the survivorship right of the donee might also be subject to the depositor's power to "alter" (change the identity of the survivorship beneficiary).

Where the account is of the "joint and survivor" type, in which each person named on the account can withdraw the account for her own benefit, deposits into the account are incomplete transfers because the depositor has a right of withdrawal. However, if a person on the account actually withdraws an amount greater than her *pro rata* share without having to account to the other account holders, the excess withdrawal is a gift from the account holders whose shares are diminished. Reg. §25.2511-1(h)(4).

3. Termination of Joint Ownership During Life

A joint-ownership arrangement might be terminated during the lifetime of the joint tenants. A termination results in a gift to the extent that the "proceeds of termination" received by a joint owner are less than what such tenant was "entitled to." The amount to which the recipient of proceeds is "entitled to" is a tax (rather than property) concept, and relates to the gift tax treatment of the creation of the joint ownership arrangement. Thus, assuming A supplied all the consideration for a severable joint tenancy held by A and B, then A and B are each "entitled to" one-half of the proceeds of termination, because the creation of the tenancy resulted in a gift from A to B of half of the consideration provided by A. If the creation involved a non-severable tenancy, the computation of the shares A and B are "entitled to" involves the use of actuarial factors appropriate for persons of the tenants' ages as of the date of termination (not the date of creation).[10] However, non-severable tenancies usually involve husband and wife, and any gifts on termination would qualify for the marital deduction, assuming the joint tenants are still married, and if the termination occurs by reason of divorce the transfer would likely be excluded under §2516 or the *Harris* doctrine, or possibly by a consideration offset.

---

9. See *Rev. Rul. 69-148*, 1969-1 C.B. 226.
10. See Reg. §25.2515-4(b).

Based on the foregoing (but ignoring divorce-related rules), a termination of a severable tenancy produces the following results:

(1) if the proceeds are split 50-50, neither party has made a gift;

(2) if the proceeds go all to the donee joint owner, the donor has made a present-interest gift of one-half; and

(3) if the proceeds revert to the donor, then the donee joint owner has made a present-interest gift of half back to the donor joint owner.

In a normal in-kind severance, with both tenants ending up as tenants in common, the proceeds received by each is half of the value of the property, resulting in no gift.

Since deposits and transfers into joint bank accounts (and street-name brokerage accounts) are incomplete transfers, what one is "entitled to" is the consideration provided by such person (plus accrued interest, dividends, and net gains). A withdrawal of less than what one is entitled to does not constitute a gift to the other, because the rest of one's share may be withdrawn later. As stated above, a gift occurs only where a party withdraws more than her share, and even then the other parties are deemed to make gifts only if their right to recover against the withdrawing party lapses, is waived, or does not exist.

A gift by all joint property owners of the entire joint tenancy property to one or more third parties simply involves a gift by each joint owner of his or her interest in the property. Assuming the tenancy was severable, each joint owner makes a gift of her *pro rata* share of the property to the donees.

C. Estate Tax Treatment of Joint-Ownership Arrangements

The estate tax treatment of "joint interests" is governed *exclusively* by §2040.[11] For this purpose, a joint interest is an interest in "property held jointly," which (under Reg. §20.2040-1(b)) refers to joint tenancies, tenancies by the entireties, and bank, bond, and brokerage accounts payable to any person named on the account or the survivor(s). Section 2040(a) applies to non-spousal joint tenancies, and §2040(b) applies to spousal joint tenancies.

A self-and-survivor bank (or brokerage) account, or a so-called Totten trust, would not be governed by §2040, because only one person has rights in the account prior to death. However, any such account would be included in the

---

11. It has been held that §2040 overrides its cognate transfer-retention cousins §§2036-2038. *Estate of Koussevitsky v. Comm'r*, 5 T.C. 650 (1945) (*acq.*). It has also been held that §2033 does not apply to a joint tenancy in specific property, on the ground that the decedent's interests in a joint tenancy expire at death. *Hernandez v. Becker*, 54 F.2d 542 (10th Cir.1931). One can speculate the extent to which §§2033, 2036-2038, and 2041 would apply if §2040 were repealed, but such speculation would be pointless, because it is assumed that §2040 is the exclusive position to apply where (and only where) a decedent was a joint tenant in a joint tenancy at death.

decedent account-owner's gross estate under §2038 (as a revocable transfer) or possibly under §2033 (on a constructive-ownership theory).[12]

1. Non-Spousal Joint Tenancies

Subsection (a) of §2040, which traces its ancestry back to the original 1916 estate tax, currently applies to joint-ownership arrangements between persons who are not married to each other.

Joint tenancies with rights of survivorship are a device to shift the ownership of property at death. Hence, it is not surprising that Congress has seen fit to provide that joint tenancy property is included in a deceased joint tenant's estate in appropriate circumstances and to an appropriate degree. Section 2040(a) follows a "transfer-retention" approach similar to that found in §§2036-2039. The interests and powers that are possessed by a joint tenant are conclusively deemed to be "strong" enough to require inclusion for that portion of the property that was "transferred" by the decedent joint tenant. Since joint tenancy property is usually acquired by purchase, a joint tenant is the "transferor" of the joint tenancy to the extent that he or she "supplied the consideration for" the acquisition and improvement of the property.

In operational terms, it follows that *the amount included in the gross estate of a decedent joint tenant under §2040(a) is simply the fraction (if any) of the joint-tenancy property or account that was "transferred" by the decedent.* Thus, where A purchases property entirely with her own funds and puts the property in the joint names of A and B with right of survivorship, the entire property is included in A's gross estate if she dies first, but nothing is includible in B's estate if he dies first. These results hold irrespective of what "interests" might be said to be owned by A and B *and irrespective of the gift tax treatment of the creation of the joint tenancy.*

The problematic aspect of §2040(a) from the practical point of view is that the entire consideration is *presumed* to have been supplied by the decedent joint tenant. Thus, no part of the property is excluded unless the decedent's personal representative can prove that the surviving joint tenant supplied part or all of the consideration. To make matters worse, under the first "provided" clause of §2040(a), the decedent's personal representative must be able to prove that any consideration that is shown to have been supplied by the surviving joint tenant was not received from the decedent by way of gift. The Service need not show any causal connection between the gift by the decedent and the use thereof by the survivor as consideration for the creation of the joint tenancy, or that the creation of the joint tenancy occurred within a certain period of time of the gift. These rules cause the creation of joint tenancies subject to §2040(a) to be a trap for the unwary: The estate of an "innocent" (i.e., nontransferor) joint tenant can be charged with the entire property.

---

12. Cf. *Northern Trust Co. v. U.S.*, 389 F.2d 731 (7th Cir.1968); *Estate of Garber v. Comm'r*, 271 F.2d 97 (3d Cir.1959); *Estate of Brooks v. Comm'r*, 50 T.C. 585 (1968) (*acq.*), holding that §2033 applied to a funded plan in which the decedent employee had withdrawal rights.

Various rules have evolved for calculating the consideration provided by the various joint tenants. Where the decedent made an *inter vivos* transfer of property in kind to the other tenant and such property was the consideration supplied by the latter, the amount of consideration attributed to the decedent is the value of the property at the time of the creation of the tenancy rather than the value at the earlier date of gift.[13] However, "income" from donated property is attributed to the donee.[14] Despite resistance from the Service, realized gains of the donee are treated as "income" attributable to the donee.[15]

A survivor who improved the property by making capital expenditures is deemed to have supplied consideration. Although there are various conceivable ways in which such consideration might be counted, Reg. §20.2040-1(a)(2) states that the amount excludible "is that portion of the entire [estate tax] value of the entire property which the consideration furnished by the other joint owner bears to the total cost of acquisition and capital additions." This "cost" approach, reaffirmed by *Rev. Rul. 81-183*, 1983-2 C.B. 180, leaves out of account the time the improvements were made and whether the improvements appreciated or depreciated at a rate differently from that of the entire property.

It is quite common for mortgages to be placed on jointly-held real property. In *Rev. Rul. 79-302*, 1979-2 C.B. 328, X and Y purchased a residence in 1974 as joint tenants for $100,000, with each of them paying $10,000 in cash, the balance of $80,000 being financed by a mortgage on which they were jointly and severally liable. Subsequently, X made all mortgage payments, in a total principal amount of $20,000, until X died in 1978, at which time the outstanding mortgage balance was $60,000. Since X and Y were jointly and severally liable on the mortgage, each of them was liable for the entire debt, but, if one of them was required to satisfy more than one-half of the debt, that tenant would be entitled to contribution from the other tenant. The Service held that the initial assumption of joint and several liability constituted a contribution by each tenant to the purchase price to the extent of one-half of the mortgage liability amount, but that subsequent payments of mortgage principal are counted as contributions of the payer. Therefore, Y's total contribution was the sum of her actual payments (here, $10,000) and one-half of the mortgage indebtedness that remained outstanding at A's death (here, half of $60,000, or $30,000). Thus, 60 percent of the estate tax value of the property was included in X's gross estate. (Also, half of the mortgage of $60,000 — $30,000 — was deductible by X's estate under §2053.)

Initially, the Service resisted the notion that the value of services could be treated as consideration provided by the survivor tenant.[16] The Service now accepts this notion, at least where the survivor and the decedent were service

---

13. See Reg. §20.2040-1(c)(4) & (5).

14. *Rev. Rul.* 79-372, 1979-2 C.B. 330 (dealing with realized gains). Compare *Tuck v. U.S.*, 282 F.2d 405 (9th Cir.1960), with *Rev. Rul.* 80-142, 1980-1 C.B. 197 (both involving stock dividends).

15. See *Estate of Goldsborough v. Comm'r*, 70 T.C. 1077 (1978) (*acq.*), *aff'd*, 49 A.F.T.R.2d (RIA) 1469 (4th Cir.1982).

16. *Rogan v. Kammerdiner*, 140 F.2d 569 (9th Cir.1944).

partners, agreeing to share the profits, and state law recognizes that the survivor has a property interest in the business.[17] This issue is now largely moot, as all of the cases dealing with this issue involved husband and wife, where consideration is no longer an issue.[18]

2. Spousal Joint Tenancies

Under §2040(b), added to the Code in 1976, an entirely different approach is adopted for joint tenancies exclusively between spouses. The rule is very simple: Upon the death of the first spouse to die, one-half of the value of the property is includible in his or her gross estate. This rule posits absolutely no significance on who "transferred" the joint-tenancy property.

The inclusion of one-half is offset by a marital deduction in an equal amount.

3. Joint Tenancies Created by Third Parties

A §2033-like "ownership" (pro-rata, or fractional interest) approach is followed where the consideration for the property is shown to have been supplied entirely by persons other than the joint tenants. See §2040(a) (the "provided further" clause). Thus, where none of three joint tenants paid consideration for their joint-tenancy interests, one-third of the value of the property is included in the gross estate of the first joint tenant to die.

4. Valuation of Included Portion

In *Estate of Young v. Comm'r*, 110 T.C. 297 (1998), the estate of a deceased spouse argued that a minority interest discount should be granted because the deceased only had a non-controlling interest, as joint tenant, in the property before death. The Tax Court held that no minority discount should be allowed because death resulted in fee simple ownership by the survivor. The Tax Court distinguished cases that granted a minority discount to a community property interest or an interest of a tenant in common where the bequeathed interest caused the legatee to end up with a fee interest or controlling interest. "The fractional interest discount, as applied in §2033, is based on the notion that the interest is worth less than its proportionate share, due in part to the problems of concurrent ownership. These problems are created by the unity of interest and unity of possession. However, at the moment of death, the co-ownership in joint tenancy is severed, thus alleviating the problems associated with co-ownership. We conclude that the Young Property is not entitled to a fractional interest discount." Id. at 316.

---

17. *P.L.R.* 7907098 (Nov. 7, 1978), citing *Berkowitz v. Comm'r*, 108 F.2d 319 (3d Cir.1939); *U.S. v. Neal*, 235 F.2d 395 (10th Cir.1956); and *Otte v. Comm'r*, T.C. Memo. 1972-76.

18. It would still be an issue for joint tenancies between husband and wife created before 1977, which are still governed by §2040(a). See *Gallenstein v. U.S.*, 975 F.2d 286 (6th Cir.1992); *Hahn v. Comm'r*, 110 T.C. 140 (1998).

5. Income Tax Basis

The percentage of the property that is included in a deceased joint owner's gross estate acquires a §1014 basis. The remaining percentage of the property has whatever basis existed prior to such death, on the theory that the survivor(s) already had acquired that percentage by purchase or gift.

D. Avoiding §2040

In order for §2040 to apply, a decedent must own an interest as joint tenant at death. Estate planners seek to avoid the possible application of §2040(a), where the parties are wealthy enough to be at risk of estate tax exposure, because of presumptions in favor of including the full value of the property in the estate of the first joint tenant to die. To avoid §2040(a), the joint tenancy might be terminated or the interest might be given to a third party.

1. Surrender Within Three Years of Death

The surrender of one's status as a joint tenant (by gift or termination) within three years of death does not cause §2040 to be applied as if the surrender had not occurred. See §2035(a), which makes no reference to §2040. In other words, the surrender is effective to avoid §2040.

2. Terminations and Transfers to Avoid §2040(a)

Suppose A and B (who are not married) desire to acquire residential real property for $100K with the entire consideration to be supplied by A, but with A intending to remove half of the property from his §2040(a) gross estate. The notion of first giving $50K to B, followed by the acquisition of the property by A and B as joint tenants, would not work because the $50K contribution of B is traceable to A, and the entire property could be included in A's gross estate under §2040(a).

A can make annual gifts of cash to B that come within the annual exclusion, and then A and B can acquire the property as joint tenants. Another possibility is for A to supply the down payment, with A and B taking a mortgage. (When A provides all of the down payment, A makes a gift to B of one-half of that amount.) Subsequently, the joint tenancy can be terminated into equal shares. This second move entails no gifts, because each of A and B is taking what they already are entitled to. Each of A and B would then own separate properties or would own 50 percent interests as tenants in common.

Alternatively, A and B could make gifts of their one-half interests to third parties (or perhaps to an irrevocable trust). Each of them would be the donor of 50 percent of the property for gift and estate tax purposes.[19]

---

19. More complex variations of this technique succeeded in *Glaser v. U.S.*, 306 F.2d 57 (7th Cir.1962); *U.S. v. Heasty*, 370 F.2d 525 (10th Cir.1966); and *Rev. Rul.* 69-577, 1969-2 C.B. 173. However, in *Estate of Hornor v. Comm'r*, 305 F.2d 769 (3d Cir.1962), a transfer of joint-tenancy property into a revocable trust was ineffective to defeat §2040(a).

QUICK QUESTIONS

1. Wilenda purchased income producing real property for $2M and had title placed in the names of Alice, Barbara, and Cristina, her three sisters, as joint tenants with the right of survivorship. On the death of Wilenda, the property was worth $3M. On the death of Alice, the property was worth $4M. On the death of Barbara, the property was worth $5M. Which one of the following statements is *TRUE*?

   A. Wilenda did not make any taxable gifts at the time of the transfer.
   B. Wilenda made taxable gifts of $2M.
   C. Wilenda made taxable gifts of $2M less three annual exclusions.
   D. Wilenda made a gift of $5M.

2. Which one of the following statements is *TRUE*?

   A. Zero is included in Wilenda's estate when she dies.
   B. $3M is included in Wilenda's estate when she dies.
   C. $4M is included in Wilenda's estate when she dies.
   D. $2M is included in Wilenda's estate when she dies.

3. Which one of the following statements is *TRUE*?

   A. Zero is included in Alice's estate when she dies.
   B. $4M is included in Alice's estate when she dies.
   C. One-third of $4M is included in Alice's estate when she dies.
   D. One-half of $4M is included in Alice's estate when she dies.

PROBLEMS, QUESTIONS, AND NOTES

1. a. What gift and estate tax results where A supplies $10,000 and B $20,000 for the year 2000 purchase of a personal residence for $30,000. The property is worth $180,000 at the death of A. Assume that A and B are not married.
   b. Same as above, except that B pays $20,000 to construct a garage on the premises in 2007.
   c. Same as (a), except that the initial the purchase price was $100,000, and $70,000 of the purchase price was financed by a mortgage loan on which A and B were jointly and severally liable. What if $10,000 of the principal of such loan had been paid by A at the time of the death of the first of them to die?
   d. Same as (a) and (b), except that A and B are married.
2. a. The creation of a joint tenancy by one joint tenant entails a gift for gift tax purposes to the other joint tenant (assuming the two aren't married). If the donee tenant dies first, there is a risk that the property will be included in

the donee's gross estate because of the §2040(a) presumptions. Upon the death of the donee joint tenant, the property comes back to the donor tenant by way of the right of survivorship. Unless the donor disposes of the property, it will be included in the donor's gross estate under §2033. If the donor died shortly after the donee, the donor's estate would be eligible for the §2013 credit on account of previously taxed transfers. However, the initial gift by the donor will not be removed from the donor's cumulative tax base under the adjusted-taxable-gift exclusion of §2001(b), because that exclusion does not apply where the property is included in the gross estate under §2033 (because what is included in the gross estate is the property, not the "gift"). Hence the same property is taxed twice to the donor tenant. This kind of double taxation of the same property occurs in any case where a donor obtains gift property back by gift, bequest, reversion, or purchase.

b. If X supplies the consideration for the purchase of property in which X and Y are joint tenants, and X dies first, X will be charged with a gift on the creation of the joint tenancy *and* the entire value of the property will be included in X's gross estate. This time the adjusted taxable gifts exclusion will be available to X's estate, because the §2040(a) inclusion in the gross estate is by reason of the *gift* (of a certain type that resulted in estate inclusion). To generalize, *the adjusted taxable gift exclusion is available for any interest in property that was the subject of a taxable gift and also included in the gross estate by reason of any of §§2036-2040.*

3. Suppose H and W acquired Blackacre as a joint tenancy for $40,000, and H dies when the property is worth $100,000. What is W's basis in Blackacre? What if Blackacre were community property? Community property with right of survivorship?

4. a. Is a self-and-survivor account included in the account owner's gross estate under §2040(a)? §2038? §2033?

   b. In the absence of §2040, would a joint-and-survivor account be includible in a decedent's gross estate under §2033? Only if the decedent contributed the entire fund? Note that the decedent could have withdrawn the entire fund during life, and that same fund is acceded to by the beneficiary. Is a right of survivorship any different (for tax purposes) than a forced heirship provision of a state probate code?

5. The Service originally took the position that a survivorship interest in joint-tenancy property could only be the subject of a qualified disclaimer under §2518 within nine months of the *creation* of the joint tenancy. But several cases, including *Kennedy v. Comm'r*, 804 F.2d 1332 (7th Cir. 1986), held that the §2518 time period should start to run as of the date of the death of the first joint tenant, on the theory that, prior to the death of the first joint tenant, the other joint tenant had no "survivorship interest" in the property on account of the fact that the decedent joint tenant could have severed the tenancy and defeated the survivorship interest. The Treasury has acquiesced, even though the rationale of these cases isn't very compelling (the survivorship interest exists but is subject to a condition subsequent). The severance interest is

separate from the survivorship interest, and must be disclaimed within nine months of its creation. In the case of joint bank (and brokerage) accounts, the survivor is deemed to have acquired no disclaimable interests at all until the depositor's death. See generally Reg. §25.2518-2(c)(4), effective for disclaimers made after 1997.

§5.3. Commercial Annuities

This section deals with commercial annuities. So-called "private annuities" are dealt with in Chapter 8.

A. *Nature and Function of Commercial Annuities*

A commercial annuity is an investment contract entered into with an insurance company or other financial institution, under which a person pays premiums in return for a promise of the company to make periodic payments (starting, usually, at a future date, such as a normal retirement age) to the person and, possibly, to the person's beneficiary, for life or possibly for a term of years. A commercial annuity may be thought of as a self-funded retirement plan that both grows (with the earning of interest) and shrinks (as payments are received) until the fund is exhausted. The idea of an annuity for one or more lives is to insure against the "risk" of living too long (and exhausting one's savings). An investor in an annuity obtains an "actuarial" return (apart from the "investment" return) by outliving one's life expectancy. Of course, there is also the risk, by dying prematurely, of an actuarial loss.

The economic essence of a fixed annuity is that the amounts receivable are a fixed (and constant) dollar amount, as opposed to a right to "income" from some source, or a right to a fixed percentage of principal. Since annuities involve "level" payments (in the manner of the typical mortgage loan) that terminate upon an ascertainable date or event, usually without a lump-sum recovery of principal at the back end, the original investment is exhausted with the passage of time, and each annuity payment consists of both an "income" component and a "principal" component for income tax purposes.

Annuities that provide for payments that vary in amount are called "variable" annuities, but otherwise, variable annuities possess the same characteristics as fixed annuities.

The following classification of annuities is relevant for the federal transfer taxes:

(1) Single Life Annuity. A single life annuity is one where payments cease upon the death of the sole annuitant (who paid the premiums).

(2) Refund Annuity. A "refund annuity" is designed to "refund" all or part of the annuitant's "principal" in case she predeceases her expected life expectancy. The refund goes to his estate or to a designated beneficiary in a lump sum.

(3) Survivor Annuity. In a self-and-survivor annuity, payments are made to the (primary) annuitant for life and then to a (survivor) beneficiary for life or for a term of years. A "joint-and-survivor annuity" is one where payments are made to two annuitants on a 50-50 basis during their joint lives, then all to the survivor for life (or a period of years).

Survivor annuities typically allow the owner to change the identity of the beneficiary. Since commercial annuities are funded insurance products, the owner is likely to have the power to make withdrawals (or borrow) up to the cash surrender value prior to the annuity starting date.

Although survivor annuities superficially resemble joint tenancies, they are not interests in specific property or in a specific fund. Instead, they are contractual arrangements having an investment flavor with (in any refund or survivorship feature) an incidental testamentary character.

B. Gift Tax Treatment of Commercial Annuities

The purchase of a commercial annuity combined with the designation of a survivor beneficiary rarely would involve a completed transfer for gift tax purposes, because any survivorship feature is either payable to the purchaser's estate or else the purchaser would retain the power to change any beneficiary designation. Also, the owner has the power to terminate or cash in the annuity, which amounts to a power to "revoke."

Nevertheless, a paid-up annuity contract can be the subject of a completed gift, perhaps to an irrevocable trust. (Such gifts are uncommon, because the primary purpose of an annuity is to insure against the primary annuitant's longevity). The gift tax value is what the issuing company would charge for the same annuity if sold to a person of the annuitant's age and sex at the time of gift.[20]

Under the "contract right" rule of Reg. §25.2503-3(a), the gift qualifies for the present interest exclusion if the donee is an individual, even though annuity payments are not to commence until the future. If the donee is an irrevocable trust, the status of the exclusion depends upon the terms of the trust. Thus, if the annuity is not to commence until a certain date, there cannot be a present interest gift unless the income beneficiary of the trust can compel the trustee to cash in the annuity and invest the proceeds in income-producing property.

C. Estate Tax Treatment of Commercial Annuities

A single life annuity is not included in the annuitant's gross estate under §2033, because, like a life estate, it expires at the annuitant's death. Of course, annuity payments received prior to death and which have not been expended on consumption have augmented the annuitant's §2033 gross estate.

---

20. See Reg. §25.2512-6(a).

Refunds (payable to an annuitant's estate) and survivor benefits amount to testamentary transfers, but they avoid inclusion under §2033 because the estate or successor does not succeed to a fund owned by the decedent but instead takes under a third-party beneficiary contract right that comes into possession at a decedent's death. Nor are these contracts covered by §2040, because they are not joint tenancies. Prior to 1954, commercial annuities with refund or survivorship features were commonly included in the gross estate of the deceased annuitant under the predecessors of §§2036, 2037, and 2038. Nevertheless, Congress added §2039(a) to the Code in 1954 because of the awkwardness of fitting annuities (and especially employee survivor benefits) within §§2036-2038. Section 2039 is modeled closely on §2036(a)(1), which typically applies to irrevocable gifts (outright or in trust) in which the donor retains the income, possession, or enjoyment of the transferred property for life (etc.). The requirements for the application of §2039 are as follows:

(1) the decedent must have been receiving annuity payments (or must have had a right to such payments commencing in the future), either alone or in conjunction with another, for life (etc.);

(2) there must be a payment or an annuity payable to any beneficiary (including the decedent's estate, as under a refund annuity); and

(3) the decedent must have been the transferor of the annuity.

There are two principal features of §2039 that deviate from §2036(a). First, under §2039(b), the "transfer" requirement is replaced by a "purchase price" concept similar to the "consideration" principle found in §2040(a). In virtually all cases the premiums will have been paid by the primary annuitant who is the decedent. However, if the annuity is community property, the decedent's spouse will be treated as having paid half of the premiums, and only half of the value of the contract will be included in the deceased annuitant's gross estate.

Second, §2039 eliminates the "retention in the property transferred" requirement found in §2036(a). Instead, §2039 only requires that the decedent's rights and the survivor's rights exist under a common "contract or agreement."

The amount includible is the value of whatever rights pass to beneficiaries multiplied by a percentage which represents the consideration supplied by the decedent. Except in the case of community property, the deceased primary annuitant is usually the one who supplied all of the consideration. The value of a refund feature is relatively easy to determine, because it is a right to a lump-sum payment. The value of a survivor annuity is the amount that the company would charge at the date of the primary annuitant's death to purchase that annuity.[21] If that amount cannot be ascertained, the "annuity" table in the actuarial tables would be used.

---

21. See Reg. §20.2031-8(a)(3), Ex. 1.

Section 2039 is fairly airtight as it applies to commercial refund and survivor annuities, and there appears to be little tax-avoidance activity in this area.

Lotteries are often structured like commercial annuities. If a lottery makes periodic payments to the winner, followed by payments to the winner's heirs or beneficiaries, the survivor benefit is included in the winner's gross estate under §2039.[22]

D. Annuity-Insurance Combinations

A possible way of avoiding §2039 might be to acquire separate single-life annuity and life insurance contracts, and then to make an irrevocable gift of the insurance policy, retaining the single life annuity. The idea would be that the proceeds of the life insurance policy would not be included in the decedent's gross estate (under §2042, the principal estate tax provision dealing with life insurance), because the decedent had parted with all rights and interests therein prior to death, and the single life annuity would not be includible because it terminates on the decedent's death. Of course, the gift of the life insurance policy would be subject to gift tax.

Just such an arrangement was considered by the Supreme Court in *Fidelity-Philadelphia Trust Co. v. Smith*, 356 U.S. 274 (1958). The facts of that case arose before §2039 was enacted, but the government contended that §2036(a)(1) applied. However, the Supreme Court disagreed, on the ground that the annuity was not retained "in the transferred property" (the insurance policy), because the annuity and insurance policy were "economically" independent contracts.

The case below dealt with virtually the same fact situation under §2039. Note that §2039(a) contains an exception for insurance on the life of the decedent.

Estate of Montgomery v. Commissioner

56 T.C. 489 (1971), aff'd per curiam, 458 F.2d 616 (5th Cir.1972), cert. denied, 409 U.S. 849.

WITHEY, *Judge*: [Decedent in May of 1964 acquired an insurance-annuity combination from National Life Insurance Co. similar to that involved in *Fidelity-Philadelphia Trust Co. v. Smith* and assigned the insurance policies to irrevocable trusts. The annuity premium was $2.2 million. The insurance pro-ceeds amount was $2 million, the premiums of which totaled about $265,000 per year, which amount was paid by the trustees from funds given to the trusts annually by decedent. Under the annuity, decedent was to receive about $272,000 per year over his remaining life. No refund of premium was to be made thereafter nor was any provision made for survivorship benefits. The decedent died in October of 1964 at age 75.]

[The parties] carried through the above as an integrated transaction.

---

22. See *Estate of Shackleford v. U.S.*, 262 F.3d 1028 (9th Cir.2001).

Respondent's contention is that the "life insurance" herein is not life insurance within the meaning of the parenthetical exception contained in §2039; that therefore the proceeds of "life insurance" policies herein are includible in decedent's gross estate [under §2039(a)].

The word "insurance" is not defined in the Code or regulations and we therefore resort to case law for its definition. The word has been discussed by the Supreme Court with respect to annuity-insurance combinations in *Helvering v. LeGierse*, 312 U.S. 531 (1941). The test in determining whether the integrated transactions before us involved life insurance is whether National in settling its obligations thereunder was exposed to a financial loss [if the decedent were to die prematurely]. It is true that on an annual basis, National was bound to pay decedent [about] $6,000 as annuity payments more than it received as premium payments on "life insurance policies," but the only risk involved was an investment risk, for it had received from decedent as the price of the annuity the amount of $2.2 million which it was free to invest, to say nothing of the so-called insurance premiums. Even invested at 1 percent, interest on that amount would far exceed the $6,000.

Having concluded [that the integrated transaction did not involve "insurance"], it is clear that §2039 applies. It is stipulated that decedent, under the annuity contract, not only possessed the right but actually did receive monthly annuity payments which ceased with the last such payment prior to his death. His grandchildren, who were beneficiaries of the two trusts, each received in trust an "other payment" in the form of insurance proceeds by reason of surviving the decedent. The transaction grew out of an understanding or agreement between decedent, National, and the trustees of the trusts which in our view fits the statutory phrase "under any form of contract or agreement."

The only authority relied on by petitioner is *Fidelity-Philadelphia Trust Co. v. Smith*. Section 2039, relating as it does specifically to "an annuity or other payment" did not exist at the date of the transaction which gave rise to that decision, and for that reason the decision is not controlling. It is true that the Supreme Court found that an insurance-annuity arrangement, to some extent the same as that before us, involved two separate items of property which were not to be aggregated under §2036(a)(1), but even though the annuity and the insurance policies here might be said to have separate entities and values, they each came into being as the result of a single integrated "form of contract or agreement" not dealt with in the Code until the advent of §2039.

E. Valuation of Lottery Payments Included Under §2039

An issue with survivor benefits under lotteries is whether the restriction on assignability justifies a discount from the actuarial (present) value of the benefit. The circuit courts are now evenly split on this issue. Upholding the use of the tables are *Negron v. U.S.*, 553 F.3d 1013 (6th Cir.2009); *Anthony v. U.S.*, 520 F.3d 374 (5th Cir.2008); and *Cook v. Comm'r*, 349 F.3d 850 (5th Cir.2003). Allowing a discount for nonmarketability are *Estate of Gribauskas v. Comm'r*, 342 F.3d 85 (2d Cir.2003), *rev'g* 116 T.C. 142, 164 (2001); and *Shackleford v. U.S.*, 262 F.3d 1028

(9th Cir.2001).[23] The facts in these cases are virtually identical: The decedent won the lottery, but died before receiving all of the installment payments.[24] Each state had legislation prohibiting the sale or assignment of the right to future lottery winnings. No state had ever defaulted on any payments to its lottery winners. The rationale of the Fifth and Sixth Circuits was that (1) §7520 requires annuities to be valued by means of the actuarial tables, (2) nonmarketability is assumed in the tables, and (3), since there was virtually no possibility that the lottery payments would not be made, there was no reason to depart from the use of the tables. "The non-marketability of a private annuity is an assumption underlying the annuity tables. For example, the value of survivor annuities payable under qualified plans (transfer of which is prohibited by ERISA); charitable remainder annuity trusts; and grantor retained annuity trusts (GRATS), which are not marketable, are determined by use of the tables." *Cook*, at 856. By contrast, the Second and Ninth Circuits held that the values calculated under the actuarial tables were so unreasonable that a discount was warranted. "The governing principle is that a departure is allowed if the tables produce a substantially unrealistic and unreasonable result." *Gribauskas*, at 88-89. "[I]f the taxpayer proves that a more realistic and reasonable valuation method exists that more closely approximates fair market value, courts are free to employ it." *Shackleford*, at 1033.

PROBLEMS, QUESTIONS, AND NOTES

1. a. Is a nonrefund single-life annuity an effective tax avoidance device? Is it includible under any of §§2033, 2039(a), or 2040(a)? Is there any situation in which one would recommend putting a substantial portion of a client's investments in this form?

   b. A "refund" annuity is purchased by Quentin, under which Quentin is to receive payments for life, starting on his 55th birthday, but if he dies before recovering his "investment" a lump sum (determined by a formula) will be paid to his estate. Assume Quentin dies before reaching the age of 55. Is the refund feature includible in his estate under §§2033 or 2039(a)?

2. a. The holding of *Estate of Montgomery* can be avoided by acquiring a life insurance policy and a single life annuity from separate companies.

---

23. *Estate of Donovan v. U.S.*, 2005-1 U.S. Tax Cas. (CCH) ¶ 50,322; 2005-1 U.S. Tax Cas. (CCH) ¶ 60,500; 95 A.F.T.R.2d (RIA) 2131 (D. Mass. 2005); and *Davis v. U.S.*, 97 A.F.T.R.2d (RIA) 332, 2006-1 U.S. Tax Cas. (CCH) ¶ 60,514 (D.N.H. 2005), *reconsideration granted in part*, 97 A.F.T.R.2d (RIA) 824 (D.N.H. 2006), judgment entered at 491 F. Supp. 2d 192 (D.N.H. 2007), are two district court decisions in the First Circuit that, on different rationales, have upheld the use of the actuarial tables. *Estate of Donovan* followed the reasoning in *Cook*. *Davis* adopted the test in *Shackleford*, but held that the decedent had not proved that the value calculated under the actuarial tables was so unrealistic and unreasonable to merit a exception.

24. *Anthony* involved the estate tax value of an unmarketable structured settlement of a personal injury claim from an auto accident; those payments were characterized as an annuity includible under §2039.

However, by acquiring them from a single company, the company would not impose a charge for actuarial risk. (Why not?) The arrangement in *Estate of Montgomery* was a bad investment for the decedent as it was. (How so?) Buying separate policies from different companies would be an even worse investment. (Why?) Since the decedent in *Montgomery* was 74 or 75 when the deal was entered into, it is evident that the $2.2M premium "for the annuity" was really the single premium for the life insurance policy. A person in her 60s (or older) would probably have to pay a single premium for either an annuity or a life insurance policy if acquired separately. In *Montgomery*, the real annuity premium was only slightly less than the annuity payment.

    b. Even if the $2M "insurance" proceeds had avoided inclusion under §2039 (or §2035(a)), would the arrangement have been an estate planning success? What is the moral of this story?

    c. An additional risk in the *Montgomery* type of scenario is posed by §2035: A gift of a life insurance policy within three years of death is ineffective to avoid §2042(2), resulting in the inclusion in the insured's gross estate of the insurance proceeds.

3. Annuity-insurance combinations spanning two or more generations are treated as the equivalent of generation-skipping trusts. §2652(b)(3).

4. A so-called "private annuity" transaction is one where parent (say) "sells" property to daughter in return for daughter's promise to pay an annuity to the parent for life. The annuity payments are set at that amount which results in the value of the annuity being equal the value of the property transferred. Thus, for gift tax purposes the transfer is for full and adequate consideration in money or money's worth. Why is §2039 inapplicable to this transaction? (Other aspects of this transaction are explored in Chapter 8.)

5. a. Survivor annuities are treated as IRD rights for income tax purposes. Hence the beneficiary simply takes over the decedent's (remaining) basis. See §§691(d) and 1014(c).

    b. After the annuity starting date, "basis recovery" is dealt with by §72(a)-(c). Basically, basis (the aggregate of net premiums paid) is "amortized" among the payments received on a ratable basis. Specifically, each annuity payment received is deemed to be a tax-free return of basis in the ratio that the annuitant's basis (referred to as the "investment in the contract") bears to the total amounts to be received under the contract (the "expected return"). The expected return is an amount equal to the annual payment under the contract times the number of years (and fractions thereof) the payments are expected to be made, calculated on an actuarial basis. The expected return amount is not discounted to present value. Both the "expected return" and the "investment in the contract" are determined as of the date the annuity payments commence (the "annuity starting date"). In the case of a "refund" annuity, an amount which represents the present value of the refund feature is subtracted from the "investment in the contract."

    c. After the entire basis has been recovered, all payments are treated as "income." If the annuitant dies before the basis has been fully recovered, the annuitant can deduct as an ordinary loss on his or her final return the amount of such unrecovered basis. See §72(b)(2) & (3).

d. Withdrawals prior to the annuity starting date are governed by §72(e). Basically, any withdrawal is deemed to come first out of income (excess of cash surrender value over the investment in the contract), with any excess coming out of principal (as a tax-free basis recovery).

§5.4. Survivor Benefits Under Employee Plans

This section deals with the transfer tax treatment of benefits payable to designated survivors of a decedent employee by an employer under a contract or plan with the employer. Such benefits are herein referred to as (employee) survivor (or death) benefits. Also discussed herein are kindred arrangements, such as individual retirement accounts (IRAs) and Social Security retirement benefits.

A. *Characteristics and Income Tax Treatment of Employee Plans and Survivor Benefits*

Employee survivor benefits arise as a matter of contract between an employee and an employer or under a "plan," the consideration being the employee's past, present, and/or future services. The survivor benefit is payable to one or more designated beneficiaries, and is often paid in the form of annuity, but might also be payable in a lump sum.

Usually, if not always, the survivor benefit is part of a package that includes a pension, retirement benefit, or other form of deferred compensation.

Employee contracts and plans providing for survivor benefits are either funded or unfunded. A *funded* plan involves employer and/or employee contributions that are regularly paid into a trust (or perhaps used to purchase annuity and insurance contracts), and the trust (or contract) is the source of payments to employees and their beneficiaries. An *unfunded* plan involves only an unsecured contractual promise to pay benefits to employees and their beneficiaries.

Benefits are either "vested" or "non-vested." A vested benefit is one that the employee (or beneficiary) has a "right" to receive, although enjoyment of the benefit may be delayed (such as when the employee reaches the age of 65 or dies). A non-vested benefit is one that can become vested only if one or more contingencies are satisfied (such as the employee not being terminated).

The basic features of contracts and plans providing for employee survivor benefits are dictated by federal law, mainly, ERISA (Employee Retirement Income Security Act of 1974, as amended), part of which appears in income tax provisions of the Internal Revenue Code. There are three main income tax categories: (1) qualified plans, (2) nonqualified arrangements, and (3) IRAs. This area is highly complex, and the description below is somewhat abbreviated.

1. Qualified Plans

A "qualified" plan is one that meets the various qualification requirements imposed by the portion of ERISA that appears as §§401-419 of the Internal Revenue Code. The purpose of Congress in enabling employers to create qualified plans was to provide an incentive, through the income tax system, for employers to provide retirement plans to broad classifications of employees. Employers are not required to offer qualified plans, but income tax benefits accrue to employers and employees under qualified plans. Since the qualification requirements are burdensome to employers, it can be said that (as a business decision) qualification serves no purpose *except* to obtain and retain employees through income tax benefits that would not otherwise be available.

The following favorable income tax treatment (relative to that of nonqualified arrangements) is obtained through qualified plans:

(1) employer contributions to the trust are *currently* deductible by the employer (up to a certain per year limit) *and* are currently excludible from the gross income of the employee;

(2) income earned by the trust is not taxed, because a qualified-plan trust is a tax-exempt entity; and,

(3) payouts are taxable to the payees in excess of basis (basis is usually zero, or low, because of the earlier income exclusions).

The actual qualification requirements (which, from the vantage of Congress, operate as a regulatory mechanism) are far beyond the scope of these materials, but (roughly speaking) they deal with such matters as the eligibility of employees, the minimum funding (and security) of plans, the methods of payout, the making of loans to participants, the portability of plans, and the termination of plans. A plan cannot be a qualified plan unless it is a "funded" plan. Qualified plans must usually provide for the early vesting of benefits and for prohibiting discrimination in favor of officers and highly compensated employees. There are also rules relating to the earliest and latest times that benefits can commence, the "rate" of payouts, and the latest time that benefits must terminate.

The default payout mode for qualified plans (other than certain defined contribution plans) is that benefits are to be paid in the form of a single life annuity. If the employee is married, benefits are to be paid in the form of an annuity for the employee followed by a life annuity for the surviving spouse. However, this latter requirement (known, somewhat inaccurately as the "joint-and-survivor annuity rule") can be waived if the employee's spouse files an informed consent. See §§401(a)(11) and 417. As previously noted in Chapter 3, such a waiver is not treated as a gift for gift tax purposes. §2503(f).

Retirement plans (qualified and nonqualified) are classified according to whether it is the contributions or the benefits that are specified. One category is the "defined benefit plan," which provides for partial-wage-placement annuity-type pension benefits according to a formula specified in advance. (A typical formula would provide an annual benefit equal to a percentage, based on years of service, of the employee's average wage for the last five years of service.) Here it is up to the employer to make contributions and investments of contributions that will produce the required benefits. The other category is the "defined contribution plan," in which the amount of the periodic contributions into the trust is specified in advance. Here, the contributions (as invested) create what is essentially a personal investment account available for retirement and beyond. (The employee bears the investment risk in a defined contribution plan.) A "section 401(k) plan" is a special kind of defined contribution plan.

2. Individual Retirement Accounts

An IRA is an investment account held in trust and managed by a financial institution or insurance company on behalf of an individual. An IRA is funded with an individual's own contributions, rather by those of an employer, but the individual can make (deductible) contributions only if employed (or self-employed). Thus, an IRA is essentially an individual-employee qualified plan for either low or moderate wage employees (due to the income phaseouts, which in 2011 allow a partial deduction for unmarried and head of household taxpayers with a modified AGI between more than $56,000 and $66,000 and for married taxpayers filing jointly with a modified AGI between more than $90,000 and $110,000 before elimination of deductible contributions at $110,000 and $66,000, respectively) or persons receiving income from personal services who are not covered by a qualified plan.[25]

The income tax treatment of an IRA parallels that of a qualified employer plan: (1) contributions by the individual to the account are deductible up to a (low) annual limit; (2) income within the account is exempt as it accumulates; and (3) payouts in excess of basis are taxable. See §§219 and 408. An account that is funded solely by deductible contributions and tax-exempt income will have a zero basis.

An individual can also make nondeductible contributions to an IRA, either by so electing "within" the deduction limitation (for 2011, $5,000, or $6,000 if over age 50) or by making contributions in excess of said limitation. Nondeductible contributions create basis that can be recovered as includible pay-outs are received. All IRA distributions will be taxed unless an individual files Form 8606 to designate contributions as nondeductible or otherwise proves that non-deductible contributions were made.

A "Roth IRA" is an individual retirement account which is the recipient of only nondeductible contributions (up to a limit), but income accruals and payouts are wholly tax free. See §408A. For 2011, if your modified AGI is more than $122,000 (unmarried or head of household) or $179,000 (married filing jointly or widow(er)), you cannot make a contribution to a Roth IRA and phaseouts begin, respectively, at $107,000 or $169,000.

There are "hybrid" arrangements that combine qualified plans and IRAs, known as simplified employee pensions (SEPs) and simplified employee accounts

---

25. See §219(b), (f) & (g).

(SEAs). Here an employer makes deductible contributions (up to a limit that is higher than a regular IRA) to an IRA. The contributions are excluded by the employee, the inside build up is tax free, and the payouts are fully taxable. See §§219(b)(2), 404(h)(1)(C), and 408(k) & (p).

3. Nonqualified Plans

A nonqualified arrangement is any arrangement other than a qualified plan, an IRA, or a Roth IRA. Nonqualified arrangements need not be funded. Such arrangements do not receive any special tax benefits and are mostly outside the scope of ERISA. They can be individually tailored to suit the needs of the parties, and are often offered only to high-ranking officers.

The income tax treatment of nonqualified arrangements basically hinges on whether the benefits are funded or nonfunded. Funded arrangements are subject to the rules of §83, by way of §402(b), which means that employer contributions are includible by the employee at the time the employee's rights first become vested (cease to be subject to a "substantial risk of forfeiture"). (Income inclusion can occur earlier than vesting under §409A.) Contributions by the employee are not deductible. The trust income of a funded nonqualified plan is taxed either to the trust or to the employer, and non-lump-sum payouts are governed by §72, which allows for basis recovery.

An unfunded nonqualified arrangement is one where the employer undertakes a contractual obligation to pay deferred compensation and/or survivor benefits in the future. Since the employee receives no "property" by reason of the contractual undertaking,[26] §83 has no application, and the income can be deferred until actual receipt (according to cash-method principles). Since the plan is nonfunded, there is no income to be taxed.

The employer can deduct contributions or pay-outs only in the year (and in the amount) they are includible by the employee. See §404(a)(5).

4. Income Tax Treatment of Survivor Benefits

Survivor benefits from all of the foregoing, when received by a beneficiary (individual, estate, or trust) following the death of the employee or account owner, are treated as income in respect of a decedent (IRD). Essentially, this simply means that the beneficiary stands in the income-tax shoes of the decedent, without any step-up in basis. Also, the beneficiary is eligible for the §691(c) income tax deduction for any estate tax attributable to the fact that the death benefit was includible in the gross estate of the employee.

Notwithstanding the foregoing, the surviving spouse of a deceased can roll over a lump-sum qualified plan benefit or an IRA benefit tax free and thereby defer income taxation into the future. See §§402(c)(9) (qualified plans) and 408(d)(3)(C)(ii)(II) (IRAs). This benefit is not obtainable under nonqualified arrangements.

---

26. See Reg. §1.83-3(c) (stating that an unfunded and unsecured promise to pay money in the future is not "property" for purposes of §83).

B. *Estate Tax Treatment of Survivor Benefits*

Under current law, employee survivor benefits can be included in a decedent's gross estate under any of §§2033, 2037, 2038, or 2039. The most important of these provisions in this context is §2039, which was expressly tailored to fit employee survivor benefits (as well as, of course, survivor annuities, discussed earlier).

1. *Survivor Benefits Under §2039*

The status under §§2036-2038 of survivor benefits (sometimes referred to as "death benefits") payable under employee plans was even more murky prior to 1955 than in the case of commercial annuities, partly because employees did not "purchase" rights to survivor benefits. Also, in many cases survivor benefits were not payable out of any pre-existing "fund." Section 2039, enacted in 1954, was intended to deal with employee survivor benefits (as well as commercial annuities). As previously mentioned, §2039 is modeled upon §2036(a)(1), but with some "tweaks." Of particular relevance here is the fact that the second sentence of §2039(b) states that employer contributions are deemed to be have been made by the employee for purposes of the "transfer requirement" of §2039.

The case below was one of the first arising under §2039 after its enactment, and it lays out many of the main features of §2039 as it applies to employee survivor benefits.

Estate of Bahen v. United States

305 F.2d 827 (Ct. Cl. 1962)

Davis, Judge.

The decedent, J. William Bahen, was born in 1905. For almost 37 1/2 years Mr. Bahen worked continuously for the Chesapeake & Ohio Ry. Co.; at this death he was the fulltime Assistant to the President. He had not retired nor was he eligible for retirement. While at the Greenbrier Hotel to attend a meeting in 1955, Bahen suffered a heart attack and died within six hours.

After Bahen's death, the C&O made payments to his widow under two plans which it had earlier established for its employees. The first was the Death Benefit Plan, adopted in 1952, which provided that, if a covered employee with more than 10 years' service died while in the company's employ and before becoming eligible for retirement, the C&O would pay a sum equal to three months' salary to his widow. The more significant arrangement was the Deferred Compensation Plan adopted in 1953 for officers. For a designated officer who was under 60 at that time, like Bahen, the C&O would pay a stated maximum sum ($100,000 in Bahen's case) at his death either before or after retirement to his widow and surviving children under 21, in 60 equal monthly installments. However, if prior to retirement the officer became totally incapacitated, the 60 installments would be made to him so long as he survived, any unpaid installment going to his widow or minor children.

Both of these plans were established by the voluntary unilateral action of the C&O. The costs were not deducted from other compensation received by Bahen. Both plans were unfunded.

A. The Deferred Compensation Plan

We first consider the Deferred Compensation Plan of 1953 under which $100,000 was paid to Mrs. Bahen in a five-year span. As we read the section and the Regulations, they demand inclusion in the estate of the proceeds of this Plan.

1. There is, initially, no doubt that the Plan, though adopted by the company unilaterally and without negotiation with the officers and employees, was a "form of contract or agreement" under the statute. This phrase is defined by §20.2039-1(b)(1)(ii) of the Regulations to include "any arrangement, understanding or plan, or any combination or arrangements, understandings, or plans arising by reason of the decedent's employment."

2. There is likewise no doubt that Mrs. Bahen received "an annuity or other payment" under the statute when she was paid the $100,000 in sixty equal installments.

3. The next problem is whether at Bahen's death there was payable to him or he possessed the right to receive "an annuity or other payment." The Deferred Compensation Plan provided that, if Bahen became totally incapacitated before retirement, the C&O would pay him the $100,000 in 60 equal monthly installments. Under both the normal understanding of the statutory words "annuity or other payment," these sums must be characterized as at least an "other payment."

4. Were these benefit payments "payable to" Bahen at his death or did he "possess the right to receive such annuity or payment?" Regulations §20.2039-1(b)(1)(ii) establish that amounts are "payable" to a decedent "if, at the time of his death, the decedent was in fact receiving an annuity or other payments, whether or not he had an enforceable right to have payments continue." Since Bahen was not receiving disability benefits when he died, this term of the statute is not satisfied. We hold, however, that at his death Bahen did "possess the right" to receive the disability payments in the future if certain conditions were fulfilled, and therefore that the alternative requirement of §2039 is met. The Regulations make clear that the decedent's interest in future benefits, even if contingent, is sufficient. Where the employer has offered a plan of this kind, the employee's compliance with his obligations to the company gives him "an enforceable right to receive payments in the future, whether or not, at the time of his death, he had a present right to receive payments." The right he possessed may have been contingent but it was not at the whim of the employer.

5. Another requirement of §2039 is that the decedent's right to receive payments must be possessed "for his life or for any period not ascertainable without reference to his death or for any period which does not in fact end before his death." For the period from when the Deferred Compensation Plan was adopted to his death, Bahen had the right to receive $100,000 in 60 installments upon his total disability prior to retirement. He thus possessed the right to receive this "annuity or other payment" for a period which did not in fact end before his death. See Reg. §20.2039-1(b)(2), Example (5), [which] is consistent with the holdings under §2036(a)(1).

6. The last element is that Bahen must have "contributed" the "purchase price" of the annuity or other payment received by Mrs. Bahen. The second sentence of §2039(b) automatically attributes the employers' contribution to

the employee "if made by reason of his employment." It is immaterial, we think, that the company did not formally make "contributions" to a separate fund, or actually purchase an annuity. Section 2039(b) does not use the words "contribution," "contributed," or "purchase price" in a narrow literal sense. The section deals with the substance of transactions, not with the mechanical way they happen to be formulated. The C&O's undertaking to make payment under the Plan was its "contribution" made by reason of the decedent's employment.

B. The Death Benefit Plan

It is a more difficult question whether the Death Benefit plan — under which the C&O paid Mrs. Bahen a sum equal to Bahen's salary for three months — is covered by §2039. Under that arrangement no benefits were payable to the decedent during his life, and if the Plan were to be judged by itself it would fall outside the ambit of the section for lack of "an annuity or other payment" to the decedent. The defendant contends that this factor is present because the words "or other payment" can include the decedent-employee's regular salary. We cannot agree. Since employees normally receive salary or wages, defendant's interpretation would effectively obliterate, for almost all employees, the express requirement of "an annuity or other payment" to the decedent.

But the Government makes another point which we do accept as bringing the Death Benefit Plan under §2039. The suggestion is that this Plan should not be viewed in isolation but must be considered together with the Deferred Compensation Plan — as if both arrangements were combined into one plan, providing two types of benefits for beneficiaries after the employee's death but only one type of benefit (disability compensation) to the employee himself. There is some factual support, if that be necessary, for looking at the two plans together, since the Death Benefit Plan was adopted in 1952 and the Deferred Compensation Plan only a year later.

The firmer legal basis is provided by the Reg. §20.2039-1(b)(2), Ex. 6, which provides: "All rights and benefits accruing to an employee and to others by reason of the employment are considered together in determining whether or not §2039 applies. The scope of §2039 cannot be limited by indirection." Effect must be given to this declaration, adopted pursuant to the Treasury's recognized power to issue regulations and not challenged by plaintiff, since it does not violate the terms or the spirit of §2039. In view of the purpose of the statute to cover a large share of employer-contributed payments to an employee's survivors, it is not unreasonable to lump together all of the employer's benefit plans taking account of the employee's death in order to decide whether and to what extent §2039 applies to his estate. There is no immutable requirement in the legislation that each plan separately adopted by a company must be considered alone. One good ground for rejecting that position is to prevent attempts to avoid the reach of the statute by a series of contrived plans none of which, in itself, would fall under the section.

Jones, Chief Judge, and Durfee, and Laramore, Judges, concur.

[Concurring opinion of Whitaker, Judge, omitted.]

The chief means of avoiding §2039 is for the employee not to retain any right to payments until death. Since few will want to avoid all "retirement" benefits, the question becomes one of what constitutes a retirement-type benefit. As noted in *Bahen*, the paradigm of a non-retirement benefit is salary.[27] In *Kramer v. U.S.*, 406 F.2d 1363 (Ct. Cl. 1969), the deceased and the employer entered into an agreement providing that the deceased be retained after retirement as a "consultant" for the same amount of his prior salary. The court (dubiously) held that this arrangement involved salary, even though the deceased was entitled to the sums whether or not services were actually performed. Apparently the court relied on the fact that the employer corporation had the "right" to demand the services of the deceased. The opposite result on very similar facts was reached in *Hetson v. U.S.*, 209 Ct. Cl. 691 (1976), *aff'g* 75-2 U.S.T.C. (CCH) ¶ 13,098 (Ct. Cl. Tr. Div.).

Another borderline situation involves the right to disability benefits. In *Estate of Bahen*, supra, the disability benefit was deemed the equivalent of a retirement benefit, because it would have been continued past retirement age and was payable even if the employee had recovered the physical capacity to work.[28] But, in *Estate of Schelberg v. Comm'r*, 612 F.2d 25 (2d Cir.1979), the disability benefits would have terminated at retirement age. Being in lieu of only salary, it was held that the "right to payments" requirement of §2039 was not satisfied.

A second way of trying to avoid §2039 is to claim that the survivor benefit was not payable by reason of "any form of contract or agreement"; that is, was essentially a gratuitous transfer by the employer. Reg. §20.2039-1(b)(1) states that an arrangement, understanding, plan, or consistent employer practice amounts to an "agreement," but there is *dicta* to the contrary.[29] In *Neely v. U.S.*, 613 F.2d 802 (Ct. Cl. 1980), death benefits were paid pursuant to a resolution of the employer's board of directors. The court held that, even if the resolutions were not binding contracts, the death benefit should be included because the beneficiary directly or indirectly (as executor) held 70 percent of the voting stock of the employer and would be able to extract the death benefit.

For §2039 to apply, the payments (once started) must continue for the employee's life (etc.). Thus, §2039 can be avoided if the employee takes the entire retirement benefit in a lump sum prior to death. However, this tactic will not work if the taxpayer has the misfortune to die before receiving the lump sum, since in that case the employee possessed the "right to receive such payment" for a period which "did not in fact end before death."[30] ERISA precludes lump-sum retirement benefits for certain types of qualified plans.

Section 2039 is not mentioned in §2035(a)(2). It would appear, therefore, that §2039 could be avoided if the employee gave up, renounced, or assigned her retirement benefit at any time prior to her death. Oddly, there appears to be no

---

27. In addition to *Bahen* itself, see *Estate of Fusz v. Comm'r*, 46 T.C. 214 (1966) (*acq.*).

28. See also *Estate of Siegel v. Comm'r*, 74 T.C. 613 (1980) (holding that disability benefits are "salary" only if confined to a period of disability).

29. See *Estate of Barr v. Comm'r*, 40 T.C. 227 (1963) (*acq. in result only*).

30. See Reg. §20.2039-1(b)(2), Ex. 5.

reported case on this issue. Perhaps employees are reluctant to give up retirement benefits payable for life. Additionally, under ERISA, rights under employee plans are usually not assignable (and cannot be seized by creditors). Finally, §2035(a)(2) does refer to §§2036-2038, which are alternate bases for including employee survivor benefits in the gross estate.

2. *Survivor Benefits Outside of §2039*

If §2039(a) does not apply, the government is not precluded from falling back on §§2033, 2036, 2037, or 2038. Subsequent to the enactment of §2039 in 1954, it has become accepted that the employee's performance of services entails an "indirect transfer" by the employee not only for gift tax, but also for estate tax, purposes. See *Estate of Fried v. Comm'r*, 445 F.2d 979 (2d Cir.1971); *Estate of Siegel v. Comm'r*, 74 T.C. 613 (1980). But, since an arrangement that fails the "income" requirement of §2039 would also fail the "retained income" requirement of §2036(a)(1), the latter section can essentially be ignored, leaving §§2037 and 2038 for consideration. To avoid both §§2037 and 2038, the employee must forego the right to change or revoke the beneficiary, and the odds that the benefit will be paid to the employee's estate must not exceed 5 percent. See *Rev. Rul. 78-18*, 1978-1 C.B. 289 (§2037); *Rev. Rul. 76-304*, 1976-2 C.B. 269 (§2038). For cases in which the issue was whether an employee's status in a business entity gave the employee the power to revoke, alter, or amend the survivor benefit, compare *Estate of Levin v. Comm'r*, 90 T.C. 723 (1988), *aff'd unpublished opinion*, 891 F.2d 281 (3d Cir.1989) (control present), with *Tully v. U.S.*, 528 F.2d 1401 (Ct. Cl. 1976), and *Kramer v. U.S.*, 406 F.2d 1363 (Ct. Cl. 1969) (control absent).

It has been held that a *funded* survivor benefit can be included in the employee's gross estate under §2033 under a "constructive receipt" theory to the extent that the employee prior to death could have withdrawn such amounts prior to death (without substantial restriction).[31] However, it is not clear to what extent these cases are still relevant, given that the cases either were decided prior to the enactment of §2039 (and the development of the indirect-transfer theory described above) or dealt with survivor benefits under qualified plans that were once excluded under §2039(c) (which was repealed in 1984). If the employee's interest expires at death, and the survivor benefit is a separate right, the arrangement fits the transfer-retention model of §§2036-2039. Section 2033 would be the appropriate provision only where the survivor (or the employer's estate) succeeds to the very same fund (as would exist in a defined contribution plan) from which the decedent employee could freely make withdrawals before death.[32]

An assignment or release by the employee within three years of death of a right to payments, a power to change the beneficiary, or a reversionary interest in the

---

31. *Northern Trust Co. v. U.S.*, 389 F.2d 731 (7th Cir.1968); *Estate of Garber v. Comm'r*, 271 F.2d 97 (3d Cir.1959); *Estate of Brooks v. Comm'r*, 50 T.C. 585 (1968) (*acq.*); *Rev. Rul. 80-158*, 1980-1 C.B. 196.

32. Cf. *Estate of Gribauskas v. Comm'r*, 116 T.C. 142 (2001) (lottery winnings payable in installments), *rev'd on valuation issue*, 342 F.3d 85 (2d Cir.2003) (lottery winnings).

employee's estate can preserve the potential application of §§2036-2038 but not of §§2033 and 2039, which are not referred to in §2035(a)(2).

3. Effect of Community Property Laws

If an employee survivor benefit is community property, then one-half of the community-property amount is excluded as not being owned or as not having been transferred by the decedent. *Rev. Rul. 75-505*, 1975-2 C.B. 364. If the decedent was unmarried during part of the period of employment or of premium payments, there is a state law issue of how much, if any, of the benefit or annuity is community property.

If the employee's spouse predeceases the employee, the deceased spouse's community property interest in the employee's rights in the employer plan is an asset of such spouse which is included in his or gross estate under §2033. Of course, the value might be very low, especially if (in the case of an employee survivor benefit) the employee's rights are non-vested.

These rules also apply to commercial annuities.

4. Gift Tax Treatment of Employee Survivor Benefits

If an employee survivor benefit is not included under any of §§2033-2039, and does not involve gifts by shareholders or partners of the business entity sponsoring the plan, it would seem logical to suppose that the employee had somehow made a gift of it during life. There is very little authority in this area. Reg. §25.2511-1(h)(10) states that a gift occurs when a person entitled to an annuity accepts a reduced annuity in return for an agreement to provide a survivor benefit. Cf. §2503(f) (exclusion where spouse waives right to survivor annuity under a qualified plan.) The notion of a completed gift presupposes an irrevocable beneficiary designation.

If the irrevocable survivor benefit is payable under a "funded" arrangement (whether or not "qualified"), there would be a gift each time the employer or employee makes a contribution into the fund. See *Rev. Rul. 76-490*, 1976-2 C.B. 300, which involved life insurance premiums paid by the employer. If the gift is made to a trust, the amount of the gift would simply be the amount transferred (since the donee would receive the accumulated income to compensate for the delay in distribution). If the gift were of a fixed future amount, the gift would be reduced to present value.[33]

In the case of unfunded benefits, an irrevocable binding contract to make a future transfer is a gift, and if the right is vested and the future amount is fixed, the right can be valued. However, it is usually the case that unfunded survivor benefits are contingent with respect to both vesting and amount. In these cases, the IRS has attempted to apply the "open gift doctrine," which treats the gift as taking place when the contingencies have been sufficiently resolved to render possible the valuation of the gift. The Service's attempt, in *Rev. Rul. 81-31*, 1981-1 C.B.

---

33. See *Rev. Rul.* 78-399, 1978-2 C.B.

475, to treat the gift as having occurred at the decedent employee's death was flatly rejected by the Tax Court in *Estate of DiMarco v. Comm'r*, 87 T.C. 653 (1986). The government declined to appeal *DiMarco*, and the IRS acquiesced in the holding that death could not fix the time of a gift for gift tax purposes. See 1990-2 C.B. 1. All of this was noted in Chapter 3. It is unclear if the open-gift doctrine can be applied in cases where the contingencies are resolved prior to death, but apparently the IRS will continue to attempt to wield the doctrine in such cases. If the doctrine does not apply, the gift must be valued at the time of the binding contract, and the value (and finality) of the gift are likely to be so contingent as to have a very low (or zero) value.

5. *Statutory Survivor Benefits*

Statutory survivor benefits, such as Social Security retirement and survivor benefits, are not subject to §2039, because they are not paid under a "contract or agreement."[34] Sections 2033-2038 would not apply for various reasons: (1) The employee has no withdrawal rights in a fund, (2) the taxes funding the benefit program are not "transfers," (3) the beneficiary designation is not under the control of the employee, and (4) benefits are not payable to the employee's estate.

PROBLEMS, QUESTIONS, AND NOTES

1. a. Vanessa, an employee of GE, is to receive a pension upon retirement at age 70 if still employed by GE. If Vanessa dies before reaching age 70, her designated beneficiary (at the moment, her husband Wayne) is to receive a lump-sum death benefit. If Vanessa dies after reaching 70, her beneficiary will receive a death benefit that diminishes in amount for each year that Vanessa lives past the age of 70. This plan is unfunded. Assume that Vanessa dies, in the alternative, (a) before reaching 70 (while still employed by GE) and (b) after reaching 70. Does §2039 apply? Would it matter if Vanessa's right to a pension vested after ten years of service? See Reg. §20.2039-1(b)(2), Ex. (3). Cf. *Estate of Wadewitz v. Comm'r*, 339 F.2d 980 (7th Cir.1964). If §2039 does not apply, would any other section apply?

    b. *Rev. Rul.* 76-380, 1976-2 C.B. 270, purporting to explain an ambiguous passage in Reg. §20.2039-1(b)(2) Ex. (6), provides that, *Bahen* notwithstanding, a qualified plan will not be combined with a nonqualified plan under the "contract or agreement" language. Both the regulation and the ruling were issued before the repeal in 1984 of the former

---

34. See *Rev. Rul. 81-182*, 1981-2 C.B. 179 (Social Security); *Rev. Rul. 76-501*, 1976-2 C.B. 267 (veteran's benefits); *Rev. Rul. 73-316*, 1973-2 C.B. 218 (Railroad Retirement Act); *Rev. Rul. 55-587*, 1955-2 C.B. 381 (servicemen in active duty). Coming to the opposite result was *Rev. Rul. 75-505*, 1975-2 C.B. 364 (Judicial Retirement System of Texas).

exclusions for survivor benefits under qualified plans and IRAs. *Rev. Rul. 88-85*, 1988-2 C.B. 333, declared various rulings, including *Rev. Rul. 76-380*, supra, to be obsolete insofar as they referred to the repealed exclusion. *Rev. Rul. 76-380* did not expressly mention the exclusion, but it is based on a case, *Estate of Brooks v. Comm'r*, 50 T.C. 585 (1968) (*acq.*), that relies wholly on the exclusion. Therefore, it should be concluded that *Rev. Rul. 76-380* (and the regulation that it purports to explain) is no longer good law. Also, the result reached in *Estate of Schelberg v. Comm'r*, 612 F.2d 25 (2d Cir.1979), would seem to be obsolete insofar as it relied on *Rev. Rul. 76-380*. No cases or IRS pronouncements dealing with facts that postdated the repeal of the exclusion have cited *Rev. Rul. 76-380*. Therefore, we conclude that qualified plans and nonqualified plans can be combined, and older authority to the contrary should be considered to be obsolete. Also, all references in the examples under Reg. §20.2039-1(b)(2) to the fact that the "plan at no time met the requirements of §401(a)" (meaning that the plan was not a qualified plan) are now irrelevant to the result reached.

2. a. What steps must be taken to avoid estate and gift tax on an employee death benefit? When, if at all, are these steps likely to be worth the risks and effort?

   b. Are qualified or nonqualified plans better adapted to transfer tax avoidance? (Qualified plans must provide for early vesting.)

   c. One of the requirements for "qualification" under §401 is that the plan must primarily benefit the employee; benefits for persons other than the employee must be merely "incidental." In *Rev. Rul. 72-241*, 1972-1 C.B. 108, the Service held that this requirement is satisfied if, at retirement, the present value of payments to other persons is less than 50 percent of the total.

§5.5. Life Insurance

Section 2042 deals with the inclusion in the *insured's* gross estate of the *proceeds* of insurance on the life of the decedent. As mentioned in Chapter 4, proceeds payable to the insured's "estate" are fully includible under §2042(1). Proceeds payable to a party or entity other than the insured's estate are fully includible in the insured's gross estate if the insured, at the moment just prior to death, possessed *any* of the *incidents of ownership* over the policy. The term "incidents of ownership" includes the following: (1) the power to cash in the policy, (2) the power to borrow against the policy's cash surrender value, (3) the power to change the beneficiaries of the policy, and (4) a possibility (worth more than 5 percent) that the policy or the proceeds would return to the insured or his estate.

Under §2035(a)(2), the transfer or release, by the insured, within three years of death of the incidents of ownership over the policy results in the inclusion of the proceeds in the gross estate of the insured.

A person can own a policy that insures the life of another person. If such (non-insured) owner dies before the insured, the value of the (unmatured) policy is included in such person's gross estate under §2033.

A. Nature of Life Insurance

Before turning to the problem of taxing life insurance under the transfer taxes, it is useful to discuss the nature of life insurance.

1. Economics of Life Insurance

Life insurance comes in two basic styles. One is "term insurance," where each year's premiums, together with the premiums of other persons in the actuarial "pool," totally cover the risk of the insured's possible death during that year. If such death occurs, the insurance company pays the "face amount" (the proceeds) to the designated beneficiary. The insurance protection ceases (lapses) when the payment of premiums ceases. As would be expected, the premiums for pure term insurance increase each year to cover the greater risk of death. (Alternatively, the premium amounts may be level, in which case the face amount would decrease each year. This is called "decreasing term," and is often marketed as "mortgage insurance.")

"Ordinary life insurance" provides for (1) lifetime protection at a fixed face amount and (2) level premium payments. The level-premium feature is achieved by overcharging the policy owner in the earlier premium years. The excess of the premium over the sum of (i) the actuarial-risk (term insurance) component and (ii) company expenses (salaries, commissions, overhead, and profit) is invested and the earnings accrue for the benefit of the owner. Such excess-premiums-plus-accrued-earnings amount is reflected in "nonforfeiture values." This term refers to the fact that, even if the owner ceases to pay premiums, a residual value remains. The most well-known nonforfeiture value is the cash surrender value, which can be withdrawn or borrowed against by the owner. Other nonforfeiture values are: (1) the right to an "extended term option," which provides insurance protection equal to the fixed face amount for a specified period of years; or (2) the right to a "reduced paid-up option," which provides lifetime term insurance protection at a reduced face amount.

The buildup of the nonforfeiture values is a form of "forced" savings. The face amount of ordinary life insurance at any point in time equals the nonforfeiture value (sometimes known as the "reserve") plus the term-insurance component. Over time, the increase in the reserve is balanced by a decrease in the term coverage. If the policy reserve should become equal to the face amount prior to the insured's death, then the policy is said to have become "fully endowed," and there is no longer any risk element. Most ordinary life insurance would become endowed at age 99 or 100; hence, it almost always "matures" upon the earlier death of the insured.

If ordinary life insurance is purchased at an advanced age, the insured may be required to pay for it with a large "single premium" almost as large as the face amount.

So-called "universal" life insurance is a variation of ordinary life insurance that offers flexibility in the size of premium payments and the ability to withdraw from the cash surrender value, but the savings are not "forced."

"Variable" life insurance is another form of ordinary life in which the reserve (and face amount) are keyed to equity funds rather than the accumulation of interest.

There are hybrid forms of insurance, such as convertible term (term insurance that can be converted into ordinary insurance without a new physical examination), level-premium term insurance (e.g., "five-year term"), and variable-universal life insurance (sometimes known as flexible-premium variable life).

2. Distinguishing Life Insurance from Other Survivor Benefits

The layperson might not see any distinction between life insurance and a survivor benefit under an annuity or employee plan, but it is necessary to make the distinction for estate tax purposes, because §2042 applies to life insurance and §2039 applies to survivor benefits (but not life insurance). The term "life insurance" as used in §2042 refers to any kind of private contractual arrangement under which a sum is paid to one or more beneficiaries, by reason of the insured's death, out of an "actuarial pool" funded by premiums paid into the pool by numerous persons as a hedge against death. As noted in *Estate of Montgomery*, supra, this definition of life insurance excludes most employee death benefits, which are made available without reference to an actuarial pool. Instead, survivor benefits under annuities and employee plans are either self-contained or calculated in inverse relation to retirement benefits paid. See *All v. McCobb*, 321 F.2d 633, 637 (2d Cir.1963), where it was stated:

> [T]he Death Benefit Plan [in this case] bears no resemblance to a life insurance program. The Plan was unfunded and the company did not make periodic contributions to it in the employee's name. The decedent in no way shifted to the company the risk that his death would come prematurely and before the company as insurer had received premiums by or on his account in a sum equal to the amount required to be paid to the beneficiary. The company in no way gambled with the decedent that he would live a long life and that it would recover by periodic assessments before his death the amount to be paid to the beneficiary. It made no difference to the company, so far as any fund was concerned, whether the decedent died prematurely or not. Nor did the company in any way undertake to distribute among a larger group of employees, on the basis of actuarial data from which the appropriate size of a terminal reserve could be computed, the risk of the premature death of a single employee. The company did nothing more than promise to pay a sum certain to a named beneficiary upon the death of a retired employee. If payments resulting from such a promise were to be regarded as insurance, the effectiveness and significance of §2039 would be greatly diminished, if not vitiated.

The fact that the employer may decide to obtain funds to satisfy its contractual obligation to pay a survivor benefit by purchasing insurance on the employee's life is irrelevant, because what counts is that the obligation to pay the benefit derives from the contract or agreement with the employee. But a distinguishable situation is presented where the employment agreement requires the employer to purchase a policy from an insurance company that, under the agreement, is itself the exclusive source of the benefits. Here the policy can be considered "life insurance" if, at the decedent employee's death, there is still an actuarial risk element. This element is deemed to exist if the reserve value (at the death of the decedent employee) is less than the (value of) the death benefit. See Reg. §20.2039-1(d).

Life insurance includes "accident insurance" that insures, *inter alia*, against the risk of death by a certain type of cause.

3. Income Tax Treatment of Life Insurance

The receipt by a beneficiary of life insurance proceeds by reason of the death of the insured is excluded from gross income under §101(a)(1). Under §101(a)(2), the situation is different if the initial owner (usually the insured) sold the policy to a third party (unless the purchaser is the insured, a partner of the insured, or a corporation in which the insured is a shareholder or officer): Here the proceeds are included subject to a basis offset.

The exclusion under §101(a)(1) does not extend to post-death income "on" the proceeds. See §101(c) & (d).

Prior to the insured's death, ordinary life insurance (that does not become fully endowed before extreme old age) possesses favorable income tax consequences relative to other investments. First, the income earned on the policy that increases the nonforfeiture values (the "inside build-up") is not taxed to the policy owner. Second, withdrawals by the policy owner from the (unmatured) policy are deemed (under §72(e)) to come first out of basis (premiums paid); only after basis is exhausted are the withdrawn amounts gross income. However, these tax benefits do not necessarily render ordinary life insurance to be a good overall investment relative to other investments.

QUESTIONS AND NOTES

1. In *Rev. Rul.* 82-5, 1982-1 C.B. 131, the Service dealt with "survivor" benefits payable to a deceased's dependents under a no-fault automobile policy. The benefits were keyed to the dependents' loss of future support from the decedent. The decedent could not change the beneficiaries, who were determined according to statute. The Service stated that it took no position on whether the benefits constituted the proceeds of life insurance (what is your view?), but that, even if life insurance was involved, §2042 did not apply because the benefits were not payable to the deceased's estate, and the decedent lacked any incidents of ownership. The Service also held that the benefits were not included under §2033 (or §2041, dealing with property over which the decedent held a general power of appointment), because the benefits didn't exist before the decedent's death.

2. **a.**   The distinction between "life insurance" and a "survivor benefit" would be involved in deciding whether, for income tax purposes, to apply §101(a).

Under §101(a), the entire face amount is (usually) excluded from income, whereas survivor benefits are treated as IRD rights (which usually means that they are included in the recipient's gross income when received).

b. This distinction may seem puzzling, because it might appear that employee survivor benefits are the functional equivalent of "insurance" in the sense that both entail testamentary transfers by way of contract. Nevertheless, life insurance derives from nondeductible premiums, so that they are "after tax" in the income system as a whole. Also, the actuarial-pool component of life insurance has multiple contributors; only the nonforfeiture-values component represents an investment by the decedent. Perhaps the key factor is that the gain in life insurance is (at least in part) analogous to the unrealized appreciation on (investment) property that escapes tax under §1014. In contrast, employee survivor benefits are a form of deferred compensation (income from services) that has never been subject to income tax. Although an investment component exists in funded employee plans, that component is considered to be incidental to the deferred compensation component.

c. Survivor benefits under commercial annuity contracts may seem closer to life insurance than to deferred compensation, since both have investment components. In fact an annuity is a pure investment by only the decedent, whereas life insurance is not. But §691(d) treats annuity survivor benefits as IRD rights. Perhaps the reason is that, if annuity survivor benefits were to obtain a §1014 basis, employee survivor benefits would universally be structured as commercial annuities. In any event, in a commercial annuity the remaining basis of the decedent (the sum of premiums paid) carries over to the survivor.

3. What is the rationale of the exception (to the income tax exclusionary rule) found in §101(a)(2), as well as the exceptions to the exception? (Can a stranger to the insured buy insurance on the insured's life?)

B. Nontax Uses of Life Insurance

Life insurance can serve to create an "instant" estate out of very little, and it can also be used to provide liquidity to an estate to pay debts and taxes. These purposes are directed to aims other than avoiding transfer taxes.

1. Revocable Insurance Trusts

A revocable *inter vivos* trust, as amended from time to time after its execution, can receive pour-overs from the insured's estate pursuant to a bequest in the will naming the trustee of the trust, as amended, as legatee.[35] A prime (nontax) advantage

---

35. The state law problems have been resolved by the Uniform Testamentary Additions to Trust Act, adopted by every state.

of this arrangement is the relative ease (in most states) of amending trusts as compared to executing codicils to wills.

The *inter vivos* trust can be named the primary or contingent beneficiary of insurance policies (and also of employee survivor benefits and annuities). Thus, an *inter vivos* trust can be the central dispositive instrument of a client's estate plan. To keep the plan up to date, it is only necessary to amend the trust. Changes in the will, life insurance policy, annuity contract, or employee benefit plan are not necessary, since they all feed into the trust, as amended from time to time.

Naming a trust as the beneficiary to receive life insurance proceeds (and annuity payouts and employee survivor benefits) may offer more post-death continuity and flexibility than alternative dispositions directly to a beneficiary, which are likely to be in a lump sum, in the form of an annuity, or under some other "settlement option" (such as the "interest only" option).

The revocable *inter vivos* trust can be funded or unfunded prior to the insured's death. If unfunded, care should be taken to satisfy the minimal state law requirement as to trust *res*. In many states, simply naming the trustee as the beneficiary of an insurance policy will satisfy the *res* requirement.[36]

An *inter vivos* trust can easily be adapted to the unusual nature of life insurance as an investment. The policies may be in the custody of either the trustee or the insured, but the trust typically provides that the trustee is absolved from any duty to pay premiums, and the insured usually retains all incidents of ownership over the policy, such as the right to change the beneficiary or make withdrawals from the cash surrender value. Other customary boiler-plate provisions: (1) require the trustee to collect the proceeds, (2) protect the insurance company by reason of its dealings with the trustee, and (3) delimit the duties and liabilities of the trustee in any suit against the insurance company.

Proceeds of insurance on the life of the insured payable to an *inter vivos* trust that is revocable or amendable by the insured is includible in the insured's gross estate under §2042(2) (and perhaps §2038 as well).

2. Using Life Insurance to Pay Estate Obligations

Life insurance can be used to achieve liquidity so that the estate can pay debts and taxes without selling assets, such as (1) assets that have sentimental value, (2) assets that cannot be sold except at a "sacrifice" price, or (3) assets that possess a special character, such as a family farm or interest in a family business.

Sometimes insurance can be made payable to (or acquired by) a person other than the estate, such as a business associate, business entity, or relative, to enable that person to purchase the asset from the estate at a fair price. If a corporation, partnership, or LLC purchases the stock, partnership interest, or equity interest owned by the decedent, it is called a "redemption." So-called "buy-sell agreements" are widely used to implement liquidity planning arrangements along

---

36. See the comment to §401 of the Uniform Trust Code.

these lines. The possible effect of such arrangements upon the valuation of estate assets was covered in Chapter 4.

Any arrangement by which proceeds of insurance on the life of the decedent are made available to the estate raises the issue of whether the proceeds are includible in the gross estate under §2042(1). That section requires the inclusion in the gross estate of the proceeds of insurance on the life of the decedent "receivable by the [decedent's] executor." This issue is important only in cases where the proceeds are not includible in the decedent's gross estate under other Code provisions, most importantly §2042(2), which applies where the insured possessed at death (or within three years of death) any of the incidents of ownership in the policy.

In *Rev. Rul. 77-157*, 1977-1 C.B. 279, the Service dealt with the §2042(1) issue where the beneficiary was a trust created by the decedent (insured), and the trustee was empowered, but not required, to use the trust funds (including the proceeds) to assist the decedent's estate, if necessary, in the payment of the obligations of the estate, in the sole and absolute discretion of the trustee. Under applicable state law (as is generally the case), the decedent's creditors could not reach the proceeds unless they were paid to the decedent's estate. (Of course, state law cannot govern the rights of the federal government, including the Service, as creditor of the decedent or the decedent's estate.) The assets of the decedent's probate estate were fully capable of satisfying the obligations of the estate without having to make any request to the trustee for additional funds, and in fact no use was made of the funds. In the Ruling, the Service stated:

Reg. §20.2042-1(b) sets forth the following:

> Section 2042 requires inclusion of the proceeds of insurance on the decedent's life receivable by the executor or administrator, or payable to the decedent's estate. It makes no difference whether or not the estate is specifically named as the beneficiary under the terms of the policy. Thus, if the proceeds are receivable by another beneficiary but are subject to an obligation, legally binding upon the other beneficiary, to pay taxes, debts, or other charges enforceable against the estate, then the amount of such proceeds required for the payment in full (to the extent of the beneficiary's obligation) of such taxes, debts, or other charges is includible in the gross estate.

Under Reg. §20.2042-1(b), quoted above, insurance proceeds are considered payable to or for the benefit of the decedent's estate to the extent that an individual beneficiary is subject to a legally binding obligation to pay taxes, debts, or other charges against the estate. Where the beneficiary is not subject to a legally binding obligation to make such payments, but may voluntarily do so, the power to so volunteer does not require inclusion in the decedent's gross estate of the proceeds payable to the beneficiary.

The circumstances of the present case involve a trustee that is empowered to use payments from the plan to assist in paying the estate's obligations and is not prohibited from doing so. Although the trustee in the present case may, in its discretion, assist the estate, (state law) relieves the trustee from any binding obligation to do so. As a result, the payments to the trustee are not payments "receivable by or for the benefit of the decedent's estate."

QUESTIONS AND NOTES

1. Section 2042(1) is probably superfluous. First, if the insured was the owner of the policy (and the proceeds were payable to the executor), the proceeds would be includible under §2033. See *Mimnaugh v. U.S.*, 66 Ct. Cl. 411 (1928), *cert. denied*, 280 U.S. 563 (1929). Cf. *Goodman v. Granger*, 243 F.2d 264 (3d Cir.1957), *cert. denied*, 280 U.S. 563 (1929) (implying that the amount included would be the proceeds). If a person other than the insured owned the policy, it would now be understood that insurance proceeds payable to the insured's estate would be includible in the insured's gross estate under §2041, since an estate designation confers on the decedent the equivalent of a testamentary general power of appointment. See the discussion of "estate remainders" in Chapter 3. This overlap can be explained by reference to the fact that the predecessor of §2042(1) was enacted in 1918, whereas the predecessor of §2041 (in this respect) was enacted in 1942.

2. a. Does the favorable result of *Rev. Rul. 77-157* hold under the same facts as the ruling, except that the benefits are in fact used by the trustee to pay the taxes? Does the result hinge on the word "receivable" (as opposed to "received")? What if the other estate assets are insufficient to pay the taxes? See *Estate of Salsbury v. Comm'r*, T.C. Memo. 1975-333.

    b. Does the *possibility* of using the proceeds to pay estate obligations fall within the "5 percent reversion" category of "incidents of ownership" under §2042(2)?

3. a. Section 2041(a)(1) will apply where insurance on the decedent's life is pledged as security for a debt of the decedent or his estate, at least to the extent the proceeds are in fact applied to satisfy such debt. See Reg. §20.2042-1(b).

    b. If the issue discussed in *Rev. Rul. 77-157* presents a problem for the estate in question, a trust receiving insurance proceeds (and employee survivor) benefits can be used to achieve estate liquidity by alternate means: (1) The estate can be authorized to sell estate assets, and the trust can be authorized to purchase them; and (2) The estate can be authorized to borrow from the trust, and the trust can be authorized to lend cash to the estate, at a suitable interest rate.

    c. These liquidity issues should be anticipated and worked out by the person drafting the will and trust.

4. In *Estate of Margrave v. Comm'r*, 71 T.C. 13 (1978) (reviewed), *aff'd* 618 F.2d 34 (8th Cir.1980), *acq. Rev. Rul. 81-166*, 1981-1 C.B. 477, the decedent (who was the insured) created a revocable trust, which was the beneficiary of an insurance policy on the insured's life owned by his wife. The IRS did not argue that the proceeds were includible under §2042(1), but four dissenting judges thought that §2042(1) applied on the theory that a revocable trust is the equivalent of an "estate" designation. Is this correct? The majority held that the insured did not possess a general power of appointment over the proceeds under §2041(a)(2), on the ground that the property was the proceeds, and that

the proceeds did not exist prior to the insured's death. Four judges disagreed on the ground that the policy existed prior to the insured's death. Which side has the better argument?

5. a. Death taxes in general, although payable by the estate representative, are ultimately borne by recipients of property according to the law of tax apportionment, which is a parallel body of law to that of who bears the burden of debts, funeral expenses, and estate administration expenses. Under the state law of tax apportionment the decedent's will (or revocable trust) usually controls, but, if the will is silent, then state law controls. The recent trend in state tax-apportionment default rules is to apportion death taxes to all taxable interests in proportion to their net values.

   b. Section 2206 of the Internal Revenue Code states that, unless the will states otherwise, the *federal* estate tax attributable to the inclusion in the gross estate of insurance proceeds can be recovered by the executor from the beneficiaries (except where the proceeds are not taxed as a result of the marital deduction). This provision overrides any state tax-apportionment default rule to the contrary.

   c. A §2042(1) problem is not raised by §2206, because it only applies to life insurance includible in the gross estate that is *not* received by the executor. In other words, an amount of federal estate tax is apportioned to the insurance proceeds only if the insurance is included under a provision other than §2042(1) itself.

   d. Section 2042(1) would not be a problem where the IRS levies on insurance proceeds received by a beneficiary under §§6324 and 6331 (or such person voluntarily pays the tax). These provisions are merely collection devices, and do not affect the question of who is ultimately liable to bear the burden of the tax. See §2205, which explicitly preserves any rights of reimbursement or contribution in favor of one against whom federal estate taxes have been collected against those who have the burden of paying the tax under the rules of tax apportionment, supra.

C. Section 2042(2)

The interpretation of §2042(2) has been somewhat clouded by a lack of clarity as to its underlying theory.

1. Possible Approaches

Concerning the issue of how life insurance proceeds (not payable to the insured's estate) *should* be treated for estate tax purposes, various possible approaches are possible.

First, the proceeds of life insurance *could* be viewed as a survivor benefit that derives from an "indirect transfer" from the premium-payer(s) to the beneficiary through the medium of the insurance company. Such an indirect transfer would be "testamentary" where (as is usually the case) the transferor could revoke or amend the policy (including the beneficiary designation). The transfer-retention approach would seem particularly appropriate where the premium-payer was the insured, because then the death benefit would emerge the very moment that the insured's interests and powers expired. Otherwise, however, the flowering of the proceeds would occur before or after the premium-payer's death. Another problem is that there may be more than one payer of premiums.

A second view would be that life insurance involves a testamentary transfer by an insured *even if no interests or powers are retained*, and perhaps even if the insured paid no premiums, because in virtually all cases the insured will have been involved in the procurement of the policy, and the proceeds spring up (wealth is created for the beneficiaries) by reason of the insured's (premature) death. However, if insured has paid no premiums, then it would seem that the insured has never made a transfer.

A third possible approach would be that the proceeds should be includible in the insured's gross estate where the decedent possessed (at death) the equivalent of an *inter vivos* general power of appointment, regardless of who paid the premiums. An insured would possess the equivalent of an *inter vivos* general power of appointment where she could appropriate the economic benefits of the policy during life (regardless of who paid the premiums).

In theory, there is no reason why two or more of the above approaches might not be followed concurrently.

2. History of §2042(2)

All of these approaches have been tried during the history of what is now §2042(2). The proceeds of life insurance were not dealt with as such by the 1916 Act. However, in 1918 Congress added the predecessor of §2042, which (in addition to what is now §2042(1)) provided for the inclusion in the insured's gross estate of the excess of the amount of proceeds (not payable to the insured's estate) over $40,000 if the insurance was "taken out" by the decedent upon his own life.

Uncertainty over the notion of "taken out" led Congress in 1942 to provide that proceeds (not payable to the insured's estate) were to be included in the gross estate of the insured where she *either* paid the premiums *or* (where another paid the premiums) possessed any incidents of ownership over the policy. (Also, the $40,000 exclusion was dropped.)

Under the first ground of inclusion, known as the "premium-payment test," there was no requirement that the decedent-insured have retained any interests or powers in the policy. The amount includible under the premium-payment test was simply the portion of the proceeds that the premiums paid by the insured bore to all premiums paid. Thus, if the proceeds were $100,000 and the insured paid $15,000 out of the $20,000 aggregate premiums, $75,000 was included.

In 1954 Congress deleted the premium-payment test, leaving the incidents-of-ownership test as the sole basis of §2042(2). The stated reason for the deletion of the premium-payment test was to allow an insured to completely avoid estate tax by transferring away all incidents of ownership in the policy and its proceeds, as could be done with retained interests and powers under §§2036-2040.

In short, there is currently no "transfer" requirement under §2042. A policy can be fully included in the insured's gross estate under §2042(2) even though the insured paid none of the premiums, if either the proceeds are payable to the insured's estate or the insured possessed any of the incidents of ownership immediately prior to his death. Saying the same thing differently, the insured can avoid inclusion under §2042(2) by divesting himself of all incidents of ownership, even though she has paid all of the premiums (unless, of course, the new owner is foolish enough to designate the insured's "estate" as beneficiary).

As will be more fully explained in §5.5.D, the assignment by an insured of the incidents of ownership within three years of death will cause the proceeds to be brought back into the insured's estate.

3. Meaning of "Incidents of Ownership"

The incidents-of-ownership concept is clearly based on a "power of appointment" concept. The issue is whether "incidents of ownership" is limited only to those powers over the policy that are the insurance equivalent of *general* powers of appointment (powers exercisable by the insured in favor of herself), or whether such idea encompasses also the insurance equivalent of *special* powers of appointment (powers exercisable by the insured only in favor of others). The case below attempts to come to grips with this issue.

Estate of Skifter v. Commissioner

468 F.2d 699 (2d Cir.1972)

Before FRIENDLY, Chief Judge, and LUMBARD and FEINBERG, Circuit Judges.
LUMBARD, Circuit Judge:

In 1961 Hector Skifter, the decedent, assigned all his interest in nine insurance policies on his life to his wife Naomi. Skifter retained no interest in the policies and no power over them. Several months later, Naomi died and left a will directing that her residuary estate, which included the nine insurance policies, be placed in trust. She directed that the income was to be paid to their daughter, Janet, for life and, upon Janet's death, there were provisions for the distribution of corpus and income to other persons. Naomi appointed Skifter as trustee and authorized him, in his absolute discretion, from time to time, to pay over the whole or any part of the principal of the trust to the current income beneficiary.

In enacting the predecessor of §2042(2), the Committee Reports of the 77th Congress acknowledged that, while the new provision introduced the term "incidents of ownership," it failed to suggest a definition of it. The Reports then went on to list the sort of powers and interests that the Congress was concerned with:

> Examples of such incidents are the right of the insured or his estate to the economic benefits of the insurance, the power to change the beneficiary, the power to surrender or cancel the policy, the power to assign it, the power to revoke an assignment, the power to pledge the policy for a loan, or the power to obtain from the insurer a loan against the surrender value.

The Treasury relied on this legislative history in promulgating Reg. §20.2042-1(c)(2):

> For purposes of this paragraph, the term "incidents of ownership" is not limited in its meaning to ownership of the policy in the technical legal sense. Generally speaking, the term has reference to the right of the insured or his estate to the economic benefits of the policy. Thus, it includes the power to change the beneficiary, to surrender or cancel the policy, to assign the policy, to revoke an assignment, to pledge the policy for a loan, or to obtain from the insurer a loan against the surrender value of the policy, etc.

It seems significant to us that the reference in the regulation for "incidents of ownership" is "the right . . . to the economic benefits of the policy," since there was no way in which Skifter could have exercised his powers to derive for himself any economic benefits from these policies. [In deleting the premium payment test in 1954], the Senate Finance Committee stated:

> No other property is subject to estate tax where the decedent initially purchased it and then long before his death gave away all rights to the property, and to discriminate against life insurance in this regard is not justified.
>
> The inference from this statement is very strong that it was the intent of Congress that §2042 should operate to give insurance policies estate tax treatment that roughly parallels the treatment that is given to other types of property by §§2036-2038 and §2041. This inference is supported by the fact that §2042(2) explicitly provides that "incident of ownership" includes a reversionary interest, and then proceeds to treat such reversionary interests in a manner closely paralleling the treatment that §2037 gives to reversionary interests in [transferred] property.

Although this legislative history is hardly conclusive, we feel that there is sufficient support to justify our conclusion that Congress intended §2042 to parallel the statutory scheme governing the interests and powers that will cause other types of property to be included in a decedent's estate. This conclusion is reinforced by the types of interests and powers that Congress indicated were exemplary of what it meant to be included within the scope of "incidents of ownership." The interests there listed are interests that would cause other types of property to be included under §2036 or §2037; and the powers that Congress discussed are also powers that would result in the property being included under §2038 or §2041.

The core of the controversy here centers on the decedent's power, as trustee, to prefer the current income beneficiary over the remainder through payment of the entire trust corpus. He did not have the power to alter or revoke the trust for his own benefit. In this regard, Reg. §20.2042-1(c)(4) provides:

> A decedent is considered to have an "incident of ownership" in an insurance policy on his life held in trust if, under the terms of the policy, the decedent (either alone or in conjunction with another person or persons) has the power (as trustee or otherwise) to change the beneficial ownership in the policy or its proceeds, or the time or manner of enjoyment thereof, even though the decedent has no beneficial interest in the trust.

The Tax Court declined to interpret this regulation so as to make it applicable here, but concluded that, since the power could not be exercised to benefit the decedent or his estate, it would not cause the proceeds to be included in his estate. If the power had been exercisable for the benefit of decedent, or for the benefit of whomever the decedent selected, it would have been necessary to include the proceeds in the estate, for there would be a powerful argument that he would have had the equivalent of a [general] power of appointment.

The Commissioner has pointed to many cases holding that a power [to invade corpus for the income beneficiary] would result in the property being included in the estate of the holder of the power. But the Commissioner's reliance on §2038 cases exposes the fatal flaw in his position. The cases he cites dealt with powers that were retained by the transferor. That is not what we have here; the power the decedent had was given to him long after he had divested himself of all interest in the policies — it was not reserved by him at the time of the transfer. This difference between powers retained by a decedent and powers that devolved upon him at a time subsequent to the assignment is not merely formal, but has considerable substance. A taxpayer planning the disposition of his estate can select the powers that he reserves and those that he transfers in order to implement an overall scheme of testamentary disposition; however, a trustee, unless there is agreement by the settlor and or beneficiaries, can only act within the powers he is granted. When the decedent is the transferee of such a power and holds it in a fiduciary capacity, with no beneficial interest therein, it is difficult to construe this arrangement as a substitute for a testamentary disposition by the decedent. Accordingly, we conclude that, although such a power might well constitute an incident of ownership if retained by the assignor of the policies, it is not an incident of ownership within the intended scope of §2042 when it has been conveyed to the decedent long after he had divested himself of all interest in the policies and when he cannot exercise the power for his own benefit.

[Judge Lumbard's opinion then noted that §2038 itself contains the phrase "(without regard to when or from what source the decedent acquired such power)," which might suggest that §2038 would apply even when the power was acquired under the will of another party.] The noted language was added to the predecessor of §2038 in 1936 in response to the decision in *White v. Poor*, 296 U.S. 95 (1935). In that case, the decedent had created a trust and conferred on the trustees the power jointly to terminate the trust. Subsequently, the decedent was appointed a successor trustee. Therefore, at death decedent possessed this power to terminate and the Commissioner attempted to apply the predecessor to §2038; but the Supreme Court held this was impermissible because decedent had not retained the power at the time of transfer but had received it later. It was for the purpose of changing this result that Congress added the emphasized language. However, this language appears never to have been applied to a power other than one that the decedent created at the time of transfer in someone else and that later devolved upon him before his death.

Because of our view that Congress did not intend §2042 to produce divergent estate tax treatment between life insurance and other types of property, we conclude that the fiduciary power that Skifter possessed at his death did not constitute an "incident of ownership" under §2042. The Tax Court was thus correct in holding that Reg. §20.2042-1(c)(4) must be read to apply to "reservations of powers by the transferor as trustee" and not to powers such as that in issue.

The Service, in *Rev. Rul. 84-179*, 1984-2 C.B. 195, modified its position and essentially went along with *Skifter*, despite having prevailed in *Rose v. U.S.*, 511 F.2d 259 (5th Cir.1975). The Ruling holds that the term "incidents of ownership" means the insurance equivalent of a general power of appointment unless the powers were "retained" by the insured in connection with a transfer of the policy or the purchase or maintenance of the policy out of the insured's own funds, in which case the broader concept of "power" found in §2038 would apply.

In another, but closely related, controversy dealing with the question of whether the "incidents of ownership" concept encompasses a mere power in the insured to affect the "time or manner of enjoyment," the Fifth Circuit held for the government. *Estate of Lumpkin v. Comm'r*, 474 F.2d 1092 (1973). In that case, the insured retained the power to elect a settlement option under which periodic payments of the proceeds (and interest thereon) to the beneficiary would be reduced, with income being, in effect, accumulated for later distribution to the beneficiary or, if she died, to her estate. In the analogous trust situation, if the settlor "retains" a power to accumulate income for ultimate distribution to the sole income beneficiary or her estate, the trust would be includible under §2036(a)(2). But then, the Third and Eighth Circuits, on facts identical to those in *Lumpkin*, held that such a power in the insurance context was not an incident of ownership. *Estate of Connelly v. U.S.*, 551 F.2d 545 (1977), *nonacq.*, *Rev. Rul. 81-128*, 1981-1 C.B. 469; *Hunter v. U.S.*, 624 F.2d 833 (8th Cir.1980). The Service has noted its disagreement with the last two cases, noting that in each of them the insured's "special power" (that would have caused inclusion if §2038 were in play) was "retained." See *G.C.M. 39317* (Dec. 12, 1984).

It is clear even in the wake of *Skifter* that §2042(2) will apply if the incidents of ownership can be exercised by the insured to benefit herself in her individual capacity (as income beneficiary or remainder of a trust), regardless of how the powers devolved upon the insured. See *Estate of Freuhauf v. Comm'r*, 427 F.2d 80 (6th Cir.1970).

A decedent-insured's right to prevent the cancellation of a life insurance policy by purchasing the policy for its cash surrender value (if his employer, whom he did not control, chose to stop paying premiums) was held not to be an incident of ownership under §2042. *Estate of Smith v. Comm'r*, 73 T.C. 307 (1979), *acq. in result in part*, 1981-2 C.B. 2. Likewise, a decedent-insured's right to convert a group policy into an individual one on the termination of his employment was held not to be an incident of ownership, on the ground that his conversion right was preconditioned on quitting his job, which made that right "too contingent and too remote" to be an incident of ownership under the statute. *Estate of Smead v. Comm'r*, 78 T.C. 43 (1982), *acq. Rev. Rul. 84-130*, 1984-2 C.B. 194. In *Estate of Beauregard v. Comm'r*, 74 T.C. 603 (1980), *acq.*, 1981-2 C.B. 1, the decedent would regain the policy once his children were 21 years old, married, became self-supporting, or left the custody of their mother. However, because the decedent-insured's contingent rights were imposed by others and were never under his control, the court analogized the right to change beneficiaries under these circumstances to a reversionary interest under §2037 and concluded that its value was below that statute's 5 percent *de minimis* ceiling.

The proceeds are includible in the estate of the insured even if the latter only possessed one of the possible incidents of ownership; it is not necessary that he possess all of them.[37] Moreover, possession of a single incident of ownership causes the entire proceeds to be included. The value as such of the incident(s) of ownership is not what determines the amount includible.[38]

Assuming that the power does constitute an "incident of ownership" over the policy, it is sufficient that the insured possessed the incident of ownership jointly with one or more other parties. Even a mere veto power over incidents of ownership held by another constitutes an incident of ownership. *Comm'r v. Estate of Karagheusian*, 233 F.2d 197 (2d Cir.1956). Compare *Estate of Rockwell*, 779 F.2d 931 (3d Cir.1985) (proceeds excluded where exercise of veto power could not have resulted in insured obtaining economic benefits).

If a life insurance policy is community property held by the insured and the insured's spouse, it is settled that the insured possesses incidents of ownership with respect to only one-half of any community-property insurance on his or her life, meaning that only half of the proceeds are includible in the insured's gross estate under §2042(2). This result follows even where the insured possessed sole community-property "management" powers over the policy. See Reg. §20.2042-1(c)(5). The theory behind this rule is that community-property management powers are possessed in a fiduciary capacity and are not to be exercised by the insured for his personal benefit at the expense of the other spouse. See *Rev. Rul.* 67-228, 1967-2 C.B. 331.

If a person other than the insured dies holding the incidents of ownership over an unmatured policy, the policy is included in such person's gross estate under §2033. The amount includible is the cost of purchasing the same policy. If (as is usually the case) such cost cannot be determined, the amount includible is the "interpolated terminal reserve" (representing any nonforfeiture value) plus the unexpired premium. See Reg. §20.2031-8(a).

Accordingly, if a life insurance policy is community property and the non-insured spouse dies first, her fractional interest in any community-property insurance, as defined by state law, is includible in her gross estate under §2033. See *Rev. Rul. 75-100*, 1975-1 C.B. 303.

If the beneficiary of a life insurance policy is two or more generations below the grantor, the death of the insured will (if the proceeds are includible in the insured's gross estate) entail a direct-skip generation-skipping transfer by the insured to the beneficiary.

---

37. See *Estate of Reifberg v. Comm'r*, T.C. Memo. 1982-70.
38. See *Rev. Rul. 79-129*, 1979-1 C.B. 306.

QUICK QUESTION

In which one of the following fact patterns is the life insurance proceeds included in the decedent-insured's estate under §2042?

A. Edith had the right to pledge the insurance policy on her life for a loan. Otherwise, Edith's husband owned the policy.

B. Fiorello purchased a life insurance policy on his life six years ago when he immediately transferred the policy to Agnes, his wife. Fiorello continued to pay the premiums on the policy.

C. David was the sole stockholder of DaDumDumDa Corp., which totally owned an insurance policy on David's life. The corporation was the beneficiary of the policy.

QUESTIONS AND NOTES

1. a. Is life insurance so inherently "testamentary" with respect to the insured that there should be no "transfer" (premium payment) *and* no requirement of any interest or power? In other words, should the proceeds be included in the insured's gross estate regardless of who purchased the policy and regardless of who owns it at the insured's death?

   b. Should the premium-payment rule be restored, or is there something about life insurance that makes the "transfer" concept awkward to apply on the basis of premium payments? Specifically, what should be the estate tax result (as a matter of policy) where the insured, *not possessing any incidents of ownership*, pays all of the premiums? The last premium only? All of the premiums except the last one? Should the result hinge on whether ordinary or term insurance is involved?

   c. Even if the premium-payment rule were restored, should it not be deemed to be superseded by the "general power of appointment" concept? Take the situation where B pays all the premiums on policies owned by the insured A. What is the basis for arguing that A is the "real" transferor?

2. a. Turning to current doctrine relating to the meaning of "incidents of ownership" (including the *Skifter* case), is it proper (given the language and history of §2042(2)) for the courts (and the IRS) to hold that the meaning of that term depends on whether the insured's possession of such incidents resulted from a "retention" transaction? Is there anything in §2042(2) that refers to how the power is acquired? Retention necessarily implies a transfer (here, the payment of premiums), yet §2042(2) was divorced from a premium-payment approach. How, then, can §2042(2) be said to incorporate the retention concept? Moreover, Congress has omitted a retention

requirement under §2038, despite its presence under §§2036 and 2037. Can one dismiss the plain text of the change to §2038 by noting that no reported case has involved a situation where the power obtained by the decedent was not created by the decedent? Besides, the observation is plainly incorrect as a matter of law. If X creates a trust appointing Y as the trustee and giving Y the power to alter the enjoyment of the income and corpus (but not naming Y as beneficiary), and Y transfers property to the trust, the portion of the trust attributable to Y's transfer is included in Y's gross estate under one or more of §§2036-2038.

   b. If *Skifter* had come out the other way, how would similarly situated persons have avoided the possibility of being subject to §2042(2)? Does an individual trustee of a testamentary trust created by another still have to worry about this issue, despite *Skifter*?

   c. Should the *Skifter* court have simply held that the §2042(2) concept of "incidents of ownership" was to be construed in light of the §2041 concept of *general* power of appointment in all cases, and that any analogy to §§2036-2038 was inapposite? Would the text or legislative history of §2042(2) mandate such a result? Preclude such a result?

   d. Does Reg. §20.2042-1(c)(4) expressly adopt a "special" power of appointment theory? How could the courts in the *Skifter* litigation have avoided treating this regulation as being dispositive? Is the regulation invalid as not being a reasonable interpretation of the statute?

3. a. Although a veto power over the use by another of a policy or proceeds might come within §2042(2), it has been held that contractual restrictions on another's exercise of powers are not sufficient to constitute an incident of ownership. *First Nat'l Bank of Birmingham v. U.S.*, 358 F.2d 625 (5th Cir.1966); *Estate of Infante v. Comm'r*, T.C. Memo. 1970-206. But see *Rev. Rul. 76-274*, 1976-2 C.B. 278.

   b. Under Reg. §20.2042-1(c)(6), incidents of ownership of a policy owned by a corporation on the life of a shareholder can be attributed to the more-than-50 percent shareholder under certain circumstances.

4. a. In *Estate of Margrave v. Comm'r*, 71 T.C. 13 (1978) (reviewed), *aff'd* 618 F.2d 34 (8th Cir.1980), which was mentioned earlier in connection with §2042(1), the decedent created a revocable trust, which was the beneficiary of an insurance policy on the decedent's life owned by his wife. On the insured's death, the proceeds were paid to the revocable trust. The Tax Court held (*inter alia*) that the decedent's power to control the trust terms did not constitute incidents of ownership, because the wife could have named another party as beneficiary of the policy. The majority characterized this situation as being one where the powers of the owner (the wife) superseded the powers of the insured (with respect to the revocable trust). Two judges dissented on the ground that the term "incidents of ownership" includes the power to dispose of the proceeds, and that incidents of ownership do not have to be vested or absolute. Section 2042(2) says "possessed at death." Is not this a situation where the insured did possess incidents of ownership (at death) subject to a condition

subsequent that never occurred? See *Terriberry v. U.S.*, 517 F.2d 286 (5th Cir.1975), *cert. denied*, 424 U.S. 977 (1976) (insured possessed incidents of ownership even though another could have revoked them). Or should incidents of ownership be limited to economic benefits obtainable by the decedent during life? Is the ability to name one's estate as beneficiary purely a testamentary power?

    b. In *Rev. Rul. 81-166*, 1981 C.B. 477, the IRS acquiescing in *Margrave*, but stated that the proceeds would be a completed transfer by the wife for gift and estate tax purposes.

5. The Uniform Simultaneous Death Act, §5, 9C Un. Laws Ann. 167, states: "Where the insured and the beneficiary in a policy of life or accident insurance have died and there is no sufficient evidence that they have died otherwise than simultaneously the proceeds of the policy shall be distributed as if the insured had survived the beneficiary." What is the transfer tax result? See *Estate of Wien v. Comm'r*, 441 F.2d 32 (5th Cir.1971) (§2033 value, not proceeds, included in estate of insured; fact of actual imminent death must be disregarded).

6.   a. The character of an ordinary life insurance policy under state law as "community" or "separate" property depends upon whether the applicable rule is the "proportionate-premium" test or the "first-premium" test. Under a first-premium regime, the payment of premiums with community property on a policy which is the insured's separate property creates a debt which is owed by the insured to the "community." In that case, the proceeds are fully includible in the insured's gross estate under §2042(2), the full amount of the debt creates an offset against the amount includible (as would any lien on property owned by the decedent), and half of the debt, which is an asset of the community and therefore half owned by the insured, is a §2033 asset of the insured. See *Rev. Rul. 80-242*, 1980-2 C.B. 276.

    b. Where the non-insured spouse died first, the amount included in the estate of the insured, who dies second, again depends on the rules of state law. Under the first-premium test, the policy either was or was not community property as of the earlier death of the non-insured. If it was community property (and assuming the non-insured spouse transferred her interest in the policy to a third party), the amount includible on the insured's death is limited to half of the proceeds. See *Rev. Rul. 75-100*, 1975-1 C.B. 303. In a state following the proportionate-premium test, the analysis is potentially complicated by the fact that premiums have been paid after the death of the non-insured spouse by the insured spouse and/ or by third parties. In *Scott v. Comm'r*, 374 F.2d 154 (9th Cir.1967), it was held that, according to California law, the proceeds were to be allocated between (a) the period up the non-insured's death and (b) the period between the two deaths. Since the policy was acquired after the marriage, the amount includible by the insured was the proceeds less half of the portion allocable to the first period. Compare *Cervin v. Comm'r*, 111 F.3d 1252 (5th Cir.1997) (different result under Texas law where claim of non-insured's estate not settled until death of insured spouse).

D. Avoiding Incidents of Ownership

An obvious way to avoid estate inclusion is for the insured to avoid possession of incidents of ownership over the policy. This might be accomplished either by a gift or by having another party acquire the policy in the first instance.

1. Gift Tax Treatment

The gift tax value of a transferred unmatured policy is based on its replacement cost rather than its cash surrender value. This rule derives from an early regulation, now designated as Reg. §25.2512-6(a), which was upheld by the Supreme Court in *Guggenheim v. Rasquin*, 312 U.S. 254 (1941). The replacement-cost rule was motivated mainly out of a concern that a donor could deplete his estate by, say, a $850,000 single premium payment for a $1,000,000 face amount policy while paying gift tax with respect to, say, $700,000 (the cash surrender value). The excess of the $850,000 over the $700,000 would go to current insurance protection, sales commissions, company costs, and company profit.

For "ordinary" life insurance, the cost of comparable contracts (if currently being sold) is the accepted measure of replacement cost. Otherwise (and more often than not where the policy has been in force for a period of time), the replacement cost is deemed to be the "interpolated terminal reserve" of the policy plus premiums already paid by the donor during the current year allocable to the unexpired premium period. The interpolated terminal reserve, which is the "source" of all nonforfeiture values in an ordinary life insurance policy, will often be close to the cash surrender value after a few years of premium payments. It cannot usually be found by inspecting the policy. The usual method of obtaining it is to inquire to the issuing company.

For pure term insurance with no reserve value, the gift tax value is simply the premium paid by the donor allocable to the unexpired period of the premium.

Of course, there is no gift of a life insurance policy where the donor retains (under the policy provisions, the terms of a trust to which the policy is assigned, or pursuant to any other arrangement) the equivalent of the right to revoke, alter, or amend the policy.

It would at first appear that the present-interest exclusion would not be available to gifts of insurance — especially term insurance — because of the futurity of enjoyment of the proceeds by the donee. However, the last two sentences of Reg. §25.2503-3(a) state:

> The term ["future interests"] has no reference to such contractual rights as exist in a bond, note, or a policy of life insurance, the obligations of which are to be discharged by payments in the future. But a future interest or interests in such contractual obligation may be created by the limitations contained in a trust or other instrument of transfer used in effecting a gift.

The first sentence in the quoted passage is the so-called "contract right exception" to the definition of "future interest." Under it, an outright gift of either ordinary or term life insurance constitutes a present-interest gift. Similarly, the payment of premiums on policies owned by another individual constitutes a present-interest gift to such owner, on the ground that the gift tax treatment of premiums follows the treatment of gifts of policies. See *Rev. Rul. 76-490*, 1976-2 C.B. 300, supra.

2. Mechanics of Gifts of Life Insurance

Avoiding estate inclusion by making a gift of a life insurance policy is sometimes easier said than done.

Commissioner v. Estate of Noel

380 U.S. 678 (1965)

Mr. Justice BLACK delivered the opinion of the Court.

Ruth M. Noel drove her husband from their home to New York International Airport where he was to take an airplane to Venezuela. Just before taking off, Mr. Noel signed applications for flight insurance policies aggregating $125,000 and naming his wife as beneficiary. Mrs. Noel testified that she paid the premiums of $5 and that her husband then instructed the sales clerk to "give them to my wife. They are hers now, I no longer have anything to do with them." The clerk gave her the policies, which she kept. Less than three hours later Mr. Noel's plane crashed. The companies paid Mrs. Noel the $125,000 face value.

[The Court first held that "accident" insurance constitutes "life insurance" insofar as it covers the risk of death by accident.]

The executors' second contention is that the decedent possessed no exercisable incident of ownership in the policies at the time of his death. This contention rests on three alternative claims: (a) that Mrs. Noel purchased the policies and therefore owned them; (b) that even if her husband owned them, he gave them to her, thereby depriving himself of power to assign them or to change the beneficiary; and (c) even assuming he had contractual power to assign the policies or make a beneficiary change, this power was illusory as he could not possibly have exercised it in the interval between take-off and the fatal crash.

The contention that Mrs. Noel bought the policies and therefore owned them rests solely on her testimony that she furnished the money for their purchase, intending thereby to preserve her right to continue as beneficiary. What she bought nonetheless were policy contracts containing agreements between her husband and the companies. The contracts granted to Mr. Noel the right either to assign the policies or to change the beneficiary without her consent. Therefore the contracts she bought by their very terms rebut her claim that she became the complete owner of the policies with an irrevocable right to remain the beneficiary.

The contention that Mr. Noel gave the policies to her and therefore was without power thereafter to assign them or to change the beneficiary stands no better under these facts. The contract terms provided that these policies could not be assigned nor could the beneficiary be changed without a written endorsement on the policies. No such assignment or change of beneficiary was endorsed on these policies, and consequently the power to assign the policies or change the beneficiary remained in the decedent.

Obviously, there was no practical opportunity for the decedent to assign the policies or change the beneficiary between the time he boarded the plane and the time he died. But the same could be said about a man owning an ordinary life insurance policy who boarded the plane at the same time or for that matter about any man's exercise of ownership over his property while aboard an airplane in the three hours before a fatal crash. It would stretch the imagination to think that Congress intended to measure estate tax liability by an individual's fluctuating, day-by-day, hour-by hour capacity to dispose of property which he owns. We hold that estate tax liability for policies "with respect to which the decedent possessed at his death any of the incidents of ownership" depends on a general, legal power to exercise ownership, without regard to the owner's ability to exercise it at a particular moment.

Mr. Justice DOUGLAS dissents.

3. Irrevocable Life Insurance Trusts

An insured can make a completed gift of an insurance policy to an irrevocable trust. Although an irrevocable insurance trust cannot be amended during the insured's lifetime, the trust may be a more suitable recipient of the policy than an individual.

It is not recommended that the grantor-insured be a trustee of the irrevocable insurance trust, even if the grantor cannot benefit himself. Recall that the *Skifter* case held §2042(2) did not apply where the insured was named trustee of his spouse's testamentary trust that contained a policy on his life. But in *Rev. Rul. 84-179*, 1984-2 C.B. 195, in which the Service accepted *Skifter*, the Service stated that an insured would be treated as possessing incidents of ownership by reason of holding "fiduciary" powers over a policy on his life that were retained by him in connection with a transfer of the policy. Nevertheless, if the irrevocable insurance trust confers insufficient dispositive discretion on the insured-trustee, it is possible that the fiduciary powers would not meet the §2038 threshold [an issue discussed in Chapter 8]. However, the Service has made no concession to this effect.

A gift of an insurance policy to a trust, or the payment of premiums on a policy owned by the trust, normally involves a gift of a "future" interest, which is not eligible for the present-interest exclusion, since an insurance policy yields no trust accounting "income" that can be distributed to a beneficiary. See Reg. §25.2503-3(c), Ex. (2). The exclusion is obtainable only if: (1) the trust requires income to be paid out currently (which is unlikely in an insurance trust) or states that specified beneficiaries can demand the income periodically, *and* (2) the trustee can be required by the beneficiaries to cash in the policy and convert the proceeds to income-producing property. See *Rev. Rul. 69-344*, 1969-1 C.B. 225. A gift of cash to an irrevocable life insurance trust, which provides beneficiaries with a demand right, qualifies for the annual exclusion under *Crummey*. If the beneficiaries do not exercise their demand rights, the cash is available for premium payments.

An issue is whether the grantor should continue to pay the premiums herself or whether income-producing assets should be transferred to the trust in order to provide funds for the trustee to pay the premiums. A disadvantage of the latter approach is §677(a)(3), which causes the grantor to be taxed on such income. This rule will not necessarily make the grantor worse off taxwise than if he kept such property, but it cancels a tax advantage that usually attaches to an irrevocable gift of income-producing property; namely, the avoidance of income tax. But if the beneficiaries are also in a high tax bracket, by paying the income tax liability the grantor is effectively transferring that additional value gift tax free.

4. Transfers Within Three Years of Death

If the taxpayer in *Estate of Noel* had succeeded in the claim that an effective assignment had occurred, the proceeds might possibly have been includible in the decedent's gross estate under the then applicable version of §2035 as a "transfer in contemplation of death." In the 1976 Act, the "contemplation of death" test was replaced by a "within three years of death" test, which surely would have snared Mr. Noel. In 1981, §2035 was amended further, and in 1997 there was a rearrangement of subsections with some slight substantive changes.

Under the current version of §2035(a) a transfer or release of an interest or power within three years of the decedent's death is "disregarded" for purposes of applying (*inter alia*) §2042. Thus, *a gift by the insured of a life insurance policy, or release by the insured of incidents of ownership therein, within three years of death, causes the proceeds to be included in the decedent's gross estate.*

Note that the §2035(c)(3) exception to §2035(a) for transfers exempt from gift tax under the gift tax annual exclusion is inapplicable to gifts of life insurance.

5. Taking Out Insurance on Another's Life

The obvious way of avoiding problems such as occurred in *Noel* or would occur under §2035 if the transfer of a policy is made within three years of death is to simply never make a transfer in the first place. In this context, "nontransfer" means that another party takes out insurance on the life of the insured.

Taking out insurance on another's life is not necessarily simple. An insurance company will only issue a policy on another's life (or agree to assignment of such a policy) to a person or entity possessing an "insurable interest" in the person's life. But a spouse, child, close relative, partner, or business of which the insured is an owner or employee, does possess the requisite insurable interest. Also, the transaction may be carried out with the involvement of the insured.

The acquisition of the policy must be effected properly. This point is illustrated by the oft-cited case of *U.S. v. Rhode Island Hospital Trust Co.*, 355 F.2d 7 (1st Cir.1966), where the father purchased an insurance policy on the life of his son, age 19, naming himself and his wife as beneficiaries. The father kept the policy in his safe deposit box and paid all premiums. However, under the policy the son was given the incidents of ownership. The wife died first, whereupon the father told the son to change the beneficiary, which the son did. The son died before the father, who received the proceeds. The government claimed that the policy was includible in the son's gross estate under §2042(2). The court agreed, saying:

> Before the Revenue Act of 1942, the tax criterion governing cases in this area was "policies taken out" by the decedent on his own life. This led to difficult problems of interpretation, which the courts resolved by creating two criteria: "payment of premiums" and possession of "incidents of ownership." The Revenue Act of 1942 eliminated the "policies taken out" language, and included an illustrative list of the kinds of rights included under "incidents of ownership." (Subsequently, the

Revenue Act of 1954 eliminated the premium payment test, leaving possession of "any incidents of ownership" as the sole criterion.) In acting this way, Congress was, we think, trying to introduce some certitude in a landscape of shifting sands. It was not trying to tax the extent of the interest of the decedent. What it was attempting to reach in §2042 was the power to dispose of property. Power can be and is exercised by one possessed of less than complete legal and equitable title. The very phrase "incidents of ownership" connotes something partial, minor, or even fractional in its scope.

Viewed against this background, what power did decedent (the son) possess? Did he have a capacity to do something to affect the disposition of the policy if he had wanted to? Without gaining possession of the policy itself, he could have borrowed on the policy, changed the method of using dividends, assigned the policy, (and) revoked the assignment. Should he have gained possession of the policy by trick (as by filing an affidavit that the policy was lost), force, or chance, he could have changed the beneficiary. In addition, his signature was necessary to a change in beneficiary, to a surrender for cash value, to an alteration in the policy. Even with this most limited power, he would be exercising an incident of ownership "in conjunction with" another.

It is no answer that decedent's father might have proceeded against him at law or in equity. The company made it clear in the contract that it bore no responsibility for the validity of an assignment, that it could pay a beneficiary without recourse, and that it was under no obligation to see to the carrying out of any trust.

While decisions against the estate of a passive but power-possessing decedent may often conflict with the honest intentions and understanding of premium-paying beneficiaries and insureds, the alternative of abandoning the insistence on the governing nature of the contract is less desirable. The drawing of a useful line would be impossible, and there would be an invitation to unprincipled estate manipulation. As government counsel has pointed out, there could always be a formally-executed side agreement under which the insured clearly surrenders to the beneficiary all his rights to the policy, such agreement to be brought to light only in the event of the decedent's dying before the beneficiary.

Assuming the policy is properly acquired by a party other than the insured, then what? If the policy owner predeceases the insured, the value of the policy (determined according to the replacement-cost method) is includible in the owner's gross estate under §2033. See *Rev. Rul. 77-184*, 1977-1 C.B. 290.

Now suppose the insured dies before the owner, triggering the payment of the proceeds. If the owner is also the sole beneficiary, the proceeds will augment the owner's potential §2033 gross estate. If, instead, a third party or a trust is named beneficiary, the payment of the proceeds to the beneficiary will constitute a "transfer" thereof by the policy owner for estate and gift tax purposes. See *Goodman v. Comm'r*, 156 F.2d 218 (2d Cir.1946). The transfer might be said to be "constructive," because the owner could have named herself beneficiary but instead allowed the proceeds to pass to others. The ultimate estate and gift tax outcome will hinge on what powers and interests, if any, that are held by the policy owner following the transfer. For example, if the proceeds are payable to a trust which is to pay the trust income to the policy owner for life, the policy owner has made a retained-interest gift of the proceeds subject to §2702, and the portion of the trust attributable to the proceeds will be included in the policy owner's gross estate under §2036(a)(1). See *Pyle v. Comm'r*, 313 F.2d 328 (3d Cir.1963).

There is no particular reason for the younger spouse to take out insurance on the life of the older spouse and to name herself beneficiary. The more straightforward approach would be for the older spouse to own the policy and name the younger spouse as beneficiary. Such an approach works just as well, because of the unlimited marital deduction.[39] Indeed, if the non-insured's spouse owns the policy on the life of the insured and dies before the insured, care would have to be exercised in disposing of the unmatured policy. If the policy is bequeathed to the insured spouse, it may qualify for the marital deduction, but in that case it will augment the insured spouse's potential gross estate and defeat any purpose of avoiding §2042(2). If the policy passes to a trust that would otherwise qualify for the marital deduction, qualification may be jeopardized by the fact that an unmatured insurance policy is non-income-producing property. If the policy is left in a non-marital-deduction trust (intended to avoid tax at the insured spouse's later death), the insured should not be named trustee, especially if, under the terms of the trust, the insured-trustee can exercise dispositive powers so as to benefit himself, because (as noted earlier) such a power will constitute an incident of ownership.

QUESTIONS AND NOTES

1. a. The wide disparity between the gift tax value of unmatured life insurance and the estate tax value of matured life insurance makes gifts of life insurance a popular form of transfer-tax reduction. Is the advantage really so significant where the donor lives out his or her full life expectancy?

   b. Gifts of term insurance seem especially attractive, since the gift tax value is insignificant and, if the gift is outright, will qualify for the present-interest exclusion. But does such a gift accomplish anything at all unless the donor dies within the current premium period?

2. a. The normal means of assigning a life insurance policy, as the *Noel* case indicates, is not by the common law method of physical delivery accompanied by donative intent, but by notification presented to the insurance company.

   b. In some cases, estates have successfully argued that imperfect assignments were effective for estate tax purposes. Thus, in *Morton v. U.S.*, 457 F.2d 750 (4th Cir.1972), a policy was taken out by the decedent on his own life

---

39. Before the advent of the unlimited marital deduction in 1982, it was not uncommon for a spouse to buy life insurance on the life of the other to avoid the marital deduction limitation.

but another person paid the premiums. The decedent then executed an irrevocable beneficiary designation, but did not purport to divest himself of all powers over the policy. It was found that, under West Virginia insurance law, the insured was under a duty not to exercise any power in derogation of the rights of the irrevocably designated beneficiary. Also, under West Virginia law, such beneficiary alone could exercise the incidents of ownership. The same approach was taken in *Watson v. Comm'r*, T.C. Memo. 1977-268, where the court held that the decedent had been issued the policy by mistake and could not exercise the incidents of ownership. And, in *Beauregard v. Comm'r*, 74 T.C. 603 (1980) (*acq.*), the court excluded the proceeds on the basis of a divorce-related court order to maintain the policy for the benefit of minor children.

c. Formerly, it was difficult for an employee to assign employer-purchased group-term life insurance. However, statutes have since been enacted in all states making such assignments possible. Coverage normally ceases upon termination of employment. In *Rev. Rul.* 72-307, 1972-1 C.B. 307, the Service conceded that the power to terminate one's employment was as an aspect of the employment relationship and hence was only incidental to the exercise of ownership rights (and, therefore, would not be considered an "incident of ownership").

3. a. Does the *R.I. Hospital Trust Co.* approach make it easier or more difficult for an insured to arrange for others to take out policies on his life? In other words, what result where B takes out a policy on A's life and A and B enter into a contract giving A the power to veto beneficiary designations and choose settlement options? Does *R.I. Hospital Trust Co.* only favor the government?

b. In "split-dollar" insurance, the employer takes out ordinary insurance on the decedent's life and proceeds to pay that portion of each premium that corresponds to the increase in the cash surrender value. The remainder of the premium is paid by the employee. On the death of the insured, the employer receives the cash surrender value, and the employee's designated beneficiary obtains the rest of the proceeds. From the employee's point of view, this arrangement amounts to "decreasing term" coverage. For estate tax purposes, the amount includible in the employee's gross estate is the proceeds less the cash surrender value just prior to the employee's death. For income and gift tax results, see *Rev. Rul.* 78-420, 1978-2 C.B. 67.

c. As already mentioned, the GST tax can apply if the insurance proceeds are subject to estate or gift tax in Generation 1 and the beneficiary is a "skip person," such as an individual in Generation 3 (a grandchild of the insured). But if a grandchild takes out insurance on the life of a grandparent, a generation-skipping transfer is avoided. The same is true if the policy is owned by the insured's child, who names her child (the insured's grandchild) as beneficiary, because here the receipt of the proceeds will involve a gift from the child to the grandchild.

E. Effect of Premium Payments

The payment of premiums by the insured on a policy owned by the insured is not a gift, and it is irrelevant under §2042. However, the payment of premiums in other scenarios can raise gift and estate tax issues.

1. Payment by the Insured on a Policy
Owned by Another

Under pre-1982 law, §2035(a) provided that the transfer of any property within three years of death brought the property back into the gross estate. Such a rule obviously applied to the transfer of the policy (and its incidents of ownership) by the insured within three years of death. Under former §2035(a), there was also authority for the proposition that the *payment of all of premiums* by the insured with respect to pure term insurance (owned by another person) within three years of death was not only a gift of the premiums but also a transfer of the *proceeds* under former §2035(a) itself (without any reference to, or incorporation of, §2042). This was sometimes referred to as the "beamed transfer [of the proceeds]" theory, a phrase taken from the leading case, *Bel v. U.S.*, 452 F.2d 683, 691-692 (5th Cir.1971), *cert. denied*, 406 U.S. 919 (1972).[40]

In 1981, Congress repealed former §2035(a) but added §2035(d)(2), which (with different language) is now §2035(a). The case below involved the question of whether *the payment of premiums* by the insured, within three years of death, on a policy taken out by another within three years of the insured's death, causes inclusion in the gross estate of the proceeds under what is now §2035(a) (and what was then §2035(d)(2)). In other words, the issue was whether the "beamed transfer" approach was overturned by the 1981 legislation.

Estate of Leder v. Commissioner

89 T.C. 235 (1987) affirmed, 893 F.2d 237 (10th Cir.1989)

WELLS, *Judge*: The decedent died on May 31, 1983. He was insured under a life insurance policy [in the face amount of $1M]. The application for the policy was signed by Jeanne Leder, as owner, and the decedent, as the insured. The policy

---

40. It appears that, in all of the cases applying the beamed-transfer theory, the insured was involved with the procurement of the policy. See *Estate of Schnack v. Comm'r*, 848 F.2d 933 (9th Cir.1988); *Detroit Bank & Trust Co. v. U.S.*, 467 F.2d 964 (6th Cir.1972), *cert. denied*, 410 U.S. 929 (1973); *First Nat'l Bank of Oregon v. U.S.*, 488 F.2d 575 (9th Cir.1973); *Kurihara v. Comm'r*, 82 T.C. 51(1984). But where the ownership of the policy by the non-insured began more than three years prior to the death of the insured, the payment of premiums by the insured did not cause any of the proceeds to be included. *First Nat'l Bank of Midland v. U.S.*, 423 F.2d 1286 (5th Cir.1970) (ordinary insurance); *Estate of Coleman v. Comm'r*, 52 T.C. 921 (1969) (reviewed) (no indication whether policy was term or ordinary insurance). See generally *Rev. Rul.* 71-497, 1971-2 C.B. 329.

initially reflected Jeanne Leder as sole owner and beneficiary. The premiums were paid by pre-authorized withdrawals from the account of Leder Enterprises, a corporation wholly owned by the decedent. All of the premiums were paid less than three years before the decedent's death. The premium payments were treated as loans made by Leder Enterprises to the decedent.

[Since 1976, section 2035(a) has required] inclusion in a decedent's gross estate of the value of property, any interest in which was transferred by him within three years of death for less than adequate and full consideration. The Economic Recovery Tax Act of 1981 ("ERTA"), added §2035(d), which applies to estates of decedents dying after 1981. Section 2035(d) nullifies §2035(a) (hereinafter the "3-year rule"), [except that] §2035(d)(2) allows the 3-year rule to be applied to a transfer of an interest in property which either (1) is included in the value of the gross estate under §2042, or (2) would have been included under §2042 had such an interest been retained by the decedent.

Petitioner asserts that unless the decedent possessed some incident of ownership of the policy at some time during the three years before his death, there was nothing for the decedent to transfer, and §2035(d)(2) is inapplicable. Respondent counters that the term "transfer" as used in §2035 refers to any transfer whether direct or indirect. Respondent's argument may be appropriate in interpreting the meaning of [former] §2035(a); however, respondent overlooks the language of §2035(d), which must be satisfied before any consideration may be given to §2035(a).

There is no more persuasive evidence of the purpose of a statute than the words by which the legislature undertook to give expression to its wishes; where these words are sufficient in and of themselves to determine the purpose of the legislation, we should follow their plain meaning. The plain language of §2035(d)(2) requires as a threshold issue that there be an interest in property under the terms of the sections it lists (e.g., §2042). Thus, in order to determine whether §2035(d)(2) applies, we must determine whether the decedent ever possessed any interest under the terms of §2042, which, as noted earlier, is the only cited section in §2035(d)(2) that potentially applies to this case. Includibility under §2042 depends upon the decedent's retention of incidents of ownership.

In the instant case we must look to the relevant state law to determine whether the decedent had any rights that might be incidents of ownership. Under Oklahoma law the decedent never possessed any contractual rights under the policy, any power to assign the policy, any express or implied power to change the beneficiary, or any power to pledge the policy to creditors. In short, he never possessed any of the incidents of ownership in the policy, regardless of his payment of premiums.

Because the decedent never possessed any of the incidents of ownership, the proceeds from the policy never could have been included in the gross estate pursuant to §2042. Thus, we hold that the exception in §2035(d)(2) is inapplicable to the proceeds from the policy and that under §2035(d)(1) the proceeds from the insurance policy are not includible in the gross estate.

After a series of further setbacks in the appeals courts,[41] the IRS has conceded the issue litigated in *Leder*. See A.O.D. *1991-012* (Jul. 3, 1991).

2. Can the Payment of Premiums Be a "Transfer" of the Proceeds Outside of §2035?

At issue is whether the "beamed transfer" theory — although now inoperative under §2035 — can be applied to find that the payment of premiums on insurance owned by another constitutes a "transfer" not just of the premiums but also of the proceeds for gift tax purposes and/or §§2036-2038. A pre-1982 case that raised the issue was *Goodnow v. U.S.*, 302 F.2d 516 (Ct. Cl. 1962). There, H had acquired a policy on his own life, which he transferred to a revocable trust, but W paid all of the premiums. On H's death, the proceeds (which were includible in his gross estate under §2042(2)) were payable to the trust, which gave W the right to the income for her life. The government unsuccessfully argued that the trust was includible in W's gross estate under §2036(a)(1) on account of the premium payments and the retained income interest. The court disagreed, suggesting that H, not W, was the real payer of the premiums (and, hence, the real transferor), because of the fact that H could have revoked the trust prior to his death.

Goodnow undermines the beamed-transfer theory by holding that the true payer of premiums, in substance, is the owner of the policy: The substance of the transaction is viewed as a gift of cash to the owner, who then pays the premiums. It can also be argued that one cannot really distinguish the cases holding that no part of the proceeds are included where the insured paid the premiums (within three years of death) on policies owned by a non-insured beyond the three-year period.[42] The rationale of these cases is that the premiums "maintain" property already owned by another. Thus, it is possible that the beamed-transfer-of-proceeds theory was not really viable and would have eventually been discarded.

Even assuming that the beamed-transfer theory possesses viability outside of §2035(a), it should not be a significant concern. Any scenario in which a person paid premiums on insurance owned by another individual or by a revocable trust would fall under the protection of *Goodnow*. If the policy was held by an irrevocable trust created by the same person who paid the premiums, that person would avoid retaining any interest or power that would set off any of §§2036-2038 and 2042. About the only danger zone would be a scenario like *Goodnow* itself but where the trust was irrevocable.

---

41. See, e.g., *Estate of Perry v. Comm'r*, 927 F.2d 209 (5th Cir.1991): *Estate of Headrick v. Comm'r*, 918 F.2d 1263 (6th Cir.1990).

42. *First Nat'l Bank of Midland v. U.S.*, 423 F. 2d 1286 (5th Cir.1970); *Estate of Coleman v. Comm'r*, 52 T.C. 921 (1969) (reviewed); *Rev. Rul. 71-497*, 1971-2 C.B. 329 (acquiescing in these results).

3. *Effect of Premium Payments by the Non-Insured Owner*

Uncertainty exists as to the proper effect, if any, of the payment of premiums *by the donee* on policies transferred by the donor within three years of death and includible in the donor's gross estate under current §2035(a).

The original source of the uncertainty was *Liebmann v. Hassett*, 148 F.2d 247 (1st Cir.1945), where the court excluded that portion of the proceeds on ordinary insurance which the donee's premiums bore to the total premiums. This case, however, was decided prior to 1954, when the premium-payment test was in effect, and would now seem to be irrelevant. Nevertheless, the Tax Court, in *Estate of Silverman v. Comm'r*, 61 T.C. 338 (1973) (*acq.*), applied (at the Commissioner's urging) *Liebmann* to the facts of a pre-1982 case arising under former §2035(a), citing Reg. §20.2035-1(e), now withdrawn, which stated that donee-constructed improvements on transferred real property are not included in the donor's gross estate under §2035. Upon appeal by the taxpayer (but not the Commissioner), the Second Circuit affirmed, 521 F.2d 574 (2d Cir.1975), but stated that, "It is not immediately apparent that payments of premiums on an existing insurance policy are 'improvements or additions to' the property here (an insurance policy), with a 'resulting enhancement' in its value." The Second Circuit then went on to state in *dictum* that the proper amount to be excluded, if anything, would be limited to the amount of premiums paid by the donee rather than a portion of the proceeds.

The Tax Court appears to have applied the *Liebmann* approach even to a post-1981 §2035 case, *Estate of Friedberg v. Comm'r*, T.C. Memo. 1992-310 (1992).[43] The post-1981 version of §2035 considered in this case (and *Leder*) took away former §2035(a) and then restored it in the case of transfers of insurance. The Tax Court accordingly thought that *Silverman* was still good law.

However, the structure of §2035 was changed again in 1997. The post-1997 version (current §2035(a)) uses language that posits a different approach, namely, that of "restoring" §2042 despite the transfer or release of incidents of ownership within three years of death. That is, §2035(a) includes what would have been included under (in this case) §2042 if the transfer or release within three years of death had not occurred. Accordingly, premiums should be irrelevant, regardless of the payer.[44]

Nevertheless, it is not clear if the Service has abandoned the *Silverman* approach. Nothing issued by the IRS after 1997 has mentioned *Silverman* one way or the other.

---

43. The §2035 issue was a subsidiary one in this case. The Commissioner's main theory was that the proceeds were included under §2042(1), because the beneficiary of the policy happened to be executor of the estate. Needless to say, that argument was a loser.

44. This result would be consistent with *Leder*, as well as with *First Nat'l Bank of Midland, Texas v. U.S.*, 423 F.2d 1286 (1970), which held that premium payments paid by the insured on policies owned by another are irrelevant under §2042 and themselves do not constitute a transfer of a portion of the proceeds under §2035. See generally Douglas A. Kahn & Lawrence H. Waggoner, *Tax Consequences of Assigning Life Insurance — Time For Another Look*, 4 Fla. Tax Rev. 381 (1999) (arguing that, at most, only the donee-paid premiums should be subtracted).

QUICK QUESTION

Two years before his death, Donald transferred a $1M life insurance policy on his life to his son Steve. Which one of the following statements is *TRUE*?

    A. Donald made a $1M gift to Steve.
    B. When Donald dies, $1M is included in his estate under §2042.
    C. When Donald dies, $1M is included in his estate under §2035.

QUESTIONS AND NOTES

1. a. The beamed-transfer theory enabled the courts in various cases to hold that the payment of premiums on pure term insurance within three years of death caused inclusion of the proceeds in the gross estate under the pre-1982 version of §2035. Without the beamed-transfer theory, a literal application of §2035 would only have brought the premiums (paid within three years of death) back into the gross estate. A doctrinal assumption in these cases was that §§2035 and 2042 were wholly separate.

   b. Were these cases wrongly decided, given that the owners of the policy could have cancelled them at any time prior to the insured donor's death? That is, was the true substance of the facts in these cases one in which the insured made a gift of cash equal to the premium amounts to the donees followed by premium payments by the donees?

   c. In all of the pre-1982 cases following the beamed-transfer theory, the policy was taken out by the third-party owner with the active involvement by the decedent insured, within three years of the decedent's death. Wouldn't a better approach have been to view these situations as involving, in substance, the taking out of the *policy* by the insured followed by a transfer *of the policy* within three years of death? Would this approach, if adopted, be able to by-pass *Leder* (and its progeny)? See *Estate of Perry v. Comm'r*, 927 F.2d 209 (5th Cir.1991).

2. a. The legislative history of the changes to §2035 in 1981 shows no "specific" awareness of reversing the result of the beamed-transfer cases. Nevertheless, there is language in the Committee Reports indicating that the prior three-year rule was being repealed except for transfers of relatively small amounts having a significant potential to remove much larger amounts from the gross estate, such as gifts of life insurance and gifts (and releases) of interests and powers falling under §§2036-2038. Textually, the post-1981 version of §2035 had effect only as it was linked to these other sections: "Paragraph (1) of this subsection [repealing the general three-year rule] shall not apply to a transfer of an interest in property which is

included in the value of the gross estate under §2036, 2037, 2038, or 2042 or would have been included under any of such sections if such interest had been retained by the decedent." Presumably, the reference to "a transfer of an interest in property" is what influenced the court in *Leder*, because premiums are not an interest in a life insurance policy, and the reference to "interest had been retained" makes no sense in the §2042 context. The 1997 changes do not seem to alter the thrust of the language as to what has to be transferred. Should courts decide these cases on the basis of pure textualism or on what Congress (likely) intended?

    b. *Leder* and its progeny removed a cloud as to how the insured should handle the payment of premiums on policies transferred to an irrevocable trust. Under pre-1982 law, the payment of premiums by the grantor-insured to the trustee (who then paid the insurance company) sometimes ran afoul of §2035.[45] These authorities would now appear to be obsolete.

    c. Does *Leder* render *Silverman* obsolete? If §2035(a) is just an adjunct to §2042, how can the payment of premiums be relevant at all?

    d. Does the 1997 change to §2035 render *Silverman* obsolete?

3. In *Rev. Rul.* 79-303, 1979-2 C.B. 332, all the premiums on H's life were paid from community property funds. H and W died simultaneously. Half of the proceeds were included in H's gross estate under §2042(2). The problem was how to treat W's one-half of the proceeds, which were paid to a third party. Since W was not the insured, §2042 could not apply. If the state law rule is that H died first, then W would have made a gift of her half of proceeds to the third-party beneficiary. The ruling held that, if the state law rule is that W died first, then half of the *proceeds* would be included under §2038. Is this holding implicitly based on the beamed-transfer theory (because, if W died first, the proceeds wouldn't have come into existence yet)? If so, is the ruling incorrect?

---

45. See *Detroit Bank & Trust Co. v. U.S.*, 467 F.2d 964 (6th Cir. 1972), *cert. denied*, 410 U.S. 929 (1973); *Kurihara v. Comm'r*, 82 T.C. 51 (1984) (reviewed) (trust is conduit for grantor premiums). But see *Hope v. Comm'r*, 691 F.2d 786 (5th Cir. 1982) (government needs to show trustee was agent in paying premiums).

CHAPTER 6

MARITAL TRANSFERS

Marital transfers (transfers by one spouse to or for the benefit of the other spouse) are a pervasive aspect of family wealth management and estate planning.

Spousal transfers raise the prospect of obtaining the gift and estate tax marital or charitable deduction, which is the principal focus of this chapter. Under the GST tax, a marital deduction would be superfluous, since a husband-wife pair are deemed to be located in the same generation as each other, regardless of their respective ages. See §2651(c)(1).

§6.1. Purpose and Effect of the Marital Deduction

The marital deduction allows a married couple to use up each spouse's exemption in full and to either (a) lower the average tax rate applicable to the couple's aggregate taxable wealth (i.e., wealth in excess of both exemptions) or (b) with proper planning, defer tax on such aggregate wealth until the death of the surviving spouse.

A. Background

Starting with the 1916 Act, husbands and wives were treated as separate tax-payers under the federal estate tax — and they still are. There is no concept of a "joint" estate tax return.

The law of marital property rights determines how property is owned by husband and wife initially, but federal tax law determines how such rights are to be characterized. The federal income and wealth transfer taxes have long treated community property as being owned one-half by each spouse,[1] as is the

---

1. See *Poe v. Seaborn*, 282 U.S. 101 (1930) (income tax); *U.S. v. Stapf*, 375 U.S. 118 (1963) (estate tax).

case with property held as a 50-50 tenancy in common by husband and wife. In the case of joint tenancies with rights of survivorship, §2040(b) provides a rule of 50 percent inclusion in the estate of the deceased spouse.

But §2034 provides that rights of dower and curtesy (as well as other inheritance rights) of a surviving spouse do not rise to the level of ownership of an interest in the other spouse's property. Thus, if H died owning Blackacre, and W has the right to a life estate in Blackacre following H's death pursuant to a dower or elective share right, the full value of Blackacre is included in H's gross estate (and any *inter vivos* gift by H of Blackacre would have been treated as a gift entirely made by H). Similarly, homestead rights and spousal-allowance rights are not excluded from a decedent spouse's gross estate. Rights of a spouse that could only have been obtained on divorce are likewise not excluded from a deceased spouse's estate, because such rights expire on the death of the deceased spouse. In all of these cases, property (and interests therein) that pass from a transferor spouse to a transferee spouse are not excluded from gift or estate tax, although they may (or may not) be deductible pursuant to the marital deduction. Of course, an initial inclusion in the transferor's tax base followed by an equal offsetting deduction produces the same end result as an exclusion. Nevertheless, it is important to keep in mind that the marital deduction is a deduction for gift and estate-included transfers, and not an exclusion.

Under a progressive rate system, or even a flat rate system with an off-the-bottom per-taxpayer exemption (or exemption equivalent), aggregate taxes are reduced where a given tax base is evenly split between two (or more) taxpayers than where the tax base is lopsidedly allocated to one taxpayer. This is as true of the federal transfer taxes as it is of the income tax. In the "old days" it was typical for the husband to enter the market — and (hopefully) accumulate wealth — and for the wife to labor in non-market settings. Under a "common law" property regime, the husband would be the owner of all of the wealth derived from his earnings, unless he gave some of it to his wife or created joint tenancies. Under a "community property" regime, in contrast, accumulated wealth (except that received by gift, bequest, or tort recovery) is "owned" 50-50 by each spouse. Thus, for estate tax (as well as income tax) purposes, a couple in a community-property state would, in the absence of the marital deduction, be typically better off than a couple in a common-law state.

Example: Assume a progressive rate schedule under which the first $500K is taxed at a 10 percent rate and the excess over $500K at a 25 percent rate. Assume that A and B, who are married, accumulate an aggregate net estate of $1M entirely from A's earnings, and that A and B die leaving all their property to their child C. If the $1M is not community property, it is all owned by A and none of it by B. Thus, the estate tax on A is $175K [$(.1 \times \$500K) + (.25 \times \$500K)$]. If the $1M is community property, however, the net estate of each of A and B is $500K, and the aggregate tax is only $100K [$2 \times (.1 \times \$500K)$].

In 1942, Congress attempted to deal with the advantage inuring to community-property couples by treating community property somewhat in the nature of joint property under §2040(a). Due to the eased pressure on revenue requirements following the conclusion of World War II, the ascendancy of a tax-cutting Republican Congress in 1946, and political pressure from community-property states, a complete overhaul of the taxation of husband and wife was undertaken in 1948, resulting in the joint-return system for the income tax and, for the estate and gift tax, repeal of the 1942 approach, restoration of the pre-1942 treatment of community property, allowance of gift splitting under §2513 for non-community-property gifts, and enactment of the marital deduction, which facilitated common-law couples' arranging their affairs to approximate the beneficial results obtained by their community-property counterparts.

The 1948 estate tax marital deduction enabled the first spouse to die (typically the husband who possessed most of the couple's wealth) to obtain a deduction — not to exceed half of the decedent's "adjusted gross estate" (gross estate less deductions under §§2053 and 2054) — equal to the value of estate-included transfers to the surviving spouse that qualified for the marital deduction. If the wealthier spouse died first, couples not possessed of community property were able to achieve the same result as under a community-property system. Community property, being already favored, was not eligible for the 1948 marital deduction.

It was more difficult to design an appropriate gift tax marital deduction. Under the community-property model, a person should be allowed to give any amount to his spouse tax free up to the point where the couple's aggregate wealth is split 50-50. Unfortunately, this approach is practically not feasible, as it would require the valuation, following any inter-spousal gift, of all property owned by both spouses. Instead, the 1948 gift tax marital deduction conferred a deduction equal to one-half of the value of a gift (before the §2503 exclusion) to one's spouse.

The 1948 marital deduction was critiqued for various reasons, one being that it cut against the desire of a majority of spouses to leave their entire estates to the surviving spouse. In 1981 the approach of the marital deduction was drastically liberalized under both the estate tax and the gift tax. The limitation on the marital deduction was completely removed, and community property became eligible for the marital deduction. The underlying philosophy of the new "unlimited" marital deduction is that husband and wife are, in a loose sense, a single taxable unit, so that transfers "within" the unit are not subject to tax. However, the single-taxable-unit idea is not carried through, because husbands and wives continue to be separate decedents under the estate tax, with separate lifetime exemptions. (If husbands and wives were really considered a single unit, then the estate tax would be imposed only on the death of the survivor, and the tax base would be the *combined* net transfers of both spouses to third parties in excess of the *combined* lifetime exemptions.)

B. Qualification Requirements

Turning to the technical aspects of the marital deduction, the gift or estate tax deduction, under §2056 or §2523 (as the case may be), is restricted to property:

(1) which "passes" from the decedent spouse to the surviving spouse (or which is a gift from the donor spouse to the donee spouse),[2]

(2) the value of which is includible in the decedent's gross estate (or would be a non-excluded gift under the gift tax),[3] and

(3) which avoids characterization as a nondeductible terminable interest.[4]

Property that passes all three tests is referred to as a "qualifying" marital deduction transfer.

1. The "Passing" and "Taxable Transfer" Requirements

The first two of these qualification rules is based on the notion that the deduction should only pertain to a transfer that would otherwise be taxable. An exclusion and deduction for the same transfer would amount to a double tax benefit. Items that would be disqualified under this rubric include life insurance proceeds payable to the surviving spouse that are not includible under §2042 (or any other provision) and the half of joint-tenancy property excluded from the decedent spouse's gross estate under §2040(b).

In the estate tax context, the "passing" requirement is not limited to probate transfers or transfers effected contemporaneously with the decedent's death. Joint ownership, life insurance, pension benefits, *inter vivos* gifts, trust transfers, and transfers effected through the exercise or non-exercise of powers of appointment will all satisfy the "passing" requirement. See §2056(c). Thus, a qualifying marital deduction estate transfer need not be a "bequest" in the literal sense.

If a surviving spouse is offered an election (under the governing instrument or state law) to take property from the decedent spouse's gross estate in lieu of what the decedent provided by way of bequest, trust interest, or whatever, the passing requirement is satisfied only for the property actually taken, rather than what could have been taken.[5] Similarly, what is actually taken under a bona fide settlement of an adversary will contest resolved by court decree will be treated as having passed to the surviving spouse.[6]

The estate tax marital deduction is reduced by any death tax payable out of the property passing to the surviving spouse and by any lien, encumbrance, or other charge on such property. This rule is separately stated in §2056(b)(4), although it is implied by the concept of "passing."[7]

---

2. §§2056(a) and 2523(a).

3. Ibid.

4. §§2056(b) and 2523(b)-(g).

5. See Reg. §20.2056(c)-2(c). A so-called "widow's allowance" for support during estate administration satisfies the passing requirement to the extent awarded. Reg. §20.2056(c)-2(a).

6. See Reg. §20.2056(c)-2(d).

7. Under the gift tax, a transfer subject to a liability amounts to a shifting of the liability from the donor to the donee and, as a general matter, constitutes consideration in money or money's worth for both income and gift tax purposes. However, if the donee is the donor's spouse, such consideration is ignored for income tax purposes on account of §1041, and is inconsequential for gift tax purposes, because (in addition to the consideration offset) the remaining "net" gift can qualify for the marital deduction.

2. *The Terminable Interest Rule*

The third qualification requirement is that the transfer *not* be a "nondeductible terminable interest." This requirement is known as the "terminable interest rule." In analyzing any transfer to a surviving spouse under this terminable interest rule, three issues must be addressed: (1) whether the interest is a "terminable" one, (2) whether the terminable interest is of the "nondeductible" type, and (3) whether any of the exceptions to nondeductibility apply.

(a) Concept of "Terminable Interest"

A "terminable interest" is an interest in property whose possession or enjoyment by the transferee is subject to a condition either precedent or subsequent, including the expiration of a period of time. See §§2056(b)(1) and 2523(b) (lead-in clauses). Thus, income interests and life estates are terminable interests, as are annuity rights, contingent remainder interests, patents, copyrights, and nonrenewable licenses. Bonds, notes, and similar contract rights are not terminable interests.[8]

It is crucial to understand that an interest is terminable if, viewing the situation *as of the moment of gift or the decedent's death*, there is *any chance* that the condition defeating or terminating the interest *might* occur in the future. Whether or not the "terminating" contingency *in fact* occurs is not at all relevant. This type of *ex ante* analysis is reminiscent of the classic Rule Against Perpetuities, without any possibility of escape under a wait-and-see approach. The purported justification of the *ex ante* approach is that qualification for the marital deduction must be determined at the date of gift or death, as the case may be.

(b) Nondeductible Terminable Interests

Once a terminable interest is identified, the next step is to determine whether it is deductible or nondeductible. A terminable interest is initially "nondeductible" where possession or enjoyment of the property would (or will) pass to a third party upon the occurrence of the condition. See §§2056(b)(1)(A) & (B) and 2523(b). The prime example of a nondeductible terminable interest is a legal or equitable life estate followed by another interest, as where W bequeaths property in trust, income to H for life, remainder to C. Another example would be a bequest from H to W "if W survives me by a period of two years, but, if she does not, then to C." In the latter case, if W failed to survive the two-year period, the bequest would go to C.

The rationale of the terminable-interest rule can now be discerned: It is to ensure that, at a minimum, a deductible transfer from one spouse to another will appear in the gift or estate tax base of the transferee spouse (unless dissipated). Thus, in the case where W transfers property to H for life, remainder to C, if H's life estate were to qualify for the marital deduction the life estate would be deductible by W (or her estate) but not includible in H's estate because it terminates at his death.

---

8. See §2056(b)(1) (flush language).

The astute observer of this example will point out that, although the income interest as such is not included in H's gross estate, the income actually received prior to death will have augmented H's §2033 gross estate. Therefore, it might be argued, the transferor spouse (W) should obtain a deduction equal to the actuarial value of the income interest bequeathed to H. However, such a rule would open the door to tax avoidance in cases where the amount deductible, which would be computed on the basis of actuarial tables, turned out to be greater than the amount actually received by the surviving spouse, either because the surviving spouse died prior to his or her life expectancy or because the net income yield was below that assumed in the actuarial tables. Of course, the opposite might turn out to be the case, i.e., the amount deductible might be less than what the surviving spouse actually receives. Nevertheless, sophisticated estate planners would set up this type of bequest only when they anticipated a tax-savings outcome. If the "beat the actuarial tables" game could be played with income interests, it could be played with even more devastating effect by employing other types of contingencies. Accordingly, the terminable-interest rule operates as a blunt instrument that simply forecloses most (if not all) tax-savings opportunities of this sort. The terminable interest rule is blunt, because it is necessary to test qualification under the marital deduction as of the time of transfer, not long after the fact.

By being a blunt instrument, the terminable-interest rule can operate to deny a marital deduction even when property is actually received by the transferee spouse. Thus, if H bequeaths Blackacre to W if she survives him by two years, the terminable interest rule bars a deduction to H's estate even though, if W in fact survives H by two years, she will receive the property outright in augmentation of her potential §2033 gross estate.[9] But, anyone knowing the terminable-interest rule would not provide for a bequest of this sort. The moral of this story is that qualification must be obtained by following the rules. Satisfying the policy of the terminable-interest rule is not good enough.

It might be thought that tax-avoidance games can still be played outside of the terminable-interest rule. Thus, if H bequeaths Blackacre to W outright, the bequest qualifies for the marital deduction even if Blackacre does not in fact appear in W's §2033 gross estate because she subsequently sells Blackacre and consumes the proceeds. But destruction of wealth always avoids the estate tax. Contingencies attached to bequests, in contrast, do not destroy property; they only affect who owns it in cases where a third party takes upon the failure or occurrence of the condition.

Suppose H takes out a self-and-survivor annuity for joint lives of H and W, and H dies first, with the value of the survivor annuity being included in the gross estate

---

9. It is not entirely clear whether a contingent bequest of this sort would satisfy the "passing" requirement. None of the examples cited under Reg. §20.2056(c)-2(b) describe such a scenario. Nevertheless, the statutory rule refers to "property interests," and a contingent bequest certainly qualifies as a property interest. Indeed, the contingent interest passes to the surviving spouse even if the bequest fails on account of the contingency. Hence, the terminable-interest rule is needed here to disallow the marital deduction in such a case.

under §2039 at value keyed to W's then life expectancy. The survivor annuity passing to W, although a terminable interest, is not disqualified, because on W's death no interest in the fund supporting the annuity passes to a third party.[10] It is true that, if W dies prematurely, the marital deduction amount (based on W's life expectancy rather than her actual lifespan) will, in hindsight, have been over-stated. But inaccurate valuation is considered to be a structural hazard of the transfer taxes. The real purpose of the terminable interest rule, therefore, is not so much to obtain accurate valuation, but rather to prevent devices that would shift wealth from W to a third party without transfer tax.

There are two per se disqualification rules that can apply to transfers that would not otherwise be disqualified. Section 2056(b)(1)(C) disqualifies (for estate tax purposes) a terminable interest that "is to be" acquired by a personal representative or trustee. Thus, if W bequeaths $100K to H with the direction that her executor buy a single-life annuity for H's life, the bequest will be disqua-lified. Second, §§2056(b)(2) and 2523(c) provide that, if a transfer to a spouse *might be* satisfied out of an asset that would be treated as a nondeductible terminable interest on its own (such as a right to rents from property included in the decedent spouse's gross estate), the marital deduction will be reduced by the value of such asset, even if such asset is not in fact used to satisfy the transfer. Because of this rule, it is standard practice to include language in the governing instrument to the effect that no such property or interest can be used to fund any transfer that would otherwise qualify for the marital deduction.

(c) The "Estate Trust"

Suppose Horacio's will creates a testamentary trust, naming the X Bank as trustee, income to Winona or accumulated in the trustee's discretion, and on Winona's death the trust assets are payable to her estate. Such a trust is known as an "estate trust." Although Winona's estate acquires a vested remainder, the current interest of Winona is contingent on the trustee's discretion, and it terminates at her death. Nevertheless, the estate trust qualifies for the marital deduction, because no third party benefits if income is accumulated and then paid to her estate upon Winona's death. The remainder in Winona's estate is considered to be a continuation of Winona herself. Moreover, that remainder assures inclusion in Winona's gross estate under §2041.

(d) Statutory Exceptions to the Terminable Interest Rule

Congress has explicitly provided for six exceptions to the terminable-interest rule.

First, under §2056(b)(3) an estate transfer that is conditioned only on the surviving spouse's surviving the decedent by six months (or less) and/or dying as the result of a common disaster (which produced the death of the decedent) qualifies for the marital deduction, but only if the divesting condition does not in fact occur (so that the surviving spouse actually receives the transfer).

---

10. See Reg. §20.2056(b)-1(g), Ex. 3; *Rev. Rul.* 76-404, 1976-2 C.B. 294.

Second, §2056(b)(5) and §2523(e) provide for an exception under both the estate and gift tax for a type of transfer referred to as a "power of appointment trust." (Actually, the arrangement need not be in trust, but virtually all transfers designed to come within this exception are made through a trust.) To qualify as a power-of-appointment trust (PAT), the trust must give the transferee spouse a right to "all of" the income for life payable at least annually *and* a *general* power of appointment (exercisable *inter vivos* or by will) exercisable by the transferee spouse "alone and in all events." The general power of appointment will cause inclusion of the property in the transferee spouse's estate and/or gift tax base under §2041(a)(2) and §2514(b) (both described in detail in Chapter 7), thereby satisfying the rationale of the marital deduction.

Third, Congress in 1981 added §2056(b)(7) and §2523(f), which refer to "qualified terminable interest property." Since, again, virtually all arrangements involving qualified terminable interest property are in trust, this exception is often referred to as the "QTIP trust" exception to the terminable-interest rule. Like the power-of-appointment trust, a QTIP trust must provide that the transferee spouse receive all of the income from the transferred property payable at least annually for life. See §2056(b)(7)(B)(ii)(I). Instead of a general power of appointment, the second requirement for qualification here is the "QTIP election," meaning that the transfer qualifies for the marital deduction only if the donor so elects on the gift tax return, or the decedent's estate representative so elects on the estate tax return. See §§2056(b)(7)(B)(i)(III) & (v) and 2523(f)(2)(C) & (4). The price to be paid for making the election is that the entire QTIP trust will be included in the estate or gift tax base of the transferee spouse under §2044 or §2519 *solely on account of the election*. (Without §2044, of course, the right to income for life would not cause the property to be includible in the estate of the transferee spouse, and without §2519, a gift of the income interest would be a lesser amount than a gift of the entire trust property.) A third requirement for qualification of a QTIP trust is that no person (such as the trustee or the transferee spouse) can have the power to appoint the QTIP property to any person other than the transferee spouse during the latter's lifetime. See §§2056(b)(7)(B)(ii)(II) and 2523(f)(3). Any such appointment would divert QTIP property away from the transferee spouse's estate and gift tax base.

In the case of both the PAT and the QTIP trust, *the value of the entire trust (or property) transfer qualifies for the marital deduction*, not just the actuarial value of the income interest transferred to the transferee spouse. Thus, the tax result is the same as for an outright transfer.

Turning to the minor exceptions, first there is §2056(b)(6), which deals with settlement options under life insurance and annuity policies, and essentially parallels the exception for PATs.

Second is §2523(d), which states (in a roundabout way) that the creation of a joint tenancy with right of survivorship (or a tenancy by the entireties) solely with one's spouse shall not be treated as a nondeductible terminable interest just because the donor spouse retains a survivorship right and a right of severance.

Finally, §§2056(b)(8) and 2523(g) give a marital deduction to a qualified interest transferred to a spouse which is followed by a remainder to charity, provided that the "charitable remainder" interest qualifies for the estate or gift tax charitable deduction under §2055 or §2522.[11] Thus, the value of the interest given to the transferee spouse is deductible as a marital deduction, and the value of the remainder interest is deductible as a charitable deduction. This vehicle will hereinafter be referred to as a marital/charitable transfer.

Sections 2056(b)(9) and 2523(h) provide that the statutory overrides to the terminable interest rule are not to result in double deductions for the same interests. An example would be a QTIP non-trust transfer of a residence or farm to one's spouse for life, remainder to charity, which would qualify both for the QTIP election for the entire value of the residence and a charitable deduction for the remainder by reason of §170(f)(3)(B)(i), which is incorporated into the estate and gift tax by §§2055(e)(2) and 2523(c)(2).[12]

(e) Elective Interests

The passing requirement, the terminable-interest rule, and concerns over valuation uncertainty all come into play with respect to interests and amounts that the surviving spouse can elect to take under state law or the terms of the governing instrument. These interests include spouse's elective share, dower and curtesy (which may entail a further election of commutation into a lump sum), "widow's allowance" awarded by a court for support during probate, homestead, an election offered by the will itself, and a settlement of a dispute involving succession.

In all of these cases, an election to take the item satisfies the "passing" requirement. If an election is not made to take the item, the passing requirement is not satisfied.

The next question is whether the availability of an election violates the terminable-interest rule either (a) because obtaining the property is contingent on the election that might be made outside of the six months' exception of §2056(b)(3), or (b) because (as is almost always the case) such rights will terminate upon W's death if she fails to make the election. The IRS has accepted the view that the requirement of having to make an affirmative election during probate and before the surviving spouse's death does not by itself render an interest terminable. Presumably, the election, which is under the control of the surviving spouse (or her personal representative), is considered to be merely procedural.[13] Thus, spousal elective shares, dower, and curtesy are not disqualified on this ground.

---

11. The qualification rules for trusts are found in §664, which requires that the sole noncharitable beneficiary (here, the transferee spouse) must have a right to a fixed amount (annuity) or a fixed percentage of the corpus (unitrust interest) payable annually for life (or a shorter period). A deduction for a charitable remainder interest not in trust is allowed only if the charitable remainder follows a noncharitable life estate in a personal residence or farm. See §170(f)(3).

12. See Regs. §§20.2056(b)-8(a)(1) & -9 and 25.2523(g)(2). Another example would be a charitable remainder unitrust, because a qualifying unitrust interest in the transferee spouse would satisfy both the marital and charitable deduction rules. See Regs. §§1.643(b)-1 and 20.2056(b)-5(f)(1).

13. See *First Nat'l Bank of Roanoke v. U.S.*, 335 F.2d 91 (4th Cir.1964); *Rev. Rul. 83-107*, 1983-2 C.B. 159. Compare *Estate of Snider v. Comm'r*, 84 T.C. 75 (1985) (Texas widow's allowance not

Similarly, the marital deduction was allowed in a case where the husband's will left his art collection in a way that allowed his wife to elect to take either a life estate or a fee in artworks she selected. *Estate of Neugass v. Comm'r*, 555 F.2d 322 (2d Cir.1977). The election had to be made within six months of the decedent's death, and it related back to such death.[14] The wife in fact elected to take the artworks in fee. It is unclear if marital deduction would be saved in a case like *Neugass* if the election could be made after the six-month period of §2056(b)(3),[15] after the estate tax return is filed,[16] after probate closes, or at an indefinite time in the future, because at some point the election right would be difficult to value (apart from the difficulty of valuing the underlying assets that are involved). Fortunately, dispositions of this type are rare, because they do not fall under any clearly recognized property rule,[17] and the same objective may be obtainable by a bequest of a larger interest coupled with a disclaimer by the legatee.

A so-called "widow's allowance" is an award by a probate court to a surviving spouse of a fixed sum or periodic payment for the purpose of supporting the surviving spouse during the period of probate. Here, the results are mixed, because state law is variable. The leading case of *Jackson v. U.S.*, 376 U.S. 503 (1964), held that a California widow's allowance was a terminable interest, stressing the fact that the allowance could not be awarded (or, if awarded, continued) to a surviving spouse who had died or remarried. However, *Jackson* did not consider whether the terminable interest was of the nondeductible type, because the taxpayer had conceded this issue on the government's (successful) motion for summary judgment in the district court.[18] It is not clear that a third party accedes to enjoyment of the same property (upon failure of the surviving spouse's claim) by reason of having received an interest therein from the decedent spouse. A widow's allowance is somewhat akin to a money claim, and is not an interest in specific property (such as a life estate).[19] Some post-*Jackson* cases have held that a widow's

---

qualified where it would be barred in whole or in part by widow's having sufficient property for her support).

14. This point apparently led the court to hold (dubiously) that there was no alternate taker under the bequest.

15. Section 2056(b)(3) only saves contingencies of a certain type that occur within six months of the decedent's death. Thus, it should have no bearing on situations not expressly covered by it.

16. See *Rev. Rul.* 82-23, 1982-1 C.B. 139 (inability to value marital bequest as of decedent's death not a bar to qualification where the amount passing to the spouse is fixed by the estate tax return date).

17. In *Neugass*, the wife's power might conceivably be called a general power of appointment, but if that is the case, then its lapse would be treated as a gift of the property (or an interest therein) from the wife to the takers in default. See §2514(b) & (e). The court in *Neugass* found that the decedent did not intend to create a power of appointment, and simply characterized the situation as an elective bequest that was not invalid under New York law.

18. The concession is noted in 347 F.2d 821, 824 (9th Cir.1963). Therefore, *Jackson* cannot be said to have decided whether the terminable interest was a nondeductible one. The regulations provide an example indicating that if W were the sole beneficiary of the decedent's estate, the interest would be deductible. See Reg. §20.2056(b)-1(g), Ex. 8.

19. If the support claim had been incurred against the decedent before death, it would have been deductible as a claim against the estate under §2053.

allowance qualifies, but on the ground that the right to it is vested under state law.[20]

The interest that can be elected must not itself be a nondeductible terminable interest. Dower and Louisiana "usufruct" interests are life estates, but they can be made to qualify pursuant to a QTIP election. But a statutory right of occupancy, such as "homestead," although it satisfies the "passing" requirement, cannot qualify, even under a QTIP election, if state law provides that the right is to terminate upon abandonment of the property, because in that case the surviving spouse loses any right to the rents and thus has no unqualified "right" to the income "for life."

3. The PAT and QTIP Trust "Income" Requirement

Under both the PAT and QTIP trust exceptions to the terminable-interest rule, the surviving spouse must be entitled to *all* of the (net) income from the trust *payable at least annually*. (This requirement does not apply to "estate trusts.") Statutes in some states *require* that income from a mandatory income trust for the transferor's spouse for life be payable at least annually.[21] The purpose of such statutes is to avoid inadvertent disqualification where deferred distributions of income would otherwise be allowable.[22]

As a bow to practicality, in the case of a testamentary trust (or an *inter vivos* trust funded by a bequest), the payments of income need not begin immediately upon the decedent's death, but may be delayed for a reasonable period of probate.[23] Under state law, estate income is treated as trust income when the estate distributes to the trust. Therefore, the income beneficiary will not "lose" his or her entitlement to such income, although its enjoyment will be delayed. However, if the trustee is *required* by the trust instrument to wait until the first month following the close of a trust accounting year before paying the income to the surviving spouse, the income requirement is not satisfied.

The term "stub income" refers to income accrued after the last distribution to the transferee spouse and such spouse's death. Stub income does not have to be distributed to the transferee spouse's estate.[24] Nevertheless, it will be included in the transferee spouse's estate under §2041 or §2044, as the case may be.[25]

---

20. E.g., *Estate of Green v. U.S.*, 441 F.2d 303 (6th Cir.1971) (Michigan); *Estate of Radel v. Comm'r*, 88 T.C. 1143 (1987). Following *Jackson* are *Estate of Abeley v. Comm'r*, 489 F.2d 1327 (1st Cir.1974) (Massachusetts); *Rev. Rul.* 72-153, 1972-1 C.B. 309 (Washington) (noting discretionary nature of allowance).

21. See Fla. Trust Code §736.08147.

22. See *Rev. Rul.* 72-283, 1972-1 C.B. 111 (deduction disallowed where trustee required by governing instrument to distribute income in January following the year that the income accrued).

23. See Reg. §20.2056(b)-5(f)(9); *Rev. Rul.* 77-346, 1977-2 C.B. 340.

24. See Reg. §20.2056(b)-5(f)(8); Reg. §20.2056(b)-7(d)(4). See also *Estate of Shelfer v. Comm'r*, 86 F.3d 1045 (11th Cir.1996) (holding that stub income was included in surviving spouse's gross estate under §2044 even though it was not payable to her estate). The default rule is, nevertheless, that stub income is payable first to a succeeding income interest or, if there is none, to the estate of the deceased income beneficiary. See Uniform Principal and Income Act (1997) §303.

25. See Reg. §20.2044-1(d)(2). In a PAT, the stub income would be subject to the transferee spouse's general power of appointment.

The regulations take the position that an illusory right to income precludes qualification. Reg. §20.2056(b)-5(f) elaborates upon this requirement in some detail with respect to the administrative powers of a trustee. This regulation is well worth reading.

In *Rev. Rul. 69-56*, 1969-1 C.B. 224, the IRS dealt with scenarios involving the traditional law of trust accounting, in which "income" essentially includes interest, dividends, and all or a portion or rents and royalties (but not capital gains and unrealized appreciation) reduced by certain charges. In one scenario presented in the Ruling, the "income requirement" was deemed to have been satisfied, where the trust instrument contained various trust accounting provisions concerning the allocation of receipts and disbursements between income and principal that were similar to those found in the then-prevailing version of the Uniform Principal and Income Act. Although the trustee was given some discretion under these provisions, such discretion was bounded by the general state law fiduciary duty of impartiality, that is, the duty to balance fairly the interests of successive beneficiaries.[26] In another scenario that satisfied the income requirement, the governing instrument conferred upon the fiduciary only a general power to determine the manner in which receipts and disbursements were to be allocated between income and principal, but again state law imposed the duty of impartiality.

The "right to income" requirement is also impacted by the investment powers of trustees. Thus, Reg. §20.2056(b)-5(f)(4) & (5) states that the income requirement is not satisfied if the trust is funded (or can be funded) with "unproductive property" (property that does not generate income in the traditional sense), unless the surviving spouse can compel the trustee to convert the nonproductive investments into productive property. Under traditional fiduciary principles, trustees in making investments were long required to invest prudently (avoiding speculative investments) and to comply with the duty of impartiality, unless the trust instrument specifically provided otherwise. Under this rubric, the typical trust portfolio held a roughly equal amount of interest-bearing obligations (bonds, notes, and mortgages) and nonspeculative stocks. Such a portfolio generally produced an income yield in the 2.5 to 5 percent range, but a portfolio of this type is barely capable (if at all) of keeping up with inflation, and this fact operates at a disadvantage to the holders of remainder interests.

In the 1990s, the "total return" concept of investing began to supersede traditional thinking about trust investments and trust accounting. The general thrust of the total-return approach is to disregard the traditional distinction between income and principal. Whereas the traditional idea of "income" was limited to such periodic receipts as interest and dividends, the total return idea looks not only to such income but also to net gains and net appreciation. Thus, in those states which have modified trust law so as to embrace (in whole or in part) the

---

26. Under the Uniform Principal and Income Act (1997), the duty of impartiality (which can be overcome by a clear intent to the contrary) is found in Uniform Principal and Income Act (1997) §103(b).

total-return concept, the trustee is allowed to invest (prudently) to maximize the total net return (such as, for example, investing in indexed stock funds) without jeopardizing the safety of principal.[27] This total economic return is then allocated fairly between the income beneficiaries and remainders. One mechanism for this allocation is the power of "equitable adjustment," which (when allowed under state law) typically operates as a two-step process, the first step being the determination of net income according to the rules concerning income and principal, and the second step being the allocation of some principal by the trustee to the net income amount, so that the sum of conventional net income and reallocated principal satisfies the duty of impartiality.[28] The other mechanism for the allocation is to convert an "income" trust to a unitrust that requires distributions to the "income" beneficiaries of an amount equal to a percentage of the value of the trust as of some specified date during the year.[29] For example, if the trust is a 4 percent unitrust and the trust (ignoring the distinction between income and principal) is worth $1M on the annual valuation date, then $40K is distributable to the income beneficiary. Of course, the trust can be set up as a unitrust at its inception.

By way of response to this change in trust law, the marital deduction "income right" regulations were amended by adding the following (found, for example, in the last sentence of Reg. §20.2056(b)-5(f)(1)):

> In addition, the surviving spouse's interest shall meet [the income requirement] if the spouse is entitled to income as determined by applicable local law that provides for a reasonable apportionment between the income and remainder beneficiaries of the total return of the trust and that meets the requirements of §1.643(b)-1 of this chapter.

Reg. §1.643(b)-1, which is also well worth reading, elaborates upon the foregoing. In addition to citing the exercise of a power of equitable apportionment, it states that a unitrust amount of 3 to 5 percent of the fair market value of trust assets will be considered to be the equivalent of "income." A unitrust, by its nature, embodies the total return concept.

An annuity (fixed-dollar payout) trust is treated as an "income" trust to the extent that the annuity amount compares to the hypothetical income yield from the trust using the interest rate under the applicable actuarial tables. Thus, if the initial trust corpus is $1M, the applicable interest rate under the tables is 5 percent, and the annuity amount is $40K per year, the surviving spouse is treated as receiving all of the income from an $800K trust.[30] As noted below, qualification might be obtainable only for a fractional share of the trust. Here, assuming that the other

---

27. See Uniform Prudent Investor Act (1994); Restatement 3d of Trusts: Prudent Investor Rule (1992).

28. See Uniform Principal and Income Act (1997) §104.

29. See Fla. Uniform Principal and Income Act (2002), §738.1041 (giving a trustee the discretionary power to convert an income trust to a 3-5% unitrust).

30. The interest rate of 5% in the tables would produce an income yield of $50K from a $1M trust. An annuity payout of $40K per year is 4/5 of such yield. A portion of a trust can qualify under the PAT and QTIP rules. In his case, 4/5 of the $1M trust qualifies.

qualification requirements are satisfied, four-fifths of the trust qualifies for the marital deduction, and four-fifths of the trust will be included in the surviving spouse's gross estate under §2044. See Reg. §20.2056(b)-7(h), Ex. 11 & 12. It appears that annuity trusts are rarely used in the marital deduction arena.

A stand-alone annuity contract (not in trust) provides for periodic payments that terminate at some point in time (i.e., upon the death of one or more beneficiaries or expiration of a term of years, or some combination of the two). Annuity contracts provide for annual payments in excess of the net economic yield, and, accordingly, each annuity payment is deemed to consist of an income and principal component. See §72(a) & (b) (income tax rule providing for ratable basis recovery). A gift or bequest of a survivor annuity contract (not in trust) is treated as wholly qualifying under the QTIP rules, since each annuity payment is, by definition, an amount greater than the income currently accrued inside the annuity contract. See §2056(b)(7)(C).

A problem arises where an annuity under an annuity contract (or its equivalent, such as a retirement plan or an IRA) is made payable to an "income only" trust for the transferee spouse: If the annuity payments are treated entirely as trust "principal," then the transferee spouse would be deprived of the income from the annuity contract, and the marital deduction for the annuity contract would be lost. The IRS responded to this problem by issuing *Rev. Rul.* 89-89, 1989-2 C.B. 231, which states that the marital deduction is not lost if (1) the income portion of each annuity payment is treated as trust income, *and* (2) the transferee spouse is entitled to the income from the "principal" portion of each annuity payment.

In a PAT, the transferee spouse can be given the income from a specific portion of the trust or a general power of appointment over a specific portion of the corpus, and in either case the corresponding portion of the trust will qualify. In a QTIP trust, the surviving spouse may likewise be given the income from only a portion of the trust or a percentage share of the income, and qualification would be limited to that portion. Alternatively, the transferee spouse may be given the right to all of the income from a trust, but the QTIP election may be made with respect to only a specific portion of the trust. A third possibility might be to give the transferee spouse a right to income in that portion of a trust to which a QTIP election is made. This scheme was allowed by the courts over the Commissioner's objection that the surviving spouse only received a contingent income interest.[31] In 1998, the Treasury added Reg. §20.2056(b)-7(d)(3) & (h), Ex. 6, which concedes this issue.

The term "specific portion" is limited to a fractional or percentage share. See §2056(b)(10). Thus, a general power of appointment (or a QTIP election) cannot be made with respect to a fixed dollar amount. (A fixed dollar amount power or election would freeze the amount that would be subject the gift or estate tax of the transferee spouse.)

---

31. See *Estate of Clack v. Comm'r*, 106 T.C. 131 (1996).

Under Reg. §20.2044-1(d) & (e), Ex. 4, a corpus distribution from a QTIP trust to the transferee spouse can be charged all to the share that qualified under the QTIP election, but only if the governing instrument so provides; otherwise, any corpus distribution shall be charged to the QTIP and non-QTIP portions on a pro-rata basis. Charging the distribution all to the QTIP share would reduce the amount includible under §2044.

4. Gift Tax Treatment of Transfers of Interests in PATs and QTIP Trusts

The aim of the PAT and QTIP trust rules might be frustrated if the amount includible at the transferee spouse's death could be reduced by gifts of trust assets, corpus distributions to third parties, or other means.

First, in neither situation can any person other than the transferee spouse be allowed to distribute or appoint any amount to a third party.[32] In the QTIP trust, not even the transferee spouse can be given such a power, but such a power (called an "*inter vivos* special power of appointment") can be given the transferee spouse under a PAT. It was once thought that an *inter vivos* special power of appointment given to the transferee spouse under a PAT allowing distributions of corpus to third parties could be exercised without gift tax exposure. However, it is now settled any such exercise would entail a gift of a portion of the transferee spouse's income interest,[33] and it would also constitute a release of the general power of appointment over corpus (and therefore be a gift of the corpus). Nor could the transferee spouse simply release the general power of appointment, because the release would be considered a "transfer" under the gift tax and, worse, would be ineffective to remove the property from the spouse's gross estate: The release would be a deemed transfer with a "retained" income interest under §2036. (The federal tax aspects of general and special powers of appointment are discussed in greater detail in Chapter 7, and retained-interest transfers are dealt with in Chapter 8.)

As mentioned above, a QTIP trust, to qualify, cannot give the spouse (or anyone else) an *inter vivos* special power of appointment. Thus, the most the transferee spouse can do is to make a gift of all or a portion of her income interest, which will constitute a gift of the same under §2511.[34] In addition, under §2519 a gift by the spouse of all *or any portion* of her income interest shall be treated as effecting an additional "transfer" by her of the *entire* remainder interest to which the QTIP election pertained. In that case, the entire property will be removed from the reach of §2044. See §2044(b)(2). Nevertheless, the portion of the deemed-transferred remainder interest attributable to any *non-assigned* income portion is

---

32. Any such power given to a person other than the transferee spouse under a PAT also would appear to violate the requirement that the transferee spouse's general power of appointment be exercisable "alone and in all events," because, if such other person could distribute corpus to third parties, then the transferee spouse's general power of appointment would be rendered contingent on the trustee's *not* exercising such power.

33. See Reg. §25.2514-1(b)(2).

34. If the transferee spouse sells all or a portion of her income interest for full and adequate consideration, the rules described in the text still apply, since §2519 is invoked by any "disposition" of the income interest. Of course, there is no "gift" of the income interest. Reg. §25.2519-1(g), Ex. 2.

includible in the spouse's gross estate under §2036, because the transferee spouse, by reason of the application of §2519, will be treated as the transferor of the remainder interest following the retained (non-assigned) portion of the income interest.

Example: H creates, by gift or estate transfer, a trust, all of the income to W for life, remainder to C, and a QTIP election is made for 80 percent of the trust. Thus, if no further action is taken by W, 80 percent of the trust will be includible in her gross estate under §2044. Suppose, however, that W makes a gift of 30 percent of her income interest (in the entire trust), at a time when the trust is worth $1M and W's income interest is worth $600K. W has thereby made a §2511 income-interest gift of $180K (30 percent of $600K). Under §2519, W is deemed to also have made a "transfer" of the entire 80 percent of the remainder that qualified for the QTIP election; namely, $320K (80 percent of $400K remainder interest). Section 2044 drops out of the picture, but 56 percent of the trust will be included under §2036 (transfer of 80 percent of the remainder retaining the income in 70 percent thereof). Also, 70 percent of the $320K remainder deemed-gift (= $224K) qualifies for the adjusted taxable gift exclusion and is removed from the cumulative tax base.[35]

A policy concern is to avoid unduly burdening the surviving spouse's separate estate with estate taxes on PAT or QTIP trust property. In the case of a PAT, the will of the surviving spouse can deal with this problem by exercising the general power of appointment in favor of her estate at least to the extent of death taxes attributable to such property. Even if the power is not exercised, the appointive property can be made to bear the burden of taxes. First, the surviving spouse's will can (if state law allows) apportion to the PAT itself the surviving spouse's estate tax attributable to the PAT. If the will is silent, §2207 (which overrides any state law default rules to the contrary) provides that the portion of federal estate taxes attributable to the possession, etc., of a general power of appointment will be borne by the power of appointment property on an "average rate" basis.

In the case of QTIP trusts, §2207A states than any estate tax triggered by §2044, or any gift tax attributable to the application of §2519 (but not of §2511), shall be paid by the trustee from the QTIP trust (and not out of other assets in the spouse's estate or by the spouse making the deemed §2519 gift). This rule can be overridden only if the will of the surviving spouse specifically countermands it.[36]

---

35. See Reg. §25.2519-1(g), Ex. 4.

36. In the case of a §2044 inclusion in the gross estate, the decedent spouse's will can specifically provide to the contrary. See §2207A(a)(2). The rule of §2207A is also found in Uniform Estate Tax Apportionment Act (2003) §3-9A-104. See *Katz v. Shirley* (In re *Estate of Klarner*), 113 P.3d 150 (Colo. 2005), holding §2207A applies to Colorado state law despite both that its state statute varies from the federal provision in that it does not require a "specific" intent to waive the restitution and that the Colorado statute applies an apportionment calculation different from the federal rule. Cf. *Hollis v. Forrester* (Ex parte *Forrester*), 914 So.2d 855 (Ala. 2005).

Any *gift* tax so paid by the trustee of the QTIP trust is "consideration" for the deemed transfer and hence is subtracted in arriving at the amount of the §2519 "net" gift.[37] Since the amount of the gift tax is dependent on the amount of the net gift, which in turn is dependent on the amount of the gift tax, a circular computation must be carried out. Thus, the results described in the example above are not completely accurate if a net gift tax was due; in that case, the §2519 gift would be reduced, as would the amount subject to §2036, and so would the amount of the §2519 gift qualifying for the adjusted taxable gift exclusion.[38]

The foregoing involvement of §§2036, 2207A, and 2519 are avoided if the spouse gives away the income only as (and after) she actually receives it, and if the trustee, pursuant to a power conferred on it by the QTIP trust, simply distributes corpus to the spouse and the spouse then gives it away. Section 2044 remains in place for the remaining corpus.

Courts have also applied a "duty of consistency," an equitable estoppel principle, to include a marital trust in the surviving spouse's estate. See, e.g., *Estate of Letts v. Comm'r*, 109 T.C. 290 (1997), *aff'd without published opinion*, 212 F.3d 600 (11th Cir.2000). That duty requires that "(a) The taxpayer made a representation of fact or reported an item for tax purposes in one tax year; (b) the Commissioner acquiesced in or relied on that fact for that year; and (c) the taxpayer desires to change the representation previously made in a later tax year after the earlier year has been closed by the statute of limitations." Id. at 297. In *Letts*, the decedent's husband's estate was closed at the time of decedent's death. His estate had taken a marital deduction in the amount of a trust for which the executor specifically did not make a QTIP election. The government had relied on the estate's representation that the trust property was not terminable interest property. Inconsistent with her husband's estate's contention, the widow's estate stated on her estate tax return that the trust property was terminable interest property. Decedent was an executrix of her husband's estate. Their son signed both estate tax returns; their daughter was a co-executor of, and signed the estate tax return for, the decedent's estate. The court found a sufficient identity between the interests of the two estates to require the application of this doctrine to require the trust's inclusion in the widow's estate. Accord *T.A.M. 200407018* (The duty of consistency applied to include the trust in the decedent's estate. Decedent's husband had claimed a marital deduction for art represented as a "pastel" in the PAT; the government relied on that representation; and the decedent's estate claimed noninclusion because the artwork was actually an oil painting.). Cf. *Estate of Posner v. Comm'r*, T.C. Memo. 2004-112.

---

37. There is no harm in making a §2519 deemed gift within three years of death: the gift tax paid by the trust under §2207 would reduce the amount includible under §2036 and would, at the same time, avoid §2035(b), since it was not paid by the transferee spouse.

38. For the consequences of a failure of the transferee spouse to collect the §2519 gift tax from the trustee, see Reg. §25.2207A-1(b).

C. *The Amount Deductible*

In general, the amount of the deduction is the value of property that is included in the tax base of the decedent and which passes from the transferor spouse to the transferee spouse in a qualified form. (Any such property is referred to hereinafter as a "marital transfer.") In the case of an estate trust, the transferee spouse receives all interests in the trust. In the case of PATs and QTIP trusts, the entire amount of the qualified transfer is deductible, not just the income interest transferred to the spouse.

Although the marital deduction amount cannot be greater than the amount included in the estate or gift tax base, it could conceivably be of a lesser amount. Cf. *Ahmanson Foundation v. U.S.*, 674 F.2d 761 (9th Cir.1981) (stock was included in gross estate at full value but the value of the charitable deduction was reduced, because the charity did not obtain the voting rights).[39]

Section 2056(b)(4)(A) provides that the marital deduction shall be reduced by any death taxes chargeable to a marital transfer. This rule can be a trap for the unwary, as where the residual bequest a marital transfer, and the tax apportionment clause of the governing instrument (unthinkingly pulled from a formbook) states that "all debts and taxes are to be charged to the residue." If the governing instrument has a tax apportionment clause at all, the clause should state that no death taxes (etc.) should be charged to transfers that qualify for the marital deduction. In the absence of a tax apportionment clause in the governing instrument, the state default rule will apply. The Uniform Estate Tax Apportionment Act provides for default apportionment of death taxes first to non-marital estate transfers,[40] precisely to avoid unnecessary reduction of the marital deduction.

Section 2056(b)(4)(B) states that the marital deduction shall be reduced by any encumbrance (such as a lien) or "any obligation imposed by the decedent with respect to the passing of such interest." The quoted "obligation" phrase was at issue in *U.S. v. Stapf*, 375 U.S. 118 (1963). The will of the husband required his widow to elect between (a) keeping her half of the community property but not receiving any bequests under the husband's will or (b) taking under the will and having her share of community debts paid off but allowing her half of the community property to pass to a trust created by the husband's will for the benefit of their children. The widow elected the second alternative. (This transaction, called a "spousal election will," is discussed at p. 444.) The Supreme Court disallowed the marital deduction, because acceptance of the marital bequests was conditioned on making a gift of her own property to the trust for the children. In effect, the bequest did not pass "to" the widow, but "through" the widow to the trust for the children.

All too often the apportionment provisions in decedent's will and revocable trust are not properly coordinated, unintentionally and unfortunately resulting in taxes or other debts being paid from the marital share and thus creating a taxable

---

39. Accord, *Estate of Chenoweth v. Comm'r*, 88 T.C. 1577 (1987).
40. See Uniform Estate Tax Apportionment Act (2003), §3-9A-103(b)(2). This rule is to apply "unless the decedent expressly and unambiguously directs the contrary."

estate. In *Estate of Lurie v. Comm'r*, 425 F.3d 1021 (7th Cir.2005), neither Lurie nor his attorney had considered the effect of Lurie's exercising a limited power of appointment from his parents' trusts, thereby creating sixteen additional trusts that were includible in his own taxable estate. Their inclusion resulted in an unexpected estate tax liability of over $12M because Lurie had already exhausted his unified credit during his lifetime. The court was therefore left to decide whether that unanticipated liability should be paid by the marital trust or by the trusts that had created the estate tax. The will plainly stated that the trust controlled the source of tax payments. Although the marital trust funding provision appeared to desire tax minimization, the trust clearly stated that taxes were to be paid from the trust without apportionment. *Lurie* is an example of thwarted intent; equitable apportionment would have better represented Lurie's goals.[41]

The "encumbrance" aspect of §2056(b)(4)(B) was at issue in the case of *Comm'r v. Estate of Hubert*, 520 U.S. 93 (1997). Allocating *debts* to the marital deduction share is not inherently disadvantageous, because the debts would be deductible under §2053 in any event.[42] However, estate administration expenses may be deducted for income or estate tax purposes, but not both. In *Hubert* the estate administration expenses were deducted for income tax purposes but were chargeable to both the principal and income of the marital trust. It was agreed that the expenses charged to principal reduced the marital deduction. The Court, however, upheld the finding below that the administration expenses charged to income did not rise to the level of a "material limitation" on the widow's right to income that would reduce the value of the deduction under Reg. §20.2056(b)-4(a). But this regulation seems directed at the "income" requirement of PATs and QTIP trusts.[43] As a result of *Hubert*, the Treasury added Reg. §20.2056(b)-4(d), which states that estate administration expenses paid by the marital share (whether out of corpus or income) always reduce the marital deduction, except in the case of estate "management" (as opposed to "transmission") expenses attributable to the marital transfer *and* not deducted for estate tax purposes under §2053. (Section 2056(b)(9) disallows double deductions for the same amounts.) As a result of the change in the regulations, it is suggested that the governing instrument prevent the deduction of administration expenses deducted for income tax purposes to be charged against the principal or income of a marital transfer, except possibly management expenses attributable to the marital transfer itself. The exception for management

---

41. An interesting situation arose in *Estate of Ferrara v. U.S.*, 94 U.S. Tax Cas. (CCH) ¶60,181, 74 A.F.T.R.2d (RIA) 6503 (1994). Ohio did not have an unlimited marital deduction like the federal statute. Because Ohio's restriction created a state estate tax that was paid from the marital share, the estate's marital deduction for federal tax purposes was accordingly reduced.

42. UPC (1990) §3-902, essentially allocates debts first to the residue, with no provision for exempting marital transfers.

43. *Hubert* had the Justices flummoxed, as they sought the answer in §2056(b)(4) and the regulations thereunder, whereas the answer really lies in the "passing" requirement. See Joseph M. Dodge, *Lifting the Shroud Obscuring* Estate of Hubert: *The Logic of the Income and Estate Tax Treatment of Estate Administration Expenses*, 3 Fla. Tax Rev. 647 (1998). The line-up in the Supreme Court was 4-3-2. The government argued that materiality wasn't relevant. The concurring opinion virtually invited clarification through regulation, and the Treasury subsequently obliged.

expenses attributable to the marital transfer (and not deducted for estate tax purposes) is that the value of property is the present value of future *net* income, and the management expenses would be incurred anyway. In contrast, estate transmission expenses are caused by the decedent's death, and are not intrinsic to the property itself.

QUICK QUESTION

Which one of the following transfers qualifies for the marital deduction under §2056?

A. Wifey willed property to Hubby; however, in the event he failed to survive the distribution of her estate, the property would go to Sonny.

B. Hannah established a testamentary trust for Curtis, her spouse, all income for life to Curtis payable semiannually, with a testamentary power of appointment over that value of the corpus that equaled the value of the corpus at Hannah's death.

C. Sam set up a testamentary trust in which all income would be accumulated until Linda's (his spouse's) death at which time Linda's estate would receive the corpus and all accumulated income.

PROBLEMS, QUESTIONS, AND NOTES

1. State whether the following inter-spousal transfers qualify for the marital deduction:

a. Wanda's will leaves $1M to Hank "if he is surviving when the probate of my estate is completed." Assume the unlikely event that the probate of Wanda's estate is in fact completed within six months of her death and that Hank, being alive, takes the $1M. See *Estate of Harmon v. Comm'r*, 84 T.C. 23 (1985).

b. Harry purchases a joint and survivor annuity for himself and Wendy, so that a fixed sum is payable monthly half and half to Harry and Wendy during their joint lives and all to the survivor until the survivor's death, at which point the annuity simply expires. (What if W dies first?)

c. Hector leaves the residue of his estate to Winny, and directs his executor to purchase, for $100K, a single life annuity for Winny. See §2056(b)(1)(C).

d. Wolf purchases Blackacre and puts it into the names of Wolf and Hanna as joint tenants with the right of survivorship. Does the result depend on which of Wolf or Hanna dies first?

    e.   Wilma leaves her residue in a testamentary trust, income to her father for his life, remainder to Hal. This arrangement is called a "spousal remainder trust." See Reg. §20.2056(b)-4(d). Under what circumstances would this device be advantageous for transfer tax purposes?

2.   One of the cardinal sins in estate planning is to effect a transfer that fails to qualify for the marital deduction and yet is includible in the transfer tax base of the transferee spouse. Such a transfer is taxed twice in the same generation.

    a.   In a PAT, the transferee's general power of appointment, whether exercisable *inter vivos* or by will, must be exercisable by him or her "alone and in all events." Thus, it is not enough that the surviving spouse be given a general power as defined in §2041(b)(1); such person must possess "more." The alone-and-in-all-events requirement raises the possibility of disaster; giving the surviving spouse a general power of appointment sufficient to include the trust in her gross estate but insufficient to qualify for the marital deduction under §2056(b)(5). See *Estate of Walsh v. Comm'r*, 110 T.C. 393 (1998) (no marital deduction where surviving spouse's benefits terminated on incompetence); *Estate of Tingley v. Comm'r*, 22 T.C. 402 (2954), *aff'd sub nom. Starrett v. Comm'r*, 223 F.2d 163 (1st Cir.1955).

    b.   The problem mentioned in (a) has arisen in various situations involving legal life estates in the transferee spouse with power in the transferee spouse to consume, such as often arises in the case of contractual ("joint and/or mutual") wills. A power to consume which does not satisfy §2056(b)(5) will nevertheless constitute a general power under §2041, unless the power is limited by an ascertainable standard relating to one or more of the transferee spouse's support, maintenance, health, and education. Characterization under state law is all-important.

    c.   An issue arises as to whether the general power of appointment is exercisable alone and in all events where the spouse has been incompetent since the date of the decedent's will. The position of the IRS is that incompetency does not bar qualification, because incompetency does not bar inclusion in the transferee spouse's gross estate under §2041. What if the trust states, "I confer upon my wife the power, exercisable so long as she is competent, to appoint the property in the trust to any person, including her estate?"

    d.   Will a power to accumulate income necessarily disqualify a PAT or QTIP trust? See Reg. §20.2056(b)-5(f)(8). See *Estate of Whiting v. Comm'r*, T.C. Memo. 2004-68 (holding for the estate because under Arkansas law the more general section of the trust allowing income accumulation upon a disability conflicted with the trust's express intent to qualify for the marital deduction and was therefore inoperative).

    e.   Is the income requirement not complied with where the trustee is empowered (or required) to:

        (1)   Retain the family residence;

        (2)   Retain life insurance policies on the surviving spouse's life;

        (3)   Retain an interest in a closely-held corporation that has never or rarely paid dividends;

(4) Invest in commercial real estate, but the trustee is required to maintain a depreciation reserve (which has the effect of reducing net rental income); and

(5) Invest in unimproved land with high appreciation potential?

Are there transfer or income tax advantages to allowing the trustee to make or keep some of these investments? What "escape hatches" are available? See Reg. §20.2056(b)-5(f)(1), (4) & (5).

3. The following deals with techniques to preserve qualification from attacks by the IRS based upon faulty planning and drafting.

   a. Operation of state law. In *Rev. Rul. 69-56*, 1969-1 C.B. 224, supra, administrative provisions in the trust which might have violated the "income" requirement were implicitly modified and limited by state law. Conceivably state law could cut against qualification. However, the trend is for state law to accommodate tax concerns.

   b. Ascertaining the decedent's intent. The case of *Virginia Nat'l Bank v. U.S.*, 443 F.2d 1030 (4th Cir.1971), involved a situation where the trust for the surviving spouse gave him an unfettered power to withdraw corpus. The trust also contained a provision that, "notwithstanding anything herein to the contrary," would have caused a forfeiture of the surviving spouse's interest if he attempted to assign it. The district court held that the "specific" language of the marital deduction trust should prevail over the "general" language of the forfeiture provision. The Fourth Circuit affirmed, but on the basis of extrinsic evidence of the testator's intent. In a similar vein is *Estate of Trunk v. Comm'r*, 550 F.2d 81 (2d Cir.1977). Traditional doctrine holds that extrinsic evidence is considered only if an ambiguity in the governing instrument is shown. This attitude may be waning. See UTC §415, allowing reformation of a trust (without a showing of ambiguity) where clear and convincing evidence shows that the settlor's intent and the terms of the trust were affected by a mistake of law or fact. A similar provision exists in UPC §2-805 for wills, but it has been adopted by very few states.

   There are numerous cases where a widow's interest is limited to amounts necessary for her to maintain her accustomed manner of living with the consequence that the courts have disallowed the marital deduction (even where the decedent appointed the widow as the sole trustee). See, e.g., *Davis v. Comm'r*, 394 F.3d 1294 (9th Cir.2005); *Estate of Aronson v. Comm'r*, T.C. Memo. 2003-189 ("as much income from such assets as she needs").

   c. Reforming the governing instrument. Section 416 of the Uniform Trust Code (2000) states:

   > To achieve the settlor's tax objectives, the court may modify the terms of a trust in a manner that is not contrary to the settlor's probable intention. The court may provide that the modification has retroactive effect.

   Virtually the same provision is found in UPC §2-806. This provision cuts against the general reluctance of courts to modify trust provisions.

However, the IRS will not give effect to a modification that is made after the taxing date. See *Rev. Rul. 73-142*, 1973-1 C.B. 405. Perhaps the possibility of a retroactive modification was thought to take care of that problem. Nevertheless, under the *Bosch* doctrine, discussed at pp. 152-153, decisions of state lower courts can usually be ignored for federal tax purposes. Thus, in Estate *of Rapp v. Comm'r*, 140 F.3d 1211 (9th Cir.1998), a surviving spouse obtained from the probate court an order modifying the decedent's will that resulted in obtaining a qualifying interest, but the modifications were disregarded for federal tax purposes. Similarly, a settlement of an estate dispute that resulted in the surviving spouse obtaining a PAT trust was not recognized when the decedent's will only gave such spouse a life estate in the first place. *Estate of Carpenter v. Comm'r*, 52 F.3d 1266 (4th Cir.1995).

d. Savings clauses. In this scenario, provisions in the will or trust that arguably disqualify the trust are contradicted by another clause in the same instrument expressing the decedent's intent to qualify for the marital deduction. Such a clause was upheld, resulting in qualification, in *Guiney v. U.S.*, 425 F.2d 145 (4th Cir.1970). A similar result was obtained in *Rev. Rul. 75-440*, 1975-2 C.B. 372, where the trustee of the marital trust was authorized to invest in insurance policies on the beneficiary's life, because another clause stated:

> Notwithstanding anything herein contained to the contrary, any power, duty, or discretionary authority granted to my Fiduciary hereunder shall be absolutely void to the extent that either the right to exercise, or the exercise thereof, shall in any way affect, jeopardize or cause my estate to lose all or any part of the tax benefit afforded my estate by the Marital Deduction under either Federal or State Laws.

But then, in *Rev. Rul. 65-144*, 1965-1 C.B. 442, the Service stated that it will not accept a savings clause that is triggered *only* upon a court's construction of a dispositive instrument so as to disqualify a possible estate tax deduction, since to hold otherwise would be to trivialize tax administration and the judicial process. Cf. *Comm'r v. Procter*, 142 F.2d 824 (1944), *cert. denied*, 323 U.S. 756 (1944) (invalidating a clause that revoked a gift if the gift was held to be taxable).

4. a. The QTIP trust, added to the Code in 1981, has far surpassed the PAT and estate trust in terms of popularity. Why do you suppose this is the case? Should the marital deduction be granted for the entire value of a trust transfer where the surviving spouse has merely an income interest and no right to, or control of, the remainder interest? *The House Ways and Means Committee Report* (H.R. Rep. No. 201), 97th Cong., 1st Sess. (1981), stated:

> Under [prior] law, the marital deduction is available only with respect to property passing . . . in specified forms which give the spouse control over the transferred property. [Accordingly,] the decedent cannot insure that the spouse will subsequently pass the property to his children. . . .

> A decedent is [now] forced to choose between surrendering control of the entire estate to avoid imposition of the estate tax at his death or reducing the tax benefits at his death to insure inheritance by his children. The committee believes that the tax laws should be neutral and that tax consequences should not control an individual's disposition of property.

Is there a natural right to a marital deduction for interests passing to third parties? Can the estate tax view husband and wife as a single unit while allowing the wealthier spouse to flaunt the single-unit concept? Is a power of a surviving spouse to take an elective share under state law an adequate escape valve?

   b. Can a lawyer represent both husband and wife, and at the same time counsel use of a QTIP trust?
   c. Would a surviving spouse be delighted to be the beneficiary of an estate trust? Is that better or worse than a QTIP trust?
   d. What potential estate and income tax advantages might inhere in an estate trust?

5. a. The surviving transferee must be the decedent's spouse at the time of death. See, e.g., *Estate of Steffke v. Comm'r*, 64 T.C. 530 (1975), *aff'd*, 538 F.2d 730 (7th Cir.1976), *cert. denied*, 429 U.S. 1022 (state court invalidation of prior divorce of surviving "spouse" rendered her marriage to decedent void); *Rev. Rul. 67-442*, 1967-2 C.B. 65 (invalidation by state court of foreign divorce restored prior marriage to decedent); *Rev. Rul. 76-155*, 1976-1 C.B. 286 (fact that person claiming as purported common-law spouse obtained modest settlement from estate does not establish fact of common-law marriage).

   b. Same-sex couples are allowed to marry in certain U.S. and foreign jurisdictions. They may qualify for a state estate tax marital deduction where the state recognizes the marriage. However, the Defense of Marriage Act (DOMA), 1 U.S.C. §7, states:

   > In determining the meaning of any Act of Congress, or of any ruling, regulation, or interpretation of the various administrative bureaus and agencies of the United States, the word "marriage" means only a legal union between one man and one woman as husband and wife, and the word "spouse" refers only to a person of the opposite sex who is a husband or a wife.

   See Patricia A. Cain, *DOMA and the Internal Revenue Code*, 84 Chi.-Kent L. Rev. 481 (2009) (attacking constitutionality of DOMA).

   c. The spouse must survive the decedent. If the order of deaths cannot be proved, one resorts to the presumption provided by state law, which is usually that the heir or legatee predeceased the decedent. See Uniform Simultaneous Death Act (1953), §§2 and 6. (What purposes does such a "presumption" serve?) Any presumption can be overridden by appropriate language in the instrument of transfer, such as, "In case it cannot be determined whether I or my spouse died first, my spouse shall be deemed to have survived me." What tax purpose does such a clause serve? See Reg. §20.2056(e)(2)(e).

§6.2. Marital Deduction Planning

This section deals with tax savings, including tax deferral, obtainable through transfers taking advantage of the gift and estate tax marital deduction.

A. Aims of Marital Deduction Planning

The basic aim of marital deduction planning is to maximize the aggregate family wealth after gift and estate taxes on both spouses.

1. Why Marital Deduction Planning Is Mostly a "Tax Game"

It is important to understand that marital deduction transfers are used for *tax* planning, and not for the nontax purpose of providing economic benefits for the transferee spouse. That is because there is no *necessary* correspondence between (1) marital deduction qualification and (2) the provision of economic benefits to the surviving spouse.

First, *qualified* transfers can deprive the transferee spouse of significant economic benefits. Consider the economic benefits *not* given to the transferee spouse (compared to ownership in fee) under the following types of qualified marital deduction transfers:

(1) single life annuity,
(2) spousal remainder trust,
(3) estate trust,
(4) PAT, and (especially)
(5) QTIP trust.

Next consider the fact that extensive economic provision can be made for one's spouse through a trust that does *not* qualify for the marital deduction. Such a trust can be set up so as to give such spouse *any or all* of the following *without subjecting the transferee spouse to significant gift or estate tax exposure*:

(1) a right to income for life,
(2) possibilities of receiving corpus (or income) according to the trustee's discretion or under dispositive "standards,"
(3) *special* powers of appointment, *inter vivos* and by will,

(4) the sole power to withdraw corpus under standards relating to health, education, support, or maintenance, and

(5) the annual (non-cumulative) power to withdraw the greater of $5K or 5 percent of corpus (a so-called a "5-and-5" power).

The first two of these items are interests or expectancies that terminate on death. The last three of them are nontaxable powers of appointment (as will be explained in more detail in Chapter 7).

A trust that provides benefits for the transferee spouse (and perhaps others as well) but does not qualify for the marital deduction (and is not includible in the transferee spouse's tax base) is usually referred among estate planners to as a "by-pass" trust, because the whole purpose for such a trust to avoid its inclusion in the transferee spouse's transfer tax base. (In dealing with clients, estate planners might refer to such a trust as a "family" trust, which reflects the likelihood that the trust has multiple beneficiaries apart from the transferor's spouse.)

In sum, a transfer that qualifies for the marital deduction does not necessarily provide "more" benefits to the transferee than a transfer that does not qualify. It follows that decisions to qualify or not qualify for the marital deduction can be made somewhat independently of decisions as to how to "provide for" such spouse. Marital deduction planning, therefore, has largely evolved into a tax game. Nevertheless, the choice within each of the qualifying and nonqualifying categories may be heavily influenced by nontax considerations.

2. Exemption Amounts and the Two-Track Estate Plan

An essential ingredient of tax planning is to use the exemption amounts of both spouses. The exemption amounts can support by-pass trusts that avoid tax *both* at the level of the transferor spouse (because of the credit keyed to the exemption amount) *and* at the level of a transferee spouse (because the transfer is in the form of a by-pass trust, as described above).

(a) The Two-Track Estate Plan

Proper utilization of both exemption amounts has had major implications for tax planning. First, it has channeled dispositions (at least those by the wealthier spouse) into a two-track scheme: (1) a "by-pass" trust to use the exemption amount and (2) marital transfers that include a trust, most likely a QTIP trust. There may well be a "package" of marital transfers that include not only a trust but also marital transfers in fee through bequests of tangible property and survivorship rights under joint tenancies, joint accounts, annuities, retirement plans, and life insurance. Similarly, there could by non-trust by-pass transfers (to children, etc.) as well. The effect of the two-trust scheme is as follows, where it is assumed that H is the owner of virtually all the wealth and that H dies first:

	Marital Transfers of H's Wealth	By-Pass Transfers of H's Wealth
H's Death	not taxed (marital deduction)	not taxed to extent of exemption
W's Death	not taxed to extent of exemption	not taxed (excluded)

(b) What if the Poorer Spouse Dies First?

The possibility exists that the poorer spouse will die first. Considering only transfer taxes, the poorer spouse's estate plan has had to be designed to make maximum use of her exemption amount. Where the poorer spouse's expected taxable estate (before the marital deduction) was less than the exemption amount, it was advised that all of her estate should be made to pass through by-pass transfers (assuming the wealthier spouse's expected estate to be above the exemption amount). Where the poorer spouse's own wealth equaled or exceeded the exemption amount, it was advised that only the excess (from a tax planning point of view, and given the named assumptions) be a candidate for marital transfers. Obviously, tax considerations could yield to a desire that tangible property pass to the surviving (wealthier) spouse. A partial "preventative measure" took the form of a clause inserted in the governing instrument of the poorer spouse stating that, "if my surviving spouse dies within 6 months of my death, then said spouse shall be deemed to have predeceased me." See §2056(b)(3).

The more pressing problem in the case of unbalanced spousal wealth (where the wealthier spouse's estate exceeded the exemption amount) was the possibility of wasting the poorer spouse's exemption (in whole or in part) in the event that the poorer spouse died first with a taxable estate below the exemption amount. Here it was advised that the wealthier spouse make inter-spousal *inter vivos* transfers in order to remove dollars from the estate of the surviving wealthier spouse and to shift dollars into (what is in effect) the "zero" bracket of the poorer spouse's taxable estate. The main inhibiting factor in making *inter vivos* marital gifts is always the nontax consideration of the possibility of divorce and consequent loss of any direct or indirect control over the property given away. Of course, if divorce occurs the poorer spouse may end up with the same amount of property in any event under the divorce decree and property settlement, but it is often difficult to predict these results in advance. If the possibility of divorce is viewed as a problem, the wealthier spouse could "hedge his bets" by making qualifying marital deduction gifts in the form of the QTIP trust, since under the QTIP trust neither the donee spouse nor the trustee has the power to dispose of the corpus to a third party during the donee spouse's lifetime.

In addition, under §2523(f)(5) the donor spouse could retain an interest in an *inter vivos* QTIP trust transfer without causing disqualification. Additionally, such retained interest does not cause inclusion of the property in his gross estate under §2036 or §2037. Nor is a later gift of such retained interest subject to gift tax, but this rule only applies if the donor's death (or the gift of the retained interest) occurs before the property is taxed to the donee spouse under §2044 or §2519. The regulations[44] discuss the following scenario: D creates an *inter vivos* irrevocable trust, income to S for life, then income to D for life, remainder to D's children, and D makes a QTIP election. If D dies before S, a portion of the trust would normally be included in D's gross estate under §2036(a)(1), but §2523(f)(5)(A) cancels out this inclusion. The trust is included in S's gross estate under §2044 upon her later death. However, if S dies before D, then the trust is included in S's gross estate under §2044, and the trust then qualifies as a deductible QTIP trust (to S's estate) because of D's secondary income interest. Since S is now the (superseding) transferor of this trust, §2036 no longer applies to include the trust in D's estate (since D is no longer the transferor). However, if S's executor makes a QTIP election for S's estate, the trust will be subject to taxation to D or D's estate under §2044 or §2519.

A disadvantage of making *inter vivos* interspousal gifts in the case of appreciated property is that the donee spouse obtains a carryover basis under §1041 rather than a possible stepped-up basis under §1014 (or §1022). This factor may weigh heavily where the poorer spouse is likely to outlive the wealthier spouse.

(c) "Portability"

The 2010 Act, §303, has significantly altered the landscape painted above by providing for the "portability" of a decedent's unused exemption amount for decedents dying in 2011 and 2012. The Act amends §2010(c) by redefining the "applicable exclusion amount" as combining the surviving spouse's "basic exclusion amount" with her "deceased spousal unused exclusion amount." Her additional exclusion amount is defined as "the lesser of (A) the basic exclusion amount, or (B) the excess of (i) the basic exclusion amount of the last such deceased spouse of such surviving spouse, over (ii) the amount with respect to which the tentative tax is determined under section 2001(b)(1) on the estate of such deceased spouse." Regarding a surviving spouse who was married more than once, portability refers only to the unused exemption of the *last* deceased spouse.

The surviving spouse may apply the additional exemption amount both to lifetime and testamentary transfers. Thus, if the deceased spouse died in 2011, having written an "I love you" will, which left everything to his surviving spouse, she could combine her own $5M exemption with his unused $5M exemption and make a total of $10M of taxable gifts or bequests before incurring any transfer tax liability. The Joint Committee gives an example that allows the surviving spouse (H2) of his deceased spouse (W) to use W's unused exclusion amount as augmented by the unused exclusion amount of W's deceased former spouse H1).[45]

---

44. Reg. §25.2523(f)-1(f), Ex. 10 & 11.

45. Jt. Comm. on Tax'n, Technical Explanation of the Revenue Provisions Contained in the "Tax Relief, Unemployment Insurance Reauthorization, and Job Creation Act of 2010" Scheduled for Consideration by the United States Senate, JCX-55-10, at 53 (". . . Wife predeceases Husband 2. Following Husband 1's death, Wife's applicable exclusion amount is $7 million (her $5 million basic exclusion amount plus $2 million deceased spousal unused exclusion amount from Husband 1). Wife made no taxable transfers and has a taxable estate of $3 million. An election is made on

The 2010 Act provides for future regulations to be issued, and it will be interesting to see if the Treasury adopts the Joint Committee's spin on portability.

In order to qualify for the increased exemption, the executor of the deceased spouse must have filed a timely estate tax return (including extensions) and made an irrevocable election specifically allowing the surviving spouse to use the decedent's unused exclusion amount.

With the adoption of portability, the problem of the earlier death of the poorer spouse can be avoided, because her unused exemption amount can be made to move to the wealthier spouse. The wealthier spouse would not need to employ a two-trust scheme for the situation where he dies first. Marital transfers alone could reduce his taxable estate to zero, and his unused exemption amount would pass to the surviving spouse. In each case, the executor of the first spouse to die must make the "portability election," even if the estate of the deceased spouse would otherwise not have to file an estate tax return.

In cases where the aggregate spousal wealth exceeds the aggregate exemption amounts, a by-pass trust of such excess would still be desirable (taxwise) to remove wealth from the surviving spouse's gross estate.

3. *Allocating Values Between Marital and Non-Marital Transfers*

From 1948, when the marital deduction was introduced, through 1981, when it was expanded into the present unlimited marital deduction, the purpose of the marital deduction was to remove geographical discrimination by permitting spouses in common-law states to "split" their estates for transfer tax purposes — an objective that had always been obtainable by spouses in community-property states by reason of the fact that community property was owned on a 50-50 basis. Estate splitting (like gift splitting) is valuable in a context of progressive transfer tax rates and exemption amounts. Since each spouse is a separate taxpayer, the couple's total property, if split, will obtain separate unified transfer tax credits and be subjected to separate rate schedules starting at the lowest marginal rates.

The primary effects of the 1981 changes were: (1) to eliminate the gift and estate tax marital deduction "limitations," and (2) to expand the list of qualifying gifts and bequests to include the QTIP and "marital/charitable" forms. A necessary by-product of eliminating the limitations was to permit tax-free inter-spousal transfers of interests in community property.

The unlimited marital deduction allows a married couple to achieve "more than" estate splitting; namely, *complete elimination of any gift or estate tax upon the transferor spouse*. Since qualifying gifts and bequests that reduce the transferor's estate tax base will, under the qualification rules, augment the transferee spouse's transfer tax base (under §§2033, 2041, 2044, 2511, and 2519), the unlimited marital deduction *can be used to obtain complete deferral of tax of the couple's aggregate wealth until the death of the second spouse*.

Wife's estate tax return to permit Husband 2 to use Wife's deceased spousal unused exclusion amount, which is $4 million (Wife's $7 million applicable exclusion amount less her $3 million taxable estate). Under the provision, Husband 2's applicable exclusion amount is increased by $4 million, i.e., the amount of deceased spousal unused exclusion amount of Wife." Id.).

In a context of a progressive rate structure, estate planners were faced with the choice of either aiming for 50-50 estate splitting (minimization of aggregate taxes) to complete elimination of tax on the first spouse to die (complete deferral of taxes). As noted above, in the case of a tax-deferral plan (and in the absence of portability), the decedent spouse's exemption would be wasted if the plan were to entail marital transfers equal to the decedent's entire net estate; accordingly, by-pass transfers aim both to use up the decedent's exemption and to avoid taxability to the surviving spouse.

Until recently, the tax rates above the exemption amount were progressive. In that context, the choice between the estate-splitting and tax-deferral approaches involved number crunching. What had to be weighed was the aggregate tax savings that could be obtained by under 50-50 estate splitting, on the one hand, and the value of tax deferral, on the other, which is the net return obtainable (up to the surviving spouse's death) on the taxes saved at the first spouse's death relative to 50-50 estate splitting. (The deferral obtainable by using the marital deduction to reduce the taxable estate to the exemption amount is essentially an interest-free borrowing from the government.) The value of deferral is a function of mainly of the period of survival by the surviving spouse, but also the nature of the assets involved (potential for appreciation, depreciation, and income yield) and their allocation between marital and by-pass transfers and predictions about the likelihood that the surviving spouse will consume (or give away) whatever is available to her. Under an assumption of survival for at least a modest period (three years) the conventional estate planning wisdom since the unlimited marital deduction was instituted in 1981 was to prefer the tax-deferral plan to the estate-splitting plan, as a general matter. Texts, manuals, and formbooks have steered estate practitioners in that direction.

For decedents dying in 2007-2009, the tax rate over the exemption-equivalent amount is a flat 45 percent; for decedents dying in 2010-2012, the tax rate is a flat 35 percent. Moreover, it seems likely that any future estate and gift tax will provide for a flat rate. Under a flat-rate-above-the exemption-amount scenario, the aggregate tax will be the same regardless of which estate(s) bear tax, and therefore there is no advantage to 50-50 estate splitting at all. *Therefore, deferral of tax is always to be preferred in large estates.* Of course, the problem of full utilization of the exemption amount remains, but that problem is easier to deal with under a portability regime. Also keep in mind that by-pass transfers avoid tax to the surviving spouse.

A discussion of various hypothetical expected estate-size scenarios follows, where "NE" means "net estate" (gross estate less deductions other than the marital deduction), and it is assumed that the exemption amount is $5M with a flat rate above that.

1. *The aggregate NEs of both spouses are not expected to exceed $5M (the "small estate" scenario).* For example, assume that H's NE is under $5M and W's NE is zero. In this case, H can leave all of his property in a credit shelter trust, with no marital transfers, and there will not be any estate tax due upon the death of either H or W. Alternatively, H can leave his entire NE to W as a marital transfer, and still no tax will be due on W's estate (under the same assumptions).

Indeed, the zero-tax "bottom line" remains the same no matter what H leaves to W in marital transfers. In short, the marital deduction is not a factor in planning small estates.

2. *The aggregate NEs of both spouses are greater than $5M but do not exceed $10M (the "medium estate" scenario).* Here, H (assumed for illustration purposes to be the richer spouse) can achieve complete tax avoidance in both estates either through portability or by a marital transfer that is at least in an amount equal to the excess, if any, of H's NE over $5M, but which does not exceed the spouse's unused exemption amount ($5M minus W's NE). Thus, if H's NE is $8M and W's NE is zero, tax can be avoided in both estates if H's marital deduction transfers are somewhere in the range of $3M ($8M − $5M) to $5M ($5M − 0). In other words, in the medium-estate scenario, it is easy to avoid tax on both estates.

3. *The aggregate NEs of both spouses exceed $10M (the "large estate" scenario).* Here, tax is unavoidable, but of course the two exemptions should be fully used up. It may be advisable for the first spouse to die (having a NE in excess of $5M) to effect by-pass transfers of the full $5M, thereby removing future economic yield from the survivor's tax base.

4. Shifting Post-Death Wealth to the By-Pass Trust

In an estate plan involving both by-pass and marital trusts, it is desirable that any growth be directed to the by-pass trust (which is not included in the surviving spouse's gross estate) and any consumption or waste be directed to the marital trust. This "secondary" tax game, in other words, is to shift post-death net economic yield from the marital-transfer property to the by-pass-transfer property. This strategy is essentially an "estate freeze" strategy for the surviving spouse's estate. This strategy can be carried through: (a) language in the instruments of transfer, (b) decisions and elections of the decedent's personal representative, (c) decisions of trustees, and (d) decisions by the surviving spouse.

First, the QTIP trust (or PAT) confers a right to "income" on the surviving spouse, and the investment policy for the marital trust might be more conservative than that for the by-pass trust. Even if it is not, there will be substantial distributions of "income" to the surviving spouse that can be consumed or made the subject of excluded gifts.

Second, the plan should facilitate the surviving spouse's ability to make gifts from the property in any marital transfer. Under a PAT, the surviving spouse can be given an *inter vivos* special power of appointment for the purpose of transferring some of the corpus to third parties. (The gift tax consequences of exercising such a power are described in Chapter 7.) In a QTIP trust, such a special power is not allowed, but the trustee can be given a power to pay corpus to the surviving spouse in its discretion under a liberal standard of invasion, and any corpus distributed could be consumed or given away in a manner that maximized the use of the §2503 exclusions.

Third, and related to the prior point, the estate plan should be set up so that the corpus of the marital trust is made available to the surviving spouse before any of the by-pass trust.

B. Post-Mortem Adjustments

If the marital transfer is made in the form of a QTIP trust, the amount of the marital deduction depends upon the QTIP election, which can be made for only a portion of the trust.

After the decedent spouse's death (and QTIP elections), the marital deduction can also be fine-tuned, in either direction, by the use of disclaimers. Of course, the requirements of §2518 must be complied with, including the rules for partial disclaimers and of no acceptance of benefits. Under §2518(b)(4)(A), a disclaimer is not disqualified under the acceptance-of-benefits principle just because the disclaimed amount falls into a by-pass trust that can distribute income or corpus to the surviving spouse.

Disclaimers can be effected by persons other than the surviving spouse in order to increase the marital deduction. However, it is likely that the trustee of the by-pass trust cannot make such a disclaimer — since fiduciaries cannot reduce or eliminate the interests and rights of others — unless all of the beneficiaries of the by-pass trust consent.

A disclaimer would be worthless if the disclaimed amount ended up with the same tax treatment. For example, nothing would be gained by W's disclaiming part of a marital deduction transfer if the disclaimed amount came back again to W in a form that again qualified for the deduction, such as by way of the intestacy statute. For this reason, it is recommended that a "disclaimer clause" should be included in the governing instrument in order to control the disposition of any disclaimed amounts and the attendant tax results.

Rev. Proc. 2001-38, 2001-2 C.B. 124, explains how to nullify a QTIP election that was unnecessary because it did not reduce the estate tax liability of the estate. By following the revenue procedure, the surviving spouse will not be subject to transfer taxes or be treated as the transferor for generation skipping transfer tax purposes. This procedure may be used when the taxable estate, without the marital deduction, is below the applicable exclusion amount or when the estate unnecessarily elected QTIP treatment for a credit shelter trust. The revenue procedure also outlines when its relief is unavailable (e.g., a partial election reducing the estate more than necessary to eliminate any estate tax liability, a reduce-to-zero formula election, or a protective election under Reg. §20.2056(b)-7(c)). See, e.g., *P.L.R.* 200226020, (CCH) IRS Letter Rulings No. 1322, p. 52 (July 2002); *P.L.R.* 200219003, (CCH) IRS Letter Rulings No. 1315, p. 9 (May 2002) (following the *Rev. Proc.*).

C. Generation-Skipping Tax Planning Involving Spouses

Either or both of the marital deduction or non-marital deduction transfers may pose issues under the GST tax. Recall that husband and wife are considered to be in the same generation for GST tax purposes regardless of any age difference. The main concern here is to make sure that the per-transferor GST "exemption" (the same as the estate tax exclusion amount) is not wasted. Each individual (and each spouse in a married couple) "has" one GST exemption that is available to allocate among generation-skipping transfers of which such individual is the "transferor." §2631(a). The donor or decedent spouse making a transfer *subject to gift or estate tax* is the *initial* "transferor" of transfers for GST tax purposes. §2652(a)(1). The transferee spouse would normally be considered the (superseding) "transferor" for GST tax purposes of all *marital* transfers, due to the fact that these transfers will be subject to estate or gift tax with respect to such transferee spouse. However, under §2652(a)(3), in the case of a QTIP transfer it is possible for initial transferor to make a "reverse GST tax QTIP election." The initial transferor spouse thereby elects to be "permanently" treated as the "transferor" of all of a QTIP trust for GST tax purposes, notwithstanding the fact that the property will appear in the transferee spouse's tax base. This election can be made notwithstanding the fact that an affirmative QTIP election has been made for estate or gift tax purposes in order to claim the marital deduction. Thus, there is no estate tax cost in making this election. The transferee spouse's consent is not required. The reverse QTIP election would be made only if the transferor's GST tax exemption is not (otherwise) fully utilized and the transferee spouse's GST tax exemption is (or can be expected to be) fully utilized.

The reverse QTIP election, unlike the estate or gift tax QTIP election, can only be made with respect to the *entire* property in a trust. Thus, it may be necessary to have two (or more) separate QTIP trusts for estate tax purposes, each of which can be the subject of a reverse QTIP election.

In a different vein, in the case of *inter vivos* gifts to third parties, a gift-splitting election for gift tax purposes is also effective for GST tax purposes. §2652(a)(2).

PROBLEMS, QUESTIONS, AND NOTES

1. Assume the following alternatives where A and B, who are married, have net taxable estates (NTEs) apart from the marital deduction as indicated. What is the amount of a desirable marital deduction transfer from A to B in each instance? All NTEs are in millions of dollars. Assume that the exemption amount is $5M and that taxable amounts are subject to a flat rate of 40 percent.

	A	B
(a)	$ 3M	0
(b)	$ 3M	$2M
(c)	$ 6M	0
(d)	$ 6M	$4M
(e)	$10M	0
(f)	$10M	$7M

2. The following have to do with drafting trust provisions with tax considerations in mind.
   a. What transfer and income tax pros and cons result from granting the surviving spouse the right to all of the income from the by-pass trust? Is there a potential estate tax advantage in doing so?
   b. Should the trustee be given a liberal power to invade the corpus of the marital trust for the benefit of the spouse? The by-pass trust?
   c. Should a PAT give the transferee spouse a testamentary or an *inter vivos* general power of appointment?
   d. Should a PAT give the transferee spouse a testamentary or an *inter vivos* special power?
3. a. Should the issue of the size of the estate tax marital deduction be decided *after* the death of the first spouse? This aim can be accomplished by leaving the entire estate of both H and W in the form of QTIP trusts and letting the executor of the estate of the first to die decide what portion will be made the subject of an election. Is there any income tax disadvantage of this arrangement compared to a scheme that has separate marital and by-pass trusts? Can this problem be avoided? See Reg. §20.2056(b)(7)(d)(3).
   b. Does putting the onus of decision making on the estate representative create fiduciary problems? How can the estate representative be protected from fiduciary liability? Is that desirable?
4. Partial disclaimers to fine-tune the marital deduction raise various issues. It is initially necessary to determine whether a partial disclaimer is valid under state law, since the alternative "transfer" type of "disclaimer" provided by §2518(c)(3) cannot take the form of a partial disclaimer. Applying the rules found in Reg. §25.2518-3, which of the following partial disclaimers are valid for tax purposes? Assume that B (the disclaimant) has the right to all of the income plus such other interests are as specified.
   a. B disclaims 30 percent of the income from a QTIP trust.
   b. Same as (a), except that B disclaims all of the income after the tenth year.
   c. Same as (a), except that the trustee can invade corpus for the benefit of B, and B disclaims the possibility of receiving corpus.
   d. Same as (c), except that B disclaims the entire income interest.
   e. The trust is a PAT in which B is given a general power of appointment by will, and B disclaims either the income interest or the general power. What if B disclaims 30 percent of either? Of both?
   f. B has both a general power by will and a special power by deed, and B disclaims either power.

§6.3. Drafting the Marital Deduction Transfer

This section will concentrate on drafting issues not already touched upon.

A. *Formula Clauses*

The aim of a formula clause is to produce just the right amount of marital and non-marital transfers as will carry out the tax planning objectives discussed in §6.2. A formula clause can carry out these objectives with precision. If (instead of using a formula clause) attempts are made to draft the marital or non-marital estate transfers in terms of fixed-dollar or percentage-share amounts, the desired result can be frustrated due to subsequent changes in the tax law or changes in the relative or absolute property holdings of the spouses. Thus, a bequest to W of "one-half of my gross estate reduced by deductions other than the marital deduction" — which would be at least plausible when H had an NE of $10M and W an NE of zero, might become pointless if H or W, or both of them, become wealthier. Similarly, a fixed monetary non-marital bequest exactly equal to the current exemption amount would be ill-advised if either (1) deductible §2053 expenses are payable out of this transfer (in which case the taxable estate will be less than the exclusion amount), or (2) other estate-included transfers, within or without the will, are made which do not qualify for the marital deduction (in which case the taxable estate will exceed the exemption amount).

1. *The Problem of Coordination*

Marital transfers can occur under the will (or elections against the will), pursuant to the terms of a trust, according to survivorship rights in property, and under beneficiary designations in contracts (annuities, employee benefit plans, and insurance policies). If there are marital deduction transfers under more than one instrument, then it is necessary to have some way of coordinating them under a formula clause in one dispositive instrument.

One means of coordination is that of consolidation of assets under a single dispositive instrument. The "standard" technique here is to use a trust (usually a revocable *inter vivos* trust) as the receptacle of all estate transfers for which this is feasible (and desired). Thus, the trust is named as the beneficiary of life insurance policies and other contract rights, and is the named legatee under the will of the estate residue. Such a trust is referred to as a "pour-over trust," and a will that leaves a bequest to an *inter vivos* trust is called a "pour-over will."[46] A trust that does not receive a will pour-over but which is named as the beneficiary of one or more life insurance policies is called an "insurance trust."[47]

Complete consolidation of assets is often not feasible, nor even desired. For example, survivorship rights exist in individuals (not trusts or estates),

---

46. *Inter vivos* trusts, as amended from time to time, can receive pour-overs pursuant to the Uniform Testamentary Additions to Trust Act, which has been adopted in all states. See UPC (1990) §2-511. Of course, a will can create a testamentary trust. Nevertheless, in some states there may be problems in naming a testamentary trust as the beneficiary of a life insurance policy, an employee benefit plan, or an IRA.

47. An *inter vivos* trust that is funded only by a beneficiary designation in an insurance policy arguably lacks a trust *res* (property interest) as generally required by trust law. However, the beneficiary designation is itself considered to be property under UTC (2000) §401, Comment.

employee benefit plans may be required to make distributions to the surviving spouse individually, and specific property (and dollar) bequests may be made under a will. Thus, in addition to (or in lieu of) consolidation of assets, coordination can be achieved by language in a will or trust formula clause that conditions the amount of the marital or non-marital transfer (as the case may be) *under that clause* to the aggregate amount of marital or non-marital transfers occurring under all other instruments. Such language looks like this:

> I give to my spouse, if [he, she] survives me an amount which, when taken together with all other interests and property that [qualify, do not qualify] for the marital deduction and that pass or shall have passed to said spouse under other provisions of this instrument or otherwise, is equal to . . .

2. *Types of Formula Clauses*

A formula clause is most likely to be of the type that will achieve tax deferral, but an estate-equalization clause is a possible option. These are discussed in turn. In either case, the formula is defined in terms of the end result that is desired.

(a) Reduce-to-Zero Formula Clause

A formula clause that attempts to achieve complete deferral of taxes is one that will produce no net estate tax, after credits, on the estate of the decedent, while at the same time fully using the decedent's full available exemption equivalent. Such a clause is often called a "reduce-to-zero" or "credit shelter" formula. *What is being reduced to zero is the estate tax after credits, not the taxable estate.* The idea is to provide for just that marital deduction which will reduce the taxable estate to that amount which will produce a tax that will be completely offset by the available credits against the estate, especially the §2010 unified transfer tax credit (which is keyed to the available exemption amount).

The formula clause can appear in either a marital transfer or a non-marital transfer, but it is more likely to occur in a non-marital transfer clause, because that clause will directly produce the desired taxable estate (the taxable estate that will produce a zero tax). In either case, it is generally desirable that any formula be worded in terms of the end result (zero net federal tax) rather than an intermediate result (such as a taxable estate equal to an amount equal to the exemption amount), because the law might change so as to change the exemption amount or replace the credit by a deduction. Also, end-result language avoids having to refer to "adjusted taxable gifts," "gift taxes payable on post-1976 taxable gifts," and "credits other than the unified transfer tax credit."

In the case of a formula *non-marital transfer*, the "taken together with" clause should refer all *nondeductible* amounts passing or payable *outside* of the formula clause itself. At the same time, the formula bequest should operate in a manner that causes the non-marital formula amount to be *increased* by any amounts payable out of the formula transfer that *are* deductible for estate tax purposes (namely, debts, administration expenses, and state death taxes). Thus, consider the following clause:

I give the X Bank, as trustee of [the by-pass] trust described below, an amount which, when (a) taken together with property included in my gross estate passing outside of this clause to any person (or payable from any source other the amount produced by this clause) that does not qualify for any federal estate tax deduction in my estate, and (b) reduced by amounts passing under this clause that qualify for any deduction allowed for federal estate tax purposes, is equal to the maximum taxable estate which, after the federal unified transfer credit and other credits available to my estate, will produce a federal estate tax of zero.

To illustrate the operation of this clause, assume an exemption amount of $3.5M, no available credits other than the unified transfer tax credit, a gross estate of $10M, no prior adjusted taxable gifts, a charitable bequest of $0.5M, and other non-marital transfers (passing outside of this instrument) of $1.5M. Debts, administration expenses, and (state death) taxes (totaling $1M) are to be paid out of the residue of the estate, which is otherwise set up to qualify for the marital deduction. Of this $1M, $0.6M is deductible for estate tax purposes and $0.4M is not (because deducted for income tax purposes). The non-marital reduce-to-zero formula by-pass clause is to produce a taxable estate of $3.5M. Under the formula set forth above, the by-pass trust will be funded in the amount of $1.6M:

$$X + (\$1.5M + \$0.4M) - \$0 = \$3.5M$$
$$X = \$1.6M$$

This correctly produces a taxable estate of $3.5M as follows:

Gross estate: $10M
        less deductions: $0.6M (§§2053 and 2057)
                            $0.5M (§2055)
                            $5.4M (§2056)
                            $6.5M total deductions
Taxable estate: $3.5M

The total marital deduction of $5.4M is the *deductible portion* of the marital residue. The "gross" marital residue is $6.4 ($8.5M passing under the instrument less $0.5M charitable transfer bequests and less the $1.6M by-pass formula non-marital transfer). This $6.4M is then reduced by the $1M in the residue that does not qualify for the marital deduction (the debts, etc.) because this $1M does not "pass" to the surviving spouse.

Alternatively, the formula may be located in a *marital-transfer clause*. Such a formula might read as follows:

I give to [my surviving spouse, to a trust qualifying for the marital deduction] an amount which, when taken together with all other interests and property that qualify for the marital deduction and that pass or shall have passed to said spouse under other provisions of this instrument or otherwise, is equal to the maximum federal estate tax marital deduction available to my estate, reduced by that amount (if any) needed to increase my taxable estate to the largest amount that will produce a zero net federal estate tax after application of all federal estate tax credits available to my estate.

What does not pass under the formula clause passes to a by-pass trust.

Again this formula works backward from a "target amount" taxable estate which will produce a tax that is reduced (exactly) to zero by all applicable credits. Assuming that only the §2010 credit is in play, this formula produces a marital transfer in an amount described as follows:

Cumulative Tax Base (apart from the formula marital transfer)
− formula marital transfer = target (exemption) amount

formula marital transfer = Cumulative Tax Base
(apart from the formula marital transfer) = exemption amount

Mostly assume the same facts as above: an exemption amount of $3.5M, no available credits other than the unified transfer tax credit, a gross estate of $10M, no adjusted taxable gifts, a charitable transfer of $0.5M, and debts (etc.) of $1M payable out of the residue (set up here as a by-pass trust) of which $0.6M is deductible for estate tax purposes and $0.4M is not (because deducted for income tax purposes). This time around, other marital transfers (outside of this instrument) are $1.5M. The marital formula transfer is: $3.9M [($10M − $0.5M − $0.6M) − $1.5M − $3.5M].

Since the formula marital amount is $3.9M, the taxable estate calculation is as follows:

Gross estate: $10M
    less deductions: $1.1M (deductions other than the marital deduction)
        $1.5M (other marital transfers)
        $3.9M (formula marital transfer)
        $6.5M total deductions
Taxable estate: $3.5M

A non-marital residue is $4.1M ($8.5M under the instrument, less the charitable transfer of $0.5M, and less the formula marital transfer of $3.9M). The non-marital residue makes payments of $1.0M, leaving $3.1M in the by-pass trust.

(b) Estate-Equalization Formula Clause

In a medium estate situation (where the aggregate spousal wealth is greater than one exemption amount but less than two exemption amounts) an "estate-equalization" formula may conceivably be desired in order to fully utilize each spouse's exemptions without unduly limiting the amount of marital transfers. A "true" estate-equalization clause has to take into account the surviving spouse's net wealth as of the date of the decedent spouse's death. However, until the case of *Estate of Smith v. Comm'r*, 66 T.C. 415 (1976) (reviewed), *aff'd per curiam*, 565 F.2d 455 (7th Cir.1977), was decided, few attorneys dared use such a formula clause out of fear that it would violate the terminable-interest rule on account of being contingent on post-death facts and events.

In *Estate of Smith*, a trust provided that, upon the death of the husband survived by his wife, the trustee was to allocate to the marital portion:

> that percentage interest in the . . . assets constituting the trust estate which shall, when taken together with all other interests and property that qualify for the marital deduction and that pass or shall have passed to Settlor's said wife under other provisions of this trust or otherwise, obtain for Settlor's estate a marital deduction which would result in the lowest Federal estate taxes in Settlor's estate and Settlor's wife's estate, on the assumption Settlor's wife died after him, but on the date of his death and that her estate were valued as of the date on (and in the manner in) which Settlor's estate is valued for Federal estate tax purposes.

It should be noted that this clause "works" if there is a progressive rate structure, but if there is a flat estate tax rate above the exclusion amounts, there are numerous allocations that would produce a zero net tax (or equal net aggregate tax amounts). Accordingly, giving the executor discretion in making a QTIP election may be the better approach to handling this situation.

In any event, the court held that an estate-equalization formula did not create a nondeductible terminable interest, even though the formula required the valuation of the widow's hypothetical net estate (that is, the net estate under the assumption that she had died on the date of the husband's death or the alternate valuation date):

> Fundamentally, respondent's argument is that because the trustee could not determine the percentage of the trust estate which should be allocated to the marital trust until [the alternate valuation date], this made the interest in property which passed to Alice contingent on the trustee's decision. In other words, if the trustee decided that no portion of the trust estate should be allocated to the marital trust [under] the equalization clause, then the marital trust would terminate or fail.
>
> We disagree. First, we believe respondent is confusing the terminable-interest rule and the determination of the value of the property interest "passing" to the surviving spouse. In our opinion an interest is not terminable under the rule simply because the value or quantity thereof cannot be determined as of the date of decedent's death. Support for this opinion is found in §20.2056(b)-4 of the regulations which recognizes that the use of the alternate valuation date might affect the amount of the marital deduction. The executor's or trustee's decision on whether to deduct administration, etc., expenses for estate tax purposes as permitted by §642(g) may also affect the value of the interest without disqualifying the interest for the marital deduction. Rather, we think the terminable-interest rule applies when the indefeasible quality of the surviving spouse's interest cannot be determined as of decedent's death. . . . Under the terms of this trust Alice had an interest which, at Charles' death, became vested and indefeasible. There was no subsequent event that could divest her of her interest in the marital portion of the trust. The trustee's obligation under the terms of the trust was fixed and it had no discretion.

The Service has acquiesced in *Estate of Smith*, Rev. Rul. 82-23, 1982-1 C.B. 139.

But *Estate of Smith* raises this issue: What if the size of a marital transfer is dependent upon a QTIP election that is wholly discretionary with the executor? The government litigated several cases in which the surviving spouse's income interest was contingent on the QTIP election. The government prevailed in the Tax Court, but was rebuffed in the courts of appeal.[48] The Treasury finally conceded this issue in 1998, when it issued Reg. §20.2056(b)-7(d)(3), T.D. 8779, 1998-2 C.B. 280.

B. Pecuniary, Fractional-Share, and Hybrid Formula Transfers

A decision must be made as to whether the formula transfer should be in the form of a "pecuniary" transfer or a "fractional-share-of-the-residue" transfer. This distinction refers to the law of wills, whereby the "residue" is the amount that is left over after all other charges and transfers, including pecuniary transfers (sometimes referred to as "general bequests"). A formula clause can also produce a "hybrid" transfer, which is a variation of a pecuniary transfer. These are considered below.

1. Pecuniary Formula

A pecuniary formula transfer provides that whatever amount is produced by the formula shall be the amount that is actually distributed to the transferee (whether an individual or trust). It follows that the amount of the transfer, determined by reference to estate tax values, does not change according to changes in asset values between the estate tax valuation date and the date of actual transfer (distribution).

Where the pecuniary formula clause funds a *marital* transfer, this potential transfer tax advantage exists: Any net appreciation in estate assets between the estate tax valuation date and the date of distribution does not augment the amount of the marital transfer — which is potentially included in the transfer tax base of the surviving spouse — but instead is diverted to the residual by-pass trust which is not taxed to the surviving spouse or her estate. In a declining market, the opposite is true: The by-pass residue bears the burden of the decline in value during the interim period between the date of death and the date the pecuniary bequest is satisfied.

A potential disadvantage of any pecuniary bequest (formula or non-formula) is that it is treated somewhat as if it were a debt of the estate. Satisfaction of an estate debt with appreciated or depreciated property produces gain or loss to the estate as an income tax entity.[49] (This possibility assumes that the governing instrument or state law allows this to occur. Nevertheless, satisfaction in kind avoids transaction costs, avoids liquidity issues, and keeps the property in the family.) To illustrate the

---

48. See *Estate of Clack v. Comm'r*, 106 T.C. 131 (1996) (and cases discussed therein).

49. See *Kenan v. Comm'r*, 114 F.2d 217 (2d Cir.1940); *Rev. Rul.* 68-392, 1968-2 C.B. 284. This rule is often referred as the "*Kenan* rule." [Section 1040 abrogates this rule in the case of assets comprising the estate of a decedent who died in 2010 and is subject to the carryover-basis rule of §1022.]

income tax consequences, if the pecuniary formula amount is $1M, and property with a basis of $980K and having an FMV $1M is used to satisfy the pecuniary formula transfer, the estate or trust would recognize gain of $20K. Of course, under §1014 the basis for assets (other than IRD and annuities) included in the gross estate will (except in the case of an ID right) be the estate tax value. Hence, the gain or loss to be recognized is limited to the appreciation or depreciation occurring between the estate tax valuation date and the date the bequest is satisfied.

In the context of a large estate, a reduce-to-zero formula will produce marital transfers that will greatly exceed the by-pass transfers. In that event, the formula pecuniary language may better be inserted in the smaller non-marital (by-pass) transfer in order to minimize the income tax exposure attributable to satisfying it with in-kind assets.

2. *Fractional-Share Formula Transfer*

In a fractional-share formula transfer, the amount to be distributed to fund the transfer is that amount ("y") which bears the same ratio to the distribution date value of the residue (of the estate or trust) as the formula amount (at estate tax values) bears to the estate tax value of the residue:

$$y = \frac{\text{formula amount}}{\text{residue (est. tax values)}} \times \text{residue (distribution date values)}$$

Unlike the pecuniary transfer, the amount actually distributed or set aside for the formula transfer is not the numerator of the fraction but rather the amount produced by applying the fraction (constituted — and frozen — by reference to estate tax values) against the distribution date values of the residue. Thus, the economic appreciation or depreciation in the estate or trust assets between the estate tax valuation date and the distribution date inures proportionately between the marital and non-marital shares of the residue. There is no opportunity here to shift interim-period wealth from the marital share to the non-marital share.

Since the estate (or trust) is not satisfying an obligation of a fixed amount, there is no "amount realized," and hence no gain or loss to the estate or trust. Nevertheless, the executor or trustee can elect to recognize gain (but not loss) in this scenario See §643(e)(3) & (4).

A fractional-share formula clause is more involved than a pecuniary formula clause. The formula itself is more elaborate, as one must define the numerator, denominator, and multiplicand. Although the "residue" appears as both the denominator and multiplicand, the two residue figures do not cancel each other out, because the residue that is the denominator of the fraction is frozen at estate tax values, whereas the residue that is the multiplicand is "at" distribution date values. For purposes of computing the deduction amount to be entered on the estate tax return the residue multiplicand is taken at estate tax values, since the deduction is computed as of the estate tax valuation date. Thus, *there is no difference in the amount deductible between the pecuniary formula transfer and the fractional-share transfer.* The primary differences between the two modes of transfer relate to: (1) the amount distributed or set aside and (2) the possible presence of gain or loss to the estate or trust.

The term "residue" is not self-explanatory. It should be specifically defined in the formula clause. It is essential that the items constituting the residue be the same for purposes of both the multiplicand and the denominator of the fraction. First, in computing the marital deduction itself the denominator and the multiplicand should cancel out, leaving the numerator of the fraction as the deductible amount. Second, circularity would result if one definition of the residue is "before" federal estate taxes and the other is "after" federal estate taxes, since the federal estate taxes cannot be determined without knowing the amount of the marital deduction, which in turn is determined by the formula clause, and so on.

In light of the foregoing, it is typically recommended that "residue" be defined as being the estate or trust assets after other transfers, debts, expenses, and taxes, as that is what is actually available for distribution or set-aside. Such a narrow definition of the residue gives the executor or trustee wide discretion in selecting assets to be used to liquidate claims, pay taxes, etc., and to constitute the residue to be distributed.

In addition, on account of the "unidentified asset" qualification rule of §2056(b)(2), the definition of the residue should exclude assets that do not qualify for the marital deduction. Alternatively, provision must be made that such assets will in fact be distributed or set aside to the non-marital share. The first alternative avoids any possible income tax issue of a taxable exchange between the shares.

As noted earlier, to the extent that the governing instrument or state law burdens the "residue" with taxes, debts, or expenses, there is a risk that the amount of the marital deduction would be reduced to the extent that the marital share of the residue is required to "share" such burden, at least to the extent that such items are not deductible under other provisions of the estate tax. This problem may be avoided if the formula itself self-adjusts for such amounts, as is the case with a reduce-to-zero formula. A definition of "residue" to be divided into marital and non-marital shares that excludes (i.e., is constituted "after") such amounts also avoids the problem. A third alternative is to provide that no portion of such items shall be payable out of the marital share but instead are to be borne entirely by the non-marital share.

Tax problems aside, the fractional share approach is advantageous in that it can be used to create marital and non-marital shares of a single trust, thereby saving trustee's fees where small trusts are involved.

A possible problem with fractional share clauses is that a division of each asset in the residue would normally be required upon the distribution date. Compliance with this mandate is virtually impossible without reducing some items to cash and thereby incurring income tax gains and losses. Moreover, a non-pro-rata allocation of assets might conceivably be deemed a taxable exchange between two trusts. These problems can be circumvented by specific language in the will and trust authorizing distributions in kind on a non-pro-rata basis, provided of course that the respective aggregate values of the property placed in the two shares are proportional.[50]

---

50. See *Rev. Rul.* 69-486, 1969-2 C.B. 159.

3. *Hybrid Formula Clause*

A third type of clause begins as a variation of the pecuniary formula clause, except that the executor or trustee is directed to satisfy such bequest with items of property "at" their estate tax values (income tax basis under §1014) rather than their distribution-date values. The idea is that the basis for income tax purposes will equal the "amount realized," so that no gain or loss to the estate or trust would result. For example, if the formula pecuniary bequest turns out to be $540K, the bequest is to be satisfied with property having an estate tax value (§1014 basis) of $540K. Such property may turn out to have a distribution date value that is greater or less than $540K.

Use of this type of clause raises estate tax issues as well, as the next item indicates.

Revenue Procedure 64-19

1964-1 Cum. Bull. 682

The Service has received inquiries concerning the amount of the marital deduction which should be allowed for a pecuniary bequest in a will or for a transfer in trust of a pecuniary amount where the governing instrument not only provides that the executor or trustee may, or is required to, select assets in kind to satisfy the bequest or transfer, but also provides that any assets distributed in kind shall be valued at their values as finally determined for Federal estate tax purposes.

Where, by virtue of the duties imposed either by applicable state law or by the express or implied provisions of the instrument, it is clear that the fiduciary must distribute assets having an aggregate fair market value at the date, or dates, of distribution amounting to no less than the amount of the pecuniary bequest or transfer, as finally determined for Federal estate tax purposes, the marital deduction may be allowed in the full amount. Alternatively, where, by virtue of such duties, it is clear that the fiduciary must distribute assets fairly representative of appreciation or depreciation in the value of all property thus available for distribution in satisfaction of such pecuniary bequest or transfer, the marital deduction is equally determinable and may be allowed in the full amount.

In many instances, however, by virtue of the provisions of the will or trust, or by virtue of applicable state law (or because of an absence of applicable state decisions), it may not be clear that the discretion of the fiduciary would be limited in this respect, and it cannot be determined that he would be required to make distribution in conformance with one or the other of the above requirements or that one rather than the other is applicable. In such a case, the interest in property passing from the decedent to his surviving spouse would not be ascertainable as of the date of death, if the property available for distribution included assets which might fluctuate in value.

The principles of *Rev. Proc. 64-19* have been applied to a reduce-to-zero non-marital formula clause.[51] Governing instruments opting for the hybrid approach have slavishly followed *Rev. Proc. 64-19*.[52] The instrument must commit itself *either* to the "minimum value" approach *or* the "fairly representative" approach, and cannot give the executor or trustee the discretion to choose between them.[53]

C. Funding Marital Deduction Transfers

In general, and "other things being equal," non-marital transfers (that will not be included in the surviving spouse's gross estate) should be funded with assets that are expected to produce the greater economic yield, and marital transfers should be funded with assets that are expected to produce the lower economic yield (especially with regards to appreciation). Funding is a function of (a) provisions in the governing instrument and (b) the proper exercise of discretion by the estate representative and/or trustee. For example, a high-yield asset such as a closely-held business interest or real estate might be the subject of a non-marital specific-bequest type of transfer (outright or in trust), and low-yield or wasting assets (such as "tangible personal property" other than collectibles) might be the subject of a specific-property marital transfer. Of course, any marital transfer should not be funded with property or interests therein which do not qualify for the marital deduction, and the governing instrument should place such assets "off-limits" for marital-transfer funding. Where a fractional share formula is used, consideration should be given to excluding nonqualifying assets from the definition of "residue." Alternatively, the residue can be defined to include such items so long as a direction is provided for allocating them all to the non-marital share.

Another common "funding" provision in the governing instrument is to exclude from marital transfers property which is eligible for the credits for pre-1977 prior gifts (§2012) and for foreign death taxes (§2014). These credits are available only where the property is subject to tax twice, but if the property is used to fund the marital deduction bequest it will not be so taxed and the credits will be wasted.[54] In contrast, a second decedent does not lose the §2013 credit just because he or she funds a marital transfer with property acquired from a close-in-time prior decedent.

Incidentally, all of the credits are applied against the estate tax (if any) "after" the unified transfer tax credit. If the second decedent uses a reduce-to-zero formula keyed only to the exemption amount, these other credits will be wasted, because

---

51. See Ltr. Ruling 8642007.

52. Under UPC (190) §3-906(a)(2), the default rule is that a pecuniary bequest must be satisfied with assets having a value, on the date of distribution, equal to the pecuniary amount. This default rule can be overridden by language in the will.

53. State law often provides a default choice for the executor. See, e.g., Fla. Probate Code §733.810(4) ("fairly representative" approach in a *Rev. Proc. 64-19* scenario).

54. A noted commentator has suggested this as a reason for keying a reduce-to-zero formula only to the exemption amount. See R. Covey, *The Marital Deduction and Credit Shelter Dispositions and the Use of Formula Provisions* (1984).

the estate tax before the §2013 credit will already be zero. Thus, the formula should operate to produce a taxable estate (in the form of by-pass transfers) that will absorb all of the available credits.

There are pros and cons with respect to using income in respect of decedent (IRD), to fund a marital transfer. On the negative side, the §691(c) deduction is lost if the IRD item is fully deductible under §2056. However, a §691(c) deduction exists only if there is a net estate tax to begin with. If a reduce-to-zero scheme is used, there will be no such tax and therefore no reason not to use IRD to fund the marital bequest. On the positive side, many IRD items consist of annuities, employee survivor benefits, deferred payments under installment sales, and periodic payouts connected with a partnership interest of the deceased spouse. Assuming that these amounts are paid outright to the surviving spouse (as opposed to being poured over into a trust), and assuming also that these items fully qualify, they are often the type of wasting asset that can be readily consumed or disposed of by the surviving spouse so as to avoid being taxed at his or her death. However, if these items are allocated to a marital trust, the ultimate disposition of them hinges on whether they are considered "income" or "principal" for trust accounting purposes.

Under state law and the governing instrument, the estate representative or trustee may have discretionary funding powers.[55] The governing instrument should provide that assets can be allocated between fractional shares of the residue on a non-pro-rata basis. Discretionary funding powers can be exercised so as to allocate low-yield or wasting assets to marital transfers. Of course the funding of a PAT or QTIP trust must be consistent with the "income" requirement.

The governing instrument might also provide that pecuniary bequests and trust transfers can be satisfied by in-kind property transfers.[56] In exercising such a power, a trustee should be on the alert as far as §267(a) is concerned. The satisfaction of a pecuniary bequest contained in a trust with depreciated property would give rise to a loss, but no deduction would be allowed.[57] This loss disallowance rule does not apply where the bequest is under the will, since an estate is not a "related party" under §267(b).

It has been widespread practice, where formula clauses are placed in a trust rather than the will, for the trust to state that the marital trust is to be set aside immediately "upon" or "at" the decedent's death, even though immediate funding of the bequest is an impossibility. In an unfunded *inter vivos* trust, such funding must await the receipt of pour-overs. In a funded *inter vivos* trust or a testamentary trust, funding must await the valuation of estate assets and the filing of a federal estate tax return. The delay in funding (and delay in income distributions) appears to violate the "entitled for life to all of the income" requirement of a PAT or QTIP trust.

---

55. UPC (1990) §3-906(a)(4) gives the estate representative the power to distribute the residue "in any equitable manner."

56. UPC (1990) §3-906(a)(2) gives the estate representative the authority (unless contradicted by the will) to satisfy pecuniary bequests in kind.

57. See §267(c)(5)-(7) ("related parties" defined to include trustee and beneficiary or trustee of related trust).

First, there is the question of whether the surviving spouse is entitled to the income from the date of death. The general rule is that estate (or trust) income accrues from the date of death for the benefit of the residuary transfer.[58] In a fractional-share bequest, such income would inure to the marital and non-marital trusts on a proportional basis. Under a pecuniary transfer, the distributee has no right to "estate income" as such, but "interest" is likely to accrue.[59] Next, the general state law rule is that the trust income interest commences at the decedent's death, even though it is not funded (or not fully funded).[60] In order to carry out this rule, estate income allocated to the trust becomes trust income when it is distributed to the trust.[61] Thus, the trust income interest relates back to the date of the decedent's death, and, accordingly, the income beneficiary (the surviving spouse) is entitled to all of the income starting at the decedent's death, even if such income might not be distributed to the income beneficiary until after the full funding of the trust.

The delayed payment of income appears to violate the "payable annually" requirement of a PAT or QTIP trust. But, thanks to *Rev. Rul. 77-346*, 1977-2 C.B. 340, this problem can be dealt without undue anxiety. This ruling holds that the "income" requirement is not violated in the case of an *inter vivos* trust where the marital trust is not set aside (funded) until the closing of the estate — which in the ruling was 18 months after the settlor's death — so long as such funding occurs within a reasonable period of time. Reg. §20.2056(b)-5(f)(9) lays down the same approach for testamentary marital trusts. Therefore, there is no need for the instrument to provide for payments of "estimated income" prior to the actual funding of the marital trust.

In *Estate of Black v. Comm'r*, 133 T.C. No. 15 (2009), the court held that where a pecuniary true worth marital trust is unfunded at the widow's death, the deemed funding date is the date of her death, which also was the date the marital trust terminated, and not the date of her husband's earlier demise.

QUESTIONS AND NOTES

1. a. Is ability to value the marital deduction transfers at the date of death a requirement of qualification (or an aspect of the terminable interest rule)? If so, why don't the elections under §§642(g) and 2032 disqualify a formula marital bequest? Because the elections are sanctioned by the Code? Because they must be made by the time the estate tax return is

58. See Uniform Principal and Income Act (1997) §202(a). A specific-property legatee "owns" the income from that property after the decedent's death, and such income is not income of the estate. See id. §201(1).
59. See id. §201(3).
60. See id. §301(a) & (b)(2).
61. See id. §302(b).

filed? Are these issues solved by the "passing" requirement? If so, is there a time limit on elections that determine how much passes to (or for the benefit of) the surviving spouse?

b. What is the qualification (or other) problem being addressed in *Rev. Proc. 64-19*? Does it involve a condition precedent to vesting? A contingency as to the amount passing? Is there a rule against "funding" discretion? Is *Rev. Proc. 64-19* still good law? (No case has explicitly tested the validity of *Rev. Rul. 64-19*.)

2. a. The concept of a reduce-to-zero formula clause raises the issue of whether estate administration expenses should be deducted for estate tax purposes or for income tax purposes. The assumption has been to deduct them for estate tax purposes, because the "minimum" estate tax rate has long been higher than the maximum income tax rate, but from 2010 to 2012 (at least) they are equal. The secondary intuition, however, is that the expenses should be deducted for income tax purposes where the estate taxes are avoided by the usual methods.

b. Section 506(b) of the 1990 UPC requires a reimbursement from income beneficiaries to principal in the following scenario: An election is made to deduct administration expenses for income tax purposes that results in the reduction of the marital or charitable deduction, which in turn results in greater estate taxes borne by principal.[62] This should rarely occur, as most estate plans will have a reduce-to-zero plan with no estate taxes. Also, the better advice is to deduct administration expenses for estate tax purposes.

c. Estate and income tax elections and decisions by a fiduciary raise a potential problem under state law insofar as the tax effects (good or bad) of the election or decision do not coincide with the economic effects. Under the doctrine of "equitable adjustment," recognized in some states, rights of reimbursement might arise. Section 506(a) of the 1990 UPC gives the executor discretionary authority to make adjustments to principal and income to counter-act any shifting of economic interests or tax benefits that arise from tax elections, decisions, and income distributions.[63]

MARITAL DEDUCTION REVIEW PROBLEM

Below are some draft clauses for a will containing marital and non-marital trusts. Your primary task is to identify the errors, both technical and judgmental, as well

---

62. Estate taxes are borne by principal. UPC (1990) §502(a)(6).
63. See Joel Dobris, *Equitable Adjustments in Postmortem Income Tax Planning: An Unremitting Diet of Warms*, 65 Iowa L. Rev. 103 (1979); *Limits on the Doctrine of Equitable Adjustment in Sophisticated Postmortem Tax Planning*, 66 Iowa L. Rev. 273 (1981).

as omissions. Not all of the tax issues relate to the marital deduction. You should also be able to explain the tax significance of whatever language in the draft trust provisions are not incorrect. Before proceeding to examine the trust language, you should review the preceding material and devise a check-list of problems that can be dealt with by proper drafting.

Assume that the decedent is much wealthier than his wife, that the formula amount is not inappropriate, and that no community property is involved.

I.

I direct that all my legal debts, and expenses of my last illness, funeral and burial expenses, and the expenses of administering my estate, together with all estate, inheritance, legacy, succession or similar duties or taxes which shall become payable in respect of any property, or interests therein, which I may own at the time of my death, and which is properly includible in my gross estate for any such taxation purposes, shall be charged to and paid from my residuary estate.

II.

I give and bequeath my household furniture, books, musical instruments, watches, jewelry, clothing and other articles of household, domestic or personal use or adornment to my wife JANET if she shall survive me by six months, or if she shall not survive me to my children who do survive me in equal shares.

III.

I give, devise and bequeath all the rest, residue and remainder of my property of whatever kind and wherever located that I own at my death or that I have any right to or interest in, including any of the foregoing gifts in this Will which for any reason fail to take effect, all of which is herein referred to as my residuary estate, to JANET, of Chicago, Illinois, and DALEY TRUST COMPANY, an Illinois banking corporation of Chicago, Illinois, as Trustees to be held, managed and distributed upon the terms, provisions and conditions as provided herein. The receipt of said Trustees for the property passing to it by this Will shall be a complete discharge and acquittance to my Executor.

A. If my spouse shall survive me by six months, the Trustees shall set aside in a separate trust (herein referred to as the MARITAL TRUST) a fraction of my residuary estate, the numerator of which is an amount equal to the maximum estate tax marital deduction allowable to my estate for federal tax purposes, reduced (but not below zero) by an amount equal to the exemption equivalent of the credits available to my estate under §§2010 and 2011 of the Internal Revenue Code of 1986 as amended, and the denominator of which is my residuary estate, but only to the extent that such amounts are allowable as a Marital Deduction for federal estate tax purposes. The Trustee shall have full power and the sole discretion to fund this trust wholly or partly in cash or kind and to select the assets which shall constitute this trust; provided, that there shall not be included in this trust any assets or the proceeds of any assets which do not qualify for the Marital Deduction for federal estate tax purposes. In addition, the Trustees shall not include in this trust any assets or the proceeds of any assets which shall be subject to both federal estate tax and foreign death taxes.

1. Commencing with the date of death of the Grantor, the Trustees shall pay all the income from the MARITAL TRUST in convenient installments to my spouse for life.

2. If, in the opinion of the Trustees, the income herein provided, together with receipts from other sources known to the Trustees, shall not be sufficient to suitably support and maintain my spouse to the extent necessary to continue to enjoy the conveniences and advantages of the standard of living to which accustomed during my lifetime, the Trustees are hereby authorized to advance to my spouse such portions of the principal of the MARITAL TRUST as the Trustees, in their sole discretion, may deem appropriate to make up such deficiencies.

3. My spouse, so long as she is not under any legal disability, shall have the power to withdraw the entire principal of said trust upon written notice delivered to the corporate Trustee.

4. JANET shall have the unrestricted right and authority to direct the disposition of the principal of this trust estate by the terms of her Last Will and Testament, so long as competent to do so, to such person or persons and in such manner as such spouse may elect; provided, however, that such power of appointment shall be exercisable only by specific reference to the power in the said Will of my spouse.

5. If JANET shall fail to validly exercise the testamentary power of appointment hereinbefore given, then upon the death of my spouse the balance of the property and estate hereof shall be added to and become a part of the principal of the RESIDUARY TRUST hereinafter established in Part B of this Article III hereof, and the trust conditions applicable shall govern the disposition of the principal and income.

B. Subject to the foregoing, all of the rest, residue and remainder of my estate shall be held in trust (hereinafter referred to as the RESIDUARY TRUST) according to the following terms and provisions:

1. The Trustees shall pay the entire income from this trust property and estate to my spouse in reasonable installments at least annually during her entire lifetime.

2. If, in the opinion of the Trustees, during the life of my said wife the income herein provided shall not be sufficient to provide for the comfort and support of my said spouse and my children, and at any time to educate my children, including a college, university, or finishing school education for each of them, or in the case of any emergency at any time befalling any of them or their dependents, such as illness, accident or extraordinary financial distress, then the Trustees are authorized to use and expend from time to time such part of the principal of this RESIDUARY TRUST estate as they may deem necessary to make up such deficiency or meet such emergency.

3. Following the death of my spouse, or upon my death, if my said spouse shall predecease me, the Trustees shall [remainder of clause omitted].

IV.

The Trustees hereunder shall have the following powers and authority in respect of all property embraced within every trust estate herein provided, viz: to take possession of the trust property, and to collect and receive the moneys, interests, profits and income arising therefrom, with full power in the Trustees to manage, invest and reinvest the same and all such trust estate in any kind of property, personal and real, including by way of illustration: bonds, interests in any amount in common trust funds maintained by the Trustees, stocks, bank accounts, real estate, life insurance policies, mortgages and other investments and property as in the discretion of the Trustees may seem most advantageous to such trust estate and the beneficiaries thereof, not being limited by any then existing laws relating to investments of trust funds.

V.

All receipts and disbursements the Trustees are authorized to make shall be credited to or charged against either income or principal as the Trustees shall determine in their sole discretion. All determinations made by the Trustees in good faith shall be final and binding upon all persons (whether in being or not) then or thereafter interested in the income and/or principal of any trust hereunder, and the Trustees shall not in any manner be held liable to any such person as a result of its determination.

CHAPTER 7

LONG-TERM TRUSTS

This chapter deals with certain tax issues relating to trusts that continue after the death of the creator and the creator's spouse, such as may arise in the context of a by-pass trust or a dynastic trust intended to last indefinitely. Those issues cluster around powers of appointment and the GST tax.

§7.1. Powers of Appointment

A power held with respect to property *transferred inter vivos by the decedent* herself is called a "retained power," and in this case inclusion of the transferred property in the transferor's gross estate is governed by §§2036-2038. In this section, the focus is on powers that are *not* retained by a donor in connection with an *inter vivos* transfer by her. Rather, the focus is on powers of an individual over property transferred (usually in trust) by another person. Such powers are referred to as *powers of appointment*. The income, estate, and gift tax consequences of the possession and exercise of powers of appointment is dealt with by §§678, 2041, and 2514.

A. Nontax Definition and Role of Powers of Appointment

A power of appointment is a nonretained power to affect the beneficial enjoyment of property. In modern practice, virtually all powers of appointment occur in the context of trusts. Powers of appointment are created by the instrument of transfer into trust. Powers of appointment do not arise by operation of law. Rights of disclaimer, statutory elections, and the ability to settle a dispute concerning succession are not powers of appointment. A power of appointment, as is the case with any power, is not subject to descent and distribution. That is, a person possessing a power of appointment cannot bequeath the power or give it away to another. A power held by a person may be given up by a "release," or it may "lapse" by its own terms. A power of appointment is not a fiduciary power, and (unless state law provides otherwise) is a wholly discretionary power, and, therefore, it need not be exercised at all. If it is exercised, the exercise is free of any possible constraint of impartiality.[1] An example of power-of-appointment language in a trust would be the following:

> The trustee [a bank] shall distribute the trust income to B for so long as B shall live. On B's death the trust shall terminate, and the trust property shall be distributed, free of any trust to C. *During B's lifetime, C shall have the power to distribute the corpus, in whole or in part, outright or in trust, to or for the benefit of my issue, but in no event shall it be exercisable in favor of C, the creditors of C, the estate of C, or the creditors of C's estate.*

In the foregoing, the person creating the trust is called the "donor" of the power. The person possessing the power (C) is called the "donee" of the power. The persons who can receive the property subject to the power of appointment (the issue of the donor) are the "objects" (sometimes referred to as "potential appointees") of the power. If the power is exercised, the persons receiving the property are the "appointees" of the power. The persons who take if the power is not exercised (in this case, B and C) are the "takers in default." The power in this example is an "*inter vivos*" power (or a power "by deed") by reason of the fact that it can be exercised only by the donee during the donee's lifetime. (A power that is exercisable only by the donee's will is called a "testamentary" power.) Finally, the power in this example is a "special" power by reason of the fact that it cannot be exercised in favor of C, C's estate, or the creditors of either. If the "but in no event" clause were omitted, *and* if C were a descendant of the donor, then the power would be a "general" power, because the donee could appoint the entire property to herself (without fiduciary constraint).

Powers of appointment are fairly common in trusts that are expected to last for a significant period of time beyond the death of the donor and the donor's spouse. Powers of appointment are provided for in trusts for three main reasons. The first is to provide for "second look" flexibility in the trust, by giving a trusted person the power to effectively alter or terminate a trust if and when changing circumstances warrant, but without imposing fiduciary constraints upon such person. The second is to favor a particular beneficiary. Finally, certain tax benefits may be conditioned on, or be obtainable through, the use of a "general" power of appointment. One example is a marital PAT, in which the transferee spouse must be given a general power of appointment (either *inter vivos* or testamentary) exercisable alone and in all events. Another example refers to qualification for the annual exclusion under §2503(c) (present-interest gifts to minors), which requires that, if the minor dies before reaching 21, the property must be payable to the minor's estate or must be subject to a general power of appointment in the minor. See §2503(c)(2)(B).

For federal tax purposes, the crucial distinction is between general and special powers of appointment. A *general* power of appointment is one where the donee of

---

1. If a trust has more than one beneficiary, the trustee shall act impartially in administering the trust and in effecting distributions. See UTC (2000) §803.

the power can appoint the trust property to herself or to her estate (or to the creditors of either). A *special* power of appointment is any power of appointment (held by any party) that is not a general power of appointment. The federal tax consequences of powers of appointment are generally visited upon a person who is a donee of a general power of appointment, as will be explained in due course.

B. Powers of Appointment Under §2033

A concept similar to that of "constructive ownership" is "constructive receipt," a recognized doctrine under the income tax with regard to cash-method taxpayers. A *general* power of appointment is a power to appoint to oneself or one's estate (or the creditors of either), and therefore is analogous to "constructive ownership." Does the constructive ownership notion result in inclusion of a property in the donee's gross estate by reason of the possession (or testamentary exercise) of a general power of appointment *under* §2033? This issue was dealt with in §4.1.B & D, and the short answer is "no." Thus, if an *inter vivos* general power of appointment is viewed as an "interest" in the property, such interest expires at death and does not descend from the donee of the power to any other person through the donee's estate or by survivorship right. If the power is exercised in favor of the donee, the property is added to the donee's wealth. If the property is exercised in favor of another, there is arguably a constructive gift by the donee to the appointee,[2] but by the time the courts came to consider the gift issue, legislative developments had overrun doctrinal development.[3]

As to a general *testamentary* power of appointment, the fund to which the power pertains pre-exists the donee's death, thereby distinguishing the situation of (say) wrongful death recoveries payable to a person's estate. It would seem therefore, that a person possessing a general testamentary power of appointment has the equivalent of a "constructive remainder interest" in the fund following his own life. However, the interest disappears on his death if the power has not been exercised in favor of his estate. In any event, the government made no attempt to tax the *possession* of a general testamentary power under the predecessor of §2033. In *U.S. v. Field*, 255 U.S. 257 (1921), the Supreme Court held that the narrow 1916 version of §2033 did not reach the *exercise* of a general testamentary power in favor of third parties, because the appointed property was not merged with her estate and fully subject to creditors claims, as the statute then required.[4] This same language was again construed restrictively in 1930 to exclude real estate

---

2. Cf. *Mallinckrodt v. Nunan*, 2 T.C. 1128 (1943) (reviewed), *aff'd*, 146 F.2d 1 (8th Cir.1945), *cert. denied*, 324 U.S. 871(income tax case).

3. See *Comm'r v. Walston*, 168 F.2d 211 (4th Cir.1948) (statutory construction); *Comm'r v. Salomon*, 124 F.2d 86 (3d Cir.1941) (relying on theory that donee was agent of donor). In 1942, Congress comprehensively legislated rules governing powers of appointment.

4. The original version of §2033 only included property of the decedent "subject to the payment of the charges against his estate and the expenses of its administration and . . . subject to distribution as part" of the estate.

not subject to estate administration.[5] The fact that §2033 was later changed to its present form has not been viewed by the courts as having rendered *Fields* obsolete. In fact, in *Helvering v. Safe Deposit & Trust Co. of Baltimore*, 316 U.S. 56, 60-62 (1942), the Supreme Court said this:

> [V]iewing [§2033] in its [historical] background, we cannot reach the conclusion that the words "interest . . . of the decedent at the time of his death" were intended by Congress to include property subject to a general testamentary power unexercised by the decedent. In *Field*, this Court held that property passing under a general power of appointment exercised by a decedent was not such an "interest" as the 1916 Act brought within the decedent's gross estate. While the holding was limited to exercised powers of appointment, the approach of the Court left little doubt that the Court regarded property subject to unexercised general powers of appointment as similarly beyond the scope of the statutory phrase "interest of the decedent."
>
> After the *Field* case, the provision it passed upon was reenacted without change. If the implications of the *Field* opinion with respect to unexercised powers had been considered contrary to the intendment of the words "interest of the decedent," it is reasonable to suppose that Congress would have added some clarifying amendment.
>
> In *Field*, this Court referred to an amendment passed in 1919, §402(e), which specifically declared property passing under an exercised general testamentary power to be part of the decedent's gross estate. The passage of this amendment, said the Court, "indicates that Congress was doubtful whether the previous Act included property passing by appointment." In the face of such doubts, Congress nevertheless specified only that property subject to exercised powers should be included. From this deliberate singling out of exercised powers alone, a Congressional intent to treat unexercised powers otherwise can be deduced. In addition, the uniform administrative practice until this case appears to have [been] contrary to what the government now urges. Because of these circumstances, we believe that a departure from the long-standing, generally accepted construction of [§2033] would override the best indications of Congressional intent.

Later in 1942 the §2033 issue was effectively rendered moot by the enactment of a separate provision that included in the gross estate property subject to any power of appointment, general or special, exercised or nonexercised, except for special powers exercisable only in favor of the donee's immediate family or charity. A similar provision dealt with the exercise or release of a power of appointment under the gift tax. However, in 1951 the 1942 changes were retroactively repealed and replaced by what are now §§2041 and 2514, which are broader than the 1919 Act but narrower than the 1942 Act.

---

5. *Crooks v. Harrelson*, 282 U.S. 55 (1930). The amendment to the predecessor of §2033 to remove the language referring to estate administration was clearly intended to overturn the result of this case, but it also undermines the basis of *Field*.

C. *Powers of Appointment Under §§2041 and 2514*

The possession, exercise, release, and lapse of a general power of appointment generally causes the property (to which the power pertains) to be subject to gift and/or estate tax.

1. *Transfer Tax Meaning of Power of Appointment*

Under the federal transfer taxes, the notion of "power of appointment" as used in §§2041 and 2514 refers only to powers held by individuals, since only individuals (and their estates) can be taxpayers. Second, the estate and gift tax sections that expressly deal with powers of appointment, §§2041 and 2514, do *not* cover any power of appointment that is *retained* by a donor in connection with an *inter vivos* transfer.[6] (Retained-power transfers are dealt with in Chapter 8.) Finally, the concept of a general power of appointment for transfer tax purposes is not limited to a power which is called a "general power of appointment" under state law. Sections 2041 and 2514 provide their own self-contained definitions of "general power of appointment," and these definitions control for federal transfer tax purposes.

Accordingly, the tax concept of a general power encompasses situations having the effect of a general power of appointment,[7] even if they are not referred to as such under the governing instrument or state law. For example, and as noted in §4.1.D, where one person confers a "remainder interest" upon another person's "estate," the latter is considered to possess a testamentary general power of appointment.[8] A power held by the holder of a legal life estate in real property to sell the property and consume the proceeds is an *inter vivos* general power of appointment, just as would be an unfettered power of a person (other than the grantor) to consume the principal of a trust. Finally, if an individual is *both* a trustee with a discretionary power to invade the corpus of a trust *and* a possible beneficiary of corpus under the same trust, such person has an *inter vivos* general power of appointment, which was possibly unintended.

2. *Estate and Gift Tax Consequences of General Powers of Appointment*

Under present §§2041(a)(2) and 2514(b), *general* powers of appointment created after October 21, 1942 are treated as follows:

(1) The *possession* at death of a general (*inter vivos* or testamentary) power of appointment causes the property to be included in the donee's gross estate. This rule encompasses the *exercise* of a general power of appointment by will, which — because a will "speaks" only at death — is necessarily "possessed" at death.

---

6. See Reg. §20.2041-1(b)(2).

7. See Reg. §20.2041-1(b)(1), stating that the term "power of appointment" is to be applied on the basis of substance and not form or nomenclature.

8. See *Keeter v. U.S.*, 461 U.S. 714 (5th Cir.1972).

(2) The *exercise* of an *inter vivos* general power of appointment, or the *release or lapse* of any general power of appointment, is treated as a "transfer" of the subject property for gift tax purposes *and* for purposes of estate tax §§2036-2038 (dealing with *inter vivos* transfers with retained interests and powers).

The possession, exercise, release, or lapse of a special power of appointment does not trigger taxation under §§2041 and 2514, except in the situation where the effect of an exercise of a special power is to release a general power of appointment or cause such a power to lapse. Also, an exercise, release, or lapse can possibly trigger a gift under §2511.

3. Transfer Tax Definition of "General Power of Appointment"

The federal transfer tax definition of general power of appointment is, obviously, central to the operation of §§2041 and 2514.

(a) In General

The tax definition of a "general" power of appointment is found in parallel estate and gift tax provisions, §§2041(b)(1) and 2514(c). A general power of appointment is a (nonretained) power of an individual to appoint property in favor of any one or more of the holder (donee) of the power, her estate, or the creditors of either. The notion of being able to appoint to oneself includes any manner of being able, under the governing instrument or state law, to withdraw, appropriate, or make an enforceable demand against money or property held by another or in trust, or to distribute the same to oneself. A *Crummey* power (see §3.5.D) is an *inter vivos* general power of appointment

A person may have a general power if the power can be exercised so as to indirectly benefit oneself. The obvious example is a power to cause the trust to pay off the donee's creditors. Similarly, a power that can be used to discharge the donee's support obligations is a general power. See Reg. §20.2041-1(c).

As mentioned above, a general power "issue" can arise if a person (who is not the trust grantor) either is a trustee with broad powers to dispose of income or corpus or is a beneficiary with powers over, or rights in, the income or corpus. It is well to be aware of this issue, and it is generally desirable to avoid inadvertently conferring an *inter vivos* general power of appointment on a person. However, there may be exceptions to the maxim of avoiding the creation of a general power, such as where a general power is a prerequisite to obtaining some statutory transfer tax benefit (such as for a PAT) or can be deployed to save transfer taxes.

(b) Exception for Powers Limited by Standards

A power to consume, appropriate, or invade corpus or income for one's own benefit would normally be a general power of appointment. However, under §§2041(b)(1)(A) and 2514(c)(1), such a power is not a general power of appointment if it is limited by an "ascertainable standard" relating to one or more of such person's "health, education, support, or maintenance."

The rationale for this exception is that the existence of standards operates so that the trustee subject to the standards is acting "pursuant to the grantor's instructions" rather than according to the trustee/beneficiary's own discretion. As a matter of trust law generally, trust beneficiaries can enforce standards in a court of equitable jurisdiction. A court can compel distributions or force the trustee to carry out the terms of the trust. In contrast, a discretionary power in a trustee is virtually immune from beneficiary lawsuits and demands, except where the trustee neglects its office, acts in bad faith, and/or abuses its discretion.[9]

It is well to keep in mind that the statutory "standards" exception to the term "general power of appointment" is not for any "ascertainable standard" but only for ascertainable standards relating specifically to "health," "education," "support," and "maintenance." *Revenue Ruling 77-60*, set out below, provides recipes for compliance.

Revenue Ruling 77-60

1977-1 Cum. Bull. 282

Under the will of decedent's spouse, the decedent was granted a life estate in certain properties, with the power to invade corpus as desired "to continue the donee's accustomed standard of living." Under applicable state law, the quoted language is not construed to impose an objective limitation on the exercise of the power of invasion granted by the donor, other than one of good faith.

Reg. §20.2041-1(c)(2) provides:

> A power to consume, invade, or appropriate income or corpus, or both, for the benefit of the decedent which is limited by an ascertainable standard relating to the health, education, support or maintenance of the decedent is, by reason of §2041(b)(1)(A), not a general power of appointment. A power is limited by such a standard if the extent of the holder's duty to exercise and not to exercise the power is reasonably measurable in terms of his needs for health, education, or support (or any combination of them). As used in this subparagraph, "support" and "maintenance" are synonymous, and their meaning is not limited to the bare necessities of life. A power to use property for the comfort, welfare or happiness of the holder is not limited by the requisite standard. Examples of powers which are limited by the requisite standard are powers exercisable for the holder's "support," "support in reasonable comfort," "maintenance in health and reasonable comfort," "support in accustomed manner of living," "education, including college and professional education," "health," and "medical, dental, hospital and nursing expenses and expenses of invalidism."

The test is the "measure of control" over the property by virtue of the grant of the power, i.e., whether the exercise of the power is restricted by definite bounds.

---

9. See UTC (2000) §814(a) (stating a discretionary power must always be exercised in good faith and in accordance with the terms and purposes of the trust and the interests of the beneficiaries).

That the amount of property that could be consumed for the benefit of the donee is not measurable or predictable is of no consequence.

A power to use property to enable the donee to continue an accustomed mode of living, without further limitation, although predictable and measurable on the basis of past expenditures, does not come within the ascertainable standard prescribed in §2041(b)(1)(A) since the standard of living may include customary travel, entertainment, luxury items, or other expenditures not required for meeting the donee's "needs for health, education or support." Nor does the requirement of a good faith exercise of a power create an ascertainable standard. Good faith exercise of a power is not determinative of its breadth.

Accordingly, the power possessed by the decedent to invade trust principal as desired to continue an accustomed standard of living was not limited by an ascertainable standard relating to health, education, support or maintenance. Therefore, the decedent possessed at death a general power of appointment under §2041.

The exception for standards relating to health, education, support, and maintenance helps to answer what would otherwise be a difficult issue; namely, that of the distinction between an *interest* of a trust beneficiary and an *inter vivos* general power of appointment of a beneficiary. The ability of a beneficiary to enforce an ascertainable trust distribution standard appears to straddle this distinction. To take a simple example, if the beneficiary has the right to withdraw the trust income annually, does the beneficiary have an income interest, or a general power of appointment over the year's income? It is an "interest" if the trustee has to pay it to the beneficiary regardless, but it is a power of appointment if the income can be left by the beneficiary in the trust and added to corpus.[10] Now consider the case where the trustee is to distribute income and/or corpus to B for B's support. Does B have something like an annuity interest expiring at death, or does B have an *inter vivos* power of appointment by reason of being able to make enforceable demands on the trustee? In the abstract, this scenario smells more of an interest than a power. If the trustee fails to comply, the beneficiary has a right akin to a money claim against the trust and trustee for the improper withholding of "required" distributions.[11] The existence of the standards exception confirms this analysis: A trustee/beneficiary who is to distribute income or corpus to herself under a standard relating to health, education, support, or maintenance possesses an interest (expiring at death) rather than a power of appointment. There is no meaningful latitude for discretion by either the trustee or the beneficiary.

A harder question is presented where a trustee is to make distributions to a beneficiary (who is not the trustee) pursuant to a distributive standard that falls

---

10. See *Ewing v. Rountree*, 346 F.2d 471 (6th Cir.1965) (beneficiary's right to demand corpus was a general power of appointment).

11. See *Marsman v. Nasca*, 573 N.E.2d 1025 (Mass. App. 1991) (executor of deceased beneficiary could recover from trust for trustee's failure to distribute corpus under "reasonable comfort and maintenance" standard).

outside of the "standards exception," especially where the standard is so broad (say, "happiness") as to open up the possibility that the beneficiary could successfully force a distribution of an unlimited amount of trust corpus. *Revenue Ruling 76-368,* below, partly answers this question.

Revenue Ruling 76-368

1976-2 Cum. Bull. 271

The decedent's spouse created a testamentary trust under which the income was payable to the decedent for life, and the remainder payable to other persons. The trustee, a bank, was authorized to invade the trust corpus and pay portions thereof to or for the use and benefit of the decedent in such manner as the trustee, in its sole and unfettered discretion, deemed advisable should the decedent be in need of funds in excess of the trust income for "health, comfort, maintenance, welfare, or for any other purpose or purposes." The trustee was directed to liberally exercise its discretionary power of invasion. Prior to the decedent's death, numerous requests had been made to the trustee for additional funds, and all such requests had been honored by the trustee.

Under Reg. §20.2041-1(b), it is provided that a power to consume or appropriate property is a power of appointment if, for example, a trust instrument provides that the beneficiary may appropriate or consume the principal. In determining whether an independent trustee's broad power of invasion can be imputed to a beneficiary, the initial step is to ascertain the scope of the decedent's rights under applicable state law.

In *Estate of Cox v. Comm'r,* 59 T.C. 825 (1973) *(acq.),* the court held that, under Texas law, the income beneficiary did not hold a power of appointment with respect to a testamentary trust which provided that, if the income was insufficient to comfortably and adequately supply the beneficiary with all comfort and necessities, then the beneficiary's comfort and necessities were to be provided for by the trustee selling trust assets. In reaching its decision that the trustee and not the beneficiary had the power of invasion, the court determined that neither the words of the will nor the extrinsic evidence indicated an intent by the testator to grant such a power to the income beneficiary. It thus decided that to attribute to the beneficiary an implied power of invasion would be inconsistent with the will provision expressly granting the trustee "sole and exclusive" management powers.

In *Security-Peoples Trust Co. v. U.S.,* 238 F. Supp. 40 (W.D. Pa. 1965), the trustee, a bank, was authorized "to advance portions of the principal of the Trust Estate to or for the benefit of [the decedent-income beneficiary and others] in such amounts, and for such purposes, as my Trustee in its discretion may deem advisable. I direct that my Trustee shall exercise liberally the power to advance principal to promote the health, comfort, maintenance or welfare of the income beneficiaries." The Government argued basically that, under Pennsylvania law, a beneficiary can compel the trustee to exercise its discretion to use trust property for the benefit of the beneficiary. The court held against the Government, stating that in the absence of a showing of necessity, and clear direction in the instrument,

Pennsylvania courts will not compel the trustee's exercise of discretion, and will support the trustee's discretion to refuse or withhold invasions of principal. The presence of additional life beneficiaries and remaindermen required the trustee to protect their interests against invasions for decedent so as to not defeat the testator's intention.

In the instant case, the trustee alone was expressly authorized to invade the trust corpus for the use and benefit of the decedent as the trustee, in its sole and unfettered discretion, deemed advisable for the stated purposes. The governing trust instrument did not give the decedent any supervening right or power, or even a conjunctive right or power, such as would indicate an intent by the testator to grant to the decedent the power to consume or appropriate the principal. While the decedent had the power to invoke a process of judicial review had the trustee, in the judgment of the decedent, failed to liberally exercise its discretionary power of invasion on the decedent's behalf, this kind of power doesn't transfer a power of invasion granted an independent trustee to the beneficiary of the trust. Accordingly, the power of invasion cannot be imputed to the decedent under §2041.

These rulings demonstrate that federal transfer tax doctrine is often closely dependent upon the law of trusts and donative transfers.[12] Indeed, federal transfer tax cases are often a good source of trust law, especially in the area of beneficiary rights.

This problem of inadvertently giving an individual a general power of appointment by naming a person as trust beneficiary and giving the same person discretionary distributive powers as sole trustee is sufficiently serious that the drafters of the Uniform Trust Code (2000) crafted a provision, §814(b)(1), that (if enacted into governing state law) amends the trust instrument by limiting the power (insofar as it pertains to distributions by the trustee to herself) in conformity to the standards exception.[13]

4. Jointly-Held Powers

If a power which looks like a "general" power is held jointly with another party, it might avoid classification as a general power. The joint-power issue arises only

---

12. If the situation is not governed by UTC §814(b)(1), the estate can argue that state non-statutory law (sometimes referring to the donor's intent) limits a power that appears not to comply with the standards exception to one that does. Such an argument succeeded in *Brantingham v. U.S.*, 631 F.2d 542 (7th Cir.1980), but the Service has specifically rejected *Brantingham*. *Rev. Rul. 82-63*, 1982-1 C.B. 135.

13. The amendment of the trust is effective as of the date of legislation, whereas a judicial modification of the trust (say, under UTC §415) is effective only as of the date of the decree. Section 814(b) refers cryptically to an "ascertainable standard," but that term is defined in UTC §103(2), which incorporates the standards exception as set out in the Internal Revenue Code. The Service has ruled that it would not recognize amendatory legislation of this type to the extent that it purported to apply retroactively *and* after federal tax consequences had already attached. At the same time, it would not treat the amendment as causing a taxable lapse of the power. *Rev. Proc. 94-44*, 1994-1 C.B. 683.

for *inter vivos* general powers of appointment, including any co-trusteeship situation where dispositive powers are involved. (A testamentary power by its nature cannot be exercised jointly.)

The estate and gift tax rules applicable to jointly-held powers created after 1942, found in §§2041(b)(1)(C) and 2514(c)(3), are based upon assumptions as to how joint holders of a power are likely to act. Nevertheless, these rules are truly rules, and not presumptions of fact, and actual facts cannot be invoked in an effort to by-pass these rules. In the discussion that follows, the word "donee" refers to the person whose power would be classified as a general power if he or she held the power alone, and the word "co-holder" refers to the other party who possesses the power jointly with the donee.

In general, if the co-holder has no personal stake in how a power is exercised, the co-holder is conclusively deemed not to be in opposition to the wishes of the donee. Hence, the co-holder's existence is ignored, and the donee is treated as possessing the general power alone. A corporation is conclusively deemed not to have a personal stake in how a power is exercised. Hence, if the co-holder of a power (a co-trustee) is a bank or trust company, the donee has a general power.

However, if the co-holder of the power happens to be creator (donor) of the power, it is conclusively presumed that the latter's concern with the property's disposition would outweigh the desires of the donee. Hence, the donee is deemed *not* to possess a general power of appointment. §§2041(b)(1)(C)(i) and 2514(c)(3)(A).

Where the co-holder is neither a corporation nor the donor of the power, the question whether a given donee possesses a general power of appointment depends upon whether the co-holder has an "adverse interest" (i.e., an interest in the trust that would be diminished by the exercise of the power in favor of the donee). See §§2041(b)(1)(C)(ii) and 2514(c)(3)(B). Here the donee is conclusively deemed not to possess a general power of appointment, the idea being that the adverse-party co-holder has a monetary incentive to veto any attempt by the donee to obtain the trust property.

In some cases, the co-holder might have an interest in the trust such that the best that could have been hoped for was to have "made a deal" with the donee to divide up the corpus. The paradigm case is where both the donee and the co-holder of an *inter vivos* general power are also objects of the power (potential appointees), but the power terminates upon the death of the donee, so that the co-holder has no chance of acceding to sole possession of the power for himself. Here the donee is deemed to possess a general power only over an *aliquot* portion of the property. §§2041(b)(1)(C)(iii) and 2514(c)(3)(C).

Revenue Ruling 79-63

1979-1 Cum. Bull. 302

The decedent's spouse created a trust under which the income was payable to the decedent for life, and the remainder was payable equally to the decedent's children or to any one of such children as the decedent might direct by will.

In addition, the trust provided that at any time during the decedent's lifetime the decedent, with the consent of C, one of the decedent's children, could direct the trustees to distribute all or any part of the trust property to anyone, including the decedent. The decedent and C were trustees of the trust and they continued in that position until the decedent's death.

Reg. §20.2041-3(c) provides, with respect to jointly-held powers of appointment created after October 21, 1942, [that] a taker in default of appointment under a power has an interest which is adverse to an exercise of the power, [but that] a co-holder of the power has no adverse interest merely because of his joint possession of the power nor merely because he is a permissible appointee under a power.

In the present case the decedent could cause the principal to be distributed during lifetime only with the consent of C. However, the interest held by C does not amount to a substantial interest in the property adverse to exercise of the power in favor of the decedent. C is a taker in default not of the lifetime power in which C has a power of consent but rather of the testamentary [special] power exercisable solely by the decedent. C would not have necessarily been in a better economic position after the decedent's death by refusing to exercise the power in favor of the decedent during the decedent's lifetime. Thus, the fact that C might survive the decedent and receive an interest in the property, if the decedent failed to exercise the testamentary [special] power, does not elevate C's interest as a consenting party of the lifetime power to a substantial adverse interest. Consequently, the decedent's power falls within the definition of a "general power of appointment." If, however, C had been the decedent's only child, C would have had a vested interest in the trust remainder that would have been substantially adverse to the exercise of the decedent's lifetime power of appointment.

The amount includible in the decedent's gross estate is the value of property subject to the general power divided by the number of holders of the power who are permissible appointees. Here C was a permissible appointee but the requirement that C consent to the exercise of the power does not raise C to the status of a co-holder of such power. Accordingly, the total value of the trust is includible in the gross estate of the decedent under §2041.

Because the "adverse party" exception to the definition of "general power of appointment" is complex, and because of the fact that the results might hinge on the (uncertain) order of the deaths of individuals, it is not recommended that this exception be relied on in drafting trust instruments. In order to avoid this problem, the Uniform Trust Code (2000) §814(c) provides that if the power to make a discretionary distribution to oneself is held jointly with another trustee, only the other trustee can effect the distribution.[14]

----

14. See *Rev. Rul. 54-153*, 1954-1 C.B. 185 (holding that a person did not have a general power of appointment where state nonstatutory law allocated to a co-trustee the power to make discretionary distributions to such person.)

1. a. The terms of the trust created by Amy confer on Barry the power to withdraw corpus for his "reasonable support, comfort, and maintenance in his accustomed standard of living, and college, graduate or professional education, including training in language, artistic and musical skills, as determined by Barry." Under local law, this power must be exercised in good faith. Does Barry possess a general power? See *Rev. Rul. 77-194*, 1977-1 C.B. 282.

    b. Same as above, except that Barry is the sole trustee and the trust provides that the trustee has the power to pay corpus to one or more of Barry, Clay, or Danielle for the purposes therein stated. See *Rev. Rul. 78-398*, 1978-2 C.B. 237 ("maintenance and medical care"); *Ltr. Rul. 7914036* ("maintain accustomed standard of living"). What effect, if any, would UTC §814 have here?

2. In each of the following, ascertain whether Zelda, as trust beneficiary, has a general power of appointment under §§2041 and 2514, by reason of being able to compel the trustee to make distributions to her.

    a. The trustee is the X Bank, and the trustee is to pay income and corpus to Zelda for Zelda's "support."

    b. Same as (a), except the trustee is to pay corpus to Zelda for her "comfort, welfare, and happiness," with power to accumulate.

    c. Same as (b), except the standards are to be applied according to the "trustee's discretion."

3. Reg. §20.2041-1(c)(1) states that an individual trustee who has the power to make distributions to a person to whom the trustee owes an obligation to support is a power to vicariously appoint to oneself. Moreover, the standards exception does not apply in such a case. (Why not?) UTC §814(b)(2) amends trusts to prohibit the exercise of such a power.

4. An unrestricted power in a person to remove the trustee *and appoint oneself* as successor trustee would amount to holding the office of trustee. Reg. §20.2041-1(b). However, being able to fire a trustee would be distinguishable, if the successor trustee has to be an unrelated and nonsubordinate party within the meaning of §672(c). See *Rev. Rul. 95-58*, 1995-2 C.B. 191. Although it might be thought that the power to fire the trustee is the power to coerce it, a trustee can be sued by other beneficiaries for breach of trust.

5. Read Reg. §20.2041-3(c). Suppose Alger creates a trust, naming Bjorn and Cesar as co-trustees with the alternative dispositive provisions described below in (a)-(b). Additionally, with respect to all of the fact patterns below, the trust provides that upon Bjorn's death, the trust is to terminate and its assets are to be distributed to Dirk. Then, consider the following alternatives, where Bjorn dies before Cesar, and, in the alternative, where Cesar dies before Bjorn. (Note: If a general power expires or is terminated during a person's lifetime, that is treated as a "lapse," which in turn is treated as the "exercise" of the power, which yet in turn is treated as a "transfer" for estate and gift tax purposes. Lapses are discussed shortly.)

    a. All the income is to be paid to Bjorn for life; corpus may be paid to Cesar in the trustees' discretion.

    b. All of the income is to be paid to Bjorn for his life, corpus may be paid to Bjorn and/or Cesar in the trustees' discretion during the lifetime of Bjorn.

6. Inclusion of the property subject to a pre-1942 power results only where there is an exercise of (a) a testamentary general power or (b) an *inter vivos* general power so that one or more of §§2036-2038 would apply treating the exercise as a "transfer." (This rule is simply a carryover of the 1918 statute discussed in *Fields* and *Helvering v. Safe Deposit & Trust Co. of Baltimore*.) A pre-1942 jointly-held power is not treated as a general power.

D. Effect of Action or Inaction by the Donee of a General Power

Taxation is triggered by the possession of a general power of appointment at the donee's death, or by its exercise, release, or lapse during the donee's lifetime. The exercise of a special power (but not its release or lapse) is capable of triggering a transfer under §2511.

1. "Possession" of a General Power

For §2041 to apply by reason of the donee's "possession" of a general power of appointment, the general power of appointment must actually be possessed at death. In the case of an *inter vivos* general power, the "at death" requirement is satisfied where the decedent held the power until it expired by reason of her death. In the case of a testamentary general power, the "at death" requirement is satisfied where property is subject to unlimited testamentary disposition by the decedent "after death," such as would occur under a power exercisable under the decedent's will in favor of the decedent's estate (or the creditors thereof) or by reason of money or property (or an interest therein) passing to the decedent's "estate."

A power of appointment is considered to exist on the date of a decedent's death even though the exercise of the power is subject to the precedent giving of notice, or even though the exercise of the power takes effect only on the expiration of a stated period after its exercise, whether or not on or before the decedent's death notice has been given or the power has been exercised.

A contingent general power is not possessed at death if the contingency did not in fact occur prior to the donee's death.[15] Thus, if Inez creates an irrevocable trust, with the income payable to Jeb for life, then remainder to Kim if living, but if Kim is not then living then remainder to Jeb's estate, Jeb dies possessed of a testamentary general power only if Kim has predeceased Jeb. However, for the contingent power rule to apply, the contingency must not be within the donee's control or, if it is within the donee's control, must possess nontax (i.e., "independent") significance.[16]

---

15. See *Estate of Gilchrist v. Comm'r*, 630 F.2d 340 (5th Cir.1980).

16. See *Estate of Kurz v. Comm'r*, 101 T.C. 44 (1993), *aff'd*, 68 F.3d 1027 (7th Cir.1995) (The Circuit Court found little of a real contingency in the case and held that "Section 2041 is designed to include in the taxable estate all assets that the decedent possessed or effectively controlled. If only a lever must be pulled to dispense money, then the power is exercisable. [Essentially,]

Inclusion under §2041 is not avoided just because the decedent lacked the legal capacity to exercise a general power of appointment by reason (for example) of minority or incompetence.[17]

As is the case under §2033, the subject *property* must be in existence at the moment of (just prior to) the decedent's death.[18] Thus, wrongful death awards payable to a victim's estate are not includible under §2041.[19] Damages that arise from an event that causes death and that survive death (such as damages relating to medical expenses and pain and suffering) are treated as existing at death.[20]

The amount includible in the gross estate by reason of possessing a general power is the value of the property subject to the power (not the value of the power itself).

2. Exercise or Release of General Power

If possession of a general power at death causes inclusion in the gross estate of the property subject to the power, then the donees of general powers would have a transfer-tax incentive to attempt to get rid of the power prior to death. This might be accomplished by "releasing" the power (giving it up), whether the power is an *inter vivos* power or a testamentary power. In the case of an *inter vivos* general power, exercising the power is a way of trying to give up the power. Thus, if the property is held in trust, the exercise of the power in a way that terminates the trust has the necessary effect of terminating the power. Similarly, the power might be exercised so as to create a wholly new trust in which the donee is lacking a general power. If an *inter vivos* general power is exercised so as to effect distributions or to merely alter the terms of the trust, a question may arise under state law as to whether the donee can exercise the power again or has exhausted the power. If the latter is the case, then the exercise would have the effect of releasing the power.

---

the regulation does not permit the beneficiary of multiple trusts to exclude all but the first from the estate by the expedient of arranging the trusts in a sequence. No matter how long the sequence, the beneficiary exercises economic dominion over all funds that can be withdrawn at any given moment." 68 F.3d at 1028, 1030).

17. E.g., *Estate of Alperstein v. Comm'r*, 613 F.2d 1213 (2d Cir.1979), *cert. denied*, 446 U.S. 918 (1980).

18. See *Estate of Margrave v. Comm'r*, 618 F.2d 34 (8th Cir.1980). However, *Margrave* misapplied the rule to the facts of that case, which involved an insurance policy on the decedent's life made payable to a revocable trust created by the decedent (which could have been amended by the decedent so as to make the proceeds payable to the decedent's estate). The basis for holding §2041 to be inapplicable was that life insurance was only an expectancy (presumably because the owner of the policy could have canceled it or named another beneficiary). But the owner did not do so, and once the decedent died the owner's power terminated. Being a beneficiary of life insurance is a property interest subject to disfeasance. See UTC §103(12) (defining "property" for trust law purposes to include a beneficiary designation).

19. *Connecticut Bank & Trust Co. v. U.S.*, 465 F.2d 760 (2d Cir.1972); *Rev. Rul. 75-127*, 1975-1 C.B. 297 (wrongful death recoveries payable to the decedent's estate).

20. See *Rev. Rul. 75-127*, supra; *Rev. Rul. 83-44*, 1983-1 C.B. 228.

Not surprisingly, §§2041(a)(2) and 2514(b) hold that release or exercise of a general power of appointment is a "transfer" for both estate and gift tax purposes. However, a qualified disclaimer of a general power under §2518 is not a release thereof.

Whether the "transfer" caused by the exercise or release of a general power is a (completed) gift for gift tax purposes, and (if so) to what extent, depends upon the nature of the powers and interests "retained" (held) in the property by the donee of the power immediately following such exercise. The same is true with regard to the estate tax significance of the exercise or release of a general power, since the resulting deemed "transfer" is "tested" with reference to the provisions of §§2036-2038 of the estate tax, dealing with transfers with retained interests and powers.

Example: Suppose Lance creates an irrevocable trust in 2001, income to Marjorie for life, giving Marjorie the unlimited power to withdraw corpus on demand at any time, remainder to Nolan on Marjorie's death. Marjorie has an *inter vivos* general power of appointment which she releases in 2006. The release is treated as a transfer by Marjorie into an irrevocable trust, income to Marjorie for life, remainder to Nolan. For gift tax purposes, Marjorie has made a gift of the property subject to a retained income interest in Marjorie, but under §2702 the retained income interest is deemed to be worth zero (if Nolan is a "family member" relative to Marjorie), resulting in a gift of the entire property by Marjorie in 2006. For estate tax purposes, Marjorie is deemed to have made an irrevocable transfer with retained income interest for life, which causes inclusion of the property in Marjorie's gross estate under §2036(a)(1) upon her death in 2009.

The *inter vivos* exercise of a general power of appointment may involve the transfer of an interest already held by the donee. Such transfer is treated under the general gift rules of §2511 rather than §2514. To illustrate, take the situation where Asim created an irrevocable trust, all the income to be paid to Becky for life, remainder to Corinna, giving Becky an *inter vivos* general power of appointment. Becky exercises the power, and causes all of the corpus to be paid outright to her friend Donna. According to Reg. §25.2514-1(b)(2), Becky has made a gift of her own income interest under §2511 and a deemed gift of the remainder interest under §2514.

3. *Lapse of General Power*

A "lapse" of a power occurs when it expires according to the terms of the governing instrument during the donee's lifetime by reason of the passage of time, the occurrence of some external event (such as the death of an income beneficiary), or the act of a third party (such as the exercise of a special power of appointment). A lapse of a general power is considered under §§2041(b)(2) and 2514(e) to be the same as a release, meaning that the donee of the power is deemed to have made a "transfer" of the property, to the extent of the lapse, for gift and estate tax purposes.

However, it is also provided in §§2041(b)(2) and 2514(e) that a "lapse" transfer is excluded from tax to the extent of the greater of $5K or 5 percent of the property subject to the power. This exemption can only apply once per calendar year, and it is separate from the gift tax annual exclusion. Thus, a person who has an annual power to withdraw trust corpus limited to the greater of $5K or 5 percent of the corpus per year is deemed not to have made any transfer upon the annual lapse of the power. A power of this type is commonly referred to as a "5-and-5 power." The 5-percent-of-corpus aspect of the rule refers to the value of corpus at the end of the year in which the lapse occurs.

Nevertheless, if the donee of a 5-and-5 power dies during a period when the power is exercisable, the donee will *possess* a general power over the amount subject to the power, and that amount will be includible under the general power "possession" rule.

Five-and-five powers are conferred upon favored beneficiaries to supplement their resources, without the beneficiaries' having to deal with the trustee and without subjecting the beneficiaries to significant gift and estate tax exposure simply by failing to exercise the power granted them. In order to take maximum advantage of the 5-and-5 rule, the power must be "noncumulative," i.e., must fully lapse every year.

Suppose instead of a 5-and-5 power the donor gives a person the annual power to withdraw $13K from the corpus. If the power goes unexercised, the donee is deemed to have made a "transfer" for gift tax purposes in each year of an amount equal to the excess of $13K over the greater of $5K or 5 percent of the then value of the corpus. For estate tax purposes (§§2036-2038), the deemed transfer by the donee is of a percentage of the trust (rather than a fixed dollar amount). Such percentage is figured by dividing the amount transferred for gift tax purposes by the value of the corpus at the end of the year in which the lapse occurred. The amount includible in the donee's gross estate, assuming of course that each "transfer" falls under one or more of §§2036-2038, would be (1) $13K (by reason of possessing the power in the year of death), plus (2) the result of multiplying the estate tax value of the corpus times a percentage which is the sum of the percentages for all prior lapse years and (3) the estate tax value of the corpus. See Reg. §20.2041-3(d)(4) & (5).

Example: Aretha creates a trust in 2006, income to Burke for life, with Burke having the noncumulative power to withdraw $20K of corpus annually. Burke dies in 2009. Assume the following values of the trust corpus:

	12/31/06	12/31/07	12/31/08	Estate Tax Valuation Date
Value of Corpus	$75,000	$120,000	$150,000	$160,000
5 Percent of Value	$ 3,750	$ 6,000	$ 7,500	(not relevant)

At the end of each of 2001, 2002, and 2003, Burke is deemed to have made the following gifts for gift tax purposes (assuming §2702 applies so as to treat Burke's retained interest in each transfer as being worth zero):

Year	Transfer	§2041(b)(2) Exclusion	Net Gift
2006	$20,000	$5,000	$15,000 ($5,000 exceeds 5% of corpus)
2007	$20,000	$6,000	$14,000
2008	$20,000	$7,500	$12,500

For estate tax purposes, Burke is deemed to have made a transfer of a fraction of the corpus at the end of each of 2006, 2007, and 2008:

Year	Net Transfer	Then corpus	Percent Transfer
2006	$15,000	$ 75,000	20.0
2007	$14,000	$120,000	11.7
2008	$12,500	$150,000	8.3

The deemed transfers by Burke in trust cause estate inclusion under §2036(a)(1), because the trust to which such transfers are deemed made provides that Burke is to receive all of the income for life. The aggregate amount includible in Burke's gross estate is $84K, which is $20K (possessed general power at death), plus 40 percent (20% + 11.7% + 8.3%) of $160K under §2036(a)(1).

The 5-and-5 exclusion is applicable to the aggregate withdrawal powers of a person during the year. The exclusion cannot be multiplied by the device of creating multiple trusts.

Recall the "Crummey power" described in §3.5.D, which is commonly used to qualify (all of) any transfer in trust for the gift tax annual exclusion. The typical Crummey power gives a beneficiary the right to withdraw the lesser of (a) an amount equal to what a given grantor gives to the trust during the year or (b) the maximum per-donee exclusion amount ($13K). It is generally understood that the beneficiary will not actually exercise the withdrawal power. The withdrawal power is typically confined to a short "window" during the year (say, the month of December). The withdrawal power is an *inter vivos* general power of appointment.

If the beneficiary dies during the "window" period, the maximum withdrawable amount is included under §2041. Otherwise, such amount is not includible, because the power was a contingent one, and the contingency did not in fact occur.

In each year the noncumulative power lapses, and the beneficiary is deemed to make a transfer for gift and estate tax purposes of an amount equal to the maximum withdrawable amount over the greater of $5K or 5 percent of the withdrawable amount. If the withdrawable amount is $13K, 5 percent thereof will be less than $650. Thus, annual transfers usually will be the maximum annual exclusion less $5K.

In creating a trust with Crummey powers, possible estate tax exposure is not a main concern, at least where the trust is expected to terminate during the beneficiary's lifetime. The main problem is perceived to be that of gift tax exposure. There are three possible ways of eliminating gift tax exposure. The first is to create a trust so that any deemed transfers by a beneficiary back into the trust will be incomplete. This result will occur if the beneficiary possesses the right to the trust income coupled with a power to alter or amend the beneficial enjoyment of the trust following such income interest.[21] This approach creates estate tax exposure for the beneficiary under §2036(a)(1) (transfers with retained income interest) and §2038 (transfer with retained power to alter, amend, or revoke). The second option is to reduce the maximum withdrawable amount to $5K, which will be fully absorbed by the 5-and-5 exclusion. This approach sacrifices full use of the annual exclusion by the grantor. The third approach uses the "hanging power" technique. The idea is that the Crummey power of the beneficiary will be "over" the maximum annual gift tax exclusion amount, but that the power will only lapse at the rate of $5K per year. Thus, the power "hangs over" to later years to the extent that it exceeds $5K in the current year.

Example: Assume the maximum annual exclusion amount is $13K. The trust does not give the beneficiary any special powers of appointment. The beneficiary has a Crummey power to withdraw the lesser of $13K per year or what the grantor contributes to the trust, but the power is to lapse at the rate of $5K per year, with the power over the excess being carried over. In 2001, the grantor transfers $13K in trust, which qualifies for the full annual exclusion of the grantor, and the beneficiary's power to withdraw $13K lapses only to the extent of $5K. The $8K (deemed) transfer by the beneficiary to the trust is an incomplete gift, because it can be revoked (withdrawn) by the beneficiary in later years. In 2002, the beneficiary can withdraw the $8K (zero grantor transfer plus $8K hanging power), and this power lapses to the tune of $5K in 2002. In 2003 the donor makes a transfer of $13K in trust, which is fully excluded, but the beneficiary has the right to withdraw $16K ($13K plus $3K hung over from the 2001 gift into trust). This power lapses to the extent of $5K, resulting in no gift by the beneficiary, and a carryover withdrawal right to 2004 of $11K.

The thought is that the contributions to the trust will stop at some time and the "hanging" amounts will be absorbed in those non-contribution years.

---

21. The income interest is a retained interest, and succeeding interests are subject to a "retained" power. Hence, there is no completed gift, and (therefore) §2702 is not a factor, due to §2702(a)(3)(A)(i).

QUICK QUESTIONS

1. In 2009, Agnes transferred property to a trust from which Barbara, her sister, received income for Barbara's life as well as an annual power to withdraw $20K. The corpus went to Carol, Barbara's daughter, at Barbara's death. Each year, Barbara allowed the power to lapse. The value of the corpus at the end of 2009 was $60K. Which one of the following statements is *TRUE*?
   A. In 2009, Barbara made a taxable gift to Carol of $7K.
   B. In 2009, Barbara made a taxable gift to Carol of $20K.
   C. In 2009, Barbara made a taxable gift to Carol of $15K.
   D. In 2009, Barbara made a taxable gift to Carol of $2K.

2. In 2009, David transferred property to a trust from which Edward, his brother, received income for Edward's life as well as an annual power to withdraw $20K. The corpus went to Frank, Edward's son, at Edward's death. Each year, Edward allowed the power to lapse. The value of the corpus at the end of 2009 was $150K. Which one of the following statements is *TRUE*?
   A. In 2009, Edward made a taxable gift to Frank of $7.5K.
   B. In 2009, Edward made a taxable gift to Frank of $20K.
   C. In 2009, Edward made a taxable gift to Frank of $15K.
   D. In 2009, Edward made a taxable gift to Frank of $12.5K.

PROBLEMS, QUESTIONS, AND NOTES

1. State the gift and estate tax consequences of the following to both the donee of the power and his or her estate:
   a. Arabella creates a trust with a corporate trustee, income to Boswell for life, remainder to Celia. Boswell also possesses the power to appoint, by written instrument delivered to the trustee, all or a portion of the trust property to any person (including Boswell or his creditors). Boswell validly exercises this power so as to change the remainder from Celia to Desmond. Assume Boswell can exercise the power again.
   b. Same as (a), but Boswell releases the power.
   c. Same as (a), except Boswell validly appoints the property in trust for his issue until his son Stefan dies, remainder to Boswell's surviving issue or if no such issue to the Community Charity.
2. What result in the problems in question 1, supra, except that Boswell possesses only a general power to appoint by will to any person or persons, including his estate or its creditors, and Boswell releases this power?
3. Ellsworth creates a trust, the income to be paid to Ellsworth's issue living from time to time, in the trustee's discretion, for 21 years, with Fritz having the

power to withdraw 50 percent of the income annually, remainder to Germaine. In fact, none of the income is paid to, or withdrawn by, Fritz. Fritz dies before the 21 years are up. Is anything includible in Fritz's gross estate? See *Fish v. U.S.*, 432 F.2d 1278 (9th Cir.1970); Reg. §20.2041-3(f), Ex. 2.

4. Petra creates a trust giving Ross a general *inter vivos* power of appointment. Ross makes an effective disclaimer under state law of the power insofar as it allows him to appoint to himself, his estate, or the creditors of either. Does Ross now hold a special power of appointment for transfer tax purposes?

5. A complete release of a pre-1942 power is not deemed to be an exercise. Neither is a partial release (conversion into a special power) if such release occurred prior to November 1, 1951. (Recall that the mere possession of a pre-1942 general power does not cause estate inclusion, see §2041(a)(1).)

6. Where the decedent/beneficiary of an IRA has the right to accelerate distributions from an IRA faster than the minimum distribution schedule selected by the creator of the IRA, the §2041 power to consume the property is a general power of appointment that will cause inclusion of the entire IRA in decedent's gross estate. *P.L.R. 199936052.*

7. To determine the value of decedent's stock, stock includible under §2033 should be combined with stock includible under §2041 because the decedent held a testamentary general power of appointment. This position is consistent with the opposite conclusion taken by the courts (e.g., *Estate of Mellinger v. Comm'r*, 112 T.C. 26 (1999)) regarding property included in the surviving spouse's estate under §2044, with respect to QTIP includible property that is not so aggregated. Section 2041 inclusion is based on ownership parallel to §2033; that is not the case with QTIP property. *Estate of Fontana v. Comm'r*, 118 T.C. 16 (2002); FSA 200119013.

§7.2. Income Tax Effects of Possessing an *Inter Vivos* General Power

In the income tax, income from property is taxed to the owner of property. Under §678, a person (other than the grantor) can be treated as the "owner" of the trust property to the extent that such person can withdraw or appropriate the trust corpus or income. Essentially, §678 applies where a person has an *inter vivos* general power of appointment over the corpus or income. (If the beneficiary can withdraw the income only, the income is attributed to the beneficiary. If the beneficiary can withdraw the corpus, all of the income, gains, and losses produced by the corpus are attributed to the beneficiary.) A trust the income from which is taxed to the beneficiary under §678 is called a "beneficiary-owned trust."

Section 678 supersedes the normal rules pertaining to the taxation of trusts and beneficiaries. However, §678 is itself superseded in cases where the *inter vivos* grantor is treated as the owner of the trust under §§671-677. §678(b). Income that is taxed to a beneficiary under §678 (or the grantor under §§671-677) is not taxed again to the actual recipient (who is deemed to be in receipt of an excludible gift).[22]

The language of §678 does not parallel that of §§2041 and 2514. There are no statutory exceptions relating to "standards" or co-holders with "adverse interests." Nevertheless, the text of §678 is explicit on the point that a person is treated as the owner of property for income tax purposes only if the power is held by such person alone. On the "standards" issue, authority is virtually nonexistent. But note that §678 applies only where a person has the power to "vest" the corpus or income in himself. Accordingly, it has been held that §678 does not apply even where a life tenant has the power to "consume" the property.[23] A *fortiori*, if the person is sole trustee having the power to pay income or corpus to himself as beneficiary, the application of §678 should be barred if the power is subject to any reasonably ascertainable standard.[24] Finally, a right of a beneficiary to enforce a standard pertaining to income or corpus should be removed even further from §678.[25]

A person is not treated as the owner of a trust simply by being able to distribute income to a beneficiary to whom the person owes a support obligation. However, any income actually distributed to such a beneficiary is taxed to the person holding the power, and any corpus so distributed is treated as a "distribution" under the "normal" income tax rules pertaining to trusts and beneficiaries. See §678(c).

Except as noted in the preceding paragraph, the exercise of a §678 power has no significance, and the release or lapse of the power would be effective to remove the holder of the power from income tax ownership of the income. However, a partial release of a §678 power will be ineffective in this regard if, after such release, the person would be treated as the owner of the trust under §§671-677 if the person were the grantor. §678(a)(2).

A §678 power can be disclaimed within a reasonable time after becoming aware of the power. §678(d). Since §678 has its own disclaimer rule, the federal transfer tax qualified disclaimer rules of §2518 do not apply in this context.

Given the highly compressed rate structure applicable under §1(e) to taxable income attributed to a trust (which usually occurs by reason of accumulating income), a grantor may draft a trust instrument so as to deliberately cause the trust to come under §678 in order to cause trust-level (i.e., undistributed) income to be taxed at the beneficiary's lower marginal rates.

§7.3. Tax Consequences of Exercising a Special Power of Appointment

A "special" power is any power of appointment that is not a general power. The *possession* of a special power has no transfer tax consequences. The exercise,

---

22. This is a gift only under the income tax. The mere *possession* of an *inter vivos* general power of appointment does not cause a gift to be made for gift tax purposes. The gift (and estate) tax consequences of such a power are governed by §§2041 and 2514.

23. See *U.S. v. DeBonchamps*, 278 F.2d 127 (9th Cir.1960).

24. See *Townsend v. Comm'r*, 5 T.C. 1380 (1945) (law prior to enactment of §678).

25. Cf. *Rev. Rul.* 76-368, p. 321.

release, or lapse of a special power lies outside of §§2041(a)(2) and 2514(b). However, the exercise of a special power can give rise to estate and gift tax consequences in the two situations laid out below.

A. Exercise of Special Power as Gift

While the exercise of a special power of appointment does not constitute a gift under §2514, there may be an issue of whether the exercise results in a gift under general gift tax principles.

Estate of Regester v. Commissioner

83 T.C. 1 (1984)

COHEN, Judge: Charles Regester (petitioner) is the personal representative of the estate of Ruth B. Regester (decedent). The issue is whether decedent made a taxable gift of her life interest in the income of a trust when she transferred the corpus of the trust through the exercise of a special power of appointment.

George L. Bignell, a resident of Michigan, died on September 29, 1973. The provisions of his will with which we are concerned created a trust as follows:

I give, devise and bequeath to my Trustee hereinafter named, IN TRUST, to dispose of the income and principal as follows:

A. He shall pay the net income thereof, at least as often as quarter-annually, to my daughter Ruth B. Regester, as long as she lives.
B. During the lifetime of my said daughter, my Trustee shall distribute the principal thereof, in whole or in part and from time to time, to or for her son Charles Regester and/or his issue, and in such proportions to or for each, as my said daughter shall appoint by instruments signed, sealed and acknowledged by her and delivered to my Trustee.
C. Upon the death of my said daughter, the remaining principal thereof and all increase and income then on hand, if any, shall be distributed as my said daughter shall by her last will and testament appoint among any one or more of the following: her son, and the issue of her son; but not the estate of my said daughter, her creditors, or the creditors of her estate.

By a trust agreement dated May 24, 1974, [Ruth's son] Charles created a trust for the benefit of his three children. By an instrument dated June 6, 1974, decedent exercised her special power of appointment over the corpus of the Bignell trust and transferred the entire amount to the trustee of the Charles Regester trust.

Powers of appointment were not taxable until 1942 when the predecessor to §2514 was enacted. Section 2514 applies only to general powers of appointment. Reg. §25.2514-1(b)(2) provides as follows:

Relation to other sections. No provision of §2514 or of [the regulations] is to be construed as in any way limiting the application of any other section of the Internal Revenue Code or of these regulations. The power of the owner of a property interest already possessed by him to dispose of his interest, and nothing more, is not a power of appointment, and the interest is includible in the amount of his gifts to the extent it would be includible under §2511 or other provisions of the Code. For example, if a trust created by S provides for payment of the income to A for life with power in A to appoint the entire trust property by deed during her lifetime to a class consisting of her children, and a further power to dispose of the entire corpus by will to anyone, including her estate, and A exercises the *inter vivos* power in favor of her children, she has necessarily made a transfer of her income interest which constitutes a taxable gift under §2511(a), without regard to §2514. This transfer also results in a relinquishment of her general power to appoint by will, which constitutes a transfer under §2514 if the power was created after October 21, 1942.

Petitioner concedes that a donee of a life estate may make a gift of an income interest in trust property. Petitioner argues, however, that the interest of decedent in the income of the Bignell trust should be treated as extinguished, and not as transferred, upon exercise of the special power of appointment. Petitioner cites *Self v. U.S.*, 142 F. Supp. 939 (1956). In *Self*, the Court of Claims [stated]:

> The [government's] argument is based on the theory that [the] donee is giving up an economic interest when he exercises the power. . . . [W]here the income beneficiary's estate is terminated by reason of the [exercise of the] power, the donor of the power is considered the transferor and the donee merely acts as his agent and gives direction to the gift pursuant to the donor's wishes.

When a person has the right to income for life and the ability to transfer that right to anyone or to retain it as long as she lives, transfer of that property without consideration gives rise to a taxable gift. Had decedent chosen to transfer her life interest to a third party prior to her exercise of the special power of appointment, she would have made a taxable gift of her life interest. The fact that she chose to convey that interest to the ultimate owner of the corpus does not disguise the fact that she chose to give her income from the trust property to another without compensation. Such a transfer is taxable irrespective of §2514.

The conceptual response to petitioner's argument that decedent's interest was terminated and not transferred is that, when the trust corpus was transferred, the income generated by the corpus was also transferred. Under the doctrine of merger, the trust would be terminated; but the enjoyment of the income continued in the hands of the transferee of the corpus.

Petitioner contends that Reg. §25.2514-1(b)(2) is invalid because it is "directly contrary to well-established case law which pre-dates the regulation." It is apparent from the discussion above that the regulation is only contrary to the *Self* case, with which we disagree, and that the substantially identical predecessor regulation pre-dated the opinion in the *Self* case. There is no basis here for holding the regulation invalid.

The Treasury, in 1981, subsequent to the taxable year involved in *Self* (and, for that matter, *Regester*) issued an amendment to Reg. §25.2514-3(e), Ex. 3; namely, the addition of the following new sentence: "Although the exercise or release of the nongeneral power is not taxable under this section, see §25.2514-1(b)(2) for the gift tax consequences of the transfer of the life income interest." See *T.D. 7776* (May 20, 1981), which stated:

> The amendment was proposed to emphasize that the *inter vivos* exercise of a nongeneral power of appointment by a life income beneficiary is not taxable under §2514, but where a consequence of the exercise is a transfer of the power-holder's life income interest, a taxable transfer occurs under §2511.

B. The "Delaware Tax Trap"

Section §2041(a)(3) of the Internal Revenue Code is unique in that the *inter vivos* or testamentary exercise of a *special* power of appointment created after October 21, 1942, can cause inclusion of the property in a donee's gross estate. The corresponding gift tax provision is §2514(d).

For one of these sections to apply, the donee must first exercise the special power. Second, such exercise must create another power of appointment "which can be validly exercised so as to postpone the vesting of any estate or interest in such property, or suspend the absolute ownership or power of alienation of such property, for a period ascertainable without regard to the date of the creation of the [exercised] power." This language obviously ties into the Rule Against Perpetuities. The Rule, and its modern statutory variants, requires vesting of all interest within a specified period of time states from the date of its creation.

Often a power of appointment can be exercised in such a way as to create future interests and powers. Notably, a special power can be exercised so as to create an *inter vivos* general power in a person who is an object of the special power. In case of such exercise, it then becomes necessary to test the validity of the interests and powers created by any appointment made pursuant to the exercise of the general power. It happens that any interest created by the exercise of an *inter vivos* general power of appointment is tested under the Rule with reference to when such power is exercised (not when the power was created or when the trust was created), because a general power by deed is treated as the equivalent of ownership. It follows that §2041(a)(3) or §2514(d) is triggered any time a special power is (validly) exercised so as to create an *inter vivos* general power in another person, because any interest created through the exercise of such general power will be tested for its validity under the Rule by reference to the date the general power is exercised (rather than the date the special power was created).

In contrast, the validity of interest created pursuant to the exercise of a testamentary general power or any special power is conventionally measured by reference to the effective date of the instrument creating the power (this rule is referred to as the "relation-back" doctrine). Here, sections 2041(a)(3) and 2514(d) are "blocked," because the validity of any interests created by exercising these will be tested under the Rule with reference to the date of the creation of the power. However, the Rule in some states (notably Delaware) is that interests created by special powers (or general testamentary powers) were to be tested with reference to the date of the exercise of such power. If this is the case, the exercise by a donee of a special power that in turn creates another special power (or a testamentary general power) would trigger §2041(a)(2) or §2514(d).

These sections would also appear to be a factor in states that have abolished the Rule entirely. Their purpose was originally to tax exercises of powers of appointment in situations where state law allowed this as a means of avoiding the Rule, which was then universal (but in different versions).[26] In such states, the exercise of any power of appointment to create another power would seem to satisfy the statutory language. (The argument against this interpretation would be that the time of the creation of the power is irrelevant in a state that has abolished the Rule. However, this argument should not prevail, given both the literal language of these provisions and their purpose to foreclose the use of perpetual trusts that avoid estate tax.) It would appear that the only way to insure against the Delaware Tax Trap in such states is for the governing instrument to prohibit the exercise of a special power to create another power. However, the creation of successive special powers of appointment would be allowed.

Choice of law issues are posed by these rules. Generally, testamentary trusts are subject to the law of the decedent's domicile. In contrast, *inter vivos* trusts can be governed by whatever law the settlor designates in the trust instrument, provided that the trust has sufficient contacts with the state whose law is to control. The usual "contact" is to name a local person or financial institution as trustee or co-trustee.

PROBLEMS, QUESTIONS, AND NOTES

1. a. Annette creates an irrevocable trust, naming a bank as trustee, income to son Bernie for life, remainder to Annette's daughter Cara, giving Cara an *inter vivos* special power to appoint (at any time) to her issue, outright or in trust. Cara exercises this power, and appoints all of the trust corpus (say, $1M) outright to her son Duncan. What gift and GST results flow from this exercise? Assume that the then (present) value of Cara's remainder interest in the trust is $375K.

    b. What transfer tax results where the donee of an *inter vivos* special power of appointment does not possess an interest but does possess a testamentary general power of appointment, and the donee exercises the special power by appointing the property outright to an object of the power?

    c. Luis creates a testamentary trust, naming daughter Martina trustee, income to Martina for life, with the corpus being payable to Martina's son Noah for his health and support needs as determined by the trustee, remainder on the death of the survivor of Martina and Noah to Luis' then surviving issue *per stirpes*. Noah suffers a severe injury and Martina distributes all of the corpus to Noah to pay medical bills. What effect does this distribution have for gift tax purposes? See Reg. §25.2511-1(g)(2).

---

26. The purpose is discussed in *Murphy v. Comm'r*, 71 T.C. 671 (1979).

2. For what it is worth, the Restatement (Second) of Property (Donative Transfers), §12.3 (illustration 6), states that a special power is "invalid" insofar as it purports to permit the donee to "extinguish" his interest through exercising the power, and that an exercise of the power entails a gift by the donee of the interest. The aim of the Restatement rule is to overturn the English common-law rule (based on the agency theory), which permitted the donee to divest himself of an interest free of the claims of his spouse and creditors.

§7.4. Giving Content to the Generation-Skipping Transfer Tax

It would be worthwhile to review §2.8, which gives an overview of the purpose and essential features of the GST tax. This section gives a more complete picture of the GST tax than was presented in §2.8.

A. *Review of Major GST Tax Features*

This review will operate by setting forth key definitions. Some details not mentioned in §2.8 are thrown in to sweeten the pot.

Generation-skipping transfer: Basically, a generation-skipping transfer is a transfer from the "transferor" to a "skip person." There are three kinds of generation-skipping transfers (defined below): (1) direct-skip transfer, (2) taxable termination, and (3) taxable distribution. See §§2611(a) and 2613.

Transferor: The person who effects the transfer by gift, bequest, or other gratuitous transfer, *provided that the transfer is subject to the gift or estate tax*. See §2652(a). A transfer is "subject to" the gift or estate tax if it is a completed gift or included in the gross estate. The fact that it does not produce any tax by reason of exclusions, exemptions, deductions, or credits is irrelevant. See Reg. §26.2652-1(a)(2). A gift-splitting election under §2513 is effective for GST tax purposes. §2652(a)(2).

Skip person: (1) an individual located in a generation that is two or more generations "below" (younger) than that of the transferor (such as a grandchild of the transferor); (2) a trust all of the "interests" of which are held by skip persons; (3) a trust in which no person presently holds an interest and which is highly unlikely ever to make a distribution to a non-skip person.[27] An individual can be a skip person without having an "interest" in the trust. A *non-skip person* is (obviously) a person that is not a skip person. A charity (which has no generation assignment) is a non-skip person.

___

27. There must be a less than 5% chance, under actuarial tables, of a distribution to a non-skip person. See Reg. §26.2612-1(d)(2)(ii). Presumably, the scenario envisioned here is one where a non-skip person (such as a charity, the grantor, the grantor's spouse, or child of the grantor) possesses a remote contingent remainder or reversion.

Interest (in trust): A person has an interest in trust if the person: (1) has a *current* right to receive distributions; (2) is not a charity and can *currently* receive (is a current permissible recipient of) distributions; or (3) is a charity and the trust is a charitable remainder annuity trust, a charitable remainder unitrust, or a pooled income fund (all as defined elsewhere). See §2652(c)(1). Thus, the holder of a noncharitable remainder interest does not possess an "interest,"[28] but a person possessing a withdrawal right does have an interest.[29] A person does *not* have an interest in trust because income or corpus *may* be used to satisfy the person's support obligations, so long as such use is discretionary (such as would be the case under a custodial arrangement).[30] See §2652(c)(3). But if the trust must currently distribute amounts for a person's support, the support obligor would have an interest.[31]

Trust: The term "trust" includes non-trust "trust equivalents" that provide for successive interests, such as legal life estates and remainders, annuity/insurance combinations, custodial accounts, joint tenancies and other arrangements with rights of survivorship, and bequests subject to any contingency that might occur more than six months after the transferor's death. See §2652(b) and Reg. §26.2652-1(b). A single trust may be treated as two or more separate trusts on account of (a) having received transfers from different transferors, or (b) providing for separate shares for different beneficiaries. See §2654(b).

Direct-skip transfer: A transfer from the "transferor" (directly) to a "skip person" (such as an outright gift or bequest to a grandchild). §2612(c).

Taxable termination: The termination (however caused) of an interest held in trust, *unless* (a) a non-skip person has an interest in the trust immediately after the transfer or (b) it is highly unlikely that a distribution can be made to a skip person in the future.[32] §2612(a)(1).

Taxable distribution: A distribution (not resulting from a taxable termination or direct skip) from a trust to a skip person. §2612(b). Section 2612(a)(2) treats certain partial termination distributions (that would not otherwise be taxable terminations due to the existence of a non-skip person as beneficiary) as partial taxable terminations.[33]

The two exceptions to the definition of "taxable termination" (combined with the fact that the definition of "taxable distribution" yields to that of "taxable termination") operate so as to limit to one the number of taxable terminations that can

---

28. See Reg. §26.2612-1(f), Ex. 12.

29. See Reg. §26.2612-1(f), Ex. 3. It is not clear whether an object of an *inter vivos* power of appointment (as opposed to a person eligible for trust distributions) has an interest.

30. Custodial arrangements for minors are described in §3.5.C. Custodial arrangements can result from bequests and life insurance as well as gifts.

31. See Reg. §26.2612-1(f), Ex. 13.

32. "Highly unlikely" means a less than 5% actuarial possibility. See Reg. §26.2612(b)(1)(iii).

33. To come under this rule, an interest must terminate by reason of the death of a descendant of the transferor, and a specified portion of the trust assets must be distributed to skip persons (or a trust exclusively for skip persons). An example would be a trust for the children of the transferor in the trustee's discretion, but if any such child dies, an aliquot share of the trust would be paid to that child's descendants. See also Reg. §26.2612-1(f), Ex. 9. In the absence of this rule, this would entail a taxable distribution, because other children of the transferor continue as beneficiaries.

occur with respect to each generation below that of the transferor. In other words, the rules are designed to produce one tax per generation. To illustrate, assume that a trust provides that the income is payable to or among all of the transferor's children or accumulated in the trustee's discretion until the death of the survivor of them, remainder to grandchildren. The children (but not the grandchildren) all possess "interests" for GST tax purposes. The death of any child is a "termination," because it is a cessation of an "interest." However, if other children (who are non-skip persons holding an "interest") are still living, the first exception comes into play. No taxable termination occurs until the death of the last survivor of the children, at which time there are no remaining non-skip beneficiaries.

The definition of "taxable termination" does not directly require that beneficial enjoyment of the property (as a result of a termination) pass to skip persons. However, the second exception requires this in a backhanded sort of way, by providing that there is no taxable termination unless there is a more than *de minimis* chance that distributions will be made to skip persons in the future. Take a trust paying income to child for life, then income to be accumulated for five years, at which time the income and corpus are to be distributed to the transferor's favorite nephew (who occupies the same generation as the child). The death of the child is a termination, but the first exception does not come into play because the nephew, although he is a non-skip person, does not possess an "interest" immediately after the child's death. However, the second exception applies because the property can never be distributed to a skip person.[34] Hence, the termination does not entail a generation-skipping transfer.

B. *Additional Rules for Identifying Generation-Skipping Transfers*

Various GST tax rules that come into play to identify the occurrence of a generation-skipping transfer, but were not mentioned earlier, are described below.

1. *Effective Date of the Tax*
The GST tax applies to transfers of a transferor made after the relevant effective date of the tax:

(1) in the case of an *inter vivos* transfer, if the transfer is complete after September 25, 1985, and

(2) in the case transfer by will or revocable trust, where the decedent or grantor dies after December 31, 1986 (unless the will or trust was executed after October 22, 1986, in which case the transfer is subject to the tax even if the transferor died before December 31, 1986).

---

34. True, if the nephew predeceases the distribution date, the nephew's children (skip persons) would end up with the property, but this fact does not negate the second exception because the nephew's remainder is vested, and therefore is included in the nephew's gross estate, and the nephew would be a superseding transferor. If the remainder were to "nephew if then living, if not to nephew's surviving descendants," then the result would hinge on whether the chance that such descendants would take is less than 5%.

Also, there is an exclusion for testamentary transfers where the governing instrument was executed before October 22, 1986, and the transferor was legally incompetent at all times thereafter. See Reg. §26.2601-1(b)(3).

Transfers before these dates never give rise to generation-skipping tax even though generation-skipping transfers with respect to them occur after these dates. However, amendments or additions to trusts after the effective date can cause all or a portion of the trust to be subject to tax. See generally Reg. §26.2601-1.

The exercise of a general power of appointment in a grandfathered GST trust may trigger GST tax. In *Estate of Gerson v. Comm'r*, 507 F.3d 435 (6th Cir.2007), a surviving spouse exercised her power of appointment in favor of her grandchildren in 2000, using a power originating from a §2056(b)(5) trust created by her deceased husband in 1975. Construing Reg. §26.2601-1(b)(1)(i) as a reasonable interpretation of the grandfather provision, the court held that the imposition of the GST tax was proper because the grandfather provision did not shield from the application of GST tax transfers of corpus pursuant to the exercise of a general power of appointment subsequent to September 25, 1985. Accord *Peterson Marital Trust v. Comm'r*, 78 F.3d 795 (2d Cir.1996). Note, however, that these two circuit court opinions conflict with the Eighth and Ninth Circuit holdings in *Simpson v. U.S.*, 183 F.3d 812 (8th Cir.1999) and *Bachler v. U.S.*, 281 F.3d 1078 (9th Cir.2002).

2. Effect of Reverse QTIP Election on the Identity of the Transferor

In the case of a QTIP trust, since the transferor and transferee spouses are by definition in the same generation (see §2651(c)(1)), a QTIP election has the effect of constituting the transferee spouse as the "transferor" for GST tax purposes after the transferee spouse is subject to tax under §2044 or the gift tax (§§2511 and 2519). However, the transferor spouse (or his estate) can elect to avoid this result, in which case the transferor of the QTIP trust will be the "transferor" for GST tax purposes. This "reverse" QTIP election does not negate the estate or gift tax QTIP election.

The reverse QTIP election was useful at a time when the GST tax exemption amount was greater than the estate and gift tax exemption amount: The reverse QTIP election allowed the transferor to fully use his GST tax exemption amount while removing the same amount from his taxable estate through a QTIP trust. After 2003, the reverse QTIP election would seem pointless in most cases, because the estate tax and GST tax exemptions are in synch. Both would normally be allocated to the by-pass trust. However, to the extent that the transferor made taxable lifetime gifts to non-skip persons, the transferor may still have a situation where her GST tax exemption exceeds her estate tax exemption.

3. Marital and Charitable Transfers

As noted already, skip and non-skip persons are defined in terms of their generational status relative to that of the transferor. The rules pertaining to generational status are found in §2651, which is sufficiently straightforward as to not warrant extended paraphrase here, except to note that any spouse of the transferor (current or former), regardless of age, is deemed to belong to the transferor's generation and, therefore, is a non-skip person.[35] It follows that a transfer to one's spouse cannot be a generation-skipping tax. Therefore, there is no need to have a "marital deduction" within the GST.

Similarly, a charity (which is neither an individual nor a trust with individual beneficiaries) cannot be a skip person. Hence, there is no need for a charitable deduction.

4. Special Rules Concerning Beneficiary Status
(a) Illusory Beneficiary Rule

The creation of a trust exclusively for one's grandchildren would normally be a direct-skip transfer. With that in mind, a transferor might seek to avoid this result by naming one of her children as a discretionary beneficiary of the trust. However, §2652(c)(2) states that an interest which is used primarily to avoid or postpone the tax is to be disregarded. Thus, if the transferor's child is an adult with substantial resources, the child may (depending on the circumstances) be disregarded, with the result that the insertion of the child will not have been effective to defeat the direct-skip rule. Under a provision of the Technical Corrections Act of 1987, the interest would not need to be "nominal" in order to be disregarded; the test would be whether the interest was inserted with the primary purpose to avoid or postpone the tax.

(b) Predeceased Ancestor Rule

This rule moves persons up a generation if their parent was dead at the time of the transfer by the transferor. For example, if the child of the transferor who is the parent of the grandchild of the transferor is dead when the transferor makes an outright bequest to the grandchild, then the grandchild is treated as a "child" of the transferor (i.e., a non-skip person), and (therefore) the bequest would not be a direct skip transfer. Similarly, an outright gift to a great-grandchild would not be a direct-skip transfer if both the intervening child and grandchild were dead when the transfer occurred. This rule, found in §2651(e), is generally available only for lineal descendants of the transferor, and is sometimes referred to as the "move-up-a-generation" rule. However, if the transferor has no lineal descendants, the predeceased parent rule applies to transfers to collateral heirs. §2651(e)(2). For example, T transfers property to T's grandniece GN. S is T's sister and the parent of N. N, deceased at the time of T's transfer, is the parent of GN. If T does not have any living lineal descendants at the time of the transfer, GN moves up a generation to one generation below T's generation, which makes GN a non-skip person. T's transfer to GN is not a GST. See Reg. §26.2651-1(c), Ex. 5.

---

35. But as explained in *T.A.M. 200150003*, T's transfers to daughters of his stepbrother were generation-skipping transfers because they were more than 37½ years younger than T. Although they were more like uncle and nieces, because the nieces were not T's lineal descendants through blood or adoption, nor related through marriage, their generation assignment was determined under §2651(d).

(c) Skips of More than One Generation

If a transfer leaps over two or more generations in one bound, there is only one generation-skipping transfer. Thus, if A makes an outright gift to a great-grandchild (and if the two intervening links in the chain are then alive), there is only one generation-skipping transfer, even though there is a double skip.[36]

It follows that simultaneous terminations of successive interests result in only a single generation-skipping transfer. Thus, if A creates a spray trust for her children and grandchildren, remainder to living great-grandchildren upon the death of the last surviving child, such death results in simultaneous terminations of the interests of both the children and the grandchildren, but there is only a single generation-skipping transfer.[37]

(d) "Transferor Moves Down" Rule for Successive Skips

A trust can be involved in successive generation-skipping transfers over time. For example, a trust might continue for several generations, if the Rule Against Perpetuities (if any) allows. In such a scenario, there would be a series of taxable terminations. As previously stated, the "inclusion ratio" stays the same throughout the trust's existence. See §2653(b)(1). For purposes of determining who is a skip person, the transferor will be deemed to move down (after a generation-skipping transfer) to the generation above the highest-generation person having an interest in the trust immediately following any such transfer. §2653(a). For example, assume that A creates a discretionary trust for children, grandchildren, and great-grandchildren to last for 90 years. While A's children are alive, distributions to the grandchildren are taxable distributions. After the last surviving child dies, the transferor is deemed to move down a generation. Thereafter, distributions to the grandchildren are no longer taxable distributions, because the grandchildren are no longer skip persons.[38]

PROBLEMS, QUESTIONS, AND NOTES

1. Identify the generation-skipping transfers (if any) in the following:
   a. An outright gift to a great-grandchild.
   b. A trust, all the income to the transferor's spouse for life payable at least annually, then all the income to or among the transferor's children and grandchildren for 21 years, remainder to the grantor's grandchildren.
   c. A trust, income to child for ten years, then income to be accumulated for a certain grandchild; when that grandchild reaches 30, the accumulated income and corpus is to be distributed to him, but if the grandchild dies

---

36. See Reg. §26.2612-1(f), Ex. 2.
37. See Reg. §26.2612-1(b)(3) & (f), Ex. 8.
38. See Reg. §26.2653-1(b), Ex. 1.

before reaching 30 the accumulated income and corpus are to be held in further trust, income to nephew for life, remainder to the transferor's then living issue *per stirpes*.

d. X in testamentary trust, unitrust interest to grandchild for life, remainder to the Z charity (assume that the charitable remainder interest qualifies for the estate tax charitable deduction in X's estate).

2. The design of the GST tax is perhaps not flawless. Consider the following.

a. Suppose A creates a trust, income to a physically disabled grandchild for 15 years, remainder to A's child C. One approach is to say that there is a direct-skip transfer to the extent of the actuarial value of the grandchild's income interest, noting that §2612(c)(1) defines a direct-skip transfer as "a transfer . . . of any interest in property to a skip person." A contrary view would be as follows: The transfer is to a trust, and a "trust" is either a skip person or not a skip person; here it *should* not be so classified because the remainder is in a non-skip person. (It would follow that payments of income to the grandchild would involve a series of taxable distributions.) In fact the trust as a whole does fall within the skip-person definition, because the child's remainder is not an "interest" for generation-skipping-tax purposes. (Why not?) So, is the amount of the direct-skip transfer the entire amount transferred to the trust (the amount received by the "transferee"; namely, the trust)? Or, is it (instead) only the actuarial value of the grandchild's interest subject to tax? The former possibility seems unfair (although it is the one taken in the instructions to the tax return), but the latter approach would create an opportunity for tax avoidance where the grandchild's actual life span is expected to be greater than his actuarial life expectancy. Treating this scenario as involving a series of taxable distributions would produce the right result.

b. Suppose that A creates a trust, income to physically disabled child C for life (expected to be short), then to grandchild G (if then living) for life, then to favorite nephew N (if living) for life, remainder to grandchildren. It turns out that C's life is short, G survives C (but not for long), and N survives both of them for many years, during which time the trust greatly appreciates. There is a taxable termination on C's death, because N (a non-skip person) has no "interest" and because G is a skip person. At that point, does A moves down a generation under §2653? If so, then the death of N would not result in a second taxable termination, despite the substantial appreciation in the trust. If not, there would be a second taxable termination, and the previously-taxed-generation rule of §2611(b)(2) would prevent double taxation of the same amount, would it not?

C. Rules Relating to the Amount of a Generation-Skipping Transfer

After a generation-skipping transfer occurs, it is next necessary to ascertain the taxable amount (the tax base).

1. Exclusions

Certain transfers are excluded in whole or in part. (The "exemption amount" is factored into the tax rate, rather than the tax base.)

(a) Transfers for Medical and Educational Purposes

Section 2611(b)(1) exempts any generation-skipping transfers that would, if made *inter vivos* by an individual, be excluded under §2503(e) of the gift tax, relating to direct payment of tuition and medical expenses. This provision is most likely to come into play in the context of a transfer that would otherwise be a direct-skip transfer or a taxable distribution.

(b) Certain Excluded Gifts

Section 2642(e) states that a direct-skip transfer which is a nontaxable gift (because excluded under §2503(b) or (e)) shall have an "inclusion ratio" of zero. To qualify for this rule, the trust must be includible in the beneficiary's gross estate (if the trust does not terminate earlier), and distributions to other persons must be prohibited.

This rule can apply to a fraction of a trust.[39]

(c) Previously-Taxed-Generation Exception

Section 2611(b)(3) states that any generation-skipping transfer shall be excluded to the extent that the property was already subject to a prior generation-skipping transfer in which the transferee was in the same or lower generation as the transferee of the current transfer (but only if the effect of this exclusion is not to avoid tax across the two transfers).

This rule would rarely come into play, due to the operation of the definitions of "generation-skipping transfer" and, especially, the "transferee-move-down" rule for multiple skips. There is no mention of this rule in the committee reports or the regulations, and it seems to have been carried over reflexively from a similar provision in the 1976 GST tax, where it served a useful purpose.[40] Assume a testamentary trust for the transferor's invalid grandchild (with a short life expectancy) for life, then for the transferor's children until the death of the survivor, remainder to the transferor's then living issue *per stirpes*. The creation of the trust is a direct-skip transfer, because the only person having an "interest" in the trust (eligibility for receiving distributions) is the grandchild. Although subsequent beneficial enjoyment is re-cycled through the children and back to other grandchildren, there is no second taxable termination, because the transferor (immediately after the direct-skip transfer) was moved down to the children's generation.[41] It is conceivable that this provision could apply to back-and-forth

---

39. See Reg. §26.2642-1(c), Ex. 2-4.
40. The 1976 GST tax (since repealed) had no move-down-a-generation rule.
41. The definitions of "taxable terminations" and "direct-skip" (by ignoring future interests) tend to trigger an "early" generation-skipping transfer, in turn causing the transferor to "move down," even though beneficial enjoyment may "move back up" in the future.

outright (non-trust) transfers of the same property,[42] but that seems unlikely, as this application would require tracing, and the federal transfer taxes generally avoid the tracing of property.[43]

If there should be any occasion where this provision is to apply, an issue would arise as whether the "to the extent that" language refers to a fractional share of the current transfer or a dollar amount. Proposed regulations under the prior generation-skipping tax took the dollar-amount approach under similar statutory language.

(d) Transfer Subject to Estate or Gift Tax

Suppose a trust is created for a child for life, with the child being given a general testamentary power of appointment, remainder to grandchild. The death of the child ordinarily would give rise to a taxable termination. But here the death of the child causes the trust to be included in the child's gross estate under §2041 due to the general power. Therefore, the generation-skipping tax becomes superfluous, at least in this case. The exclusion comes by way of §2652(a), which defines a "transferor" as the person most recently subject to estate or gift tax. Since the child is now the transferor, the grandchild is now a non-skip person.[44]

The result would be different if D created a QTIP trust for surviving spouse S for life, remainder to grandchildren, and it is assumed that a QTIP election is made but not a reverse QTIP election. Here the trust is included in S's gross estate under §2044, and S becomes the superseding transferor, but now there is a direct-skip generation-skipping transfer from S to the grandchild (instead of a taxable termination in relation to D as the transferor).[45]

The §2611(b)(1) exemption is potentially important for planning purposes. In certain cases it might be preferable to subject the property to estate or gift tax in the hands of a beneficiary who is in lower estate and gift tax rate brackets (or who has not used up all of his or her unified transfer tax credit) rather than have the property be subject to GST tax. Accordingly, it might be desirable to create testamentary general powers of appointment — perhaps contingent on objective facts pertaining to the donee's transfer tax situation at death.

---

42. Donor makes gift of artworks to grandchild, grandchild dies and grandchild's estate passes back to donor-grandparent by will or inheritance, and donor-grandparent bequeaths her estate to other grandchildren, resulting in two direct-skip transfers of the same property.

43. The most closely-analogous provision (the §2013 estate tax credit for amounts taxed to a prior decedent) does not require tracing. The only other area where tracing is a possible issue is that of identifying the provider of consideration for a joint tenancy under §2040(a), and here §2040 provides presumptions. Also, in the case of anything other than unique long-lived tangible property, tracing is pointless, because cash is fungible, and other property is liquid or has a short life.

44. Reg. §26.2612-1(b)(1)(i) holds that a transfer subject to estate or gift tax cannot be a taxable termination. In light of the statement in the text, which is based on a change in the Code in 1988 (see S. Rep. No. 100-445, 100th Cong., 2d Sess. 367 (1988)), this sentence would appear to be superfluous. Considering that the statement only refers to a taxable termination, it would not preclude the existence of a taxable distribution or direct-skip transfer with respect to the superseding transfer.

45. See Reg. §26.2652-1(a)(5), Ex. 3.

(e) Consideration Offsets

Section 2624(d) states that the tax base shall be reduced by "the amount of" any consideration provided by a transferee for a generation-skipping transfer. The consideration-offset concept (having to do with "replenishing" a donor's potential estate) doesn't fit easily into the GST tax scenario, because a generation-skipping arrangement, by definition, doesn't avoid the transferor's estate or gift tax. Nothing is said as to who is to receive the consideration, and there are no regulations to explain this provision. Perhaps the idea is that a "purchase" cannot be a gratuitous transfer. In any event, the "amount of" language would appear to limit the consideration offset to a dollar amount rather than to a fraction of the transfer constituted as of the (possibly earlier) date when the consideration was received.

2. Valuation

Valuation is of the amount transferred. Estate and gift tax valuation rules and principles would apply. With respect to the question of whether the transfer itself can affect the value (e.g., by carving up the property into minority interests), the focus is on the value received by the transferee, in the case of taxable distributions and direct-skip transfers, which suggests that gift tax principles would apply. In the case of taxable terminations, it appears that estate tax principles would apply, because the reference is to "all the property" subject to the termination.

Normally, the property is valued at the time of the generation-skipping transfer. If direct-skip property was included in the transferor's gross estate, both an alternate-valuation-date election and an election to use special-use valuation under §2032A will be effective also for GST tax purposes. §2624(b). If a taxable termination coincides with, and is triggered by, the death of an individual, an alternate-valuation-date election can be made, for generation-skipping tax purposes only, in conformity with the rules of §2032 (requiring, *inter alia*, that the election reduce the tax base and the tax). §2624(c).

3. Transmission Costs

In the case of a taxable termination, the taxable amount is reduced by (trust) administration expenses (etc.) occasioned by the transfer. §2622(b). In the case of a taxable distribution, there is a reduction equal to any expenses of the transferee caused by the imposition of the GST tax. §2621. No adjustments are made to direct-skip transfers.

4. Effect of the GST Tax on the GST Tax Base (and the Gift Tax Base)

Does the GST tax itself reduce the tax base? In the case of a taxable termination, the tax, although paid out of the trust (or other property), is not a deduction from the tax base. In other words, the tax base is tax-inclusive. The same is true of a taxable distribution, by virtue of the fact that the tax base is what the transferee receives (before the tax), with the tax to be paid by the transferee. See §2603(a)(1). To illustrate, assume a distribution of $100K to a grandchild of the grantor and a tax rate of 45 percent. The tax ($45K) is based on the before-tax amount of $100K, but the transferee ends up with a net benefit of $55K. (If the trust, instead of the transferee, pays the GST tax, the taxable amount is increased by such tax. See §2621(b).)

The situation with direct-skip transfers is different, because, although the tax base is again the amount received by the transferee, the tax is to be paid by the transferor. §2603(a)(3). Thus, if D makes an *inter vivos* gift of $100K, the GST tax of $45K is paid by D. The tax base is not $145K. This result is similar to that obtained under the federal gift tax, which applies to the same transfer. But then the gift tax base (what the donee receives) would omit both the gift tax and the GST tax. Accordingly, Congress, to prevent discrimination in favor of gift (as opposed to estate-included) direct-skip transfers, added §2515 to the gift tax. *Section §2515 provides that any GST tax on a direct-skip gift transfer is itself a taxable gift for gift tax purposes.* (In effect, this rule imposes the gift tax "before" any GST tax on the same transfer, which is consistent with the other possible scenarios.)

In the case of a direct-skip *estate* transfer, the GST tax is payable by the decedent transferor's estate, and §2603(b) states that the GST tax is to be charged to the amount transferred, unless the governing instrument *specifically* dictates otherwise. Where the GST tax is charged to the bequest, then the amount of the before-tax bequest has to be increased to take the tax into account. A bequest (charged with the GST tax) would need to be $145K to effect an after-tax transfer to the legatee of $100K. Nevertheless, charging the GST tax to the direct-skip bequest does not render the tax base as being tax inclusive, because the tax is still *computed* with reference to what the transferee receives ($100K), not the sum of the amount received and the tax itself.

D. *Implications of Tax Base Rules for Planning*

Initially, direct-skip transfers appear to be favored (relative to taxable terminations and distributions) because the tax base is tax-exclusive. The advantage of a tax-exclusive tax base was pointed out (in comparing the gift tax to the estate tax) in §2.5.C.2. Where the tax base is tax-exclusive, the transferor parts with a smaller amount to move a "target sum" to the transferee than under a tax-inclusive tax.[46] Nevertheless, a complete picture of options requires consideration of the application of the estate and gift tax to the same transfer. It happens that the estate or gift tax is deemed to be imposed "before" the GST tax. Otherwise, there would be little or nothing left for the transferee!

The table below shows how much a transferor must part with, under alternative assumptions, to move $100x into the hands of a transferee after all federal transfer taxes. In all cases the applicable tax rate is assumed to be 45 percent, and that all exemptions and exclusions have been exhausted. There

---

46. How much does a transferor have to part with to move $1M to a transferee after tax, assuming a 45% rate? If the tax base is tax inclusive, it takes $1.818M ($1.818M less $0.818M tax = $1M). If the tax base is tax exclusive, it is $1.45M ($1M to transferee, $0.45M as tax).

are no separate descriptions of taxable distributions, because the latter are taxed the same as taxable terminations, since both are tax inclusive under the GST tax. Where the tax base is tax inclusive, the tax will be 45 percent of the amount parted with. When the tax base is tax exclusive, the tax rate will be 31 percent of the amount parted with $(45/145 = 0.31)$. It is assumed that the tax base does not increase between the date of transfer and the date of any taxable termination. It is also assumed that the estate tax due is entirely paid out of the bequest. "GT" means subject to gift tax, "ET" means subject to estate tax, "DS" means direct-skip transfer, and "TT" means taxable termination. All numbers are rounded to the nearest whole number.

Table 7-1
Transfer Efficiency

	Form of Transfer			
	(1) GT DS	(2) ET DS	(3) GT TT	(4) ET TT
Amount Parted With	$210x	$264x	$264x	$331x
Rate	.31	.45	.31	.45
Tax	−65x	−119x	−82x	−149x
GST Tax Base	145x	145x	182x	182x
Rate	.31	.31	.45	.45
GST Tax	−45x	−45x	−82x	−82x
Net to Transferee	$100x	$100x	$100x	$100x

The "amount parted with" is the "net to transferee" plus the sum of both the GST tax and the estate or gift tax. In columns (1) and (2) involving direct-skip transfers, the computations are essentially made from the bottom up; the GST tax is 45 percent of the amount received by the transferee. The fact that the $45x GST tax on the "GT DS" in column (1) is treated as a taxable gift under §2515 simply means that it, plus the $100x received by the transferee, is the amount subject to a 45 percent gift tax (= $65x). In columns (3) and (4), the GST tax is 45 percent of the amount then in the trust ($182x).

For each mode of generation-skipping transfer (direct skip, taxable termination), the gift tax mode, not surprisingly, is 20 percent cheaper than the estate tax mode. It is also the case that for each of the estate and gift modes, the direct-skip transfer is 20 percent cheaper than the taxable termination transfer!

The table above appears to disregard the time-value of money. A tax paid now (under a direct-skip transfer) is more burdensome than the identical tax paid later (as in a taxable termination). However, it is a stretch to assume that the tax base (and the tax) will not change over time. Assuming a flat tax rate, there is no time-value-of-money disadvantage if the tax base appreciates at the same rate as the discount rate. It is unlikely that a trust would appreciate at the same rate as the discount rate, due to: (1) the trustee's duty of impartiality, (2) the tendency to maintain a nonrisky (and low-return) investment portfolio, and (3) the fact that trust accumulations are subject to high income tax rates. However, a given trust could appreciate at a healthy rate, or the tax rate itself might change. In short, it is hard to make generalizations based solely on the timing of the tax.

E. Effect of the Exemption Amount on Planning

The foregoing analysis fails to take into account the exemption amount.

1. Operation of the Exemption Amount

The GST exemption amount factors into the GST tax rate applicable to generation-skipping transfers with respect to a particular trust or property. Recall that the tax rate (the *applicable rate*) is the (percentage) rate obtained by multiplying the maximum federal estate tax rate by the *inclusion ratio* applicable to the transfer. §2641. The "inclusion ratio" is the percentage obtained by subtracting the *applicable fraction* (really, percentage) from the number "1" (i.e., 100%). §2642(a)(1). The "applicable fraction" (i.e., the *exclusion percentage*) is obtained by dividing the *GST exemption amount* allocated to transfer by the value (at the time the transferor effects the transfer) of the amount transferred (but net of death taxes recovered from the transfer and any amounts qualifying for the gift or estate tax charitable deduction). See §2642(a)(2). The "GST exemption amount" of a transferor (to be used over her lifetime) is equal to the current estate tax exemption amount. §2631(c). This amount (a fixed dollar amount) is to be *allocated* by the transferor among various GST transfers. See §§2631(a) & (b) and 2632.

If the exemption amount allocated (by the transferor) to the net transfer equals the net transfer, the rate applicable to that transfer is zero, because the numerator of the exclusion ratio will equal the denominator (resulting in 100%), and "100% minus 100%" is zero (percent).

2. Effect of the Estate Tax on the Exemption Amount

From Table 7-1, and disregarding the possible advantage (or disadvantage) of delaying the tax, it is apparent that the *inter vivos* direct-skip transfer is the cheapest to effectuate, whereas the estate-initiated taxable termination is the most expensive. However, the analysis undertaken in Table 7-1 assumed that the transfer-tax exemption amounts have been fully exhausted, so that all transfers are fully taxable. The analysis in Table 7-1 leaves out of consideration the effect of the exemption amount under the GST tax, as well as the fact that any *estate tax* charged to the transfer reduces the amount of the exemption amount needed to exempt the transfer from GST tax. Table 7-2 (otherwise based on the same assumptions as Table 7-1) assumes full taxation under the estate or gift tax (i.e., that the estate and gift tax exemption has otherwise been used up), and shows the maximum amount that can fund a generation-skipping transfer that produces a GST tax of zero.

Table 7-2
Maximum Exempt GST Tax Transfers

	Form of Transfer			
	(1) GT DS	(2) ET DS	(3) GT TT	(4) ET TT
Gift or Bequest	$ 3.5M	$ 6.36M	$ 3.5M	$ 6.36M
– *Estate Tax* @ *45%*	0	−2.86M	0	−2.86M
GST Denominator	3.5M	3.5M	3.5M	3.5M
Exemption Allocation	3.5M	3.5M	3.5M	3.5M
GST Tax	0	0	0	0
Gift Tax @ 45%	−1.575M	0	−1.575M	0
Net to Transferee	$ 3.5M	$ 3.5M	$ 3.5M	$ 3.5M
Cost to Transferor	$ 5.075M	$ 6.36M	$ 5.075M	$ 6.36M

The results here are somewhat different than in Table 7-1. Here, *there is no difference between direct-skip transfers and taxable terminations within either the gift tax mode or the estate tax mode.* Gifts are still more efficient than bequests for either direct-skip transfers or taxable terminations. (The other side of the coin is that an exemption allocated to a bequest shields a larger bequest amount than an exemption allocated to a gift.)

3. Leveraging the Exemption

Tables 7-1 and 7-2 assumed no growth in the value of a given trust between the time of its creation and the time of the first taxable termination. What if there is significant growth? The "inclusion ratio" is constituted at the time of the gift or bequest. *The "inclusion ratio" that is attached to the transfer from its inception stays with that transfer forever.* §2653(b). That rate is applied against the value of the generation-skipping transfer at the time of such transfer (if later than the date the transferor parted with the property). Thus, if A creates a trust, income to A's children until the death of the survivor, remainder to A's then living issue, and A (at the time the trust is created) allocates her exclusion amount to the trust in an amount sufficient to produce an applicable GST tax rate of zero, and the value of the trust is $10M when the taxable termination occurs at the death of the last survivor of A's children, the taxable termination results in zero tax! This phenomenon is referred to as "the leveraging of the GST exemption." If the applicable rate were 20 percent (instead of zero), the tax would be $2M.

It is worth noting that where the trust bears the generation-skipping tax in a generation-skipping taxable termination (and the inclusion ratio is greater than zero), the second sentence of §2653(b)(1) provides that the amount of such tax will reduce the denominator of the fraction used to determine the inclusion ratio that will be applied to subsequent taxable terminations and distributions.[47] This rule operates to decrease the taxable portion of future generation-skipping transfers.

The leveraging effect suggests that the GST tax exemption be allocated to transfers that are long-term and expected to appreciate over time.

4. Allocating the GST Tax Exemption

Section 2631 states that the transferor (or his executor) can allocate the GST tax exemption among transfers as desired, but that any such allocation (once made) is irrevocable. The choice of the transferor (and the transferor's executor) is subject to several default rules.

Section 2632(b) states that the exemption is allocated automatically so as to completely exempt direct-skip gifts on a first-come first-served basis, unless the transferor elects otherwise on a Form 709.

Next, §2632(c) provides a similar rule for *inter vivos* gifts to any GST trust that are not direct-skip gifts (called "indirect skips"). The term "GST trust" means a trust that could have future taxable distributions or taxable terminations, but there are exceptions to the definition of "GST trust" for trusts that might significantly shrink (due to corpus distributions), might (or will) be included in a beneficiary's gross estate, and are split-interest charitable trusts. A transferor can elect to treat a trust as a "GST trust" even if it is not.[48]

Gift transfers not governed by a default rule can receive allocations pursuant to the filing of a Form 709. Such allocations can be made after the transfers, but such late allocations are prospective only (except as allowed by §2632(d)).[49] Prior allocations cannot be reduced.[50] The inclusion ratio is reconstituted at the date of the late allocation.[51] Hence, a late allocation would be disadvantageous (relative to an earlier allocation) if the trust property has appreciated since the date of the transfer.

Any unallocated GST exemption amount remaining at the transferor's death can be allocated by the executor, but if the executor fails to do so the unused exemption is allocated first to direct-skip transfers triggered by the transferor's death. See §2632(e).

It might be desirable for the transferor to add a clause to her will either specifying in detail how the allocation is to be made or authorizing the personal representative to make the allocation in its discretion or under a maximum-reduction-in-aggregate-tax standard.

---

47. The statute refers to "regulations prescribed by the Secretary," but there are no such regulations.

48. See Reg. §26.2632-1(b)(3).

49. Section 2632(d) allows a retroactive allocation where a generation-skipping transfer is caused by the (premature) death, during the transferor's lifetime, of a non-skip person (who falls within a certain degree of relationship to the transferor) who lies in a generation below that of the transferor.

50. See Reg. §26.2632-1(b)(4).

51. See Reg. §26.2642-2(a)(2) & -4.

It is a common tax-planning device to create two trusts, one for non-skip persons (to which trust no exemption is allocated) and the other exclusively for skip persons (to which the exemption is allocated to the greatest degree possible). The first trust allows (and encourages) corpus distributions to non-skip persons. (An exemption allocation to such a trust would be wasted, because distributions to non-skip persons do not benefit from the GST tax exemption.) The second trust, which perhaps has an inclusion ratio of zero, accumulates income and grows fat while the first trust takes care of non-skip beneficiaries, thereby fueling the leveraging effect.

In *Notice 2001-50*, 2001-34 I.R.B. 189, the IRS issued guidance on requests for an extension of time to make a GST tax §2642(b)(1) and (2) exemption allocation and a §2632(b)(3) and (c)(5) election. According to the Notice, §301.9100-3, which requires a taxpayer to establish that he acted in good faith and that the relief will not prejudice the government's interests, is applicable to these requests. A request for relief should follow the procedures for a private letter ruling request (see §5.02 of *Rev. Proc. 2001-1*, 2001-1 I.R.B. 1, 28).[52]

5. *Estate-Includible Completed Gift Transfers*

If a completed gift transfer is of the type that would be included in the gross estate of the transferor, the inclusion ratio is constituted at the end of the estate tax inclusion period (ETIP), which is the earliest to occur of (a) the transferor's death, (b) the time that the transfer would cease being includible in the gross estate,[53] or (c) the date of a generation-skipping transfer with respect to the property. See §2642(f). The effect of this rule is usually to increase the denominator of the exclusion ratio, and thereby to "require" an increased exemption allocation. Basically, exemption allocations to a transfer of this type are effective only as of the close of the ETIP period. Therefore, it is generally not desirable to allocate an exemption amount to such a transfer prior to the close of the ETIP period.

This rule also discourages the creation of trusts of this type in the first place.

6. *Effect of Having Two or More Transferors*

If an *inter vivos* transfer is made by co-owners (as would occur if community property were the subject of the transfer), or if gift splitting is elected under §2513, or if a "partial" reverse generation-skipping-tax QTIP election is made, then a separate inclusion ratio is figured with respect to each transferor. If husband and wife make a gift of $2M in community property, each can allocate all of his or her exemption to his or her tax base so as to exempt the entire transfer from generation-skipping tax. (Each transferor, however, can exempt only his or

---

52. *P.L.R.200118037* (despite the passage of several years, the government granted an extension of time for the trustee of the marital trust to make a reverse QTIP election under §2652(a)(3) for the GST tax).

53. This rule is applied without regard to §2035. An example would be where the transferor retains the income until age 70 (which would cause inclusion in her gross estate under §2036(a)(1) if she dies before reaching 70) and she survives her 70th birthday. Section 2036(a)(1) drops off, and the transferor's 70th birthday would be the "inclusion ratio date" for GST tax purposes.

her portion of the tax base; exemption amounts are not transferable among married transferors even with the 2010 adoption of portability for estate tax purposes.) Similarly, the §2503 tax exclusion can be doubled with respect to a given transfer by means of gift-splitting under §2513 or through a gift of community (or co-owned) property.

F. Powers of Appointment and the GST

The possession and exercise of powers of appointment can produce consequences under the GST.

1. Giving a General Testamentary Power of Appointment to Beneficiaries

A person who is subject to estate or gift tax under §2041 or §2514 becomes the "transferor," superseding the original transferor, and the designation of "skip persons" and "non-skip persons" (and the imposition of the GST) is altered (or eliminated) accordingly. Indeed, Reg. §26.2612-1 goes further by stating that a taxable termination cannot occur if the property is subject to estate or gift tax at such time.

Example: Renee creates a testamentary trust, income to son Spike for life, then to such persons (including Spike's estate) as Spike appoints by will, but in default of such appointment to grandchild Tino. If Spike did not possess a general power of appointment, there would be a taxable termination upon Spike's death, because the property would then pass outright to a skip person (Tino), who is two generations below the generation of the transferor (Renee). However, Spike's general power of appointment causes the property to be included in Spike's gross estate, and that renders Tino into a "non-skip person," because Tino is only one generation below Spike, the "superseding" transferor. Thus, upon Spike's death there is no taxable termination and no GST.

This rule is based on the idea that the GST is "not needed" if the estate or gift tax is imposed with respect to the intermediate generation.

For planning purposes, giving a beneficiary a general power of appointment saves transfer taxes only if the beneficiary can avoid estate or gift tax on account of the beneficiary's unused unified transfer tax credit. (Otherwise, the trust would be subject to estate tax rather than GST tax.) Accordingly, a *testamentary* general power would be used for this purpose, because the unused credit can be ascertained at the beneficiary's death. Moreover, the instrument might be drafted so that the power only exists *to the extent of* such beneficiary's unused credit. Such a power is called a "springing" power. Springing powers can be given to multiple beneficiaries, perhaps in multiple generations.

2. Effect of the Exercise of a Special Power of Appointment

The exercise of a special power can trigger, delay, accelerate, or eliminate the operation of the GST tax.

Example: Artemis creates an irrevocable trust, naming the Troy State Bank as trustee, income to son Bruno or accumulated during Bruno's life, and upon Bruno's death remainder to Artemis' daughter Corinna, giving Bruno an *inter vivos* special power to appoint to his issue. If the power is not exercised, Bruno's death does not result in a taxable termination, since Corinna is a non-skip person. Bruno, however, does exercise this power, and appoints all of the trust corpus outright to his daughter Dorothy. This appointment causes a taxable termination for GST purposes, since Dorothy is a skip person (relative to the transferor, Artemis).

Similarly, the appointment of all of the trust property to a person who is a non-skip person (relative to the transferor) can eliminate possible exposure to the GST.

F. Basis Adjustments

If a taxable termination occurs at the same time and as the result of the death of an individual, the basis of the property transferred obtains a step-up or step-down in basis to its value at the time of transfer, in the manner of §1014. However, if the inclusion ratio is less than 1.0, any step-up or step-down in basis is diluted by multiplying it by the inclusion ratio. If the inclusion ratio is zero, there would be no step-up or step-down in basis. See §2654(a)(2).

Example: Assume a taxable termination occurs at the death of a child of the transferor, the value of the property is $1M, its aggregate basis just prior to the taxable termination is $400K, and the inclusion ratio is 0.6. In that case the basis after the taxable termination is $760K ($400K initial basis plus 0.6 times the would-be step-up of $600K).

In any case other than a taxable termination resulting from an individual's death, the property obtains a basis adjustment equal to the GST tax attributable to the excess (if any) of the property's value over its basis just prior to the transfer. See §2654(a)(1), which is modeled on §1015(d)(6) (adjustment to basis for appreciated property subject to gift tax).

Example: Assume the property has a basis of $400K, a value at the time of the generation-skipping transfer of $1M, and the generation-skipping tax is $200K. The basis following the transfer is $520K ($400K initial basis plus 0.6 times $200K). The 0.6 is the unrealized appreciation divided by the value just prior to the generation-skipping transfer.

The statute does not clearly state what happens in the case of a direct-skip transfer. If such transfer is included in the transferor's gross estate, it will receive a §1014 step-up or step-down basis wholly apart from the GST tax. In the case of a direct-skip gift of property which had appreciated up to the time of gift, the property obtains an upwards basis adjustment first under §1015(d)(6) and then under §2654(a)(1), but these adjustments cannot cause the basis of the property to exceed its value.

G. Postscript: The Perversion of the Concept of a GST Tax: How the Present Tax Encourages the Making of Generation-Skipping Transfers

Although the purpose of a generation-skipping tax is ostensibly to create parity between a succession of outright transfers, on the one hand, and generation-skipping trusts on the other,[54] the current GST actually creates a tax incentive to establish generation-skipping trusts. This incentive is generated by the GST exemption, which is "in addition to" the estate and gift tax exemption. The effect of the GST exemption is to double (at least) the value of gratuitous transfers from generation to generation that escape transfer tax. Thus, assume an individual (X) who begets a lineage that has one descendant per generation. Assume further that these descendants create no net wealth of their own, and live entirely off of the income from the endowment created by X, who dies with a taxable estate of $9,863,636. After the estate and gift tax credit (having an exemption equivalent of $3.5M), the tax will be $2,863,636, leaving $7M after tax. Half of this amount will pass outright (and intact) from generation to generation, without estate tax, due to the estate and gift tax credit. The other $3.5M is put into a generation-skipping trust, which is forever free of GST tax (as well as gift and estate tax) on account of the separate GST tax exemption amount.

On the one hand, a weak GST tax may be viewed as being preferable to no GST tax at all. On the other hand, it appears that enactment of the current GST tax in 1986 created an incentive for states to abolish (or weaken) their Rule Against Perpetuities. In any event, an effective GST tax would have no "internal" exemption, but would play off unused estate and gift tax exemptions of individuals "connected with" the trust. But that approach, which was followed in the (repealed) GST tax that was in effect from 1976 to 1986, was considered (rightly or wrongly) to be too difficult to design effectively. The problem is that the unused exemptions would be those of persons in skipped generations, and those persons may not have benefited (directly or indirectly) from the trust.

Basically, a GST tax is incompatible with an estate and gift tax system, which is a tax on gratuitous property transfers by individuals. The concept of a property transfer presupposes fee ownership (or possession of cash) at some point. A GST tax is, at best, a tax on "partial" ownership, and, at worst, on no ownership at all. It is not surprising, therefore, that the task of finding a solution to the problem of designing an effective GST tax has proven elusive.

Under an accessions tax, an individual would have a personal lifetime exemption that would be used up (on a first-come, first-served basis) against all gratuitous receipts, from whatever (generational) source. By the very nature of an accessions tax (which taxes only actual receipts of cash or property but not

---

54. The equity rationales for a GST tax are questioned in Joseph M. Dodge, *Comparing a Reformed Estate Tax with an Accessions Tax and an Income-Inclusion System, and Abandoning the Generation-Skipping Tax*, 56 S.M.U. Law Rev. 551 (2003). Although the estate planning bar had opposed earlier attempts to enact a GST tax, no such opposition has appeared since the enactment of the present GST tax in 1986.

acquisitions of present or future interests), there is no generation-skipping "problem" to begin with.

1. a. The notion that a GST tax should reach outright gifts and bequests (not in trust) is controversial. The objection is that no intermediate-generation person has received a benefit from such a transfer. Another way of stating the matter is that it is inequitable to tax outright transfers differently solely on account of the (generational) identity of the transferor.

    b. The 1976-1986 GST tax did not reach direct-skip transfers (nor did prior proposals). As a result, an inducement existed for the "layering" of separate trusts for different generations of beneficiaries. Taxation of direct-skip transfers mostly put a stop to this technique. However, the current GST tax creates an inducement to create a separate trust for the benefit of non-skip persons.

2. a. Another controversial feature of the current GST tax is the "leveraging effect," under which the exemption expands (or contracts) as the trust expands or contracts. Presumably, the leveraging effect is based on the notion that direct-skip transfers should be put on a parity with taxable terminations (and distributions). Given that the exemption amount is that "of" the transferor (rather than that of beneficiaries), leveraging was seen as necessary. However, assigning the exemption to the transferor was a second-best approach to obtaining exemptions from unused estate and gift tax exemption amounts. If the exemption amount allocated to a trust is seen as belonging to the trust (rather than the transferor), is leveraging really required as a matter of equity or neutrality? Assigning a fixed-dollar exemption amount to a trust (as a replacement for the inclusion-ratio approach) would also simplify matters: The exemption would simply be applied against taxable distributions and taxable terminations.

    b. Analytically, leveraging is distinct from the rule that the inclusion ratio (which can be zero) stays with the trust forever. This rule is even more controversial than that of leveraging, which could be confined to the first taxable termination (or distribution). The "forever" rule has created an inducement to create dynastic trusts, which in turn has created pressure to relax the Rule Against Perpetuities. Proposals have been made to limit the "forever" rule. One suggestion would have the exclusion ratio increase to 1.0 after 90 years. (Can Congress adopt such a change that is applicable to existing irrevocable trusts? What if state law allows a trust to be reformed for tax reasons?)

3. The material above has omitted discussion of rules governing successive transfers to the same trust, pour-overs to a trust from another trust, and the division of a trust into multiple trusts. By way of crude generalization, the rules are

designed so that these kinds of events cannot be used to alter prior exemption allocations.

    a.   In the case of an outright addition to a trust, the "applicable fraction" (exclusion ratio) is reconstituted immediately after the trust. The numerator is the sum of: (1) the exemption amount allocated to the current transfer and (2) the excludible portion of the trust property as of the moment just prior to the transfer (i.e., the "prior" exclusion fraction times the then-value of the property). The denominator is the sum of (1) the value of the property "involved in such [current] transfer" and (2) the value of the property in trust just prior to the current transfer. See §2642(d).

    b.   A similar rule (only in reverse) applies in the case of a pour-over to another trust. The "nontax portion" of the pour-over shall be treated as an allocation of an exemption amount to the receiving trust. See §2653(b)(2).

    c.   If a trust is divided into separate trusts, the exclusion ratio would normally carry over. However, it is possible to sever a trust into fractional shares in a way that one trust ends up with an exclusion ratio of zero and the other with an inclusion ratio of 1.0. See §2642(a)(3).

4. a.   Section 164(a)(5) allows an income tax deduction for any federal GST with respect to distributions which are treated as current "income" to the distributee under the federal income tax rules (as opposed to trust accounting rules).

    b.   The §691(c) income tax deduction for the estate tax attributable to IRD rights has a GST tax counterpart: The deduction is that portion of the GST tax (triggered by a person's death) that is attributable to the inclusion in the GST tax of income items which were not included in the income of the trust until after the taxable termination or direct-skip transfer. See §691(c)(3).

    c.   Section 6166(i) provides for the deferred installment payment of any GST tax attributable to an interest in a closely-held business in connection with an estate-included direct-skip transfer, if the transferor's estate qualifies for §6166.

    d.   Section 303(d) provides that closely-held stock constituting more than 35 percent of the value of a generation-skipping transfer occurring as the result of an individual's death can be redeemed to pay generation-skipping tax so that the redemption will be treated as a "sale" (with basis offset) rather than a "dividend."

5. a.   Section 2603(b) charges the GST tax to the property transferred, unless the governing instrument provided otherwise by specifically referring to the GST tax. Any state-law tax apportionment statute or rule to the contrary would be disregarded. Recall that any GST tax paid by the trust on a taxable distribution is treated as an additional taxable distribution, because the distributee is the one liable for the tax. §2621(b).

    b.   Under §2662(a), the person who is liable for payment of the GST tax is also the person who is required to file the return. The return is to be filed: (1) for a direct skip (other than *from* a trust) on or before the due date for the corresponding estate or gift tax return, and (2) in other cases by the 15th day of the fourth month of the returner's taxable year.

c. The standard gift tax return (Form 709) devotes portions of itself to the GST tax on direct-skip gift transfer. In addition, the instructions to the Form 709 state that a gift which is not a direct-skip transfer can have an exemption amount allocated to it by attaching a "Notice of Allocation" statement.

d. Section 2662(b) authorizes the Treasury to require information returns. Conceivably, such returns might be required with respect to non-direct-skip transfers in trust, transfers from an estate or trust to another trust, or arrangements that are the equivalent of generation-skipping trusts.

e. Other than the foregoing, there are no separate statutory provisions that are specifically applicable to the GST tax as such. Section 2661 states that those provisions of Subtitle F (§6001 *et seq.*, relating to procedure and administration) as are applicable to the gift tax shall be applicable to the GST tax, except that those provisions of Subtitle F as are applicable to the estate tax shall apply to generation-skipping transfers occurring "at the same time as and as a result of" a person's death.

§7.5. Income Taxation of Subchapter J Trusts and Their Beneficiaries

This section discusses the income taxation of trusts (and their beneficiaries) where the trust is neither a "beneficiary-owned trust" (as described in §7.2) nor a "grantor trust" (as described in §8.4). In the case of beneficiary-owned trusts and grantor trusts, the trust is not a taxpayer, and the trust income (etc.) is attributed directly to an individual (a beneficiary having a sole *inter vivos* general power of appointment, or the grantor, as the case may be). In those cases, the trust (in other words) is a "conduit" or "pass-through" entity. A trust which is neither a beneficiary-owned trust nor a grantor trust is known as a "Subchapter J trust."

A. Overview

A Subchapter J trust is treated as a taxpayer (a taxable entity), much in the manner that an "estate" is treated as a taxable entity for income tax purposes. See §4.3. Stated as a broad generalization, the trust is taxed (under the §1(e) rate schedule) on the excess (if any) of trust ordinary net income for the year over "distributions" for the year, plus trust net capital gains for the year, and beneficiaries (as a group) report ordinary gross income in an amount which is the lesser of (a) aggregate "distributions" received by them for the year or (b) the trust ordinary net income for the year. Of course, there are modifications and exceptions to this general pattern, but the basic idea is that net ordinary income and net capital gains are initially computed at the trust level, and then all or a portion of such net ordinary income (and much less often, net capital gain) is "moved" to the beneficiaries on account of (and not in excess of) distributions to such beneficiaries.

B. *Trust Net Income*

The first step in figuring out the tax consequences of a Subchapter J trust is to figure the trust's net income for the trust taxable year. Under §644, the trust's taxable year shall be the calendar year. (That is, a fiscal year cannot be chosen.) Of course, a trust can have a short initial taxable year (ending on December 31) or a short final taxable year (beginning on January 1).

In general, the trust's *net* income is computed in the same manner as for an individual. §641(b). The trust's net income is gross income less deductions (other than the distribution deduction and specific exemption, which are taken "later" in arriving at trust *taxable* income). Deductions for trust administration expenses are taken under §212(1) and (2). As "investment" deductions, they can be "miscellaneous itemized deductions" subject (under §67) to a 2-percent-of-AGI "floor," unless the expenses are unique to trust administration. See §67(e); Prop. Reg. §1.67-4(b) (2007). In *Knight v. Comm'r*, 552 U.S. 181 (2008), the Supreme Court held that a trust's investment counseling fees were not unique to trust administration.

Any income tax deductions for depletion and depreciation are allocated between the trust and the beneficiary in accordance with the disposition of trust accounting income. However, if the trustee maintains a "reserve" for trust accounting purposes,[55] the deductions are allocable first to the trust to the extent of the reserve, and if the deductions exceed the additions to the reserves such excess is allocated pursuant to the preceding sentence.[56]

A trust's charitable deduction is allowed under §642(c), described at the end of §8.3, rather than §170.

C. *How Trust Income Is Shifted to Beneficiaries*

Moving to a more technical way of describing how the Subchapter J rules work, Subchapter J trust is taxed on its trust net income for the year, supra, *less* the "distribution deduction" for the year, and *less* the flat exemption (which is $100 or $300). *The amounts reportable as income by the distributees (as a group) equal the trust's distribution deduction for the taxable year.* This deduction/inclusion scheme operates to shift net income from the trust to the distributees (as a group). The aggregate amount taxed to the trust and to the distributees cannot exceed the trust net income, supra.

---

55. The term "reserve" refers to a reduction in net trust accounting income equal to some percentage of a depreciable (or depletable) asset's original net cost. The effect of keeping a reserve is to reduce net income that can be distributed to income beneficiaries. The reduction in (distributable) income results in the accumulation of cash income, and nondistributed cash income is added to corpus. A reserve is a way of achieving impartiality between income and corpus beneficiaries of a trust that is heavily funded with wasting assets, because (in the absence of the reserve) all the cash would be distributed currently and the corpus would waste away.

56. See §§167(d) and 642(f); Reg. §1.167(h)-1(b).

Both the distribution deduction and the amounts reportable by distributees are the *lesser of* (a) aggregate "distributions" for the year or (b) distributable net income (DNI) for the year. See §§651, 652(a), 661(a), and 662(a). The "lesser of" aspect of the rule precludes the creation of a tax loss at the trust level by reason of the making of excess distributions. At the same time, it prevents distributees (as a group) from having income in excess of trust net income (which is the theoretical ceiling for trust DNI). "Distributions" and "DNI" are terms of art.

"Distributions" means actual distributions of money and property during the trust's taxable year, but not distributions to charity, and not distributions specified by the trust of specific property or a specific sum of money payable in three or fewer installments (unless payable only from trust income). See §663(a). As with an estate, distributions during the first 65 days of the trust taxable year may, at the election of the trustee, be allocated (deemed to have been made) in the prior taxable year of the trust. See §663(b). If a "distribution" is made in kind, the amount of the distribution is an amount equal to the income tax basis of the trust in the property, unless the trust recognizes gain or loss on the distribution, in which case the amount of the distribution is the fair market value of the property. See §643(e). It should be noted that any loss on such a deemed sale would not be recognized under §267(a)(1), because a trustee and a beneficiary are "related parties" under §267(b)(6).

The concept of DNI places a limit upon the distribution deduction and the amount includible by the beneficiaries. The definition of DNI starts with trust net income,[57] and the definition of DNI functions so that neither the distribution deduction nor the amounts included by distributees can exceed trust net income. Conceptually, DNI is designed to resemble (somewhat) trust accounting net income (which is what a trust can distribute to its "income" beneficiaries). Accordingly, in computing DNI, trust net income is reduced by net capital gains if (1) the net capital gains of the current year are properly allocated to corpus (following the conventional rule of trust accounting) *and* (2) the net capital gains for the current year are "not paid, credited, or required to be distributed to any beneficiary during the taxable year." See §643(a)(3). The allocation of net capital gains to corpus for trust accounting purposes means that they cannot be distributed to "income" beneficiaries. The issue then arises as to whether net capital gains (for the current year) are deemed to be paid (etc.) to a person who receives a corpus distribution during the current year. This and other related questions are dealt with by Reg. §1.643(a)-3. In general, net capital gains of the current year (allocated to corpus) are *not* included in DNI just because corpus is distributed to a beneficiary in the same year. However, the opposite result will occur where:

> (1) the trust terminates during the year,
> (2) the trust instrument states that the proceeds of sale of a particular asset are to be distributed to a beneficiary,

---

57. See §643(a)(1) & (2) (defining DNI initially as trust taxable income disregarding the distribution deduction and the trust exemption amount).

(3) the trustee makes a practice of distributing to beneficiary the exact net proceeds of asset sales,

(4) capital gains are treated as constituting a portion of a unitrust distribution.

The foregoing typically operate to exclude (i.e., subtract) net capital gains and losses in computing DNI. Where this occurs, net capital gains will be taxed to the trust, because the reduction in DNI for net capital gains will reduce *pro tanto* both the distribution deduction and the aggregate amount included by distributees.

In a similar vein, §643(a)(4) holds that extraordinary dividends and taxable stock dividends are excluded from the DNI computation if they are properly allocated to trust corpus. However, this rule only applies to "simple" trusts, described below.

Although some gross income items allocated to corpus are excluded from the DNI computation, deductions (other than those for capital losses) are not excluded by reason of being properly charged against corpus for trust accounting purposes.[58] This rule prevents the wasting of deductions, as can be illustrated by an example in which ordinary trust (gross, and trust accounting) income is $22K, §212 deductions of $2K are allocated to corpus, and that the resulting trust accounting income of $22K is distributed to B. In this example, DNI is $20K, since the deductions are subtracted in computing DNI despite being a reduction of corpus. The trust taxable income is zero ($22K gross income *less* $2K §212 deductions *less* $20K distribution deduction), and B reports gross income of $20K. In effect, B obtains the benefit of the deduction, even though the expense (that gave rise to the deduction) did not reduce the "income" distribution. If the $2K had not reduced DNI, the trust taxable income would still be zero ($22K less $2K less $22K distribution deduction; however, the distribution deduction cannot produce a loss at the trust level), and B would report $22K. Thus, $22K would be subject to tax, even though the net income "pie" was only $20K.

D. *Allocation of Income Among Beneficiaries*

An amount equal to the distribution deduction is reported as income by the distributees as a group. As a broad generalization, the reportable income (limited by trust DNI) is allocated among the distributees in proportion to the amount of "distributions" received by them, and not on a first-come first-served basis.[59] However, the precise operation of the allocation rules presupposes that note be made of the distinction between simple trusts and complex trusts. As a definitional matter, a "simple trust" is a trust that (1) is required to distribute all of its trust accounting income currently, (2) does not in fact make any corpus distribution during the year, and (3) does not provide for any payments or set-asides for

---

58. The deductions reduce trust net income, which is the starting point for the DNI computation.

59. See §§652(a) and 662(a).

charities. A "complex trust" is any trust which is not a simple trust. (An estate is treated as a complex trust.)

One (trivial) consequence of this distinction is that simple trusts (and complex trusts which are required to distribute all income currently) obtain a $300 specific exemption, whereas other Subchapter J trusts receive only a $100 specific exemption. Recall that an estate receives a specific exemption of $600. Recall also that only simple trusts can benefit from the rule excluding from DNI extraordinary dividends and taxable stock dividends allocated to corpus.

The main significance of the distinction between simple and complex trusts is that simple trusts are governed by the deduction/inclusion rules of §§651 and 652, whereas complex trusts (and estates) are governed by those of §§661 and 662. There is actually little difference between the two sets of rules *except for the fact that the complex-trust provisions make a distinction between first-tier and second-tier distributions*. A first-tier distribution (from a complex trust) is any amount of trust accounting income required to be distributed currently during the year. Regulations amended in 2004 treat a unitrust interest of 3-5 percent of corpus as an income interest.[60] Another regulation treats a required annuity distribution as a first-tier distribution to the extent of available income.[61] A second-tier distribution is any proper distribution which is not a first-tier distribution. See §661(a)(1) & (2).

The point of the distinction between first- and second-tier distributions is that first-tier distributions draw out the trust DNI for the year first, and only the remaining trust DNI is drawn out by second-tier distributions. Additionally, the DNI allocable to each tier is allocated among that tier's distributees in the ratio of distributions (of the relevant tier) received. This allocation principle also applies in the case of simple trusts, where there is only one tier. Allocations of DNI are only necessary where distributions (within a tier) exceed the DNI allocable to that tier.

Example: To illustrate these rules, assume that the trust in question is required to pay 50 percent of the trust net income to B, and that the trustee is authorized to pay income and or corpus among B, C, or D in the trustee's sole discretion. For the trust's taxable year, trust accounting net income is $40K, DNI is $36K, and $28K is distributed to each of B, C, and D. Of the $28K distributed to B, $20K (50 percent of trust accounting net income) is a first-tier distribution from a complex trust. Since the first-tier distribution is less than trust DNI, all $20K is reportable as income by B. The remaining DNI of $16K (being less than aggregate second-tier distributions) is allocated among B, C, and D according to the ratio of second-tier distributions, which is an 8-28-28 ratio, with the result that $2K, $7K, and $7K (= $16K) are reportable by B, C, and D respectively as second-tier distributions. Thus, although each beneficiary receives the same amount, B has to pay tax on

---

60. See Reg. §1.643(b)-1 (2004). This regulation defines "income" (really, "trust accounting income") under §643(b), which is frequently referred to in Subchapter J, as in the definitions of "simple trust" and "first-tier distribution."

61. See Reg. §1.662(a)-2(c).

$22K (total), while C and D must pay tax on only $7K each (=$36K DNI total). These results hold true regardless of when the various distributions were made during the taxable year.

The rules for identifying first- and second-tier distributions prevent a trustee from manipulating the income tax results to distributees by cherry-picking the source of distributions. First-tier distributions are amounts required *by the trust instrument* to be paid out of trust accounting income, and all other distributions are second-tier distributions, regardless of whether the trustee uses income or corpus as the source of the distribution.

There is a "separate share" rule for trusts under §663(c), which provides that separate shares of a trust will be treated as separate trusts solely for purposes of computing DNI, the distribution deduction, and amounts reportable by beneficiaries. The separate shares are not treated as separate trusts for rate and exemption purposes.

The various facts necessary to perform the relevant computations (trust net income, trust DNI, total "distributions" to various beneficiaries) can only be performed at the end of the trust's taxable year. Accordingly, the last day of the trust's taxable year is the date of reckoning for not only the trust but also for the beneficiaries receiving distributions during the year (and possibly the first 65 of the next taxable year). The distributees are (in effect) deemed to receive distributions and their allocable share of trust DNI at the end of the trust's taxable year.[62] If both the trust and the distributee report on a calendar year basis (which is almost always the case), the income of the trust attributed to a beneficiary for (say) the year 2012 is the income (etc.) that was realized by the trust in 2012.

The trustee (or, in the case of an estate, the executor) is required to file a return for the trust (Form 1041) *and* information returns for the distributees (see §6034A) by April 15 of the year following the taxable year of the trust (if the taxable year is a calendar year).

E. *The Conduit Principle*

The "character" of items included in DNI and reportable by distributees (as net capital gains, net tax exempt income, foreign-source income, etc.) is passed through from the trust to the distributees according to the "conduit" principle. Thus, if any net capital gains are included in DNI, the beneficiaries receiving the capital gains portion of the DNI will report net capital gains on their individual returns. Normally, any special "character" items that make up DNI will be allocated to the various distributees on a pro-rata basis, but, if the governing

---

62. In the unlikely event that the trust and distributee are on different taxable years, the distributee reports her allocable share of trust income in the distributee's taxable year in which the trust taxable year ends. See §§652(c) and 662(c). Thus, if a trust is on a calendar year and the distributee is on a fiscal year ending June 30, the trust income (for the trust's entire taxable year ending on 12/31/01) is reportable by the distributee in her taxable year ending on 6/30/02.

instrument allocates any character item to a specific distributee, that allocation will be respected for tax purposes.[63] See §§652(b) and 662(b).

Perhaps the most common type of character income that enters into DNI is interest from state and local government bonds that is exempt from income tax under §103. This kind of character income causes additional rules to apply that have not previously been mentioned. Of course, exempt interest, although included in trust accounting income, is not included in gross income for income tax purposes. At the same time, expenses allocable to such income cannot be deducted for income tax purposes. See §265(a)(1). Since trustee's fees are (normally) not specifically allocable to any particular income, they are pro-rated between included income and exempt interest (that is included in trust accounting income), and the portion allocated to exempt interest is disallowed.[64] The amount of net exempt interest (exempt interest reduced by the disallowed deduction amount) is added to DNI, pursuant to §643(a)(5). At this point, net tax exempt interest, being included in DNI, is eligible to be passed through to distributees. However, in order to prevent this tax-exempt item from being deductible to the trust (as a component of the distribution deduction), the distribution deduction is deceased by such net tax-exempt amount. See §§651(b) and 661(c).

Example: Assume that a trust is required to distribute "income" to B annually. In the year in question, the trust receives $80K of includible interest and $20K of exempt interest, and incurs trustee fees of $5K, of which $4K is deductible for income tax purposes ($5K × 80/100). Trust accounting income is $95K, and trust net income is $76K ($80K gross income less four-fifths of the trustee fees). DNI is $95K: $76K + $19K (the net tax exempt interest). B "reports" $95K (DNI and "distributions" are the same), but $19K is net tax-exempt interest, leaving $76K as net included income. The trust's distribution deduction is $76K ($95K – $21K), leaving trust taxable income of zero.

What if the trust provided that income could be paid to B or accumulated in the trustee's discretion, and the trustee (using the same facts as above) distributes $57K to B and accumulates $38K? The items constituting the DNI should be pro-rated between the distributed income (57/95 = 60%) and accumulated income (40%). In that case, the distribution deduction would be $45.6K [$57K – (.6 × $19K)], leaving trust taxable income of $30.4K (ignoring the exemption). B's distribution would be included in the amount of $45.6K. Total taxable income (ignoring the trust exemption amount) would be $76K.

---

63. Any "special allocation" of a character item, to be given income tax effect, must be *required* by the governing instrument, and must have an effect that is independent of tax consequences. See Reg. §1.652(b)-2.
64. See Reg. §1.643(d)-2(a)(2).

1. Assume a testamentary trust incurs the following during the taxable year: Interest and dividends received by the trust are $50K (assume that dividends are not a special "character" item); the trust realizes capital gains of $10K, which are allocable to corpus; and trustee's commissions of $2K are allocated all to income.

   a. Compute the taxable income of the trust and the amount (and character) of the amount reportable by B, assuming that the trust instrument requires that all of the trust income be distributed to B annually, with the trustee having the power to invade corpus for B's benefit in its discretion, and that the trustee distributes only the trust "income" to B.

   b. What result if, instead, the trustee distributes $70K to B?

   c. Same facts as (a), except the trustee has discretion to pay income to B or accumulate it, as well as the power to invade corpus, and in fact $30K is distributed to B out of the proceeds of the sale of securities that produced the capital gain of $10K.

   d. Same facts as (a), except $10K out of the $50K interest and dividends is tax-exempt interest under §103, and (accordingly) $400 out of the $2K commissions cannot be deducted by reason of §265(a).

   e. Same facts as (a), except that the trust terminates near the end of the taxable year, and that B receives the same "income amount" as in (a), and the remainder C receives $800K in cash and property.

2. a. For planning purposes, accumulations of ordinary income in a Subchapter J trust are considered to be generally undesirable. Why is this so? How can a trustee effectively accumulate income without running into this problem?

   b. How can the "65-day rule" of §663(b) be used to save income taxes?

   c. A beneficiary receiving distributions from a trust has to report income that is characterized as "unearned" income. What issue does that raise, and for whom?

   d. How can the concept of first- and second-tier beneficiaries be used for tax planning purposes?

   e. The §663(a)(1) rule for bequests of fixed sums of money or specific property, although available in theory, is less likely to come into play for trusts than for estates. Does a required annuity pay-out come within this rule? What about a direction that the beneficiary receive half the trust corpus upon reaching the age of 35? How can this rule be used in a trust context? When, if at all, would it be desired?

   f. Would maintaining a depreciation or depletion reserve be advantageous for income tax purposes?

   g. Assuming distributions during a year equal or exceed DNI, is there any income tax advantage in allocating administration expenses to corpus (rather than income), assuming such an allocation is allowed?

3. a. Trusts are required to pay estimated tax where a trust income tax liability is foreseeable. Under §643(g), the trustee can elect to treat any portion of the estimated tax payment as having been made by the beneficiary, in which case the amount of such tax payment shall be treated as a "distribution" to the beneficiary (potentially deductible to the trust and includible by the beneficiary); the deemed distributee will be able to apply the same amount as a credit against individual income tax liability.

    b. Under §643(e), multiple trusts created by a grantor and the grantor's spouse can be treated as a single trust by the IRS for rate and exemption purposes if they have substantially the same primary beneficiary or beneficiaries.

CHAPTER 8

GIFTS WITH RETAINED INTERESTS AND POWERS

This chapter is mainly about *inter vivos* transfers with retained interests and retained powers (other than the power to revoke, which was covered in §§3.3.A and 5.1). This chapter also covers split-interest charitable gift and estate transfers. The estate tax provisions scrutinized in this chapter are mainly §§2036, 2037, and 2038, which were briefly mentioned in §2.2.C and from time to time in Chapter 5 (mainly by way of the explanation of the derivation of §2039 from §2036(a)(1)). The gift tax aspects of retained-interest gifts (including an explanation of the actuarial tables) was briefly covered in §3.4.C.

This general topic has traditionally been considered earlier in the course and in more depth than is the case here. The enactment of §2702 in 1990 drastically rendered this topic into more of a specialist one, because §2702 virtually "prohibits" the making of such "traditional" retained-interest gifts as those with retained life estates, income interests, and reversions. Nevertheless, a few types of retained-interest gifts are still "permitted."

§8.1. Estate Tax §§2036-2038

The estate tax rules are considered first, because the significance of the gift tax rules (especially §2702) can best be grasped by how they combine with the estate tax rules. Here is found a careful examination of §§2036(a), 2037, and 2038(a)(1), and related provisions. Where these provisions "catch" an *inter vivos* transfer in their net, all (or a portion) of the estate tax value of the transferred property is included in the gross estate of the transferor. These provisions are densely packed with doctrine. Each phrase has a history and a "technical" meaning.

A. Overview

This material is an overview of §§2036-2038, beginning with a brief history, continuing with a list of the "elements" that these sections have in common, and concluding with prototypical examples that illustrate their application.

1. Brief History of §§2036-2038

Under an estate tax (not backed up by a gift tax) in which the gross estate is constituted only by property owned (or constructively) at death, an obvious form of avoidance would be the *inter vivos* transfer of a testamentary nature. Accordingly, the 1916 estate tax law contained a provision that included *inter vivos* transfers "intended to take effect in possession or enjoyment at or after [the transferor's] death." This provision, which was borrowed from similar state inheritance tax provisions, has since evolved into §§2036-2039. (Separate clauses in the 1916 estate tax caused inclusion of "transfers in contemplation of death" and of survivor interests in joint tenancies.) All of §§2036-2040 are based on a common theory: Where a decedent transferred property and retained certain significant interests or powers in the property, the property transferred warrants being included in the transferor's gross estate at its estate tax value.

The evolution of the 1916 provision into present §§2036(a), 2037, and 2038(a)(1) is mainly a story of Congress's reaction to Supreme Court decisions during the period 1930 to 1949. Since 1949, these provisions have changed little, and, doctrinal development has been relatively stagnant since the mid-1970s.

Although the 1916 Act provision referring to transfers intended to take effect at the transferor's death was somewhat vague, two early Supreme Court cases from the late 1920s construed the 1916 language to require that the transferor retain an interest in, or power over, the transferred property.[1] Also, "intended" was construed to refer to the objective operation of a transfer, rather than to the transferor's subjective intent. Stated crudely, a transfer was deemed to take effect at a transferor's death by reason of the expiration (at the transferor's death) of an interest or power retained by the transferor. That is, an *inter vivos* transfer has a testamentary character where the transferor has not divested himself of all incidents of ownership in the property. This basic idea was explicitly incorporated into §§2036-2038. However, these sections do not actually require *total* divesture of incidents of ownership. Hence, it is necessary to inquire into the precise reach of these sections.

In 1924, perhaps out of concern with state court interpretations of similar language in state inheritance taxes, Congress enacted what is now §2038(a)(2), which requires inclusion in the gross estate of *inter vivos* transfers where the transferor has the power at death to revoke, alter, or amend the transfer. Transfers that can be revoked, altered, or amended by a transferor are almost always *inter vivos* transfers in trust (or "declarations of trust"). Section 2038(a)(1), enacted in

---

1. *Shukert v. Allen*, 273 U.S. 545 (1927); *Reinecke v. Northern Trust Co.*, 278 U.S. 339 (1929).

1936 in response to two 1935 Supreme Court decisions,[2] added (1) the word "terminate," (2) the phrase "(in whatever capacity exercisable)," and (3) the phrase "(without regard to when or from what source the decedent acquired such power)."[3]

In 1930, the Supreme Court held (unexpectedly) that a transfer (in trust) with a reserved income interest in the transferor escaped inclusion under the 1916 "take effect at death" provision.[4] The 1930 national elections (in the wake of the economic collapse that had begun in 1929) moved Congress toward the left, and in 1931 the new Congress enacted the predecessor of §2036(a), which not only overturned the result of the case just mentioned, but added what is now §2036(a)(2) (referring to a retained power to affect beneficial enjoyment of the property or income).[5] A more considered version was produced in 1932, that (1) replaced "income" by "right to income" in subsection (a)(1), (2) added in subsection (a)(2) the phrase "either alone or in conjunction with any person," and (3) added "or for any period not ascertainable without reference to [the transferor's] death." Section 2036 has since not been changed in substance, except for the addition in 1978 of §2036(b) (referring to the retention of the right to vote transferred stock in a controlled corporation), which overturns the result of a 1972 Supreme Court case.[6] Recall that §2039, dealing with survivor annuities and survivorship benefits under employer plans, was a 1954 spin-off from §2036.[7]

After enactment of the predecessors of §§2036 and 2038, the "take effect at death language" of the 1916 Act continued, but was basically confined to situations where the transferor retained a reversionary interest in the transferred property (usually in trust). This language was construed expansively by the Roosevelt Court in a string of decisions[8] that prompted the 1949 Congress to finally replace the 1916 language by a more detailed provision that was in turn replaced in 1954 by what is now §2037.

The various statutory changes described above (and others) were made to be prospective only. *Cases and rulings on facts preceding the effective dates of these statutory changes should be approached with caution, as they are based on different statutory language (and interpretations thereof) than is presently in force.* "Old" irrevocable transfers (before 1954) should be examined with an eye to the possibility that some version of prior law applies to them. Nevertheless, in the interests

---

2. *Helvering v. Helmholz*, 296 U.S. 93 (1935) (power to terminate not a power to "revoke"); *White v. Poor*, 296 U.S. 98 (1935) (transferor acquired power by being appointed trustee by third parties).

3. This history is recounted in §5.1.

4. *May v. Heiner*, 281 U.S. 238 (1930).

5. This provision was enacted by way of Joint Resolution (by-passing committee procedures), and signed by President Hoover later in the same day (March 3, 1931) that the Supreme Court decided cases that re-affirmed *May v. Heiner*, supra note 4. *May v. Heiner* was later overruled by the Supreme Court itself in *Comm'r v. Estate of Church*, 335 U.S. 632 (1949).

6. *U.S. v. Byrum*, 408 U.S. 125 (1972). See §9.1.

7. See §5.3.C.

8. *Helvering v. Hallock*, 309 U.S. 106 (1940); *Comm'r v. Estate of Church*, 335 U.S. 632 (1949); *Estate of Spiegel v. Comm'r*, 335 U.S. 701 (1949).

of concision and clarity, prior law is generally ignored in this book except as is necessary to explain current law, and cases arising under prior law are presented or excerpted herein only where they are deemed relevant to current law.

2. *Elements Required for Inclusion Under §§2036-2038*

Application of any of §§2036-2038 to include an *inter vivos* transfer in the transferor's gross estate requires that *all* of the following conditions be satisfied:

1. The decedent must have made an *inter vivos* "transfer" of property;
2. The transfer must not have been for full and adequate consideration in money or money's worth;
3. The decedent must have possessed an interest or power of the type described in any of §§2036-2038;
4. Such interest or power must have been possessed by the decedent "at" death (however, the transfer or relinquishment of such interest or power within three years of death is ineffective, under §2035(a), to defeat the application of §§2036-2038);
5. Except in the case of §2038, the power or interest described in §§2036-2038 must have been "retained" by the decedent in connection with the transfer (i.e., held back in connection with the transfer); and,
6. Such interest or power must be "in" the transferred property itself.

The concepts of "*inter vivos* transfer" and "consideration" have been explored in their gift tax setting in Chapter 3. Material on these topics is included in this chapter only as it uniquely relates to the estate tax.

B. *The Interests and Powers that Trigger §§2036-2038*

The material below discusses the interests and powers that, if held by the transferor at death (etc.), cause any of §§2036-2038 to apply.

1. *Prototypical Situations*

The student might better grasp §§2036-2038 by being initially introduced to the "core" scenarios that are covered by these sections. The student should examine the "fit" of the relevant statutory language to the scenario presented. Additionally, the scenarios described below are considered to be "basic" and straightforward applications of the statutory provisions.

1. *Transfers where the decedent retained the "right to the income" or "the possession or enjoyment" of the transferred property for life (etc.). §2036(a)(1).* Thus:

(i) Arnold deeds a remainder interest in Blackacre to Camille, while retaining a legal life estate. The legal life estate entitles Arnold to possession or enjoyment of Blackacre. The entire value of Blackacre as of Arnold's death is included in Arnold's gross estate.

(ii) Arnold irrevocably transfers securities in trust, naming an independent trustee, income to Arnold for life, remainder to Camille on Arnold's death.

Arnold has "the right to the income" from the transferred property. The value of the *entire trust* as of Arnold's death is included in Arnold's gross estate.

2. Transfers where the decedent retained the power to affect the beneficial enjoyment of the income from the property. §2036(a)(2). Thus:

(i) Doris creates an irrevocable trust, *naming herself as trustee*, with the income to be paid to Emma or Emily in such amounts and proportions as the trustee decides *in its discretion* for a period of 30 years, remainder to Ferdinand. Doris dies before the 30-year period has expired. Doris (the transferor) has a discretionary power (as trustee) to alter the beneficial enjoyment of the income. (It is immaterial that Doris cannot distribute the income to herself.) This power is retained for a period "which does not in fact end before her death." The value of the entire trust as of Doris's death is included in her gross estate.

(ii) Gertrude creates an irrevocable trust, *naming herself as trustee*, with the income to be paid to Hilary or accumulated as the trustee decides *in its discretion*, and on Hillary's death remainder to Ivan. The retained power to accumulate income is a power to shift income away from Hillary to Ivan, since accumulated income is (unless the trust provides otherwise) added to corpus, which eventually passes to Ivan (or Ivan's successors). The value of the entire trust as of Gertrude's death is included in her gross estate, assuming Gertrude dies before Hillary. (If Hillary dies first, the trust terminates, and Gertrude's power lapses.)

Note that, in the examples above, the retained power to designate the enjoyment of the income causes the *entire property* to be included in the transferor's gross estate.

3. Transfers where the decedent retained a reversion worth more than 5 percent of the amount transferred <u>and</u> where possession or enjoyment of the property was contingent on surviving the decedent. §2037. Thus:

(i) Jason creates an irrevocable trust, naming a corporate trustee, income to Kevin for life, then reversion to Jason if living, but if Jason is not then living, remainder to Lennox. Section 2037 requires not only that the transferor retain at least a 5 percent reversionary interest, but also that "possession or enjoyment of the property can ... be obtained only by surviving the decedent." This second ("survivorship") requirement has been construed to mean something like "possession or enjoyment is conditioned (in some way) on the transferor's death." Here, Lennox cannot come into possession of his remainder interest unless the transferor (Jason) dies before Kevin.[9] The death of Jason is a "necessary" (if not "sufficient") condition for Lennox to obtain possession

---

9. These facts are essentially the same as those in *Helvering v. Hallock*, 309 U.S. 106 (1940), and are the same as in Reg. §20.2037-1(e), Ex. 3.

or enjoyment. Jason clearly has a reversion. The "5 percent test" is applied at the moment before Jason's death but without reference to the fact of Jason's actual death. At this testing moment, the value of the reversion is the value of the trust times the actuarial factor representing the chances that Jason would have outlived Kevin (if they had both enjoyed their life expectancies) *and* times the remainder factor for Jason's then age.[10] (In most cases, it's best to request the IRS to figure this out![11]) If Jason dies before Kevin, and if Jason's reversion is worth more than 5 percent at the moment just prior to Jason's death, the value of Lennox's remainder interest (as of Jason's death) is included in Jason's gross estate. Kevin's remaining income interest is not included under §2037, because that interest is not contingent on Jason's death. Although Jason had a reversion, it is not includible under §2033 (or §2037), because it expired at Jason's death. (If Kevin were to die before Jason, Jason will acquire the trust property in fee simple, and §2037 would cease to be relevant.)

(ii) Mort enters into an (irrevocable and nonamendable) arrangement with his employer that, upon Mort's death, a survivor benefit will be paid to Nakeesha, if Nakeesha survives Mort. The law of donative transfers provides that the absence of a beneficiary (a situation that would occur if Nakeesha does not survive Mort) results in a reversion to the transferor. Such a reversion is called an "implied" (as opposed to an "express") reversion. In this case (if Nakeesha predeceased Mort), the survivor benefit would be paid to Mort's estate. Clearly, Nakeesha has to survive Mort in order to take. Mort's estate (a continuation of Mort) has a reversion. If, at the time of Mort's death (but ignoring the time of his actual death) Mort had a greater than 5 percent chance of outliving Nakeesha, the entire survivor benefit is included in Mort's gross estate under §2037.[12]

The amount includible under §2037 is not the value of the reversion but rather the value of interests of which the possession or enjoyment can be obtained only by surviving the decedent. The word "only" is the basis of the so-called "alternate contingencies" exception: If the beneficiary *could have* obtained (but did not obtain) possession or enjoyment through the occurrence of a (not unreal) contingency other than the transferor's death, §2037 is avoided.[13] An example would be where a remainder could take in possession on the earlier to occur of the transferor's death or the expiration of 12 years from the date of transfer.[14]

---

10. See Reg. §20.2037-1(c)(3) & (4).

11. See *Rev. Rul.* 76-178, 1976-1 C.B. 273.

12. This hypothetical is virtually identical to that found in Reg. §20.2037-1(e) (Ex. 2), and is identical to that posed in *Rev. Rul.* 78-18, 1978-1 C.B. 289.

13. See Reg. §20.2037-1(b).

14. See Reg. §20.2037-1(e), Ex. 6. The exception pertains to what could have happened, not what actually happened. In the text hypothetical, it operates if the decedent dies before the 12-year period has expired (that is, the remainder *could have* come into possession as the result of the alternate contingency). If the remainder actually takes into possession before the decedent's

Along similar lines, the last sentence of §2037(b) provides that §2037 is avoided if possession or enjoyment could have been obtained through the exercise of an *inter vivos* general power of appointment that was exercisable at the time of the transferor's death. Although this exception appears to be simply an iteration of the application of the alternate-contingencies exception,[15] it was thought (when enacted) to pertain to the reversionary-interest concept, and indeed it is placed in §2037(b), which elaborates on the "5 percent reversionary interest" requirement. Specifically, this sentence was enacted in 1949 to overrule a 1945 Supreme Court decision that held (in effect) that a reversion existed at a transferor's death despite the possibility of its disfeasance by the exercise of a general power of appointment.[16] This statutory exception has become superfluous due to the enactment in 1954 of the "more than 5 percent" rule for reversions, because a reversion that can be cut off by the act of another party has negligible market value (and would be incapable of actuarial valuation). Indeed, the Service has ruled that the existence of even an *inter vivos* "special" power of appointment causes the reversion to be worth less than 5 percent of the value of the property.[17]

4. *Transferred interests that can be revoked, altered, amended, or terminated by the transferor.* §2038(a)(1). Thus:

> Ollie creates an irrevocable trust, naming a corporate trustee, income to Priscilla for life, remainder to such persons as Ollie appoints by written instrument delivered to the trustee during his lifetime, but in default of such appointment to Quentin. If Ollie dies before Priscilla, the (actuarial) value of the remainder interest (as of Ollie's death), which Ollie could have altered, is included in Ollie's gross estate.
>
> Section 2038 requires inclusion only of the interests to which the power pertains.

Note generally that the retained interest or power (often referred to as "the string") operates strictly as a triggering mechanism. *In no case is the amount includible under §§2036-2038 the value of the retained interest or power itself.*

Note also that "the property" (in cases involving trusts) to which the interest or power must pertain is the trust itself, not the cash or property initially transferred into the trust.

2. *Holding the String at Death*

Under §2038, the transferor must actually hold the power at death, *or* have held the power earlier but have relinquished it within three years of death. Section

---

death because of the expiration of the 12-year period, §2037 would not include that interest, because it is *already* in possession as of the transferor's death.

15. This rule seems to be redundant to the alternate-contingencies exception. However, the survivorship requirement (in which such exception is embedded) refers to acquiring possession or enjoyment "through ownership of such interest," a little-noticed phrase that would exclude the status of being an object of a power of appointment.

16. *Goldstone v. U.S.*, 325 U.S. 687, 692 (1945).

17. *Rev. Rul.* 79-117, 1979-1 C.B. 305.

2038(b) provides that inclusion cannot be defeated by "notice giving" or "delayed effect" provisions relating to the power.

Section 2037 requires that the transferor own a reversionary interest (worth more than 5 percent of the corpus) at death (the moment just prior to death).

Section 2036(a) requires that the transferor's interest or power must be retained "for his life, or for any period not ascertainable without reference to his death or for any period which does not in fact end before his death." The concept of a period "not ascertainable without reference to his death" would cover such a scenario as "until 90 days before the settlor's death."[18] The phrase "which does not in fact end before his death" would cover the situation where the transferor retains the income for 20 years, but dies in year 19.

3. *Assigning or Releasing the String Within Three Years of Death*

Under §2035(a), a transfer or release of an interest or power within three years of death will *not* be effective to avoid any of §§2036-2038.

The case below dealt with the predecessor of §2035(d), which currently states that "subsection (a) [of §2035] . . . shall not apply to any bona fide sale for an adequate and full consideration in money or money's worth." The then predecessor of §2035 included in the gross estate the value of "transfers in contemplation of death."

United States v. Allen

293 F.2d 916 (10th Cir. 1961)

Before MURRAH, Chief Judge, and BRATTON and BREITENSTEIN, Circuit Judges.
MURRAH, Chief Judge.

Maria Allen created an irrevocable trust in which she reserved the income for life, the remainder to her two children. When she was 78 years old, the trustor-decedent was advised that her retention of the life estate would result in the corpus being included in her gross estate. With her sanction, counsel began searching for a means of divestiture, and learned that decedent's son, Wharton, would consider purchasing his mother's interest. At that time, the actuarial value of the retained life estate was approximately $135,000 and the corpus was valued at some $900,000. Wharton agreed to pay $140,000 for the interest, believing that decedent's actual life span would be sufficient to return a profit to him. [The court below found that the transfer was in contemplation of death.]

Our narrow question is whether the corpus is removed from a decedent's gross estate by a transfer [in contemplation of death] at the value of the reserved life estate. Must the consideration be paid for the interest transferred, or for the interest which would otherwise be included in the gross estate?

---

18. See Reg. §20.2036-1(b)(1)(i).

In one sense, the answer comes quite simply — decedent owned no more than a life estate, could not transfer any part of the corpus, and received no more than the [value of the] interest transferred. It would thus seem to follow that the consideration was adequate.

It does not seem plausible, however, that Congress intended to allow such an easy avoidance of the taxable incidence befalling reserved life estates. This result would allow a taxpayer to reap the benefits of property for his lifetime and, in contemplation of death, sell only the interest entitling him to the income, thereby removing all of the property which he has enjoyed from his gross estate. It seems certain that in a situation like this, Congress meant the estate to include the corpus of the trust.

[Concurring opinion of Breitenstein, J., omitted.]

Is *Allen* still good law? The statute in effect for the transaction in *Allen* stated that a transfer (not for full consideration) in contemplation of death (later, within three years of death) was included in the gross estate. In 1981 the statute was changed so that the transfer itself was no longer to be included, but that the transfer (or release) of a retained interest or power within three years of death would not be effective to avoid §§2036-2038. The statute was slightly revised in 1997, so that current §2035(a) states that the gross estate shall include the full value of property even though the string was transferred or released within three years of death. The "consideration exception" does not state what the sale is "of." Also, the exception is located in a separate subsection, rather than (as in §§2036-2038) being found in a parenthetical expression immediately following the word "transfer." The subsection (d) exception is to "subsection (a)," which states the *result* of full inclusion, rather than to (a)(1), which refers to the "transfer" (or release) of the string. Indeed, the concept of full and adequate consideration for the release of a power makes no sense, because a power has no actuarial value. *Allen* has been a well-known case since it was decided, and, if *Allen* were no longer good law, §2035(a) would be easily avoided. Therefore, all things considered, it is reasonable to conclude that the consideration necessary, under §2035(d), to avoid any of §§2036-2038 must equal at least the value (at the time of "sale") of the interests that would have been includible under these sections in the absence of the sale.[19]

The "partial" consideration received in an *Allen*-type transaction would, under §2043(a), qualify as an offset (deduction) against the amount includible.

Section 2035(e) cryptically states that any distribution from a revocable trust (as described in §676) created by the decedent "shall be treated as a transfer made directly by the decedent." Prior to the enactment of this language in 1997, the IRS had argued that such a distribution operated not only to complete the transfer for gift tax purposes but also to relinquish the revocation power for estate tax purposes, triggering inclusion of the distributed property in the gross estate (and without the

---

19. *Allen* was cited with approval in *Estate of D'Ambrosio v. Comm'r*, 101 F.3d 370 (3d Cir.1996), *cert. denied*, 520 U.S. 1230 (1997), a case reaching a possibly incompatible result.

benefit of the gift tax annual exclusion). Section 2035(e) operates to foreclose this argument. Thus, the distribution is simply a gift transfer by the decedent within three years of death, which is not includible in the gross estate, but does not entail the release of any power. (Any net gift tax on such gift is, of course, included in the gross estate under §2035(b).)

4. Contingent Interests and Powers

Section 2038 requires that the transferor *actually hold* the power (to revoke, alter, amend, or terminate) at the transferor's death (really, the instant just prior to death). Thus, if the transferor's possession of a power is contingent on an event that has not occurred prior to the transferor's death, then §2038 does not apply.

In contrast, §2037 is all about contingencies. The transferor's reversionary interest is usually contingent. Section 2037(b)(2) states that a reversionary interest includes "a *possibility* that the property transferred by the decedent *may* return to him or his estate, or (2) *may be subject to a power of disposition by him.*"[20]

A contingent *power* of disposition over corpus has the same status as the possibility of obtaining corpus. It is stated in §2037(b) that such a contingent power is to be valued (under the 5 percent rule) as if it were a contingent interest.

The difference between §§2037 and 2038 can be illustrated by an irrevocable trust created by X, income to Y for life, then, if X is living at Y's death, to such of X's issue as X appoints by written instrument delivered to the trustee within six months of Y's death, but in default of such appointment to Z. If X predeceases Y, §2038 is avoided, because X never came into possession of the contingent power, but X's contingent power satisfies §2037 so long as (treating the power as if it were a reversionary interest) it is worth (at X's death) more than 5 percent of the trust.[21]

Contingent income interests and powers over income have been held to satisfy §2036(a).[22] An example is where A creates an irrevocable trust, income to B for life, then income to A for life (if A outlives B), remainder to C, and A predeceases B. In this case, the amount includible under §2036(a) is the value of the trust (at A's death) reduced by the value of B's outstanding income interest.[23]

An interest or power held by the transferor is not negated merely by the possibility that it could have lapsed, or have been cut off, by an event or by an act of another party.[24] However, such a possibility would diminish or destroy the value of a reversionary interest under §2037.

---

20. This sentence codifies the result of *Philadelphia-Fidelity Trust Co. v. Rothensies*, 324 U.S. 108 (1945).

21. See *Costin v. Cripe*, 235 F.2d 162 (7th Cir.1956) (property included, although the transferor could not appoint to himself).

22. See Reg. §20.2036-1(b)(3); *Estate of Farrel v. U.S.*, 553 F.2d 637 (Ct. Cl. 1977).

23. See Reg. §20.2036-1(b)(1)(ii). The regulation states that this result flows from the phrase "for any period not ascertainable without reference to [the transferor's] death." This analysis is puzzling. The transferor retained the "right" (to future enjoyment of the income) "for life."

24. See *Goldstone v. U.S.*, 325 U.S. 687 (1945).

5. *Relations Among §§2036-2038*

Sections 2036 and 2037 are mutually exclusive. Section 2036 covers transferor interests in, or powers over, *income* (or *current* possession or enjoyment), whereas §2037 covers situations where the *future* possession or enjoyment of *corpus* is conditioned on the decedent's death, and the possibility that the decedent might obtain income (or the power over income) in the future is expressly excluded from the term "reversionary interest" as defined in §2037(b).

An illustration of the disconnect between §§2036 and 2037 is an irrevocable trust created by D, income to E for life, with an annuity of $10K per year to D payable out of corpus, with the trust to terminate on the later to occur of D's death or E's death, remainder to F. Since the income is payable to a person other than the grantor, §2036(a)(1) does not apply. However, the right to corpus is a reversionary interest (that is probably worth more than 5 percent as of D's death, unless D is then at a very advanced age). The survivorship requirement is satisfied (and the alternate contingencies exception avoided) insofar as the value of both E's income interest and F's remainder interest is subject to shrinkage while D is alive.

There is some uncertainty in this type of case as to the amount includible, which is supposed to be the value of interests that are contingent on surviving the decedent. It has been held that the amount includible is the actuarial value of the grantor's corpus annuity (valued as of the moment of his death but ignoring the actual fact of death).[25] It has also been held that the entire corpus is included if there was (at the grantor's death) a greater than 5 percent chance that the grantor would have consumed the entire corpus.[26] Arguably, neither of these results is compatible with the language of §2037, which basically states that *if* the grantor retains a reversionary interest worth more than 5 percent, the entire interest that is contingent on surviving the decedent is includible.[27] In a trust of this sort, it is *possible* that the entire corpus could be devoured by corpus distributions if the grantor lived long enough.

Sections 2037 and 2038 are also mutually exclusive, as noted earlier, because §2037 (insofar as it covers powers at all) refers to contingent powers, whereas §2038 requires the power to be possessed by the decedent at death.

---

25. *Bankers Trust Co. v. Higgins*, 158 F.2d 957 (2d Cir.1947); *Estate of Klauber v. Comm'r*, 34 T.C. 968 (1960), *nonacq.*, 1964-2 C.B. 8.

26. *Estate of Valentine v. Comm'r*, 54 T.C. 200 (1970).

27. In *Spiegel v. Comm'r*, 335 U.S. 701, 707 (1949), dealing with the predecessor of §2037, the Court stated:

> The question is not how much is the value of a reservation, but whether after a trust transfer, considered by Congress to be a potentially dangerous tax evasion transaction, some present or contingent right or interest in the property still remains in the settlor so that full and complete title, possession or enjoyment does not absolutely pass to the beneficiaries until at or after the settlor's death.

Of course, statutory changes have made the value of the reversion relevant, but only as to whether §2037 is triggered.

Sections 2036(a)(2) and 2038 frequently overlap, because the power to designate current enjoyment or income is also the power to alter the enjoyment of such current interest.

If property (or an interest therein) is included in a person's gross estate under two or more Code provisions, the same amount is not counted more than once in the gross estate. The amount includible is the largest amount includible under any of the relevant sections. Thus, if a person has a retained power over the income of transferred property, the value of the unexpired income interest would be includible under §2038, but since §2036(a)(2) requires the *entire* trust to be included in such a case, that section, not §2038, ultimately controls.

QUICK QUESTION

Sally created a trust with $5M that provided income to her son Ted for life, remainder to her grandson Victor. Sally retained the power to invade the trust corpus for the benefit of Ted. Which one of the following statements is *FALSE*?

A. Sally has made a completed gift of the income interest only.
B. When Sally dies, the value of the trust corpus is included in her estate under §2038.
C. When Sally dies, the date of death FMV of the trust is included in her estate under §2036.
D. At Ted's death, there is a taxable termination, subjecting the trust to GST tax.

PROBLEMS, QUESTIONS, AND NOTES

1. a. In *Comm'r v. Estate of Holmes*, 326 U.S. 480 (1946), involving the pre-1936 version of §2038, X created a trust, naming himself as trustee, income to Y for 15 years, remainder to Y if living but if not to Y's issue, with X having the power to terminate the trust and pay the corpus to Y if living. The Court held that X's power to invade corpus was one to "alter": Although Y was both income beneficiary and primary remainder, a premature termination would have precluded the possible future enjoyment of the trust by Y's issue. This result is not controversial.

    b. In *Lober v. U.S.*, 346 U.S. 335 (1953), also involving the pre-1936 version of §2038, the facts were essentially the same as in *Holmes*, except that the remainder was "to Y or his estate." Although here the income beneficiary and the remainder were as identical as is legally possible, the Court again held that the grantor retained a power to "alter." Thus, the 1936 addition of the word "terminate" turned out to be superfluous, at least in this type of case.

c. Under the influence of *Lober*, a retained power of the grantor to accumulate income (without a power to invade corpus) is considered a power to alter beneficial enjoyment under §2036(a)(2), *even where the remainder is the same person (or such person's "estate") as the income beneficiary.*[28]

d. However, where a settlor/trustee has the power to invade corpus for the benefit of an income beneficiary (who is not identical to the remainder beneficiary), and thereby has the power to "alter" the remainder interest, it has been held that she does not have the power to alter or "terminate" the income interest, because the economic enjoyment of the income beneficiary can only be enlarged by the exercise of the power to invade corpus.[29] Therefore, the value of the outstanding income interest is not includible under §2038. In addition, on these facts there is no power to designate (i.e., change the identity of) the persons who shall enjoy the income. Therefore, §2036(a)(2) does not apply.[30]

2. a. How can a reversionary interest be worth zero for §2033 purposes but at the same time be worth something for purposes of the 5 percent test under §2037(a)(2)? The answer is that the valuation under §2033 takes account of the grantor's actual death. Thus, if the reversion lapses or is cut off at A's death, it is worth zero under §2033. But under §2037 the valuation is undertaken *at the moment just prior to A's actual death, disregarding the fact of such death.* See §2037(b) (second sentence); Reg. §20.2037-1(c)(3). Thus, if A creates an irrevocable trust, income to B for life, reversion to A if living, but if not to C, and A predeceases B, A's reversion is worth zero under §2033 but under §2037 it has positive value, because (at the moment just *before* A's death *and disregarding the fact A failed to outlive B*) A *could have* outlived B, and this possibility is capable of actuarial calculation. The 5 percent rule was added to weed out *de minimis* (accidental) reversions.

b. Although §2037 is something of a tough nut to crack (and has accumulated a vast amount of doctrine), it is also relatively unimportant in current practice. It is now fairly unusual to create an irrevocable trust with an express reversion. Such a trust is no longer effective to shift income for income tax purposes, if the grantor has a 5 percent reversion (or the grantor's spouse has a 5 percent remainder).[31] See §§672(e)(1) and 673. Accidental (implied) reversions arise where the grantor fails to convey away all interests in the property, but many accidental reversions will

---

28. See *Leopold v. U.S.*, 510 F.2d 617 (9th Cir.1974).

29. See also §2503(b)(1) (second sentence) (stating that the present-interest gift exclusion is not lost in such a scenario).

30. See *Walter v. U.S.*, 341 F.2d 182 (6th Cir.1965).

31. Under prior law, a reversion after ten years did not cause the trust income to be attributed to the grantor, and reversionary-interest trusts were common income-shifting devices.

flunk the more-than-5 percent requirement, and others will occur in the context of transfers that flunk the "survivorship" requirement. In situations where §2037 is a concern, reversions can be avoided by "tying up" all contingencies relating to interests in corpus. The most certain way of doing this is to provide a "gift over" (substitute gift) to a charity if all contingent remainders fail. The alternative of providing for a vested remainder, or even a gift over to a person who is not required to survive all prior estates, is frowned upon, because a remainder interest of this type is included in such person's probate and §2033 estates.[32]

3. Analyze the following irrevocable *inter vivos* transfers under §§2033, 2035, and 2036-2038:

   a. Allison in trust, naming herself as trustee, income to Bart or accumulated in the trustee's discretion until Bart reaches 30 (or dies before reaching 30), remainder to Bart or his estate (and Allison dies before Bart reaches 30).

   b. Craig in trust, naming himself as trustee, income to Darlene for life, remainder to Erich, with the trustee having the power to pay or distribute all or any of the corpus to Darlene in the trustee's sole discretion (and Craig dies before Darlene).

   c. Frankie in trust, naming an independent trustee, income to Guy for life, remainder to Helen if living, but if not reversion to Frankie (and Frankie dies before Guy). Does the answer depend on whether Helen is alive at Frankie's death?

   d. Inger in trust, naming an independent trustee, income to be accumulated during the life of Inger, remainder to the then living issue of Inger's mother. Inger dies at age 70 survived only by her nephew Jan (age 60).

   e. Karl in trust, naming an independent trustee, income to Linda for life, then to Mickey for life, and on Mickey's death remainder to Nigel, but if Mickey is not living at Linda's death then remainder to such persons as Karl designates by his will, and in default of such appointment to Nigel, and Karl dies before Linda. Does it matter if Mickey is still alive at Karl's death?

4. a. If the same series of transactions as in *Allen* had occurred after 1990, the retained income interest would be disregarded for gift tax purposes by reason of §2702. Thus, the gift of only a remainder interest in property (following an income interest) is treated as a gift of the entire property. The ultimate effect of §2702 will be dealt with in §8.2.

   b. A person who sells a retained (carved-out) income interest (as in *Allen*) would end up with ordinary income (as opposed to capital gains) and no basis offset whatsoever. Basically, the sales proceeds would be viewed as an acceleration of ordinary income.[33]

5. It is sometimes suggested that taxing retained-*interest* transfers at death creates unnecessary complications to the system, and that it would be better to tax transfers of this type only at the time of gift, disregarding retained interests. Such a rule is called an "easy-to-complete rule." Section 2702 indeed has the effect of taxing many retained-interest gifts in full at the time of transfer, but §§2036-2038 are still on the books. Below are arguments against an easy-to-complete rule.

   a. If simplification is the goal, it can be achieved just as easily by taxing all retained-interest transfers only at the date which is the earliest to occur of (a) the date the transferor no longer has such interest or (b) the date of the transferor's death. Such a rule is referred to as a "hard-to-complete rule."

   b. In a tax with a high exemption, and assuming that the exemption does not increase as fast as the general rate of appreciation in the economy, tax-payers systematically gain by an easy-to-complete rule. Additionally, death is a matter of public record, whereas gifts (which generally are not) can easily fly below the IRS radar screen.

   c. Taken to its extreme, an easy-to-complete rule would allow a person to declare a gift of the present value of her expected estate at the date of death. If such declaration were made at an early enough age, the value of such an early gift would fall within the exemption in virtually 100 percent of cases. (The present value of $100M after 80 years, at a 5 percent annual discount rate, is about $202K.)

   d. A hard-to-complete rule would benefit taxpayers in cases where the prop-erty (corpus) can come back to the taxpayer pursuant to a power to revoke, a reversion, a decision of a trustee, or a power of appointment lodged in another. An easy-to-complete rule would result in double taxation, because "recovered" gift property would also appear in the donor's §2033 estate. There is presently no mechanism to avoid or mitigate this type of double taxation, and any mechanism that might be devised to avoid double taxation would be complex and hard to apply.

   e. In a retained-income transfer, a hard-to-complete rule accurately values what is transferred from the donor to the transferee. Assume that A creates a trust with $1M, income to A for life, remainder to B, and assume that B can sell the remainder interest. Treating the gift amount as being $1M drastically overstates what B actually obtains at the date of gift. Treating this transfer only as a gift to B of the actuarial value of the remainder interest is problematic for three reasons. First, as explained in §3.4.C, actuarial valuation disregards changes in value of the underlying property between the date of gift and the date that B obtains possession. Correct valuation of a remainder interest in property assumes that the value of the

---

33. See *Comm'r v. P.G. Lake, Inc.*, 356 U.S. 260 (1958).

property at a fixed future date can be known, but (of course) such knowledge is unavailable. Second, in its reduction-to-present-value aspect, the use of actuarial tables, apart from possible inaccuracies, actually misconceives the transaction. It treats B as an investor by attributing the subsequent increase in B's remainder interest (that occurs solely with the passage of time) as if it were wholly a return on B's own investment, but in fact B has invested nothing, and this gain is due solely to the fact that A, by carving out and reserving the income from the same property, has created a situation in which value shifts from A's retained income interest to B's remainder interest solely on account of the passage of time.[34] That is, in this type of transaction, A has set up a transaction under which a series of automatic value transfers from A to B must necessarily occur with the passage of time. Third, use of actuarial values creates an opening for opportunistic behavior: If A's personal health situation (actual prospect of longevity) is subpar, the use of actuarial tables will understate the gift in present-value terms, and only short-lived donors will utilize this transaction if this particular legal rule is in force. A hard-to-complete rule taxes the transfer at exactly the value as received by B and as parted with by A. In the unlikely scenario where B sells her remainder interest, the amount of the sales proceeds can fix the gift from A to B.

f.   Under an accessions tax, retained-interest transfers do not create a design problem. Transferees simply include distributions in their tax bases as such distributions are received (as opposed to when an interest is acquired).

C. The Neutering of the Concept of a Taxable Retained Power

This material examines doctrine, mostly developed by the courts, that (in the main) has significantly diluted the concept of a "taxable" retained power that can trigger §§2036-2038.

1. Jointly-Held Powers

The general default rule at common law was that co-trustees must act unanimously. Where this is the case, a trustee has effective veto power over the acts of the other trustee(s). The trust instrument (or the law of a particular state) may hold otherwise, and say that the trustees may act by majority vote or that one trustee may make decisions as to certain matters.[35]

---

34. To use a simplified example, assume that A makes a gift of property worth $10K to A for two years, remainder to B. At a 5 percent annual discount rate, the present value of A's interest is $930 and the present value of B's interest is $9,070. After 1 year (at the same discount rate), the value of A's interest decreases by $450, and B's remainder interest increases by the same amount. At the end of the second year, the shift in value is $480. This analysis ignores the change in value of the underlying property.

35. See UTC §703(a).

Regardless of applicable trust law, a power of a grantor is not immunized from §§2036-2038 by reason of being held jointly by the transferor with one or more other persons.[36] That is the case (at least under §§2036(a)(2) and 2038) even where the co-holder of the power has an interest adverse to the exercise of the power in favor of the transferor,[37] and can block action by the transferor.[38] In contrast, §2037 would probably be defeated by an adverse-party co-holder of the power,[39] and possibly by a non-adverse party co-holder possessing a veto power.[40]

2. The Helmholz Doctrine

In *Helvering v. Helmholz*, 296 U.S. 93 (1935), the grantor of an irrevocable trust was also a beneficiary thereof, and the trust provided that all of the beneficiaries could get together to terminate the trust, at which time the corpus would be divvied up by the beneficiaries. The government argued that the grantor had retained the power to revoke in conjunction with other parties under the predecessor of §2038(a)(2), apparently on the theory that the beneficiaries could have agreed to re-vest the property in the grantor. The majority opinion on this point is confused, but the safest reading of the case is that it held that a power to terminate was not the same as a power to revoke, alter, or amend. The Court then observed:

> The general rule [of state law] is that all parties in interest may terminate the trust. The clause in question added nothing to the rights which the law conferred.[41] Congress cannot tax as a transfer intended to take effect in possession or enjoyment at the death of the settlor a trust created in a state whose law permits all the beneficiaries to terminate the trust.

In the companion case of *White v. Poor*, 296 U.S. 98 (1935), the grantor created a trust that, *inter alia*, gave the trustee the power to terminate the trust and re-vest the property in the grantor. The grantor was not the original trustee, but was later appointed trustee. The Court held that the trust was not includible,

---

36. Sections 2036a(a)(2) and 2038 include the phrase "either alone or in conjunction with any person."

37. In *Helvering v. City Bank Farmers Trust Co.*, 296 U.S. 85 (1935), the Supreme Court (by a 5-to-4 margin) construed §2038(a)(2) as applying even where the co-holders of the power did have an adverse interest. Indeed, it has been held that a mere veto power over the decisions of others is considered a power that is within the scope of §§2036(a)(2) and 2038. E.g., *Ducharme v. Comm'r*, 164 F.2d 959 (6th Cir.1947); *Rev. Rul.* 70-513, 1970-2 C.B. 194.

38. See *Estate of Yawkey v. Comm'r*, 12 T.C. 1164 (1949).

39. See *Reinecke v. Northern Trust Co.*, 278 U.S. 339 (1929) (under the 1916 "take effect at death" provision, which was the predecessor of §2037, an adverse party co-holder of a retained power defeated inclusion in the gross estate).

40. See *Estate of Klauber v. Comm'r*, 34 T.C. 968 (1960) (*nonacq.*) (the court assuming *arguendo* that any co-holder would defeat §2037).

41. Both the statement of the state law rule and its application to the facts of *Helmholz* were somewhat ambivalent. The rule is that all parties in interest can, if the grantor consents, terminate the trust. See UTC §411(a). In *Helmholz*, the power was not given to all beneficiaries, nor was it given to the grantor as such.

because the grantor did not reserve the power in herself, even though the statute did not require any such reservation or retention.

Both holdings are questionable as a matter of statutory interpretation, but these interpretations were made in the shadow of a constitutional (Due Process) objection; namely, that both transfers were wholly complete, without any reservation of a power, before the effective date of the predecessor of §2038(a)(2). In fact, both decisions held unanimously that a construction in favor of includibility would have resulted in an unconstitutional application of the statute to the facts.

The enactment of the predecessor of §2038(a)(1) in 1936 added the word "terminate," which could have been (but was not) construed to overturn the result of *Helmholz*, since the power in *Helmholz* was a power to terminate, whereas that in *White v. Poor* was a power to revoke (re-vest in the grantor). The same 1936 Act also added the phrase "(without regard to when or from what source the decedent acquired such power)," which was clearly meant to overturn the result of *White v. Poor*, but could also be viewed (by way of the phrase "or from what source") as overturning *Helmholz* as well.

Despite this confusion, current Reg. §20.2038-1(a)(2) states that §2038 does not apply "if the decedent's power could be exercised only with the consent of all parties having an interest (vested or contingent) in the transferred property, and if the power adds nothing to the rights of the parties under local law." *Helmholz* is no longer considered to stand for the proposition that a power must be expressly "reserved" for it to fall within §2038(a)(1).[42] Therefore, the legacy of *Helmholz* probably boils down to the proposition that an irrevocable trust will not be subject to §2038 solely because a state law procedure exists to terminate or modify the trust that involves the grantor's participation together with that of all other interested parties. A holding to the contrary would mean that no *inter vivos* trust could avoid §2038 (unless it expressly, and effectively, opted out of all such procedures), a result that could not have been intended by Congress.[43]

3. Vicarious Powers

An issue is whether the grantor of an *inter vivos* trust can avoid the "powers" provisions of §§2036-2038 by naming another party as trustee, where it is expected

---

42. Section 2038(a)(2), the provision at issue in the cases, contains no effective date for the transfer, presumably because the transfer itself would have been incomplete when made (where the power to revoke, alter, or amend was reserved). Note that §2036(a)(1), enacted in 1936 to overturn the results of one or both of these cases, is only effective for transfers made after June 22, 1936. Hence, the Due Process issue that existed in the two cases no longer exists as far as §2036(a)(1) is concerned.

43. A problem could arise under the regulation if there is a state law procedure or mechanism that requires the participation of the grantor and allows termination or modification of dispositive provisions without participation of *all* interested parties. Under §§412, 415, and 416 of the UTC, a court can modify the terms of the trust for various specified reasons, but §410(b) states that any such proceeding is to be commenced by a beneficiary or trustee. Thus, the grantor (as grantor) is not an interested party in these types of proceedings, whereas the grantor is a necessary party to the "consent-termination" proceeding referred to in Reg. §20.2038-1(a)(2). Thus, the UTC appears to avoid non-compliance with the regulation. The larger moral is that state law reform efforts cannot ignore federal transfer tax doctrine.

that the other party will be compliant with the grantor's wishes in exercising a dispositive power over income and/or corpus.

It has long been held that another trustee's powers will not be attributed to the grantor just because the trustee is a non-adverse party, or even the grantor's spouse, child, or friend.[44] Nevertheless, it has been stated in dictum that a trustee's powers will be attributed to a grantor who in fact has dominated and controlled the trustee.[45] And it appears to be settled that the trustee's powers will be attributed to the grantor if the grantor can fire the trustee at will *and* appoint herself as successor trustee. Regs. §§20.2036-1(b)(3) and 20.2038-1(a). The case below involved the "gray area" where the grantor could fire the trustee, but could not appoint himself as successor trustee.

Estate of Wall v. Commissioner

101 T.C. 300 (1993)

NIMS, *Judge*: The single issue for decision is whether property held by three irrevocable inter vivos trusts created by the decedent, Helen S. Wall (Mrs. Wall), is includable in her gross estate under §2036(a)(2) or §2038(a)(1) because in creating the trusts Mrs. Wall reserved the right to remove the sole trustee, a corporation, and appoint a successor corporate trustee.

Rev. Rul. 79-353, 1979-2 C.B. 325, addresses the precise question presented here. *Rev. Rul. 79-353*, first notes that the courts have held that the reservation by the settlor of the power to substitute himself as trustee is equivalent to reservation by him of the trustee's powers. *Mathey v. U.S.*, 491 F.2d 481 (3d Cir.1974). However, *Rev. Rul. 79-353* next holds that "Thus, reservation by the settlor of the power to remove the trustee at will and appoint another trustee is equivalent to reservation of the trustee's powers." The foregoing conclusion disregards the fact that the discussion which preceded it dealt exclusively with a settlor's reserved power to appoint himself. The underlying assumption of *Rev. Rul. 79-353* is that even a corporate trustee will be compelled to follow the bidding of a settlor who has the power to remove the trustee; otherwise the settlor will be able to find another corporate trustee which will act as the settlor wishes. In other words, says respondent, under these circumstances the settlor has the *de facto* power to exercise the powers vested in the trustee.

Under established principles of the law governing trusts, a trustee would violate its fiduciary duty if it acquiesced in the wishes of the settlor by taking action that the trustee would not otherwise take regarding the beneficial enjoyment of

---

44. See *Comm'r v. Irving Trust Co.*, 147 F.2d 946 (2d Cir.1945) (compliant trustee); *Estate of Ballard v. Comm'r*, 47 B.T.A. 784 (1942), *aff'd*, 138 F.2d 512 (2d Cir.1943) (grantor's wife was trustee); *Estate of Sherman v. Comm'r*, 9 T.C. 594 (1947) (reviewed) (*nonacq.* on other issues) (related party).

45. See *Estate of Klauber v. Comm'r*, 34 T.C. 968, 973 (1960) (reviewed) (§2037).

any interest in the trust, or agreed with the settlor, prior to appointment, as to how fiduciary powers should be exercised over the distribution of income and principal. The trustee has a duty to administer the trust in the sole interest of the beneficiary, to act impartially if there are multiple beneficiaries, and to exercise powers exclusively for the benefit of the beneficiaries. See, e.g., Bogert, Law of Trusts and Trustees, sec. 543, at 217 (2d ed. 1993) ("Perhaps the most fundamental duty of a trustee is that he must display throughout the administration of the trust complete loyalty to the interests of the beneficiary and must exclude all selfish interest and all consideration of the interests of third persons.").

In irrevocable trusts such as those under scrutiny, the trustee is accountable only to the beneficiaries, not to the settlor, and any right of action for breach of fiduciary duty lies in the beneficiaries, not in the settlor. The trustee's duty of sole fidelity to the beneficiary remains the same regardless of whether or not distributions are discretionary and whether or not limited by a standard such as one related to health, education, support in reasonable comfort, and the like. In the absence of some compelling reason to do so, which respondent has not shown, we are not inclined to infer any kind of fraudulent side agreement between Mrs. Wall and First Wisconsin as to how the administration of these trusts would be manipulated by Mrs. Wall.

We hold that Mrs. Wall did not retain such an ascertainable and enforceable power to affect the beneficial enjoyment of the trust property.

In *Rev. Rul.* 95-58, 1955-2 C.B. 191, the IRS revoked *Rev. Rul.* 79-353.

In *Estate of Farrel v. U.S.*, 553 F.2d 637 (Ct. Cl. 1977), the grantor of a trust containing a discretionary power over income did not possess the power to remove the trustees but did possess the power to appoint herself trustee in case a vacancy occurred for any reason. The court held that the "contingent" power over the income possessed by the grantor fell within §2036(a)(2), relying on this passage from Reg. §20.2036-1(b)(3):

> With respect to such a power, it is immaterial whether the exercise of the power was subject to a contingency beyond the decedent's control which did not occur before his death (e.g., the death of another person during the decedent's lifetime).

Section 2038 did not apply because the power was not actually possessed at death.

4. *Powers of Independent Significance*

The notion of "power of independent significance" (a term, by the way, that has not been used in any estate tax case, regulation, or ruling) is a "power" held by the transferor that relates to some activity "outside" of the trust in question but which indirectly, or "incidentally," can affect the beneficial enjoyment of the trust. (The term echoes the wills and estates "doctrine of acts of independent significance," which holds that an act is not a testamentary act — that would be invalid for lacking the formalities of will execution — if it can be explained as having significance apart from controlling the devolution of property after the actor's death.)

Estate of Tully v. United States

528 F.2d 1401 (Ct. Cl. 1976)

Before DURFEE, Senior Judge, and DAVIS and KUNZIG, Judges.
KUNZIG, Judge.

Before his death, Tully was employed by Tully and DiNapoli, Inc. (T&D), a [corporation the stock of which was] owned 50% by decedent and 50% by DiNapoli. On July 1, 1959, Tully, DiNapoli, and T&D entered into a contract whereby T&D promised to pay death benefits to the Tully and DiNapoli widows. On March 7, 1964, Tully died. T&D paid his widow the $104,000 called for in the contract.

Tully did transfer an interest in the death benefits to his wife by executing the 1959 contract, [which] looked to Tully's past and future services to T&D for consideration. Tully in substance, if not in form, made a gift of a part of his future earnings to his wife. However, Tully did not keep a power to "alter, amend, revoke or terminate" the death benefit transfer. There was no express reservation of such power in either the 1959 or 1963 contracts and no indication in the record of any other express agreements in which Tully obtained a §2038(a)(1) power.

[The court first dealt with the argument that Tully's 50% stock ownership of T&D gave him unfettered power to change the death benefit plan to suit his own tastes. This argument is defeated by the Supreme Court decision in *U.S. v. Byrum*, 408 U.S. 125 (1971), which held that shareholder control — which mainly resides in the ability to elect the Board of Directors (which in turn would decide dividend policy) — was not a power to alter beneficial enjoyment of a trust that held the corporate stock.]

Moreover, the death benefits are not includible in Tully's gross estate despite the fact that Tully might have altered, amended, revoked, or terminated them in conjunction with T&D and DiNapoli. A power expressly exercisable in conjunction with others falls within §2038, but "power" as used in this section does not extend to powers of persuasion. If §2038(a)(1) reached the possibility that Tully might convince T&D and DiNapoli to change the death benefit plan, it would apply to speculative powers. In addition, if §2038 applies to situations where an employee might convince an employer to change a death benefit, it would sweep all employee death benefit plans into the gross estates of employees. We find that Congress did not intend the "in conjunction" language of §2038 to extend to the mere possibility of bilateral contract modification.

The death benefits here were to be paid based on decedent's annual salary. From this, defendant reasons that up until the time of his death, Tully could have accepted lesser compensation or terminated his employment in order to alter or revoke the death benefits. In practical terms, we reject this possibility. This is not a factor which rises to the level of a §2038(a)(1) "power." An employee might accept lesser compensation or terminate his employment for a myriad of reasons, but to conclude that a motive for such action would be the death benefit plan itself is not only speculative but ridiculous.

Finally, it might be argued that Tully could have divorced his wife to terminate her interest in the death benefits, but again such an argument reduces the term "power" to the speculative realm. A man might divorce his wife, but to assume that he would fight through an entire divorce process merely to alter employee death benefits approaches the absurd.

The *Byrum* case, mentioned in *Tully*, might itself be cited as an example of the power-of-independent-significance doctrine. In *Byrum* the grantor's retained power to vote stock that was transferred to the trust entailed responsibilities other than the control, for its own sake, over the flow of dividends to the trust as a means to shift enjoyment between income and remainder beneficiaries.

Other authorities can be said to fall within this doctrine. An irrevocable trust naming after-born children as income beneficiaries involves a retained "power" to alter beneficial enjoyment through the grantor's ability to produce or adopt more children, but in Rev. Rul. 80-255, 1980-2 C.B. 272, the Service held that §2036(a)(2) did not apply in such a case, on the ground that the decision to have children was an act of independent significance. And, in Rev. Rul. 75-415, 1975-2 C.B. 374, a power to terminate one's college education was disregarded in a gift tax setting for the same reason.

5. Administrative Powers

It would seem that a trust grantor could name herself as trustee without running afoul of §§2036(a)(2) and 2038 of the estate tax, so long as she has not retained any power to accumulate or sprinkle income or invade corpus. In the case set forth below, however, the government argued that the grantor retained the equivalent of powers to accumulate income and invade corpus due to the administrative powers he held as trustee. "Administrative" (as opposed to "dispositive") powers of a trustee have to do with the management of the trust. The particular powers involved in this case were the power to select investments and the power to allocate receipts and disbursements between "income" and "principal" (known as the "trust accounting power"). This issue arises only in cases where the trustee is directed to pay "income" to one or more beneficiaries, and where the income beneficiaries are different from remainder beneficiaries. Income beneficiaries desire that net income be maximized, and remainder beneficiaries prefer that net economic return inure to corpus. "Income" (really, net income) is determined under the law of trusts, not the federal income tax law or principles of business accounting. Under traditional trust accounting law, "income" includes interest and dividends, but net capital gains (and unrealized appreciation and depreciation) inure to corpus. Income beneficiaries prefer investments in bonds. Corpus beneficiaries prefer investments in growth stocks that don't pay dividends. There are fiduciary-law issues as to how to allocate costs, such as trustee fees and taxes, and whether income from wasting assets should be charged with (reduced by) depreciation or depletion.

Old Colony Trust Co. v. United States

423 F.2d 601 (1st Cir.1970)

Before ALDRICH, Chief Judge, and McENTEE and COFFIN, Circuit Judges.
ALDRICH, Chief Judge.

The sole question in this case is whether the estate of a settlor of an *inter vivos* trust, who was a trustee until the date of his death, is to be charged with the value of the [trust] by virtue of reserved powers. Article 7 [of the trust] gave broad administrative powers to the trustees, with discretion to acquire investments not normally held by trustees, and the right to determine what was to be charged or credited to income or principal. It further provided that all decisions made by the trustees in good faith should be conclusive on all parties, and stated that the trustees were empowered, "generally to do all things in relation to the Trust Fund which the Donor could do if living and this Trust had not been executed." The government claims that these [clauses] meant that the settlor-trustee had "the right to designate the persons who shall possess or enjoy the [trust] property or the income therefrom" within §2036(a)(2) and possessed a power "to alter or terminate" within §2038(a)(1).

If *State Street Trust Co. v. U.S.*, 263 F.2d 635 (1st Cir.1959), was correctly decided, the government must prevail. There this court held against the taxpayer because broad powers similar to those in Article 7 meant that the trustees "could very substantially shift the economic benefits of the trusts between the life tenants and the remaindermen." We accept the taxpayer's invitation to reconsider this ruling.

Trustee powers given for the administration of the trust must be equitably exercised for the benefit of the trust as a whole. Restatement Trusts 2d §§183 & 232. With all respect to the majority of the then court, we find it difficult to see how a power can be subject to control by the court, and exercisable only in what the trustee fairly concludes is in the interests of the trust and its beneficiaries as a whole, and at the same time be an ownership power.

The government's position, to be sound, must be that the trustee's powers are beyond the court's control. Under Massachusetts law, however, no amount of administrative discretion prevents judicial supervision of the trustee. Thus in *Appeal of Davis*, 67 N.E. 604 (Mass. 1903), a trustee was given "full power to make investments in such manner as to them shall seem expedient, it being my intention to give my trustees the same dominion and control over said trust property as I now have." In spite of this language, and in spite of their good faith, the court charged the trustees for failing sufficiently to diversify their portfolio. We do not believe that trustee powers are to be more broadly construed for tax purposes than the probate court would construe them for administrative purposes. We hold that no aggregation of purely administrative powers can meet the government's amorphous test of "sufficient dominion and control" so as to be equated with ownership.

[The court went on, however, to find that the settlor-trustee had retained dispositive powers under other provisions of the trust instrument which caused inclusion of the trust under §§2036(a)(2) and 2038.]

The rule of *Old Colony Trust Co.*, supra, that retained administrative powers do not rise to the level of the type of powers contemplated by §§2036(a)(2) and 2038, was essentially approved by the Supreme Court in *U.S. v. Byrum*, 408 U.S. 125 (1972), discussed below.

As to the law of trusts, a trustee generally has a duty of impartiality among beneficiaries and classes of beneficiaries (such as income beneficiaries and remainder beneficiaries). Any discretion given to the trustee concerning managing the trust would be subject to this overriding duty. See UTC §803. (The trust instrument can expressly override and modify this duty, and direct or permit that certain beneficiaries be favored.) In addition to the duty of impartiality, the trustee must administer the trust in good faith and with a view towards the interests of the beneficiaries. See UTC §801.

Until the 1990s, a trustee subject to a duty of impartiality between income beneficiaries and remainders was likely to choose a "balanced" portfolio consisting of fixed-income and appreciating investments. This strategy typically produced an "income" yield in the 3-4 percent range, with any net appreciation inuring to the remainder interest. But this strategy also constrained investment choice, and both income and remainder beneficiaries were unhappy.

In the 1990s, a reform movement sought to free trustees from rigid investment constraints by moving towards a "modern portfolio theory" model, in which the controlling idea is "total economic return," which views as unsound the distinction between traditional "income" (interest, dividends, etc.) and accretions to corpus (net realized gains and net appreciation). These efforts bore fruit in the Restatement Prudent Investor Rule (1992), its Uniform Trust Code counterpart, and the 1997 revision of the Uniform Principal and Income Act. Revisions of state trust accounting law sympathetic to this trend can follow one of two routes. One is to deem annuity (fixed dollar payouts) and unitrust interests (payouts equal to a fixed percentage of corpus valued annually) to be "income" interests. Some states even allow a trustee to convert an existing "income" trust to a 3-5 percent unitrust. Annuity and unitrust interests effectively remove trustee discretion to shift beneficial enjoyment through the exercise of administrative powers. The other path, taken by the revised Uniform Principal and Income Act, is to allow trustees to allocate principal amounts to "income" in appropriate circumstances and amounts so as to equitably balance the interests of income and remainder beneficiaries.

6. *The Power to Control Business-Entity Distributions*

Suppose A makes a gift of SmallCorp stock to B, with B being forbidden to assign the stock during B's lifetime, with A having the power (through control of SmallCorp) to control the flow of dividends and/or to liquidate the corporation. Oddly, the government never claimed that such a gift (assuming A died before B) was includible in A's gross estate under §2036(a)(2) or §2038.[46]

---

46. The government had litigated similar cases where the gift tax annual exclusion was at issue. See §3.5.B.

In *U.S. v. Byrum*, 408 U.S. 125 (1972), the decedent owned more than 50 percent of the stock in a family corporation and transferred some of the stock to an irrevocable trust, naming a corporate trustee, with income beneficiaries and remainders. The decedent retained the voting rights in the stock, and these voting rights, when combined with his voting rights in nontransferred stock, allowed the transferor to control the flow of dividends into the trust. The trust was locked into the stock as its sole investment, as the trustee was prohibited from selling it. The government argued for the inclusion of the trust in the gross estate under both §2036(a)(1) (on the theory that retained voting rights were retained "enjoyment") and under §2036(a)(2) (on the theory that the decedent's power to control the flow of dividends amounted to a retained power to accumulate income for the benefit of the remainder). The Court decided in favor of the taxpayer, with a scathing dissent by Justice White.

The majority opinion on the §2036(a)(2) issue was based on the notion that the decedent's power was an "administrative power" on account of the fact that it related to trust investments, and then stated that administrative powers lay outside of §§2036(a)(2) and 2038, relying on a very early case (under a different statutory provision)[47] that did not really come to grips with the issue,[48] followed by the unsupported (and dubious) claim that estate planners had relied continuously on that case.[49] Against the argument that the decedent effectively had retained the power to accumulate the trust income, the Court majority said that such power was constrained by a general fiduciary duty under corporate law. However, such a duty is as general as that which bounds the dispositive discretion of a trustee. The better argument would be that the Board of Directors, not the controlling shareholder, has control over dividend policy, and the Board would set dividend policy by considering the welfare of the corporation rather than according to the beneficial enjoyment of the trust.

As to the §2036(a)(1) issue, the Court held that voting rights did not rise to the level of "possession or enjoyment," which connotes economic benefits.

In response to *Byrum*, Congress enacted §2036(b) in 1976, and amended it in 1978. Section 2036(b) overrides only the §2036(a)(1) result of *Byrum* in cases where the decedent, immediately after the transfer and during the three-year period ending on the decedent's death (but applying the stock attribution rules of §318), had the right to vote 20 percent of the voting power. This change is narrow in scope, and leaves the §2036(a)(2) holding of *Byrum* intact.

---

47. The governing statute was the "intended to take effect at death" language of the 1916 Act, which was then construed to require a power to revoke or a retained reversion in the settlor.

48. *Reinecke v. Northern Trust Co.*, 278 U.S. 339 (1929). The issue of administrative powers was a minor issue in this case, and the Court brushed it aside with the observation that a trust is not included in the settlor's estate merely because the settlor is trustee.

49. In fact, the government had won the trial court decision in the *State Street Trust* case, 160 F. Supp. 877 (D. Mass.), on March 19, 1958, nine months before the *Byrum* trust was created. After *State Street Trust* was affirmed (in 1959), Byrum could have surrendered his voting rights in the transferred stock. The estate planning community took *State Street Trust* very seriously, and altered language in trusts to take it into account. *Old Colony Trust*, supra, did not overrule *State Street Trust* until the *Byrum* litigation was well under way.

7. *Dispositive Powers Limited by Standards*

Here consideration is given to the situation involving an irrevocable trust created by the grantor *naming herself trustee or co-trustee*, with income or corpus to be distributed to or among one or more beneficiaries for their "support," "maintenance," "comfort," or other "standard" as determined by the trustee. Here the grantor has a "dispositive" (distributive) power over income or corpus, and the issue is whether this constitutes a right to designate beneficial enjoyment under §2036(a)(2) or a power to "alter" under §2038.

United States v. Powell

307 F.2d 821 (10th Cir.1962)

Before PHILLIPS, PICKETT and LEWIS, Circuit Judges.
PHILLIPS, Circuit Judge.
On June 4, 1932, Leonidas Powell created an irrevocable living trust. The trust instrument designated Powell and the Fourth National Bank in Wichita as cotrustees. The trust instrument provides, in part, as follows:

Fifth: If, at any time during the continuance of this trust, it is necessary or advisable to use some portion of the principal for the maintenance, welfare, comfort or happiness of the Grantor's wife or daughters, or for the education of Grantor's said daughters, the Trustee is hereby authorized and empowered to use so much of the principal as in the discretion of the Trustee is necessary or advisable to be used to meet such conditions, and provided that the Trustee shall deem that the purpose for which the payments are to be made, justifies the reduction in the principal of the trust properties.

The taxpayers called five witnesses. In its findings of fact the court, in part, found:

> 11. Paragraph Fifth of the trust was intended by the settlor to mean only that distributions might be made to his wife and two daughters from the corpus of the trust if, but only if, such use of the corpus were required to maintain them in the conservative mode of living to which they had been accustomed during his lifetime, and that as used by Mr. Powell the word "happiness" in the phrase "maintenance, welfare, comfort or happiness" was intended to mean, and must be equated with, basic maintenance and welfare, not with "pleasure" or subjective "delight."

The court concluded that the power to invade the corpus did not reserve to the settlor the power to "alter, amend, revoke, or terminate" the trust within the meaning of §2038.

There is nothing in the context in which the term "happiness" is found, or in the instrument as a whole, that indicates an intent that it should be given a broader connotation than its usual and ordinary meaning. The usual and ordinary meaning of "happiness" is "a state of well-being characterized by relative permanence." Webster's New International Dictionary. It is synonymous with "comfort" or "welfare." Macmillan's Modern Dictionary. In its ordinary sense "happiness" has the characteristic of permanence or endurance, as distinguished from pleasure, which is transitory.

Of course, the exercise of discretion to invade the corpus with liberality and in accordance with the wishes of a beneficiary is not a power restricted by a fixed standard. Here, on the contrary, the trust instrument indicated that the power should be exercised with restraint and only when the purpose justified a reduction of the corpus. In the following cases the quoted language was held to provide an ascertainable and judicially enforceable standard [for invading principal]: *Ithaca Trust Co. v. U.S.*, 279 U.S. 151 ("necessary to suitably maintain her in as much comfort as she now enjoys"); *Hartford-Connecticut Trust Co. v. Eaton*, 36 F.2d 710 (2d Cir.) ("which the trustee may deem necessary or advisable for her comfortable maintenance and support"); *Berry v. Kuhl*, 174 F.2d 565 (7th Cir.) (for "treatment, support or maintenance"); *Lincoln Rochester Trust Co. v. Comm'r*, 181 F.2d 424 (2d Cir.) ("as may be necessary for her proper care, support and maintenance"); *Blodget v. Delaney*, 201 F.2d 589 (1st Cir.) ("any amount in their discretion for her comfort and welfare"); *Estate of Frew v. Comm'r*, 8 T.C. 1240 ("in the trustees' sole discretion, for the proper maintenance and support of said beneficiary"); *Estate of Wetherill v. Comm'r*, 4 T.C. 678 (for "care, maintenance and support"); *Estate of Elmer v. Comm'r*, 6 T.C. 944 (for "comfortable support").

We conclude that the provisions in the trust instrument giving the trustees power to use the corpus "for the maintenance, welfare, comfort or happiness" of the beneficiaries and for the "education" of the daughters, established an ascertainable, external, and judicially enforceable standard [subject to the] supervision and control of the courts of Kansas in the exercise of their equity powers. Hence, the authority given the trustees to invade the corpus did not give the settlor the power to alter the trust within the meaning of §2038.

In *Powell*, the court was simply applying an established doctrine that a grantor/trustee's dispositive power limited by an ascertainable standard does not fall within §2036(a)(2) or §2038. The doctrine was initiated in the case of *Jennings v. Smith*, 161 F.2d 74 (2d Cir.1947). The rationale of the doctrine is basically that the existence of the standards renders the identity of the trustee irrelevant. The beneficiaries can enforce the standards, which limits the trustee's discretion.

However, the reach of the doctrine cannot be stated with any precision, and one must consult the cases, which are numerous (and include some cases not involving §§2036-2038). Additional cases finding a limited and ascertainable standard include: *Leopold v. U.S.*, 510 F.2d 617 (9th Cir.1975) (support, education, maintenance, and general welfare); *Estate of Ford v. Comm'r*, 450 F.2d 878 (2d Cir.1971) (support, maintenance, education, welfare, and happiness); *Estate of Hays v. Comm'r*, 181 F.2d 169 (5th Cir.1940) (best interests of beneficiary); *Estate of Bell v. Comm'r*, 66 T.C. 729 (1976) (*acq.*) (well-being and maintenance in health and comfort); *Estate of Budd v. Comm'r*, 49 T.C. 468 (1968) (*acq.*) (care, support, and medical attention); *Estate of Wier v. Comm'r*, 17 T.C. 409 (1951) (*nonacq.*) (support, maintenance, and education for the beneficiaries' interests and advantage).

Grudgingly, the Service has conceded the validity of the *Jennings v. Smith* doctrine in principle. See *Rev. Rul. 73-143*, 1973-1 C.B. 407.

Nevertheless, the government has won a few of the cases involving retained powers purportedly limited by standards: *Merchant's Nat'l Bank of Boston v. Comm'r*, 320 U.S. 256 (1943) (happiness); *Old Colony Trust Co. v. U.S.*, supra (beneficiaries' best interests); *Newton Trust Co. v. Comm'r*, 160 F.2d 175 (1st Cir.1947) (use and benefit); *Industrial Trust Co. v. Comm'r*, 151 F.2d 592 (1st Cir.1945), *cert. denied*, 327 U.S. 788 (1946) (pleasure); *Estate of Cutter v. Comm'r*, 62 T.C. 351 (1970) (necessary for the benefit of the beneficiary); *Estate of Yawkey v. Comm'r*, 12 T.C. 1164 (1949) (*acq.*) (best interests of beneficiary).

For gift tax purposes, the rule is that a retained-power gift is complete if the donor's power is subject to a "fixed or ascertainable standard." See Reg. §25.2511-2(c). This term is not elaborated upon, although presumably this rule is designed to catch any transfer that avoids estate tax on the same ground. Reg. §25.2511-1(c)(2), which deals with the situation where a trustee having a beneficial interest in a trust makes a distribution to another beneficiary, states that there is no gift if the trustee's power is limited by a "reasonably fixed or ascertainable standard," and goes on to say:

> [A] power to distribute corpus for the education, support, maintenance, or health of the beneficiary, for his reasonable support and comfort, to enable him to maintain his accustomed standard of living, or to meet an emergency, would be a [reasonably fixed or ascertainable] standard. However, a power to distribute corpus for the pleasure, desire, or happiness of a beneficiary is not such a standard. The entire context of a provision of a trust instrument granting a power must be considered in determining whether the power is limited by a reasonably definite standard. For example, if a trust instrument provides that the determination by the trustee shall be conclusive with respect to the exercise or nonexercise of a power, the power is not limited by a reasonably definite standard. However, the fact that the instrument is phrased in discretionary terms is not in itself an indication that no such standard exists.

Note that the "standards exception" for retained dispositive powers is looser and less precise than that for nonretained dispositive powers (powers of appointment). In the latter area, the statute excludes all special powers of appointment but only general powers that are limited by standards relating specifically to health, education, support, and maintenance.

QUESTIONS AND NOTES

1. a. Why are powers of trustees who are children, spouses, friends, and relatives of the grantor (generally) not attributed to the grantor? Compare the "grantor trust" provisions under the income tax (§§671-677), where interests and powers held by a grantor's spouse, by "related or subordinate" parties, or even independent trustees are (under various scenarios)

attributed (in effect) to the grantor. But an "adverse party" co-holder of a power, although ignored under §§2036(a)(2) and 2038, can alter the tax results under the grantor-trust income tax rules, the gift tax, and §§2037 and 2041. The grantor-trust rules under the income tax are dealt with in §8.3.

b. If §2036(a)(2) applies to contingent powers, does it apply in cases where the grantor could be appointed as trustee by a court or a third party (rather than by the grantor)? Should the governing instrument bar such an appointment?

c. Is *Tully* right in characterizing decedent's power to alter or terminate (together with DiNapoli and T&D) as being one of "persuasion?" Does §2038 apply only when the decedent and others possess the power jointly *as trustees*? If not, is there any difference between getting trustees to agree on a decision as opposed to non-trustees? Should *Tully* have simply relied on *Helmholz*?

d. The facts of *Estate of Siegel v. Comm'r*, 74 T.C. 613 (1980), resembled those of *Tully*, but the Tax Court here held for the government on the ground that the employment contract specifically provided that its terms could be modified by the mutual agreement of the employee and the employer. The court held that this provision "added something" that was not present under the law of contracts; namely, the ability to cancel the rights of a third-party beneficiary.

2. a. Just how would the exercise of a power over trust investments and trust accounting decisions shift enjoyment between income and remainder beneficiaries? In any event, as a result of *Old Colony* and *Byrum*, a virtual per se rule exists to the effect that "administrative" powers *always* lie outside of §§2036-2038. In this context, investment powers and trust accounting powers are not to be exercised in a way that unduly favors income beneficiaries over corpus beneficiaries, or vice versa, unless the trust states otherwise.

b. One might think that a similar rule would apply to a grantor/trustee's dispositive discretion. However, the duty of impartiality does not really prevent unequal or disproportionate distributions where distributions are to be made according to the trustee's discretion. It only imposes such *de minimis* duties as good faith, honesty, lack of personal bias, due consideration of the status and needs of the beneficiaries, and forbearance from the abuse of discretion. Besides, if dispositive discretionary powers were immune from §§2036(a)(2) and 2038 because of the existence of such minimal constraints, then those sections would be shrunk to the point of invisibility (except for a power of revocation).

c. Did the court in *Powell* go too far in reading "happiness, welfare, and comfort" to be mere "glosses" on "maintenance?" Didn't that leave the grantor/trustee a lot of leeway in the making of corpus distributions? Would a remainder beneficiary have been able to prevent a liberal exercise of discretion to invade corpus? (The beneficiaries in *Powell* were also the natural objects of the grantor/trustee's bounty, and would hardly have risked disinheritance by bringing such a suit while the grantor was alive.)

d. *Powell* was a "straight" standards case. An "intermediate" scenario would exist where the trust specifies one or more standards but the trustee is expressly given discretion in implementing it. An example would be a direction to distribute income "for the support, comfort, and maintenance of B as the trustee in its sole discretion shall determine." This type of clause would not totally deprive the beneficiaries of any remedy. An equity court could compel the trustee to conform to the standards if the trustee simply failed to exercise any judgment, acted arbitrarily, abused its discretion, or acted dishonestly or in bad faith. However, the trustee's exercise of discretion will not be second-guessed by a court so long as the distributions are anywhere within the range of what a reasonable person would distribute under the applicable standards. Although this type of case arguably expands the grantor/trustee's discretion, it appears that it is not governed by a different set of estate tax rules, nor does it appear that this type of case has generated a more pro-government set of outcomes.

e. Cases involving distributive standards present facts that are scattered over at least two dimensions: (1) the precision of the standards themselves, and (2) the degree of trustee discretion in administering them. A possible third dimension is the relevance of the mental state of the beneficiary (as in "comfort," "welfare," and "happiness"), as opposed to the judgment of the trustee. A multidimensional distribution of facts is not conducive to a one-dimensional (yes-or-no) legal rule. In this area, courts are being asked to draw a line in quicksand.

f. If a rule is difficult or costly to administer, one must ask if the rule itself is worth the effort. Thus, should the Code be revised so that retained powers of disposition (other than powers to revoke) would not cause a gift to be incomplete, and would not cause inclusion in the gross estate? Would a completed-gift rule for such transfers mismeasure the amount or value of gratuitous transfers (as would be the case with retained-interest transfers)?

g. Under an accessions tax, retained powers would be irrelevant. Only distributions to parties (other than the grantor) would be taxable.

3. a. The retained-power cases acutely raise the issue of whether the federal tax law really needs to be dependent on the law of trusts or (in other areas) on the law of future interests. Does dependence on state law render the tax law easier to understand? Does it create greater certainty and predictability? Would it violate the Constitution if tax rules relating to the timing of a taxable transfer differ from property-law rules?

b. Of particular note in *Powell* was the trial court's reliance on extrinsic evidence to "construe" the standards used in the trust. The prevailing norms of interpretation for wills and trusts are (despite some relaxation in recent years) the "plain meaning" and "four corners of the governing instrument" rules, see Restatement of Trusts 2d, §38(2) & (4), stating that (absent duress, fraud, mistake, or some other basis for rescission or reformation) extrinsic parol evidence is not to be admitted to contradict, supplement, or vary the terms of a written trust. Nevertheless, extrinsic evidence of various kinds can be admitted to resolve "ambiguities." Was there any real ambiguity in the standards used in the *Powell* trust? If so, does such ambiguity exist for all such dispositive standards? Should a dictionary be used? Should state courts evolve "rules" of interpretation in this area? See, e.g., *Pyle v. U.S.*, 766 F.2d 1141 (7th Cir.1985) (under Illinois law, "comfort" means "maintain in accustomed standard of living").

   c.   Is not the use of extrinsic evidence in a tax case likely to be self-serving and wholly one-sided? Is there not a "whipsaw problem" in allowing the admission of extrinsic evidence to construe trust terms to mean something other than they appear to mean? Should there be "federal law" as to the meaning of dispositive standards in tax cases?

4.   The existence of a power of invasion of corpus in a trustee, with or without standards, may raise issues under other Code provisions.

   a.   Assume A creates a trust, income to B for life, remainder to C, with the trustee having the discretionary power to invade corpus in favor of B. Upon C's death (prior to that of B), the amount includible in C's estate under §2033 would probably be zero, on the theory that no buyer would willingly purchase a remainder contingent on the unfettered will of another. But in *Estate of Gokey v. Comm'r*, 72 T.C. 721 (1979), the court found that a remainder interest of this type did possess an ascertainable value where the power of invasion was limited by an ascertainable standard ("B's support needs").

   b.   An income interest transferred from a decedent to another person can provide the basis of a §2013 credit against the estate tax of the income beneficiary (if the latter dies within ten years of the death of the first decedent), provided that the income interest can be valued. If the trustee can invade corpus for the benefit of a person other than the income beneficiary, the credit will be lost, unless (perhaps) the power is limited by ascertainable standards. See *Holbrook v. U.S.*, 575 F.2d 1288 (9th Cir.1978).

5.   a.   One of the arguments raised by the *Byrum* majority was that the concept of "control" (over a non-trust entity's distribution policy) was too vague and amorphous. Section 2036(b) responds to this by defining control in mathematical terms.

   b.   Does *Byrum* dictate the result in a case where a person owns personal-use assets, transfers them to a holding company (perhaps an LLC), gives the equity interest in the holding company to a donee, and continues to use the assets? This and other devices based on transfers of interests in non-trust entities are discussed in Chapter 9.

D. The "Retention" of an "Interest" (or Power) Under §§2036 and 2037

The overriding theme of this subsection is that the concept of a possessory interest, a "right to income," or a "reversionary interest" under §§2036(a)(1) and 2037 is often hard to disentangle from the concept of "retention," which is a common requirement of both §§2036 and 2037 (but not of §2038).

The term "retention" basically means "to hold back something" in connection with a transfer. It is a failure of a transferor to convey all of the incidents of ownership to others, resulting in some incidents of ownership "staying with" the transferor.

1. Meaning of "Retention" in Connection with Outright Transfers

In the case of outright transfers, "retention" is contrasted with the situation where a donee voluntarily makes a "gift back" (of some type) to the transferor. Thus, if Spencer gives Valhalla to Thurman outright, and Thurman gratuitously allows Spencer to occupy Valhalla until Spencer's death, Spencer has not retained possession of Valhalla, and §2036(a)(1) is avoided. Here is a case of this general type.

Estate of Linderme v. Commissioner

52 T.C. 305 (1969)

TANNENWALD, Judge: Emil Linderme, Sr., executed a quitclaim deed for his residence on September 7, 1956 in favor of his sons, Emil Jr., Fred, and Edwin, which was recorded in the Deed Records. The deed was then delivered to Emil Jr. Since he acted as custodian of his father's papers, he placed the deed in a file maintained in the decedent's name, where it remained until the decedent's death. No Federal gift tax return was filed. The other two brothers were not made aware of the deed until after the death of Emil Sr.

Emil Sr. continued to live alone in the house without paying rent. Each of his sons at all times maintained residences independently. Emil Sr. continued to receive the bills for, and paid with his own funds, the taxes, insurance premiums, maintenance expenses, and all other expenses relating to the property, until he entered a nursing home in March 1963. Thereafter, the property remained vacant. The Linderme brothers never discussed the sale or rental of the property until after their father's death, [which occurred in October 1964].

Petitioner insists that respondent's assertion of the applicability of §2036(a)(1) constitutes an unwarranted attempt to create a statutory presumption of retention of "possession and enjoyment" from the mere fact of occupancy by the decedent from the time of the quitclaim deed in 1956 until his removal to a nursing home. We do not thus interpret respondent's position. Rather, we understand respondent to argue that, based upon an evaluation of all the facts and circumstances herein, there are adequate grounds for inferring an agreement or understanding on the part of decedent and his three sons sufficient to bring the transfer within the sweep of §2036(a)(1).

Decedent continued in exclusive possession of the residence until he entered the nursing home. The residence was unoccupied from that time until his death about a year and a half later. There was neither consideration of any sale or rental of, nor any effort to sell or rent, the residence during that interval, thus indicating that the property was being held available for decedent's possible return. From the date of the quitclaim deed until his death, decedent's funds were used to pay all the expenses relating to the property.

It is neither necessary that the proscribed retained interest he expressed in the instrument of transfer nor necessary that the decedent have a legally enforceable right to possession or enjoyment.

A significant element [in the cases in which taxpayers prevailed] seems to have been the fact that there was no withholding of occupancy from the donee. In the absence of such withholding, the continued co-occupancy of the property by the donor with the donee was considered, in and of itself, an insufficient basis for inferring an agreement as to retained possession or enjoyment. In the instant case the decedent continued to occupy the residence to the exclusion of the donees or anyone else whose status stemmed from their rights to the property. That occupancy was as much an "economic benefit" as if decedent had rented the property and obtained the income therefrom.

On the basis of the entire record herein, we are satisfied that, beyond the mere existence of the family relationship and the mere occupancy of the premises, decedent did have an understanding whereby he retained the exclusive use of the residence until death.

A "retention" in connection with an outright (non-trust) transfer of property normally requires an agreement or understanding with the transferee that the transferor receive back possession, enjoyment, or the right to rentals. Such an agreement or understanding may be inferred (or at least suspected) from the actual possession of enjoyment of transferred property or the rents therefrom, and at that point the burden is often thrown upon the taxpayer to show that there was no agreement or understanding.

Cases and rulings like *Linderme* are common.[50] However, in *Estate of Gutchess v. Comm'r*, 46 T.C. 554 (1966) (reviewed), *acq.*, Rev. Rul. 70-155, 1970-1 C.B. 189, the Tax Court refused to apply §2036(a)(1) where the donor and donee were husband and wife. The court held that, in a husband-wife situation, an agreement or understanding would not be implied from the sole fact of continued occupancy by the donor spouse together with the donee spouse, which is a "natural" arrangement.[51] Perhaps the *Gutchess* case can be said to involve a "retention of independent significance." Presumably, the continuation of

---

50. *Guynn v. U.S.*, 437 F.2d 1148 (4th Cir.1971); *Estate of Kerdolff v. Comm'r*, 57 T.C. 643 (1972); *Estate of Honigman v. Comm'r*, 66 T.C. 1080 (1976); *Estate of Tehan v. Comm'r*, T.C. Memo. 2005-128. But see *Estate of Wells v. Comm'r*, T.C. Memo. 1981-574.

51. Accord *Union Planters Nat'l Bank v. U.S.*, 361 F.2d 662 (6th Cir.1966).

marriage would not be dictated solely by the donor's scheme to continue living in the house.

The Service takes the position that co-occupancy does not (except in the husband-wife situation) automatically insulate the donor from §2036. See *Rev. Rul.* 78-409, 1978-2 C.B. 234. Also, in *Estate of Hendry v. Comm'r*, 62 T.C. 861 (1974), §2036(a)(1) was held to apply, despite the co-occupancy of the house by husband and wife, because the husband retained the rents from the land. Thus, it would be risky for farming and ranching couples to rely on *Gutchess*.

If a donor of property leases it back from the donee, by prearrangement, for a fair rental, there has been no retention of a possessory interest or an income interest under §2036, since the donee is obtaining the (full) income from the property. *Estate of Barlow v. Comm'r*, 55 T.C. 666 (1971) (*acq.*). However, in *Estate of DuPont v. Comm'r*, 63 T.C. 746 (1975), a gift-leaseback of a ranch ran afoul of §2036(a)(1), because the rent was pegged at its value as grazing land, not at its fair rental value according to its highest and best use. Another factor cited was the fact that the rent was "frozen" under an unduly long-term lease. *DuPont* suggests that a gift and leaseback of agricultural or ranch land is, depending on local conditions, risky (to say the least) as far as §2036(a)(1) is concerned. See also *Estate of Maxwell v. Comm'r*, 3 F.3d 591 (2d Cir. 1993) (rental payment by transferor lacked substance because it merely offset interest payment from the donee to the transferor).

2. Retention in Trusts for the Benefit of the Settlor

It is in the context of discretionary trusts for the settlor that the retention concept often becomes tangled up with the concept of what *interest* is required to trigger §§2036 and 2037. A perfect illustration is the case set forth below, involving the predecessor of §2037.

Commissioner v. Irving Trust Company

147 F.2d 946 (2d Cir. 1945)

Before SWAN, A. HAND, and CHASE, Circuit Judges.

AUGUSTUS N. HAND, Circuit Judge:

The decedent, Hugh M. Beugler, established an inter vivos trust [on] October 22, 1927. It was provided that:

> The Trustee may from time to time in its absolute discretion, and as often as it deems advisable, pay over, transfer, convey, assign and deliver to the settlor all or any part of the principal of the said trust fund, at all times retaining, however, a sufficient Principal Fund to provide the income to be paid to [the settlor's ex-wife].

The trustee never paid any portion of the principal of the trust to Beugler.

The question is whether the trust must be included in decedent's gross estate as a transfer intended to take effect in possession or enjoyment at or after his death within the meaning of §302(c) of the Revenue Act of 1926 which was the law in effect at the time the trust was created [and was the predecessor to present §2037].

The settlor disposed of the corpus and left no legally enforceable rights in himself either by way of reversion or otherwise. Whatever the trustee did not grant to him of its own free will would ultimately pass either to the settlor's issue or in default of issue to [his heirs]. The power was in no respect the property of the settlor but had been vested in the trustee. It was purely discretionary with the latter and the settlor could not cause it to be exercised for his benefit.

In *Bankers Trust Co. v. Higgins*, 136 F.2d 477 (2d Cir.1943), there was a provision in an inter vivos trust that deficiencies in income might be taken out of principal so far as might be necessary to maintain the income to the trust beneficiaries at $60,000 per year. Inasmuch as it was possible to estimate the probable yearly income of the trust, and thus to compute, by the application of mortality tables, the maximum amount of principal necessary to meet the pre-scribed payments to the beneficiaries, this court held that this maximum amount of principal should be included in the estate of the settlor.

In *Blunt v. Kelly*, 131 F.2d 632 (1942), the Third Circuit required an inclusion in the settlor's estate of the corpus of a trust which under the terms of the trust might be used for the support and maintenance of the settlor if, in the opinion of the trustee, the necessity should arise.

In each of these two decisions the inclusion was based on the right of the settlor to require payments to be made out of the trust fund in order to meet his financial needs or to be made on his behalf because of other circumstances set forth in the trust instrument and independent of the mere will of the trustee.

In the case at bar, the discretion of the trustee was absolute, and no court could compel its exercise.

A case similar to *Bankers Trust v. Higgins* and *Blunt v. Kelley*, except that it involved §2036(a)(1) (instead of §2037), is *Estate of Boardman v. Comm'r*, 20 T.C. 871 (1953), *acq.*, 1954-1 C.B. 3. In that case Carolyn Boardman created an irrev-ocable trust, naming a corporate trustee, under which the trustee was to make such distributions from income and principal to Carolyn "during her life, as the Trus-tees deem necessary for her comfort, support and or happiness." Practically all of the income of the trust up to the death of Carolyn was distributed to her sooner or later, and none of it was distributed to any other person. The Tax Court included in the trust in Boardman's gross estate, saying:

> The Trustees were directed to consider her "happiness" as a basis for distribu-tions, and this was presumably the basis on which actual distributions were made. The trustees could not resist her demand for the income, as necessary to her happiness, under the provisions of the trust even though it was not all necessary for her comfort and support.

Returning to *Irving Trust*, was it a "retention" case or a "reversionary interest" case? The current version of §2037(b)(1) defines the term "reversionary interest" to mean "a possibility that property transferred by the decedent ... may return to him or his estate." It cannot be denied that the *Irving Trust* scenario fits squarely into this language. Whether such a reversion is worth more than 5 percent is a separate question. Also to be noted is the fact that the possibility of receiving corpus would not have reduced the amount of the gift, because that possibility would not have been susceptible of actuarial valuation.[52] But the language of §2037 trumps the gift tax rule, and Reg. §20.2037-1(c)(3) states that, if (as here) actuarial tables cannot be used, then general valuation principles are to be used (meaning the "willing-buyer, willing-seller" test). Nevertheless, *Rev. Rul. 79-117*, 1979-1 C.B. 305, is perhaps relevant. That ruling held that the 5 percent test (under §2042(2)) was not satisfied where the insured's reversion could have been defeated by the exercise, by the insured's spouse, of her power to change the beneficiary of the policy.

The next case was positioned in relation to §2036(a)(1) in the same way as *Irving Trust* was positioned under §2037.

Estate of Skinner v. United States

316 F.2d 517 (3d Cir.1963)

Before Biggs, Chief Judge, Ganey, Circuit Judge, and Sheridan, District Judge. [Judge Sheridan sat in this case but took no part in its decision.]

Biggs, Circuit Judge:

On March 5, 1936, the decedent, Maria M. Coxe Skinner, then unmarried and a Pennsylvania resident, set up a trust providing that the trustees were "To collect the interest, income, dividends, and profits from the real estate * * * during the life of the said Maria M. Coxe (Skinner and) to pay the net income of the said estate, or so much thereof as (the) Trustees, may, in their sole and absolute discretion, deem proper under all the circumstances for the comfortable support, and maintenance of the said Maria M. Coxe," [with directions as to income not distributed to Maria].

In 1936 Mrs. Skinner filed a federal gift tax return in which she excluded from the value of the assets transferred to the trust an amount which in her view represented the value of the life estate retained by her under the terms of the trust agreement. The Internal Revenue Service denied the exclusions, stating: "In view of the absolute discretionary power vested in the Trustees, it is considered that you did not reserve a life estate in the trust, and the amount of the income that may be paid to you by the trustees is not susceptible of an accurate determination." As a result, additional gift tax was paid by Mrs. Skinner in 1938.

During her lifetime, Mrs. Skinner received all income from the trust. She died on January 12, 1953. The Commissioner held that the corpus was includible in Mrs. Skinner's taxable estate, allowing the estate, however, a credit for the gift tax paid by her in 1938.

The decision of the [the District Court, which held for the government,] was rested primarily on the conclusions expressed by us in *Estate of McNichol v. Comm'r*,

---

52. See Reg. §25.2511-1(e) (incorporating the *Robinette* rule), discussed in §3.4.C.2.

265 F.2d 667 (3d Cir.1959), *cert. denied*, 361 U.S. 829 (1959). [There] the decedent-settlor executed general warranty deeds to income-producing real estate for the benefit of his children. The deeds reserved no interest in the property to the decedent. However, there was a contemporaneous oral agreement between him and his children whereby he was to receive the income from the property until his death. Because of this oral agreement the Commissioner determined that the decedent had retained sufficient interest to sweep the property into his gross estate. The court below made a finding of fact, based on an inference drawn from the circumstances, [namely,] that Mrs. Skinner thought she had retained a life estate when she created the trust and demonstrated this when she filed her gift tax return for the year 1936, and that she actually did receive the income from the trust for life. The operative facts as found by the court below were not clearly erroneous and were fully supported by the evidence.

We realize, as did the court below, that to some degree at least it was breaking new and perhaps dangerous ground in reaching this decision. [District] Judge Layton stated: "The court is aware that the holding in this case places a heavy burden upon the estate of a settlor of a discretionary trust to avoid the inference of secret prearrangements with the trustee when the settlor has in fact received all income during his life." See 197 F. Supp. at 730. However, every case of this sort must stand on its own facts, and the practice of assuming that a trustee, corporate or otherwise, is necessarily independent of the *cestui* whom he represents, need not be followed invariably but may be rebutted by circumstances.

The judgment will be affirmed.

In *Estate of McNichol*, cited by *Estate of Skinner*, the decedent conveyed income-producing real estate to his children, but continued to receive the rents from the properties until his death. The court upheld inclusion based on an inference of an oral understanding with his children. In the course of its opinion, the court of appeals stated:

Petitioners argue that [the predecessor of §2036(a)(1)] is inapplicable to a transfer with a retained income interest unless that interest is reserved in the instrument of transfer. This argument is based upon the statutory provision that the income must be retained "under" the transfer. This is too constricted an interpretation to place on the statute. The statute means only that the life interest must be retained in connection with or as an incident to the transfer.

Next, petitioners point out that the statute speaks of the retention of "the right to the income." Emphasizing the word "right," petitioners argue that Congress has decreed that [§2036(a)(1)] is applicable only if a transferor reserves to himself an enforceable claim to the income. Since, according to petitioners, the statute of frauds of Pennsylvania would foreclose judicial enforcement of the oral understanding between the decedent and his children, petitioners conclude that the decedent had no "right" to the income from the property.

It is not necessary for us to delve into Pennsylvania law. While state law creates legal interests and rights, it is the federal law which designates which of these interests and rights shall be taxed. In seeking to discover the type of transfers at which [§2036(a)(1)] is aimed, the words "right to the income" are not entitled to undue emphasis. The statute deals with two things: retention of "possession or enjoyment" and retention of "the right to the income." The history of the statute discloses that "the right to the income" clause was not intended to limit the scope of the "possession or enjoyment" clause. The [Joint Resolution] of 1931 included for the first time express language taxing property which had been transferred *inter vivos* with a lifetime retention of "the possession or enjoyment of, or the income from" the property. This amendment said nothing about the "right to" income. The words "right to" were inserted for the first time by the 1932 amendment. This insertion was to make clear that Congress intended that the statute should apply to cases where a decedent was entitled to income even though he did not actually receive it. H.R. Rep. No. 708, 72d Cong., 1st Sess. 46-47; S. Rep. No. 665, 72d Cong., 1st Sess. 49-50. Hence, the "right to income" clause, instead of circumscribing the "possession or enjoyment" clause in its application to retained income, broadened its sweep.

The conclusion is irresistible that the petitioners' decedent "enjoyed" the properties until he died. He who receives the rent in fact enjoys the property. Enjoyment as used in the death tax statute is not a term of art, but is synonymous with substantial present economic benefit. Under this realistic point of view the enjoyment of the properties which the decedent conveyed to his children was continued in decedent by prearrangement and ended only when he died.

Skinner and *McNichol*, won by the government, seem to require either a retention of a right under the instrument of transfer or under a side agreement, even in the case of a trust that provides for discretionary distributions to the settlor. In that respect, the cases under §2036(a)(1) are not inconsistent with the *Irving Trust* case.

The authorities set forth above involve a third-party trustee. If the grantor herself is the trustee of a discretionary trust for her own benefit, then she has the *de facto* "right" to the income and/or the power to revoke the corpus.[53]

3. Indirect Retention by a Settlor Through the Rights of the Settlor's Creditors

The next case is a gift tax case, but it has obvious implications for the estate tax as well.

Outwin v. Commissioner

76 T.C. 153 (1981), acq., 1981-1 Cum. Bull. 2

DAWSON, *Judge:* We must decide whether the transfers by the petitioners to their respective discretionary trusts in 1969 constituted completed gifts. In the present cases the discretionary trusts are irrevocable under the terms of the written trust agreements. In each instance the grantor may receive lifetime distributions of trust income or corpus only in the "absolute and uncontrolled discretion" of the

---

53. See *Estate of Helfrich v. Comm'r*, 143 F.2d 43 (7th Cir.1944).

trustees. The trustees are empowered to distribute the entire corpus to the grantor even though such distribution results in the termination of the trust. Additionally, the trust agreements require the grantor's spouse to give his or her prior written consent in an individual capacity to any such distributions. Upon the death of the grantor the surviving spouse acquires the right to mandatory distributions of trust income on at least an annual basis, plus distributions of principal in the unfettered discretion of the trustees. The grantor's spouse is also given a special testamentary power of appointment over the corpus.

Where the trust agreement specifies, as here, that distributions to the settlor are to be made in the absolute discretion of the trustees, with no enforceable standard provided, the transfer is generally held to be complete for gift tax purposes. A different result obtains, however, where state law permits creditors of the settlor-beneficiary to pierce the trusts for satisfaction of claims.

In *Paolozzi v. Comm'r*, 23 T.C. 182 (1954), the taxpayer created a trust under the terms of which the trustees were authorized to pay her so much of the trust income as they in their absolute discretion determined to be in her best interest. Under Massachusetts law, the creditors of a settlor-beneficiary of a discretionary trust could reach for satisfaction of claims the maximum amount which the trustee could pay to the settlor or apply for her benefit. Thus, we concluded that the taxpayer could at any time obtain the economic benefit of the trust income simply by borrowing and then forcing her creditors to look to her interest in the income for a source of repayment. On this basis we held that the gift was incomplete to the extent of the value of her life estate.

Respondent does not dispute the correctness of *Paolozzi*. Rather, he seeks to distinguish [it] on the ground that discretionary distributions from the trusts herein require the prior individual consent of the grantor's spouse, who is also a remainderman beneficiary thereof. We disagree.

A strong public policy [exists] in Massachusetts against persons placing property in trust for their own benefit while at the same time insulating such property from the claims of creditors. That policy would be easily frustrated if creditors were prevented from reaching the trust assets merely because the settlor's spouse is given an interest in the trust and the right to veto discretionary distributions which might deplete that interest. It is not unreasonable to assume that, because of the marital relationship, the settlor could anticipate the complete acquiescence of his spouse in any discretionary distributions which he might receive, regardless of their effect on her interest as a remainderman. Thus, in the absence of unforeseen circumstances, such as divorce, the possibility of a spousal veto in such situation may be at best a remote possibility. This is particularly true in the present cases, where the fact that each spouse has the right to veto distributions from the other's discretionary trust(s) could discourage the exercise of that authority through fears of reprisal.

Respondent, however, argues that the interest of the grantor's spouse as a remainderman beneficiary makes him or her truly adverse in spite of the marital relationship. He [cites] gift tax authorities which hold that a power in the grantor to revoke or alter a trust does not render a gift incomplete if the power is exercisable only in conjunction with a person having "a substantial adverse interest" in the trust. Reg. §25.2511-2(c) & (e); *Camp v. Comm'r*, 195 F.2d 999 (1st Cir.1952). *Camp* indicates that the grantor's spouse may qualify as an adverse party if he or she possesses a direct legal or equitable interest in the trust property. Yet, while this may be true for gift tax purposes, it does not necessarily follow that the concept is relevant in determining the rights of creditors under state law respecting assets placed in a discretionary trust for the settlor's own benefit. In the latter case the principal concern is not whether a completed gift has occurred, but rather whether a transfer in trust will be permitted to shield the grantor's assets from the claims of present or future creditors. In that context we think the veto power held by the grantor's spouse would be ineffective to shelter the discretionary trust assets from such claims, even though the spouse qualifies as an adverse party under general gift tax principles.

We hold, therefore, that creditors of the petitioners could reach the assets of the discretionary trusts, and under the holding of *Paolozzi* the petitioners have failed to surrender dominion and control over the trust assets.

In *Estate of Paxton v. Comm'r*, 86 T.C. 785, 818 (1986), it was held that the corpus of a self-settled discretionary trust was includible under §2036(a)(1) because the settlor's creditors could reach the income.

The Massachusetts creditor's rights rule cited in *Outwin* is also the general rule in the United States. See UTC §505(a); Restatement of Trusts 3d, §58(2).[54]

The state law rule cited above is not universal however. Accordingly, a settlor has been held not to have an interest where her creditors could not reach a trust under the particular circumstances.[55] Recently, some states (notably Alaska and Delaware) have passed legislation that takes the opposite approach to the Restatement and Uniform Trust Code. Statutes of this type enable settlors to create what are called "domestic asset protection trusts." Where the creditors of the settlor cannot reach the income or corpus of the trust, then the transfer would be a completed gift, since whatever is retained by the donor is not capable of valuation using actuarial principles. *Rev. Rul.* 77-378, 1977-2 C.B. 348.

4. Retaining an Interest Vicariously: Trusts for the Support of the Settlor's Dependents

A special kind of creditor of the decedent is a person to whom the decedent owes support obligations. Reg. §20.2036-1(b)(2) states:

> The use, possession, right to the income, or other enjoyment of the transferred property is considered as having been retained by or reserved to the decedent to the extent that the use, possession, right to the income, or other enjoyment is to be applied toward the discharge of a legal obligation of the decedent, or otherwise

---

54. In accord with *Outwin* and *Paolozzi* is *Comm'r v. VanderWeele*, 254 F.2d 895 (6th Cir.1958) (Michigan).
55. See *Estate of Uhl v. Comm'r*, 241 F.2d 867 (7th Cir.1957) (Indiana); *Herzog v. Comm'r*, 116 F.2d 591 (2d Cir.1941) (New York).

for his pecuniary benefit. The term "legal obligation" includes a legal obligation to support a dependent during the decedent's lifetime.

It follows that a potential problem arises under §§2036(a)(1) and 2037 whenever a trust is created for the "support," "maintenance," and benefit of a person who is a legal dependent of the grantor.

Estate of Chrysler v. Commissioner

44 T.C. 55 (1965), acq. in result only, 1970-2 C.B. xix,
rev'd on other issues, 361 F.2d 508 (2d Cir.1966)

ARUNDELL, *Judge*: [In 1945 and 1946, decedent created identical irrevocable trusts for his daughter Helen and his son Jack, naming three individuals as co-trustees.] The trust for the daughter provided in part:

> The Trustees shall pay over the net income to Helen F. Chrysler, daughter of the Grantor, during her life; provided, however, that as long as she shall be a minor, the Trustees shall use and apply so much of the net income and any accumulated income of the trust as the Trustees shall deem advisable for her maintenance, education and support; and the Trustees shall accumulate the balance of such income during the minority of said Helen F. Chrysler; and upon her attaining the age of twenty-one years the Trustees shall pay over to her all accumulations of income; or if said Helen F. Chrysler shall die before attaining the age of twenty-one years, all accumulations of income shall be paid over to her estate.

[Decedent died while both children were still minors.] None of the income of either trust was used for the maintenance, education, or support of the beneficiary during decedent's lifetime and all such income was accumulated.

Respondent argues that: "These trusts were an effective instrumentality through which the decedent could discharge his legal obligation to support his children. Decedent could have availed himself at any time until his death to have the income applied for the support of his children."

The above argument is not supported by the facts. Decedent could not have availed himself at any time until his death of having the income applied for the support of his children. This could only be done in the discretion of the three trustees. Decedent was not one of the trustees.

The facts in the cases principally relied upon by the respondent involve facts entirely different from the instant case. In *Comm'r v. Estate of Dwight*, 205 F.2d 298 (2d Cir.1953), the husband decedent had created two trusts to pay the income to his wife and children for *their "support and maintenance."* [To the same effect is *Estate of Lee v. Comm'r*, 33 T.C. 1064 (1959).]

In the instant case, the decedent could not direct the trustees to apply any of the income for the maintenance, education, and support of the minor beneficiaries. Sole discretion as to whether any income of the trusts was to be so applied rested and remained in the trustees. The trust instruments specifically provided that only "so much" of such income "as the Trustees shall deem advisable" shall be so used, and the balance accumulated.

We think the facts in the instant case are more like those in *Estate of Douglass v. Comm'r*, 143 F.2d 961 (3d Cir.1944). The decedent in that case created a trust for the benefit of his minor child. In the trust instrument decedent gave the trustees permission to apply the income to the extent that the trustees "may deem necessary for the education, support and maintenance of said minor." In denying the Commissioner's claim, the court said in part:

> There is certainly an important difference of fact between a trust set up for the very purpose of providing for the settlor's legal obligation to his wife and the one in which disinterested trustees have an option to apply a portion of the income for the support of the settlor's minor child.
>
> We hold that the respondent erred in including [the trusts] in the decedent's gross estate.

Chrysler was followed in *Estate of Mitchell v. Comm'r*, 55 T.C. 576 (1970), and the Service has acquiesced, 1971-2 C.B. 3.

Compare *Estate of Gokey v. Comm'r*, 72 T.C. 721 (1979), where a trust for the "support, care, welfare, and education" of the settlor's minor child was held to be includible under §2036(a)(1). The court found that, under Illinois law, the words "care," "welfare," and "education" referred to the child's accustomed standard of living and, therefore, merely restated the concept of "support."

Sections 2036(a) and 2037 "drop off" if the settlor survives to the age the child reaches the age of majority, because then the settlor's vicarious interest in the trust will have terminated prior to the settlor's death.

Is the analysis any different if the trusts are created under a divorce or legal separation? Any alimony-type obligation to an ex-spouse is typically discharged by a property transfer (perhaps in trust), and in that case the ongoing support obligation ceases, and §§2036 and 2037 would not be applied on account of the payments to the ex-spouse. The issue would then be whether the *inter vivos* transfer is exempt from gift tax under §2516, the *Harris* doctrine, or on account of consideration received (where it is recognized that a release of a support right, but not an inheritance right, counts as consideration in money or money's worth). See §3.1.B.4. (If an estate tax deduction issue should arise under §2053, §2043(b)(2) operates to treat transfers from an estate to the decedent's ex-spouse as a deductible claim if the requirements of §2516 are satisfied.).

In contrast to spousal support obligations, child support obligations cannot be discharged by a lump-sum transfer (into an irrevocable trust), as courts retain *in personam* jurisdiction over the support obligor. Section 2516(2) exempts the support obligation from gift tax (if the requirements of §2516 are satisfied), to which the *Harris* doctrine would be a back-up. However, there is no equivalent exemption from estate tax: Section 2043(b)(2), supra, does not apply for purposes of §§2036-2038 (or in relation to obligations to support minor children). Thus, the issue would continue to be whether trust language providing for distributions to minor children creates a retained interest in income and/or corpus. In *Comm'r v. Estate of Dwight*, 205 F.2d 298 (2d Cir.1953), which was cited in *Chrysler*, the trust (executed pursuant to a divorce settlement for the decedent's minor children) was included under §2036. It is, therefore, probably not advisable to create a child support trust as a means of satisfying one's ongoing child support obligation resulting from a court decree, but instead to simply pay child support directly.

5. Transfers to a Trust Created by Another

A retention occurs if X transfers money or property to a pre-existing trust created by Y that provides X with the requisite interest or power. Thus, if Jack had created a trust, income to Ken for life, remainder to Lewis, and *Ken* transfers securities to this trust, Ken has made a transfer with a retained income interest inherent in the terms of the trust, and the portion of the trust attributable to Ken's transfer is included in his gross estate on his death. Such a scenario is typical of spousal election wills, used in community-property states: The surviving spouse transfers her half of the community property to a testamentary trust (created under the decedent spouse's will) that provides for an income interest (and perhaps a special power of appointment) for the surviving spouse. Here the surviving spouse is treated as retaining the income interest (and power to affect beneficial enjoyment).[56]

A more complex variation is that of "reciprocal trusts," where there are two transferors.

United States v. Estate of Grace

395 U.S. 316 (1969)

Mr. Justice MARSHALL delivered the opinion of the Court.

Decedent was a very wealthy man at the time of his marriage to the late Janet Grace in 1908. Janet Grace had no wealth or property of her own, but, between 1908 and 1931, decedent transferred to her a large amount of property, including the family's Long Island estate. Decedent retained effective control over the family's business affairs, including the property transferred to his wife. She took no interest and no part in business affairs and relied upon her husband's judgment. Whenever some formal action was required regarding property in her name, decedent would have the appropriate instrument prepared and she would execute it. On December 15, 1931, decedent executed a trust instrument, hereinafter called the Joseph Grace Trust. The trustees were directed to pay the income of the trust to Janet Grace during her lifetime. On December 30, 1931, Janet Grace executed a trust agreement, hereinafter called the Janet Grace trust, which was virtually identical to the Joseph Grace trust. The trust properties included the family estate and corporate securities, all of which had been transferred to her by decedent in preceding years.

---

56. E.g., *Estate of Vardell v. Comm'r*, 307 F.2d 688 (5th Cir.1962).

The trust instruments were prepared by one of decedent's employees in accordance with a plan devised by decedent to create additional trusts before the advent of a new gift tax expected to be enacted the next year. Janet Grace, acting in accordance with this plan, executed her trust instrument at decedent's request.

Janet Grace died in 1937; decedent died in 1950. The Joseph Grace trust was reported as a nontaxable transfer, and the Janet Grace trust was reported as a trust under which decedent held [only an income interest]. The Commissioner included the amount of the Janet Grace trust in decedent's gross estate.

The doctrine of reciprocal trusts was formulated in response to attempts to draft instruments which seemingly avoid the literal terms of §2036, while still leaving the decedent the lifetime enjoyment of his property. The doctrine dates from *Lehman v. Comm'r*, 109 F.2d 99 (2d Cir.1940), *cert. denied*, 310 U.S. 637 (1940). In *Lehman*, decedent and his brother owned equal shares in certain stocks and bonds. Each brother placed his interest in trust, [giving] the other the right to withdraw $150,000 of the principal. If the brothers had each reserved the right to withdraw $150,000 from the trust that each had created, the trusts would have been includible in their gross estates as interests of which each had made a transfer with a power to revoke. The Second Circuit ruled that the effect of the transfers was the same as if the decedent had transferred his stock in trust and had reserved the right to withdraw $150,000.

[In this case,] the Court of Claims was divided over the requirements for application of the doctrine. The majority held that the crucial factor was whether the decedent had established his trust as consideration for the establishment of the trust of which he was a beneficiary. The court ruled that decedent had not established his trust as a *quid pro quo* for the Janet Grace trust. It therefore found the reciprocal trust doctrine inapplicable. The court recognized that certain cases had established a slightly different test for reciprocity. Those cases inferred consideration from the establishment of two similar trusts at about the same time.

We agree with the dissent that the approach of the Court of Claims majority places too much emphasis on the subjective intent of the parties and for that reason hinders proper application of the estate tax laws. Inquiries into subjective intent, especially in intrafamily transfers, are particularly perilous. Second, there is a high probability that such a trust arrangement was indeed created for tax-avoidance purposes. And, even if there was no estate-tax-avoidance motive, the settlor in a very real and objective sense did retain an economic interest while purporting to give away his property. Finally, it is unrealistic to assume that the settlors of the trusts, usually members of one family unit, will have created their trusts as a bargained-for exchange for the other trust. "Consideration," in the traditional legal sense, simply does not normally enter into intrafamily transfers.

For these reasons, we hold that application of the reciprocal trust doctrine is not dependent upon a finding that each trust was created as a *quid pro quo* for the other. Such a "consideration" requirement necessarily involves a difficult inquiry into the subjective intent of the settlors. Nor do we think it necessary to prove the existence of a tax-avoidance motive. As we have said above, standards of this sort, which rely on subjective factors, are rarely workable under the estate tax laws. Rather, we hold that application of the reciprocal trust doctrine requires only that the trusts be interrelated, and that the arrangement, to the extent of mutual value, leaves the settlors in approximately the same economic position as they would have been in had they created trusts naming themselves as life beneficiaries.

Applying this test to the present case, we think it clear that the value of the Janet Grace trust must be included in decedent's estate. It is undisputed that the two trusts are interrelated. They are substantially identical in terms and were created at approximately the same time. Indeed, they were part of a single transaction designed and carried out by decedent. It is also clear that the transfers in trust left each party, to the extent of mutual value, in the same objective economic position as before. Indeed, it appears, as would be expected in transfers between husband and wife, that the effective position of each party vis-à-vis the property did not change at all. It is no answer that the transferred properties were different in character. For purposes of the estate tax, we think that economic value is the only workable criterion. Joseph Grace's estate remained undiminished to the extent of the value of his wife's trust and the value of his estate must accordingly be increased by the value of that trust.

[Mr. Justice Stewart did not participate. Mr. Justice Douglas would have dismissed the writ of *certiorari* as having been improvidently granted.]

The reciprocal trust doctrine potentially encompasses any of §§2036-2038 where there are "crossed" interests or powers. See (in addition to *Lehman*, supra) *Estate of Hill v. Comm'r*, 229 F.2d 237 (2d Cir.1956) (§2037); *Estate of Bischoff v. Comm'r*, 69 T.C. 32 (1977) (§§2036(a)(2) and 2038).

However, some lower court decisions have taken a narrow view of *Estate of Grace*. In *Estate of Levy v. Comm'r*, T.C. Memo. 1983-453, crossed trusts avoided the reciprocal trust doctrine even though the trusts were identical, except for the fact that one transferor acquired, under the trust created by the other, a special power of appointment. And, in *Estate of Green v. Comm'r*, 68 F.3d 151 (6th Cir.1995), the court refused to apply the doctrine to a crossed-powers case. Both decisions relied on the following passages from *Estate of Grace*: (1) "[The doctrine requires] that the arrangement, to the extent of mutual value, leaves the settlors in approximately the same economic position as they would have been in had they created trusts naming themselves as life beneficiaries;" and (2) "It is also clear that the transfers in trust left each party, to the extent of mutual value, in the same objective economic position as before."

Contrary to these cases, we see nothing in *Estate of Grace* to suggest that it is limited to cases arising under §2036(a)(1). The first quoted sentence is simply an application of the doctrine to the facts presented in *Grace*. The second quoted sentence cannot be taken literally to mean that the transfers must leave the economic position of the transferors unchanged, because the trusts in *Grace* both made completed gifts of the remainder interests! The language, especially the phrase "to the extent of mutual value," only requires that each transferor end up with the same interest or power which it granted to the other (and which would cause inclusion in the gross estate).

Furthermore, these cases overlook the fact that *Estate of Grace* did not create the reciprocal trust doctrine. It only lowered the evidentiary threshold for its application in certain situations. The issue in reciprocal-trust cases, as with "retention" cases generally, is whether the interest or power acquired by the decedent/transferor in the trust created by the other party was a random "gift back" or whether it was a condition of the decedent's transfer. If it was a condition of the decedent's transfer, then the interest or power was "retained." The only issue should be one of fact. Really, these cases merely pose the "agreement or understanding" issue in a different context. Reciprocal trusts are surely subject to the following sentence in Reg. §20.2036-1(c)(1)(i):

> An interest or right is treated as having been retained or reserved if at the time of the transfer there was an understanding, express or implied, that the interest or right would later be conferred.

6. Effect of Interest Retained on the Amount Includible

The retention concept bears on the amount includible. Thus, if the transferor retained an interest (or power) in only a portion of the property, the amount includible is only that portion of the property to which the interest (or power) pertained.[57] Thus, if Garina creates a trust, 40 percent of the income to Garina for life, the rest being accumulated, remainder to Hiram, only 40 percent of the trust is includible under §2036(a)(1). Similarly, if in a §2037 case the reversion extends only to a portion of the trust, then that portion, less outstanding income interest therein, would be includible.[58]

Section 2036(a)(1) requires inclusion of the entire property where the transferor retains the "income" from the property. What is the includible amount if the transferor retains a right to an annuity or a "unitrust interest" (right to fixed percentage of corpus as valued annually)? This issue is dealt with by Reg. §20.2036-1(c)(2), issued in 2008. First, it is clear that that a retained annuity or unitrust satisfies the "possession or enjoyment, or right to income" language of §2036.[59] Second, the amount includible is the amount (not to exceed the value of the trust) necessary to yield the required payment stream (using the §7520 interest rate determined as of the transferor's death). In the case of an annuity payment, the amount is the annuity amount (adjusted for frequency of payments) divided by the §7520 interest rate (not to exceed the principal). The arithmetic is more complicated in the case of a unitrust interest. If the annuity or unitrust amount cannot be paid without depleting principal, the transferor is deemed to have retained all of the income from the property, and the entire corpus would be included.

7. Can Inter Vivos Transfers Avoid Both Gift and Estate Tax?

The fact that there are separate doctrinal rules under the gift and estate taxes raises the issue of whether, cheating apart, a transfer can avoid both gift tax and estate

---

57. See Reg. §20.2036-1(c)(1)(i).
58. See Reg. §20.2037-1(d).
59. See T.D. 9414, 2008-2 C.B. 454.

tax by reason of retained interests and powers. There is no statutory rule (that would be akin to §2044) holding that a transfer that avoids gift tax must be included in the gross estate solely by reason of having avoided gift tax on account of one or more retained interests and powers. At the same time, the IRS will not be blind to the possibility of inconsistent results. The estate tax return is required to disclose all gifts made within three years of death and all gifts *whenever made* (except outright non-trust transfers) worth more than $5K.[60] In any dispute concerning the inclusion of a trust in the gross estate, the prior gift tax treatment of the transfer will be revealed.

There is no duty to take consistent positions as to the gift and estate tax results of a given transfer. On the Commissioner's part, such a duty would be pointless, because double taxation of the same transfer under the gift and estate tax is often required by doctrine, and, where it occurs, is mitigated by (1) the exclusion from the cumulative tax base for post-1976 taxable gifts included in the transferor's gross estate (the "adjusted taxable gifts exclusion") and (2) the §2012 credit for taxes paid on pre-1977 gifts. The taxpayer is free to make all nonfrivolous legal arguments under both the gift tax and estate taxes. Nevertheless, in the cases (involving retained interests and powers) won by the taxpayer on estate tax issues, it appears that the taxpayer had earlier reported a completed gift. In some of the government estate tax victories, the taxpayer failed to report a completed gift. These observations suggest that gift and estate tax doctrine "works out" in virtually all cases to snare a gratuitous transfer at least once. In some cases, gift tax doctrine has been "adapted" to "fit" estate tax doctrine. An example is the second sentence of Reg. §25.2511-2(c), which states that a gift is complete if the donor has a dispositive power that is "a fiduciary power limited by a fixed or ascertainable standard." In other scenarios, as noted already, a transfer can be both a completed gift and included in the gross estate, but the estate-tax computation mechanism prevents double taxation.

As a practical matter, the government only cares about inconsistent gift and estate tax results if it loses (or anticipates losing) an estate tax controversy. At that point, it would want to see if the gift tax issue relating to the same transfer can be considered. (Considering the gift tax issue would be advantageous for the Service even if no gift tax would be owed, because adjusted taxable gifts use up the unified transfer tax credit.) If the statute of limitations has not run out on the gift tax issue, the IRS can try to obtain an admission or determination that a taxable gift was made (and to attempt to assess any resulting gift tax deficiency). The normal period of limitations is three years from the filing of a gift tax return, but the period is six years if the unreported items exceed 25 percent of the value of reported items.[61] However, the statute of limitations does not begin to run against the government on gifts (for which a return is required) unless (1) a gift tax return is filed for the year of the gift, (2) the return is not fraudulent, *and* (3) *the gift item is disclosed on the return*.[62] See §6501(c)(1)-(3) & (9).

---

60. See Reg. §20.2018-3(c)(7).

61. See §6501(a) & (e)(2) (these rules apply for both estate and gift taxes).

62. This rule was added by the Taxpayer Relief Act of 1997. Previously, the disclosure of specific items was only required for certain gifts subject to §2702, which itself had only been enacted in 1990. A related change was the addition of §2001(f), which bars the revaluation (for purposes of

If the statute of limitations has run against the government, the issue is then whether the government can re-open the gift issue if it has been determined that the gift property is not included in the gross estate. However, the so-called "mitigation provisions" of the Code, §§1311-1314, which address certain inconsistent result scenarios under the income tax, do not apply to inconsistent gift and estate tax determinations.[63]

That mainly leaves the doctrine of *equitable recoupment* as the government's only procedural opening if the gift tax statute of limitations has run. Equitable recoupment arises when a single transaction, item, or taxable event is subject to two inconsistent determinations. The doctrine was applied to tax litigation in *Bull v. U.S.*, 295 U.S. 247 (1935), which held that certain partnership profits were post-death income of an estate, and should not have been (but were) included in the gross estate of a decedent partner. Hence, the income tax taxpayer was entitled to a credit (offset) against additional income tax in an amount equal to the overpaid estate tax, even though the statute of limitations had run on the estate tax issue. But in *U.S. v. Dalm*, 494 U.S. 596 (1990), the Court emphasized that equitable recoupment was basically a defense to a money claim, and could not be the basis of a separate suit by a party that had suffered two inconsistent determinations.[64] Thus, equitable recoupment by the government would have to be pursued in the estate tax proceeding itself.

The proper scenario for applying equitable recoupment is illustrated by *Estate of German v. U.S.*, 7 Cl. Ct. 644 (1985). There, a Maryland donor in an *Outwin*-like situation filed a gift tax return but claimed that the gift was incomplete on the theory that the donor's creditors could reach the trust income and corpus. After the statute of limitations had expired with respect to the gift tax issue, the donor died. The executor included the trust in the gross estate on the estate tax return and then filed a claim for refund, alleging that the trust was not includible under §§2036(a)(1) and 2038 on the ground that the donor's creditors could *not* reach the trust income and corpus. The Claims Court agreed with the estate on the merits of the estate tax issue, and granted the refund claim, but the government was granted an "offset" against the refund claim in an amount equal to the (barred) gift tax that should have been paid on the initial transfer under the same interpretation of Maryland law.[65]

---

computing the estate tax) of gifts on which the statute of limitations had run. (Previously, such revaluation had been possible.)

63. See §1312 (omitting gift and estate tax inconsistency from the list of "circumstances of adjustment" that can be made despite the running of the statute of limitations).

64. Although it was once thought that the Tax Court could not apply the equitable recoupment doctrine, that is no longer the case. *Estate of Branson v. Comm'r*, 264 F.3d 904 (9th Cir.2001), *cert. denied*, 535 U.S. 927 (2002).

65. Accord, *Estate of Buder v. U.S.*, 436 F.3d 936 (8th Cir.2006) (holding that the government was entitled to the defense of equitable recoupment for unpaid estate taxes in the husband's estate due to the allowance of a marital deduction for a faulty QTIP election — although the court first discounted that amount to reflect that a charity and a daughter, not parties to the litigation or beneficiaries of the trust, would have borne some of the husband's estate tax liability. However, the court denied the government interest on the unpaid estate taxes because the government knew of the erroneous QTIP election and could have timely recovered the deficiency.).

A conceivable weapon in tax litigation is that of *equitable estoppel*. In *Estate of German*, the government claimed (as an alternative to equitable recoupment) that the refund claim should be wholly denied (and the trust included in the gross estate), notwithstanding the underlying merits, under an equitable estoppel theory, alleging that taxpayer's counsel made a false representation to the effect that the transfer was an incomplete gift. The Claims Court (7 Cl. Ct. at 646) stated the doctrine as follows:

> Equitable estoppel is ordinarily invoked when because of representations by the taxpayer, relied on by the government, the latter allows the period of limitations on assessment of a tax properly due to pass without a statutory notice of deficiency. But it is an equitable doctrine and requires misrepresentations of fact, reliance thereon, and detriment to the government which cannot otherwise be corrected.

The Claims Court refused to apply this doctrine on the facts: The taxpayer's counsel did not make a knowing misrepresentation of "fact" that was detrimentally relied upon by the government. Legal positions, even if erroneous, are not misrepresentations of facts.[66]

QUICK QUESTION

David established a trust with $2M and with the following terms: income to David for his life, then income to David's wife Essie for her life, remainder to Flora, David and Essie's daughter. Which one of the following statements is *TRUE*?

A. David made a taxable gift of only the remainder interest to Flora.
B. If Essie dies before David, when David dies, only the value of Flora's remainder interest will be included in David's estate.
C. If Essie survives David, when David dies, nothing will be included in David's estate.
D. If Essie survives David, when David dies, the full date of death FMV of the trust will be included in David's estate, with the possibility of Essie's interest qualifying for the QTIP marital deduction.

QUESTIONS AND NOTES

1. a. A power or interest can be "retained" simply by failing to transfer all interests in the property. Thus, in *Estate of Cooper v. Comm'r*, 74 T.C.

---

66. See *Ross v. Comm'r*, 169 F.2d 483, 496 (1st Cir.1948).

1373 (1980), the taxpayer transferred bonds to a trust but kept the interest coupons. The taxpayer died before the bonds matured. The bonds were included under §2036(a)(1). The same result occurred in *Estate of Nicol v. Comm'r*, 56 T.C. 179 (1971), where the decedent entered into a crop rental agreement on farmland, and then gave the farmland to his daughter (subject to the crop lease).

b. There are cases applying §2036(a)(1) solely on the basis of the fact that the transferor in fact continued to enjoy the income from the property, with the tacit acquiescence of the donees, even though there was no agreement or understanding as to the duration of such an arrangement. See *Estate of Lee v. U.S.*, 59 A.F.T.R.2d (RIA) 1251 (6th Cir.1987); *Carpenter v. U.S.*, 243 F. Supp. 993 (W.D. Okla. 1965);

c. In other cases, the courts find that continued enjoyment is circumstantial evidence of an "implied" agreement. See *Strangi v. Comm'r*, 417 F.3d 468 (5th Cir.2005) (distributions from family limited partnership); *Estate of Thompson v. Comm'r*, 382 F.3d 367 (3d Cir.2004) (same); *Estate of Reichardt v. Comm'r*, 114 T.C. 144 (2000) (same, stating that heavy burden is on taxpayer to disprove implied understanding, where family members make the decisions). In *Estate of Paxton v. Comm'r*, 86 T.C. 785 (1986), the court found, on the basis of a few distributions from a discretionary trust to the settlor, an implied agreement that the trustee (a relative) would pay income to the settlor on demand. It is also worth stating that none of the cases require that the agreement or understanding be legally enforceable.

d. The cases noted in items (b) and (c) above look like "sham conveyances," and in some of them the transfers were not reported for gift tax purposes. Should inclusion in such cases be obtained under §2033 (instead of §2036(a)(1))?

2. a. In our opinion, the issue of retention is analytically separate from that of the quality of the settlor's interest under §§2036(a)(1) and 2037(b). In the case of a discretionary trust for the benefit of the settlor, the possibility of receiving corpus is a reversionary interest under §2037 (although possibly not worth more than 5 percent) and the possibility of receiving income satisfies the "possession or enjoyment or right to income" requirement of §2036(a)(1), for the reasons stated in *McNichol*.

b. As to retention, a side agreement should be required in connection with an outright gift, but not in the case of a trust which names the settlor as discretionary beneficiary of income or corpus. Where the very instrument of transfer names the settlor as corpus or income beneficiary, it is hard to say that the settlor has given everything away. Moreover, the trustee of an *inter vivos* trust (unlike the donee of an outright transfer) has no economic interest in withholding distributions. Thus, an agreement should not be required for a finding of a "retention." Thus, we think that *Irving Trust* was wrongly decided. Nevertheless, an agreement or understanding has been found in most of the cases, and in many others a retention would be found on the basis of the rights of the settlor's creditors.

c. If our approach were adopted, an issue would be the amount includible.
In a §2037 case, all interests that would be diminished if corpus were
distributed to the settlor would be included if the 5 percent test is satisfied.
In a §2036(a)(1) case involving a trust, the amount included should be
that percentage of the property that is obtained by dividing the income
received by the settlor over the total income. Cf. *Rev. Rul. 79-109*, 1979-1
C.B. 297 (one-twelfth of the value of a vacation property was includible
where donor used the same for one month out of the year). However, if it
appeared that the settlor could effectively obtain income from a "discretionary" trust on demand, the entire value of the trust should be included.

3. a. In a reciprocal trust with "crossed" income interests, each grantor appears
to be making a gift to the other of an income interest. According to a ruling
issued by the Service in 1969 in a related fact situation, one of these
income-interest gifts is considered to be for full and adequate consideration, and the other income-interest gift will be net of a consideration
offset. See *Rev. Rul. 69-505*, 1962-2 C.B. 179. A simpler approach would
have been to apply the retained-interest analysis posited by *Estate of
Grace*.[67] In any event, §2702 applies to retained-interest transfers involving "family members," and it should clearly apply to transactions like
Estate of Grace, since Reg. §25.2702-2(a)(3) defines "retained" to mean
(an interest) held by the same person both before and after the transfer in
trust. A retained interest that triggers §2702 cannot also be claimed as a
consideration offset that would negate §2702.[68] (This result is implicit in
Estate of Grace itself, where no consideration offset was allowed against
the amounts includible under §2036.) Thus, where §2702 applies, *Rev.
Rul. 69-505* should be considered to be obsolete.

b. The amount included in the gross estate in a crossed-income-interest
scenario (as in *Estate of Grace*) should be based first on what the decedent
transferred, which is the attempted depletion of the transferor's §2033
estate, and secondarily by the "retained" interest. Thus, if the initial transfer by W to W's trust was three-fourths of the amount transferred by H to
H's trust, then three-fourths of the value of H's trust should be included in
H's estate (because H retained three-fourths of an income interest relative
to the amount he transferred), and all of the value of W's trust should be
included in W's gross estate. However, the Service, in *Rev. Rul. 74-533*,
1974-2 C.B. 293, held instead that the amount included in H's gross estate

---

67. Suppose that A and B each create trusts with $10M, income to the other for life, remainder
to C, and that the actuarial factors for income interests are 0.5 for A's life and 0.6 for B's life (B being
the younger of the two). Under the approach of *Rev. Rul. 69-505*, A has given B and C interests worth
$6M and $4M respectively, and B has given A and C interests worth $5M and $5M respectively. After
consideration offsets, A has made a net gift to B of $1M, as well as a gift to C of $4M, and B has made
no net gift to A and a net gift of $4M to C. If A and B were deemed to have simply retained the interest
received from the other, their net gifts would be $5K and $4K respectively.
68. An income interest that triggers inclusion under §2036(a)(1) cannot also be a consideration
offset that would partially negate §2036(a)(1).

was the full value of W's trust at H's death, and that three-fourths of the value of H's trust at W's death was included in W's gross estate.

4. It is hard to generalize as to whether a retention can occur "by operation of law."

    a. The *Outwin* case may be said to have involved a retention by operation of law. Another operation-of-law situation occurs under §2037 where a trust grantor fails to tie up all dispositive contingencies, resulting in the grantor having an "implied reversion." Should all contingencies in fact fail, the trustee will hold the property in resulting trust for the transferor and his successors.

    b. In *Gutchess*, supra, the government made the argument that the donor (H) who transferred his personal residence to W "retained" the occupancy thereof by operation of law because, under domestic relations law, he could not be evicted from the property unless W obtained a court order for good cause shown. The Tax Court majority dismissed this argument as not amounting to a retention "under" the transfer. The Tax Court now appears to limit *Gutchess* to its facts. *Estate of Hendry v. Comm'r*, 62 T.C. 861, 876 (1971). Moreover, the ongoing marriage relationship that underlay co-occupancy possessed "independent significance."

    c. *Estate of Wyly v. Comm'r*, 610 F.2d 1282 (1980), *acq. in result, Rev. Rul. 81-221*, 1981-2 C.B. 178, involved a rule found in Texas, Louisiana, and Idaho under which the income from separate property is community property. The government argued that any gift by H to W (or vice versa) involved a transfer with retention of half of the income, resulting in half of the property being included in the donor's gross estate. The Fifth Circuit, relying mostly on *Gutchess*, stated (overbroadly) that a retention by operation of law per se avoids §2036.

5. a. For income tax purposes, discretionary trusts for the benefit of the grantor (or of the grantor's spouse) are treated as grantor-owned trusts, except where an adverse-party trustee has to consent to the distributions. §§676(a) and 677(a).

    b. In *Douglas v. Willcuts*, 296 U.S. 1 (1935), the Supreme Court held that distributions to an ex-wife from a trust created by the husband to fund the husband's ongoing support obligations were income to the husband. The result of this case was overturned by the enactment of §682, so that the distributions are to be taxed to the wife. This rule (which does not apply to child support payments) parallels that for "tax alimony" paid directly under §§71 and 215.

    c. Under §677(b), a grantor is not treated as the owner of a trust merely because income *may* be applied or distributed for the support of a beneficiary (other than the grantor's spouse) of the grantor. However, income that is actually so distributed is taxed to the grantor.

6. In *T.A.M. 200407018*, decedent's husband's estate (i.e., the estate of the first spouse to die) had claimed a marital deduction under §2056(b)(5) for the value of a painting that his estate represented to have been included in a QTIP trust. When the decedent (the surviving spouse) died, her executor claimed that the

item really should have passed under a non-marital bequest and therefore was not included in the surviving spouse's gross estate under §2044. The executor's claim was factually correct, but the statute of limitations had run on the husband's estate, barring a correction of the error. The IRS applied the duty of consistency doctrine (treating the estates of husband and wife as being in privity) and included the item in the wife's gross estate. The duty-of-consistency doctrine (quasi-estoppel) does not require willful misrepresentation. Accord, Estate of *Letts v. Comm'r*, 109 T.C. 290 (1997).

E. The Requirement that the Retained Interest (or Power) Be "in" the Property Transferred

The interests and powers described in §§2036-2038 as being retained or held by the grantor must exist "in" the same property that was transferred. In the case of property transferred in trust, the "property" means the trust estate as it might be constituted from time to time, not the actual cash or assets initially transferred to the trust, which may have been sold, distributed, or otherwise disposed of by the trustee prior to the decedent's death.

The requirement that the interest be retained "in" the transferred property most frequently arises under §2036(a). A general strategy for avoiding that section is to detach an annuity right from transferred money or property. The two most common situations where this is attempted involve (a) the segregation of annuity and survivorship rights and (b) the private annuity transaction.

1. Segregation into Separate Funds

One might try to avoid §2036(a)(1) by creating two separate funds. One fund would provide only a benefit payable upon death. The death benefit might be provided by a life insurance policy or, alternatively, by an irrevocable trust that accumulates income until the grantor's death. The other fund would be a single-life annuity that provides periodic payments to the grantor of the trust for the grantor's life, at which point the annuity would be exhausted. The combination of a right to periodic payments together with a death benefit bears a strong economic resemblance to a §2036(a)(1) transfer. The case below involved just such an arrangement.

Fidelity-Philadelphia Trust Co. v. Smith

356 U.S. 274 (1958)

Mr. Chief Justice WARREN delivered the opinion of the Court.

In 1934 decedent, then aged 76, purchased a series of annuity-insurance combinations. Three single-premium life insurance policies, at face values of $200,000, $100,000, and $50,000, were obtained without the requirement of a medical examination. As a condition to selling each life insurance policy, the companies required decedent also to purchase a separate, single-premium, non-refundable single-life annuity policy. The premiums for each insurance and annuity policy were fixed at regular rates. The size of each annuity, however, was calculated so that in the event the annuitant-insured died prematurely the [pre-paid] annuity premiums, less annuity payments already made, would combine with the companion [pre-paid] insurance premiums, plus interest, to equal the amount of insurance proceeds to be paid. Each annuity could have been purchased without the insurance policy for the same premium charged for it under the annuity-insurance combination.

In the year of purchase, decedent assigned all rights and benefits under the insurance policies to the Fidelity-Philadelphia Trust Company as trustee [of an irrevocable trust]. A gift tax was paid by the decedent.

It is conceded by the parties that the question of whether the proceeds should be included in the estate is not determinable by the federal estate tax provision dealing with life insurance proceeds. Cf. *Helvering v. LeGierse*, 312 U.S. 531. [*Editor's note*: Even if the policies were treated as "life insurance," the proceeds would have avoided inclusion under §2042 because the decedent-insured did not possess "incidents of ownership" at death.] The Government contends that the annuity payments until death were income from property transferred by the decedent through the life insurance policies [under §2036(a)(1)]. The Government's position is not well taken.

To establish its contention, the Government must aggregate the premiums of the annuity policies with those of the life insurance policies and establish that the annuity payments were derived as income from the entire investment. This proposition cannot be established. Admittedly, when the policies were purchased, each insurance-annuity combination was the product of a single, integrated transaction. However, the parties neither intended that, nor acted as if, any of the transactions would have a quality of indivisibility. Regardless of the considerations prompting the insurance companies to hedge their life insurance contracts with annuities, each time an annuity insurance combination was written, two items of property, an annuity policy and an insurance policy, were transferred to the purchaser. The annuity policy could have been acquired separately, and the insurance policy could have been, and was, conveyed separately. The annuities arose from personal obligations of the insurance companies which were in no way conditioned on the continued existence of the insurance contracts.[8] Quite clearly the annuity payments arose solely from the annuity policies. The use and enjoyment of the annuity policies were entirely independent of the insurance policies. Because of this independence, the Commissioner may not, by aggregating the two types of policies into one investment, conclude that by receiving the annuities, the decedent had retained income from the insurance contracts.

---

8. Where a decedent has transferred property to another in return for a promise to make periodic payments to the transferor for his lifetime, it has been held that these payments are not income from the transferred property. [Citations omitted.] In these cases the promise is a personal obligation of the transferee, the obligation is usually not chargeable to the transferred property, and the size of the payments is not determined by the size of the actual income from the transferred property.

Mr. Justice Burton, with whom Mr. Justice Black and Mr. Justice Clark join, dissenting.

It seems to me that this case is indistinguishable from one in which a settlor places a sum in trust under such terms that he shall receive the income for life, and the principal shall be payable to designated beneficiaries upon his death. As the principal, in that event, would be includable in the settlor's estate for estate tax purposes, so here the proceeds of the insurance policies should be included in this decedent's estate.

A life insurance policy would be preferred to an irrevocable accumulation trust as the mechanism to provide a survivor benefit, because accumulated income in a trust is subject to high marginal trust income rates, whereas the "inside build-up" in a life insurance policy avoids income tax.

2. Private Annuities

Another situation raising the "in the property transferred" issue is the so-called "private annuity," which is alluded to in footnote 8 of the *Fidelity-Philadelphia Trust Co.* majority opinion. The private annuity transaction is one where a person transfers property to a person who is a natural object of the transferor's bounty in return for a promise by the transferee to pay an annuity to the decedent for life.

A private annuity resembles an installment sale of the property, except that the payments are to terminate at the transferor's death. Indeed, the private annuity closely resembles the self-canceling installment note (SCIN), described at §3.1.A.4. As a practical matter, the Service has no reason to assert gross estate inclusion of the transferred property under §2036(a)(1) in cases where the total payments to be ultimately received by the transferor can be expected to exceed the value of the property transferred plus a reasonable rate of return thereon. And, of course, §2036(a) by its own terms excludes any transfer made for full and adequate consideration in money's worth. (Nor would such a transfer result in a gift for gift tax purposes.) With these points in mind, the typical private annuity transaction would be structured so that the payment level would be set high enough so that the consideration (the annuity promise) would equal or exceed the value of the property transferred. The annuity promise is valued using the relevant annuity table under §7520.

Nevertheless, if the transferor dies well before his or her actuarial life expectancy, the §2033 gross estate of the transferor will not in fact have recovered sufficient annuity payments to make up for the transfer of the property. In such a case, the Service may attempt to apply §2036(a)(1). Here is such a case.

Fabric v. Commissioner

83 T.C. 932 (1984)

Sterrett, *Judge*: Mollie P. Fabric died testate on February 21, 1977. On May 31, 1974, the decedent was hospitalized, suffering from multiple medical problems. Decedent was treated and released on July 3, 1974. During the first nine months of 1975, the decedent had severe chest pains, which were alleviated only with nitroglycerine. On September 5, 1975 the pains had increased in their intensity, resulting in hospitalization. Medical tests revealed that she had a blockage in a coronary artery. The decedent underwent coronary artery bypass open-heart surgery on September 24, 1975. Prior to the surgery, the decedent's physicians predicted that she had a 60 to 75 percent chance of survival. Decedent survived the surgery, but on October 8, 1975 decedent had a permanent intravenous pacemaker inserted. Decedent was discharged from the hospital on October 11, 1975. During [the rest of] 1975, the decedent [suffered from] retention of excessive fluid in the chest and lungs. The decedent entered the hospital in December 1975 to have this condition treated. After the decedent was discharged, her follow-up care was entrusted to Dr. Morton Diamond, a cardiologist practicing in Hollywood, Florida. Even with decedent's medical problems, Dr. Diamond was of the opinion that as of the latter part of 1975 and as of January 1976 he would have expected the decedent to live easily several years, possibly even in excess of 5 years.

Decedent was hospitalized on January 6, 1977 because of congestive heart failure. The decedent was hospitalized for the last time on February 11, 1977, and died on February 21, 1977 from congestive heart failure. Decedent's death occurred approximately 1 year and 5 months after her September 24, 1975, operation.

In September 19, 1975, five days prior to her September 24, 1975 operation, the decedent executed numerous documents. These documents included her will, a foreign trust, and an annuity agreement with the trustee of the trust. The trust was initially funded with $750. It was irrevocable and the decedent did not retain any control over it. Decedent did send the independent trustee, Cayman Nat'l Bank, a letter expressing her desire that the trustee consult with her sons and her attorney with respect to investments. This letter, however was merely precatory and we attach no legal significance to it. So long as the decedent was living, no distributions could be made to the beneficiaries.

In accordance with the annuity agreement, Cayman Nat'l Bank agreed to pay decedent $2,378.48 per week for the rest of her life. The annuity was a fixed obligation and was not dependent on the trust's income. Its amount was determined by use of the [gift tax actuarial tables]. In consideration for the Bank's promise, decedent agreed to transfer assets to the trust totaling $1,150,000 in value. Under the laws of the Cayman Islands, the Bank was liable to the full extent of its assets for paying the annuity in the event the trust assets had been exhausted.

The critical issue is whether the disputed transaction is to be treated as an annuity, or a retained life estate in the transferred properties [under §2036(a)(1)]. This issue has been addressed in the income tax context by this Court in *Lazarus v. Comm'r*, 58 T.C. 854 (1971), *aff'd*, 513 F.2d 824 (9th Cir.1975), and *La Fargue v. Comm'r*, 73 T.C. 40 (1979), *aff'd in part and rev'd in part*, 689 F.2d 845 (9th Cir.1982). [Although these cases dealt with issue of whether the trust income should be taxed to the transferor under §677(a),] their rationale is fully applicable to the case at bar.

In *Lazarus*, pursuant to a comprehensive plan, taxpayers established a foreign trust for the benefit of family members. Taxpayers then entered into an annuity agreement with the trust whereby they transferred stock to the trust in exchange for the trust's promise to pay them $75,000 a year for life. As part of the prearranged plan, the trust sold the stock to a corporation for a nonnegotiable promissory note, which provided for annual interest payments of $75,000. We found that an annuity had not been purchased. Rather, the transaction was a transfer of the stock to the trust with a reservation of the right to have the annual income of $75,000 distributed to taxpayers. The only source of the payments to taxpayers was the income from the property they had transferred to the trust.

In *La Fargue*, taxpayer transferred various assets to a trust in return for equal annual payments for life from the trust. While there was not any precise tie-in between the income of the trust and the annuity payments, this Court did mention that the transferred property was the sole source of the annuity payments to taxpayer. There also was no relationship between the present value of the purported sales price and the fair market value of the transferred properties. This Court ruled that the transfer of assets was not a sale or exchange for an annuity but rather a transfer in trust with a reserved interest. The Ninth Circuit reversed, holding that [various] "informalities" did not justify looking through the formal terms of the annuity agreement.

In the instant case, respondent insists that the decedent failed to purchase an annuity. He alleges that the annuity agreement was not financially guaranteed by the trustee, and accordingly all payments were to be charged to the transferred property. This case is appealable to the Ninth Circuit, which reversed us in *La Fargue*. We find that the facts here are substantially similar to those in *La Fargue*. Therefore, given our decision in *Golsen v. Comm'r*, 54 T.C. 742, 757 (1970), *aff'd*, 445 F.2d 985 (10th Cir.1971), *cert. denied*, 404 U.S. 940, we believe that we are compelled to hold that the decedent entered into a valid annuity agreement. We express no opinion with respect to whether, aside from the *Golsen* rule, we would follow *La Fargue*.

The next issue is whether the decedent erred in using the actuarial tables set forth in [the regulations] in valuing her annuity. Respondent maintains that the decedent's physical condition at the time she entered into the annuity agreement should have been considered.

The actuarial tables are provided as an administrative necessity and their general use has been readily approved by the courts. In exceptional circumstances courts will permit departure from the tables. Respondent cites various Tax Court decisions [which] permitted departure from use of the tables. In the majority of these opinions it was shown that the individual's maximum actual life expectancy was 1 year or less. At the time of decedent's execution of the annuity agreement, it was not established that her maximum life expectancy was 1 year or less. Furthermore, the uncontroverted testimony of decedent's physician was that as of late 1975 decedent should live several more years, possibly even 5 more years. Only where death is imminent or predictable will departure from the tables be justified.

On the last point dealt with in *Fabric*, the literal language of §7520(a) — which was enacted in 1988 (subsequent to *Fabric*) — appears to require the use of the actuarial tables in *all* relevant cases (not expressly excepted). However, the regulations under §7520, which were promulgated in 1995 and modified in 1999, provide that the tables are not to be used (or are to be modified) in certain situations. One such situation involves mortality:

> The mortality component . . . may not be used . . . if an individual who is a measuring life is terminally ill at the time the gift is completed. [A]n individual who is known to have an incurable disease or other deteriorating physical condition is considered terminally ill if there is at least a 50 percent probability that the individual will die within 1 year. However, if the individual survives for 18 months or longer after the date the gift is completed, that individual shall be presumed to have not been terminally ill unless the contrary is established by clear and convincing evidence.

See Reg. §25.7520-3(b)(3), which is followed by an example involving a private annuity transaction.

The regulations (and the example) do not consider the ability of the promissor to make the payments for the annuitant's full life expectancy. However, if the promissor had no independent financial resources, it is hard to see how there could have been a "bona fide sale for full and adequate consideration." In that same vein, an annuity trust that is expected to expend the entire corpus before all payments can be made must be re-calculated as an annuity "with the term of years determined by when the fund will be exhausted by the annuity payments." See Reg. §25.7520-3(b)(2)(v), Ex. 5(ii). This exception to the use of the tables confirms the result in *Estate of Froh v. Comm'r*, 100 T.C. 1 (1993), *aff'd in an unpublished opinion*, 46 F.3d 1141 (9th Cir.1995). In *Froh*, a gift tax case, the parties agreed that the gas reserves, and hence the income stream, would be exhausted before the end of the term of the trust. Therefore, the court reasoned, the percentage factor in Table B of the gift tax regulation should not be used to value the gift of the term interest in the property. The regulations provide a method to determine whether that condition exists in a particular situation. See Reg. §20.7520-3(b)(2)(i).

PROBLEMS, QUESTIONS, AND NOTES

1. Suppose Julio, with $1M in hand, invests $660K in a nonrefund nonsurvivor annuity that returns $75K a year (income plus principal) for life. The other $340K is placed in an irrevocable trust, income to be accumulated until Julio's death, at which time the trust is to terminate and its assets are to paid over, free of trust, to Kelsey if then living, but if not to Lance if living. Julio dies after several years, at which time the trust is worth $1.1M, and the annuity is worth zero.
   a. Might the trust be includible in Julio's estate under §2037? Cf. Reg. §20.2037-1(e), Ex. 2. What steps can be taken (in advance) to assure that §2037 will not apply?

    b.   Does the literal language of §2036(a)(1) bar its application in this scenario? Why shouldn't the "value of the property transferred" be construed to mean both the annuity premium and the trust transfer, at least where the two transfers are part of a single transaction? Has Julio retained the possession or enjoyment of the transferred property?

    c.   Does this arrangement save transfer taxes compared to the case where a §2036(a)(1) trust had been created with $1M, producing net income of $75K per year, and the trust being worth $1.1M at Julio's death? Is the arrangement described above "abusive?" Under what economic assumptions would it be advantageous?

    d.   Does it make sense that §2036(a)(1) be so easily avoidable? Are there nontax reasons that would make one hesitate to use this kind of arrangement?

2.   Economically, a combination of a life insurance policy and a single life annuity is a "straddle" position with respect to the same risk; namely, the death of the annuitant-insured. Life insurance is a hedge against the risk of premature death, and a single life annuity is a hedge against living too long (and exhausting one's personal funds).

    a.   The straddle (integrated transaction) analysis was invoked in a prior case involving virtually identical facts, *Helvering v. Le Gierse*, 312 U.S. 531 (1941), to show that the arrangement as a whole was not "life insurance" subject to §2042, because the arrangement as a whole did not involve a "bet" against premature death. *Le Gierse* did not consider the applicability of §2036(a)(1). The holding of *Le Gierse* meant that the transaction in *Fidelity-Philadelphia Trust Co.* could not be analyzed under §2042, which left §2036(a)(1) as the only provision that might have caused inclusion in the gross estate.

    b.   Does the "straddle" analysis suggest that the two transactions in *Fidelity-Philadelphia Trust Co.* should have been integrated (treated as a single transaction) subject to §2036(a)(1)? If the risks are offsetting, the transaction as a whole is a simple investment. In fact, the total premiums paid by the decedent in *Fidelity-Philadelphia Trust Co.* amounted to exactly $230K, and the annual annuity payments totaled $7,466, which is a rate of return of 3.25 percent.[69] In 1934, that would have been a reasonable income return from a trust.[70] Since the insurance company would not have issued the insurance policies without the annuity policies, of what relevance is the fact that the premium for the annuity policy was that which would have been paid by an arm's-length purchaser? All of the

---

    69. These facts are not revealed in either the decision of the Supreme Court or that of the Court of Appeals for the 3d Circuit, 241 F.2d 690, but can be gleaned from the decision of the district court, 142 F. Supp. 561 (E.D. Pa. 1956).

    70. The rate of return on AAA corporate bonds in 1934 was about 4.2 percent. Trusts and insurance products entail management costs.

insurance company obligations were contractual and payable out of its general funds.

3. **a.** The transaction described in *Fidelity-Philadelphia Trust Co.* would now result in inclusion in the gross estate (of the insurance proceeds) under §2039, which is similar to §2036(a)(1) except that the "in the property" requirement is replaced by an "under the same contract or agreement" requirement, where annuities or pension rights are involved. See *Estate of Montgomery v. Comm'r*, 56 T.C. 489 (1971), *aff'd per curiam*, 458 F.2d 616 (5th Cir.1972), *cert. denied*, 409 U.S. 849, set out in §5.3.D. Section 2039 was enacted in 1954, subsequent to the death of the decedent in *Fidelity-Philadelphia Trust Co.*

   b. Can an annuity-insurance combination be structured in a way that would avoid §2039?

   c. Would §2039 apply to separate-fund situations other than annuity-insurance combinations?

   d. Although §2039 ostensibly applies to "annuities," the Service has not attempted to apply §2039(a) to *private* annuities, presumably because there is no identifiable "annuity or other payment receivable by any beneficiary by reason of surviving the decedent," as required by §2039.

4. According to footnote 8 of *Fidelity-Philadelphia Trust Co.*, the characteristics of a private annuity that would avoid §2036(a)(1) are: (1) "the promise is a personal obligation of the transferee," (2) "the obligation is usually not chargeable to the transferred property," and (3) "the size of the payment is not determined by the size of the actual income from the transferred property."

   a. Taking the last factor first, although a tie-in between the annuity amount and the income of the trust should suggest inclusion under §2036(a)(1), the absence of a tie-in should not, in itself, negate it, because "possession or enjoyment" can take a form other than "income." Reg. §20.2036-1(c)(2), issued in 2008, clearly states that retained annuity and unitrust interests trigger §2036(a)(1), the only issue being the amount includible. Thus, if the annuity amount is less than the "table" income yield, the amount included under §2036(a)(1) would be only a portion of the property transferred.

   b. In the private annuity scenario, the annuity payments will exceed the "table" income yield. That portion of the payments that equals the "table" income yield cannot be consideration in money's worth that would wholly negate §2036(a)(1), because the retained income is what triggers §2036(a)(1) in the first place. But the excess of the value of the annuity promise over the value of the "income" right (which is the value of the "principal" component of the annuity) should be viewed as "consideration in money or money's worth" supplied by the promissor. Traditionally, the consideration has been treated as being "partial." See *Estate of Greene v. U.S.*, 237 F.2d 848 (7th Cir.1956). Whether this consideration would be "full and adequate" is considered at §8.1.F.2.

   c. Private annuities only make economic sense if the transferor/annuitant is expected to underperform her actuarial life expectancy. In that scenario, and if actuarial tables are used, the consideration for the transferred amount is overvalued relative to what the transferor ends up receiving. Under the §7520 regulations, the IRS is stuck with having to use the actuarial tables except in cases of imminent death. Actuarial tables are based on statistics for the entire population, and are really not representative of the small population that uses private annuities.

d. The securing of the annuity promise by the transferred property is one way in which the annuity could be held to be "chargeable to the transferred property." There is ample *dicta* and textbook statements to this effect,[71] but no modern §2036(a)(1) cases are on point. Substantial control over the trust property might also result in estate inclusion.[72]

e. If the source of the annuity is designated to be solely the transferred property or the income therefrom, §2036(a)(1) should apply (with the appropriate consideration exclusion or offset). The more difficult case is where the transferred property is the "first" source of the payments backed up by a "personal" obligation of a promisor to make the payments if the property (and the income) should be exhausted. *Fabric* appears to be such a case. Cases apparently to the contrary of *Fabric* include *Estate of Greene v. U.S.*, 237 F.2d 848 (7th Cir.1956), and *Estate of Schwartz v. Comm'r*, 9 T.C. 229 (1947). The IRS can claim that, in a particular case, the "back-up" promise lacks substance (e.g., if the promissor is an individual with no other assets and an unproven earning capacity). See *Mitchell v. Comm'r*, T.C. Memo. 1982-185 (gift tax case).

5. There are numerous income tax issues raised by private annuities.

a. The first issue is whether the transferor is treated as the "owner" of the transferred property under §671, which in turn hinges on whether a trust is involved and, if so, whether the transferor (or the transferor's spouse) is receiving, or might receive in the future, the income "from the property." See §677(a). The analysis used here is essentially the same as would be used in a §2036(a)(1) case, but without any general "control" issue.

b. Assuming the transferor is not treated as the owner under §677(a), the income tax aspects of (1) the property transfer and (2) the receipt of payments is detailed in *Rev. Rul. 69-74*, 1969-1 C.B. 43. As noted above, the private annuity exchange bears a strong resemblance to an installment sale. In the ruling, the Service held that the annuitant recognized gain on whichever was less, the value of the property transferred or the value of the annuity obligation received, less the annuitant's basis in the property. Moreover, such gain is deferred to accord with the receipt of annuity payments, but it is not treated as an "installment sale" under §453. Each annuity payment is, therefore: (1) part pro-rated gain on the exchange, (2) part tax-free return of capital under §72(b), and (3) part

---

71. See *Estate of Bell v. Comm'r*, 60 T.C. 469 (1973) (reviewed) (income tax case).
72. See *Bixby v. Comm'r*, 58 T.C. 757 (1972) (*acq.*).

ordinary income (to the extent that the annuity payment exceeds the return-of-capital and deferred-gain components).

c.   However, case law has held that if the annuity obligation is secured by the property transferred, an escrow, or (presumably) a trust, the gain is recognized all in the year of sale and the annuitant's investment in the contract for purposes of §72 is increased accordingly. See *212 Corp. v. Comm'r*, 70 T.C. 788 (1978) (reviewed).

d.   The promissor receives no income tax deductions for his, her, or its troubles.[73] Of course, that is not a problem if the promissor is not subject to U.S. tax, as was the case in *Fabric*.

F. The Requirement of a Transfer for Less than Full Consideration

Sections 2036-2038 all require that the decedent have made a transfer of the property for less than full and adequate consideration in money or money's worth.

1. Inter Vivos Transfer by the Decedent

In order for any of §§2036-2038 to apply, there must have been a "transfer" by the decedent during life. This requirement is premised on the notion that §§2036-2038 are a back-up to §2033, which cannot apply to property that has been transferred away by the decedent during life.

Property transferred by persons other than the decedent cannot be included in the decedent's gross estate under §§2036-2038. Thus, a basic issue in the estate tax (as well as in the gift tax, infra) is to identify the "real" transferor.

(a) Multiple Transferors

If there is more than one transferor in a situation where any of §§2036-2038 might apply, the maximum amount includible in the estate of a decedent under any of §§2036-2038 is the estate tax value of that portion of the property that can be traced to transfers by the decedent. In most situations, however, tracing is impossible. Where a trust or other entity is involved, the original assets that were transferred are likely to have been replaced or exhausted.

In *U.S. v. O'Malley*, 383 U.S. 627 (1966), the Supreme Court was faced with the issue of whether accumulated income was includible, along with the corpus, under §2036(a)(2). The estate argued that only the corpus was "transferred" by the grantor. The Court, in a rather murky opinion, included the accumulated income.

---

73. See §1275(a)(1)(B) (annuity promise not a debt for various purposes); *Bell v. Comm'r*, 76 T.C. 232 (1981), *aff'd per curiam*, 668 F.2d 448 (8th Cir.1982) (no interest deduction if no "indebtedness"; unsecured private annuity obligation not a debt); *Dix v. Comm'r*, 46 T.C. 796 (1966), *aff'd*, 392 F.2d 313 (4th Cir.1968) (no interest deduction); *Rev. Rul. 72-81*, 1972-1 C.B. 98 (annuity payments constitute nondeductible capital expenditures for acquisition of property).

The accumulated income derived from the amount transferred by the decedent. There was no other individual transferor to the trust in question.

Where tracing is not feasible, the maximum amount includible under any of §§2036-2038 is the estate tax value of the property times a fraction, the numerator of which is the amount transferred by the decedent and the denominator of which is the amount transferred by all transferors. Thus, if A transfers $75x and B $25x into a trust, all of the income to be paid to A for life, and upon A's death the estate tax value of the trust is $400x, the maximum amount includible in A's gross estate is $300x. This approach is the one followed under §2040(a) in the case of joint tenancies with right of survivorship (not involving husband and wife exclusively).

A common dual-transferor situation arises whenever community property is the subject of a transfer. Each spouse is the transferor of one-half of the property for purposes of §§2036-2038. The decedent's personal representative has the burden of proof of showing the extent to which the property transferred was community property. If the decedent died in a "common law" state, the task of tracing present property back to its alleged community-property origins may be rather difficult.[74]

The community-property situation is distinct from gift splitting under §2513. *Gift splitting for gift tax purposes does not alter the identity of the transferor for estate tax purposes.* Thus, if H creates a trust, income to H for life, remainder to C, and H and W file a *gift-splitting election*, H is the "transferor" of the entire trust for estate tax purposes, and the full estate tax value thereof is included in H's gross estate under §2036(a).

(b) Indirect and Constructive Transfers

The notion of "transfer" under the estate tax, as well as under the gift tax, encompasses "indirect" and "constructive" transfers of the type discussed in §3.2. Recall that the indirect-transfer concept has been frequently applied to employee death benefits that avoid inclusion under §2039. Under §2039 itself, contributions by an employer are treated as having been made by the employee (or by the employee and the employee's spouse if community property is involved).

A "constructive" transfer occurs where the decedent never actually possessed the property in question but had the right to acquire it and allowed such right to terminate or lapse, with the result that the property remained (or ended up) in the hands of another. If the decedent continued to possess an interest or power in the property until his death, §§2036-2038 might apply. Situations in which constructive transfers might occur include disclaimers, settlements of will contests, and contractual wills. (However, a disclaimer that qualifies under §2518 is deemed not to be a transfer by the disclaiming party.) The exercise, release, or lapse of a general power of appointment during life also, conceptually speaking, involves a constructive *inter vivos* transfer, but in this case §2041(a)(2) expressly cross references to §§2035-2038. The lapse of a *Crummey* power (see §§3.5.D and 7.1.D) is but one example of a constructive transfer under §2041. Recall that a lapse of a general

---

74. See, e.g., *Chase Nat'l Bank v. Comm'r*, 225 F.2d 621 (8th Cir. 1955).

power of appointment is not deemed to be a transfer to the extent of the greater of $5K or 5 percent of the maximum amount that can be appointed.[75]

NOTES

1. In a reciprocal trust scenario the amount includible should not exceed the estate tax value of the trust transferred by the decedent. (If the trust created by the other party was smaller in amount than the trust created by the decedent, the amount included should be reduced on the ground that the "retained" interest or power pertained to such smaller trust.)

2. a. In a non-trust transfer (e.g., a transfer of real estate with a retained life estate), improvements made by the transferee would be excluded. Presumably, the amount excluded would be the portion of the estate tax value of the property attributable to the improvements.

   b. If the transferee laid waste to the property (above and beyond normal economic depreciation), it is unclear if the amount includible would be reduced by such waste. (In a trust scenario, poor investments by the trustee would reduce the amount includible. Thus, in *Howard v. U.S.*, 125 F.2d 986 (5th Cir.1942), involving a trust included under a §2038, the amount included was the actual property in the trust at the decedent's death.) In *Estate of Humphrey v. Comm'r*, 162 F.2d 1 (5th Cir.1947), *cert. denied*, 332 U.S. 817, it was held that the entire amount of cash transferred in contemplation of death was includible, even though by the time of the transferor's death the transferees had dissipated most of it. However, this holding is probably limited to former §2035 and cases where the transferor retains no "string." See *Estate of DeWitt v. Comm'r*, T.C. Memo. 1994-552.

3. Trusts funded with community property raise various issues under state law and the federal gift and estate taxes.

   a. The first state law issue is which spouse has the legal power to effect a transfer of community property into an *inter vivos* trust. State law may require both spouses to join in the transfer, especially in the case of real property. Otherwise, the spouse who is the "manager" of the particular community property can make the transfer without joinder by the other spouse. This state law issue, however, has no bearing on the federal transfer tax result: If community property is transferred (by one or both spouses) each spouse is the transferor of half of the property.

   b. In cases where one spouse had the power to transfer the community property to a trust, an issue may arise as to whether the transfer can be

---

75. See §2041(b)(2); *Fish v. U.S.*, 432 F.2d 1278 (9th Cir.1970) (incompetency of holder of power held to be immaterial; also, the 5 percent referred to the income subject to the withdrawal power, not the corpus).

set aside by the other spouse under such doctrines as "illusory trust" or "fraud." Various defenses might exist to such a claim, such as consent, ratification, or laches. Since the possibility of a set-aside can only be established by litigation, and is highly dependant on the facts, such possibility is not considered to be a power of revocation or a general power of appointment for transfer tax purposes, and would not negate the initial transfer.

c. Another state law issue is who, if anybody, has the power to revoke a trust funded with community property. The prudent thing to do is to spell this out in the trust instrument.

(i)   If one spouse only has the power to revoke and vest all of the property in himself as separate property, an issue is whether property transferred to the trust immediately changes its character from community property to that of the separate property of the power holder. A conversion would operate as a present gift by the other spouse to the spouse holding the revocation power. However, such a conversion is unlikely to be implied under state law.[76] Alternatively, if there is no present gift but the power-holding spouse can vest the property in himself, the spouse having the power would possess a general power of appointment over the other spouse's half interest in the property (as well as the power to revoke his half of the community property).

(ii) Another possibility is to give each spouse the right to revoke as to one-half of the property during their joint lives. This might operate to presently convert the community property into equal portions of separate property, a conversion which — although it would not entail any gift for gift tax purposes — would remove the property from the community-property basis rule of §1014(b)(6).

(iii) A third possibility, under the terms of the trust or state law, is that the trust (and its property) continues its character as community property, and that any revocation would not alter that status. If the trust terminates upon the death of the first spouse with half going to the surviving spouse and the other half to third parties, the half going to the survivor will be deemed to be the survivor's own share of the community property, and the half going to third parties will not qualify for the marital deduction in the decedent spouse's estate. But if the trust terminates with all of the property passing to third parties, the survivor will be deemed to have made a gift of her half to the third parties. If the community-property trust continues after the death of the first spouse, the decedent will be treated as having made an estate-included transfer of his share and the survivor as having made an *inter vivos* transfer of her share as of the decedent spouse's death.

---

76. See *Katz v. U.S.*, 382 F.2d 723 (9th Cir.1967) (California law).

2. *Transfers for Consideration in Money or Money's Worth*

Sections 2036-2038 all assume an *inter vivos* transfer that was gratuitous in nature. A transfer, otherwise includible under these sections, made in exchange for full and adequate consideration in money or money's worth is excluded, as the property transferred has been fully replaced with money or other property. This result is codified in the parenthetical phrase referring to full and adequate consideration found in §§2036(a), 2037(a), and 2038(a).

If consideration in money or money's worth is given, but it is not "full and adequate," such partial consideration reduces the amount includible pursuant to §2043(a).

(a) What Qualifies as Consideration in Money or Money's Worth

The concept of consideration in money or money's worth has already been discussed in the context of the gift tax. See §3.1.A.1. The concept of "money or money's worth" derives from the necessity for the consideration to constitute wealth that would augment the transferor's potential §2033 gross estate. Thus, the estate and gift tax concept of consideration in money or money's worth is distinguishable from the broader concept of consideration under the law of contracts. Thus, if A conveys property to B on condition that B create an irrevocable trust that gives A an income interest for life, A has made a transfer for consideration in the contract-law sense (which results in A being the "real" transferor of a §2036(a)(1) trust under the indirect transfer doctrine), but the consideration provided by B, being a mere promise, is not in the form of money or money's worth.

The surrender of a claim against the transferor generally constitutes consideration in money's worth. However, the release by a spouse (or future spouse) of inheritance rights is not considered to be valid consideration, because such a release does not increase the transferor's wealth. See §2043(b)(1). But a release of support rights is treated as consideration in money or money's worth by analogy to any other release of a current debt or other current liability of the transferor. See *Rev. Rul.* 78-379, 1978-2 C.B. 238.

To qualify for estate tax purposes, the consideration must be given by the person who acquires the interests that would (but for the exclusion) be included in the gross estate. See *Estate of Keller v. Comm'r*, 45 T.C. 851 (1965). Thus, if A creates a trust, income to B for life, then to A if living, but if not to C, A has made a transfer of the §2037 variety. If B paid consideration to A in an amount equal to the value of B's income interest, this consideration does not negate the application of §2037, since B's life estate would be excluded from B's gross estate in any event. (However, the consideration would be full and adequate for gift tax purposes.) By way of contrast, if A creates a trust, income to A for life, remainder to C, consideration given by C for the transfer of the remainder interest to C qualifies for estate tax purposes.

If a person supplies consideration in excess of what she receives, the excess consideration may (or may not) be treated as an indirect gift by the consideration provider to another beneficiary of the trust. See *Rev. Rul.* 77-314, 1977-2 C.B. 349.

The consideration must not constitute the very element that causes inclusion under §§2036-2038 in the first place. See *U.S. v. Past*, 347 F.2d 7 (8th Cir.1965).

These points can be illustrated by a reciprocal trust scenario involving crossed income interests, such as that presented in *Estate of Grace*, supra. Suppose that A creates a trust with $1M, income to B for life, remainder to C, and B creates a trust with $800K, income to A for life, remainder to C, and that A and B are the same age. The income interest received by A (from B) does not qualify as consideration *for estate tax purposes*, because that interest is the very thing that causes §2036(a)(1) to apply in the first place (resulting in inclusion in A's gross estate of 80 percent of the value of A's trust). The income interest received by B (from A) causes all of B's trust to be included in B's gross estate. The problem is how to account for the excess consideration coming from A's trust to B (the value of an income interest in $200K). This excess amount should not reduce the amount included in B's gross estate, because it is not an indirect transfer from A to C. Instead, it should be treated as a simple net gift from A to B.

Prior to the enactment of §2516, there were numerous cases posing complex consideration issues involving trusts created by a husband for an ex-wife and children that were included under §2036 or §2037.[77] An issue in many of these cases is whether any excess consideration provided by the wife (in the form of her surrender of support rights) should have been treated as indirect transfers by the wife to adult child trust beneficiaries through the husband's trust, in which case the excess consideration would reduce the net amount included in the husband's gross estate.

(b) When Is the Consideration to Be Valued?

The fact that consideration is received at the time of transfer for interests that are included in the gross estate at the transferor's death raises the issue of how to "match" a gift-date value with death-date value. The matching approach determines whether consideration is "full and adequate," as opposed to "partial." There are three conceivable approaches to matching consideration to estate tax values:

(1) Consideration would be fixed at its gift-time value and compared to the estate tax value.

(2) Consideration would be traced forward and valued at the estate tax valuation date.

(3) The consideration would be matched with the gift tax value of the amount transferred. If the consideration equals (or exceeds) the amount transferred, the transfer would be treated as being "full and adequate." Otherwise, the amount included would be the "non-sale fraction" of the transfer:

$$\text{amount included} = \frac{(\text{gift value} - \text{less consideration})}{\text{gift value}} \times \text{estate tax value}$$

---

77. See, e.g., *Spruance v. Comm'r*, 60 T.C. 141 (1973), *aff'd*, 505 F.2d 731 (3d Cir.1974); *Estate of Glen v. Comm'r*, 45 T.C. 323 (1966) (reviewed); *Estate of Hartshorne v. Comm'r*, 48 T.C. 882 (1967); *Estate of Nelson v. Comm'r*, 47 T.C. 279 (1966), *rev'd on other grounds*, 396 F.2d 519 (2d Cir.1968); *Rev. Rul.* 77-314, 1977-2 C.B. 349.

To state the matter briefly, the third approach is used to "test" whether consideration is "full and adequate," but, if it is not, the first approach is used, thanks to the case set forth below.

United States v. Righter
400 F.2d 344 (8th Cir.1965)

Before BLACKMUN, GIBSON and HEANEY, Circuit Judges.
BLACKMUN, Circuit Judge.

The decedent, Edna, died December 27, 1961. Edna's threatened contest of [her sister's] will was settled with the execution of an agreement and of a trust indenture on January 18, 1950. Pursuant to the provisions of these instruments Edna transferred to the trustee her 316 shares in a corporation and two nephews transferred to the trustee 158 shares of the same stock. The 474 shares comprised the corpus of the trust. The indenture provided that Edna was to be paid the dividends so long as she lived, and that upon her death the stock was to be distributed to the nephews.

Except for her receipt of consideration, the 316 shares Edna transferred to the trust would be fully includible under §2036(a)(1) because of her retention of the right to the income therefrom. The 316 shares were valued as of the [estate tax] valuation date at $379,200. The measure of the shares' includability in Edna's gross estate is, under §2043(a), only "the excess of the [estate tax] value of said shares over the value of the consideration received therefor by decedent." The consideration received was the interest for her life in the 158 shares transferred by the nephews. How that consideration is to be valued is our problem.

From the inception of the trust in 1950 until her death in 1961, Edna received from the trust dividends on the 158 shares in the amount of $229,890. According to [actuarial] tables utilized by the Service, the present worth on January 18, 1950, of a life estate in a fund consisting of the 158 shares, for a female of Edna's age, was $35,773. The District Court concluded that the includible transfer is to be reduced by the total Edna received from the trust, that is, $229,390. We disagree and reverse.

The estate's argument is that the statute, when it speaks of "the consideration received therefor by the decedent," is plain, simple language and means precisely what it says, that is, receipts by the decedent, which here consist of the dividends on the 158 shares. This reasoning is said to be buttressed by the facts that the value of property subject to federal estate tax is always determined as of the date of death or optional valuation date and that the use of mortality tables is unnecessary here where what Edna received is susceptible of exact proof.

We hold that the statute means consideration received by the transferor-decedent as of the date the transfer for the insufficient consideration is made, not as of the subsequent date of the decedent's death. A number of factors support this conclusion:

1. The transaction was in January 1950. That is when the opposing transfers were effectuated by Edna and by the nephews. In this sense, we read the statutory

words "consideration received" in the present tense, not as "income received on the consideration property as long as the decedent lives."

2. Admittedly, the use of the transfer date for evaluating the consideration and the use of the death date for evaluating the includible property may produce, on occasion, a strange or curious result. This may happen when the consideration property is a fee interest and substantially changes in value between the transfer date and the estate tax valuation date. But the facts may cut either way. The difficulty, if there be one, lies in the statute. There is nothing improper or unusual, in tax law, in having death tax consequences flow from a pre-death event and, at the same time, in having valuation directed to the date of death or optional valuation date.

3. The estate's argument that "consideration received" is to be measured by total life income is necessarily at cross purposes with the determination of when a transfer, within the statute's language, "is not a bona fide sale for an adequate and full consideration in money or money's worth." That determination can only be made at the time of the transfer and cannot be deferred and made to hang on future fortuitous circumstances of longevity and of income.

4. It is evident, we think, that had Edna died soon after the inception of the trust and before any dividends were received by the trustee, or if the trust corpus were nonproductive, the estate would not be conceding that no consideration was received by Edna for the property she transferred. Yet this is the result compelled by a rule which measures consideration by lifetime receipts.

5. Valuation by measuring income may lead to difficulties in practice. What if the consideration property is destroyed or lost or given away or dissipated or rendered nonproductive? In the situation where no trust is present, it is possible, perhaps likely, that the decedent would sell and not retain the consideration property. And if sold, do we have a tracing problem which must be resolved before "consideration received" can be measured or is consideration then to be the income plus the sale price?

The points made in the *Righter* opinion do not justify rejection of alternative (3) (the pro-rata-transfer approach), which fixes the estate-inclusion fraction at the date of gift. However, the taxpayer in *Righter* did not advance that approach,[78] and in *Magnin v. Comm'r*, 184 F.3d 1074 (9th Cir.1999), it was flatly rejected on the ground that the text of §2043(a) mandated the *Righter* approach.[79] The *Righter* rule for measuring partial consideration is now well-entrenched, despite its inconsistency with testing "full and adequate" at the date of the gift transfer.

---

78. The pro-rata sale approach was apparently used in the early case of *Helvering v. U.S. Trust Co.*, 111 F.2d 576 (2d Cir.1940). *Nourse v. Riddell*, 143 F. Supp. 759 (S.D. Cal. 1956), used an actual-income approach in a full-and-adequate consideration case. In *Estate of Vardell v. Comm'r*, 307 F.2d 688 (5th Cir.1960), it was stated that the measure of partial consideration was the lesser of the gift tax value of the income interest or the actual income received.

79. Anticipating *Righter* in explicitly rejecting an actual-income approach was *Estate of Gregory v. Comm'r*, 39 T.C. 1012 (1963).

(c) "Full and Adequate" in Relation to What?

If a transfer is made for "full and adequate" consideration, §§2036-2038 are completely barred. Intense controversy has arisen over the situation where a grantor has created a trust, retaining a current-enjoyment interest for life (or a term of years), and has received consideration from the remainder equal to the actuarial value of the remainder interest. Basically, this amounts to a sale of a remainder interest accompanied by retention of a current-enjoyment interest. The issue, dealt with in *Estate of D'Ambrosio* set out below, is whether the consideration is "full and adequate" if it equals the value of the remainder interest, as opposed to the value of the entire property.

Estate of D'Ambrosio v. Commissioner

101 F.3d 309 (3d Cir.1996), cert. denied, 520 U.S. 1230 (1997)

Before COWEN, NYGAARD and LEWIS, Circuit Judges.
NYGAARD, Circuit Judge.

Decedent owned, inter alia, one half of the preferred stock of Vaparo, Inc.; these 470 shares had a fair market value of $2,350,000. In 1987, at the age of 80, decedent transferred her remainder interest in her shares to Vaparo in exchange for an annuity which was to pay her $296,039 per year and retained her income interest in the shares. According to the actuarial tables set forth in the Treasury Regulations, the annuity had a fair market value of $1,324,014. The parties stipulate that this was also the fair market value of the remainder interest.

Section 2036(a) effectively discourages manipulative transfers of remainder interests which are really testamentary in character by "pulling back" the full, fee simple value of the transferred property into the gross estate, except when the transfer was "a bona fide sale for adequate and full consideration." The issue is whether the sale of a remainder interest for its fair market value constitutes "adequate and full consideration" within the meaning of §2036(a). Appellant argues that it does. The Commissioner takes the position that only consideration equal to the fee simple value of the property is sufficient. Appellant has the better argument.

The Tax Court and the Commissioner rely principally on *Gradow v. U.S.*, 11 Cl. Ct. 808 (1987), *aff'd*, 897 F.2d 516 (Fed. Cir.1990); *Estate of Gregory v. Comm'r*, 39 T.C. 1012 (1963); *U.S. v. Allen*, 293 F.2d 916 (10th Cir.1961). We find these cases either inapposite or unpersuasive.

In *Allen* [set out at §8.1.B.3], the decedent set up an irrevocable *inter vivos* trust in which she retained a life estate and gave the remainder to her children. Apparently realizing the tax liability she had created for her estate under the predecessor of §2036, she later attempted to sell her retained life interest to her son for an amount slightly in excess of its fair market value. After she died, the estate took the position that, because decedent had divested herself of her retained life interest for fair market value, none of the trust property was includable in her gross estate. The Court of Appeals disagreed, holding that consideration is only "adequate" if it equals or exceeds the value of the interest that would otherwise be included in the gross estate absent the transfer.

Allen, however, is inapposite, as the Commissioner now concedes, because it involved the sale of a life estate after the remainder had already been disposed of by gift, a testamentary transaction with a palpable tax evasion motive. This case, in contrast, involves the sale of a remainder for its stipulated fair market value. Nevertheless, we agree with its rationale that consideration should be measured against the value that would have been drawn into the gross estate absent the transfer.

Gregory presents a closer factual analogy to D'Ambrosio's situation. *Gregory* was a "widow's election" case involving the testamentary disposition of community property. Typically in such cases, the husband wishes to pass the remainder interest in all of the marital property to his children, while providing for the lifetime needs of his surviving spouse. In a community property state, however, half of the marital property belongs to the wife as a matter of law, so he cannot pass it by his own will. To circumvent this problem, the will is drafted to give the widow a choice: take her one-half share in fee simple, according to law, or [allow] her half of the community property [to pass to a trust created by her husband's will] in exchange for a life estate in the whole. Put another way, she trades the remainder interest in her half of the community property in exchange for a life estate in her husband's half.

In *Gregory*, the widow exchanged property worth approximately $66,000 for a life estate with an actuarial value of only around $12,000; by the time she died eight years later, the property she gave up had appreciated to approximately $102,000. The Tax Court compared the $102,000 outflow to the $12,000 consideration and concluded that the widow's election did not constitute a bona fide sale for an adequate and full consideration.

We believe that the *Gregory* court erred in its analysis, although it reached the correct result on the particular facts of that case. Rather than evaluate the adequacy of the consideration at the time the decedent dies, we will compare the value of the remainder transferred to the value of the consideration received, measured as of the date of the transfer. In *Gregory*, the $12,000 the decedent received was grossly inadequate against the value of the property she transferred, regardless of the valuation date. The court was therefore correct that the transfer was not for adequate and full consideration. Because of that gross inadequacy, however, the holding of *Gregory* does not extend to the issue now before us: whether, when a remainder is sold for its stipulated fair market value, the consideration received is inadequate because it is less than the fee simple value of the property.

The facts in *Gradow* were similar to those in *Gregory*; both are "widow's election" cases. [There] the court focused on the statutory language of §2036:

[T]here is no question that the term "property" in the phrase "The gross estate shall include . . . all property . . . of which the decedent has at any time made a transfer" means that part of the trust corpus attributable to plaintiff. If §2036(a) applies, all of Betty's former community property is brought into her gross estate. Fundamental principles of grammar dictate that the parenthetical exception which then follows — "(except in case of a bona fide sale . . .)" — refers to a transfer of that same property, i.e., the one-half of the community property she placed into the trust.

We cannot agree with the *Gradow* court's conclusions that "property" refers to the fee simple interest and that adequate consideration must be measured against that value. Rather, we believe that the clear import of the phrase "to the extent of any interest therein" is that the gross estate shall include the value of the remainder interest, unless it was sold for adequate and fair consideration.

The *Gradow* court also believed that its construction of §2036 was "most consistent" with its purposes. The Tax Court in this case was persuaded that decedent's sale of her remainder interest was testamentary in character and designed to avoid the payment of estate tax that otherwise would have been due. It noted particularly that the transfer was made when decedent was eighty years old and that the value of the annuity she received was over $1 million less than the fee simple value of the stock she gave up. [However,] it is not our role to police the techniques of estate planning by determining, based on our own policy views and perceptions, which transfers are abusive and which are not. That is properly the role of Congress, whose statutory enactments we are bound to interpret.

Even looking at this case in policy terms, however, it is difficult to fathom either the tax court's or the Commissioner's concerns about the "abusiveness" of this transaction. A fee simple interest is comprised of a life estate and a remainder. Returning to the widow's election cases, assume that the surviving spouse's share of the community property is valued at $2,000,000. Assuming that she decides not to accept the settlement and to keep that property, its whole value will be available for inclusion in the gross estate at death. Next, assume that same widow decides to sell her remainder and keep a life estate. As long as she sells the remainder for its fair market value, it makes no difference whether she receives cash, other property, or an annuity. All can be discounted to their respective present values and quantified. In sum, there is simply no change in the date-of-death value of the final estate, regardless of which option she selects.

Assume that a decedent sells his son a remainder interest in Blackacre, which is worth $1 million in fee simple, for its actuarial fair market value of $100,000 (an amount which implicitly includes the market value of Blackacre's expected appreciation). Decedent then invests the proceeds of the sale. If the rates of return for both assets are equal and decedent lives exactly as long as the actuarial tables predict, the consideration that decedent received for his remainder will equal the value of Blackacre on the date of his death. The equivalent value will, accordingly, still be included in the gross estate. Moreover, decedent's son will have only a $100,000 basis in Blackacre, because that is all he paid for it. He will then be subject to capital gains taxes on its appreciated value if he decides to ever sell the property. Had Blackacre been passed by decedent's will and included in the gross estate, the son would have received a stepped-up basis at the time of his father's death or the alternate valuation date. We therefore have great difficulty understanding how this transaction could be abusive.

Because we conclude that the tax court erred as a matter of law when it determined that the consideration received by Rose D'Ambrosio for her remainder interest was not adequate and full, we will reverse and remand for it to enter judgment in favor of the estate.

Cowen, Circuit Judge, dissenting.

The Tax Court's opinion is supported by well-established case law and the plain language of the Internal Revenue Code. It should be affirmed.

The majority holds that under section 2036(a), "adequate and full consideration" must be provided merely for that portion of the taxpayer's property interest actually transferred, rather than for the full value of the property that is the basis for the ongoing income interest. The majority excludes from the computation of "full and adequate consideration" the value of decedent's life interest in the transferred stock, on the grounds that D'Ambrosio retained that interest. When a taxpayer makes a transfer with a retained life interest, the powerful arm of section 2036(a) pulls into the gross estate the full value of the transferred property, not merely the value of the remainder interest.

The majority accepts the view of the estate that the decedent "sold" only the remainder interest to Vaparo. This view of section 2036 sanctions tax evasion: It enables strategic segmentation of the property into multiple interests, with "adequate and full consideration" now required only for a specific transferred segment, rather than the indivisible whole. Such an interpretation of section 2036(a) thwarts its very purpose, enabling taxpayers to avoid paying estate taxes on property while retaining the income benefits of ownership.

The estate asserts that the Tax Court erred because it misunderstood or disregarded the "economic reality" of a sale of a remainder interest. To the contrary, it was precisely the Tax Court's awareness of the economic realities of a retained interest transaction that led it to follow well-established law. Executrix D'Ambrosio alleges that if the Decedent had retained and invested the dividends from the Vaparo Stock and from the annuity payments received during her life, the potential value of her gross estate as a result of the sale would be worth no less on the date of her death, than if she had never sold the remainder interest in the Vaparo Stock. This view ignores the very reason for section 2036(a). Its purpose is precisely to prevent taxpayers from retaining the practical benefits of asset ownership during their lifetime while divesting themselves for estate tax purposes of a portion of that property. As the court in *Gradow* correctly explained:

> [The "economic reality" argument] flies squarely in the face of the Supreme Court's analysis as to the assumptions and purposes behind 2036(a). The Court has taught that §2036(a) is a reflection of Congress' judgment that transfers with retained life estates are generally testamentary transactions and should be treated as such for estate tax purposes. The fond hope that a surviving spouse would take pains to invest, compound, and preserve inviolate all life income from half of a trust, knowing that it would thereupon be taxed without his having received any lifetime benefit, is a slim basis for putting a different construction on §2036(a) than the one heretofore consistently adopted.

11 Cl. Ct. at 815-816.

D'Ambrosio has been followed by the Fifth and Ninth Circuits. *Wheeler v. U.S.*, 116 F.3d 749 (5th Cir.1997); *Estate of Magnin v. Comm'r*, 184 F.3d 1074 (9th Cir.1999).

According to the trust that D created and to which she transferred $10M, income is to be paid to Auntie Anti for life, and corpus at Anti's death to D; but if D is not then living, corpus to Bravado, D's daughter. When D dies before Auntie Anti, which one of the following statements is *FALSE*?

A. D has made a completed gift of $10M, less an annual exclusion for Anti's income interest.

B. Because there is a beneficiary (Bravado) who must survive D in order to receive the property, the survivorship requirement of §2037 is met.

C. D has retained a reversionary interest includible under §2033.

D. If the value of D's reversionary interest at D's death is more than 5 percent of the value of the trust corpus, the date of death FMV of Bravado's remainder interest is included in D's estate under §2037.

QUESTIONS AND NOTES

1. a. Did the consideration in *Righter* meet all of the tests for qualification? In *Righter* and *D'Ambrosio*, the life estate or annuity received would not, as an interest, be includible in the transferor's gross estate under §2033, because it expired at the decedent's death. Nevertheless, this fact did not disqualify such interest as consideration. Why not?

   b. *Righter* was a "partial consideration" case under §2043(a). Virtually no observer agrees with the result as a matter of logic or theory. Does the language of §2043(a) mandate the *Righter* result? Reg. §20.2043-1(a) states that "only the excess of the fair market value of the property (as of the applicable valuation date) over the price received by the decedent. . . ." Is this formulation unambiguous?

2. a. Both *Gradow* and *D'Ambrosio* take the position that the consideration, to be full and adequate, should match the value of the property transferred. Of what significance, then, is the phrase in §2036(a) "to the extent of any interest therein of which?" Does it refer to what the decedent transferred, or does it refer to the interest that is included in the gross estate? In a §2036(a)(1) scenario, what is "transferred?" Is it the fee or is it the remainder interest? What is the amount included? Is it the fee or the remainder interest?

   b. The majority opinion in *D'Ambrosio* relies on actuarial tables, as well as present-value and compound-interest concepts: The present value of the consideration received (for the remainder interest) would, if invested, equal the value of the fee at the time the transferor's lifetime is expected to end. However, this analysis leads to the conclusion that §2036(a)(1) serves no purpose, because the gift tax, after all, would reach the value of the remainder interest in accordance with mortality tables and present-value analysis. The whole point of §2036(a)(1) is to avoid giving the date-of-transfer facts any finality. If §2036(a)(1) did not exist, retained-enjoyment-interest transfers would be opportunistically used by donors expecting to underperform their statistical life expectancies (as is the case with private annuities). Reduction to present value allows wealth transfers to be brought under the exemption amount.

c. The majority opinion in *D'Ambrosio* states that the actuarial value of a remainder interest includes future appreciation. This statement is misleading. It is true that the *current* value of any property is (presumably) the discounted present value of all future returns, including appreciation. But the actuarial tables simply divide such *current* value into two components, the income interest and the remainder interest, on the basis of standard assumptions. The value of a remainder interest in property is the current value of the property times the actuarial factor for a remainder interest, and such factor is simply the number 1.0 discounted to the present for the period of the measuring life at the discount rate provided by the table. In other words, the value of a remainder interest under the tables *assumes no appreciation at all* (and that *all* economic return, at the assumed rate, goes to the "income" interest). But a trust is typically operated so that some economic return is shifted from current income to appreciation.

d. The higher the discount rate, the lower the value of remainder interests. The discount rate assumed under the actuarial tables issued under §7520 is 120 percent of the applicable federal mid-term rate (AFR), which is keyed to fixed-yield U.S. government debt obligations. Thus, even assuming no appreciation to corpus, remainder interests are systematically undervalued by the gift and estate tax actuarial tables, and the consideration needed to fully "pay for" such an interest would also be undervalued.

e. Can *D'Ambrosio* really be reconciled with *Allen*? Wouldn't the same kind of time-value-of-money analysis employed in *D'Ambrosio* lead to the conclusion that there was no tax avoidance in an *Allen*-type situation?

3. Transfers for consideration "look like" sales or exchanges, and as such numerous income tax issues are raised. These are only sketched here. For purposes of illustration, assume a sale of a remainder interest such as occurred in *D'Ambrosio*.

a. The "buyer" of the remainder interest would have a basis in his or her interest equal to the greater of "cost" or her §1015 basis (but not the sum of the two). See Reg. §1.1015-4. The §1015 basis of the remainder (for purposes of determining gain or loss) would, in turn, be an amount equal to the §1015 basis for the property as a whole times the actuarial factor for a remainder interest following a measuring life of the seller's age at the time the buyer sells the remainder interest. See Reg. §1.1015-1(b); *Rev. Rul.* 77-413, 1977-2 C.B. 298.

b. The retained income interest, if *not* in trust, is a wasting asset that could be amortized by the transferor were it not for §167(e), which disallows amortization deductions. If the transfer is in trust, the income would be taxed to the transferor under §677(a), with no amortization deduction with respect to the income interest.

c.   If the sale of the remainder interest were for an annuity or other periodic-payment consideration, it would appear that the possibility of deferring any gain would be governed by the authorities applicable to private annuity transactions.

4.   The following material, dealing with spousal election wills, will probably be of direct interest only to students expecting to practice in a community-property jurisdiction.

a.   Prior to the enactment of §2702 in 1990, a typical "spousal election will" involving community property involved an *inter vivos* transfer by the surviving spouse of her share of the community property into a trust created under the husband's will with retained income interest "in exchange" for an income interest in the deceased spouse's share of the community property. Essentially, the surviving spouse exchanges a remainder interest in her share of the community property for an income interest in the deceased spouse's share.[80] The remainder interest usually is conferred on the couple's issue. In the scenario just described, the surviving spouse's share will be included in her gross estate under §2036(a), pending any consideration exclusion or offset.

b.   A preliminary issue is whether this transaction should be treated as "a bona fide sale" for consideration in money's worth. In a community-property jurisdiction, either spouse can "disinherit" the other spouse (refuse to bequeath any amount to the surviving spouse). There is no election against the deceased spouse's will. Thus, by accepting the arrangement, the surviving spouse is obtaining something that she is not entitled to, in conjunction with creating a §2036(a) transfer (giving up a remainder interest in her own share of the community property). Thus, for estate tax purposes, the transaction is more like a sale or exchange than one of coincidental gratuitous transfers.[81]

c.   A possible problem with treating the income interest in the husband's share as "qualifying" consideration is that the consideration is not provided by the persons obtaining the remainder interest. But then, the deceased spouse can be said to be making an indirect bequest through the surviving spouse to the remainders: The surviving spouse is given an

---

80. See *Comm'r v. Siegel*, 230 F.2d 339 (9th Cir.1957) (gift tax); *Estate of Vardell v. Comm'r*, 307 F.2d 688 (5th Cir.1962) (estate tax); *Estate of Christ v. Comm'r*, 54 T.C. 493 (1970), *aff'd*, 480 F.2d 171 (9th Cir.1973) (income tax).

81. In *Helvering v. Butterworth*, 290 U.S. 365 (1933), the Supreme Court held that a wife taking a lesser interest under her husband's will than she had under a common-law-state elective share statute was an estate beneficiary and not a purchaser of an income stream. *Butterworth* was "distinguished" by the Tax Court in *Estate of Christ*, supra, on the ground that the surviving spouse in the community-property situation is giving up an interest in her own property, rather than choosing between alternative forms of inheritance rights.

income interest "on condition" that the surviving spouse give up a remainder interest in her own property. To the extent that the deceased spouse is the real transferor of this remainder interest, the surviving spouse is not its transferor. This indirect-transfer analysis produces the same result as consideration-offset analysis.

d. The indirect-transfer analysis was adopted by the Supreme Court in *U.S. v. Stapf*, 375 U.S. 118 (1963), as the basis for disallowing the marital deduction (to the estate of the deceased spouse) by reason of §2056(b)(4). At the same time, none of the *deceased spouse's* property will be included in the surviving spouse's estate, because she only has an income interest in the deceased spouse's share of the community property.

e. The aim of the spousal election will is that the surviving spouse's share of the community property will avoid full inclusion under §§2036-2038 on account of a consideration exclusion or offset. If the *D'Ambrosio* approach becomes generally accepted, the possibility that the surviving spouse's estate will avoid §2036(a) entirely will be increased. However, the value of an income interest for the life of the surviving spouse in the deceased spouse's share (the consideration received) would normally be relatively small in amount, unless the surviving spouse is expected to outlive the deceased spouse by a significant period of time.

f. Section 2702, enacted in 1990 (and discussed shortly) has emerged as an obstacle to the traditional spousal election will device. However, that section can be avoided if the surviving spouse retains the power to "alter" the remainder interest in her share of the community property. See §2702(a)(3)(A)(i) & (B). (In that case, there is no completed transfer of either the income interest or the remainder interest in the surviving spouse's property.) But that poses a new issue (apparently not yet squarely decided): If the surviving spouse has given nothing away (in the eyes of the gift tax), how can she be receiving consideration in a sale transaction? In *Robinson v. Comm'r*, 675 F.2d 774 (5th Cir.1982), *cert. denied*, 459 U.S. 970, it was held that, in just this scenario, the consideration received by the surviving spouse could not be treated as being "for" her later release of her retained power to alter (which completed the gift of the remainder interest). Moreover, the Fifth Circuit (675 F.2d at 781 n. 20) intimated that there would be no consideration offset for estate tax purposes if the power had not been released.[82]

g. An income tax issue arises under the spousal election will device on account of the fact that the consideration is a "carved out" income interest in the deceased spouse's community-property share. There is strong authority from outside of the spousal election will situation to the effect that a sale of a carved-out income interest yields a zero basis offset and

---

82. Cf. also *Steinman v. Comm'r*, 69 T.C. 804 (1978) (no consideration offset when transferor retained both income interest and *general* testamentary power of appointment).

ordinary income to the transferor. See *Comm'r v. P.G. Lake, Inc.*, 356 U.S. 260 (1958).

§8.2. Section 2702 and Its Impact on Retained-Interest Gifts

This section reviews the gift tax and GST treatment of transfers with retained interests, and discusses the manner in which double taxation of such transfers under the estate and gift tax is mitigated.

Assuming that §2702 does not apply, the value of a gift shall be reduced by the (actuarial) value of any retained interest(s) calculated by using actuarial tables. *However, if the retained interest is incapable of being valued under actuarial tables, its value cannot be subtracted. Robinette v. Helvering*, 318 U.S. 184 (1983); Reg. §25.2511-1(e). If an interest (otherwise capable of actuarial valuation) is subject to a retained power to revoke, alter, or amend, it shall be treated as a retained interest for purposes of the foregoing. For a more elaborate explanation of these rules, see §3.4.C.

A. Section 2702

Section 2702, applicable to gift transfers made after October 8, 1990, operates to override the foregoing rules in many situations to the detriment of the donor, and significantly alters the calculus of a donor contemplating a retained-interest gift.

1. Basic Operating Rule

Where §2702 applies, the retained interest will be worth zero for gift tax purposes, resulting in a deemed gift of the retained interest! §2702(a)(2)(A). Thus, if D creates an irrevocable trust, income to D for life, remainder to R, §2702 operates so as to treat D as having made a gift of the retained income interest (as well as of the remainder interest). Since the actual income received (if not consumed) will augment A's §2033 gross estate, §2702 may be said to have the effect of taxing the same "thing" twice.

The deemed-gift retained interest does not qualify for the annual exclusion, because it is not "really" a present-interest gift. See Reg. §25.2502-2-6(c), Ex. 1.

Following the same "logic," it appears that a deemed gift of a retained interest under §2702 cannot be split with one's spouse under §2513. See Reg. §25.2702-6(a)(3) (referring to gift splitting on subsequent transfer of retained interest).

If any deemed-gift retained interest is subsequently made the subject of a gift (or included, as an interest, in the transferor's gross estate), the amount of the later gift or estate transfer is reduced (but not below zero) by the earlier §2702 deemed gift of the same interest. See Reg. §25.2702-6. Thus, if D creates a trust, income to D for life, remainder to R, D is initially treated as having made a gift of the entire fee interest in the property. If D makes a later gift of her retained income interest, this mitigation rule would apply. But it would not apply if D died without having made this later gift, since the retained income interest is not (as an interest) included in D's gross estate under §2033 or §2036(a)(1), because it expired at D's death.

2. *Why §2702 Was Enacted*

Section 2702 was enacted in 1990 to "do away" with the device called the grantor retained income trust (GRIT), which was considered to be abusive. In a typical pre-1990 GRIT, D (age 55) creates an irrevocable trust with (say) $1M, retaining the income for (say) 25 years, remainder to R. If the applicable federal rate (AFR) for the month of the gift is 5 percent, one would use the 6 percent tables (because 120% of 5% is 6%) for determining remainder interests for a term certain, and the value of the remainder interest after 20 years would be $233K. Assume that D dies 26 years later at age 81. Since D outlived the 25-year term of the trust, the GRIT would avoid inclusion in D's gross estate, because the retained income interest lapsed before D's death. (Even though the lapse occurred within three years of D's death, §2035(a) is avoided, since a lapse is not a "transfer" under §2035(a).) The GRIT could have been be set up and/or operated so as to obtain an "appreciation return" rather than an "income return." Suppose at D's death the trust is worth $3.2M. D would have removed this amount from her gross estate but has only been charged for a gift of $233K! Although D would have received the income from this trust, the "income" yield could have been suppressed in favor of appreciation.

Congress could have dealt with this perceived abuse by treating this transfer as being incomplete for gift tax purposes until the retained income interest expires. In that case, D would be charged with a delayed gift of about $3M at the end of the 25-year trust period. But Congress instead chose to enact §2702, which treats D as having made an up-front (*ex ante*) gift of $1M. In transfer tax jargon, Congress opted for an easy-to-complete rule (as opposed to a hard-to-complete rule) under the gift tax.

3. *Prerequisites for Applying §2702*

The following requirements must be satisfied under §2702(a)(1) for §2702 to apply in the manner described:

1. There must be an *inter vivos* transfer in trust. A non-trust transfer also comes under §2702 if there are successive interests. See §2702(c). A transaction in which two family members purchase successive interests in property from a third party (the "joint purchase" situation) is treated as if the person ending up with the life or term interest was the "transferor" of the entire property (with any cash provided by the other party being treated as a partial consideration offset). §2702(c)(2).
2. The transfer (of the nonretained interest) must be to or for the benefit of a "member of the transferor's family," which is defined in §2704(c)(2) to include the transferor's spouse, descendents or ancestors of the transferor or transferor's spouse, the transferor's brothers and sisters, and spouses of any of the foregoing.

3. An interest must be retained by the grantor or "any applicable family member," which term is defined in §2701(e)(2) to include the grantor's spouse, the ancestors of the grantor and grantor's spouse, and spouses of such ancestors. According to the regulations, in order to be "retained" (by an "applicable family member") the interest must be held by such person both before and after the transfer. Thus a transfer by D in trust, income to D's spouse for life, remainder to D's issue, does not fall within §2702. See Reg. §25.2702-2(a)(3) & (d)(1), Ex. 3.

The retained interest can be a term interest, an interest for life, a reversion, or a remainder retained by the grantor, or any of the foregoing subject to the grantor's power to revoke, alter, or amend. See Reg. §25.2702-2(a)(4) & (d)(1), Ex. 6.

4. Explicit Exceptions to §2702

Apart from the implicit exceptions (such as where the donees are not family members), there are various explicit statutory exceptions to §2702.

(a) Incomplete Gifts

An "incomplete gift" is not subject to §2702. An incomplete gift is one where all interests are subject to a retained power to revoke, alter, or amend. The regulations also treat as an incomplete gift any transfer in which one or more interests are retained and all other interests are subject to a retained power to revoke, alter, or amend. Thus, if D creates a trust, income to D for life, then to such of D's issue as D appoints by will, the transfer is treated as being wholly incomplete and not subject to §2702. See Reg. §25.2702-2(d)(1), Ex. 4.

Section 2702(a)(3)(B) states that the term "incomplete gift" means any transfer that would not be treated as a gift "whether or not consideration was received for such transfer." This sentence is intended to mean that any consideration given for a nonretained interest shall be treated as "partial consideration" with respect to the entire transfer. Thus, if D creates an irrevocable trust with $1M, income to D for life, remainder to R, and R gives D cash consideration equal to the then value of the remainder interest, then the "wholly-incomplete transfer" exception does not apply, and D is treated as having made a gift of $1M reduced by the consideration received from R. See Reg. §25.2702-4(d), Ex. 2. Thus, the *D'Ambrosio* approach to consideration under §2036(a)(1) is expressly rejected for purposes of §2702!

(b) Retained Qualified Interest

A retained interest that is a *qualified interest* is subtracted from the amount of the gift at its actuarial value. §2702(a)(2)(A). A "qualified interest" is an annuity interest, a unitrust interest, or a vested remainder (reversion) following an annuity or unitrust interest. §2702(b). See Reg. §25.2702-2 for additional qualification rules pertaining to qualified interests.

The rationale for the qualified-interest exception is that qualified (annuity and unitrust) interests can be accurately valued, and cannot be manipulated (diluted) as can retained "income" interests (or reversions following income interests).

A transfer with a retained qualified annuity interest for a term of years is called a grantor retained annuity trust (GRAT). A transfer with a retained qualified unitrust interest for a term of years is called a grantor retained unitrust (GRUT).

(c) Personal Residence Trust

Section 2702(a)(3)(A)(ii) excepts from §2702 a trust "all the property in which consists of a residence to be used as a personal residence" by the grantor. See Reg. §25.2702-5(b) for the requirements for a personal residence trust (PRT).

The regulations also provide that a qualified personal residence trust (QPRT) shall be treated as a PRT. A QPRT is a more flexible device than a "straight" PRT.

(d) Nondepreciable Tangible Personal Property

Section 2702(c)(4) cryptically states that a (retained) term interest in tangible personal property shall be subtracted from the value of the gift of such property, but at a value based on the willing-buyer willing-seller test (rather than its actuarial value), "if the nonexercise of rights under [such term interest] would not have a substantial effect on the valuation of the remainder interest." It turns out that this phrase (mainly) refers to nondepreciable tangible personal property whose value is (relatively) unaffected by its use, i.e., artworks, although it could apply to other collectibles, precious metals, and jewelry. See Reg. §25.2702-2(c) & (d)(2).

B. GST Tax Treatment of Retained-Interest Transfers

Under §2642(f), any *inter vivos* transfer of the type that would be included in the donor's gross estate shall be treated as having been transferred for GST purposes at the later date which is the earliest to occur of (1) the transferor's death, (2) such time as the property ceases to be "includible" in the donor's gross estate, or (3) such time as a generation-skipping transfer is made with respect to such property. This period is called the estate tax inclusion period (ETIP). See Reg. §26.2632-1(c). The delaying effect of this rule impacts (and would usually increase) the amount of the GST exemption that would need to be allocated to this transfer to completely shield it from the GST.

C. Applying the Adjusted Taxable Gift Exclusion

Unification of the gift and estate taxes in 1976 was achieved by treating the taxable estate as if it were the decedent's "last" taxable gift. Thus, the estate tax base is a "cumulative" tax base that includes all of the decedent's taxable wealth transfers before and at death. See §2001(b)(1), which requires that the tax, using the §2001(c) rate schedule, be figured on a tax base consisting of the taxable estate and "adjusted taxable gifts." Only post-1976 taxable gifts are included in the definition of "adjusted taxable gifts." And not all post-1976 gifts are included. In order to prevent double-counting the same gifts in the cumulative tax base, the term "adjusted taxable gifts" is defined in the last sentence of §2001(b) to *exclude* gifts of interests which resulted in the inclusion of such interests in the transferor's gross estate under any of §§2035-2040. The rule by which twice-taxed interests are removed from the "adjusted taxable gifts" total is referred to as the "adjusted taxable gift exclusion."

The adjusted taxable gifts exclusion has the effect of "retroactively" removing the gift tax value of a twice-taxed transfer from the cumulative tax base for purposes of figuring the estate tax. Thus, interests that are subject to both gift and estate taxes to the same person are ultimately reckoned at their estate tax values rather than their gift tax values. This fact embodies a principle that estate-inclusion rules have priority over gift tax rules. This principle holds whether the value of the twice-taxed property has appreciated or depreciated after the date of gift.

The adjusted taxable gifts exclusion only applies to gifts of property or interests therein that are included in the gross estate *by reason of the form of transfer* (i.e., under §§2036-2040). The exclusion does not apply in cases where the property is included in the transferor's §2033 gross estate because of having received the property (or its economic yield) back by gratuitous transfer or purchase, as a trust distribution, or as a payment under a contract right.

Example: Suppose D creates a trust with $1M, income to herself for life, remainder to R (a "family member"). Assume that the retained income interest is worth $760K and that the remainder interest has a value of $240K. There is a deemed gift of $760K under §2702 and an actual (future interest) gift of $240K under general gift tax principles. Upon D's death, the trust is worth $2.3M, which amount is fully included in D's gross estate under §2036. Since the *remainder interest* transferred to D was subject to both the gift tax and (by reason of the form of transfer) the estate tax, the $240K taxable gift is removed from the total of adjusted taxable gifts. The deemed gift of the income interest under §2702 is not excluded, because such income interest is not included in the gross estate under §2036 (that is, by reason of the form of transfer). Although the *actual income* received by D will have augmented D's §2033 gross estate, the §2702 deemed gift of the income *interest* does not fall within the adjusted taxable gifts exclusion. (If the rule were otherwise, §2702 would have no permanent effect.) Thus, the §2702 deemed gift of $760K "stays in" the cumulative tax base as an adjusted taxable gift, the $240K remainder-interest gift is "pulled out" of the cumulative tax base, and the same remainder interest is included in the gross estate at its estate tax value of $2.3M.

Example: This time assume that D transfers $1M to an irrevocable *inter vivos* trust, creating the following interests: income to B for life ($613K), then reversion to D if living ($87K), but if not to C ($300K). The interests given to B and C are actual gifts, and the interest retained by D is a deemed gift under §2702. D dies before C, and D's reversion is then worth zero under §2033 but was sufficient to cause §2037 to apply. The trust is still worth $1M at D's death, but the amount includible under §2037 is $900K (assuming that B's outstanding income interest is then worth $100K). "Adjusted taxable gifts" include: (1) $600K ($613K reduced by the annual exclusion of $13K), because B's income interest was not included in D's gross estate, and (2) $87K, the deemed gift of the reversion, which also was not included in D's gross estate. The remainder-interest gift to C is not included as an adjusted taxable gift, because it is included in the gross estate under §2037 at $900K.

NOTES

1. Section 2702(a)(3)(A)(iii) authorizes the Treasury to add further exceptions to §2702 under regulations. The Treasury has so far made exceptions for (*inter alia*) certain transfers involving deductible charitable interests, transfers of remainder interests following a retained interest which consists solely of the possibility of receiving discretionary distributions from an independent trustee, and a trust in which the sole transferred interest is to an ex-spouse that is exempt from tax under §2516. See Reg. §25.2702-1(c)(3)-(8).
2. Section 2702 has essentially "killed" retained-interest transfers other than GRATs, GRUTs, qualified personal residence trusts, and retained-interest transfers to non-family-member donees.
   a. The risk posed by the creation of a GRAT or GRUT is that the transferor might die before the expiration of the term interest, causing §2036 to apply. The fact that the transferor has an annuity or unitrust interest (rather than an income interest) affects the amount included, as explained in §8.1.D.6. See Reg. §20.2036-1(c).
   b. GRATs and GRUTs are "allowed," because the valuation of annuity interests and unitrust interests is considered to be far more accurate than the valuation of income interests. Annuity and unitrust payouts are "fixed" (as a dollar or percentage amount). Income amounts are "variable" and are susceptible to the investment and trust accounting decisions of trustees.
   c. A unitrust interest operates so that the unitrust beneficiaries and the remainders "share" in net growth (or shrinkage). Of course, net growth occurs only if the unitrust payout rate is less than the total economic return. Otherwise, the trust can shrink, and the unitrust beneficiary and the remainders will share in the decline, but the corpus will never reach zero on account of a unitrust interest. Unitrust interests are valued under Reg. §1.664-4(e)(7).
   d. An annuity interest resembles a "debt" claim against the trust, leaving the remainder as the "residual" interest. The annuity beneficiary essentially has "first claim" on trust assets, especially if the annuity payout rate is high (5 percent or more) relative to initial corpus. If the payout rate is high enough, there is a possibility that corpus will be exhausted and that the remainders will get nothing. However, if the annuity payout rate is low (3 percent or less), net growth in the trust will inure entirely for the benefit of the remainders. GRATs are more often used than GRUTs, because the annuity amount can be set high enough to reduce the value of the remainder interest (the gift amount) to zero (or near zero). However, Reg. §25.7520-3(2)(i) & (v) (Ex. 5), issued in 1999, requires recalculation

(reduction in value) of an annuity that is likely to exhaust the fund before the annuity term expires.

e.   Reg. §§25.2702-3(b) & (c) were amended in 1999 to state that the "[i]ssuance of a note, other debt instrument, option, or other similar financial arrangement in satisfaction of the" annuity or unitrust amount does not constitute payment. The purpose of the amendment was to prevent such arrangements from constituting "qualified interests" because they distort the payment of the transferor's retained interest by delaying the payments to him or her without requiring adequate interest to preserve a current value equivalent. (The regulations provide a transition rule for trusts created before September 20, 1999. The interest will be treated as a qualified interest under §2702(b) if the notes, etc., are not used to satisfy annuity or unitrust payment obligations after that date and if any note previously used is paid in full by December 31, 1999, as well as any option is paid in cash or other trust assets equal to the greater of the required annuity or unitrust payment plus interest (under §7520) or the fair market value of the option.)

f.   In *Estate of Walton v. Comm'r*, 115 T.C. 589 (2000), *acq.*, Notice 2003-72, 2003-2 C.B. 964, the court invalidated then Example 5 of Reg. §25.2702-3(e), holding that an interest retained for the shorter of the grantor's life or a fixed term of years that would be paid to her estate for the rest of the fixed term in the event of her earlier death was the functional equivalent of a fixed term and was therefore a qualified interest. The court decided that the example was more like a fixed-term interest in accord with the legislative history of the statute than like a reversionary interest, which was more likely to cause an interest to be undervalued. The regulation was re-written to conform to the court's holding in *Walton*.

g.   In *Walton*, the court held that the two-year annuity interest retained by the taxpayer in each GRAT was a qualified interest, which led many to conclude that the court implicitly approved the taxpayer's use of short-term "zeroed out" GRATs. This form of GRAT results in no taxable gift since the retained value of the annuity interest equals the value of the transferred remainder interest.[83] Although the actual GRAT investment in *Walton* created a shortfall in annuity payments and did not produce any tax-free gift to the children (remaindermen), that investment failure was limited to the two year term and to that particular GRAT, thus resulting merely in a lost opportunity cost. The two-year term is also favorable because it limits the risk of the taxpayer's death within the GRAT term and thus the application of §2036. The Joint Committee proposed imposing a minimum ten-year term requirement for a GRAT. *Description of Revenue Provisions Contained in the President's Fiscal Year 2010 Budget Proposal — Part One: Individual Income Tax and Estate and Gift Tax*

---

83. Some estate planners advise clients to generate a small taxable gift in order to trigger the running of the statute of limitations on the transfer.

Provisions (JCS-2-09), Joint Committee on Taxation (Sept. 8, 2009) at 149, but that restriction was not incorporated in the 2010 Act.

h. In *Cook v. Comm'r*, 269 F.3d 854 (7th Cir.2001), the court affirmed the Tax Court's decision that, to qualify as a GRAT, under Reg. §25.2702-3(e) (Ex. 6), the remainder interest must be fixed and ascertainable at the creation of the GRAT. Because the remainder interests were conditioned on the spouse's surviving the grantor and remaining married to the grantor, they did not satisfy this requirement. The spousal income interests also violated the durational requirements of Reg. §25.2702-3(d)(3). Accord, *Focardi v. Comm'r*, T.C. Memo. 2006-56. Cf. *Schott v. Comm'r*, 319 F.3d 1203 (9th Cir.2003), *rev'g*, T.C. Memo. 2001-110. On February 24, 2005, the IRS issued final regulations under §2702, effective as of July 26, 2004. *T.D. 9181*, 70 Fed. Reg. 9222. Expressly refusing to adopt *Schott* in these regulations, Treasury explained that §2702 was enacted not only to prevent valuation difficulties, but also to prohibit the valuation inaccuracy "present when the value of a retained interest is increased through the use of a joint and survivor (or two-life) annuity or unitrust interest if there is no certainty that the survivorship interest will ever be paid."

3. a. Since any post-1976 taxable gift will appear in the cumulative tax base either as an "adjusted taxable gift" or as part of the taxable estate, and since an estate tax is figured "on" the cumulative tax base, it is necessary to provide a "credit" against the §2001(b)(1) tax for any gift taxes already paid or due on such gifts, since otherwise the gifts will have been taxed twice. Accordingly, under §2001(b)(2) there is a "credit" against the tax on the cumulative tax base for the actual gift tax (net of credits) on all post-1976 gifts (not just those included in the definition of "adjusted taxable gift").

b. Section 2001(b)(2) states that the amount subtracted for post-1976 taxable gifts is the tax (after credits) that "would have been payable" on such gifts if the §2001(c) rate schedule as of the date of the decedent's death had been applicable to such gifts. This rule prevents a taxpayer from retroactively obtaining the benefit of any rate reductions that occurred after the year of gift (and which are in effect at the date of death). The after-credit aspect of the rule is not changed, i.e., one still refers to the credit in effect at the time of gift.

c. Recall that pre-1977 gifts are not included in the §2001(b)(1) cumulative estate tax base. In lieu of the §2001(b)(2) "credit," §2012 provides a credit against the estate tax with respect to gift taxes on pre-1977 gifts included in the gross estate.

4. Gifts which are subject to gift tax but are also subject to estate tax labor under certain disadvantages relative to their being subject to either estate or gift tax alone, despite the adjusted taxable gift exclusion.

a. First, the taxable gift "temporarily" uses up all or part of the transferor's unified transfer tax credit, which could have better been used to avoid current tax on gifts that are not destined to be included in the gross estate.

b. Another disadvantage occurs where the gift was split with the transferor's spouse under §2513. In that case, all of the transferred property is included in the transferor's gross estate, gift splitting notwithstanding. Nevertheless, the net gift tax paid by the transferor's spouse by reason of gift splitting is deemed to have been paid by the transferor for purposes of §2001(b)(2). §2001(d). The problem lies in the fact that the gift deemed made by the transferor's spouse remains in the latter's cumulative tax base as an adjusted taxable gift, and this adjusted taxable gift will have pushed the spouse's own transfers into higher marginal rate brackets. (This rule does not apply where the property is included in the decedent's gross estate only under §2035(a). See §2001(e).)

5.   Under a "realization" accessions tax, an accession would occur only upon a distribution (as opposed to the acquisition of a trust interest). Therefore, actuarial tables would not be used, and rules like §2702 would not exist.

§8.3. Split-Interest Charitable Transfers

Gifts and estate-included transfers to charity are deductible from the gift and/or estate tax base if the transfer qualifies for the deduction. In the case of gifts, there is also a possible income tax deduction. Fee simple gifts clearly qualify. However, most of the doctrine and planning relating to charitable transfers has revolved around split-interest charitable transfers. In the early days of the estate and gift tax, a split-interest charitable transfer was deductible to the extent of the value of the charitable interest (such as a remainder interest, an income interest for a term of years, or an annuity interest) if said charitable interest was susceptible to actuarial valuation. In 1969, Congress (being concerned with valuation abuses), drastically restricted the types of charitable interests that could qualify for the deduction.

Split-interest charitable transfers are considered at this point because a deductible charitable interest resembles an excludible retained interest. Also, the qualification rules enacted in 1969 were the model for the "qualified retained interest" rules of §2702.

A. Background

As far as state law is concerned, there are three distinctive (and interrelated) features of charitable trusts. The first is that such a trust can be perpetual, i.e., it is not subject to the Rule Against Perpetuities. The second is that it is not subject to the rule that a "private" trust is void where the beneficiaries are indefinite and unascertainable. Instead, a charitable trust must be devoted to purposes beneficial to the community, such as charity, education, the promotion of health, the advancement of religion and morality, the furtherance of governmental purposes, and so on, where an indefinite number of persons may be benefitted. Since there are no ascertainable beneficiaries, the trust is enforceable by the state attorney general. The third distinctive feature arises from the first two: Since a charity can have perpetual life with reference to stated charitable purposes, it might outlive such purposes. In that case the trust may be "reformed" under the doctrine of *cy pres* if such can be accomplished within the general charitable intent of the settlor.

A charity may also be organized as a corporation rather than a trust, with the same characteristics as noted above. A corporation may be preferred to a trust because it is easier to facilitate control through a Board of Directors who can arrange for their successors without court involvement and can adopt and alter bylaws to implement management functions.

For federal income tax purposes, "charitable" trusts and corporations (i.e., those described in §501(c)(3)),[84] as well as other organizations (such as fraternal lodges, veterans organizations, and so on), are exempt from income tax, except with respect to unrelated business and unrelated debt-financed income. Also, a §501(c)(3) organization which is a "private foundation" (which is not an "operating foundation") is subject to a tax of 2 percent on net investment income.[85]

Individuals make charitable transfers for philanthropic and tax reasons. A given charitable transfer may produce deductions under the income, gift, and/or estate taxes, and can avoid generation-skipping tax. Take, for example, an irrevocable trust created by A, income to A for life, with the trust to terminate on A's death and the corpus to be paid to a designated charity. If this transfer were to "qualify" under the various deduction rules, the present transfer of the charitable remainder interest would produce an income tax deduction in the year of transfer (under §170), as well as a gift tax deduction (under §2522). In both cases, the deduction would be based upon the present value of the charitable remainder interest computed by reference to actuarial factors. Since the value of A's retained interest is not a gift, the transfer in question will involve no gift tax exposure whatsoever. (Section 2702 would not apply in this example because there is no transfer to a family member.) This trust would also be included in A's gross estate under §2036(a)(1), but the inclusion would be offset by a charitable deduction for estate tax purposes (under §2055). Finally, since a tax-exempt organization is

---

84. A §501(c)(3) organization ("charity" in the tax sense) is a trust or corporation organized and operated exclusively for religious, charitable, educational, scientific (including medical), literary, etc., purposes, subject to certain restrictions relating to politics and profit taking.

85. §4940. Private foundations may be subject to penalty excise taxes on account of self-dealing (with grantors or managers), failing to distribute income currently, failing to dispose of controlled businesses, undertaking speculative investments, and expending funds on certain travel and study grants, lobbying, and other political activity. See §§4940-4945. A "private foundation" is defined by §509(a) to be any §501(c)(3) organization which is not: (1) a "public" charity (an organization described in §170(b)(1)(A)); (2) an organization receiving more than one-third of its support from the public (rather than from investment income); or (3) an organization devoted to testing for public safety. Roughly speaking, then, a private foundation is a charity founded by gifts and bequests from wealthy individuals (or a family), which is supported primarily by investment income, and which is not a church, school, hospital, or similar noncultural institution. Also, gifts to private foundations are treated less favorably for income tax purposes both under the "cut-down" rules and the percentage limitations. A private "operating foundation" is one that, *inter alia*, spends substantially all of its income for its exempt function; that is, to operate a program or activity as opposed to making grants to or through other tax-exempt organizations.

deemed to occupy the same "generation" as the grantor,[86] there would be no generation-skipping transfer. The end result would be that the transferor will have obtained a lifetime income tax benefit at no transfer tax cost and without having given up current enjoyment of the property. (In fact, a charitable remainder interest following an income interest does not qualify for the income and gift tax charitable deductions, but that problem could have been remedied by having the charitable remainder interest follow a qualified annuity or unitrust interest for A's life.)

B. General Qualification Rules

Unlike the income tax charitable deduction, *there is no dollar or percentage limitation on the charitable deduction for gift and estate tax purposes.* (However, there is a limitation, expressed as a percentage of adjusted gross income, for income tax purposes.[87] Additionally, the income tax charitable deduction for an item of appreciated property may be the property's income tax basis, rather than its value.[88])

The deduction cannot exceed the amount of the completed gift (otherwise subject to gift tax) or must be included in the transferor's gross estate.[89] However, it is possible that the deductible value can be less than the amount included in the transfer tax base. See *Ahmanson Foundation v. U.S.*, 674 F.2d 761 (9th Cir.1981) (minority discount imposed for deduction purposes but not for estate-inclusion purposes).

The gift or estate tax deduction cannot exceed the value of the interest "passing" from the transferor to a charity.[90] To obtain the deduction, the charity must be of the type listed in the relevant deduction provision (§§170(c), 2055(a), and 2522(a), as the case may be), and the transferred amount must be used exclusively for charitable purposes.[91]

---

86. See §2651(f)(3). See also the definition of "skip person" in §2613.

87. See §170(b), which limits the aggregate income tax deduction to 50 percent, 30 percent, or 20 percent of the taxpayer's adjusted gross income for the year, depending on the nature of the donee organizations and, in some cases, of the property contributed. The amount of the gifts in excess of the limitations can be carried forward for five years.

88. See §170(e), which applies, *inter alia*, where the appreciated property would not produce long-term capital gains to the transferor if sold, e.g., because the asset is inventory or some other non-capital asset, or is held for less than one year. In the case of appreciated long-term capital gains property, the deduction is again equal to basis, but there are several important exceptions which facilitate, for example, the giving of artworks to museums, securities to colleges, and land to churches.

89. §2055(d) (estate tax). The rule is implicit in §2522(a) (stating that the deduction must be for a "gift").

90. The deduction has been disallowed in cases involving bequests to individuals bound by a vow of poverty to turn over their property to a religious order. See *Estate of Lamson v. U.S.*, 338 F.2d 376 (3d Cir.1963).

91. Also, the donee must be organized and operated so that no portion of its earnings inure to the benefit of a private individual, and the donee must not attempt to influence legislation or political campaigns. See §§2055(a)(2)-(4) and 2522(a)(2)-(4).

In the case of an estate transfer, any items payable out of a charitable transfer (such as taxes, debts, and administration expenses), under the governing instrument or the default rules of state law, reduce the charitable deduction. Nevertheless, some of these items (state death taxes, claims against the decedent, and administration expenses not deducted for income tax purposes) may well be independently deductible for estate tax purposes.[92]

There is no statutory "terminable interest rule" as such. Nevertheless, an estate transfer that is contingent or conditional is disallowed on the basis that it is not susceptible of valuation as of the date of the decedent's death, unless the condition or contingency is "so remote as to be negligible."[93]

C. Charitable Remainder Trusts

The basic idea of a charitable remainder trust is that individuals possess current-enjoyment interests that occur prior to a remainder in the charity. The noncharitable "lead" interest may be retained by the grantor or given to one or more other individuals, such as children of the grantor. There are three types of qualifying charitable remainder trusts: (1) the charitable remainder annuity trust, (2) the charitable remainder unitrust, and (3) the pooled income fund.[94] Other charitable remainder trusts, such as a charitable remainder income trust, do not qualify. The basic idea, as with §2702, is that annuity and unitrust interests are less susceptible to valuation abuse than income interests. Strict compliance with the qualification rules is required. It would be tedious to set out all of the qualification rules; only the essentials will be noted here. Nevertheless, in practice, the full array of qualification rules should be mastered.

1. The Charitable Remainder Annuity Trust (CRAT)

The definition of a qualifying charitable remainder annuity trust (CRAT) is the same for income, gift, and estate tax purposes, and is set forth in §664(d)(1) and the regulations thereunder. A fixed sum of money, equal to or greater than 5 percent of the initial value of the corpus, must be paid at least annually to one or more noncharitable beneficiaries (living at the time of the creation of the trust) for the life or lives of such beneficiaries or for a term of years not greater than 20. The fixed sum may be expressed as a specified dollar amount or as an amount generated by a formula (such as "6% of the initial value of the corpus as finally determined for federal tax purposes"). No payments other than the annuity amount may be made to the individual beneficiaries. In other words, the trustee cannot be given the power to invade the corpus of the trust except insofar as that is

---

92. See Reg. §20.2055-3(b)(3), stating that estate "management" (as opposed to "transmission") expenses attributable to (and paid from) the charitable share reduce the charitable deduction, unless such expenses are separately deducted under §2053.

93. Reg. §20.2055-2(a); *Rev. Rul.* 70-452, 1970-2 C.B. 199.

94. §§170(f)(2)(A), 2055(e)(2), and 2522(c)(2).

necessary to fulfill the annuity payout requirement.[95] A CRAT may not receive additional contributions from anyone.[96]

The Service will disallow the deduction for the charitable remainder interest if the probability that a noncharitable (annuity) beneficiary will outlive the payout of all of the trust assets exceeds 5 percent. This situation could arise from an overly high payout rate or from a too low rate of return on the corpus.[97] This rule derives from the regulation (previously alluded to) disallowing the deduction where the charitable interest is subject to a nontrivial condition or contingency.

2. *The Charitable Remainder Unitrust (CRUT)*

Under a charitable remainder unitrust, as defined in §664(d)(2) & (3), a fixed percentage of the net fair market value of assets computed annually, which percentage must not be less than 5 percent (or more than 50 percent), is paid to the current beneficiaries.[98] The determination of value can be made at any time during the year, so long as the practice is consistent.

In most other respects, the CRUT is subject to the same qualification rules as the CRAT. In both cases, the deduction is disallowed unless the value of the charitable remainder is at least 10 percent of the trust's initial value.[99] While the income interest of either a CRUT or a CRAT may be subject to a qualified contingency, the value of that interest will be computed without reference to that contingency.[100]

Unlike a CRAT, the CRUT instrument may allow for income payments in any year to be the lower of the trust's income or the above computed income amount (a NICRUT)[101] and may allow for the total of any excess fixed percentage amounts to be paid to the noncharitable beneficiary in later years (a NIMCRUT).[102]

---

95. If such an interest is inadvertently provided under the governing instrument, it should be disclaimed. The flush language of §2055(a) provides the termination of a power of invasion of corpus (prior to its exercise) no later than the date for filing the estate tax return has the effect of a qualified disclaimer.

96. Reg. §1.664-2(b) ("A trust is not a charitable remainder annuity trust unless its governing instrument provides that no additional contributions may be made to the charitable remainder annuity trust after the initial contribution. For purposes of this section, all property passing to a charitable remainder annuity trust by reason of death of the grantor shall be considered one contribution." Id.). This subsection of the regulation was adopted on August 22, 1972, in *T.D.* 7202, 1972-2 C.B. 313.

97. See *Rev. Rul. 77-374*, 1977-2 C.B. 329.

98. Alternatively, the trust may provide for distribution of the lesser of the trust income for the year or the unitrust amount, provided that shortfalls in the unitrust amount shall be made up in later years when the trust income exceeds the unitrust amount. See §664(d)(3).

99. §664(d)(1)(D).

100. I.R.C. §664(f)(1) & (2). A "qualified contingency" is "any provision of a trust which provides that, upon the happening of a contingency, the payments described in paragraph (1)(A) or (2)(A) of subsection (d) (as the case may be) will terminate not later than such payments would otherwise terminate under the trust." I.R.C. §664(f)(3).

101. I.R.C. §664(d)(3)(A). A NICRUT, or a NIOCRUT, is an acronym for a net income (only) charitable remainder unitrust.

102. I.R.C. §664(d)(3)(B). A NIMCRUT is an acronym for a net income with a makeup provision charitable remainder unitrust.

3. *The Pooled Income Fund*

A pooled income fund is defined in §642(c)(5) as a trust managed by the donee charity, to which a number of private donors irrevocably transfer property. The donors can retain an income interest in themselves and/or other individual beneficiaries (living at the date of gift) for their lives. The pooled income fund is essentially a fundraising device for colleges and other large charities which offers to save the prospective donor transaction and administrative costs. A donor or noncharitable beneficiary may not be a trustee of the pooled income fund. Also, the fund cannot invest in tax-exempt bonds.

Unlike the annuity trust or unitrust, the income interest is determined by the actual rate of return on the fund's investments.

Upon the death of the designated beneficiary, the charity withdraws assets equal in value to the share of the fund from which the beneficiary derived income.

For purposes of computing the deduction, the assumed rate of return is the highest rate of return enjoyed by the fund in any of the three years prior to the gift. If the fund has not been in existence for three years, the rate shall be assumed to be 6 percent or such rate as shall be prescribed by the Service.

4. *GST Tax Issues*

Since the charitable remainder is deemed to occupy the same generation as the grantor, the charity is a "non-skip person" and, therefore, the termination of the last noncharitable interest cannot constitute a taxable termination or taxable distribution. Nor can the initial transfer to a charitable remainder trust involve a "direct skip" transfer, even if the noncharitable beneficiaries are all "skip persons." Since the transfer is in trust, there can be a direct-skip transfer only if the trust itself is a skip person, but that is impossible, because a trust can be a skip person only if all "interests" are held by skip persons (but the charity, a non-skip person, has an interest)[103] or else no distribution can ever be made to a non-skip person (such as a charity).[104] There could, however, be a generation-skipping transfer where the first noncharitable beneficiary occupied a generation below that of the grantor and was succeeded by a second noncharitable beneficiary in a lower generation still.

5. *Income Taxation of the Charitable Remainder Trust*

As to the income taxation of the charitable remainder trust (if not the pooled income fund), the rules of §664 supersede those of the rest of Subchapter J. Under §664(b), the noncharitable distributees report first the gross income for the current year (plus unreported income accumulated in prior years), then the gains for the current year (and for prior years), then exempt income of the current year (and for prior years), and finally tax-free trust corpus. The amounts so reportable for the current year cannot exceed the amount of the distributions received by noncharitable beneficiaries for the year.

---

103. A qualified charitable remainder trust is deemed to possess an "interest" for generation-skipping purposes even though such interest is not current. See §2652(c)(1)(C).

104. See §2613(a)(2).

The trust itself is not subject to tax on undistributed income under §1(e). See §664(c). Therefore, the trust obtains no deduction for accumulated income and capital gains which will (or might) be eventually paid to the charitable remainder.

6. Direct Charitable Annuities

Here, the donor transfers money or property to a charity in exchange for a promise by the charity to pay a sum certain at least annually. Although this transaction resembles a charitable remainder trust, it is essentially that of a "private annuity." Because the annuity is not payable out of the transferred property, this type of arrangement is not viewed as a split-interest transfer, and (accordingly) the qualification rules as to charitable remainder trusts do not apply.

The income tax aspects of this transaction will be governed by the private annuity rules, except that there will be up-front income and gift tax deductions to the extent that the value of the property transferred exceeds the value of the annuity promise.[105]

D. Charitable Lead Trusts

A charitable lead trust is the reverse of a charitable remainder trust; here, an income interest is given to the charity and one or more remainder interests are given to noncharitable persons.

1. Qualification

Like the charitable remainder trust, the lead interest (here that of the charity) must receive a guaranteed annuity (which may take the form of a formula percentage of the initial corpus) or a unitrust interest (fixed percentage of the yearly value of the corpus). Unlike the charitable remainder trust, here the amount or percentage need not equal or exceed five or any other specified percent of the corpus. The amounts must be paid annually to the charity for a term of years (or for a measuring life). No payments may be made during the period of charitable use to any noncharitable beneficiary whether out of income or corpus.

Charitable lead annuity trusts and unitrusts are referred to as CLATs and CLUTs respectively.

2. Estate and Gift Tax Deduction

The principal advantage of a charitable lead trust is that a large estate or gift tax deduction can be taken presently without the trust assets' being transferred outside of the family.

In the case of CLAT, it would appear that a deduction of 100 percent of the assets' value could be obtained if the annuity rate is high enough or the payout

---

105. The annuity promise is valued under Reg. §1.72-9. See *Rev. Rul.* 72-438, 1972-2 C.B. 38; *Rev. Rul. 80-281*, 1980-2 C.B. 282.

period long enough.[106] However, in 1999 the Treasury amended Reg. §25.7520-3(b)(2)(i), which states that an annuity will not be valued at 100 percent if the fund is likely to be exhausted (under the assumption that any measuring life can live to age 110). Example 5 of Reg. §25.7520-3(b)(v) gives an example of a CLAT funded with $1M and paying an annuity of $100K to a charity for the life of the donor, age 60, and concluding that the annuity is worth only about $880K (rather than $1M).

A charitable lead unitrust interest can never generate a 100 percent deduction, because the amount paid to the charity is always a percentage (far below 100 percent) of the corpus that exists from time to time.

3. Generation-Skipping Tax Treatment

The creation of the charitable lead trust cannot be a direct-skip transfer for the same reason as applies to a charitable remainder trust. However, the expiration of the charitable interest will be a taxable termination if all interests are then held by skip persons.

The denominator of the "exclusion ratio" applicable to generation-skipping transfers is to be reduced by an amount equal to any gift or estate tax charitable deduction, thereby increasing the exclusion ratio. §2642(a)(2)(B)(ii)(II).

4. Income Tax Treatment

No income tax deduction with respect to an *inter vivos* charitable lead trust is allowed unless the grantor is deemed to be the owner of the trust property pursuant to §671.[107] In this case, later payments by the trust to the charity are not deducted (again) by the grantor, even though the trust income is taxed to the grantor.

E. Non-Trust Partial Interests

In general, non-trust gifts of income, remainder, or other partial interests[108] do not qualify for the gift, estate, or income tax charitable deductions.[109] However, there are exceptions provided by §170(f)(3)(B).

First, a remainder interest in a personal residence or farm can qualify. The value of such interest is to be determined by discounting to the present the value of the property after reduction by imputed depletion or (straight-line) depreciation to the date the remainder is expected to come into possession.[110]

---

106. The "standard" way of valuing annuities is to multiply the annuity payment by the (adjusted) annuity factor found in the appropriate actuarial table.

107. See §170(f)(2). If the grantor ceases to be treated as the owner of the trust, the previously deducted amount (reduced by the discounted value, at the time of the transfer, of amounts actually paid to the charity) is "recaptured," i.e., included in the grantor's gross income.

108. Allowing a charity to use an asset rent-free is a "partial interest" for which no deduction is allowed.

109. §§170(f)(3)(A), 2055(e)(2), and 2522(c)(2).

110. See §170(f)(4).

The gift must be of a remainder interest in the property, not in the proceeds from the sale of the property.[111] Also, a non-trust gift of a remainder interest in the furnishings does not qualify.[112]

A second permissible form of non-trust qualifying gift is one of an undivided portion of the donor's entire interest in property (and the proceeds thereof). Such transfers must take the form of a fractional share or percentage of the property. A copyright is treated as separate property apart from the work of art to which it pertains for purposes of the transfer tax charitable deductions.[113] A related rule (described in the Notes at the end of §3.1.A) is that a loan of an artwork to a museum is treated as a non-gift for gift tax purposes.[114]

The third category of qualifying gift is a "qualified conservation contribution" as defined in §170(h). This section covers remainders and perpetual easements (etc.) in real property granted to governmental units or (public) charities to be used exclusively for conservation purposes, as specifically defined in §170(h)(4). A gift of one's entire interest in real property, as reduced by a retained "qualified mineral interest" as defined in §170(h)(6), also qualifies. The amount deductible is the loss in value of the property to the donor.[115] Conservation easements are discussed in §4.4.C.2 in conjunction with the §2031(c) valuation discount for qualified conservation easements.

PROBLEMS, QUESTIONS, AND NOTES

1. a. It must be emphasized that in order to qualify a split-interest transfer for the deduction, the trust instrument must conform to the relevant statutes and regulations. When a charitable split-interest in trust is not established in one of the prescribed formats such as a CRT or CLT, the taxpayer receives no deduction for his gift to charity.[116] Not only must the trust instrument satisfy certain requirements, but also the trust must actually make its mandatory payments.[117] These strict rules for charitable split-interests in

---

111. *Rev. Rul. 77-169*, 1977-1 C.B. 286

112. *Rev. Rul. 76-165*, 1976-1 C.B. 279.

113. §§2055(e)(4) and 2522(c)(3).

114. See §2503(g).

115. See *Rev. Rul. 76-376*, 1976-2 C.B. 53.

116. See, e.g., *Galloway v. U S.*, 492 F.3d 219 (3d Cir.2007); *Estate of Johnson v. U.S.*, 941 F.2d 1318 (5th Cir.1991); *Estate of Edgar v. Comm'r*, 74 T.C. 983 (1980), *aff'd*, 676 F.2d 685 (3d Cir.1982).

117. See *Estate of Atkinson v. Comm'r*, 309 F.3d 1290, 1296 (11th Cir.2002) Although the CRAT was required to make annuity payments to the decedent during her life, the facts showed "that the estate produced no copies of these [supposedly sent] checks or the cover letters that supposedly accompanied the checks to Atkinson, nor did the annuity trust's ledger reflect any outgoing annuity payments to Atkinson during her lifetime." Id. at 1292. Referring to the Tax Court opinion, the circuit court explained that the payout requirement "ensures that the trust does not accumulate untaxed wealth for charities, which would sidestep the income distribution requirements of private foundations." Id. at 1294.

trust must be met even where there is no valuation manipulation potential. In *Galloway v. U.S.*, 492 F.3d 219 (3d Cir.2007), the decedent had left his property in trust to two charitable beneficiaries and to two noncharitable beneficiaries. Under the plain meaning of the statute, that meant the trust had to be in one of the prescribed statutory forms, which concededly it was not. Under the terms of the trust, half of the value of the trust was to be distributed on January 1, 2006, one-fourth to each beneficiary, and the remaining assets in the trust were to be distributed the same way ten years later.[118] The circuit court acknowledged that the denial of deduction, although the proper result, was "unfortunate" since there was little opportunity for abuse. "Each beneficiary of the Trust, charitable and noncharitable, shares equally in the risk of loss and the benefit of good investing as each beneficiary receives an equal share in the property." Id. at 224. Although the decedent had literally created a defective charitable split-interest trust, *Galloway* is a case where none of the interests had to be valued by means of the actuarial tables.

b.   Sample clauses for charitable remainder trusts, charitable lead trusts, and pooled income funds are found in various revenue procedures. (See, e.g., *Rev. Proc.* 2003-53 through 60, 2003-2 C.B. 230 *et seq.* (CRAT); *Rev. Proc.* 2005-52 through 59, 2005-2 C.B. 326 *et seq.* (CRUT); *Rev. Proc.* 2007-45, -46, 2007-29 I.R.B. 89, 102 (CLAT); *Rev. Proc.* 2008-45, -46, 2008-30 I.R.B. 224, 238 (CLUT).) See Richard L. Fox, *A Guide to the IRS Sample Charitable Remainder Trust Forms*, 33 ETPL 13 (2006) (criticizing some aspects of the government forms and suggesting some alternatives).

c.   In 1984, Congress permanently amended the split-interest provisions to allow taxpayers a limited post-death ability to comply with the strict rules. To be a "qualified reformable interest," either all payments must be expressed as specific dollar amounts or a fixed percentage of the fair market value of the trust property (I.R.C. §2055(e)(3)(C)(ii)) or a judicial proceeding must be initiated by "the 90th day after the last date (including extensions) for filing the [estate tax return]." (I.R.C. §2055(e)(3)(C)(iii)(I).)[119]

---

118. 492 F.3d at 220. Moreover, the trust also provided that if an individual is not alive at the distribution date(s), "his or her share will be distributed to the remaining beneficiaries in equal parts." Id.

119. Deficit Reduction Act of 1984, Div. A, The Tax Reform Act of 1984, Pub. L. No. 98-369 §1022, 98 Stat. 494, amending I.R.C. §§170(f), 664(f), 2055(e), and 2522(c). See H. R. Rep. No. 98-861, at 757, 1242 (1984) (Conf. Rep.) ("The House Bill provides a permanent rule permitting reformation of charitable split-interest trusts if certain requirements are satisfied. Under this provision of the house bill, the relative values of the charity and the noncharity interests in the trust may not vary by more than 5 percent as a result of the reformation. Additionally, unless the reformation proceedings are begun within 90 days after the due date of the federal estate tax return (or the first trust income tax return if no estate return is due), the trust must, as executed, provide for an annuity trust or unitrust amount. . . .").

     d. Any truth to the following criticisms of the 1969 required charitable split-interest trust formats?[120] (1) A CRT allows the donor to avoid income taxes by timing the donor's deduction before the actual charitable gift; (2) a NICRUT and a NIMCRUT serve as unintentional and gratuitous retirement saving and deferral devices; and (3) a CLT allows a settlor to avoid transfer taxes on gifts to noncharitable beneficiaries.

     e. Under §4947(a)(2), a split-interest charitable trust is subject to statutory provisions applicable to "private foundations" other than §4940 (the 2 percent tax on net investment income) and §4942 (the tax on failure to distribute income currently). In addition, under §508(e) the trust must contain certain language relating to these provisions. These rules do not constitute the trust as a private foundation.

2. a. B owns a Picasso and makes a gift of it to the local art museum, a "private operating foundation," but retains the picture in his home for his lifetime. Is this transaction subject to §2702? Does it qualify for the various charitable deductions? If not, is there any way in which B can obtain an income tax charitable deduction for this item, while yet retaining possession of the property during his life?

     b. The tax-planning game in the case of split-interest charitable transfers is to arrange matters so that the charitable gift is over-valued (and the non-charitable gift undervalued). What are the optimal economic and family conditions for achieving this result?

     c. An appealing goal is to obtain a large up-front income tax deduction for a split-interest charitable transfer. However, there are various Percentage-of-Adjusted-Gross-Income "ceilings" on the charitable deduction allowed in a year, which depend on the status of the donee organization and whether the property is appreciated property. See §170(b). In some cases, a five-year carry-forward of unusable deductions is available. See §170(d)(1). In the case of a charitable lead trust, it might be advantageous to avoid the up-front deduction (how does one do this?), because one could keep the property until death and make annual charitable donations. For this reason, most charitable lead trusts would be contained in wills or estate-included trusts with the aim of achieving estate tax savings.

3. The conservation type of outright charitable transfer can be used to benefit the very wealthy. Assume that Madison owns a 400-acre horse farm in Middleburg, Virginia. Carving out a five-acre tract for herself (which includes the personal residence and outbuildings), Madison gives an easement to the county government to be used perpetually for scenic enjoyment and the protection of natural environmental systems. The deduction is not lost on account of the fact that Madison continues to derive enjoyment from the property by: (a) enjoying its scenic vistas and the privacy provided by it (the land itself need not be open to the public), (b) by taking walks through

---

120. See Wendy C. Gerzog, *The Times They Are Not A-Changin': Reforming the Charitable Split Interest Rules (Again)*, 85 Chi.-Kent L. Rev 849 (2010).

the property, or (c) running her horses and cattle on the land with the permission of the county.[121] In *Stoller v. Comm'r*, T.C. Memo. 1987-275, the taxpayer purchased property for $315K. Two years later he created a scenic easement and successfully claimed an income tax deduction for $1,065K based on the loss in value attributable to surrendering development rights. Taxpayer retained the right to use the property for personal use, and the public was not granted physical access to the property. Accord, *Glass v. Comm'r*, 124 T.C. 258 (2005). Cf. *Options to Improve Tax Compliance and Reform Tax Expenditure* (JCS-2-05), Joint Committee on Taxation (Jan. 27, 2005) at 277, 281, 283 (proposal to eliminate the deduction for façade and conservation easements relating to personal residence properties and requiring recapture for resumption of personal residence use).

4.   a.   If a trust is deemed to be owned by the grantor under §671 (discussed in §8.4), the income and deductions are attributed to the grantor. Thus, any distributions to the charity would be potentially deductible by the grantor under §170. However, in the case of an *inter vivos* charitable lead trust, an up-front deduction for the charitable lead interest is allowed only if the trust is deemed owned by the grantor under §671, and in that case (to prevent double deductions) actual distributions to the charity are not deductible under §170.

   b.   Assuming that the *inter vivos* (charitable lead) trust is not owned by the grantor, the rules of Subchapter J apply. There, current distributions to charity from the trust (or an estate) out of "gross income" are deductible under §642(c)(1), in lieu of the normal §170 deduction. The §642(c) deduction for trusts and estates is not subject to either the cut-down rule or the percentage limitations found in §170.

   c.   It is worth mentioning that an estate (but not a post-1969 trust) can claim a deduction under §642(c)(2) for "gross income" (including capital gains) permanently accumulated ("set aside") for the benefit of a charity.[122] This rule would most frequently come into play where the residuary bequest is outright to a charity.

   d.   A Subchapter J trust or estate does not obtain an income tax charitable deduction for charitable distributions or set-asides from *corpus*. Nor are such distributions or set-asides treated as "distributions" for Subchapter J purposes.[123] The idea is that any items to be paid out of corpus are to be deducted (if at all) for estate tax purposes, and items to be paid out of income are to be deducted (if at all) for income tax purposes, but that nothing paid to a charity is to be deducted for both estate and income tax purposes.

---

121. See Reg. §1.170A-14(d)-(f).

122. A similar rule exists under §642(c)(3) for pooled income funds.

123. §663(a)(2). A "distribution" has the effect of shifting income from the estate or trust to the distributee. But since a charitable distributee is exempt from income tax, any such shifting would cause income to disappear from the system.

§8.4. Income Tax Treatment of Transfers with Retained Interests and Powers

In the case of an *inter vivos* trust, the grantor may be treated as the "tax owner" of the trust property. It is a basic maxim of income taxation that the "owner" (or "deemed owner") of property is taxed on the net income therefrom. Accordingly, to the extent that the grantor is treated as the owner of an *inter vivos* trust, the income, expenses, losses, etc., incurred by the trust are attributable directly to the grantor. In that case, neither the Subchapter J rules described in §7.5 nor the "beneficiary-owned trust rules" (i.e., §678) described in §7.2 apply. See §§671 and 678(b).

According to §671, whether (and to the extent that) the grantor is deemed to be the owner of an *inter vivos* trust created by the grantor is to be determined *exclusively* under the rules provided in §§672-677, and not under any general "control" or "substantial ownership" theory. The "grantor trust rules" of §§671-677 rules are the income tax counterparts of the estate and gift tax rules (including §2702) pertaining to *inter vivos* transfers with retained interests and powers. The statutory grantor trust rules apply only in the case of trusts. Non-trust transfers are presumably governed by case law applying a control or substantial ownership theory.[124]

The *content* of the income tax grantor trust rules differs from the estate and gift tax rules in many respects. In general, the rules lean heavily towards holding that the grantor is the owner of the trust property. The rules (except for §676) were enacted only in 1954, and are more elaborately "statutory" (less encrusted by regulation and case law) than the estate and gift tax rules. It again would be tedious (and unnecessary) to attempt to describe every rule found in §§672-677. Nevertheless, here is an overview. The grantor is deemed the income tax owner of an *inter vivos* trust during any period (during the grantor's lifetime) where:

(1) the trust is revocable by the grantor, or a non-adverse party can "re-vest" title to the property in the grantor (see §676);

(2) the grantor possesses a more-than-5 percent reversion (§673);

(3) the grantor will *or may* receive income or corpus *currently or at some time in the future*, or the income can be used to pay premiums on insurance policies on the life of the grantor or the grantor's spouse (§677);

(4) an "administrative" power exists in the grantor or a non-adverse party that (to state the matter with a broad brush) overrides normal fiduciary constraints (see §675); or

(5) any "dispositive" power is held by the grantor or a non-adverse party, but there are three levels of exceptions. One set of (narrow) exceptions applies even to powers held by the grantor or a non-adverse party. See §674(b). A second exception is for a power to allocate income limited by a reasonably definite external standard if held by a person other the grantor (or spouse living

---

124. *Helvering v. Clifford*, 309 U.S. 331 (1940); *Helvering v. Horst*, 311 U.S. 112 (1940); *Comm'r v. Sunnen*, 333 U.S. 591 (1948); *Estate of Alperstein v. Comm'r*, 80 T.C. 331 (1983).

with the grantor). See §674(d). The third exception is for powers over income or corpus held by an "independent trustee," which term excludes the grantor, the grantor's spouse, and any "related or subordinate party subservient to the grantor" as defined in §672(c). See §674(c).

For purposes of the foregoing, *a power or interest held by the grantor's spouse is attributed to the grantor.* "Spouse" means the grantor's spouse when the trust was created, and the grantor's current spouse. See §672(e).

From the brief overview of the rules set forth above, it is evident that a power held by an adverse party (even if it might be exercised for the benefit of the grantor or grantor's spouse) will generally not cause the grantor to be treated as the owner. The concept of "adverse party" is defined in §672(a) and Reg. §1.672(a)-1, and is essentially the same as for gift tax purposes. A trustee is not an adverse party simply by reason of being a trustee. A beneficiary (or holder of a general power of appointment) is likely to be an adverse party, but perhaps only as to a portion of the trust. Since a power (or interest) held by the grantor's spouse is attributed to the grantor, such spouse cannot be an adverse party.[125]

It is possible that the grantor might be treated as the owner of only a portion of the trust. For example, assume that a corporate trustee (a non-adverse party) has the discretion to pay income to the grantor or to B in its sole discretion for so long as B shall live, and on B's death the trust is to terminate and its assets distributed free of trust to C. So long as both the grantor and B are alive, the power to pay income to the grantor falls within §677(a)(1). The trustee properly allocates capital gains and losses to "corpus." Here the grantor is taxed on the "ordinary" income of the trust under §677(a), whether or not any of it is actually paid to the grantor, but the capital gains and losses are taxed to, or deducted by, the trust, since, being allocated to corpus for trust accounting purposes, they never increase or decrease the amounts potentially payable to the grantor.

To prevent double taxation of the same income to both the grantor and the beneficiaries or the trust, amounts received by the beneficiaries or the trust are treated as tax-free gifts from the grantor under §102.

It is not necessarily a bad thing for a trust to be a grantor trust. In a trust that accumulates (or can accumulate) ordinary income, the accumulated income would, if the trust is taxed as a "subchapter J trust" (see §7.5), be taxed under the highly compressed rate schedule of §1(e). In that case, it would probably be better if the trust is a grantor trust (or perhaps a beneficiary-owned trust), at least if the grantor (or beneficiary having a sole general *inter vivos* power of appointment) is in a lower income tax bracket than the trust. Even if the trust cannot accumulate income, it is possible that the grantor (or "beneficiary owner") might be in a lower

---

125. Section 672(c)(1) states that the grantor's spouse is a related or subordinate party only if living with the grantor. This rule might be seen as conflicting (potentially) with the rule of §672(e) that attributes a power held by the grantor's spouse to the grantor. That is, could a spouse not living with the grantor be treated as an "independent trustee" under §674(c)? This seems unlikely, given that §672(e) was enacted at a later date than §672(c).

income tax bracket than the actual distributee. An *inter vivos* trust that is constructed deliberately to be a grantor trust for income tax planning purposes is sometimes called an "intentionally defective grantor trust."

PROBLEMS, QUESTIONS, AND NOTES

1. The grantor trust rules offer good opportunities to test a person's ability to read the Code carefully, and perhaps to consult the regulations.
    a. Evaluate the following under §§673, 674, and 677(a): Ambrose, age 46, creates an irrevocable trust, naming the X Bank as trustee, income and/or corpus to child Buffy, age 18, for her support, education, health, and comfort in the trustee's discretion, with any income not so used to be accumulated and added to corpus, and upon Buffy's death the trust is to be paid over to Ambrose's wife Amber (currently age 40) if living, otherwise to Cleo. Capital gains are allocable to corpus. If the trust is a grantor trust, how would it be revised to lose such status?
    b. Assume the defects in (a) are cured. Can any of the following be trustee instead of the X Bank: (1) Ambrose, (2) Amber, (3) Buffy, (4) Cleo, (5) Ambrose's brother, or (6) Ambrose's other child Bea?
    c. Under §677(b), if the grantor owes a support obligation to the beneficiary, any income distributions that actually discharge all or part of the grantor's support obligations will be taxed to the grantor. But the income will not be taxed to the grantor just because income *could be* distributed to such beneficiary.
2. a. The original version of the grantor trust rules "allowed" an income-shifting trust to last for ten years, followed by a reversion in the grantor. In 1986, §673 was amended by replacing the ten-year rule by the 5 percent rule, and 672(e) was added providing (*inter alia*) that a remainder in the grantor's spouse would be treated as a reversion in the grantor. The enactment of §2702 has the effect (usually) of treating a reversion as a completed gift for gift tax purposes. These developments have pretty much "killed" a reversionary-interest trust as an income-shifting device.
    b. Can you think of any trust which is a grantor trust but which is a completed gift? In what scenario might this be a desirable result?
    c. Can you think of any trust which is a nongrantor trust yet is incomplete for gift tax purposes?
    d. Should the estate and gift tax rules be conformed to the income tax grantor trust rules? Along these lines, in 2001 Congress enacted §2511(c), which was to have taken effect upon repeal of the estate tax (and the GST tax), but it was repealed by the 2010 Act. Section 2511(c) stated that an *inter vivos* transfer into trust shall be treated as a completed gift unless it is treated as *wholly* owned by the grantor (or grantor's spouse) under the income tax grantor trust rules.

§8.5. How Should Transfers with Retained Interests and Powers Be Treated Under the Transfer and Income Taxes?

Transfers with retained interests and powers have generated a vast body of exceedingly complex doctrine that is not completely harmonized among the estate tax, the gift tax, and the income tax. There has long been discussion of the possibility of reforming (and simplifying) these rules. In the case of the transfer taxes, the issue is often put as whether *inter vivos* transfers with retained interests and powers be subject only to gift tax under an "easy to complete" rule or only to estate tax (or possible later gift tax) under a hard-to-complete rule. The material that follows presents our "take" on this issue.

A. *Revocable Transfers*

Perhaps the most easily justified hard-to-complete rule is that for revocable transfers. On an intuitive level, if such transfers were treated as completed gifts, but later revoked, the property would (unless consumed) appear in the donor's gross estate or be the subject of a later gift.

Although conceivably the system might provide that revocable transfers are complete but at the same time provide an exclusion or deduction from the gross estate for previously-taxed transfers that were later revoked, it would be hard to trace gross estate assets back to revoked amounts. Section 2012, which provides an estate tax credit for gift taxes on pre-1977 gifts included in the gross estate, illustrates some of the complexities of such an approach, which would also create a long-term recordkeeping problem.

A revocable transfer is essentially the same as the interest-free demand loan in the *Dickman* case, §3.1.A.5. The "present value" gift approach doesn't work. The transfers occur only over time as assets are released to third parties. Death is the final release. Both the timing and the measurement of completed transfers can be accurately ascertained only as, when, and to the extent that the donor's string on the property is cut. This is precisely the manner in which the gift and estate taxes treat revocable transfers.

B. *Transfers with Retained Reversions*

Somewhat the same considerations apply to *inter vivos* transfers with retained reversions (which are covered by §2037), although here the property might (or will) "come back" to the transferor on the occurrence of objective contingencies (rather than by the exercise of the transferor's will). Objective contingencies are often (although not universally) capable of valuation under actuarial principles, which is not the case for the possible exercise of a person's unfettered will. Thus, in this situation it may be worth "trying on" an easy-to-complete rule to see if it can work.

Different approaches might be appropriate for transfers with vested reversions and for transfers with contingent reversions. A "vested" reversion is one that does not expire at the transferor's death. A contingent reversion might fail on the transferor's death or on the occurrence of some other event.

The vested reversion situation could be handled in a straightforward manner, as follows. The gift amount would be the value of the property as reduced by the value of the reversion. Essentially, this represents the value of the interest that is parted with. If the reversion comes into possession prior to death, the property will augment the transferor's potential §2033 gross estate. Otherwise, the date-of-death value of the reversion will be included in the gross estate under §2033. Regardless, it would be incorrect to "exclude" the amount of the earlier gift from the gross estate, because there really was a depletion of the transferor's potential gross estate in an amount equal to amounts received by the donees of the current enjoyment interest during the transferor's lifetime. The problem here lies with use of the actuarial tables in valuing that gift. The tables may have operated inaccurately. The fact that actuarial tables *can* be used to assign a present value to a gift of a future interest is not a compelling justification for the position that they *should* be used, at least if a better approach is available. Indeed there is a better approach (at least for trusts), which would be to treat retained-vested-reversion transfers the same as revocable transfers under a hard-to-complete approach. Under this approach, distributions from the trust to third parties during the transferor's lifetime would be gifts. In the case of a non-trust transfer, the choice would be between using actuarial tables or else imputing distributions so long as the current-enjoyment interest is outstanding.

Inter vivos transfers with retained *contingent* reversions are what are usually covered by §2037. Section 2037 is the most opaque and difficult of all of the gross estate inclusion provisions. Treating these as revocable transfers seems appropriate in cases where the reversion has a more than trivial chance of occurring before the transferor's death. But then, if the possibility that the reversion will occur is remote, it might make sense to apply an easy-to-complete rule. In that case, if the reversion came into possession, the gift would be removed from the adjusted taxable gifts total, but if the reversion vested (without coming into possession) the reversion would be treated as having a zero value for estate tax purposes.

C. Transfers with Retained Income Interests

The traditional view has been that such a transfer "looks" testamentary, because the donor does not part with possession or enjoyment until death. However, it can be argued that the gift tax is capable of taxing the remainder interest when that interest is irrevocably given away. One can simply use actuarial tables to value that interest. Although the actuarial tables may turn out to be wrong in a given case, they should average out in the long run.

The rejoinder is that only a few persons in the population make transfers of this type. This poses the problem of "adverse selection." In this context, the problem is that transferors who can take advantage of an easy-to-complete rule will make transfers of this type, and those who cannot won't. The goal of the aggressive estate planner in this situation would be make a gift of a remainder interest that would be undervalued relative to what the holder of the remainder interest actually receives. The remainder interest is necessarily undervalued if the retained interest is overvalued relative to what the transferor receives back.

Actuarial tables are "present value" tables. The valuation of an interest under the tables is a function of these factors:

1. Life expectancy. The longer the life expectancy, the lower the value of a remainder interest. Thus, a remainder interest is undervalued if the transferor dies prior to his or her actuarial life expectancy. There are two possible ways in which this can be anticipated. First, family and personal medical history may indicate a relatively short life expectancy for the individual relative to the population. Second, the tables used for estate and gift tax purposes are "unisex" tables, meaning that the life expectancy built into the tables is systematically overstated for males.

2. Discount rate. The higher the discount rate, the lower the present value of remainder interests. The discount rate used in the tables is 120 percent of the federal mid-term rate. This discount rate seems systematically too high in the usual economic environment, where the income return from trusts averages 3-5 percent.

3. Expected economic return. The expected return is also set at 120 percent of the mid-term federal rate. However, the tables assume that all of this return is "income" and that none of it is added to corpus. In fact, the typical trust over time yields a modest "income" return (3-5 percent), with the rest of the return being allocated to corpus (as net capital gains or as net unrealized appreciation). In a retained-income trust, it may be understood that economic return is to be obtained with an eye to augmenting corpus rather than producing income. Indeed, the grantor may herself be the trustee and able to control investment decisions.

These points in themselves do not wholly undermine the case for an easy-to-complete rule. The valuation rules could be "straightened out" so as to yield a higher value for remainder interests. But this approach would still offer opportunities for manipulation (although less commonly). Congress in 1990 took the more draconian approach of §2702: Treat the retained income interest as being worth zero (except in certain cases) for gift tax purposes, resulting in a gift of the entire property. But this solution goes too far the other way, because it treats the decedent as having made a gift of substantial amounts that will return to her potential §2033 gross estate.

Again the better solution appears to be the hard-to-complete rule, under which the property would be subject to estate or gift tax upon the expiration of the transferor's retained interest (whether at death or during life). Section 2036(a)(1) is consistent with this norm as far as it goes, but it does not apply where the retained interest expires prior to the transferor's death (which may well be the case where a GRAT or GRUT is involved). Unlike present law, there would be no reason to treat the initial transfer as involving any kind of gift.

A hard-to-complete rule would eliminate controversies over the transfer tax treatment of discretionary or "standards" trusts for the benefit of the settlor.

D. *Retained-Power Transfers*

Here, unlike the situations described above, there is no possibility that the property (or its economic yield) will return to the transferor. Thus — and contrary to current doctrine — an easy-to-complete rule seems *prima facie* correct, at least for transfer tax purposes. Here the only argument in favor of a hard-to-complete rule is that wealthy transferors don't have any real use for the property or its yield but would derive equivalent satisfaction from possessing the power to control the beneficial enjoyment of the property. This argument is a kind of "ownership in substance" argument. However, the transfer taxes are all about the transfer of wealth, not the retention of subjective enjoyment relating to transferred wealth. Moreover, any concept of "substantial retained ownership" raises problems of degree. At what point is retained control so significant as to justify a hard-to-complete rule? Such a situation is likely to produce either arbitrary statutory rules or else is likely to breed endless "facts and circumstances" litigation. It can even produce both, because litigants will attempt to "move" a given situation from one category to another.

An easy-to-complete rule would eliminate issues revolving around co-trustees and "adverse parties."

E. *Income Tax Rules*

Basically, for transfer tax purposes, a retained-interest transfer (broadly defined to encompass almost any possibility that the income or corpus would return to the grantor) would be subject to a hard-to-complete rule. The income tax rules could, if desired, be easily conformed to this approach by eliminating existing exemptions relating to adverse parties. However, the proposed easy-to-complete rule for retained-power transfers would be incompatible with the traditional income tax policy that income from property should be attributed to the person who controls the property.

CHAPTER 9

ADVANCED VALUATION ISSUES

This chapter covers classic entity estate tax freezes, the use of entities (especially family limited partnerships, or FLPs) to create valuation discounts, and the use of rights and restrictions (lapsing or nonlapsing) to affect tax valuations. Particular attention will be paid to the effectiveness of §§2701 and 2704 to curb the effectiveness of these devices.

§9.1. The *Byrum* Case

The "seed" from which much of the material in this chapter has evolved is *U.S. v. Byrum*, 408 U.S. 125 (1972). In *Byrum*, the decedent owned between 71 percent and 88 percent of the total voting stock of three corporations, and transferred amounts of such stock to an irrevocable trust such that, after the transfer, he owned 59 percent, 42 percent, and 35 percent of the total stock of each corporation, respectively, with the trust owning 12 percent, 46 percent, and 48 percent of the stock in the same corporations. The trustee was a bank, but the decedent individually retained the powers to (1) vote the transferred shares, (2) veto the sale or transfer of trust assets and approve reinvestments, and (3) remove the trustee and appoint a corporate successor trustee.

The beneficiaries of the trust were the decedent's children and grandchildren. The trust instrument gave the trustee discretion to distribute income and/or principal to the beneficiaries according to standards.

Byrum's estate planning goal was to remove stock from his gross estate at its current gift tax value, while using his retained control over the corporation to increase the value of the stock given to the trusts. (Another possible goal, not considered by the Supreme Court, could have been to create minority interest discounts in the decedent's retained stock in two of the three corporations.)

The government first argued that the decedent retained the power to accumulate the income from transferred property within the meaning of §2036(a)(2) by his ability to vote the transferred shares together with his nontransferred shares so as to control dividend policy and prevent dividends from being paid to the trust. Failure to pay dividends would presumably increase the earnings base of the corporation, and thereby increase the value of the stock held by the trust. Moreover, this power was locked in, due to the fact that the decedent could prevent the trustee from disposing of the shares. The Court rejected the government's §2036(a)(2) contention on two grounds.

First, the Court relied on a supposedly ironclad rule that retained "administrative" powers fall outside of the scope of §§2036(a)(2) and 2038. The fact that there was no such well-established rule at the time *Byrum* was decided has been commented upon at p. 393. Even if there had been such a rule, *Byrum* was a case of first impression with respect to the facts and theory advanced by the government. The Court merely concluded that administrative powers were involved, without analyzing whether in substance the powers were really "administrative" or "dispositive." Although the decedent's "retained" powers under the trust instrument pertained to the trust's sole investment, the decedent (unlike previous cases involving retained administrative powers) was not exercising these powers in a trustee capacity subject to the general constraint of impartiality. In fact, a controlling shareholder owes no meaningful fiduciary duty with regard to the payment of dividends.

The second ground of decision was one of "supervening cause" (that precluded the decedent from having the "right" to accumulate income), and this ground played out on two levels. First, the majority noted that the Board of Directors, not the decedent as controlling shareholder, had control over the payment of dividends. The Board, although serving at the will of the decedent, was said to be constrained by fiduciary duties owed to the corporation and minority shareholders, who were (apparently) unrelated to the decedent. However, the decision of the Board to pay or not to pay dividends essentially falls under the "business judgment rule," and a decision not to pay dividends will not be overturned by the courts unless there is bad faith or an abuse of discretion.[1] But such a minimal constraint on the discretionary dispositive power of a *trustee* does not prevent the application of §2036(a)(2) or §2038.

The Court majority avoided dealing with the question of whether a more-than-50 percent shareholder can effectively control Board decisions by stating that a less-than-50 percent shareholder might have *de facto* control over a Board, so that a "control test" would be too hard to apply on a case-by-case basis. But only a more-than-50 percent shareholder can have any "right" to control a Board. The effect of the majority's theory is to immunize a decedent from §§2036(a)(2) and 2038 in any case where control is exercised through a non-trust entity. The majority opinion suggested that holding for the government would somehow "discriminate" against closely-held business interests, but the Court's holding just as surely discriminates in favor of them, since it is just such holdings through which control can be most readily exercised.

---

1. The scope of the power to pay "excessive" dividends is not really at issue. That would pose a §2038 issue, which the government did not raise.

The second level of the "intervening cause" theory is that the independent trustee of the trust could decide to pay or accumulate income, or distribute corpus, and this power could be exercised so as to thwart any power retained by the decedent. However, the only power that would thwart the decedent's power to accumulate income would be the power to invade corpus, but the decedent could have prevented the invasion of corpus by objecting to any disposition of the trust assets, which was constituted almost entirely of the transferred stock! Additionally, the trustee's power to invade corpus was limited by ascertainable standards relating to support, health, education, and need. Finally, the Court simply ignores prior authority to the effect that §2036 is not negated just because a third party had a power to defeat the decedent's retained interest or power, unless the decedent's interest or power was in fact defeated prior to his death.

The government also argued that the right to vote transferred stock amounted to retained "enjoyment" under §2036(a)(1). The Court sensibly held here that "enjoyment" referred to substantial economic benefits, not subjective utility.

Byrum was controversial, to say the least, and in the Tax Reform Act of 1976 Congress intervened. Oddly, it did so by overturning the result under §2036(a)(1), not §2036(a)(2). Section 2036(b), added by the 1976 Act, states that a retained right to vote transferred stock of a controlled corporation shall be deemed to constitute "enjoyment" under §2036(a)(1). A corporation is deemed "controlled" by the decedent if at any time within three years of death the decedent, after applying the §318 attribution rules, had the right (either alone or in conjunction with any person) to vote stock possessing at least 20 percent of the combined voting power of all classes of stock.

Section 2036(b) was applied in *Rev. Rul.* 80-346, 1980-2 C.B. 271, which held that an oral agreement with the trustee requiring the latter to obtain the grantor's approval before voting the stock came within §2036(b).

In *Rev. Rul. 81-15,* 1981-1 C.B. 247, the Service acknowledged that the *Byrum* holding under §2036(a)(2) survived the enactment of §2036(b). It follows that §2036(a)(2) does not apply where the grantor can control the flow of dividends with respect to transferred stock by reason of the voting control residing in stock not transferred by the grantor. This is easy to arrange: The transferred stock can be stock that has no voting rights. Gifts of nonvoting equity are what characterizes entity estate freezes, discussed shortly.

QUESTIONS AND NOTES

1. In *Chambers v. Comm'r,* 87 T.C. 225 (1986), the court held that a *Byrum*-type trust was a completed gift for gift tax purposes. The court felt bound by the *Byrum* analysis, so that the right to control dividends on transferred stock did not amount to a power to "alter" beneficial enjoyment. Since there is no gift tax counterpart to §2036(b), this holding suggests that a transfer with retained voting rights will be subject to both gift and estate tax, although the gift will be taken out of the cumulative tax base under the adjusted-taxable-gifts exclusion.

2. a. The retention of the right to vote transferred shares would reduce the value of the gift, especially if the donee lacks control or the possibility of forming a control coalition. Lapsing voting rights would not be an asset of the transferor's §2033 estate, because they lapse at the transferor's death.

   b. Where (as was the case in *Byrum*) the retained right to vote stock is personal to the decedent, and (therefore) lapses on his death, such lapse will constitute a gross estate inclusion under §2704(a)(1), enacted in 1990, if the decedent and members of the decedent's family control the entity both before and after the decedent's death. The theory is that the lapse entails a shift in value from the decedent to the owners of the equity interest, and this is the measure of the amount includible. See §2704(a)(2). In *Byrum*, the government made nothing of this point.

   c. If an asset that is included in the gross estate is subject to a restriction that lapses at the decedent's death, the restriction (that would arguably depress the value of the asset) is disregarded under general valuation principles. That is, the asset is valued without regard to the restriction. See §4.4.D & E. Section 2704(a) applies to cases where the underlying asset is not already included in the gross estate. If the lapse occurs during the person's lifetime, it is treated as a gift for gift tax purposes.

   d. In the case of a gift with a retained current-enjoyment interest (such as would fall under §2036(a)), the retained interest is a right that loses value with the passage of time (and lapses "finally" at or before the death of the donor), effecting a shift of value to the interests following the retained interest. In other words, sections 2036(a) and 2704 are based on the same fundamental insight. However, §2704(a) does not apply to lapses of current-enjoyment interests generally, but is limited to lapses of voting and liquidation rights. Section 2704 is discussed in connection with liquidation rights in §9.4.A.

3. Speaking of liquidation rights, if a person has sufficient voting control of a corporation to force a liquidation, the value of such person's stock is no less than the person's share of the net value of the corporation's underlying assets. See *Estate of O'Connell v. Comm'r*, 640 F.2d 249 (9th Cir.1981); *Estate of Jephson v. Comm'r*, 87 T.C. 297 (1986). Should this approach be applied to the stock owned by a decedent at death where the power to force a liquidation derives from aggregating the voting rights of the decedent in transferred stock (includible under §2036(b)) and nontransferred stock (includible under §2033)? Cf. *Rev. Rul. 79-7*, 1979-1 C.B. 294 (transferred shares includible under former version of §2035 combined with nontransferred shares, resulting in a denial of a minority-interest discount).

4. a. If *Byrum* had come out the other way under §2036(a)(2), would a transfer of stock or a partnership interest be includible under §2036(a)(2) on account of the transferor's control of the corporation or partnership derived from nontransferred equity or domination of management? What feature(s) of §2036 would prevent such inclusion? Would §2038 also be avoided? If so, what planning vistas are revealed?

b. *Byrum* can be criticized for overrating the fiduciary constraints imposed on majority shareholders relative to minority shareholders. At least the minority shareholders in *Byrum* were not family members, and the corporations carried on businesses (as opposed to being incorporated investment portfolios). In *Northern Trust Co. v. Comm'r*, 87 T.C. 349 (1986), the Tax Court cited a controlling shareholder's "fiduciary duty" to the minority shareholder as a basis for reducing the claimed minority-interest discount.

c. In a family limited partnership (FLP), the other equity-holders are family members, and the assets are typically of an investment (rather than a business) character. In such a scenario, does *Byrum* insulate from §2036 a decedent who maintains unlimited control of the assets he has transferred to that partnership? *Byrum* was distinguished in *Estate of Strangi v. Comm'r*, T.C. Memo. 2003-145, *aff'd*, 417 F.3d 468 (5th Cir.2005) (*Strangi II*), where the court held that the "intrafamily fiduciary duties within an investment vehicle" like the FLP in *Strangi* did not rise to the substantial and substantive obligations found in the business framework of *Byrum*. It was also noted that *Byrum* involved an independent corporate trustee that was solely authorized to determine payments of income or principal to or for the beneficiaries.

§9.2. Section 2701 and Entity Estate Freeze Transactions

The term "estate freeze" in its broad sense refers to any scheme whereby the older generation's retained assets (or interests therein) are "frozen" in value while the appreciation potential inherent in the same assets is transferred at minimal transfer tax cost to the younger generation. Examples of estate freeze techniques previously encountered include GRATs, private annuities, installment sales, and sales of remainder interests: The older generation ends up with a creditor interest and the younger generation ends up with the appreciation-potential asset or equity interest.

The material below deals with *"entity* estate freezes" wherein the underlying property is a "business" entity (corporation, partnership, or LLC) rather than a trust. The typical classic entity estate freeze transaction involves a scenario where the decedent owned voting common stock in a closely-held corporation, and during life causes the corporation to undergo a "recapitalization" in which the decedent ends up with (a) preferred stock (a "senior" equity interest) with a high dividend payout rate and (b) common stock with residual dividend rights (a "junior" equity interest). The common stock, which embodies the appreciation potential, is made the subject of a gift, and the fixed-income preferred is held until death. The fixed-income preferred stock will have a value equal (or almost equal) to the pre-recapitalization value of the original common stock, and the "new" common stock (the junior equity) will have a very low (or zero) value. The tax planning aim of the classic entity estate freeze is that the retained preferred stock should maintain a steady ("frozen") value for purposes of §2033, and the appreciation potential (inherent in the junior equity) will be removed from the gross estate at minimal gift tax cost.

A. *Status of Entity Estate Freezes Under §2036(a)*

The case below dealt with an attempt to include the gifted junior equity interest in the donor's gross estate under §2036(a)(1).

Estate of Boykin v. Commissioner

Tax Court Memorandum Decision 1987-134

KORNER, *Judge*: The sole issue presented here for decision is whether decedent John G. Boykin retained either a right to income from, or the enjoyment of, voting stock that he transferred to a family trust for the benefit of his children such that the value of the stock is includable in his gross estate under section 2036(a)(1).

Findings of Fact

This case involves stock of Tensaw Land & Timber Company, Inc. ("Tensaw") that the decedent transferred to a trust for the benefit of his children. Tensaw is an Alabama corporation that was incorporated on November 6, 1937. [Decedent's father, Frank Boykin, controlled Tenshaw.] Frank W. Boykin died in early 1969. At the time of his death Tensaw had only one class of stock, voting common ("voting stock"). Forty thousand shares of the voting stock were issued and outstanding. [Decedent and his 3 siblings each owned 7,000 shares.]

On October 7, 1969, Tensaw amended its articles of incorporation. The amendment authorized the board to issue 150,000 shares of nonvoting stock. Contemporaneously with the adoption of the amended articles, Tensaw issued to the owners of the voting stock 3.75 shares of the nonvoting stock for each share of voting stock. Tensaw's amended articles of incorporation granted the nonvoting shares a preference with respect to liquidating distributions and dividends. Each share of the nonvoting stock was granted a right to receive ten times the dividends paid by Tensaw on each voting share.

On October 8, 1969, [decedent transferred all of his voting shares to an irrevocable trust] for the benefit of the children of decedent.

Opinion

The issue for decision is whether decedent retained either the right to income from, or the enjoyment of, the voting stock that he transferred to the trust for the benefit of his children such that the value of the stock is includable in his gross estate under section 2036(a)(1). Respondent bases his argument that decedent retained the right to income from, and the enjoyment of, the voting stock [by reason of] the dividend rights of the nonvoting stock that decedent retained. According to respondent, by retaining the nonvoting shares, decedent in fact "earned dividends from the equity in [Tensaw] attributable to the voting stock transferred in trust." Respondent reasons that the effect of the dividend rights enjoyed by the nonvoting shares was that decedent retained "nearly all the income from the transferred property" and that "this retention of income constituted a retention of the enjoyment of the transferred voting common stock or a right to income from the transferred stock."

Although it is apparent that decedent transferred property — the voting shares — it is equally apparent that he retained no right to the income from the transferred property.

It is important to recognize at the outset that shareholders have no legal title to a share of corporate earnings and assets until a dividend is declared or a division is made on the winding up or dissolution of the corporation. The corporation itself is the owner of its earnings and assets. Shareholders have the right to receive dividends on their stock only after the dividends have been declared, and only if their receipt of the dividends is consistent with their rights as shareholders.

When decedent gave his voting shares to the trust for the benefit of his children on October 8, 1969, he transferred with the voting shares the right to receive all dividends and liquidating distributions that were subsequently declared on them. The only rights decedent retained were those accorded to the Tensaw nonvoting shares he retained, which were separate and distinct rights from the rights enjoyed by the voting shares that he transferred.

Respondent points to *Estate of Cooper v. Comm'r*, 74 T.C. 1373 (1980), and *Overton v. Comm'r*, 6 T.C. 304 (1946), affd. 162 F.2d 155 (2d Cir.1947), to support his argument that decedent retained an interest in the voting shares. In *Estate of Cooper*, a decedent retained the interest coupons from bearer bonds that she transferred to a trust for her grandchildren. This Court held that the value of the bonds was includable in the decedent's gross estate as the decedent had retained the income from the transferred bonds. In *Overton*, a common shareholder caused his corporation to reissue his stock into two classes. He transferred the class B shares to his wife. The class B shares had a right to receive only $1 per share of distributions of the corporation's capital, yet received dividends of $150.40 a share in the six years after he transferred them to his wife. This Court considered the amount of dividends that the class B shares received in proportion to the liquidation value of the shares and concluded that the reissuance of two classes of stock was in substance simply a device to shift income from one taxpayer to another. We accordingly held that the dividends paid on the class B shares were taxable to the class A shares.

Neither *Estate of Cooper* nor *Overton* supports respondent's position in this action. This is not a case such as *Estate of Cooper* in which a taxpayer has attempted to reduce his estate by transferring an asset while retaining the bare right to the income therefrom. As we have already discussed, Tensaw's voting shares were separate and distinct from its nonvoting shares. When decedent transferred his voting shares he gave up the right to receive the dividends to which those shares subsequently became entitled as well as the assets those shares might subsequently receive in a liquidation of Tensaw. This is similarly not a case such as *Overton* in which a taxpayer has attempted to shift income by creating a class of stock that has been paid dividends that represent an excessive return on the liquidation value of the shares. Neither class of Tensaw's stock was designed to be paid dividends that represent an excessive return on the liquidation value of the shares. By prohibiting Tensaw's board from declaring dividends on the voting shares until Tensaw's net worth was sufficient to redeem all nonvoting shares at their $100 per share call price, Tensaw's articles of incorporation guaranteed that dividends would not be paid on the voting shares until those shares had a positive liquidation value. The dividends paid on the nonvoting shares, which reached $6.50 a share in the year after decedent's death, do not represent an excessive return on their $100 a share liquidation value. The fiduciary duties of the trustees of the family trusts to the trusts' beneficiaries, and of the directors of Tensaw to the voting shareholders, limited Tensaw's ability to pay dividends to the nonvoting shares that represented an unreasonable return on their $100 per share call price. See *Chambers v. Comm'r*, 87 T.C. 225, 235 (1986).

This is a case in which a taxpayer transferred his entire interest in shares of stock and retained no right to income from or the enjoyment of the shares. We therefore hold that no part of the value of the voting stock is includable in decedent's gross estate under section 2036(a)(1).

B. Entity Estate Freezes Under §2701

Congress responded to *Boykin* by enacting §2036(c) in 1987. Clause (1) of that section essentially provided:

> In General — For purposes of subsection (a), if
>
> > (A) any person holds a substantial interest in an enterprise, and
> > (B) such person in effect transfers after December 17, 1987, property having a disproportionately large share of the potential appreciation in such person's interest in the enterprise while retaining an interest in the income of, or rights in, the enterprise,
>
> then the retention interest shall be considered to be a retention of the enjoyment of the transferred property.

After intense lobbying by the estate planning bar, Congress in 1990 retroactively repealed §2036(c) and replaced it by §2701, which is applicable to gifts made after October 8, 1990. According to the Senate Report to the 1990 Act:

> The committee believes that an across-the-board inclusion rule is an inappropriate and unnecessary approach to the valuation problems associated with estate freezes. The committee believes that the amount of any tax on a gift should be determined at the time of the transfer and not upon the death of the transferor. Moreover, the committee is concerned that the statute's complexity, breadth, and vagueness posed an unreasonable impediment to the transfer of family businesses. The committee also is concerned that many taxpayers have refrained from legitimate intrafamily transactions because of the uncertainty over the scope of its rules.

Section 2701, the replacement for §2036(c), basically treats the gift of the common stock (the junior equity) in a *Boykin*-type situation as a gift for gift tax purposes of *both* the common *and* the preferred stock (the senior equity) of the donor. See §2701(a)(1) & (3). (This approach is basically the same as that for retained-interest transfers under §2702, discussed at §8.2.) With the repeal of §2036(c), *Boykin* would continue to preclude inclusion of the transferred common stock in the donor's gross estate.

Example 1: Deirdre owns 100 percent (100 shares) of the common stock of Zany Corp., with an aggregate value of $100K, and causes a recapitalization that replaces each common share by one share of nonvoting common and 1 share of voting preferred having a $1K par value that is to pay an annual dividend at a rate of 7 percent. Deirdre gives 80 common shares to Eli. Deirdre claims that the 100 shares of preferred stock possess a value of $100K, so that the common shares (and the gift to Eli) have a zero value. Assuming that the requirements for the application of §2701 are satisfied, Deirdre is treated as having made a gift of $80K to Eli (the value of 80 percent of the preferred *and* common stock). Assume that on Deirdre's death the preferred stock, which is included in her gross estate under §2033, is worth $87K. Since the same stock has already been treated as a gift to the extent of $80K, only $7K is included in Deirdre's gross estate under §2033. See §2701(e)(6) (calling for "proper adjustment" upon subsequent disposition of retained senior equity interest). The 20 percent common stock holding of Deirdre is included at its fair market value.

However, if the retained senior equity is a "distribution right which consists of a right to receive a qualified payment" (hereinafter called a "qualified payment right" [QPR]), then such retained senior equity is not to be treated as being worth zero, but is to be valued under conventional valuation principles. In other words, a QPR is not treated as being part of the gift. §2701(a)(3)(C). A QPR is defined as a fixed-rate cumulative dividend right (or its equivalent). See §2701(c)(3).

In cases where the retained distribution right is a QPR, the gift of the common stock would be treated as having a value no less than an amount which is equal to 10 percent of the total value of *all* stock interests multiplied by the percentage of the total *common* stock that is represented by the gift. §2701(a)(4).

Example 2: Same facts as Example 1, except that the retained preferred stock is a QPR. Hence, Deirdre is treated as having made a gift of only 80 shares of common stock, but such shares will be treated as being worth (no less than) $8K (despite actually being worth zero). The retained preferred would be included in Deirdre's gross estate at its full $87K value.

The concept of QPR is based on the idea of a guaranteed payout that is analogous to an annuity or unitrust interest. If distributions with respect to a QPR are not made on schedule, any disposition (by gift or at death) of the retained senior equity triggers an additional gift or bequest of any accrued but unpaid distributions, the theory being that such amounts (accumulations inside the entity) have caused a shift in value away from the retained senior equity to the transferred junior equity. See §2701(d).

A transferor can irrevocably elect to have a QPR treated as a non-QPR or (if not inconsistent with the controlling instruments) can elect to treat a non-QPR as a QPR, but in the latter case the value of the QPR cannot exceed its market value. See §2701(c)(3)(C); Reg. §25.2701-2(d), Ex. 5.

Section 2701 is not limited to gifts of common stock in corporations but also encompasses gifts of junior equity interests in any other type of business entity, including partnerships and LLCs. Here are some other rules pertaining to §2701, many of which are designed to limit its application to family-controlled closely-held entities:

1. The transfer to the junior equity must be to a "member of the transferor's family," as defined in §2701(e)(1), referring to the transferor's spouse, descendents, the transferor's spouse's descendents, and spouses of any such descendents.
2. The senior equity must be retained (held) by the transferor or any "applicable family member," as defined in §2701(e)(2) to refer to the transferor's spouse, ancestors, the transferor's spouse's ancestors, and spouses of any such ancestors.
3. Equity held by any entity shall be deemed to be "indirectly" held by individuals. See §2701(e)(3).
4. Transfers of junior equity interests are beyond the reach of §2701 if market quotations for such equity are readily available on an established securities market or if such market quotations are available for the retained senior equity interest. See §2701(a)(1) (second sentence) & (2)(A).
5. Section 2701 does not apply unless the transferor and "applicable family members" (including siblings and descendents thereof) possess "control" (taking attribution rules into account) of the entity immediately before the transfer. Control is defined as holding 50 percent or more ("by vote or value") of the company's stock; 50 percent or more of the partnership's capital or profits interests; or, in a limited partnership, any general partnership interest. See §2701(b)(2).
6. A retained "liquidation, put, call, or conversion right" (other than a right that "must be exercised at a specific time and at a specific amount") cannot be a QPR (because it is not a "distribution right"), and thus has a zero value. See §2701(c)(1)(B)(ii) & (c)(2)(B)(i). If a QPR is subject to one or more put, call, liquidation, or conversion rights, the QPR will be valued at the lowest amount consistent with the maximum exercise of such rights. See §2701(a)(3)(B); Reg. §25.2701-2(a)(3) & (5) (calling this the "lower of" rule).

PROBLEMS, QUESTIONS, AND NOTES

1. a. Does an entity estate freeze transaction entail the *passive* shifting of value from a retained interest to gifted interest over time, in the manner of a retained-interest transfer? If not, was §2036(c) an appropriate response? Does an entity estate freeze disguise an *active* shifting of value subsequent to the gift? If so, is it of the type that can be reached by the gift tax?

b. Would entity estate freezes exist apart from the transfer taxes? Certain similar transactions were allowed by §2036(c) and are allowed by §2701: gifts of equity in an entity where the transferor has (a) a right to receive an annuity or pension from the entity or (b) a creditor interest evidenced by debentures, bonds, or debt instruments. What is "special" about retained "senior equity" (preferred-stock-like interests)?

c. Under *Robinette v. Helvering*, 318 U.S. 184 (1943), codified in Reg. §25.2511-1(e), a retained interest is treated as being worth zero if it cannot be valued according to generally accepted valuation principles. Could the government have applied this rule to entity estate freezes in cases where the retained distribution rights were shaky or contingent?

2. Alex owns all of the stock in company A, with a market value of $1.5M. The company is re-capitalized so that Alex owns $1M worth of preferred stock (1,000 shares of $1K par value preferred bearing an annual noncumulative dividend of $100 per share) and 1,000 shares of voting common stock, the latter of which he transfers to Bonnie, his daughter.

a. Does §2701 apply to Alex's transfer? What is the value of his gift to Bonnie?

b. Can Alex obtain a better result without amending the corporate instruments? How? See Reg. §25.2701-1(e), Ex. 2.

3. Amelia owns all of the stock in company AM, with a market value of $1.5M. She holds 1,000 shares of $1K par value preferred bearing an annual cumulative dividend of $100 per share (with a value of $1M) and all of AM's 1,000 shares of voting common stock. Amelia has the right to "put" all of the preferred stock to AM at any time for $900K. She transfers the common stock to Bart, her son, and keeps the preferred. What is the value of her gift to Bart? See Reg. §25.2701-2(a)(5).

4. Company C (owned by the donor's daughter and son-in-law) contributes 1 percent of the assets of partnership P in return for a 35 percent partnership interest. A trust (the interests of which are owned by the donor and her spouse) contributes 99 percent of P's total assets in return for a 65 percent partnership interest. The partnership agreement provides that proceeds from capital transactions must be distributed to the limited partner to the extent of its capital contribution, with any additional proceeds to be distributed to the partners in proportion to their partnership interests. In *T.A.M. 199933002*, the Service first held that, under the attribution rules of §2701(e)(1)(B) & (b)(2)(B), the donor was deemed to control 100 percent of P. Second, the Service held that §2701 can apply to newly formed entities. The third holding was that the donor's interest was senior to C's interest because of the distribution preference. Accordingly, the donor had effectively transferred a (34 percent) equity interest in P to a family member while she retained an applicable retained interest. See also *P.L.R. 200138028* (involving the formation of an FLP, with the retention of a QPR *and* a liquidation right, resulting in the application of the "lower of" rule of §2701(a)(3), which is illustrated by Reg. §25.2701-2(a)(5)).

§9.3. Family Limited Partnerships

A family limited partnership (FLP) is simply a limited partnership of which all the interests therein are owned by family members.

A. Use of FLPs (and Other Entities) to Obtain Valuation Discounts

Typically, the taxpayer has mostly liquid assets (such as marketable securities and cash) that are converted to illiquid ones through the transfer of those assets to a holding company, which can be a corporation, LLC, or partnership, in return for equity interests in such company.[2] Any equity interest in such an entity would obtain a lack-of-marketability discount. The FLP is the entity of choice, because the FLP agreement can contain (and state law can impose) restrictions on liquidation, assignment, and alienation (to thwart creditors, including divorce creditors). These restrictions operate to keep the plan intact and to further depress the value of the equity interests. In addition, gift giving by the creator of the entity often includes the transfer of minority interests and, after *inter vivos* gifts, a decedent often holds a minority share in the FLP when she dies. Lack-of-marketability and minority discounts are briefly discussed at §4.4.B.

In contrast to the income tax, there are no look-through (entity disregarding) statutory provisions under the transfer taxes.[3] There is a rule that an equity interest transferred by a person who can unilaterally liquidate the entity is to be valued (at a minimum) with reference to the underlying asset values of the entity,[4] but this rule can be avoided in the case of a corporation by reducing one's voting control and in the case of a partnership by imposing restrictions on the liquidation of the entity or the liquidation (redemption) of an equity interest.

In principle, if the entity is a sham, interests in the entity would be disregarded, and the equity-holders would be treated as owning the underlying assets, thereby

---

2. Case law bears out the description in the text: an FLP is formed primarily with liquid assets by using the FLP form. By being poured into an FLP, the assets are transformed into FLP interests that are illiquid and devalued. See, e.g., *Estate of Korby v. Comm'r*, 471 F.3d 848 (8th Cir.2006), *aff'g*, T.C. Memo. 2005-102 and 2005-103 (cash, stocks, and bonds); *Estate of Thompson v. Comm'r*, 382 F.3d 367, 370 (3d Cir.2004) (marketable securities and a note receivable); *Estate of Rosen v. Comm'r*, T.C. Memo. 2006-115 (cash and marketable securities); *Estate of Harper v. Comm'r*, T.C. Memo. 2002-121 (marketable securities and a note receivable). Real estate is also often contributed to an FLP. See, e.g., *Bigelow v. U.S.*, 503 F.3d 955, 959 (9th Cir.2007); *Estate of Abraham v. Comm'r*, 408 F.3d 26 (1st Cir.2005), *aff'g*, T.C. Memo. 2004-39; *Estate of Erickson v. Comm'r*, T.C. Memo. 2007-107 (marketable securities and real estate); *Estate of Schutt v. Comm'r*, T.C. Memo. 2005-126 (Alabama timberlands, marketable securities, and cash).

3. Under the income tax, the income of a "C corporation" that is a personal holding company (PHC) is subject to an additional 15% tax on undistributed personal holding company income. See §541. The idea is that this penalty tax will force the PHC to distribute dividends. Entities treated as partnerships (partnerships and LLCs) are subject to pass-through income taxation, as are Subchapter S corporations. See also §§951 and 954 (pass-through taxation to U.S. shareholders of PHC income of controlled foreign corporation).

4. See *Estate of O'Connell v. Comm'r*, 640 F.2d 249 (9th Cir.1981); *Estate of Jephson v. Comm'r*, 87 T.C. 297 (1986).

losing any discounts that would have attached if the entity had been recognized. However, as will be demonstrated, the courts hardly ever find that an entity is a sham.

FLPs are widely used to obtain valuation discounts, which appear to fall in the 30-60 percent range.[5] The *Kelley* case below offers a good description of the typical FLP scenario and its attendant valuation discounts.

Estate of Kelley v. Commissioner

Tax Court Memorandum Decision 2005-235

VASQUEZ, *Judge:* The sole issue for decision is the fair market value of Webster E. Kelley's (decedent) 94.83-percent interest in a family limited partnership [FLP].

In December 1999, the estate employed Appraisal Technologies Inc. (ATI) to prepare a valuation of decedent's interests in these closely held entities. ATI concluded that a 53.5% valuation discount was applicable. Respondent contends that the estate is entitled to a 25.2% discount.

Market Value Before Discounts

There are three common approaches to measure the interest in a closely held entity: the income approach, the net asset value (NAV) approach, and the market approach. Value is determined under the income approach by computing a company's income stream. Value is determined under the NAV approach by computing the aggregate value of the underlying assets as of a fixed point in time. Value is computed under the market approach by comparison with arm's-length transactions involving similar companies. [The] NAV method is generally an appropriate method to apply when computing the value of a nonoperating entity. The parties agree that the value of the FLP's assets on the valuation date, decedent's date of death, was $1,226,421, consisting of $807,271 cash and $419,150 in certificates of deposit and no liabilities. Therefore, we use this as the NAV.

Minority Interest (Lack of Control) Discount

Pursuant to the partnership agreement, a buyer of all or any portion of the transferred interests would have limited control of his investment. [As stated in *Peracchio v. Comm'r*, T.C. Memo. 2003-80: "For instance, such holder (1) would have no say in the partnership's investment strategy, and (2) could not unilaterally recoup his investment by forcing the partnership either to redeem his interest or to

---

5. "According to IRS estate and gift tax attorneys, who review and audit Federal estate tax returns, and various private-sector studies of valuation discounting, recent discounts of FLP interests fall between 30 percent and 60 percent." Martha Britton Eller, *Which Estates Are Affected by the Estate Tax?: An Examination of the Filing Population for Year-of-Death 2001*, 25 Stat. Inc. Bull. 185, 197 (Summer 2005).

undergo a complete liquidation."] A hypothetical willing buyer would account for this lack of control by demanding a reduced price; i.e., a price that is below the NAV of the pro rata share of the interest purchased in the FLP. A minority discount will therefore apply in this case where a partner lacks control.

In determining the minority discount for the FLP, we believe a correct analysis would be to take the arithmetic mean of all of the closed-end [mutual] funds, as shareholders in closed-end funds lack control [of the underlying fund investments]. [As stated in *Peracchio*, supra: "The idea is that, since such shares (by definition) enjoy a high degree of marketability, those discounts must be attributable, at least to some extent, to a minority shareholder's lack of control over the investment fund."] Although we find neither expert particularly persuasive on this issue, we will apply a 12-percent discount on the grounds that (1) respondent has effectively conceded that a discount factor of up to 12% would be appropriate, and (2) petitioner has failed to prove that a figure greater than 12% would be appropriate. See *Peracchio v. Comm'r*, [supra] (using a 2% minority discount factor for the "cash and money market funds" asset category of a family limited partnership).

Marketability Discount

A discount for lack of marketability is appropriate in valuing the interests in the FLP, as there is not a ready market for partnership interests in a closely held partnership.

There are several ways to determine a marketability discount. Two of the most common include the initial public offering (IPO) approach and the restricted stock approach. IPO studies compare the private-market price of shares sold before a company goes public with the public-market prices obtained in the IPO of the shares or shortly thereafter. Restricted stock studies compare private-market prices of unregistered (restricted) shares in public companies with the public-market prices of unrestricted but otherwise identical shares in the same corporations. A variant of the restricted stock approach, the private placement approach, attempts to isolate the effect that impaired marketability has on the discount determined under the restricted stock approach. This Court has concluded that the private placement approach is appropriate where the interest to be valued was part of an investment company, as the assessment and monitoring costs would be relatively low in the case of a sale of an interest in that company. The FLP is an investment company, as 100% of its assets consist of cash and certificates of deposit.

We are not persuaded by ATI's recommendation of a 38% marketability discount, as the restricted stock studies referred to in ATI's expert report examine mostly operating companies, and there are fundamental differences between an investment company holding easily valued and liquid assets (cash and certificates of deposit) and operating companies. We are also not persuaded by [the government expert's] recommendation of a 15% marketability discount.

In *McCord v. Comm'r*, 120 T.C. 358 (2003), [later reversed on other issues, 461 F.3d 614 (5th Cir.2006)], we focused on the Bajaj study and found that a 20% marketability discount was appropriate for interests in a family limited partnership classified as an investment company. Dr. Bajaj divided the private placements into three groups: the 29 lowest discounts, the middle 29 discounts, and the 30 highest discounts. The low discount group, with a discount of 2.21%, is dominated by registered private placements which did not suffer from impaired marketability. The high discount group, with a discount of 43.33%, is dominated by unregistered private placements which, unlike the sale of an interest in an investment company, have relatively high assessment and monitoring costs. As these characteristics do not reflect the characteristics of an investment company, we concluded in *McCord*, as we do here, that the partnership is in the middle discount group, and a discount of 20% is applicable. In *Lappo v. Comm'r*, T.C. Memo. 2003-258, we found that a 21-percent initial discount was appropriate for an interest in a family limited partnership consisting of marketable securities and real estate subject to a long-term lease. We then made a further upward adjustment of 3% to the marketability discount for characteristics specific to the partnership, including: The partnership was closely held with no real prospect of becoming publicly held; the partnership was relatively small and not well known; there did not exist a present market for the partnership interests; and the partnership had a right of first refusal to purchase the interests. As these characteristics are similar to the characteristics in the FLP [here], we find that a 3-percent upward adjustment is applicable.

Therefore, we hold that the fair market value of the 94.83-percent limited partnership interest is $788,059, computed as follows:

Total NAV	$1,226,421
94.83%	1,163,015
Less: 12%	− 139,562
	1,023,453
Less: 23%	− 235,394
	$ 788,059

NOTES

1. The so-called "minority" (lack of control) discount discussed in *Estate of Kelley* is really a separate discount (apart from the minority-interest discount and the lack-of-marketability discount). Even the term "lack of control" discount is somewhat misleading. What was lacking in *Estate of Kelley* was not control over the *enterprise* but lack of control over its *assets*, in the sense that the decedent could not treat the assets as his own or obtain a share of the assets by causing a liquidation (redemption) of his FLP interest (i.e., exchanging his FLP interest for a corresponding share of the underlying assets). Restrictions on redemption are typical of FLPs, and raise issues under §2704, discussed at §9.4. The inability to exchange one's equity in an FLP for a share of the underlying assets is what renders an FLP analogous to a mutual fund, except (of course) that mutual fund shares are actively traded on securities markets.

2. a. Congress could (and perhaps should) enact a look-through rule for family investment holding companies. Under a look-through rule, the donor or decedent would be deemed to own his or her pro-rata share of the investment assets held by the entity, thereby precluding various valuation discounts. There is ample precedent under the income tax for identifying passive investment income and assets. See §§469, 543, and 954(c).

    b. It has been suggested that it would be unconstitutional for Congress to impose a wealth transfer tax on an amount significantly greater than an asset's actual value at the time of transfer. The constitutional basis for the wealth transfer taxes is that they are "indirect" (i.e., excise) taxes not subject to apportionment among the states in accordance with population. The unconstitutionality argument would probably be based on the Fifth Amendment Due Process Clause. The Due Process argument appears to be weak. First, the value is there, and can be reached by liquidating the entity. Second, the loss of value is brought about by the acts of the taxpayer.

    c. Often FLPs are created near the end of an individual's life and/or at a time of illness or incapacity, implicitly suggesting an estate planning motive.[6] See, e.g., *Abraham* (Alzheimer's disease); *Erickson* (88 years old and Alzheimer's disease); *Korby* (Mrs. Korby had Alzheimer's disease, and Mr. Korby was 80 years old with heart problems); *Rosen* (88 years old and "in failing health"); *Thompson* (93 years old). However, the existence of a tax-avoidance motive does not usually cause an FLP to be disregarded. In *Kimbell v. U.S.*, 371 F.3d 257 (5th Cir.2004), *vacating and remanding*, 244 F. Supp. 2d 700 (N.D. Tex.), the decedent was 96 when, two months before her death, she created her FLP with a term of 40 years. The Fifth Circuit held that the FLP would be recognized if the transaction was not a sham or a disguised gift.

    d. A less draconian approach than a look-through rule would be to amend §2035 so as to treat any assets transferred to an FLP within three years of a decedent's death as being directly owned by the decedent. See Walter Schwidetzky, *Last Gasp Estate Planning: The Formation of Family Limited Liability Entities Shortly Before Death*, 21 Va. Tax Rev. 1 (2001).

B. Status of FLPs Under §2036(a)

The government's goal in trying to apply §2036(a) upon the formation of an FLP is to cause the inclusion of the assets transferred to the FLP in the transferor/decedent's gross estate. Inclusion of the assets (rather then the equity interests in

---

6. "Estates of decedents 90 and older reported the largest average FLP holdings, about $1.4M per estate, while estates of decedents under 50 reported the smallest average FLP holdings, $630,700 per estate. These youngest decedents were still accumulating wealth at the time of their deaths and certainly had not begun to consider asset divestiture plans, such as the formation of FLP's and the 'gifting' of FLP interests." Eller, supra note 5, at 197.

the FLP) precludes the availability of valuation discounts. But, since the (discounted) equity interests are also included in the gross estate under §2033, how is double taxation avoided? If the government is successful in including the underlying assets in the gross estate under §2036(a), the discounted equity interest received will constitute a *partial* consideration offset under §2043(a) against the amount included under §2036(a). For example, if D transfers assets worth $1M to an FLP in return for a partnership interest having a discounted value of $400K, then the net amount included under §§2036(a) and 2043(a) is $600K, and the amount included under §2033 is $400K (assuming no value change in the equity interest up to the time of D's death), which adds up to $1M.

The possible factual basis for applying §2036(a) to an FLP scenario would be that the transferor, after the formation of the FLP, continues to enjoy and/or control the FLP assets in his personal capacity (as opposed to, *per Byrum*, his capacity as FLP equity-holder or manager).

The substantive §2036(a) issue often is entangled with two other issues: (1) whether the entity is a sham (in which case the undiscounted value of the assets is included under §2033, and §§2036 and 2043 don't come into play) and (2), if the entity is not a sham but §2036(a) applies, whether the decedent's transfer of assets to the entity is a "bona fide sale for a full and adequate consideration" (which wholly negates the application of not only §2036(a) but also of the gift tax, rather than being a partial consideration offset). These issues are easily confused or co-mingled, as will become evident by a perusal of the material below.

In *Estate of Reichardt v. Comm'r*, 114 T.C. 144 (2000), diagnosed with terminal cancer, the decedent, together with his children, created an FLP a year before he died, with decedent's revocable trust as the FLP's general partner. Decedent formally transferred all of his assets to the FLP, but, as the only one to sign partnership checks and documents, decedent continued to manage and enjoy his property in the same way he had done before the FLP transfers. The Tax Court applied §2036(a) on account of the commingling of partnership assets with the decedent's personal assets and the decedent's continued enjoyment of the property. (The government might have cited the same facts in an attempt to show that the partnership was a sham, but it did not.) The court brushed off the consideration issue, saying there was no "sale." Presumably, the partnership interests were treated as not existing apart from the assets. Accord, *Estate of Schauerhamer v. Comm'r*, T.C. Memo. 1997-242; *Estate of Harper v. Comm'r*, T.C. Memo. 2002-121 (here the government raised the sham-entity theory, but the court did not reach it, because it held for the government on the §2036 and sale issues).

In a court-reviewed opinion, *Estate of Strangi v. Comm'r*, 115 T.C. 478 (2000) (*Strangi I*), the government relied solely on a sham-partnership theory, which the Tax Court rejected on the ground that the FLP agreement had legal effect and would have affected dealings with third parties. Thus, the court held that the property included in decedent's estate was the limited partnership interest and not the assets transferred to the partnership. The Tax Court also held that no gift resulted just because the value transferred to the FLP by the decedent exceeded the value of the FLP interest received by reason of valuation discounts, because this loss of value to the decedent did not cause a corresponding transfer of wealth to other family members. The Fifth Circuit, 293 F.3d 279 (5th Cir.2002), affirmed these holdings, but remanded to allow the government to advance a §2036 argument. On remand, in *Strangi II*, T.C. Memo. 2003-145, *aff'd*, 417 F.3d 468 (5th Cir.2005), the Tax Court held that the decedent retained income from the transferred assets and the power to control partnership distributions, causing inclusion under §2036 (a)(1) & (a)(2) of the date-of-death value of the transferred assets, rather than of the (discounted) FLP interest. The factual basis for this conclusion was that the decedent's son-in-law (Gulig), an estate planner, devised the entire scheme after the decedent's health deteriorated, and after he was appointed the decedent's attorney-in-fact. The FLP was managed by Stranco, a corporation owned by the decedent and his children, but Gulig was the manager of Stranco and (thereby) of the FLP. The FLP paid decedent's medical, nursing care, and funeral expenses and the estate's debts, administration expenses, taxes, and even a bequest to decedent's sister. The Tax Court held that the bona fide sale exception did not apply, because the arrangement amounted to a mere "recycling" of the decedent's wealth through a different form.

As a result of the *Strangi* litigation, it is evident that a taxpayer can avoid the sham-partnership theory but then run afoul of §2036(a).

C. *The Bona Fide Sale Exception Under §2036(a)*

As already noted, a bona fide sale for adequate and full consideration in money or money's worth is excluded from the application of §2036, and would also avoid gift tax. The policy behind the exception is that where there is a substitution of assets (i.e., merely different assets of equal value replacing the transferred assets) in the decedent's estate, her estate is not diminished. Yet, with FLP discounts amounting to roughly 50 percent, how can the FLP equity interests constitute "adequate and full consideration" for the assets transferred?

Estate of Thompson v. Commissioner

382 F.3d 367 (3d Cir.2004)

Before SCIRICA, Chief Judge, ROSENN and GREENBERG, *Circuit Judges.*
SCIRICA, *Chief Judge*:

[The Court affirmed a holding of the Tax Court, T.C. Memo. 2002-246, that §2036(a) applied on the ground that there was an implied agreement that the transferred assets would be available for the decedent's personal use. It was noted that the transfer of assets to the FLP virtually stripped the decedent of assets to support himself. The remainder of the opinion deals with the bona fide sale exception.]

The estate claims decedent's transfer of liquid, marketable securities and other assets to the FLP reduced the value of those assets by 40% because of the resulting lack of control and marketability. In one sense, claiming an estate tax discount on assets received in exchange for an *inter vivos* transfer should defeat the §2036(a) exception outright. If assets are transferred inter vivos in exchange for other assets of lesser value, it seems reasonable to conclude there is no transfer for "adequate and full consideration" because the decedent has not replenished the estate with other assets of equal value. See *Wheeler v. U.S.*, 116 F.3d 749, 762 (5th Cir.1997) ("[U]nless a transfer that depletes the transferor's estate is joined with a transfer that augments the estate by a commensurate (monetary) amount, there is no 'adequate and full consideration' for the purposes of either the estate or gift tax.").

That said, the Tax Court has held that the dissipation of value resulting from the transfer of marketable assets to a closely-held entity will not automatically constitute inadequate consideration for purposes of §2036. See *Harper v. Comm'r*, T.C. Memo. 2002-121 (noting partnership interests may constitute "adequate and full consideration" if there is also a "potential [for] intangibles stemming from pooling for joint enterprise"); *Stone v. Comm'r*, T.C. Memo. 2003-309 (concluding the lack of marketability discount applied to limited partnership interests does not, on its own, result in inadequate consideration for purposes of §2036). Nonetheless, we believe this sort of dissipation of value in the estate tax context should trigger heightened scrutiny into the actual substance of the transaction. Where, as here, the transferee partnership does not operate a legitimate business, and the record demonstrates the valuation discount provides the sole benefit for converting liquid, marketable assets into illiquid partnership interests, there is no transfer for consideration within the meaning of §2036.

We conclude decedent's transfers to the FLP do not constitute "bona fide sales" within the meaning of §2036, although for somewhat different reasons than the Commissioner suggests. The Commissioner argues there was no "bona fide sale" in this case because decedent "stood on both sides of the transaction" as transferor and a limited partner of the family partnerships. The Commissioner's position is supported by several cases which have concluded that a "bona fide sale" requires an arm's length bargain. [Citations omitted.] As a practical matter, an "arm's length" transaction provides good evidence of a "bona fide sale," especially with intra-family transactions. But some courts have also found a bargained-for exchange in the family context when the interests of individual family members were sufficiently divergent. See, e.g., *Bank of New York v. U.S.*, 526 F.2d at 1012 (3d Cir.1975) ("Even a family agreement, although achieved without apparent bitterness, has been regarded as bargained for when members of the family had interests contrary to those of other family members."); *Stone, supra* (finding an arm's length bargain in intrafamily transaction where each family member retained independent counsel).

Neither the Internal Revenue Code nor the governing Treasury Regulations define "bona fide sale" to include an "arm's length transaction." Regulation §20.2036-1(a) defines "bona fide sale for an adequate and full consideration" as a transfer made "in good faith" and for a price that is "adequate and full equivalent reducible to a money value." Based in part on an interpretation of this regulation, the Court of Appeals for the Fifth Circuit concluded a "bona fide sale" only requires "a sale in which the decedent/transferor actually parted with her interest in the assets transferred and the partnership/transferee actually parted with the partnership interest issued in exchange." See *Kimbell v. U.S.*, 371 F.3d at 257 (5th Cir.2004). We similarly believe a "bona fide sale" does not necessarily require an "arm's length transaction" between the transferor and an unrelated third-party. Of course, evidence of an "arm's length transaction" or "bargained-for exchange" is highly probative, but we see no statutory basis for adopting an interpretation of "bona fide sale" that would automatically defeat the §2036 exception for all intra-family transfers.

We are mindful of the mischief that may arise in the family estate planning context. But such mischief can be adequately monitored by heightened scrutiny of intra-family transfers, and does not require a uniform prohibition on transfers to family limited partnerships.

The facts here are distinguishable from those Tax Court cases which have denied the "bona fide sale" exception after finding decedent "stood on both sides of the transaction." Here, by contrast, both the formation and funding of the Partnerships involved substantial participation by decedent's family members and their respective spouses. However, while a "bona fide sale" does not necessarily require an "arm's length transaction," it still must be made in good faith. See Reg. §20.2043-1(a). A "good faith" transfer to a family limited partnership must provide the transferor some potential for benefit other than the potential estate tax advantages that might result from holding assets in the partnership form. Even when all the "i's are dotted and t's are crossed," a transaction motivated solely by tax planning and with "no business or corporate purpose . . . is nothing more than a contrivance." *Gregory v. Helvering*, 293 U.S. 465, 469 (1935). "To hold otherwise would be to exalt artifice above reality and to deprive the statutory provision in question of all serious purpose." As discussed in the context of "adequate and full consideration," objective indicia that the partnership operates a legitimate business may provide a sufficient factual basis for finding a good faith transfer. But if there is no discernable purpose or benefit for the transfer other than estate tax savings, the sale is not "bona fide" within the meaning of §2036(a).

After a thorough review of the record, we agree with the Tax Court that decedent's inter vivos transfers do not qualify for the §2036(a) exception because neither the Thompson Partnership nor Turner Partnership conducted any legitimate business operations, nor provided decedent with any potential non-tax benefit from the transfers.

GREENBERG, *Circuit Judge, concurring.*

I join in Chief Judge Scirica's opinion in this case without reservation but want to add a few thoughts with respect to the issue of whether we are dealing with transfers for "adequate and full consideration in money or money's worth." Preliminarily on this point I think that Chief Judge Scirica gets to the heart of the matter by noting that "[i]n one sense, claiming an estate tax discount on assets received in exchange for an *inter vivos* transfer should defeat the §2036(a) exception outright [for][i]f assets are transferred *inter vivos* in exchange for other assets of lesser value, it seems reasonable to conclude that there is no transfer for 'adequate and full consideration' because the decedent has not replenished the estate with other assets of equal value." Therefore, a transfer of $1,000,000 in assets will be for an adequate and full consideration if it is for $1,000,000 in money. If a transfer is for property then the "money's worth" of the property should be of the same value as money received for the transferred property would have had to have been, *i.e.*, $1,000,000.

In this case, inasmuch as the transfers were not for money the exception can apply only if the transfers were for property that can be regarded as being for "money's worth." Yet one of the motivations for the transfers was that there would be a substantial discount, claimed by the estate to be 40%. To me nothing could be clearer than a conclusion that if the discount was justified (even if in a lesser percentage than the estate claimed) in a valuation sense then the decedent could not have received an adequate and full consideration for his transfers in terms of "money's worth."

[Judge Greenberg made three additional points. First, the Commissioner was not making inconsistent arguments by stating there was a lack of "adequate and full consideration" for §2036 purposes "while acknowledging that the decedent did not make taxable gifts upon the creation of the partnerships." There was no gift on the transfer of assets to the partnership because the value that decedent lost on creating the partnership didn't go to anyone else. Secondly, the court's holding should not be applied in "routine commercial circumstances" with "legitimate businesses." Accordingly, section 2036(a) shouldn't be interpreted "in a way that will impede the socially important goal of encouraging accumulation of capital for commercial enterprises." Thirdly, Judge Greenberg rejected that part of *Estate of Stone v. Comm'r*, T.C. Memo. 2003-309, in which the Tax Court discredited, as effectively eliminating the bona fide sales exception of §2036, the government's argument that a transfer of assets for a proportionate partnership interest is not adequate and full consideration. In connection with that last point, Judge Greenberg criticized the *Kimbell* decision, stating: "*Kimbell* does not take into account that to avoid the recapture provision of §2036(a) the property transferred must be 'replaced by property of equal value that could be exposed to inclusion in the decedent's gross estate' . . . on a 'money or money's worth' basis."]

Judge ROSENN joins in this concurring opinion.

———————————

In the next case, the Tax Court, in a reviewed decision, ignored the *Thompson* concurrence.

Estate of Bongard v. Commissioner
124 T.C. 95 (2005) (reviewed)

GOEKE, *Judge*: [The decedent was a skilled and experienced businessman who started his own corporation, Empak. He transferred all his remaining shares in that corporation to a holding company, WCB Holdings, L.L.C. The next day decedent transferred all of his non-voting shares in WCB Holdings to an FLP in return for a 99% equity interest. The formation of these entities each entailed "transfers." As to the "bona fide sale" exception, there are two components, first, that there be a bona fide sale, and second, that it be for a full and adequate consideration in money or money's worth. After discussing some the Tax Court's prior cases, the opinion continued.]

The Court in *Estate of Stone v. Comm'r*, T.C. Memo. 2003-309, held that the bona fide sale exception in §2036(a) was satisfied. In *Stone*, the decedent had operated a successful closely held business for a number of years and created five family limited partnerships. We rejected the Commissioner's argument that the formation of each of the family limited partnerships was not "motivated primarily by legitimate business concerns." A reason for employing the limited partnership concept was to resolve the Stones' children's concerns. There were significant intrafamily disputes with regard to the Stones' assets which led to litigation.

The adequate and full consideration prong was also deemed satisfied. All partners in each partnership received interests proportionate to the fair market value of the assets they each transferred, and partnership legal formalities were respected. We rejected the Commissioner's argument that valuation discounts attached to the partnership interest the decedent received precluded the adequate and full consideration prong from being satisfied. We reasoned that the Commissioner's argument effectively read "out of §2036(a) the exception that Congress expressly prescribed when it enacted that statute." We found that the partnerships had economic substance as a joint venture for profit in which there was a genuine pooling of property and services.

In the context of family limited partnerships, the bona fide sale for adequate and full consideration exception is met where the record establishes the existence of a legitimate and significant nontax reason for creating the family limited partnership, and the transferors received partnership interests proportionate to the value of the property transferred. The objective evidence must indicate that the nontax reason was a significant factor that motivated the partnership's creation. A significant purpose must be an actual motivation, not a theoretical justification.

By contrast, the bona fide sale exception is not applicable where the facts fail to establish that the transaction was motivated by a legitimate and significant nontax purpose. A list of factors that support such a finding includes the taxpayer standing on both sides of the transaction, the taxpayer's financial dependence on distributions from the partnership, the partners' commingling of partnership funds with their own, and the taxpayer's actual failure to transfer the property to the partnership.

In *Kimbell v. U.S.*, 371 F.3d 257, 258 (5th Cir.2004), the Fifth Circuit separated the bona fide sale exception into two prongs: (1) Whether the transaction qualifies as a bona fide sale; and (2) whether the decedent received adequate and full consideration. The court first examined the adequate and full consideration language and set forth an objective inquiry. The court stated that the proper question in examining the adequate and full consideration prong was whether the sale depleted the gross estate. The Court of Appeals disagreed with the District Court's determination that a sale between members of the same family cannot be a bona fide one. A transaction between family members is, however, subjected to heightened scrutiny to ensure that it is not a sham or disguised gift. Applying its test to the facts, the Court of Appeals held in *Kimbell* that the *pro rata* partnership interest the decedent received was adequate and full consideration. The court also found that the decedent's transfer met the bona fide sale exception because the partnership was in actual possession of the assets transferred, partnership formalities were satisfied, she retained sufficient assets outside of the partnership to meet her personal needs, some of the assets contributed were active business assets, and she had nontax business reasons for creating the partnership.

Recently, the Court of Appeals for the Third Circuit, in *Estate of Thompson v. Comm'r*, 382 F.3d 367 (3d Cir.2004), focusing on the adequate and full consideration language, stated that an *inter vivos* transfer in exchange for assets of a lesser value should trigger heightened scrutiny into the substance of the transaction. The Third Circuit found that neither partnership engaged in transactions rising to the level of legitimate business operations that provided the decedent with a substantive nontax benefit.

[Applying the foregoing, the court held that the decedent's transfer of Empak stock to WCB Holdings satisfied the exception to §2036(a) because WCB Holdings was founded to pool the family's Empak stock within one entity as part of a larger plan to attract new corporate investors or to fuel "a corporate liquidity event." However, regarding the transfer of WCB Holdings units to the FLP, the court was unable to find a significant nontax motive. There was no change in investment strategy once the FLP was created and the estate's claims of additional credit protection, of facilitating the decedent and his wife's post-marital agreement, and of enhancing the decedent's gift-making plans were insufficient nontax motives. "BFLP also never diversified its assets during decedent's life, never had an investment plan, and never functioned as a business enterprise or otherwise engaged in any meaningful economic activity." Finally, it was found that there was an implied agreement that the decedent would continue to enjoy the FLP assets, thereby satisfying §2036(a).]

Laro, J., concurring in result. The majority applies its test in lieu of deeply ingrained case law that conditions satisfaction of the "bona fide sale for an adequate and full consideration in money or money's worth" exception on the transferor's receipt of property equal in value to that of the property transferred by the transferor. In other words, under that caselaw, the adequate and full consideration exception may apply only where the transferor's receipt of consideration is of a sufficient value to prevent the transfer from depleting the transferor's gross estate.

I disagree with both prongs of [the majority's] test. I believe that a transferor satisfies the adequate and full consideration exception in the context of a transfer to a partnership only when: (1) The record establishes either that (i) in return for the transfer, the transferor received a partnership interest and any other consideration with an aggregate fair market value equal to the fair market value of the transferor's transferred property, or (ii) the transfer was an ordinary commercial transaction (in which case, the transferred property and the consideration received in return are considered to have the same fair market values), and (2) the transfer was made with a business purpose or, in other words, a "useful nontax purpose that is plausible in light of the taxpayer's [transferor's] conduct and useful in light of the taxpayer's economic situation and intentions."

Halpern, J., concurring in part and dissenting in part. I believe that the majority has strayed from the traditional interpretation of the bona fide sale exception by incorporating into the exception an inappropriate motive test ("a legitimate and significant nontax reason"), and by concluding that a partnership interest "proportionate" to the value of the property transferred constitutes adequate and full consideration in money or money's worth.

[T]o establish that the transfers were for full consideration, petitioner must, for each transfer, establish that the value of the property transferred by decedent did not exceed the cash value of the property received by him. By the explicit terms of section 25.2512-8, Gift Tax Regs., the resulting inquiry is limited to an economic calculus, and there is no room for any inquiry as to the transferor's (decedent's) state of mind. Yet the majority makes his state of mind critical. Certainly, decedent's state of mind (i.e., his intent) is important in determining whether the ordinary-course-of-business exception applies (was the transfer "free of any donative intent"), but once it is determined that the transfer in question was not made in the ordinary course of business, intent is no longer relevant to the determination of whether the transfer was for full consideration.

I also disagree with the implication of the majority opinion that, in the context of a transfer to an entity (here, transfers to both a limited liability company and a family limited partnership), the full consideration requirement can be met by a showing that the transferor received an entity interest (e.g., a limited partnership interest) proportionate to the value of the property contributed to the entity. While an inquiry as to proportionality may have some bearing on whether the transfer was in the ordinary course of business, within the meaning of Reg. §25.2512-8 (e.g., was at arm's length), I fail to see how proportionality aids the inquiry as to whether the value of the property transferred exceeded the cash value of the consideration received in exchange. Here, because of the presence of donative intent, the transfers cannot be considered in the ordinary course of business.

Finally, as I read the majority's approach to the bona fide sale exception, the majority has added to the exception the requirement that the taxpayer show that the decedent's transfer to the entity was motivated "by a legitimate and significant nontax purpose." If, indeed, that is the majority's approach, then even if an objective analysis indicates that the transferor received full consideration, the bona fide sale exception presumably would not be satisfied if a subjective analysis reveals that the transaction did not have a legitimate and significant nontax purpose. According to the majority, indicators of the lack of such purpose include (1) that the transferor stood on both sides of the transaction, (2) commingling of the transferor's and the transferee's funds, and (3) the failure of the transferor actually to make a transfer. Certainly, the "bona fide sale" portion of the bona fide sale exception would exclude transfers that were shams or based on illusory consideration.

In *Estate of Bigelow v. Comm'r*, 503 F.3d 955 (9th Cir.2007), the Ninth Circuit, while appearing to follow *Bongard*, upheld a Tax Court decision that the purported nontax motives for the transaction were unreal.

QUESTIONS AND NOTES

1. In our opinion, the courts (especially the Tax Court) have made a mess of this area.

    a. The "proportionality" test for full and adequate consideration is easily satisfied, and essentially puts the burden on the government to discredit the taxpayer's alleged motives. We agree with the opinions of Judges Laro and Halpern in *Bongard*.

    b. A plain reading of the text indicates that a "bona fide sale" does not, by itself, insulate a transaction from §2036(a). The bona fide sale must be for full and adequate consideration in money or money's worth, which is purely an objective comparing-of-values test. Business motive is irrelevant. A transfer of liquid assets for a discounted equity interest would fail to satisfy the exception, and would constitute only partial consideration.

    c. Courts that hold that full and adequate consideration isn't required if the shortfall amounts to economic waste appear to be relying on the gift tax notion that the gift is what the donees receives. See *Rev. Rul. 93-12*, 1993-1 C.B. 202, set forth at §3.4.B, holding that a donor owning 100 percent of the stock of a corporation obtained minority discounts when making five gifts of 20 percent interests to family members. This move overlooks the fact that the estate tax rule is the opposite (it's the value of what the decedent had), and these FLP cases involve §2036(a), which includes the transfers in the gross estate. Stated abstractly, the issue is whether gift tax or estate tax valuation principles apply in cases involving §§2036-2038. In essence, the material in this unit is an unconscious "replay" of the controversy dealt with in *Estate of D'Ambosio*, p. 438.

    d. Would "bona fide sale" then be stripped of any significance? No, because here the estate tax would be construed *in pari materia* with the gift tax, specifically, Reg. §25.2512-8, which states that a transaction in the ordinary course of business would be excluded even if the value of the consideration turned out to be objectively inadequate.

    e. The expression "bona fide" literally means "good faith" in Latin. A transaction among family members *could* be bona fide if the family members acted at arm's length in negotiating an arrangement. And, of course, the transfer could be for full and adequate consideration. No reasonable reading of the exception would make it impossible for intra-family transactions to satisfy it.

    f. Until the line of cases culminating in *Bongard*, motive was never determinative of the outcome, and would not have invalidated a transaction in which the values exchanged were equal.

    g. Disproportionality is indicative of a disguised gift, if the interests of other family members are enhanced. Proportionality does not establish equality of values, only that the values *could* be equal.

    h. It seems to us that the majority opinion in *Bongard* conflates the issues of (1) sham entity, (2) retained enjoyment, and (3) the consideration exception. More generally, it elevates language in court decisions over the plain language of the statute.

2. a. In our view, none of the following rationales for forming an FLP (if proved) would lead to the conclusion that the bona fide sale exception applies: gift giving, estate planning, income tax savings, protection against creditors, protection of assets in case of divorce, promoting family harmony, teaching younger family members about investing, centralized asset management, and keeping the assets in the family. Some of these facts might show a business purpose for forming the entity that would be sufficient to resist a sham-transaction claim by the IRS, but none shows an arm's-length transaction in commerce, and most cut against arm's-length characterization.

   b. In *Stone*, the court delineated what it referred to as business motivations for forming the decedent's FLP: All of the five FLPs functioned "as joint enterprises for profit" in which the children provided active management; one of the aims was to align the children's bequests with assets they were interested in, and to protect the decedent from possible mismanagement and dissipation. Even if one or more of these count as "business" reasons, business purpose is irrelevant under §2036(a), and is only "preliminary" to the bona fide sale issue. The court also noted the parents' good health, the independent counsel for each adult child, each partner's receipt of an FLP interest proportionate to his contribution, the respect of FLP legal formalities, and the decedents' retention of sufficient assets to maintain their lifestyle. To what legal issues, if any, are these facts relevant?

   c. In *Kimbell*, it was held that the exchange was a bona fide sale that had been entered into for substantial business and for other nontax motivations, including protection against liability for environmental contamination. The court underlined that the oil and gas properties were a continuation of a business her late husband had established in the 1920s; the partnership protected the Kimbells from creditors to a greater extent than could be accomplished through their living trust; pooling assets under a single management would reduce administrative costs; the partnership could preserve the property in case of divorce, as had been an issue during one of the grandson's divorce; her son's ill health; the agreement's provision for the resolution of all disputes through mediation or arbitration. The court de-emphasized the facts that the sale was between family members, and without negotiation. Citing *Stone*, the court explained that the inquiry should be focused on three facts: (1) whether the partners' partnership interests were proportionate to the value of the assets each partner contributed; (2) whether the contributed assets were properly credited to each partner's capital accounts; and (3) whether, on the partnership's dissolution or termination, each partner would receive distributions reflective of his/her capital account. To what estate tax issues, if any, do these facts bear?

   d. In *Kimbell*, the FLP's oil and gas interests constituted 11 percent of its assets. Of that 11 percent, 71 percent were "working interests" as opposed to passive royalty interests. The vast majority of interests in *Kimbell* were liquid: cash, notes, and securities. The court considered the other assets necessary for maintaining the oil and gas interests. How can liquid assets equal to 90 percent of the enterprise be "necessary" to operate the other 10 percent? In *Estate of Shurtz v. Comm'r*, T.C. Memo. 2010-21, an FLP was upheld despite the need for active management of only about 16 percent of the FLP assets.

3. a.   Despite *Bongard*, *Kimbell*, and *Stone*, the government has prevailed in a number of the cases purportedly following these authorities. Besides *Bongard* itself (on the FLP-formation issue) and *Thompson*, the government prevailed in *Korby v. Comm'r*, 471 F.3d 848 (8th Cir.2006), *aff'g*, T.C. Memo. 2003-103 (Tax Court did not believe that asset protection was a significant motivation); *Estate of Bigelow v. Comm'r*, 503 F.3d 955 (9th Cir.2007), *aff'g*, T.C. Memo. 2005-65 (same; no evidence of significant creditor claim); *Estate of Jorgenson v. Comm'r*, T.C. Memo. 2009-66 (managing investments after death is not a significant nontax reason); *Estate of Erickson v. Comm'r*, T.C. Memo. 2007-107 (same); *Estate of Rector v. Comm'r*, T.C. Memo. 2007-367 (the following are not significant nontax reasons: gift giving, managing investments that do not require active management, diversification of investments that actually remain the same, and credit protection that is ineffective for a general partner and factually unnecessary). In *Bigelow*, the Ninth Circuit distanced itself from the *Kimbell* proportionality test, stating that there either has to be a meaningful pooling of interests or assets or the transferor must receive a significant nontax benefit. In *Erickson*, pooling of interests was insufficient because of the absence of a significant nontax benefit. Along similar lines is *Estate of Rosen v. Comm'r*, T.C. Memo. 2006-115.

    b.   The government has also lost some cases, most notably: *Estate of Schutt v. Comm'r*, T.C. Memo. 2005-126 (motive to lock in certain investments deemed to be significant nontax motive); *Estate of Black v. Comm'r*, 133 T.C. 15 (2009) (preserving controlling stock interest for benefit of the family held to be significant nontax benefit); *Estate of Mirowski v. Comm'r*, T.C. Memo. 2008-74 (transfer to LLC upheld on basis of pooling-of-assets motive, even though most of the assets, other than some patent rights, were passive).

    c.   In institutional terms, the Tax Court has attempted to seize control of this issue by characterizing it as basically a factual one, which (if the relevant court of appeals agrees) means that reversal is unlikely except for "clear error." The overall effect is to give Tax Court judges effective discretion in deciding cases that hinge on the existence of significant nontax motives (which, in principle, must be "real," and not merely "theoretical"). An example of such judicial discretion is the decision in *Mirowski*, supra, where the Tax Court accepted the taxpayer's purported justifications at face value and summarily rejected (without even specifying them) the government's arguments and authorities. Accordingly, outcomes are unpredictable, and fact-intensive trials are commonplace.

D. Indirect Gifts of FLP Assets and the Step-Transaction Doctrine

One can make gifts "through" an entity, such as an FLP, in three ways. First, one can make a direct gift of an equity interest owned by the donor. Second, under Reg. §25.2511-1(h)(1), when an equity-holder makes a transfer of money or property to the entity, without receiving debt or equity in return, she makes an indirect gift to the other equity-holders. Third, gifts occur on the formation of the entity when a person contributes money or property to an entity and receives back a disproportionately small equity interest, resulting in disproportionately larger equity interests for family members.

Once a gift is identified, the follow-up issue is whether the gift is of an equity interest (which obtains entity-related valuation discounts, including minority-interest discounts) or whether the gift is of all or a portion of the underlying (undiscounted) assets. Not surprising, this issue depends on the facts. A court may find a gift of undiscounted assets if (a) the sequence of events is unclear or "wrong," or (b) if, pursuant to the application of the step-transaction doctrine, intermediate steps in a sequence of events are disregarded for tax purposes.

Jones v. Comm'r, 116 T.C. 121 (2001), illustrates the correct sequence to ensure that the taxpayer is making a gift of a discounted partnership interest and not of the assets themselves. First, the taxpayer contributed assets to his FLP. The interest received was proportional to his contribution, which was properly reflected in his capital account. Therefore, the formation of the FLP did not increase any of the other partners' FLP interests. Later that same day, he transferred a large part of his partnership interest to his five children, through a carefully documented order of events that enabled the decedent's gifts to benefit from FLP discounts.

In contrast, in *Shepherd v. Comm'r*, 283 F.3d 1258 (11th Cir.2002), *aff'g*, 115 T.C. 376 (2000), it was held that the taxpayers had made an indirect gift of land and not a gift of a discounted partnership interest.[7] Although the deed purported to transfer the land to the partnership, it was not effective until the partnership was created on the next day. Because there was no recipient in existence on August 1 to receive the gift, the gift was effective on August 2, just after the partnership was established. Gifts are valued according to what the donor parts with, not according to how the donee receives it (in this case, as an enhanced-value partnership interest).

Likewise, in *Senda v. Comm'r*, 433 F.3d 1044 (8th Cir.2006), *aff'g*, T.C. Memo. 2004-160, the Eighth Circuit upheld the Tax Court's finding that the taxpayers had not produced sufficient evidence that their contributions of stock to two FLPs preceded their transfer of FLP interests to their children. In *Senda*, the taxpayers had depended on unreliable after-the-fact documents, such as tax returns and two letters faxed to their tax advisors, which the court held did not conclusively determine the order of the transactions. Accord, *Linton v. U. S.*, 638 F. Supp. 2d 1277 (W.D. Wash 2009), *aff'd* in part and *rev'd* in part and remanded ____ F.3d ____ (9th Cir.2011). (The circuit court in *Linton* held that the government was not entitled to summary

---

7. The land itself obtained a discount by reason of being a 25% undivided interest in the hands of the donor.

judgment on the indirect gift issue as there was contrary evidence in the record regarding when the taxpayers intended to make their gifts.[8])

Where the donor has carefully documented the "proper" sequence events — namely, (1) FLP formation, (2) transfers of assets to the FLP, (3) adjustment of only the donor's capital account, and (4) only then the transfer of his FLP interests — the government may still assert that the step-transaction applies. Under that doctrine, a court can collapse a series of steps to view them as one transaction. The step-transaction doctrine, a substance-over-form principle, comes in three versions. Under the "binding commitment" test, the doctrine applies if the taxpayer is legally bound to carry out the sequence of moves. At the other end of the spectrum is the "end result" test, which depends only on the intent of the parties as they commence the sequence. The intermediate version is the "inter-dependence test," which requires the court to determine whether the various steps would only be legally meaningful "as part of the larger transaction."[9] In *Senda,* supra, the Eighth Circuit held that the Tax Court had properly used the step-transaction doctrine to determine the character of the transferred property as the stock (not the partnership interest) and that the Tax Court's findings that the transactions were integrated and concurrent were thoroughly corroborated by the facts. While the taxpayers contended that application of the doctrine is restricted to identifying the donor or donee in a gift tax case, the appellate court cited two of its own decisions to the contrary.[10]

However, in *Holman v. Comm'r,* 130 T.C. 170 (2008), *aff'd,* 601 F.3d 763 (8th Cir.2010), and later in *Gross v. Comm'r,* T.C. Memo. 2008-221, the court refused to apply the step-transaction doctrine to find that the taxpayer had made indirect gifts of the assets they had transferred to their FLPs. In *Holman,* the court applied the "interdependence" test, and found that, although the taxpayers created the FLP to make gifts of their FLP interests to their children, the transactions effec-tuating the gifts had legal effect even without the taxpayers' gifts. Accordingly, it was found that the FLP was formed before gifts were made of interests therein. The court emphasized the fact that the value of the FLP interests fluctuated for a period of five days prior to the gifts, during which period the taxpayers bore the risk of those valuation changes. Likewise, in *Gross,* the court held that the step-transaction doctrine did not apply because 11 days separated the final transfers of the transferor's stock to her FLP and her gifts of partnership interests to her daughters, and because the stocks were all, or virtually all, "heavily traded, relatively volatile common stocks."

---

8. The Ninth Circuit in *Linton* also reversed the district court's granting summary judgment to the government on the application of the step transaction doctrine. The circuit court held that the record was insufficient to apply the doctrine under any of its three tests.

9. See *Penrod v. Comm'r,* 88 T.C. 1415 (1987) (corporate reorganization case under the income tax).

10. *Estate of Schuler v. Comm'r,* 282 F.3d 575 (8th Cir.2002); *Sather v. Comm'r,* 251 F.3d 1168 (8th Cir.2001). In *Schuler* and *Sather,* the Eighth Circuit had applied the reciprocal-trust doctrine to deny additional annual exclusions for gifts made by the taxpayer and his brother to each other's children. The court considered the step-transaction doctrine to be a variant of the doctrine of substance over form, which included the reciprocal-transaction doctrine.

In a case of first impression, *Pierre v. Comm'r*, 133 T.C. 24 (2009) (reviewed), the government advanced a novel theory for treating gifts of interests in an entity (in this case, an LLC with a single equity-holder) as gifts of its underlying assets. In 2000, a wealthy friend gave the taxpayer Suzanne Pierre, a New York resident, $10M in cash. She then organized Pierre Family LLC. Under the "check the box" regulations,[11] the single-member LLC was to be treated as a "disregarded entity," rather than as a C corporation or pass-through entity. Shortly after forming the LLC, Pierre created two trusts, one to benefit her son and the other, her grand-daughter. Somewhat later, Pierre contributed cash and marketable securities to her LLC, and shortly thereafter she transferred her interest in the LLC equally to the two trusts. The government contended that, since the entity is ignored "for federal tax purposes" under the check-the-box regulations, the taxpayer should be treated as having made transfers of cash and stock to the trusts, even though the LLC was a valid separate entity from the taxpayer under New York law.

The Tax Court, in a reviewed decision, rejected the government's theory, essentially on the ground that the property rights to be valued under the federal transfer taxes are initially determined by state law, and that the check the box regulations were created to simplify the classification of entities for income tax purposes. In this case, they allowed a single-member entity to be treated as identical to that owner.[12] According to the Tax Court majority, the regulations were not intended to affect how the transfer of interests in a validly formed LLC should be taxed for federal gift tax purposes. Specifically, the regulations related to the *classification* of acknowledged entities, which matters because of the various income tax regimes that can apply to entities, not to whether an entity will be ignored.

In a concurring opinion (joined by all but one of the majority judges), Judge Cohen stated that the regulation was ambiguous because it uses "for federal tax purposes" and not "for *all* Federal tax purposes." Judge Cohen also stated that the term "disregarded" was ambiguous. Judge Cohen continued by arguing that, unless specifically over-ridden by *Congress* (which was not the case here), the prevailing valuation rule is the willing-buyer willing-seller test, and a willing buyer of the LLC equity interest could not ignore the legal incidents of LLC status under state law.

In his dissent, Judge Halpern stated that the regulations provide that the consequence of disregarding a single-owner LLC is that "its activities are treated in the same manner as a sole proprietorship, branch, or division of the owner."[13] Thus, for all tax purposes, the LLC's activities are treated the same as those of a sole proprietorship. Moreover, although there is no requirement that income and gift tax provisions must be interpreted *in pari materia* with gift tax provisions, Judge Halpern noted that there was nothing in the definitions of terms used in the check-the-box regulations that indicates that those terms should have different meanings for purposes of the income and gift tax provisions of the Internal Revenue Code.

---

11. See Reg. §§301.7701-1(a)(1) and 301.7701-3(a) & (b).
12. Reg. §301.7701-3(a) & (b)(1)(ii).
13. Reg. §301.7701-2(a).

Judge Kroupa, the trial judge in *Pierre*, separately dissented on the ground that the check-the-box regulations state that "for federal tax purposes" the single-member LLC should be "disregarded." She accused the majority of "either ignoring the plain language of the regulation or silently invalidating it."

In a supplemental opinion to *Pierre*, T. C. Memo. 2010-106, the donor (who began by owning 100 percent of the LLC stock) made gifts to the two trusts of 9.5 percent interests, and then (on the same day) "sold" 40.5 percent interests to each trust in return for a promissory note. The donor thereby hoped to get away with being treated as only having made two 9.5 percent gifts. However, the Tax Court applied the step-transaction doctrine to treat the transaction as two gifts of 50 percent interests, each of which was reduced by the value of the note, on the ground that there was no nontax reason to separate the gift and sale components of the transaction with respect to each trust.

The step-transaction doctrine may be invoked in almost any gratuitous-transfer scenario. In *McCord v. Comm'r*, 461 F.3d 614 (5th Cir.2006), *rev'g*, 120 T.C. 358 (2003) (reviewed), discussed at §3.4.D, the donors made gifts of their interests in an FLP in January of 1996, under a formula wherein any excess of the value of an FLP interest over a fixed amount was to go to charity, but the FLP had a call right to repurchase the FLP interest the charity had received, and in fact it exercised that right shortly after the gift was made. Judge Laro, dissenting from the Tax Court's reviewed decision, would have applied the step-transaction doctrine to limit the charitable deduction to what the charity received on redemption. See 120 T.C. at 429. Some of the facts relied upon by Judge Laro were: the transaction contemplated that the charities would be out of the picture shortly after the gift was made; the transfers of the partnership interests to the charities were subject to a call provision that could be exercised at any time; the call provisions were exercised almost contemporaneously with the transfers to the charities; the call price was significantly below fair market value; the charities never obtained a separate and independent appraisal of their interests; neither charity ever had any managerial control over the partnership; the charities agreed to waive their arbitration rights as to the allocation of the partnership interests; and the other donees were at all times in control of the transaction. However, none of the other opinions in the case addressed this theory.

QUICK QUESTION

In light of case law in the FLP area, which one of the following statements is *FALSE*?

A. A healthy 96-year-old may successfully establish an FLP.
B. An FLP may be successfully established solely with marketable securities.
C. The proper order of events to avoid an indirect gift of FLP assets is to give FLP interests to children and then transfer stock to the FLP, carefully increasing the children's capital accounts for the stock transfers.

D. An FLP interest is valued typically with lack-of-marketability and minority discounts in the aggregate between 30-60 percent.

1. **a.** To avoid disqualification for entity-interest discounts, before making gifts of interests in that entity to the transferor's family members, do estate planners merely need to ensure that the transferor's asset contribution to the entity is proportionate to the interest received back and that the contribution is properly reflected in his or her capital account?

   b. The cases holding that indirect gifts are made of the underlying assets might appear to be contrary to *Rev. Rul. 93-12*, 1993-1 C.B. 202, set forth at §3.4.B. That ruling held that a donor owning 100 percent of the stock of a corporation obtained minority discounts when making five gifts of 20 percent interests to family members. But the issue in the cases is exactly "What property does the donee receive (assets or an equity interest)?"

   c. An examination of the cases suggests that the step-transaction doctrine has been applied only where the two transactions occur virtually simultaneously and where a court has otherwise found an indirect gift in fact from the unclear or unfavorable evidence of the sequence of the two transactions of contributing assets to the family LLC or FLP and the transfer of interests in that family entity. If so, do the cases tell us anything beyond the obvious point that the donor has the burden of proving that she made a gift of an interest in an entity (rather than of its underlying assets)? Does the step-transaction doctrine add anything to the picture? Stated differently, might a court apply the step-transaction doctrine to a case where the formation of the entity clearly preceded the gift of the interests in the entity?

2. **a.** Turning to *Pierre*, the check-the-box regulations are issued under Code §7701(a)(2) & (3), which define "corporation" and "partnership" for purposes of the Code to "include" certain cognate entities. The lead-in language of §7701(a) includes the clause, "where not otherwise distinctly expressed or manifestly incompatible with the intent thereof, the term [corporation, partnership] includes. . . ." None of the basic gift tax Code provisions (§§2501, 2511, and 2512) refer to corporations or partnerships. This observation raises the question of whether the regulation, if construed to alter accepted gift tax valuation rules, would be valid as applied to the transfer taxes. Could the Treasury issue regulations under §§2031, 2512, and 7701 that disregard the entity status of family holding companies generally?

   b. In response to the foregoing, the dissenting opinions contended that §7701 is ambiguous, and therefore that the regulations are valid under the *Chevron* doctrine of administrative law.[14] Assuming that §7701 is ambiguous and that the *Chevron* doctrine applies, does this argument aid in construing the regulation, in light of the lead-in language of §7701? Aren't the check-the-box regulations themselves ambiguous with respect to gift and estate tax valuation? If they are unambiguous, there is then the issue of how they can be reconciled with the willing-buyer, willing-seller test, which also exists per regulations, but is long-standing, and has been assumed to be the "general" valuation principle by numerous Code provisions, Supreme Court decisions, and published rulings. Is it significant that there was no contemporaneous amendment to the estate and gift tax regulations? (By way of contrast, the increased use of the unitrust prompted changes in both the income and transfer tax regulations relating to the definition of "income.")

c. There is little doubt that the purpose of the check-the-box regulations was to classify entities (especially, LLCs) for purpose of the various income tax regimes available to entities. Can such a purpose be cited to restrict what might otherwise be viewed as unambiguous (broad) language? In *Estate of Hubert v. Comm'r*, 520 U.S. 93, 118 (1997), an estate tax valuation case, a plurality of the Supreme Court stated:

> [W]e may not totally ignore the plain language of a regulation or ruling because the entity promulgating it did not *really* want to have to adopt it. See *Connecticut Nat. Bank v. Germain*, 503 U.S. 249, 253-254 (1992) ("We have stated time and time again that courts must presume that a legislature says in a statute what it means and means in a statute what it says there"); *West Virginia Univ. Hospitals, Inc. v. Casey*, 499 U.S. 83, 98 (1991) (rejecting argument that "the congressional purpose in enacting [a statute] must prevail over the ordinary meaning of statutory terms").

For what it's worth, this passage undercuts the methodology used by some courts in the past to narrowly construe estate-inclusion provisions: *Estate of Skifter* (p. 241); *Field* and *Safe Deposit & Trust Co. of Baltimore* (p. 316).

d. In *Estate of Hubert*, it was held that the statute and regulation in question did not resolve the factual issue presented (i.e., were ambiguous as applied), so that the Tax Court's application of these provisions to the facts before it (in a way contrary to the Commissioner's position) had to be affirmed. In effect, the Commissioner was precluded from construing an ambiguous regulation (and statute) through taking a litigating position, leaving it up to the Tax Court to decide the case.

e. Judge Halpern, in dissent, cited *McNamee v. Dept. of the Treasury*, 488 F.3d 100 (2d Cir.2007), which he read as holding that federal law, in the

---

14. See *Chevron U.S.A. Inc. v. Natural Res. Def. Council, Inc.*, 467 U.S. 837 (1984) (where a statute is ambiguous, certain high-level administrative pronouncements control). Most recently, *Mayo Foundation for Medical Ed. and Research v. U.S.*, 562 U.S.____(2011) held that *Chevron* applies to tax and to §7805 regulations.

form of the check-the-box regulations, did indeed define the property rights and interests transferred. While state law protected Mr. McNamee from his LLC's liabilities, the check-the-box regulations allowing him to avoid double income taxation also made him liable for federal employment taxes. The majority in *Pierre* characterized *McNamee* as only holding that a state cannot interfere with the way federal tax law imposes its liabilities.

§9.4. Section 2704: Voting and Liquidation Rights and Restrictions

Section 2704, enacted in 1990, deals with two separate valuation issues involving family-controlled entities. One provision, §2704(a), treats the lapse of voting or redemption rights as a gift or estate transfer. The other, §2704(b), operates to disregard certain restrictions on liquidation of the entity.

For these sections to apply, the taxpayer, together with members of the family, must own (with the application of the attribution rules found in §2701(e)(3)): (a) a general partnership interest in a limited partnership, (b) at least 50 percent of the capital or profits interest in a partnership, or (c) at least 50 percent of the stock (by vote or value) of a corporation. The term "member of the family" refers to any of the taxpayer's spouse, the taxpayer's proximate relatives (ancestors, decedents, and siblings), and any spouse of any such proximate relative. See §2704(c). An entity that satisfies one of the control tests is referred to below as a "family-controlled entity."

A. *Section 2704(a): Lapsing Redemption and Voting Rights*

Congress enacted §2704(a) primarily to change the result of *Estate of Harrison v. Comm'r*, T.C. Memo. 1987-8. In *Harrison*, the decedent owned a limited partnership interest. During life, he had the right to dissolve the partnership and obtain his share of the underlying assets, but this right lapsed at his death. Citing the principle that estate tax valuation looks forward,[15] the Tax Court held that the value of the limited partnership interest that passed at death was the lower value of the interest without the right to dissolve the partnership.

Section 2704(a) causes the lapse of a voting or liquidation right in a family-controlled entity to be a transfer subject either to gift or estate tax.[16] The amount of the transfer is determined by subtracting the value of interests owned by the right holder and "members of her family" immediately after the lapse (treating all such

---

15. See §4.4.D & E, with the leading authority being *U.S. v. Land*, 303 F.2d 170 (5th Cir.1962), in which the court disregarded a restriction that lapsed at death. In *Land*, disregard of the lapsing *restriction* increased the value. In *Harrison*, disregard of a lapsing *right* decreased the value.

16. See Reg. §§25.2704-1(a)(1), (b), & (c)(1).

interests as held by one individual) from the value of all interests owned by them before the lapse (treating the rights as being nonlapsing).[17] The term "liquidation right" is defined essentially to mean "redemption" right; that is, a right (a "put" right) to have the entity acquire the holder's equity interest.[18] (A right to dissolve a partnership causes the partnership interest to be exchanged for the holder's share of the entity's assets, and would satisfy this definition.)[19] The term "voting right" includes not only the right to vote on entity matters but also the right of a general partner to participate in management.[20] The Treasury is given the authority by §2704(a)(3) to issue regulations to extend the operation of §2703(a) to rights other than voting and redemption rights, but it has not yet done so.

The source of the right, or the trigger of the lapse, may be state law, the entity's charter or bylaws, an agreement, or other source.[21] The term "lapse" means not only its usual meaning but also "restricted or eliminated." A right doesn't lapse just because a person transfers (by sale, gift, or death) the interest to which such right attaches. Thus, a liquidation right in a corporation is not deemed to lapse just because a person held such a right by virtue of 100 percent voting control, and loses the ability to liquidate the corporation by transferring stock to another.[22]

Under Reg. §25.2704-1(c)(2), a lapse of a redemption right does not cause §2704(a) to apply in any of the following cases:

(1) the holder and family members cannot (immediately after the lapse) liquidate the holder's interest, but (disregarding any restriction on liquidation described in §2704(b)) could have liquidated it prior to the lapse;[23]

(2) the right was previously valued under §2701, and there would be double taxation after adjustments under Reg. §25.2701-5; or,

(3) the lapse occurs only because of a change in state law.[24]

The first of these exceptions is somewhat opaque, but presumably exists because a lapse of a liquidation right under the governing instrument would not effect a "transfer" if the interest cannot be liquidated after the lapse because of a non-self-imposed restriction on liquidation. This rule is illustrated by Example 6 of Reg. §25.2703-1(f), in which D was a general partner that had a unilateral liquidation right that lapsed at death, but the partnership agreement prevented D's surviving family members from liquidating the partnership after D's death. However, the

---

17. See §2704(a)(2); Reg. §25.2704-1(d).

18. See Reg. §25.2704-1(a)(2)(v).

19. See Reg. §25.2704-1(f) (Ex. 5), which closely resembles the facts in *Harrison*.

20. See Reg. §25.2704-1(a)(2)(iv).

21. See Reg. §25.2704-1(a)(4).

22. See Reg. §25.2704-1(c)(1) & (f) (Ex. 7) (no lapse where 100% shareholder makes gift of 30% interest, thereby becoming unable by himself to cause a corporate liquidation, which requires an 80% vote, because the donee does not lose the right to join the donor in voting for a liquidation).

23. See Reg. §25.2704-1(c)(2)(i)(B). This regulation further provides that the inability to liquidate immediately after the lapse is determined under state law, as modified by the entity's governing instruments, but does not take into account any restrictions described in §2704(b).

24. "[A] change in the governing instrument of an entity is not a change in state law." Reg. §25.2704-1(c)(2)(iii).

exception does not apply in Example 6, because (in the absence of the agreement) state law would have allowed such liquidation. In other words, the liquidation restriction was self imposed. If state law would have barred the liquidation, then the restriction would not be self-imposed, and §2704(a) would not apply.

The conference agreement provided two straightforward examples illustrating the treatment of lapsing voting or liquidation rights under §2704(a):

Example 6. Parent and Child control a corporation. Parent's stock has a voting right that lapses on Parent's death. Under the conference agreement, Parent's stock is valued for Federal estate tax purposes as if the voting right of the Parent's stock were nonlapsing.

   Example 7. Father and Child each own general and limited interests in a partnership. The general partnership interest carries with it the right to liquidate the partnership; the limited partnership interest has no such right. The liquidation right associated with the general partnership interest lapses after ten years. Under the conference agreement, there is a gift at the time of the lapse equal to the excess of (1) the value of Father's partnership interests determined as if he held the right to liquidate over (2) the value of such interests determined as if he did not hold such right.

PROBLEMS

1. Before her death, Alma owned all of Better Company preferred stock, which represented half of the total voting power of the company (the other half resided in the company's common stock). According to the company's bylaws, the voting rights of the preferred stock lapsed at Alma's death. Alma's children owned 40 percent of the common stock and unrelated third parties owned the rest. Does §2704(a) apply at Alma's death? See Reg. §25.2704-1(f), Ex. 2.

2. According to the bylaws of Clearly Company, voting rights of transferred stock are halved after a transfer but totally restored five years later. Danny owned 60 percent of the company stock before his death, and his family owned the remaining 40 percent. When Danny died his stock, with the reduced voting rights, devolved to his children. Does §2704(a) apply at Danny's death? See Reg. §25.2704-1(f), Ex. 3.

3. Elaine owns 84 percent of Frankly Company, which requires a minimum of 70 percent of the voting shares to liquidate. She gives half of her stock in equal amounts to her three children. Does §2704(a) apply to Elaine's gift? See Reg. §25.2704-1(f), Ex. 4.

4. Gary owns all of Hardly Company, which he recapitalizes by exchanging his common stock for voting common and for nonvoting, noncumulative, preferred stock. The preferred shares carry a ten-year put right to sell the stock to the Company for its par value. Gary gives the common stock to his grandchild Izzy in a transfer subject to §2701, according to which the retained put right

obtains a zero value. Gary's daughter, Jane, owns the preferred stock when the put right lapses. Does §2704(a) apply when the put right lapses? See Reg. §25.2704-1(f), Ex. 8.

B. Section 2704(b): Transfers Subject to Restrictions on Liquidating the Entity

Section 2704(b)(1) provides that the value of a partnership or corporate interest in a family controlled entity must be determined by disregarding any "applicable restriction," which is defined in §2704(b)(2) as one which effectively limits the entity's ability to liquidate, and which either:

(a) lapses at any time after the transfer, or
(b) is subject to a right of removal (in whole or in part) by the transferor, the transferor's estate, or any members of his family, alone or together.[25]

However, crucially, the term "applicable restriction" excludes:

(1) a restriction imposed by law; and
(2) a commercially reasonable restriction arising from non-related-party financing transaction.[26]

The first of these exceptions has largely emasculated §2704(b), because many states have enacted laws that impose onerous restrictions on liquidating certain kinds of entities, such as FLPs.

Section 2704(b)(4) gives specific authority for regulations to be promulgated to disregard other restrictions for valuation purposes, but no such regulations have been issued.

The conference agreement provided the following illustration of the application of this statute:

Example 8. Mother and Son are partners in a two-person partnership. The partnership agreement provides that the partnership cannot be terminated. Mother dies and leaves her partnership interest to Daughter. As the sole partners, Daughter and Son acting together could remove the restriction on partnership termination. Under the conference agreement, the value of Mother's partnership interest in her estate is determined without regard to the restriction. Such value would be adjusted to reflect any appropriate fragmentation discount.[27]

In the next case, the government contended that §2704(b) prevented the donors from discounting for lack of marketability the value of the FLP interests they had transferred to several grantor retained annuity trusts (GRATs) and to their children.

---

25. See Reg. §25.2704-2(b).
26. §2704(b)(3).
27. See H.R. Rep. No. 101-964, 101st Cong., 2d Sess. (1990) (Conf. Rep.), at 1137-1138.

Kerr v. Commissioner

113 T.C. 449, 459 (1999), aff'd, 202 F.3d 490 (5th Cir.2002)

Jacobs, *Judge*: Petitioners argue that the provisions of the partnership agreements do not constitute "applicable restrictions" because: (1) The provisions do not restrict liquidation of the partnerships within the meaning of section 2704(b)(2)(A); and (2) the university's interests in [the FLPs] demonstrate that the Kerr family did not have the ability unilaterally to lift any restrictions on liquidation within the meaning of §2704(b)(2)(B)(ii). In the alternative, petitioners assert that any restrictions on liquidation in the partnership agreements are excepted from the definition of an "applicable restriction" pursuant to §2704(b)(3)(B). We agree.

In what we view as an expansion of the exception contained in §2704(b)(3)(B), the Secretary promulgated Reg. §25.2704-2(b), which states in pertinent part: "An applicable restriction is a limitation on the ability to liquidate the entity (in whole or in part) that is more restrictive than the limitations that would apply under the state law generally applicable to the entity in the absence of the restriction." Thus, the question arises whether the partnership agreements involved herein impose greater restrictions on the liquidation of KFLP and KILP than the limitations that generally would apply to the partnerships under State law.

The partnership agreements states in pertinent part that the partnerships shall dissolve and liquidate upon the earlier of December 31, 2043, or by agreement of all the partners. Petitioners direct our attention to TRLPA section 8.01, which provides that a Texas limited partnership shall be dissolved on the earlier of: (1) The occurrence of events specified in the partnership agreement to cause dissolution; (2) the written consent of all partners to dissolution; (3) the withdrawal of a general partner; or (4) entry of a decree of judicial dissolution. We conclude that §10.01 of the partnership agreements does not contain restrictions on liquidation that constitute applicable restrictions within the meaning of §2704(b), because Texas law provides for the dissolution and liquidation of a limited partnership pursuant to the occurrence of events specified in the partnership agreement or upon the written consent of all the partners, and the restrictions contained in §10.01 of the partnership agreements are no more restrictive than the limitations that generally would apply to the partnerships under Texas law.

The Obama administration's 2010 Budget Proposal included the following proposed change to §2704(b), which (however) was not included in the 2010 Act:

> Since the enactment of section 2704(b), new State statutes providing for more restrictive liquidation rights, as well as regulatory and judicial interpretations of section 2704(b), arguably have limited the provision's effectiveness in curbing inappropriate marketability discounts. The proposal modifies section 2704(b) to create a category of "disregarded restrictions" that would be ignored when valuing an interest in a family-controlled entity transferred to a member of the family if, after the transfer, the restriction will lapse or may be removed by the transferor and/ or the transferor's family. The proposal provides that the transferred interest would

be valued by substituting for the disregarded restrictions certain assumptions to be specified in regulations. The proposal provides that disregarded restrictions would include limitations on a holder's right to liquidate that holder's interest in the family-controlled entity that are more restrictive than a standard to be specified in regulations. A disregarded restriction also would include a limitation on a transferee's ability to be admitted as a full partner or holder of an equity interest in the entity. In determining whether a restriction may be removed by one or more members of the family after a transfer, certain interests held by charities or others who are not family members would be deemed to be held by the family. Such interests are to be identified in regulations. Under the proposal, regulatory authority is granted, including the ability to create safe harbors under which the governing documents of a family-controlled entity could be drafted so as to avoid the application of section 2704 if certain standards are met.[28]

PROBLEMS, QUESTIONS, AND NOTES

1. a. Kermit owns 60 percent of the voting interests in Lollipop Company, whose bylaws prohibit the company's liquidation for ten years, after which liquidation requires approval of 60 percent of the voting interests. Without this provision, state law requires 80 percent voting interest approval to liquidate. During the ten-year period, Kermit gives the stock to his son Mortimer. How should Kermit's gift be valued? See Reg. §25.2704-2(d), Ex. 3.

    b. Olivia and her children Poppet and Quincy are partners in the OFLP, wherein each owns both general and limited partnership interests. Any general partner has the right to dissolve OFLP at any time. As part of a loan agreement with Rupert, Olivia's relative, all partners agree that OFLP may not be liquidated without the Rupert's consent until the loan is repaid. During this period, Olivia gives to each child one-half of both of her partnership interests. How should Olivia's gifts be valued? See Reg. §25.2704-2(d), Ex. 4.

2. a. Did the 2010 proposal lack sufficient specificity? Would it have been subject to the "overinclusiveness" criticism of former §2036(c)? Was it underinclusive, because the §2704(b) proposal only dealt with liquidation restrictions (which cause nonmarketability discounts to apply)? Was the proposal unnecessary, given the Secretary's power under §2704(b)(4)? Is a better approach simply to eliminate the state-law exception?

    b. The 2010 proposal also described several measures dealing with the appropriateness of minority discounts attaching to transfers between family members in a family-controlled entity. "For example, one recently

---

28. *Description of Revenue Provisions Contained in the President's Fiscal Year 2010 Budget Proposal — Part One: Individual Income Tax and Estate and Gift Tax Provisions* (JCS-2-09), Joint Committee on Taxation (Sept. 8, 2009) at 140-142.

introduced bill, the Certain Estate Tax Relief Act of 2009, would deny a minority discount in connection with the transfer of an interest where the transferee and members of the transferee's family together have control of the entity."[29] Another possible approach to minority discounts is to deny discounts for self-created minority interests, such as gifts of minority interests out of a controlling interest. However, once again, there was no provision dealing with minority discounts in the 2010 Act.

---

29. Id. at 144, *citing* in n. 232, H.R. 436, *Certain Estate Tax Relief Act of 2009* (111th Cong., 1st Sess.).

TABLE OF CASES

Italic page numbers indicate principal cases

TABLE OF STATUTES

TABLE OF REGULATIONS

TABLE OF REVENUE RULINGS AND REVENUE PROCS.

Italic page numbers indicate principal revenue rulings

TABLE OF PRIVATE LETTER RULINGS AND TECHNICAL ADVICE MEMORANDA

Italic page numbers indicate principal rulings

Revenue Ruling 59-60

1959-1 C.B. 237

SUBJECT MATTER: SECTION 2031.-DEFINITION OF GROSS ESTATE

APPLICABLE SECTIONS:

26 CFR 20.2031-2: Valuation of stocks and bonds.

In valuing the stock of closely held corporations, or the stock of corporations where market quotations are not available, all other available financial data, as well as all relevant factors affecting the fair market value must be considered for estate tax and gift tax purposes. No general formula may be given that is applicable to the many different valuation situations arising in the valuation of such stock. However, the general approach, methods, and factors which must be considered in valuing such securities are outlined.

§1. Purpose.

The purpose of this Revenue Ruling is to outline and review in general the approach, methods and factors to be considered in valuing shares of the capital stock of closely held corporations for estate tax and gift tax purposes. The methods discussed herein will apply likewise to the valuation of corporate stocks on which market quotations are either unavailable or are of such scarcity that they do not reflect the fair market value.

§2. Background and Definitions.

.01   All valuations must be made in accordance with the applicable provisions of the Internal Revenue Code of 1954 and the Federal Estate Tax and Gift Tax Regulations. Sections 2031(a), 2032 and 2512 (a) of the 1954 Code require that the property to be included in the gross estate, or made the subject of a gift, shall be taxed on the basis of the value of the property at the time of death of the decedent, the alternate date if so elected, or the date of gift.

.02   Section 20.2031-1(b) of the Estate Tax Regulations and section 25.2512-1 of the Gift Tax Regulations define fair market value, in effect, as the price at which the property would change hands between a willing buyer and a willing seller when the former is not under any compulsion to buy and the latter is not under any compulsion to sell, both parties having reasonable knowledge of relevant facts. Court decisions frequently state in addition that the hypothetical buyer and seller are assumed to be able, as well as willing, to trade and to be well informed about the property and concerning the market for such property.

.03   Closely held corporations are those corporations the shares of which are owned by a relatively limited number of stockholders. Often the entire stock issue is held by one family. The result of this situation is that little, if any, trading in the shares takes place. There is, therefore, no established market for the stock and such sales as occur at irregular intervals seldom reflect all of the elements of a representative transaction as defined by the term "fair market value."

§3. Approach to Valuation.

.01   A determination of fair market value, being a question of fact, will depend upon the circumstances in each case. No formula can be devised that will be generally applicable to the multitude of different valuation issues arising in estate and gift tax cases. Often, an appraiser will find wide differences of opinion as to the fair market value of a particular stock. In resolving such differences, he should maintain a reasonable attitude in recognition of the fact that valuation is not an exact science. A sound valuation will be based upon all the relevant facts, but the elements of common sense, informed judgment and reasonableness must enter into the process of weighing those facts and determining their aggregate significance.

.02   The fair market value of specific shares of stock will vary as general economic conditions change from "normal" to "boom" or "depression," that is according to the degree of optimism or pessimism with which the investing public regards the future at the required date of appraisal. Uncertainty as to the stability or continuity of the future income from a property decreases its value by increasing the risk of loss of earnings and value in the future. The value of shares of stock of a company with very uncertain future prospects is highly speculative. The appraiser must exercise his judgment as to the degree of risk attaching to the business of the corporation which issued the stock, but that judgment must be related to all of the other factors affecting value.

.03   Valuation of securities is, in essence, a prophesy as to the future and must be based on facts available at the required date of appraisal. As a generalization, the prices of stocks which are traded in volume in a free and active market by informed persons best reflect the consensus of the investing public as to what the future holds for the corporations and industries represented. When a stock is closely held, is traded infrequently, or is traded in an erratic market, some other measure of value must be used. In many instances, the next best measure may be found in the prices at which the stocks of companies engaged in the same or a similar line of business are selling in a free and open market.

§4. Factors to Consider.

.01   It is advisable to emphasize that in the valuation of the stock of closely held corporations or the stock of corporations where market quotations are either lacking or too scarce to be recognized, all available financial data, as well as all relevant factors affecting the fair market value, should be considered. The following factors, although not all-inclusive are fundamental and require careful analysis in each case:

a. The nature of the business and the history of the enterprise from its inception.
b. The economic outlook in general and the condition and outlook of the specific industry in particular.
c. The book value of the stock and the financial condition of the business.
d. The earning capacity of the company.
e. The dividend-paying capacity.
f. Whether or not the enterprise has goodwill or other intangible value.
g. Sales of the stock and the size of the block of stock to be valued.
h. The market price of stocks of corporations engaged in the same or a similar line of business having their stocks actively traded in a free and open market, either on an exchange or over-the-counter.

.02   The following is a brief discussion of each of the foregoing factors:

(a) The history of a corporate enterprise will show its past stability or instability, its growth or lack of growth, the diversity or lack of diversity of its operations, and other facts needed to form an opinion of the degree of risk involved in the business. For an enterprise which changed its form of organization but carried on the same or closely similar operations of its predecessor, the history of the former enterprise should be considered. The detail to be considered should increase with approach to the required date of appraisal, since recent events are of greatest help in predicting the future; but a study of gross and net income, and of dividends covering a long prior period, is highly desirable. The history to be studied should include, but need not be limited to, the nature of the business, its products or services, its operating and investment assets, capital structure, plant facilities, sales records and management, all of which should be considered as of the date of the appraisal, with due regard for recent significant changes. Events of the past that are unlikely to recur in the future should be discounted, since value has a close relation to future expectancy.

(b) A sound appraisal of a closely held stock must consider current and prospective economic conditions as of the date of appraisal, both in the national economy and in the industry or industries with which the corporation is allied. It is important to know that the company is more or less successful than its competitors in the same industry, or that it is maintaining a stable position with respect to competitors. Equal or even greater significance may attach to the ability of the industry with which the company is allied to compete with other industries. Prospective competition which has not been a factor in prior years should be given careful attention. For example, high profits due to the novelty of its product and the lack of competition often lead to increasing competition. The public's appraisal of the future prospects of competitive industries or of competitors within an industry may be indicated by price trends in the markets for commodities and for securities. The loss of the manager of a so-called "one-man" business may have a depressing effect upon the value of the stock of such business, particularly if there is a lack of trained personnel capable of succeeding to the management of the enterprise. In valuing the stock of this type of business, therefore, the effect of the loss of the manager on the future expectancy of the business, and the absence of management-succession potentialities are pertinent factors to be taken into consideration. On the other hand, there may be factors which offset, in whole or in part, the loss of the manager's services. For instance, the nature of the business and of its assets may be such that they will not be impaired by the loss of the manager. Furthermore, the loss may be adequately covered by life insurance, or competent management might be employed on the basis of the consideration paid for the former manager's services. These, or other offsetting factors, if found to exist, should be carefully weighed against the loss of the manager's services in valuing the stock of the enterprise.

(c) Balance sheets should be obtained, preferably in the form of comparative annual statements for two or more years immediately preceding the date of appraisal, together with a balance sheet at the end of the month preceding that date, if corporate accounting will permit. Any balance sheet descriptions that are not self-explanatory, and balance sheet items comprehending diverse assets or liabilities, should be clarified in essential detail by supporting supplemental schedules. These statements usually will disclose to the appraiser (1) liquid position (ratio of current assets to current liabilities); (2) gross and net book value of principal classes of fixed assets; (3) working capital; (4) long-term indebtedness; (5) capital structure; and (6) net worth. Consideration also should be given to any assets not essential to the operation of the business, such as investments in securities, real estate, etc. In general, such nonoperating assets will command a lower rate of return than do the operating assets, although in exceptional cases the reverse may be true. In computing the book value per share of stock, assets of the investment type should be revalued on the basis of their market price and the book value adjusted accordingly. Comparison of the company's balance sheets over several years may reveal, among other facts, such developments as the acquisition of additional production facilities or subsidiary companies, improvement in financial position, and details as to recapitalizations and other changes in the capital structure of the corporation. If the corporation has more than one class of stock outstanding, the charter or certificate of incorporation should be examined to ascertain the explicit rights and privileges of the various stock issues including: (1) voting powers, (2) preference as to dividends, and (3) preference as to assets in the event of liquidation.

(d) Detailed profit-and-loss statements should be obtained and considered for a representative period immediately prior to the required date of appraisal, preferably five or more years. Such statements should show (1) gross income by principal items; (2) principal deductions from gross income including major prior items of operating expenses, interest and other expense on each item of long-term debt, depreciation and depletion if such deductions are made, officers' salaries, in total if they appear to be reasonable or in detail if they seem to be excessive, contributions (whether or not deductible for tax purposes) that the nature of its business and its community position require the corporation to make, and taxes by principal items, including income and excess profits taxes; (3) net income available for dividends; (4) rates and amounts of dividends paid on each class of stock; (5) remaining amount carried to surplus; and (6) adjustments to, and reconciliation with, surplus as stated on the balance sheet. With profit and loss statements of this character available, the appraiser should be able to separate recurrent from nonrecurrent items of income and expense, to distinguish between operating income and investment income, and to ascertain whether or not any line of business in which the company is engaged is operated consistently at a loss and might be abandoned with benefit to the company. The percentage of earnings retained for business expansion should be noted when dividend-paying capacity is considered. Potential future income is a major factor in many valuations of closely-held stocks, and all information concerning past income which will be helpful in predicting the future should be secured. Prior earnings records usually are the most reliable guide as to the future expectancy, but resort to arbitrary five-or-ten-year averages without regard to current trends or future prospects will not produce a realistic valuation. If, for instance, a record of progressively increasing or decreasing net income is found, then greater weight may be accorded the most recent years' profits in estimating earning power. It will be helpful, in judging risk and the extent to which a business is a marginal operator, to consider deductions from income and net income in terms of percentage of sales. Major categories of cost and expense to be so analyzed include the consumption of raw materials and supplies in the case of manufacturers, processors and fabricators; the cost of purchased merchandise in the case of merchants; utility services; insurance; taxes; depletion or depreciation; and interest.

(e) Primary consideration should be given to the dividend-paying capacity of the company rather than to dividends actually paid in the past. Recognition must be given to the necessity of retaining a reasonable portion of profits in a company to meet competition. Dividend-paying capacity is a factor that must be considered in an appraisal, but dividends actually paid in the past may not have any relation to dividend-paying capacity. Specifically, the dividends paid by a closely held family company may be measured by the income needs of the stockholders or by their desire to avoid taxes on dividend receipts, instead of by the ability of the company to pay dividends. Where an actual or effective controlling interest in a corporation is to be valued, the dividend factor is not a material element, since the payment of such dividends is discretionary with the controlling stockholders. The individual or group in control can substitute salaries and bonuses for dividends, thus reducing net income and understating the dividend-paying capacity of the company. It follows, therefore, that dividends are less reliable criteria of fair market value than other applicable factors.

(f) In the final analysis, goodwill is based upon earning capacity. The presence of goodwill and its value, therefore, rests upon the excess of net earnings over and above a fair return on the net tangible assets. While the element of goodwill may be based primarily on earnings, such factors as the prestige and renown of the business, the ownership of a trade or brand name, and a record of successful operation over a prolonged period in a particular locality, also may furnish support for the inclusion of intangible value. In some instances it may not be possible to make a separate appraisal of the tangible and intangible assets of the business. The enterprise has a value as an entity. Whatever intangible value there is, which is supportable by the facts, may be measured by the amount by which the appraised value of the tangible assets exceeds the net book value of such assets.

(g) Sales of stock of a closely held corporation should be carefully investigated to determine whether they represent transactions at arm's length. Forced or distress sales do not ordinarily reflect fair market value nor do isolated sales in small amounts necessarily control as the measure of value. This is especially true in the valuation of a controlling interest in a corporation. Since, in the case of closely held stocks, no prevailing market prices are available, there is no basis for making an adjustment for blockage. It follows, therefore, that such stocks should be valued upon a consideration of all the evidence affecting the fair market value. The size of the block of stock itself is a relevant factor to be considered. Although it is true that a minority interest in an unlisted corporation's stock is more difficult to sell than a similar block of listed stock, it is equally true that control of a corporation, either actual or in effect, representing as it does an added element of value, may justify a higher value for a specific block of stock.

(h) Section 2031(b) of the Code states, in effect, that in valuing unlisted securities the value of stock or securities of corporations engaged in the same or a similar line of business which are listed on an exchange should be taken into consideration along with all other factors. An important consideration is that the corporations to be used for comparisons have capital stocks which are actively traded by the public. In accordance with section 2031(b) of the Code, stocks listed on an exchange are to be considered first. However, if sufficient comparable companies whose stocks are listed on an exchange cannot be found, other comparable companies which have stocks actively traded in on the over-the-counter market also may be used. The essential factor is that whether the stocks are sold on an exchange or over-the-counter there is evidence of an active, free public market for the stock as of the valuation date. In selecting corporations for comparative purposes, care should be taken to use only comparable companies. Although the only restrictive requirement as to comparable corporations specified in the statute is that their lines of business be the same or similar, yet it is obvious that consideration must be given to other relevant factors in order that the most valid comparison possible will be obtained. For illustration, a corporation having one or more issues of preferred stock, bonds or debentures in addition to its common stock should not be considered to be directly comparable to one having only common stock outstanding. In like manner, a company with a declining business and decreasing markets is not comparable to one with a record of current progress and market expansion.

§5. Weight to be Accorded Various Factors.

The valuation of closely held corporate stock entails the consideration of all relevant factors as stated in section 4. Depending upon the circumstances in each case, certain factors may carry more weight than others because of the nature of the company's business. To illustrate:

(a) Earnings may be the most important criterion of value in some cases whereas asset value will receive primary consideration in others. In general, the appraiser will accord primary consideration to earnings when valuing stocks of companies which sell products or services to the public; conversely, in the investment or holding type of company, the appraiser may accord the greatest weight to the assets underlying the security to be valued.

(b) The value of the stock of a closely held investment or real estate holding company, whether or not family owned, is closely related to the value of the assets underlying the stock. For companies of this type the appraiser should determine the fair market values of the assets of the company. Operating expenses of such a company and the cost of liquidating it, if any, merit consideration when appraising the relative values of the stock and the underlying assets. The market values of the underlying assets give due weight to potential earnings and dividends of the particular items of property underlying the stock, capitalized at rates deemed proper by the investing public at the date of appraisal. A current appraisal by the investing public should be superior to the retrospective opinion of an individual. For these reasons, adjusted net worth should be accorded greater weight in valuing the stock of a closely held investment or real estate holding company, whether or not family owned, than any of the other customary yardsticks of appraisal, such as earnings and dividend paying capacity.

§6. Capitalization Rates.

In the application of certain fundamental valuation factors, such as earnings and dividends, it is necessary to capitalize the average or current results at some appropriate rate. A determination of the proper capitalization rate presents one of the most difficult problems in valuation. That there is no ready or simple solution will become apparent by a cursory check of the rates of return and dividend yields in terms of the selling prices of corporate shares listed on the major exchanges of the country. Wide variations will be found even for companies in the same industry. Moreover, the ratio will fluctuate from year to year depending upon economic conditions. Thus, no standard tables of capitalization rates applicable to closely held corporations can be formulated. Among the more important factors to be taken into consideration in deciding upon a capitalization rate in a particular case are: (1) the nature of the business; (2) the risk involved; and (3) the stability or irregularity of earnings.

§7. Average of Factors.

Because valuations cannot be made on the basis of a prescribed formula, there is no means whereby the various applicable factors in a particular case can be assigned mathematical weights in deriving the fair market value. For this reason, no useful purpose is served by taking an average of several factors (for example, book value, capitalized earnings and capitalized dividends) and basing the valuation on the result. Such a process excludes active consideration of other pertinent factors, and the end result cannot be supported by a realistic application of the significant facts in the case except by mere chance.

§8. Restrictive Agreements.

Frequently, in the valuation of closely held stock for estate and gift tax purposes, it will be found that the stock is subject to an agreement restricting its sale or transfer. Where shares of stock were acquired by a decedent subject to an option reserved by the issuing corporation to repurchase at a certain price, the option price is usually accepted as the fair market value for estate tax purposes. See Rev. Rul. 54-76, C.B. 1954-1, 194. However, in such case the option price is not determinative of fair market value for gift tax purposes. Where the option, or buy and sell agreement, is the result of voluntary action by the stockholders and is binding during the life as well as at the death of the stockholders, such agreement may or may not, depending upon the circumstances of each case, fix the value for estate tax purposes. However, such agreement is a factor to be considered, with other relevant factors, in determining fair market value. Where the stockholder is free to dispose of his shares during life and the option is to become effective only upon his death, the fair market value is not limited to the option price. It is always necessary to consider the relationship of the parties, the relative number of shares held by the decedent, and other material facts, to determine whether the agreement represents a bona fide business arrangement or is a device to pass the decedent's shares to the natural objects of his bounty for less than an adequate and full consideration in money or money's worth. In this connection see Rev. Rul. 157 C.B. 1953-2, 255, and Rev. Rul. 189, C.B. 1953-2, 294.

Index